NEW AGE BIBLE VERSIONS

G.A. RIPLINGER

Bill Stubblefield
PO Box 85
Nicholasville KY
40340

I owe a very special debt of gratitude to my family and to Cheryl for the typesetting of this book.

 Published by A.V. Publications Corporation, P.O. Box 280, Ararat, VA, USA 24053

First printing, 1993
Sixth printing, 1995

ISBN 0-9635845-0-2
Library of Congress Catalogue Card Number 93-92561
Printed in the United States of America

Note to the reader: 1) All editions and printings of the NIV and NASB et al. are not the same. 2) The NIV and NASB do not have identical wording because each is copywritten. Space permits only one example, often that of the NASB, but heresy occurs in other versions as well, worded in a slightly different way.

For additional copies or a free catalogue of materials contact:

1-800-435-4535

Publications Corporation

P.O. Box 280 • Ararat Virginia, USA 24053

Hear ye, and give ear; be not proud: for the LORD hath spoken. . .

But if ye will not hear it, my soul shall weep in secret places for your pride; and mine eye shall weep sore, and run down with tears, because the LORD'S flock is carried away captive.

Jeremiah 13:15, 17

For I testify unto every man that heareth the words of the prophecy of this book, If any man shall add unto these things, God shall add unto him the plagues that are written in this book:

And if any man shall take away from the words of the book of this prophecy, God shall take away his part out of the book of life, and out of the holy city, and from the things which are written in this book.

Revelation 22:18-19

It may be the most important book ever written. . .Unparalleled. . .stunning expose.

Texe Marrs

I must under God renounce every attachment to the *New American Standard.* . .I'm afraid I'm in trouble with the Lord. . .We laid the groundwork; I wrote the format; I helped interview some of the translators; I sat with the translator; I wrote the preface. . .

I'm in trouble; I can't refute these arguments; its wrong, it's terribly wrong; it's frighteningly wrong; and what am I going to do about it?. . .I can no longer ignore these criticisms I am hearing and I can't refute them. . .

When questions began to reach me at first I was quite offended. However, in attempting to answer, I began to sense that something was not right about the NASV. Upon investigation, I wrote my very dear friend, Mr. Lockman, explaining that I was forced to renounce all attachment to the NASV. . .The product is grievous to my heart and helps to complicate matters in these already troublous times. . .The deletions are absolutely frightening. . .there are so many. . .Are we so naive that we do not suspect Satanic deception in all of this?. . .

I don't want anything to do with it. . .

[T]he finest leaders that we have today. . .haven't gone into it [the new version's use of a corrupted Greek text], just as I hadn't gone into it. . .That's how easily one can be deceived. . .I'm going to talk to him [Dr. George Sweeting, then president of Moody Bible Institute] about these things. . .

[Y]ou can say the *Authorized Version* [KJV] is absolutely correct. How correct? 100% correct!. . .

If you must stand against everyone else, stand.

Dr. Frank Logsdon

TABLE OF

Contents

PART FOUR CHRIST OR ANTICHRIST

THE MEN & THE MANUSCRIPTS

PART ONE THE MEN

PART TWO THE MANUSCRIPTS

PART THREE BACK TO THE FUTURE

EPILOGUE

APPENDICES

NOTES

NIV, NASB, et al.		KJV
men	2 Pet. 1:21	holy men
angels	Matt. 25:31	holy angels
brethren	I Thess. 5:27	holy brethren
prophets	Rev. 22:6	holy prophets
apostles and prophets	Rev. 18:20	holy apostles and prophets
Spirit	John 7:39	Holy Ghost
Spirit	I Cor. 2:13	Holy Ghost
Spirit	Matt. 12:31	Holy Ghost
Spirit	Acts 6:3	Holy Ghost
Spirit	Acts 8:18	Holy Ghost

INTRODUCTION

[Y]e have perverted the words of the living God.
Jeremiah 23:36

This book is what reporters refer to as a 'scoop'. Much digging in libraries and manuscripts from around the world has uncovered an alliance between the new versions of the bible (NIV, NASB, Living Bible and others) and the chief conspirators in the New Age movement's push for a One World Religion. Unlike the sensational or emotion-ridden fogging of the facts which could accompany such a disclosure, this book objectively and methodically documents the following discoveries, which stunned the author as they will the reader.

1. The New Age movement's expressed goal of infiltrating the evangelical church and gradually changing the bible to conform to its One World Religion is evident in the current new versions. Their words and doctrines prepare the apostate church of these last days to accept the Antichrist, his mark, image, and religion—Lucifer worship.

2. This has taken place because the editors of the new

versions, as well as the authors of the Greek editions, manuscripts, lexicons and dictionaries used in their compilation, hold beliefs which an orthodox Christian would find shocking. Research opens the door exposing them in seance parlors, mental institutions, prison cells and courtrooms for heresy trials. A few examples include:

•The Greek text used to translate the NIV, NASB and others was an edition drastically altered by a Spiritualist (one who seeks contact with the dead through seances), who believed he was in the "new age."[1] Two other 'new' version editors were also involved in spiritualism.

•The NIV's chief editor vaunts his version's heresy saying:

> This [his own translation] shows the great error that is so prevalent today in some orthodox Protestant circles, namely the error that regeneration depends upon faith. . .and that in order to be born again man must first accept Jesus as Savior.[2]

> [F]ew clear and decisive texts that declare that Jesus is God.[3]

•The NASB's progenitor, called "the mediator between East and West" by his colleagues, was an instrumental member of the 'gathering' which *East-West Journal* calls the kick off event for the New Age movement and "East West Synthesis."[4] This new version editor referred to his alterations of the articles of faith saying:

> The changes thus far. . .are in the right direction. . .and should contain the germs of a new theology.[5]

•A surprising number of new version editors have permanently lost their ability to speak (five and still counting).

•Insanity marked another prominent new version editor whose commitments to mental institutions served as bookends to a life fraught with derangement and hallucinosis.

•The reference dictionary used by new version editors to research Greek etymology was edited by Hitler's propaganda 'high priest', who was later tried and found guilty of war crimes as an accessory in the death of millions.

3. Contrary to advertising claims, the new versions are *more* difficult to read than the KJV, according to research using the Flesch-Kincaid Grade Level Indicators.

4. A 'new' Christianity is emerging from the new versions which substitute riches for righteousness, a crown for a cross, and an imitation for a new creation.

5. The few Greek manuscripts underlying new versions contain yet unreleased material which is an exact blueprint for the antichrist's One World Religion. A complete translation of these is being called for by new version editors and New Agers alike. This 'new' version could be the final "universal bible" called for by U.N. Assistant Secretary General Robert Muller.

Why this Book?

This book is written in loving concern for those who are 'victims' of these versions. Unsuspecting Christians have been carried off by an ancient chariot, resurrected and given a fresh coat of paint by Madison Avenue. (Is that Latin for 'hail the new'?) It appears that there is a vast difference between the press publicity and the product. This chasm, characteristic of the coming antichrist-Big Brother era, was called 'Newspeak' by George Orwell. It is built of soap bubbles which burst at the slightest touch of analysis. The documentation herein will scatter to the wind many false arguments and confident conclusions. After this evidence is made public, new versions will keep afloat only on the hot air of emotion and preconceived prejudice.

Kent State University has always been a hot-house creating a climate of open discussion and debate. This has cultivated creative thinking (e.g., the liquid crystal) and also a crop of cults and classrooms providing pulpits for professors preaching New Age consciousness. Each year brings a swell of students who eagerly swallow the sophistry of the 'sage on the stage'. After a decade in this climate, as a Christian and a professor, plied with questions, a bombshell hit as a young man asked, "Is the fall, recorded in Isaiah 14 about Lucifer [as the KJV and Hebrew text indicates] or Jesus, the morning star, as the NIV and NASB imply?" Practiced perception pointed to the latter as a mislaid page from the podium of the New Age sages surrounding me. This prompted a six year research project into new bible versions, Greek editions and manuscripts, commencing with over 3000 hours of word-for-word collation of the entire New Testament. This groundwork was inspired by Herman Hoskier, the world's pre-eminent manuscript scholar who observed:

> Rough comparison can seldom, if ever, be of any real use, the exact collation of documents, ancient or modern with the Received Text, is the necessary foundation of all scientific criticism.

The Lord graciously provided me access to documents, as well as research time not typically available to busy pastors, seminary students, and Christians. The investigation focused heavily on the *New American Standard Version* (NASB), a F.E. (formal equivalency) version popular among pastors, and the New International Version (NIV), a D.E. (dynamic equivalency) version growing in popularity in evangelical circles. (A review of those versions which tend to translate 'esoteric' Greek manuscripts, like papyrus 46 or Manuscript D, showed them unlikely candidates for use by Christians—i.e., *Today's English Version* (TEV), *Good News for Modern Man*, *The New American Bible*, the *Jerusalem Bible*, and the *New Revised Standard Version.*)

Scientists marvel at how children are conformed to the physical likeness of their parents through several microns. They hold formulas several feet long which contain the complex genetic code to create 60 trillion highly differentiated cells. If God put the key to one's passing physical life in such a perfect and complex format, can you imagine how intricately and carefully the key to eternal life—conformed to the image of his Son—would be? As with the genetic code, one change sets off a series of alterations which makes the 'new born' unlike instead of like his parents. The changes, additions and omissions discovered in the new versions have affected the health of the body of Christ and taken it step by step away from the image of God.

OVERVIEW

The Message, the Men and the Manuscripts

ONE

The Mandate: Infiltrate

And they worshipped the dragon which gave power unto the beast: and they worshipped the beast, saying, Who is like unto the beast? Revelation 13:4

Souls snagged in a spiritual region remote from reason, will one day give way—sliding headlong down into Satan's dark chambered church. These chaff choose a pew. (He'll hew one for YOU too.) Friend and foe are "falling away," down the steep slippery stairs, framed by the archfiend—to the Church of Chapter 13.

Satan's barred by a small book from his quest for the throne. When opened it unleashes a wall of words—graven in stone.

It is written, Thou shalt worship the Lord thy God and him only. . .Luke 4:8

NIV, NASB et al.		**KJV**
worship	Phil. 3:3	worship God

Wanting to weaken this wall, Satan slips out stone after stone, hoping not to be known.

Satan cometh immediately and taketh away the word. . . Mark 4:15

To begin, he removes the rubblestone of sin and the keystone of salvation. The cornerstone of Jesus Christ and the capstone of his second coming are cut. These words once withdrawn leave loopholes for skeptics and portholes for postulators. Taken together these breaches become windows with wide-angle lenses, taking in the "broad way" of these "last days." The stones piled high become props for his lie. Widening and deepening gaps give way, as scattered stones lay—like stepping stones to Satan's sought after throne. The word of God so discomfit, becomes a bridge to the bottomless pit.

His goal is to trap souls, so he adds key words, like keyholes. Page after page these open his hatchway to the New Age. Slipping in the side door of Satan's church, using these keys, the ushers of apostasy bring souls from the nave to their knees, as a chorus of New Agers sing:

> We are one world. We now need a world religion. We are entering a New Age.[1] *Toward a New World Religion*

> I would suggest a meeting of the world's religions. . .My great personal dream is to get a tremendous alliance between all major religions and the U.N. . .a completely new world in the making, a new age.[2]
> Robert Muller U.N. Asst. Sec. General

> I predict that in our lifetime we will see the rise of essentially a New World Religion.[3] Jean Houston

> [E]stablish a church based on universal principles.[4]
> Unity-in-Diversity Council

> The reorganization of the world's religions. . .[is] for the new world religion.[5] Alice Bailey

In Asia and Africa, Satan has cleared footpaths to his throne through the paganism that grips much of the globe today. Visions of this "angel of light" light the way for the masses in South and Central America, Mexico, Spain, Italy, Ireland, and half of Europe and North America. Finally, he has set in motion a current to carry the communist and 'Christianized' cultures to the coming 'conversion'. A storyteller, weaving "cunningly devised fables" will lull this group to sleep. As the New Age's nanny admits:

> [T]he war. . .will be fought with mental weapons in the world of thought.[6]

Antics with Semantics

The "beast's" own books betray his scheme to use bibles as building blocks for his bridge back to Babel—its One World Government and One World Religion. God split this league by dividing the languages. So Satan sees *words*, welding East and West, as the only weapon in his war to win the world. His legion carrying this common language is called 'The New Age Movement'. *The Encyclopedia of Occultism and Parapsychology* divulges Satan's secret in their definition of "the New Age," calling it a "largely semantic revolution."[7] ('Semantics' means changes in the meaning of words.) Lola Davis, another semantic soldier writes in *Toward a World Religion for the New Age*:

> When an appropriate common vocabulary is developed, each group can help toward a World Religion.[8]

Already inside the church, the wife of Episcopal Bishop James Pike echoes:

> [We need]. . .one vocabulary and one way of talking so that we won't have the split we have had for so many years.[9]

Since both Western 'Christians' and Eastern mystics are moving along a semantic bridge—meeting in the middle—in spiritual Babylon, their troops are trumpeting two trends.

TREND ONE

Oriental mystics, traveling West via the New Age Movement, are adopting Christian terms for their occult ideas and identities. (Some years ago the leading New Age newsletter [Lucis Trust, United

Nations Plaza] called for volunteers to help find acceptable Christian counterparts for New Age words.) So now 'Buddha', 'Krishna', and Lucifer become 'The Lord', 'The Christ', and 'the One'. Occult initiation becomes 'baptism', the beginning step on their 'Way'. *Los Angeles Times* writer, Russell Chandler, observes:

> New Age metaphysical groups often co-opt the language and trappings of the traditional Christian church, thereby making newcomers feel more comfortable in their transition to alternate forms of belief or practice.[10]

A book about Luciferic initiation made its way to the bestseller's list. Its author, Whitley Striber, called it *Communion* to make it more easily acceptable. "Infiltrating the New Age Into Society," an article in a New Age journal admits:

> One of the biggest advantages we have as New Agers is, once the occult, metaphysical New Age terminology is removed, we have concepts and techniques that are very acceptable to the general public. So we can change the names and in so doing, we open the New Age door to millions who normally would not be receptive.[11]

The New Age Dictionary by Alex Jack, editor of the popular *East-West Journal*, gives New Age definitions for Christian terms. He boasts, "[T]his book is only the beginning in the direction of unifying. . .East and West."[12] The left column gives some of his New Age definitions, while the column on the right shows how new versions are changing to conform to the New Age.

NEW AGE DICTIONARY	NEW VERSIONS
the Holy Spirit: a spirit that is whole	Substitute man's spirit for the Holy Spirit.
Christ: any fully realized person	Drop 'Jesus' from Christ.

NEW AGE DICTIONARY	NEW VERSIONS
Sanat: [Satan scrambled] Lord of the World	Use 'Lord' alone dropping the identity of Jesus or Jehovah.
Lucifer: the morning star	Call Lucifer "the morning star."
the dragon: a great beneficent being; a symbol of wisdom	Drop half of the references to "the dragon."
devil: great strength	Omit connection between Lucifer and the devil.
daemon: demigod	Transliterate *daemon* as demon, dropping its connection with devil.
Sin: Sumerian Moon God	Omit scores of references to sin.
love: sexual passion or desire[13]	Substitute 'love' for 'charity'.

The New Age scheme to use Christian words to veil their 'venom' has not gone unnoticed by cult watchers. Moody's book *Satan's Evangelistic Strategy for This New Age* lists several ways in which Satan works. One method is to "use language to disguise your identity." Others have observed:

> This new theology can be confusing with its apparent new definitions for words that have long established meaning.[14]
> Dave Hunt *Beyond Seduction*

> What the bewildered Christian fails to understand is that the cultist redefines orthodox terminology to suit his own belief system.[15] Bob Larson *Larson's Book of Cults*

> Satan, the real master of the New Age, delights in mysterious code words and phrases because they allow his agents, when questioned, to escape public censure by hiding behind a verbal mirage.[16] Texe Marrs *Dark Secrets of the New Age*

> Christians can be disarmed since these terms are part of their own vocabulary.[17]
> Elliot Miller *A Crash Course on the New Age*

TREND TWO

Western word warriors traveling east on the semantic bridge have matched moves with the mystics. Since Buddha, Krishna, and Lucifer became 'the Christ', 'the Lord', and 'the One', editors riding the new version bandwagon east have changed Jesus and Jehovah to 'the Christ', 'the Lord' and 'the One'—all a response to the call for a common language and the crowning of the Nameless God of occultism. *The Metaphysical Bible Dictionary*, a standard source for New Age beliefs, chides those who refuse to join the new age/new version move to replace personal names with impersonal titles.

> Those who personalize God, Christ, Devil, and localize heaven and hell are the Pharisees of the present time.[18]

In this New Age 'name game', new versions have substituted 'titles' which transport the reader immediately to a list of Satan's latest poison pen names. The rock scene sings of Lord Satan (Venum) who's "a new god" and "a star from the east" (Wang Chung). New Agers refer to Lucifer as "the One," "the Spirit of the Age" and a "divine being." Now new versions point readers to Satan instead of God.

SUMMARY: THE NAME GAME	
KJV/Christianity	**New Versions/New Age**
Lucifer	morning star
Jehovah	Lord
Holy One of Israel	One
Holy Ghost	Spirit
Lord Jesus Christ	Lord
Godhead	divine being

As the following quotes reveal, the 'New' age and 'New' versions are merely resurrecting the serpent worship of history's Gnostics, Egyptians, magicians, and witches.

> In ritual magic there is a doctrine of the Incommunicable Name, the hidden name of the god. It is believed that this god keeps his name secret in order that no one may gain power over him.[19]

> The god of witchcraft's name is kept a secret.[20]

> In Egypt, for example, the concept of the "Concealed Name" was extremely common.[21]

> In Gnostic thought, the concrete is resolved into the abstract. **Personal names** are replaced by terms of philosophy; mythological figures are changed into qualities and attributes and events into cosmic processes. [Hence, the personal name Jehovah becomes the attribute 'Lord'.] In many religions the god represents a **thing** such as Aeolus, as the personification of the wind. [Hence, the personal name Lucifer becomes a thing, 'morning star'.][22]

This book will document in detail hundreds of New Age philosophies which have gained entry into the church via the new versions. Like the pinhole in the ozone which over the last 100 years has stretched into a wide puncture, the slit in the "bottomless pit," which allowed liberalism to leak into the *Revised Version* of 1881, has now become a streaming spout, spreading mysticism out through the *New International Version* and *New American Standard Version.* The new versions give a picture of the widening apostasy. And like a photographic negative, it is a dim view. When held up to the light of God's word, it is clearly discernable that they are pictures of the coming One World Religion. Line by line the face of Jesus Christ and Christianity has been changed—first to a caricature and finally to the face of Antichrist.

When the picture is fully developed, a final edition *'New Revised International Version'* will be the culmination of a progressive plan described in *Dark Secrets of the New Age*. Its author reveals:

> 1. Satan recognizes that a bible is needed to control the masses. The development of a New Age Bible is among his top priorities.

> 2. The New Age has pledged to develop a world Bible [which]. . .will affirm the 'truths' to be found in Hindu,

> Buddhist, Sufi Moslem and other Eastern Mystical religions.
>
> 3. The New Age Bible will be the unholy vessel into which the Antichrist will pour these doctrines of devils. It will incorporate the major doctrines of the [One World] religion.
>
> 4. The devious strategy that seems to be paying off for the New Age is that of revising or updating the Bible to make it more 'meaningful to modern times'. It will not be necessary to stage a direct frontal attack on Christianity. The Bible of the Christians and Jews will surely be revised and 'objectionable passages. . .will be removed.
>
> 5. The church will all be unified in doctrine and ritual. . . Antichrist will seize world political and economic power . . .establish a One World Religion and One World Government.[23]

The pressure to change the bible to conform to this One World Religion is conceded by 'insiders' on new version projects.

> Certain words have gathered theological significance through the years and to change them might be to **change doctrine**. . .Do the changes in meaning come from new evidence or simply **new theology**.[24]
>
> Lewis Foster, NIV and NKJV Committees

> [T]he question of good or bad translation is no longer a linguistic one but a **doctrinal** one.[25]
>
> John Kohlenberger *The N.I.V. Concordance*

The plumb line for heresy and orthodoxy is given by cult expert Bob Larson who says:

> The basic fault of cults is that they demote God, devalue Christ, deify man, deny sin and denigrate scripture.[26]

Those five heresies summarize my findings regarding new versions. This leads me to direct the reader to heed Josh McDowell's warning in *Understanding the Cults*.

> Beware of any group or individual that changes essential doctrine.[27]

Gordon Lewis, Christian apologist and cult expert, notes that the New Age 'word game' "makes the bible endorse what its writers emphatically opposed."[28] The following chart is an overview of the New Age words and doctrines found in new versions. The words are direct quotations from each version. Documentation follows in this book.

Are new versions preparing mankind to receive the Antichrist and "worship the dragon"?

KJV	VERSE	NASB (NIV) et al.
Jesus	Luke 24:36	he
Jesus	Matt. 4:18	He
Jesus	Mark 2:15	He
Jesus	Mark 10:52	Him
The kingdom of God	Matt. 6:33	His kingdom
God	Rev. 21:4	He
God	I Tim. 3:16	He
God	Gal. 1:15	He
God	Matt. 22:32	He
the name of the Lord	Acts 22:16	His name
the spirit	I Cor. 14:2	his spirit
his Father's name written in their foreheads	Rev. 14:1	His name and the name of His Father written on their foreheads (see Rev. 14:11!)
worship God	Phil. 3:3	worship (see Rev. 9, 13, 14, 16)

WHO IS GOD?		
KJV	**NEW VERSIONS**	**NEW AGE/ LUCIFERIANS**
He	The One	The One
The Holy One	The One	The One
The Holy Spirit	The Spirit	The Spirit
Jehovah	The Lord	The Lord
Our Father	The Father	The Father
Lord Jesus Christ	The Christ	The Christ
The Godhead	divine being	divine being
God	a God	a God

WHO IS:		
KJV	**NEW VERSIONS**	**NEW AGE/ LUCIFERIANS**
Lucifer? Satan	OMIT	a God called the Virgin
the dragon? Satan	OMIT	a God called the Virgin
the Force? Satan	OMIT	a God called the Virgin
Mary? a virgin	the Virgin	a Goddess called the Virgin
Diana? devil	OMIT	a Goddess called the Virgin
devils? devil	demons	demons (Gods and Goddess)
Satan? devil	OMIT	Jehovah
WHO IS THE MORNING STAR?		
KJV	**NEW VERSIONS**	**NEW AGE**
Jesus Christ	Satan	Satan

ANTICHRIST OR CHRIST?		
KJV	**NEW VERSIONS**	**NEW AGE/ LAST DAYS**
Jesus	he	he
Christ	him	him
Jesus Christ	the Christ	the Christ
King of saints	King of nations	King of nations
God	he; the Great Power	he; the Great Power
The kingdom of God	His kingdom	His kingdom
The name of the Lord	His name	His name

ONE WORLD RELIGION OR CHRISTIANITY:		
KJV	**NEW VERSIONS**	**NEW AGE/ LAST DAYS**
his Father's name in their foreheads	his name. . .in their foreheads	his name. . .in their foreheads
[those who worship an image are] too superstitious	[those who worship an image are] very religious	[those who worship an image are] very religious
the image of him	the image of the One	the image of the One
visions he has not seen	visions he has seen	visions he has seen
a new earth	a new age	a new age
end of the world	end of the age	end of the age
(the enemy) MYSTERY BABYLON	(the enemy) BABYLON	(the enemy) BABYLON
fruit of the Spirit	fruit of the light	fruit of the light
keep under my body	beat my body	beat my body
Pray: Our Father, which art in heaven. . .thy will be done as in heaven so in earth. . .but deliver us from evil.	Father (omit remainder)	Father (omit remainder)

WHO IS JESUS CHRIST?		
KJV	**NEW VERSIONS**	**NEW AGE**
The Lord Jesus Christ	Jesus	Jesus
Jesus Christ	the Christ	the Christ
Jesus	him	him
Christ	he	he
God	he	he
Son of God	Son of man a son of the gods	Son of man a son of the gods
Son	servant	servant
the Son	a Son	a Son
the Saviour	a Savior	a Savior
the way	a way	a way
good master	teacher	teacher
Alpha and Omega	OMIT	OMIT
equal with God	OMIT	OMIT
God	OMIT	OMIT
the creator	OMIT	OMIT
(co-eternal with God)	OMIT	OMIT
virgin born	OMIT	OMIT
rose from the dead	OMIT	OMIT
ascended into heaven	OMIT	OMIT

WHAT IS MAN?		
KJV	**NEW VERSIONS**	**NEW AGE**
ignorant	unaware	unaware
vile	humble	humble
a little lower than the angels	a little lower than God	a little lower than God
OUR ATTITUDE SHOULD BE:		
I abhor myself	my conscience is clear	my conscience is clear

WHY DID CHRIST DIE?		
KJV	**NEW VERSIONS**	**NEW AGE/ LUCIFERIAN**
for us	OMIT	OMIT
FOR WHOM DID CHRIST COME?		
men	men on whom his favor rests	men on whom his favor rests

HOW ARE WE SAVED?		
KJV	**NEW VERSIONS**	**NEW AGE/ HUMANISM**
—	how hard it is	how hard it is
by grace	OMIT	OMIT
through his blood	OMIT	OMIT
the gospel of Christ	a gospel	a gospel
the door	a door	a door
the word	a message	a message
believe	obey	obey
faith	faithfulness	faithfulness
believe in him	believe	believe
Lord, Jesus	OMIT	OMIT
THEN WE ARE:		
saved	are being saved	are being saved
DESTINATION OF THE UNSAVED		
KJV	**NEW VERSIONS**	**NEW AGE/ HUMANISM**
hell	grave	grave
hell	death	death
fire	OMIT	OMIT

CHARACTERISTICS OF THE CHRISTIAN LIFE		
KJV	**NEW VERSION/ NEW CHRISTIANITY**	**NEW AGE/ HUMANISM**
pure	adequate	adequate
Rejoice	proud	proud
righteous	prosperous	prosperous
take up the cross	OMIT	OMIT
[grow] by the word	OMIT	OMIT
give with simplicity	give with generosity	give with generosity
follow	imitate	imitate
not with outward adorning	outward adorning	outward adorning
ATTITUDE TOWARD ENEMIES		
KJV	**NEW VERSIONS**	**HUMANISM**
bless	OMIT (you. . .bastard)	OMIT (you. . .bastard)
do good	OMIT (go to hell)	OMIT (go to hell)
forgive	OMIT (you son of a bitch)	OMIT (you son of a bitch)
'EXPRESSLY' FORBIDDEN		
KJV	**NEW VERSIONS**	**NEW AGE**
murder	OMIT	OMIT
fornication	OMIT (its "natural")	OMIT
whoremongering	OMIT	OMIT
blasphemy	OMIT	OMIT
bear false witness	OMIT	OMIT

GOD'S ATTITUDE TOWARD CHRISTIANS		
KJV	**NEW VERSIONS**	**NEW AGE/ LUCIFERIANS**
servants	slaves	slaves
chastened	punished	punished
humble	humiliate	humiliate

New versions have touched the palate of bible readers giving them a taste of the New Age. Like a cake's ingredients, mysticism is mixed so thoroughly with Christianity that it is not easily discernable, except to those who have tasted the forbidden fruit before. Consequently, New Agers like Shirley MacLaine say, "The bible is very metaphysical." Mystics can now say "[T]he bible confirms New Age views," as *Mystery Mark of the New Age* reveals.[29] New versions have incited a shift in doctrine within some Christian circles that has not gone unnoticed by mystics and occultists. Starhawk, a self-proclaimed witch remarks:

> I am very glad to discover such movement within Christian churches that is sympathetic to the pagan spirit.[30]

Author of *Toward a World Religion for the New Age* has also tasted the forbidden fruit before and points out the origin of Christianity's "changes in teaching."

> [Christianity] demonstrates changes in teaching. . .which are related to the ageless wisdom taught in Egypt. . .early Greek philosophy and in the mystical schools. . .and in most esoteric groups.

Naive Christians pass over the esoteric terminology and philosophy in new versions because, as Moody's *Agony of Deceit* points out:

> [T]hey are unaware that they are repeating the errors of the past. Because they do not understand Greek philosophy or Oriental mysticism, or 19th century theosophy [Luciferianism], they do not know how seriously they have been affected by such thinking.[31]

Caught up or Falling away?

> Let no man deceive you by any means for that day shall not come except there come a falling away first.
> II Thessalonians 2:3

Players drop—captured pawns of the black-hearted chessman who makes his move across checkered bibles. His deadly dart escapes view. But Genesis 3 provides a clue to those who say, "The devil surely could not have infiltrated new versions of THE BIBLE!" Yet, "We are not ignorant of his devices." (II Corinthians 2:11) His point of attack (the words of God), his method (subtlety), and his vehicle (the tree of knowledge [Ph.d]), successfully served as "devices" to snare his prey—so they continue today.

His subtlety today is called a "softening up process" by the author of the *Lucifer Connection*.[32] New Age spokesmen reveal their mandate and their method:

MANDATE:
Change those aspects of religion. . .which delay the full manifestation of planetary unity. . .[33]

The New Group of World Servers "Objectives",
(U.N. Plaza, N.Y.)

METHOD:
The collusion is so **low-key** that no one notices.[34]

The Aquarian Conspiracy

Present religions will begin to **make changes** and **evolve** into. . .the World Religion. . .We need to **synthesize** the major religions with a World Religion for the New Age.[35]

Toward a World Religion for the New Age

[T]he dominant straight society has apparently **not recognized** the pervasiveness of the new consciousness culture. Perhaps this is just as well as far as polarization between the old culture and the new one has been avoided. If the New Age movement does become a target of alarmed forces. . .it will offer a. . .target very hard to identify.[36]

Donald Keys "Planetary Citizens"

Progressive simplification and unification will. . .have taken place in the religious field.[37]

Most New Agers, however teach that the new will overcome the old by a **gentle process** of ecumenical unity and absorption of the religions into one another. . .The New World Religion will contain all the common elements of all religions.[38]

The Lucifer Connection

> The new spirituality does not reject the earlier patterns of the great universal religions. . .they will not be forced out of existence in the New Age, they will be **absorbed into** the New Age.[39]
>
> If the final planetary synthesis of the Eastern and Western Spiritual traditions is to be realized. . .Eastern mysticism must be **incorporated into** traditional Christianity.[40]
>
> Peter De Cappens, New Age editor

Yet new versions omit all three clues describing Satan's devices.

Method: "creep into" II Tim. 3:6
Means: "by any means" II Cor. 11:3
Moment: "at his will" II Tim. 2:26

The Method: Men and Manuscripts Corrected or Corrupted?

It is natural to perceive certain discrete phenomena, such as apostasy in the next pew or a version that's new, without placing it within a broader scheme, both historically and geographically. Each time the reader turns a page in this book, he will be pulling back the curtain of time, revealing the concealed wires on the marionettes who are setting the stage for the New Age. The unsound doctrines in new versions cannot be examined without realizing that they are only symptoms of a disease that was contracted years ago.

New versions (and the 'new' church they are producing) owe their occult bend to their underlying Greek text, a novelty produced in the 1870's by B.F. Westcott, a London Spiritualist. Secular historians and numerous occult books see him as 'the Father' of the current channeling phenomenon, a major source of the "doctrines of devils" driving the New Age movement.

His British Ghostly Guild became the training grounds for much under-the-table hand holding between his students and London's Madame Helena P. Blavatsky, another Spiritualist and then editor of *Lucifer* magazine. Christian cult watchers aptly call her "the seamstress who cut the pattern for the harlot's new dress."[41] She was to become, as *Los Angeles Times* magazine says, "godmother of the New Age movement."[42] The editor of the *New Age Dictionary*

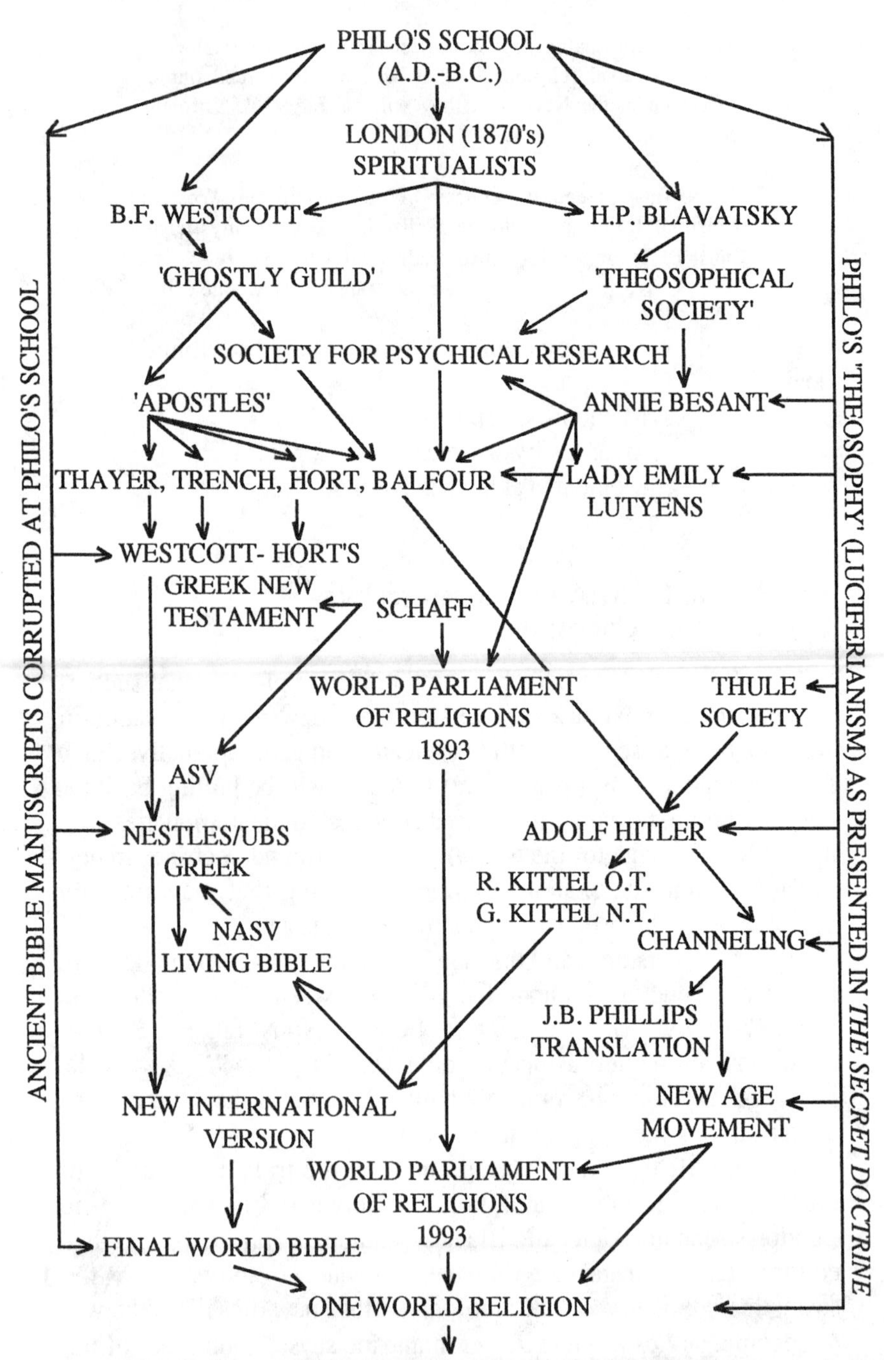

'and they worshipped the dragon' Revelation 13

calls her the "midwife of the New Age."[43] New Age leader Vera Alder says:

> H.P. Blavatsky was one of the foremost to resurrect the ancient Mystery Teachings and interpret them for our time in a set of books which have become the Bibles, as it were, of the modern metaphysician or occultist.[44]

Since both Westcott and Blavatsky, through their occult involvement, signed up for service in Satan's Church, he has used them as his two arms. She has offered her writing arm to usher in the friends of the Bride of Satan, the whore (Revelation 17). Her writing has wrapped up society's non-conformists (Hitler, Sirhan Sirhan) in her wizard's cape, capturing them for Satan's kingdom. Westcott, working as a 'priest' in the Church of England, will wed Satan to the harlot church. With his sheep's clothing, he has pulled the wool over the eyes of churched-conformists.

The Encyclopedia of the Unexplained says Blavatsky exhumed her Luciferian doctrines from Philo's School in Alexandria, Egypt.[45] This same school also produced manuscripts of the Old and New Testament—altered to conform to their esoteric teachings. The graveyard haunts of Westcott's 'Ghostly Guild' brought up these very manuscripts and used them to alter the traditional Old and New Testaments. New versions mimic the New Age because they both made their debut on the same stage—at Philo's School.

As spiritualists (necromancers) both Westcott and Blavatsky recognized the esoteric tone given New Testament manuscripts produced within hearing distance of Philo's school. Both believe these were 'corrected' not corrupted versions. Blavatsky's books (with subtitles like 'Holy Satan') join Westcott in sounding the death bell for the KJV—the real bible. She blows Westcott's 'spiritualist trumpet' saying:

> That which for nearly 1500 years was imposed on Christendom as a book, of which every word was written under the direct supervision of the Holy Ghost; of which not one syllable nor a comma could be changed without sacrilege, is now being retranslated, revised and **corrected** and **clipped** of whole verses, in some cases of entire chapters.[46]

> [The] London Committee for the Revision of the Bible. . .show[s] the origin of the bible to be occultism. . .and pagan.[47]

Westcott's then "shocking" Greek New Testament slowly infiltrated the liberal seminaries during the first half of this century and today floods the bookstores under 'New' version covers. James Webb, author of *The Occult Underground* and *The Occult Establishment* is among a string of historians tying Westcott's work to the "Occult Revival." He observes:

> It is to restate a truism that what is avant-garde for one generation is taught to the next in the schools [seminaries]. By the third generation, it has become an accepted part of the unperceived assumptions on which everyday life is based.[48]

Even the *NIV Concordance* editor concedes that this century's versions are a deviation from the text type used, as Blavatsky said, "for nearly 1500 years." He acknowledges, "A century ago—even a half century ago. . .nothing seriously threatened these standards."[49] Noting their deviation from the traditional text, one NIV editor yields, "Certain verses that. . .have traditionally been thought to be part of Holy Writ, were in the judgement of the translators, not present. . ."[50] Wheaton professor, Dr. Gordon Fee, comments on the "clipped" character of all versions except the Authorized Version (KJV).

> The contemporary translations as a group have one thing in common: they tend to agree against the KJV. . .in omitting hundreds of words, phrases and verses.[51]

The NIV has 64,098 less words than the KJV. Manuscripts and Greek New Testaments produced according to the "revise" rule of Philo's school are markedly different from the great mass of N.T. manuscripts (over 5000) used to produce the KJV. J.B. Phillips, *another* Spiritualist *and* new version editor, acknowledges this "vast" difference in his forward to the *NASB Greek-English Interlinear New Testament.*

> You will see how and why a modern translation produces vastly different verbal results.[52]

The *vast* difference between this Greek text type and most, mirrors the vast difference between paganism and Christianity. Yet they have become, in Webb's words, ". . .an accepted part" of liberal N.T. scholarship. The mandate to infiltrate has been followed so fully that these altered manuscripts are referred to today as *"the originals"* by Luciferians *and* liberal N.T. scholars.

LUCIFERIAN	NIV EDITORS
"This 'Pagan' view was shown in the original[s]. . .the English translation [KJV] being worthless."[53]	The KJV is "misleading. . .erroneous. . .corrupted by errors."[54]
"The King James Version; as it is translated, has no resemblance whatever to the originals."[55] Blavatsky	"The King James Version. . . changed the originals. . . "[56] Palmer
	"[T]he Textus Receptus contains so many significant departures from the original manuscripts of the various New Testament books that it cannot be relied on as a basis for translation."[57] Youngblood

What spurs them to concur? The uncanny parallel between what these 'New' editors brew and Lucifer's 'New' Age view, will be uncovered herein through scores of quotes—matched as if hatched by the same name. This job, says Bob Larson, is Satan's:

> There is a striking harmony in the way all false belief systems view truth. This is to be expected because all ideologies which are contrary to scripture originated from the same source—Satan.[58]

Discoveries into Darkness

The "vast" shift in the contents of the New Testament, moved by Westcott's graveyard manuscript 'discoveries', marks the beginning of a series of 'digs', around the tree of knowledge and down to the bottomless pit. "Science and recent discoveries" will be utilized to 'authorize' Satan's diabolical enterprise—the New World Bible. New Age leader, Vera Alder, forecasts:

> [F]rom all archaeological archives. . .and the illuminations of modern science and discovery. . .the Research Panel would develop a new 'Bible' of a World Religion which will be the basis of future education.[59]

To equalize the pagan and 'Christian' elements in this synthesized religion, two groups of documents arise. *Toward a World Religion for a New Age* reveals:

> In this century religious data previously unavailable has been found. Among these are[:]
>
> [1] the Dead Sea Scrolls
>
> [2] Christian writings deleted from the bible during the 4th century
>
> Probably much of this knowledge could be advantageously used in synthesizing the major religions with a World Religion for the New Age.[60]

Item [1], the scrolls from the Dead Sea, are merely shed debris—the skins of the python who crushed the souls of this ancient sect. Their burial served as protection, lest this occult infection spread, leaving others 'spiritually' dead. Unearthed from the sand at Satan's hand, they are being given life by much media hype. These scrolls will squeeze souls into submission to the serpent's lies—all while promising, "to make one wise."

Item [2], the "Christian writings deleted from the bible during the 4th century," are *the very manuscripts now* being used to "correct," as Luciferians say, the New Testament and create new versions. These manuscript types (*Aleph*, B, D, papyrus 75, 45 et al.)

were rejected by a growing and discerning Christian body—almost immediately after their creation by the 'friends of Philo'. "Deleted" also were their extra books such as *The Shepherd of Hermas* and *The Epistle of Barnabas*. Both paint a scene which will be seen when Satan's Church of Chapter Thirteen convenes (see chapter 40). New Agers, like Davis, also recognize the esoteric qualities of these "deleted" manuscripts. Their ability to synthesize pagan and Christian ideas drew the liberal churchmen who circled the table of the 'new' Greek and 'new' version committees. Inch by inch, Davis' "deleted" manuscripts have become, in the words of editor Bruce Metzger, the "discovered" manuscripts.[61] *Dark Secrets of the New Age* cautions concerning this revision strategy:

> The bible that is developed by the antichrist will be applauded as fully in keeping with the high tech age. Further, New Age citizens will be told that New Age scriptures can be changed when ever new scientific discoveries suggest revisions are needed.[62]

The New Order "shall deceive MANY."

Alder's bait, the scrolls and "deleted writings,"will be used to re-'educate' members of Satan's emerging global state. On her slate for its magistrate is the New Age candidate—antichrist. She continues:

> Who will this superman be? There is surely only One who would be suitable—the Christ. . .he will build an integrated **new world order**. Orthodoxy as we now know it would have ceased to exist.[63]

The two pallbearers who carried orthodoxy out of the church also christened the "new order's" name. First "Blavatsky. . .broke the ground for the creation of the new order," then Westcott seeded the soil with tares and tales of a "progressive" "new order."[64] These weeds have gradually gained ground and today grip Presidential policy and public opinion. They are also choking the church, cautions Constance Cumby. Gleaning from the plan in Rifkin's *Emerging Order*, she concludes:

> The evangelical church would be the primary instrument to bring the new world order to birth.[65]

The confiscation of the bible by the antichristian world system has begun. Zondervan, the world's largest publisher of the NIV, has just been taken over by the secular publisher Harper Collins. The American Bible Society now titles and seals bibles for worldwide distribution with the insignia—*Good News for a New Age* or 'God's Word for a New Age'.(see Plate) At this moment even the evangelical churches glue the mortar which will bind the new order. The NIV clears the way, in Hebrews 9:10, then the NEB spears the prey.

> [T]he old order is gone and a new order has already begun.
> II Corinthians 5:17 (NEB)

In church after church, on channel after channel, new versions are becoming sanctified by custom. "Everybody's doing it," quip Christians in spiritual adolescence. Basing the decision of what bible to use on church 'customs' or personal experience is a move to the New Age mind set. Margot Adler, a modern witch, says:

> Most Neo-pagan religions. . .are based on. . .custom and experience rather than the written word.[66]

Concordance editor, John Kohlenberger, points out the three most common reasons for selecting a version of the bible: 1) friends and fellowship, 2)finances, 3) and finally, research.

> Those with a theological investment in a given translation can make the choice a matter of faith and fellowship. And those with an economic investment in a given translation can help muddy the waters with half-truths and overstatements. Unless you simply want to accept someone else's opinion second hand, you must do a bit of research.[67]

Promoting new versions, magazine ads and media preachers together present a fog accompanied by a bull horn. The blare fills the air allowing feelings (not facts) to fan Philo's ancient ash heaps and their heresies. Scholar Dean John Burgon observes:

GOD'S WORD
FOR A NEW AGE

> The Sacred Text has none to fear so much as those who feel rather than think.[68]

A world of shared misconceptions often surrounds both the 'man on the street' and the man of letters. True researchers know that the popular press serves poorly as a research tool; primary sources must be examined. The popular reference work *Words About the Word,* published by Zondervan, will serve as an example. It asserts that 1) The "doctrinal problems" in the KJV are discussed in *The English Bible from KJV to NIV.* 2) The orthodoxy of new version editors, regarding the inerrancy of scriptures, can be seen in such autobiographies as J.B. Phillips'. 3) A comparison of verses indicates that the new versions exceed the KJV in references to the deity of Christ. Upon checking the books and verses given, which few do, it is discovered that *no* "doctrinal problems" are listed, Phillips *flatly denies* a belief in the inerrancy of scriptures, and the verses cited are *not* representative of the deity issue at all. Yet, for most, the false *impressions* remain.

This book and others, like linguistic expert Dr. Wilbur Pickering's recent *The Identity of the New Testament Text,* break through this maze of multiplied misinformation. His documentation proves the highly misleading nature of the Greek text and critical apparatus underlying new versions. He set the stage for this, the final page, closing 'the cover' on new versions.

The Old Testament priests were given the responsibility of preserving the scriptures which were written by the prophets (Deuteronomy 31). When Christ died, the veil of the temple was torn; the priesthood then passed to *all* who come to God through faith in Jesus Christ (I Peter 2:16). As priests, believers now are charged with safeguarding the scriptures written by the apostles. Lewis Foster, a member of both the NIV and NKJV Committees reflects the elitism among liberal scholars who say the issue is "beyond the sight of the average reader."[69] It is the purpose of this book to bring the subject *within* their sight, re-arming them to "fight the good fight."

> Prove all things: hold fast that which is good.
> I Thessalonians 5:21

The Message

PART ONE

They Worshipped The Dragon

TWO

Praying to a New God: Lucifer, the god of this world

II Cor. 4:4

praying to a new god

You better start praying
to a new god.
they're saying the devil's
got a new job.
it's another second coming
like it or not
you better start
praying to a new god.
start praying,
what are you afraid of
there's a big world. . .
they've all come to see
a star from the east.
is he man or beast?
decide
feel like I'm crucified,
still I'm not satisfied
start praying to a new god
praying on the freeway, airwaves
. . .at the back door
on the dance floor,
start praying to a new god.[1]

This handful of lines from the huge hit recording hammers away at hearers in the 90's. They crow, ". . .the devil's got a new job," as a new god, but students of the word of God recognize his timeworn attempt.

> They sacrificed unto devils, not to God; to gods whom they knew not, to **new gods**. . .And when the Lord saw it, he abhorred them, because of the provoking of his sons, and of his daughters. . .They chose new gods; then was war in the gates. Deuteronomy 32:17,19; Judges 5:8

Pounding to penetrate this generation, Satanic lyrics have drifted from the 'metalica' to the 'middling' music market. This shift from the counter-culture to the common place has likewise occurred as the philosophies of the "Occult Underground," as James Webb called it, have been transported by fellow travelers into the recent bible versions.[2] Their "star from the east" is reverberating on the pages of all of the new bible versions; the repercussions thunder as we witness the "falling away."

The Doctrine of Satan: The Name Game

> "How art thou fallen from heaven, O Lucifer, son of the morning!" how art thou cut down to the ground, which didst weaken the nations!
> For thou hast said in thine heart, I will ascend into heaven, I will exalt my throne above the stars of God: I will sit also upon the mount of the congregation, in the sides of the north: I will ascend above the heights of the clouds; I will be like the most High.
> Yet thou shalt be brought down to hell, to the sides of the pit. They that see thee shall narrowly look upon thee, and consider thee saying, Is this the man that made the earth to tremble, that did shake kingdoms, that made the world as a wilderness, and destroyed the cities thereof; that opened not the house of his prisoners?" Isaiah 14:12-17

In Lucifer's boastful cry, "I will be like the most High," discontentment weighs on every word; the anointed cherub wanted an identity change. The new persona he wished to pursue included the response of worship from whomsoever would. This is seen in his appeal to Jesus Christ to "fall down and worship me," recorded in Matthew 4:9. Unfortunately his ambition will be fulfilled, as seen in Revelation 13:4, "and they worshipped the dragon." Revelation 12:9 identifies, "the great dragon [as]. . .that old serpent, called the Devil, and Satan."

The public relations campaign required to transform the public's image of Satan, from his true evil character to one which would inspire worship, is monumental. It pivots upon the transformation of his identity.

Historically, Isaiah 14 has been used as *the* singular biography of Lucifer, shedding unique light upon the "mystery of iniquity." In verse twelve Lucifer is in heaven; in verse fifteen Satan is in hell. The intervening verses expose his pride in the five "I wills," each a rung in his descent into hell. ("I will," is also the official motto of the U.S. city sporting zip code 60606. In 1966, this same city hatched the NIV.)

These passages must be the object of Satan's rancor and consequently his opposition. They reveal his arrogance (verse 13 and 14), his responsibility for much of the world's misery (verse 17) and his end (verse 15 and 16). He is indicted as soundly in Ezekiel 28, but is unnamed and designated "the anointed cherub."

His ambition is to be "like the most High" and these verses sweep away that illusion, presenting him transparently. To hold that he would not grapple with the word "Lucifer" until it was securely removed from such an unflattering context and replanted into a "like-the-most-High" context, is naivete. *Fait accompli*, the feat is accomplished in all new bible versions; the KJV remains uncorrupted.

NIV	NASB	KJV
How you have fallen from heaven O **morning star**, son of the dawn. . .but you are brought down to the grave.	How you have fallen from heaven O **star of the morning**, son of the dawn. . .you will be thrust down to Sheol.	How art thou fallen from heaven, O **Lucifer**, son of the morning!. . . Yet thou shalt be brought down to **hell**.(Is. 14:12,15)

Twentieth century versions have removed the name Lucifer, thereby eliminating the *only* reference to him in the entire bible. The word Lucifer then falls to the realm of the poets and writers of mythology and ceases to be an identifiable character of biblical origin. He is thereby divorced from the truth concerning himself. In John 8:44 Jesus said, "the devil. . .is a liar, and the father of it." He can now have whatever characteristics he desires.

"Morning Star" Not In Hebrew

The change in new versions does not spring from the original Hebrew language, but from the 'theology' of the new version editors. The NIV's wording parallels *exactly* the view expressed by NIV committee member R. Laird Harris. He asserts that Isaiah 14 is not about "Lucifer" and his descent to "hell," but about a king from Babylon and his interment in the "grave."[3]

The NIV's version of Harris' view is one link in a chain tied to New Age Luciferian H.P. Blavatsky, who like the new versions and new theologians, denies the fall of Lucifer. Blavatsky writes the script for the 20th century scribes saying:

> Now there are many passages in the Bible that prove on their face, exoterically, that this belief was at one time universal; and the two most convincing are Ezekiel 28 and Isaiah 14. Christian theologians are welcome to interpret the great War before Creation. . .if they so choose, but the absurdity of the idea is too apparent.[4]

An examination of the original Hebrew will dispel any illusion that "morning star" is an acceptable substitute for the word "Lucifer." The Hebrew is "*helel, ben shachar*," which is accurately translated, "Lucifer, son of the morning." The NIV and NASB give an English translation *as if* the Hebrew said, "*shachar kokab, ben shachar*" or morning star, son of the morning (or dawn). Yet the word for star (*kokab*) appears nowhere in the text. Also 'morning' appears only once, as the KJV shows, not twice as new versions indicate. The word *kokab* is translated as 'star' dozens of other times by NIV translators; morning or dawn is likewise used hundreds of times. New version editors know *boqer kokab* is 'morning star' since it is used in Job 38:7. If God had intended to communicate 'morning star', he could have repeated it here. The word he chose, *helel*, appears nowhere else in the Old Testament, just as "Lucifer" appears nowhere else.

Why "Morning Star"?

The matching of Lucifer with the morning star rises not from the Hebrew bible but from classical mythology, a fount of bitter water not intended by God as our "fountain of living waters" (Jeremiah 17:13). Reference works concede that the switch is based on ". . .classical mythology for the planet Venus."[5] Just because Satan has convinced the heathen world to connect him with Venus, the morning star, is no basis for the repetition of that "myth" by Christian scholars. But II Timothy 4:3, 4 says the time for myths has come.

> For the time will come when they will not endure sound doctrine; but after their own lusts shall they heap to themselves teachers, having itching ears; And they shall turn away their ears from the truth, and shall be turned unto fables. [*muthos*: from which we get the word 'myths']

Who is the "Morning Star"?

The ultimate blasphemy occurs when the "morning star" takes "Lucifer's" place in Isaiah 14. Jesus Christ is the "morning star" and is identified as such in Revelation 22:16, 2:28 and II Peter 1:19. With this slight of hand switch, Satan not only slyly slips out of the picture but lives up to his name "the accuser" (Revelation 12:10) by attempting to make Jesus Christ the subject of the diatribe in Isaiah 14.

The NASB compounds its role as malefactor by placing the reference, II Peter 1:19, next to Isaiah 14:12 to solidify the notion that the passage refers to Jesus Christ rather than Lucifer.[6] In using this reference the NASB becomes the willing marionette, costumed in sheep's clothing, of ravenous wolves like New Age Rosicrucian leader R. Swineburn Clymer. His occult treatise concurs with the new versions' perversions regarding the daystar. He concludes,

> In this one short sentence is stated most clearly one of the greatest occult truths. [7]

Lucifer's Spar To Be "The Morning Star"

With an eye to be ". . .like the most High" (Isaiah 14), Lucifer has tried to infer that he is the "Morning Star." Spanning the gamut from the compendium on black magic, *The Secret Teachings of All Ages* by Manly P. Hall, to the increasingly popular *New International Version* of the bible, the "Morning Star" is used as a synonym for Lucifer. Hall comments:

> The pentagram is used extensively in black magic. . .it signifies the fall of the Morning Star.[8]

Blavatsky echoes, "[T]he pentagram. . .is the Morning Star."[9] In the *Theosophical Glossary*, used as a major resource of dogma by the New Age we read:

> [T]he Christian savior is made to say of himself in Revelation XVI:22, [sic] I am the bright morning star or Lucifer.
>
> The Christians. . .without suspecting the real meaning. . . greeted the Morning Star, Venus, Lucifer. The Trinity. . . was in truth composed of the Sun (the Father). . .Venus (the Holy Ghost), . . . and Lucifer, as Christ, the bright and morning star. The Verbum (the Word) and Lucifer are one. . .[10]

One hundred years ago, Blavatsky's Theosophical Society promoted Krishnamurti, a young Hindu, as "the star from the east" and "the second coming" of Christ. Today the "prince of the power of the air" propagandizes to a new generation through the radio air waves that "a new god. . .is a star from the east. . .another second coming." The sounds have reached the United Nations Plaza where Lucis Trust re-echoes the 'new version' of the facts.

> Lucifer as here used means. . .the morning star and has no connection whatsoever with Satan. . .[11]

Prior to the "falling away" and apostasy of this current generation of scholars, there was a general consensus that Christ alone was the day star. The old *Commentary: Critical and Explanatory of the Old Testament* by Robert Jamieson foretold the current name game.

> Daystar: a title truly belonging to Christ and hereafter to be assumed by antichrist.

Likewise timeworn (1913) *The Pulpit Commentary: Isaiah* by H.D.M. Spence states:

> [T]he title daystar is truly Christ's but will be confiscated by the antichrist of whom Babylon is a type and mystical Babylon is a forerunner. And Satan will assume it, who is the spirit that energizes the heathen world power Babylon, that now energizes the apostate church and shall at last energize the secular antichrist. . .and his champion the false prophet.

Stages Of Initiation

The first step in Satan's public relations campaign was to remove his name from the indictment in Isaiah 14, which is the only historical non-fictional documentation of his true nature. Evidently it was much easier to excise the one word "Lucifer," than to retain it and replace the remaining verses of chapter 14 with the compliments he has currently deceived New Age leaders into penning.

New Age and esoteric literature is replete with references to levels of initiation as a part of their theory of the evolution of consciousness. Overheard on one of my infrequent research visits to the local New Age bookstore was the comment by the owner to a customer selecting a book, "I don't know if you are ready for that; you'd better start with something that doesn't shock a beginner."

Expectedly, there are a number of different levels of esoteric understanding among New Agers regarding the identity of Lucifer and Satan.

The following five steps represent Satan's progressive and gradual image-transforming campaign.

STEP ONE

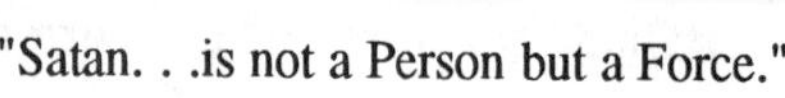

The Denial of the Existence of Satan.

"Satan. . .is not a Person but a Force."
Pike, *Morals and Dogma*

"The Devil is a metaphysical abstraction."
"There have never been any Devils or disobedient angels."
Blavatsky, *Isis Unveiled, The Secret Doctrine*

"According to the New Age doctrine. . .Satan is a mere collective thought form." Carr, *Lucifer Connection*

"[T]he devil [is] the flesh and its desires."
Clymer, *The Science of the Soul*

"Devil: the mass of thoughts. . .that fight against the truth." Filmore, *Metaphysical Bible Dictionary*

Agreeing with these esoterics are the editors of the 'New' Greek New Testament from which all new versions are translated. Reflecting "an age when the personality of Satan is freely called in question," both Westcott and Hort assert that the devil is not a person but a general "power of evil."[12]

STEP TWO

The Assertion that Lucifer and the Devil are Separate and Distinct Entities

One Luciferian confesses:

> It must be recognized that he takes mighty precautions against being recognized as the Prince of Darkness.[13]

As a part of his identity crisis Satan has historically hidden behind the name and identity facades of the heathen pantheon. Among the list of thousands of names he has used are the Hindu Kali and Shiva, as well as the Greek Hermes and Roman Hermas, Heosphorus, Phosphorus and Pan. The apostle Paul peeks behind this pagan parade observing, "[T]hat which is offered in sacrifice to idols. . .they sacrifice to devils" I Corinthians 10:19-20.

Ancient writings such as the *Book of the Secrets of Enoch* and the essays of Pythagoras made a distinction between Lucifer and Satan which migrated into the writings of New Age godmother H.P. Blavatsky. The current adoption of her belief that "Lucifer has never been the name of the Devil" has been noted by New Age observers.[14]

> Why then is the world still confused about the Luciferic roots of the New Age. In part this comes about as a result of the New Ager's absurd contention that though Lucifer is lord, he is not Satan. Satan is said to be a figment of the Christian imagination. Lucifer is not Satan. Lucifer is a good angel.[15]
>
> Marrs, *Dark Secrets of the New Age*

> The Lucifer of the New Age is not the Lucifer of the bible. Lucifer is thus misidentified and given a positive image in the New Age. . .New Agers have divorced Satan and Lucifer. Many of them believe that Satan is a myth invented by the church in the Middle Ages.[16]
>
> Carr, *The Lucifer Connection*

The following definitions from two patently New Age dictionaries expose this movement's blatant adoption of Step 2.

> *Metaphysical Bible Dictionary:* day-star (Lucifer). . .The passage in Isaiah regarding the day-star or Lucifer. . .is supposed to be Satan. . .this is a mistake; the text has no such inference. . .[I]n II Peter 1:19 day-star is symbolic of the Christ lights springing up in individual consciousness.[17]

> *The Dictionary of Angels:* Lucifer ('light giver') erroneously equated with the fallen angel [Satan] due to a misreading of Isaiah 14:12. . .The name Lucifer was applied by St. Jerome and other Church Fathers. Milton . . .Vondel. . .Blake. . .and Meredith [helped create his wrong identity]. Actually Lucifer. . .is the brightest angel, even the Child of Light.[18]

Step 2 has seized some seemingly traditional groups. Albert Pike issued the following instructions to the Masons.

> Yes, Lucifer is God. . .The doctrine of Satanism is a heresy; and the true and pure philosophic religion is the belief in Lucifer. . .you may repeat it to the Brethren of the 32nd, 31st, and 30th degrees: The Masonic religion should be. . .maintained in the purity of the Luciferian doctrine.[19]

Perhaps the most shocking aspect of Step 2, the alleged distinction between Lucifer and Satan, is its appearance in the majority of 'Christian' reference books. We would expect as much from New Age sources, but pseudo-scholarship and what appears to be much copying from each other, has Christians parroting the New Age line.

Lucifer has been removed from most bible dictionaries and commentaries. If he appears at all, the reference quickly assures the reader that Lucifer is not Satan. The accompanying samples will stun the reader, showing the theological effect of the removal of Lucifer's name from new versions. They are evidence for Carr's claim that "New Age ideas infiltrate the church and appear under a Christian impremature."[20] They remind readers of Kurt Koch's warning in *The Devil's Alphabet:* "He operates through the latest scientific methods."[21]

The following reference books were *not* found in liberal or neo-orthodox bookstores but in essentially fundamental-type stores or church libraries. They were the only books offered, for the most part, in the reference section.

REFERENCE BOOK	AUTHOR	Citation under heading "Lucifer" or Isaiah 14	
International Bible Commentary	F.F. Bruce (editor)	"[I]t is ***inappropriate*** to the passage to think Satan is meant."	p. 732

REFERENCE BOOK	AUTHOR	Citation under heading "Lucifer" or Isaiah 14	
Harper's Bible Dictionary		"[T]he connection was made ***erroneously*** between Lucifer and Satan."	p. 582
Eerdman's The Bible Dictionary		Lucifer is **not** included in this dictionary. They refer the reader from 'Lucifer' to 'daystar' (Jesus Christ) saying, "another name for morning star. II Peter 1:19, Revelation 2:28. Some commentators link the idea with an ancient ***myth*** about the banishment of a *divine* person."	p. 267
Smith Bible Dictionary		"[F]rom Jerome downward it referred to Satan."	
The New Standard Bible Dictionary	Funk and Wagnel, Editor, M. W. Jacobs	Lucifer is **not** included. They refer the reader to 'daystar' which states, "[Applied to Lucifer **and** Christ.]"	p. 173
Dictionary of the Bible	McMillian Pub., (ed. McKenzie)	Lucifer is **not** included.	
Who's Who in the Old Testament	Joan Connery	Lucifer is **not** included.	

REFERENCE BOOK	AUTHOR	Citation under heading "Lucifer" or Isaiah 14	
Interpreter's One Volume Commentary on the Bible		"The theme of the downfall is vividly elongated in a ***mythological*** picture. The tyrant is likened to the Day Star." [blasphemy!]	p. 341
Dictionary of Proper Names and Places in the Bible		"[S]cholars argue that Isaiah 14:12 should be interpreted as a reference to a Canaanite **myth**."	p. 657
Hurlbert's Handy Bible Encyclopedia	Jesse Hurlbert	"[T]he word has **nothing** to do with the devil."	p. 207
Interpreter's Bible Dictionary		"[T]he meaning of what the tyrant has done is set forth in the ***myth*** of Helal. . .another *mythological* element is the mount of assembly."	p. 261
Twentieth Century Bible Commentary	Davies Richards	Lucifer is **not** included.	

The trend to ignore the KJV's Lucifer/Satan connection is shared by Luciferians and new version editors. Both Blavatsky and NIV, NKJV committee member Lewis Foster steer readers away from the bible and toward sources such as these commentaries.

LUCIFERIAN	NEW VERSION EDITOR
"The English [KJV] translation of the bible can never be relied upon."[22]	"[I]t demands the aid of a good commentary to study the meaning of the passage."[23]

Constance Cumby has observed the fruit of this burgeoning trend in the Christian community.

> "Interestingly, as many New Age groups work to extol Lucifer's name, there has been a parallel movement within Christianity to clear his name and disassociate him from any Satanic identity."24

Lest his character be maimed, Satan stole his *new* name—another move in his game.

NASB, NIV et al		KJV
OMIT	Luke 4:8	Get thee behind me, Satan

Challenging those who profess the changes in new versions do not affect any major doctrines, Herbert Lockyer's classic *All the Doctrines of the Bible* calls Isaiah 14, "The biography of the devil [where]. . .Lucifer. . .becomes Satan." He observes the current dilemma:

> How shocked all true. . .believers. . .were to read that Dr. Ramsey, when Archbishop of Cambridge, answered Cambridge undergraduates' question about Satan, he said, 'I do not draw from the bible the inference that there is an individual monarch of evil.' One wonders from what kind of Bible the genial Archbishop reads. It must be one from which all references to a personal devil. . .have been expurgated. [T]he Archbishop of Canterbury, ecclesiastical head of the Church of England cannot find the devil in his bible.25

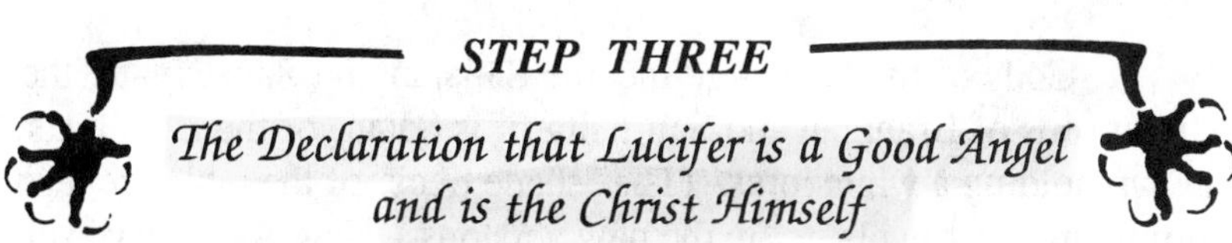

STEP THREE

The Declaration that Lucifer is a Good Angel and is the Christ Himself

Garnishing his name with adulation is the next step. Higher levels of initiation embrace this tenet which seems to be held by a quickly growing circle of occult elitists. This slippery descent into the "depths of Satan" begins with buttery blandishments by New Age high priestess H.P. Blavatsky.

> Lucifer represents. . .Life. . .Thought. . .Progress. . . Civilization. . .Liberty. . .Independence. . .Lucifer is the Logos. . .the Serpent, the Savior.[26]

David Spangler, contributing editor of *New Age Journal* assents:

> Lucifer. . .is an angel of God's love. . .the angel of man's inner evolution. . .[He] prepares man in all ways for the experience of Christhood. Christ is the same force as Lucifer.[27]

Vaulting themselves into unparalleled profanity New Agers like Benjamin Creme address Lucifer as, "the sacrificial lamb."[28] Channeller J.Z. Knight transmits, "[I]n Lucifer lies divinity."[29] Alice Bailey concurs, "Lucifer is the Ruler of Humanity."[30]

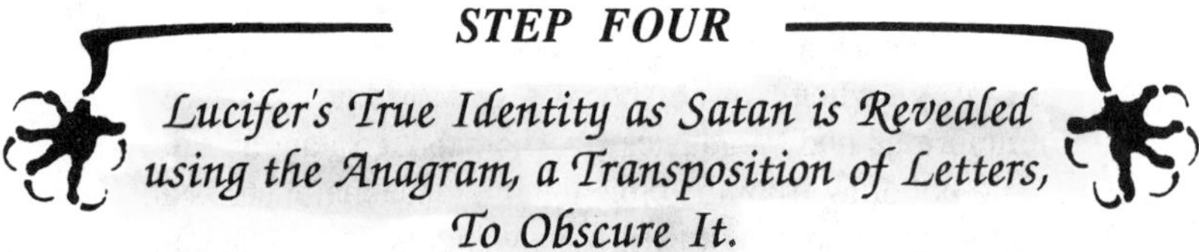

'Blinds', as esoterics call them, include scrambling the letters of a name to hide the true meaning of a word from the uninitiated. They confide:

> The name isn't important. It is the letters.[31]

Gods of the New Age include Sanatan and Sanatsiyata, the Hindu sons of Brahman and San-tisita (it is Satan) of the Buddhists, shown holding a white lotus. (The "shade trees" of the bible are also turning into "lotus plants" in the new versions.) New Agers say each name is "concealed anagrammatically,"[32] "and are aliases,"[33] and are "an anagram used for Occult purposes."[34] "Satan," "it is Satan," and the like are clearly meant. Constance Cumby reports Sanat Kumara is being touted as "our God" by New Age leaders Benjamin Creme, David Spangler, Church Universal and Triumphant and the California Association of Sananda and Sanat Kumara. (Is Santa, the great usurper of Christ's attention at Christmas, an anagram? "Ole Nick" is listed among the fallen angels or devils in the *Dictionary of Fallen Angels*. Scholars concur that Christ was born in the fall on the 4th day of the feast of tabernacles. December 25 is actually "the feast in honor of the birth of the son of the Babylonian queen of heaven, later called Saturnalia by the heathen Romans."[35])

STEP FIVE

The Bare Facts are Revealed; The Rhetoric is Gone. It is Satan Himself Behind All of the Cosmetic Semantics.

[T]he four previous steps have seen Satan, with the aid of the New Age and not diminished by the new bible versions and commentaries, create a web of subterfuge, each thread designed to obstruct man's path to the truth expressed in Isaiah 14. To speed the cultural transition from Step 1 to Step 5, New Age leaders quote from the book of Jude and conclude, "Paul, Peter, and Jude. . .reverenced Satan."[36] They finally disclose to their 'most advanced' initiates that Isaiah 14 *is* about Lucifer and Luke 10:18 *is* about Satan.

> [O]ne of the most hidden secrets. . .involves the so called fall of Angels. Satan and his rebellious host. . .will thus prove to have. . .become the direct Saviors and Creators of divine man. . . .Thus Satan, once he ceases to be viewed in the superstitious spirit of the church, grows into the grandiose image. . .It is Satan who is the God of our planet and the only God. [The last line sits on a page headed 'Holy Satan.'] Satan [or Lucifer] represents. . .the Centrifugal Energy of the Universe. . .this ever-living symbol of self-sacrifice for the intellectual independence of humanity.[37]

Too Close for Comfort

Those who have embraced Step 5 stand perilously close to the church and the culture as a whole. The previous quotation was not written by the Son of Sam or any of the other counter-culture dementia who are known to follow Satan. It was penned by the celebrated midwife of the twentieth century New Age movement, who assisted the 'doctors' who delivered today's new versions. Her friend, Anna Kingsford, the wife of a clergyman whose church sponsored these new versions, founded a group called "Esoteric Christianity." Her book, *The Perfect Way*, includes an appendix entitled, "The Secret of Satan." Summarizing her views she says:

> Among the Gods is none like unto him. . .Many names hath God given him. . .Stand in awe. . .speak his name with trembling. . .blessed and sanctified is the Angel of Hades, Satan.

It would seem that protrusive worship of Satan would be beyond the conscionable in our culture. One would expect it to be reserved for obscure groups like the Yezidyes of East Turkey. Yet children's games like Skeltor bring such ideas close to home. Just prior to sitting down to write this paragraph, I was drawn to the window by the sounds of a small group of young teenagers. Overheard was a repeated rhyme, ". . .the devil in me, the devil in me." They were all clothed entirely in black, a sight quite ominous in itself. Soon their disappearance into an upstairs room of a neighbor's home was followed by the flash of a light which silhouetted an image flanked by two black candles.

A generation earlier, the full moon accompanied young teenagers to football games on such a night. Questioning Christian students who attend the same high school elicited stories of a girl who writes 'I love Satan' on the walls of the school and another who interrupts classes singing 'I'll kill your baby'. Tragically, Step 5 has impregnated this brood of nestlings; the seeds will incubate until Revelation 13:4 is hatched.

The "devils. . .and hateful bird" of Revelation 18:2 have perched, as well, among the well-feathered nests of our society. Observed during a visit to the home of the granddaughter of one of the nation's most famous and wealthy industrialists was a large collection of very hand-worn Satanic and occult books accompanied by several black candles. Her comment that the volumes had belonged to her famous grandparents was accompanied by her extraordinary interest in discussing all of their fine points. A subsequent visit by her to my home, was abruptly cut short upon her discovery that I was a Christian. It sprung her from her seat without comment and propelled her out of the door, never to be seen by me again. This 'disappearing act' must be hereditary. Her 'father' vanished from Isaiah 14 and Luke 4, as well.

Rich and poor have given Satan the nod as his New Age prods have a new generation, "praying to a new god."

THREE

Your Father, the Devil

John 8:44

Or Our Father Which Art in Heaven

Luke 11:2

Praying to a new god

Praying to a new one,
how is it done?
Leave out the Son.
Then change a few words,
maybe every third,
'til the subject is blurred
and the prayer is transferred?

New Agers invoke "a father" (John 8:44), a Jesus and a spirit (II Corinthians 11:4). But they do not follow the formula prescribed by God of praying to "Our Father," in the name of Jesus Christ through the Holy Spirit. New versions, as well, use formulas of their own, so that prayers take a path to 'the new god's' throne.

Perhaps the most shocking discovery of my research was the admission by the New Age movement and esoteric community that there is, in fact, an occult version of the "Our Father" and that it has found its way into Luke 11:2 in the new versions.

KJV	NIV, NASB, et al.
Our Father **which art in heaven** Hallowed be thy name Thy kingdom come **Thy will be done, as in heaven, so in earth** Give us day by day our daily bread And forgive us our sins; for we also forgive everyone that is indebted to us. And lead us not into temptation; **but deliver us from evil** Luke 11:2-4	Father hallowed be your name your kingdom come Give us each day our daily bread Forgive us our sins for we also forgive everyone who sins against us. And lead us not into temptation

The bold sections on the left indicate the words and sections which have been removed from the prayer in all modern versions, such as the NIV, NASB, *Living Bible,* NRSV, *Good News for Modern Man, New Century Version, The New American Bible,* and *The New Jerusalem Bible.* They are *the* very words which distinguish "Our " Father "in heaven" who "delivers us from evil" from "your father the devil," who is "the god of. . .this present evil world."

New Age Confession

The use of the term 'Father' by occultists and New Agers, when addressing their god, should be no surprise since Satan's goal is to be "like the most High." A close examination of New Age writings reveals their plan to portray their 'preying' wolf in sheep's clothing. Alice Bailey instructs the movement's inner core as follows:

> The general public will regard it as a prayer to God transcendent. They will not recognize Him yet as immanent in his creation.[1] Alice Bailey

Eliphas Levi's *Dogma and Ritual of High Magic* distinguishes between the original "Our Father" and the shortened version used by esoterics and new versions.

> [There is an]. . .occult version of the Paternoster [Latin for 'Our Father']. . .There were originally two ways of doing it. . .one reserved for the . . .initiate. . .the other for the profane.[2]

The heading "The Real Paternoster" blazes across the pages of one of H.P. Blavatsky's books, as does "Holy Satan." She confesses that the Father of the New Age is, as she puts it:

> "Holy Father of Evil, Sainted Satan."[3]

With jaded joy, she boasts that this 'Father's' version has stepped into the new bible versions—cradled by her second century mentor Marcion, then carried to the twentieth century by bible critic B.F. Westcott.

> Finally we may add that modern bible criticism, which unfortunately became active and serious toward the end of the last century, now generally admits that Marcion's text of the only gospel he knew anything about—that of Luke, is far superior and far more correct than that of our present Synoptics. We find in *Supernatural Religion* the following startling sentence: 'We are, therefore, indebted to Marcion for the correct version even of the 'Lord's Prayer'.[4]

New Age Bible Interpretation outlines how Marcion's followers used the shortened Lord's Prayer.

> [E]arly Christians used this prayer in the following manner to attract the beneficent down-pouring of the great celestial Hierarchies.[5]

Marcion, or the "beast," as he was called by second century Christians, describes 'the Father' of these "great celestial hierarchies" in his *Philosophumena, The Revelation of Marcion.* (emphasis mine)

> [F]irst its Father. . .the Kabalistic Ain Suph. . . manifest[ed] itself in the form of the Invisible *One*. The Supreme Tetrad [meaning four] came down unto him. . .in a *female form*. . .the Silence, the Father.[6] [Marcion and Blavatsky's 'Father' uses the title 'One' and appears in a female form, a clue this book will pursue in Chapters 5, 6 and 7.]

New Ager Blavatsky analyzes this flurry of words, this "Father," the female image, and Marcion's theology.

> This is as plain as ancient esoteric secrecy could make it.[7]

> Marcion viewed Jesus neither as King or Messiah. . .[He] maintained the fallaciousness of the idea of an incarnate god.[8]

> [He] taught that Deity had to be viewed under the symbol of four. . .[and] gave out more of the esoteric truth than any other Gnostic.

> This teaching of Marcion was that of the early Kabalists and is *ours*. [the New Age's] This Father alone is the God of spirit. . .To compare him with the subordinate and Sinaitic Deity is an error. Did Jesus ever pronounce the name of Jehovah? Never![9]

Marcion's mischief was recorded by his contemporaries—Christians such as Tertullian, Epiphanius and Irenaeus. The latter said:

> Wherefore also Marcion and his followers have betaken themselves to mutilating the scriptures, not acknowledging some books at all; and curtailing the gospel according to Luke; and the epistles of Paul, they assert that these alone are authentic, which they themselves shortened.[10]

More recently and of equal weight are the comments by Dean John Burgon. Internationally respected for his renowned scholarship, he writes of "heretical depravation" and "scandalously corrupt Greek texts" used by the committee and new versions for their Lord's Prayer.[11]

> Marcion's mutilated recension of S. Luke's gospel. . .the Lord's Prayer. . is exhibited by codices Aleph, A, B, C, D. . .[T]hey are never able to agree among themselves as to any single various reading. . .of 32 (out of 45) words. . .Besides omitting the eleven words which B omits jointly with Aleph, Drs. Westcott and Hort erase from the Book of Life those other 11 words which are omitted by B only. And in this way it comes to pass that the mutilated condition to which the scalpel of Marcion the heretic reduced the Lord's Prayer some 1730 years ago (for the mischief can all be traced back to him) is palmed off on the Church of England. . .as the work of the Holy Ghost![12]

A Deeper Look

An analysis of each of the deleted or retained sections follows to show 'why' and 'how' New Agers use their version of the Lord's Prayer.

"Our"

"Our" must be removed since it is a clear witness against the New Age belief in the 'universal fatherhood' of God. The concept that God is Father to all, without the adoption that occurs at the new birth, is a maxim of the New Age and the soapbox on which many liberal churches pose.

The bible, however, speaks of mankind's distinct division into two camps, described by Jesus to the Pharisees.

> I speak that which I have seen with my Father: and ye do that which ye have seen with your Father. . .If God were your Father, ye would love me. . .Ye are of your father the devil. John 8:38, 42, 44

This disdain for a father which is "ours" alone is repeated throughout the new versions, based upon the "scandalously corrupt" Greek minority texts. The following examples are given.

KJV		NEW VERSIONS
my Father	John 10:29,30,32	**the** Father
my Father	John 14:28	**the** Father
our fathers	Acts 3:25	your fathers
our Lord	Gal. 1:3	**the** Lord
God and **our** Father	I Thess. 1:3	our God and Father
God himself and **our** Father	I Thess. 3:11	our God and Father
God **our** Father	I Thess. 3:13	our God and Father
God **our** Father	2 Thess. 1:2	God **the** Father
God **our** Father	I Tim. 1:2	God **the** Father
our Lord Jesus	Philem. 1:25	**the** Lord Jesus
our Lord Jesus **Christ**	Rev. 22:21	**the** Lord Jesus
(The epistles of Paul use the term 'the' Father after their first chapters distinguish him as 'our' Father.)		

In Ephesians 3:14, the corrupt Greek text also omits the words denoting 'which' Father:

KJV	NASB
I bow my knees unto the Father **of our Lord Jesus Christ**	I bow my knees before the Father.

"Father"

This title is in the new versions since, as the following examples illustrate, it has been used from Babylon to the present to identify Satan, the 'father' of the occult family of religions. Blavatsky reveals, "The initiates alone understood the secret meaning of the term "Fathers."[13]

Ancient

Babylon: Makes multiple references to "the father." (see writings of Eudemus)

Egypt: Reveals the connection between the serpent and the pagan "father" calling forth, "Osiris. . .great favorite of thy father Ra, **Father** of Fathers. . .attached the **serpent** on thy head. . ."

The Egyptian Book of Hermes also speaks of the "Breath of the Father." [A] fiery **dragon** appears to Hermes and says, "I am thy God. I am far older than the concealed deity. I am God the **Father**."

The Egyptian Funeral Rituals found among the hymns of the *Book of the Dead* says, "I have made my soul come and speak with his Father. . ."

India: Brahman is called "Father of men."

Plato: Wrote of his "Father Aetha," "the Fashion and Father of all things."

Rome: Built temples to the god, "Janus, Father of the world," says *Bryant's Mythology*.

Mexico: Yzona, "the Father."

Mithraism: Called its leader Pater Patrum, or "Father of Fathers."

Time of Christ

Simon, the Magician: Preached, "One Father, unknown to all," according to Irenaeus, *Clementine Homilies*, I., xxii, p. 118.

Gnostics: Referred to "Father Ennoea" and "the uncreated Father." Used "Septre of the Father" as a secret password.

Nazarenes: Worshipped "Father Abatur."

Basilideas: Worshipped "the unnamed Father." (See Chapter 28 regarding the new versions' omission of Jehovah.)

Occult Revival

Rudolf Steiner: Wrote an entire book entitled, "The Our Father [Lucifer]."

Eliphas Levi: Calls necromancers to invoke, "Vouchsafe to be present O Father of All. . .Glory be to the father of life." (*Dogma and Ritual of High Magic*)[14]

Madame Blavatsky: Four "Fathers"

1. Satan:
   "**Satan** the Serpent of Genesis. . .the real creator and benefactor, the **Father** of Spiritual Mankind."[15]
   "The Great Serpent Jupiter. . .the Dragon of Life, the Father."[16]
2. The **devils** or fallen angels:
   "[T]he **Fathers**, the lower angels, are all nature spirits."[17]
3. The initiator:
   "During the mysteries. . .the initiator was called Father. Furthermore, the hierophant, the discloser of the Petroma, was called 'Father'."[18]
4. The sun:
   "**Lucifer**, as Christ, the bright and morning star. . .the **Father** is the Sun. . ."[19] [Arthur C. Clark, popular author of *2001 Space Odyssey* and *2010* writes in the latter of a sun, named Lucifer, appearing to bring peace to the earth.]

Alice Bailey: Speaking of the anti-Christ she says, "[H]e is closer to the Father and to the One. . .[H]e had to re-institute the Mysteries of Initiation in such a form that they would prove the basis of a new world religion, [worshipping] The Father, the Lord of the World." "We are all Gods, all the children of the One Father."[20]

R. Swineburn Clymer: Writes, "There are those throughout the world who have been here before and now belong to the Invisible Brotherhood, the Hierarchies of the Illuminated. . .[T]hey have dedicated themselves to the works of the Father."[21]

Charles & Mildred Filmore: Deny an external "Father" yet say, "We have identified ourselves with the Father-Mind."[22]

Current New Agers

Benjamine Creme: Says, "Sanat Kumara. . .is our Father."[23]

David Spangler: Looks forward to "a vast initiatory process [with] life in the Solar Father." (*Conscious Evolution: Personal and Planetary Transformation*)

Meher Baba, Baba Paramahansa: Use the term *Baba*, meaning 'Father' as part of their name. The former is guru of Peter Townshend of the "Who" rock group. The latter is John Denver's 'Father' guru.[24]

Harold Sherman: Authored New Age book, *How to Use the Power of Prayer*. Suggests readers pray, "Great Spirit. . .Dear Father."[25]

World Healing Meditation (prepared by the Planetary Commission): "I and the Father are one and all that the Father has is mine. In truth I am the Christ of God."[26]

Encyclopedia of Occultism and Parapsychology: Suggests New Age necromancers, "[O]pen the bible and wait for the spirit to come saying, 'Vouchsafe to be present, O Father of All, and thou thrice mighty Hermes Conductor of the Dead. . .Glory be to the Father.'"[27]

Why do new version editors use the occult version in Luke11:2? The preceding history noted that both the *Dogma & Ritual of High Magic* and the *Occult Encyclopedia* recommended the use of the term "Father of All" or "All-Father" to necromancers (spiritualists who seek contact with the dead). Followers of Hermes do likewise. Do new versions use the occult version of the Our Father because *the* editor of the 'New' Greek New Testament underlying all new versions was also a spiritualist, who communed with the "All-Father" and founded the 'Hermes Club'?"[28] (See Chapter 30.) Fellow spiritualists recognize their affinity with new versions saying Jehovah is not 'the Father'.

> [T]he bible [new version] has never made any secret of it. Only the text of the Protestant English Bible [KJV] is, as usual, in disagreement with those. . .versions more concordant with truth and fact.[29]

"Which Art In Heaven"

This critical phrase distinguishes the identity of the Father being worshipped because it delimits and defines his dwelling place.

> ". . .heaven; for it is God's throne" Matthew 5:34

> ". . .children of your Father which is in heaven." Matthew 5:45

> "[T]here came a voice from heaven saying. . .Thou art my beloved Son." Mark 1:11

God is in heaven; the 'god of this world' is not. As Jesus reports in Luke 10:18, ". . .I beheld Satan as lightning fall from heaven." "Which art in heaven" has therefore fallen "as lightning" from the pages of the new versions. (Not only in Luke 11 but also in John 3:13 where Christ "who is in heaven" is omitted based on a few Greek manuscripts corrupted by those who agreed with Apolinarius that Christ was not God before the incarnation.)

A God "in heaven" is also not consistent with New Age pantheists who write:

> We should pray the Lord's prayer, 'Our Father is within us in secret, not in heaven.' The kingdom of God and of heaven is within you, says Jesus, not outside.

> [T]he effect of abandoning a logical Pantheism. . .[was] to build a prop for lazy man, a merciful Father, in Heaven.[30]

"Hallowed Be Thy Name"

This phrase is used by the New Age to invoke a spirit, to affirm one's own godhood or perhaps to doxologize one of the 'Fathers' of the New Age. Like the new versions, the *New Age Bible Commentary's* exposition on the use of the Lord's Prayer eliminates the "our" and "which art in heaven," beginning:

> '*Hallowed be thy name*': Invocation of the masculine pole of spirit. Will, through the planet of divinity Neptune, to the Hierarchy Aries, who gave the first initial impulse of motion.[31] [The pitch fork used as a symbol for the astrological sign Neptune and seen accompanying him in drawings is among several elements which some historians have used to associate Neptune and Satan.]

Unity's *Metaphysical Bible Dictionary* tells New Agers to pray, "Father, Hallowed be thy name," just like the new versions.

> In true prayer we. . .turn our attention within to the very center of our being, where the Father dwells. . .In order that the creative law of words [magic] may be fulfilled, we must pray, 'Father, Hallowed be thy name.' Here is recognition of the all-inclusive and completeness of Divine-Mind.[32] [Along with their dismissal of "Our. . . which art in heaven," they then go on to interpret esoterically the remaining verses in Marcion's dehydrated Lord's Prayer.]

"Thy Kingdom Come"

> If **Satan** also be divided against himself, how shall **his kingdom** stand. . .no doubt the **kingdom of God** is come upon you. Luke 11:18-20

The currently popular heavy metal rock group *Kingdom Come* gives venomous voice to the serpent who coils "all the kingdoms of the world" (Luke 4:5,6). His kingdom comes—crushing its prey—invoked by those who choose to be charmed. The *Dogma & Ritual of High Magic* rattles their chant:

> [T]he initiate, carrying his hand to his forehead, said, 'To thee'; then he added, 'belong'; and continued carrying his hand to his breast, 'the kingdom. . .throughout the generating cycles—Tibi sunt Malchut et Geburah et chesed per aeonas'.[33]

The battle royal rages between "his kingdom" and the "kingdom of God." New versions commit high treason, and for no reason, since the earliest manuscript, P45, and the majority of Greek manuscripts agree with the KJV.

NIV, NASB		KJV
his kingdom	Luke 12:31	the kingdom of God

'His kingdom' cannot bear the Lord's Prayer of Matthew 6 to mix 'the kingdom' with "Our Father which art in heaven." So here comes the leaven—new versions omit sentence seven!

NIV		KJV
OMIT	Matt. 6:13b	For thine is the kingdom, and the power and the glory, for ever, Amen.

This is a sin since it's in 99 out of 100 Greek N.T. documents, 3rd century manuscripts like the Sahidic version and Apostolic Constitution, and the 4th century writings and versions of Chrysostom, Ambrose, Isidore, the Gothic, Ethiopic, Cureton's Syriac, Harkleian, Armenian and Georgean. Paul repeats it in II Timothy 4:18, as well.

New Agers pray "thy kingdom come" along with Alice Bailey who channeled Djwhal Khul saying:

> The objective of the new social order, of the new politics, the new religion is. . .to bring in the Kingdom. . .

Of antichrist.

"Thy Will Be Done In Earth As It is In Heaven"

This entire line is taken out of new versions based upon the scantiest manuscript evidence imaginable. The majority of Greek texts and even the corrupt manuscripts retain it, with the exception of Vatican MS. NO. 1209, which does not contain Revelation, Titus, I and II Timothy, and Hebrews 9:14-13:25 either. The explicitness of this verse leaves little room for interpolation. By removing this line and the 'heaven' of the first line, "heaven" has been completely eliminated from the Lord's Prayer.

The "will" of "heaven" is in opposition to that "will" spoken of frequently by the New Age. Alice Bailey's New Age sickle has pruned "the Branch of righteousness" (Jeremiah 33:15) to match new versions, saying:

> 'Father, Thy will be done' is the answer 'flung back' from 'the Father's house. . .where the will of God is known. . .Shamballa of the esoterics. . .where reigns the Christ.'[34]

The Great Invocation of the New Age speaks of "the centre where the Will of God is known." This "centre" is not heaven and their God is, by their own admission, Satan. New Age manual, *The Keys of Enoch,* speaks of obeying the image which comes from "The Father" so that we will not err in fulfilling the "Father's will."[35] Even Reverend Moon organizes his followers in prayer sessions "to bring about Moon's will on earth."[36]

Heaven is out; the centre, the image, Reverend Moon, and Shamballa are in.

"Give Us This Day Our Daily Bread"

This phrase is preserved in the new versions. Satan's offer of material benefit in exchange for worship is seen in Luke 4.

> All this power will I give thee and the glory of them: for that is delivered unto me; and to whomsoever I will I give it. If thou therefore wilt worship me, **all** shall be thine.

In this devil's bargain, the worshipful prelude, "Father, Hallowed be thy name," is an overture which anticipates recompense. Jeremiah 44 describes such a correlative relationship between the female idol, "the queen of heaven" and the wayward Hebrews.

> [W]e make her cakes to worship her. . .But since we left off to burn incense to the queen of heaven, and to pour out drink offerings unto her, we have wanted **all** things.

Answered prayer is not necessarily an indicator of fellowship with the true God.

"And Forgive Us Our Sins; For We Also Forgive Everyone That is Indebted To Us."

Kathryn Paulsen's, *The Complete Book of Magic and Witchcraft* cites a Satanic ritual:

> Grant that I may be cleansed by this water from all my sins. . .[37]

Although this seems peculiar, Satan's desire to be "like the most High" extends to masquerading as a forgiver and destroyer of sins, so this line is kept in the corrupt versions.

Esoteric Christianity, says:

> Stand in awe of him and sin not: speak his name with trembling. . .For Satan is the magistrate of the Justice of God. . .[38]

Even the Hindu Krishna sect exclaims, "Hari Krishna!" 'Hari' means "sin destroyer."

"Lead Us Not Into Temptation"

A phrase which has a very straight forward meaning to Christians, is adopted by the esoteric community and given a cryptic meaning. These words are included in the new versions because, as *New Age Bible Interpretation* inform us, this phrase was used by Marcion's followers as,

> . . .the invocation of the desire nature through Venus.[39]

Blavatsky gives her endorsement to this line:

> 'Lead us not into temptation' is addressed by man to the terrible spirit of duality in man himself.[40]

"But Deliver Us From Evil"

This final line is uprooted from the text and jettisoned away, in company with all of the references to 'heaven'. Words like good and evil, heaven and hell, paint a picture which is too black and white for the New Age which sees the world in varying shades of grey. The new versions don't present an "evil world," as seen in Galatians 1:4, but an "evil age." They believe this 'evil Age' of Pisces will soon become their glorious 'Age' of Aquarius.

Regrettably, when the New Age Great Invocation chants, ". . .seal the door where evil dwells, "the Holy Father of Evil" is sealing them *in* 'with,' rather than delivering them "from" evil. Isaiah 14 warned that Satan ". . .opened not the house of his prisoners."

New Versions Halt Prayer

God's formula of praying to the Father, in the Son's name, through the Holy Spirit is totally circumvented in new versions. They call for prayer directly to the Son or to the Father, but not in Jesus' name.

NIV, NASB, et al.		KJV
If you ask **me** anything in my name, I will do it.	John 14:14	If ye shall ask anything in my name I will do it.

(The preceding verse states that the prayer is answered "that the Father may be glorified in the Son," yet new versions omit the Father.)

If you shall ask the Father for anything he will give it to you in my name.	John 16:23	Whatsoever ye shall ask the Father **in my name**, he will give it you.

In addition, prayer, especially fervent prayer, is omitted seven times from new versions. (John 14:16, 17:9, 15, 20, Luke 21:36, Acts 1:14 and James 5:16) Other examples, like the following abound.

NIV, NASB, et al.		KJV
keep on the alert	Mark 13:33	watch and pray

Prayer's powerful partner—fasting—also disappears in new versions.

NIV, NASB, et al.		KJV
OMIT	Matt. 17:21	this kind goeth not out but by prayer and fasting.
OMIT	2 Cor. 6:5	in fastings
OMIT	2 Cor. 11:27	in fastings
this kind can come out only by prayer	Mark 9:29	This kind can come forth by nothing, but by prayer **and fasting**
devote yourself to prayer	I Cor. 7:5	give yourselves to **fasting and** prayer
Four days ago I was praying	Acts 10:30	Four days ago I was **fasting**. . .and. . . prayed

This tendency to short circuit man's prayer life is a reflection of some new version editors' unbiblical beliefs. Edwin Palmer, NIV chairman believes that prayer should be directed to the Holy Spirit.[41] Origen, the editor of the Greek manuscripts used for new versions agreed.[42]

Confusion regarding prayer is pervasive today in Christian circles. Kenneth Copeland says, "Pray to yourself."[43] Others 'claim' or 'demand' answer to prayer, unaware that this is the exact method used by esoterics. Alice Bailey urges them to "lay your demands before God."[44]

Finally: "[T]hey worshipped the dragon"

Speaking at the occult Arcane School, Robert Muller, esoteric and Asst. Sec. General of the United Nations, told of his efforts to unite East and West with "world prayers." (Already in place is U.N. Rule 62 which requires this group to pray.) Muller suggests:

> The prayer, Our Father, which the Christ has given us, remains as valid as ever.[45]

"Integrating Eastern and Western Prayer" is promoted by one Catholic publication. Their advertisement, which follows, integrates the Lord's Prayer with yoga, meditation and the *chakras* of India. [i.e., the serpent coiled at the bottom of the spine][46]

THE LORD'S PRAYER

INTEGRATING EASTERN AND WESTERN PRAYER

Louis Savary

Savary used modern Scripture studies to analyze the seven petitions of the Our Father. He takes these seven petitions and makes a remarkable correlation with the seven energy centers of the East (chakras). He explains how these petitions and chakras describe various postures before God.

The final stereo cassette has two centering meditations using the petitions and specially designed music by Steve Halpern.

4 cassettes (3 hrs., 20 min.) with study guide in vinyl album

AA0391 **$32.95**

Final cassette (40 min.) sold individually

AA0394 **$8.95**

Legions of mainline churches, which are Christian in name only, recite the Lord's Prayer every Sunday as a part of their liturgy. As the apostasy of the last days reaches its culmination, these church members will pick up the new 'Bibles' provided in the pews, and recite Luke 11:2, so artfully carved by Marcion to match his diabolical theology. They will finally fulfill the biblical prophecy. . .

> [A]nd they worshipped the dragon.
> Revelation 13:4

FOUR

The Dragon,

That Old Serpent, Which is the Devil and Satan

Revelation 20:2

The fiery dragon, first emblazoned on the Gate of Ishtar in ancient Babylon, was to journey round the girth of God's earth. He soon parched a path in the orient whose aftermath scorched souls from pole to pole. His fiery breath still speaks death, yet in today's New Age, he's all the rage. One New Age observer says, "One finds the dragon gracing everything from newsletters to jewelry."[1] His migration to America is marked by a posh West Coast restaurant where patrons dine beneath a life-size dragon (designed by leading architect Frank Ghery). The dragon's inroads corrode the children, as books like the *Dragon ABC*, *Dragon Dance* and *The Dragons of North Chittendon* call kids on a voyage to a mirage.

When Satan escaped Isaiah 14 and Luke 4:8, he slipped out the 'dragons' in between. The weight of this drama and its details are diminished as new versions dismiss "the dragon's" role and depose him from over half of the 34 bible verses. The NIV omits 20 references, while the NASB drops 18. Again, the clues vanish and the culprit escapes detection, while scribes like the NIV's Edwin Palmer admit their "uncertain" position.[2] The NIV even had to unload the episode where Satan meets his last abode.

"[H]e shall slay the dragon." Isaiah 27:1

"The great dragon was cast out, that old serpent called the Devil, and Satan, which deceiveth **the whole world**." (Revelation 12:9) Richard Roberts, traveling partner of Joseph Campbell (*The Power of Myth*), reports on the pervasive worship of the dragon worldwide. This image of international scope is skipped in the "international" version.

Robert's remarks relating to the nature of this dragon bear remembering by the reader as this book further investigates Satan's name game.

> As far as I've been able to determine, every culture contains a mythology of a serpent or dragon which represents the ancient and formidable Goddess of nature.[3]

FIVE

The One vs. the Holy One

The Sexless 'One'

Hath a nation changed their gods? Jeremiah 2:11

C*hanging of the Gods* by New Age author Naomi Goldenberg asserts:

> God is going to change. . .we women are going to bring. . .the end of Him.[1]

God does not change, but new versions try to transfigure him as they translate. The NASB and other new versions "brings the end of **Him**" changing the words "he" and "Son" to "the One." (The word in all Greek texts is always masculine, not neuter.)

	NASB (NIV et al.)	KJV
Luke 10:16	rejects the One	despiseth him
Luke 12:5	the One	him
Matt. 13:37	The one	He
Matt. 24:13	the one who endures	he
John 4:25	One	he
John 6:46	the One	he

	NASB (NIV et al.)	KJV
John 7:18	the one	his
John 9:37	He is the one (NIV)	it is he
John 15:21	the One	him
John 12:45	he who beholds me beholds the One (NIV)	he that seeth me seeth him
I Cor. 15:28	the One	unto him
Acts 7:38	the one	he
Acts 10:21	the one (NIV)	he
Acts 10:42	this is the One (NIV)	it is he
Acts 22:9	the One	him
Col. 3:10	the image of the One	him
Heb. 5:7	tears to the One	unto him
Heb. 7:21	the One	him
Rev. 2:1	The One	he
Rev. 1:18	the living One (NIV)	he that liveth
I Pet. 1:15	One who	he which

Books like *Sensuous Spirituality*, by avowed lesbian NIV editor Virginia Mollenkott, echo the New Age movement's hopes to replace the 'he' of Christianity with the neuter 'One' of Hinduism. InterVarsity Press warns:

> The One must move from the avante garde fringe to the very heart and mind of society. The whole society must be brought into harmony with the One as the New Consciousness produces the New Age.[2]

'The One' is being smuggled into Christianity, concealed under the cover of new bible versions like the NKJV. 'The One's' masquerade is betrayed by the **800 blanks** which occur where the underlying Greek or Hebrew word should be given in the *NASB Exhaustive Concordance*. If 'the One' does not come from the original Greek or Hebrew, what is its source? *The Encyclopedia of Mysticism and Mystery Religions* [Mystery Babylon?] unravels the 'mystery':

> *One:* Term for the Ultimate. . .in many mystical religions and philosophies.[3]

The New Age resurrects the mystery religions revealing 'the One's' three fold meaning.

> 1. 'The One' or 'the Only One' is Lucifer, the angel of this planet's evolution.
> 2. 'The One' or 'the Living One' is all of reality as described in pantheism or monism.
> 3. 'The Coming One' or 'The Mighty One' is Lord Maitreya's New Age Christ [antichrist].

New versions harbor all three aspects of the 'Mysteries'. This section will show *some* of these 'stowaways' and displays the New Age piracy piloted by new version editors and currently floating under 'the bible' banner.

The One: Lucifer

Mystery Babylon is foreseen in Revelation chapter 13. The mystery religions convene—

> And they worshipped the dragon. (Revelation 13:4)

The dragon's name is the same 'One' which slips in 'til it grips. The rebels worship the dragon with 'the bible' on their lips. Arch-Luciferian Madame Blavatsky lists a litany of names for this 'being of sin' in her book *The Secret Doctrine.*

> The Dragon of Wisdom is the One
> The One and the Dragon
> Great One. . .Lucifer
> Lucifer is one
> Sanat. . .For he is One
> The Fiery Serpent. . .is but One
> One ever hidden. . .Sat
> One Reality—the Nameless Sat
> Pan,. . .the One and Great All. . .theology makes him the Devil!
> Pan is the One
> a virgin Kumara. . .the Mysterious One[4]

'The One' is so central to Luciferian teaching that the entire first chapter of the *Secret Doctrine* is a discussion of 'the One'. This title is so pervasive in the book that it covers an entire page in her index.

Lucifer's cry—to "be like the most High" (Isaiah 14:14) is seen in his claims to the divine names—'god' (II Corinthians 4:4) 'Christ' (I John 2:22), 'prince' (Matthew 12:24), 'king' (Job 41:34), 'lord' (Matthew 10:25) and 'one' (Matthew 13:19, I John 2:13, 14, 3:12, 5:18). The last, "the wicked one" is a sharp contrast to "the Holy One," the title God uses to identify himself. The Hebrew word *qadash,* meaning 'holy', is translated "Holy One" (even in Isaiah 57:15 where the two words are split). Satan is not holy and therefore can claim only the name 'One'. Blavatsky agrees saying 'the One' applies neither to the "creator nor to the Father of our modern monotheists," nor their "Holy One."[5]

God also identifies himself as "the Holy One of Israel" to distinguish himself from "the god of this world" (II Corinthians 4:4). The religions "of this world" identify their "god" as "the One," not the "Holy One of Israel."

Rig Veda:	"That which is One the wise call it in diverse manner."[6]
Egyptian Funeral Ritual:	"I am the Great One."[7]
The Aquarian Conspiracy:	"In the infinite One. . .the God of Force."[8]
Qur'an 112:	"Allah is One." [Mohammed means Praised One; the expected Madhi is the Guided One.][9]
Bhagavad Gita:	"the Blessed One"[10]
Tibetian Buddhism:	"The Great One"[11]
Druzes:	"the One Supreme"[12]

Cults, channelers, and gurus worship 'the One' [the dragon] as well.

Association for Research and Enlightenment (Edgar Cayce):	"The One Source"[13]
Worldwide Church of God (Herbert W. Armstrong):	"the One. . .you can become God"[14]
Church Triumphant and Universal (Elizabeth Clare Prophet):	"Sanat [Satan] Kumara, the Great One."[15]
Science of Mind Church (Terry Cole-Wittaker):	"the One-beyond-ism"[16]
Unity (Ernest Ramsey):	"For the Glory of One"[17]
Channelers: Neil Cohen, John Randolf Price:	"the Beloved and Radiant One" and "the Awakened One"[18]
Bhagwan Rajneesh:	"the Blessed One"[19]
Eckankar:	"the Divine One"[20]

Author of *Toward A World Religion for the New Age* sees the same 'One' wrapping the world.

> Similarities in the religions may be attributed to their being based on revelations from the One.[21]

Blavatsky admits 'the One' is not "the Holy One of Israel" saying:

> One is not Jehovah.
> The Jewish Deity is. . .never the One Absolute All.
> No God. . .called Jehovah. . .can be the One.
> The One is superior to Elohim.
>
> [T]he Unknown Unmanifested One, since it abounds in both sexes is—male and female—nor yet the Christian 'Father' as the latter is a male and not androgyny.[22]

The NIV's Mollenkott says, "To refer to God Herself seems to me a humanly just way of referring to the One who is neither male nor female."[22] New versions again parrot pagans like Blavatsky saying, "the One" is not Jesus Christ.

> It is not the **One** unknown ever present God in Nature. . . that is rejected, but the God of human dogma and his humanized 'Word'.[23]

	NASB (NIV, et al.)	KJV
John 1:14,18	the One and Only (NIV)	the only begotten Son
Luke 9:35	My Chosen One (chosen is in a few MSS)	my beloved Son
John 6:69	Holy One of God*	Christ, the Son of the living God
John 4:42	this **One** indeed is the Savior of the world	this is indeed the **Christ**, the Saviour of the world

*(Luke 4:34 reveals that only the devils call Jesus the 'Holy One of God'.)

Yet Intervarsity's *Understanding the New Age* points out:

> [T]he presuppositional antithesis between Christ and the One could not be sharper. [24]

New 'International' Versions adopt 'the One' of the nations and nix the God of Israel.

	NASB (NIV et al.)	KJV	GREEK	NEW AGE
Mark 12:32	he is **One**; and there is no one else besides Him	there is one **God** and there is none other but he	The word 'God' is omitted from the minority Greek text.	Stating that there is no one **else** beside God is Pantheism.
Matt. 19:17	There is only **One** who is good	There is none good but one, that is **God**	Minority text omits "God" and "there is none good."	Substitute the 'One' for 'God'.

	NASB (NIV et al.)	KJV	GREEK	NEW AGE
Luke 23:35	His Chosen **One** (NIV, Living Bible)	the chosen of **God**		The speakers are mocking Christ.

The One or the Son

The dismissal of "he" and "Son" for "the One" in new versions makes them copies of *The Occult Catechism* which reads:

> Question: 'What is it that ever is?'
> Answer: 'The One is. . .the Father and Mother.'[25]

This virus, spawned now in new versions, is spreading in some 'Christian' bookstores and spotting works by (Frs.) John Powell and Matthew Fox with "the mother-father. . .he/she God" and "the Kingdom/Queendom of God." Years earlier, before new versions, a reader only saw such sentiments in obscure esoteric works like Mary Baker Eddy's *Rudimentary Divine Science*:

> God is the everpresent I am filling all space. . .the one Mother-Father.[26]

The NIV Story, by NIV editor Burton Goddard (p. 65), says stylists like Mollenkott made "significant changes" to the NIV text. She says, "Happy and aligned with the One are those who find their home in the breathing; to them belongs the inner kingdom and queendom of heaven."[26] Remember—"The One must move from the avante garde fringe to the very heart and mind of society."

NIV's the One and Only: Satan

Why are the 3 titles used by the NIV *identical* to the 3 titles used by Luciferian Mme. Blavatsky? Historians affirm the title belongs to Satan.

LUCIFERIAN	NIV	KJV
"the One and Only"[27]	"the One and Only"	"the only begotten Son" (John 1:14,18)
"only One"[28]	"only One"	"God" (Matt. 19:17)
"Only One"[29]	"Only One"(f)	"God" (John 5:44)

Variations of this title occur elsewhere also.[30]

LUCIFERIAN	NEW VERSIONS	KJV
"One-Only One"[31]	"only one. . .the One" (NASB) "only one. . .the one" (NIV)	"one" (James 4:12)
"the One and Only God"[32]	"the *one* and only God" (NASB)	"God" (John 5:44)

NIV chief Edwin Palmer asserts that the terms 'one' and 'only' are "modern and elegant" substitutions.[33] But historians have regarded the title as 'old and evil'. Layard's *Babylon and Nineveh* (London, 1853) traces the origin of the 'One Only' to *the serpent* "the one Only God of the Babylonians."[34] MACROBIUS, *Saternalia* written in A.D.1521 confirms the historical association of the term "one only" with Satan.

> a serpent. . .According to the fundamental doctrine of the mysteries [is]. . .the **one only** god. . .Satan, then was recognized as the **one only** god.[35]

The title, according to "Asiatic Researches" (London, 1806) was a "wicked perversion of the title of the true God." Lowth and other Orientalists have written of the perverse "rites of the ONLY ONE."[36] Another author notes the universal adoption of the title by pagan religions worldwide and its depiction by the symbol of the dragon or serpent.

> But all the multiform divinities with which the Pagan world abounded. . .at the bottom they recognized only *Adad*, the One God. . .each of these figures was only an emanation of the Same Great Being or Only One.[37]

Harnack's *History of Dogma* cites the title 'One and Only' in a strictly non-Christian context. The third century Arians adopted the title for God to affirm their denial of the deity of Jesus Christ. Scholars contest that Arianism's "language was borrowed from Origen," the progenitor of the few Greek manuscripts which sometimes use the title 'the One'. Harnack cites one of the eight tenets of Arianism as:

> The characteristic of the One and Only God is solitude.[38]

The title has grown and spread down through history, seeded in American soil by Johnny Appleseed. His tracts promoted 18th century mystic Emmanuel Swedenborg whose "communication with spirits" revealed, "The universe is an image of God. . .the one only."[39] Today the title finds itself planted in the mystical and esoteric section of the library, in books like Rice's *Eastern Definitions*, where "the One and Only Reality" matches "the Nameless Sat" [Satan].[40] Now 'the One and Only' is shooting up in Detroit—as the name of its diabolical street gang leader. In this hot house, missionary Joseph K. Hicks sees the fruit of the seeds of the "one" and "only" and they are neither "modern" nor "elegant."

Number One

'The One' has crossed the tracks, so to speak, from street gangs and Satanists to society as a whole. The semantic rail system of the New Age has carried the term as its chief cargo. One author agrees saying:

> The root idea of the New Age is oneness, unity, and wholeness—the One for all.[41]

The *Los Angeles Times* religious editor observes:

> The New Age bottom line can be stated in three words. . .All is One.[42]

Virtually all exposés on the New Age Movement observe that 'the One' is *this* movement's object of worship. Books like Intervarsity's *Unmasking the New Age* identify 'the One' as the god of the New Age over 100 times (in a book of only 192 pages). Its chapter and subject headings echo the New Age theme: "The Rise of the One," "Putting the One to Work," "Pluralism and the One," "All Religions are One," and "Challenging the One." To neophyte New Agers 'the One' does not represent Lucifer but merely the following world views.

> *Monism*: The philosophical doctrine that there is only one reality in existence and that all things are parts of or composed of this reality.
>
> *Pantheism*: The doctrine that reality involves a single being of which all things are modes, moments, members, appearances or projections. . .the whole of reality itself, are God.[43]

Both monism and pantheism are technically called *Visistadvaita* qualified non-dualistic Hinduism, as developed in the 11th century by Ramaniya. Scholars describe it as an "elastic" philosophy because it accepts *all* gods and theologies. It states, "The One Power manifests itself in various ways."[44] This schizophrenic philosophy is perfect for the New World Religion which will try to embrace and marry the many religions of the world.

Benjamin Creme writes in *Reappearance of the Christ* :

> [T]he new world religion will be based [on] God Transcendent and of God Immanent within every form of life.[45]

The New 'International' bibles are as "elastic" as the cosmology which has infiltrated them—pleasing the pantheists with the neuter Hindu 'One' on some pages, then pandering to the 'less evolved' Judeo-Christian tradition on other pages.

Today the great majority who have fallen sway to 'the One' have never picked up Lao Tse's book *Tao Teh Ching,* nor would they classify themselves as pantheists on religious preference cards. Yet, through cultural osmosis, they have adopted a view of the universe that is saturated with 'the One'. Hollywood's *The Empire Strikes Back* and *Star Wars* paint scenographic pictures of Lao's *ki* or force.

Douglas Groothius points out, "The social credibility granted to science is being employed to empower the One for all."[46] Intellectuals are being prodded down the primrose path to pantheism's 'One' by Planck's quantum physics, Gabor's holographic theories and books by Fritjof Capra like *The Tao of Physics.* A study of college students on 48 campuses identified a greater proportion who believe God and the material world are one and the same, than believe in the Christian view of God as a distinct supernatural 'Being'.[47] These students are merely mirroring textbooks laced with the views of Thoreau, Emerson, Spinoza, Schelling and Schopenhauer, all professing the "oneness underlying all phenomena."

The word 'One' may have brought to mind "the Holy One of Israel" to a past generation, but a shift in semantics is mirroring the move from a Christian to a humanistic culture. This shift is not accidental, but part of what esoteric Alice Bailey called 'the Plan'. She said, "This type of transcendent. . .creator must be shown to be false."[48] So showing up side by side on bookstore shelves are books like *The Dream of the Earth* and new versions, both urging Christians to drop 'the Son' for 'the One'.

This New Age god of pantheism is not a personal God but a **number**. They assert:

> God is a number endowed with motion. . .the essence of which is eternally One, formless, sexless. . .We refuse to see that which monotheists call a personal anthropomorphic God.[49]

Readers will not "see" a "personal God" in many new version entries since his person has been replaced by a number.

NASB (NIV)	KJV
One	God, Christ, Son, he, Most High, majestic, righteous, straight, strong, and just, etc.

Like the Gnostics of old, New Agers refer to this force or ultimate reality as 'one' because the number denies any duality or distance between 'god' and man. When deity is ascribed to this 'one' reality, it becomes a proper name 'the One'. New versions transform the Greek words *heis* (used elsewhere correctly as "one jot," "one of his disciples," etc.) to 'the One', giving the New Age god greater visibility and accommodating a broader range of 'religionists'. (Now that Zondervan is owned by Harper San Francisco "all things are possible," if they are profitable.)

	NASB	**KJV**
John 1:26	among you stands One	. . .one
Matt.23:8-10	One is your teacher One is your father	one. . . one. . .
John 8:50	One	one
Rom. 5:17	the One	by one
Rom. 5:19	the One	one
Rev. 4:2	One	one (italics)

"The Living One"

The tenets of pantheism are often expressed in esoteric circles by referring to the 'one life' or the living planet. Note how this living 'One' moves from the "avante garde fringe to the very heart of society."

Step 1	*Luciferian:*	"There is **ONE LIFE**, eternal, invisible." [50] (Blavatsky)
Step 2	*New Age:*	"He is closer to the **One Universal Life** than ever before. . .the basis of the New World Religion." [51] (Bailey)
Step 3	*New Greek New Testament Editor:*	"[T]he **one life** is fulfilled in many parts." [52] (Westcott)
Step 4	*New Version Committee (NIV):*	"[T]here is One Ultimate Interrelational Being who undergirds. . .everything that lives."[52] (Mollenkott)

Step 5	*New Versions:*	**"the living One"** Luke 24:5 (NASB) **"the living One"** Rev. 1:18 (NIV, *Living Bible*) ('One' is not in *any* Greek text.)
Step 6	*Apostate 'Christianity':*	"[A] new human community for. . .the manifestation of that **life**-giving, **life**-enhancing **Universal One**." (World Council of Churches, "Ministerial Foundation in a Multi-Faith Milieu")

Lest anyone contend that the new versions and New Greek editors are not presenting a pantheistic philosophy, a detailed description of their 'one life' philosophy follows:

> To me it appears that the Spirit is teaching us now above all things the unity of life, of all things, of all beings, of the seen and of the unseen. . . We view. . .men as disconnected, but this is simply a consequence of our limited powers. To God all life that is truly life is one. . . There can be no doubt that the uniform tendency of recent research is to establish in many unexpected ways the closeness of the connections by which we are bound one to another. In proportion as we know more fully, this connection is found to be more powerful and far reaching. It is the element—one element—in the idea of life which has been revealed to us in this age. . .the little life which is now my own is part of a vaster life.[53]
>
> Westcott

> [T]he relation of parts to wholes pervades the invisible no less than the visible world, and beneath the individuality which accompanies our personal lives lies hidden a deeper community of being as well as feeling and action.[54]
>
> Hort

> The monism I'm talking about assumes that god is so all-inclusive that she is involved in every cell of those who are thoughts in her mind and embodiments of her image.[54]
>
> Mollenkott

Even NIV translator Larry Walker applauds the rejection of the Hebrew Old Testament for the *Ugaritic* wherein the gods of pantheism preside.

> The god named Yam (sea) was not recognized in the KJV. . .but is reflected in some of the new translations. . .'Sea' in JB (Job 7:12). . .The NIV does not contain the divine names Yam or Mot, but it does refer to Death in Job 26:6, 28:22 where it is personified.[55]

The National Catholic Register calls (Fr.) Thomas Berry, author of *The Dream of the Earth,* "the acknowledged leader of a massive shift in consciousness as Christians [?] begin to see the Earth as the revelation of God."[56] This massive shift received its impetus from the esoterics and is being fostered by new versions who seem to agree that: 1.) the creation is a manifestation and revelation of the One, its creator. 2.) "All" will finally be gathered back into the One.

LUCIFERIAN	'NEW' GREEK EDITORS	NEW VERSIONS
"Everything originated in the One. . .the Creator."[57] Blavatsky	"One who is the Creator."[58] Hort	"the creation waits eagerly for the revealing. . . the creation. . . **its own will**" (NASB, NIV, et al.) Rom. 8:19, 20, 21
LUCIFERIAN	**'NEW' GREEK EDITOR**	**NEW VERSION**
"All merge into the One itself"[59] Blavatsky	"[A]ll. . .is gathered up without loss of personality in One. . .God in all things and all things in God."[60] Westcott	"[I]n that day the LORD will be the *only* one, and His name *the only* one." NASB (Zech. 14:9)

The Coming One: The Executioner!

The Hindu belief that God is in *all* things leads logically to the notion that it is he who is inspiring every action in the world—both good and *evil. A Reasoned Look at Asian Religions* describes pantheism and its denial of free will.

> Each individual is a part of the cosmic process. No man chooses his actions; they are determined for him.[61]

NIV chief, Edwin Palmer also flatly denies free will and, at his own admission, "accepts the most illogical matters possible." He takes what he calls his "mystical faith" to its illogical limits; Madame Blavatsky is there to meet him.[62]

NIV EDITOR	LUCIFERIAN
"God is the one. . .God is all in all. . .There is none other beside him. He controls the thoughts and activities of all men. Is Sin within the Plan of a Holy God? Yes. All things are in the plan of God. . .even our sin and evil. . .If sin were not in his plan, then he would no longer be almighty. There would be forces outside of him. All things are foreordained by God: the moving of a finger. . .the opening of a window, the mistake of a pianist while playing—even sin. . .The Bible describes man as utterly passive in the whole matter."[63]	"He is the One. . .But if the homogeneous One is no mere figure of speech. . . [he] must contain in itself the essence of both good and evil. If God is Absolute. . .whence comes Evil or D'Evil if not from the. . .Absolute. We are forced to accept the emanations of good and evil. . .as offshoots of the same trunk of the Tree of Being or to resign ourselves to the absurdity of believing in two eternal absolutes."[64]

If God judges men by their actions, they must be free to act. Palmer's conclusions are *truly* "illogical." His denial of free will is seen in his NIV. He says his change in I Thessalonians 1:4 "suggests the opposite" of the KJV.[65]

NIV and NASB et al.		KJV
He has chosen you	I Thess. 1:4	your election of God
If anyone is to go into captivity, into captivity he will go.	Rev. 13:10	He that leadeth into captivity, shall go into captivity.
everyone whose name has not been written from the foundation of the world	Rev. 13:8	the Lamb slain from the foundation of the world

Islam has recently adopted this view and the evil which has ensued has had global effects. They believe:

> [E]verything that happens results from God's choosing it to happen. When a man acts, God creates in him the will, the power and the intention to act.[66]

Charles Manson, agreeing with Palmer, Blavatsky and the Moslems asks, "If God is One, then what is bad?"[67] One Intervarsity editor observes:

> Few people realize Charles Manson was immersed in the One for all. . .This is the great mystery—the ultimate paradox with which Eastern religions perpetually wrest. If the ultimate truth. . .is that in this one, all opposites including evil are eternally reconciled then have we any right to blame Charles Manson. . . Both Mark Satin and Jerry Rubin speak of legitimate experiences where good and evil dissipate into 'the One'.[68]

Those, like Manson, Blavatsky and the NIV's Chief, Edwin Palmer, who see God as 'the One'—driving both evil and good—"call evil good" (Isaiah 5:20). They are setting the stage for the slaughter of those who are saved during the tribulation. Jesus forewarned:

> Yea, the time cometh, that whosoever killeth you will think that he doeth God service. John 16:2

The Hindu 'bible', the *Bhagavad Gita* meaning 'Song of the Divine One', is currently *very* popular among New Agers. It is a lengthy tale in which 'the One' tells Arjuna to be "utterly passive" (to use Palmer's words) as he kills in God's service. 'The One', that is, the universe, is merely 'cleansing itself'. *Dark Secrets of the New Age* says,"[T]he Christian's failure to trust the One will be fatal," as the bible foretold:[69]

> [B]eheaded for the witness of Jesus, and for the word of God, and which had not worshipped the beast, neither his image, neither had received his mark upon their foreheads, or in their hands. Revelation 20:4

Can you just imagine how the following new verses could be plucked out of context and used to encourage worship of the image of the beast, and murder in his "service." In the NASB 'the One' is God (II Thessalonians 2:4); he has an image; and he beheads those whom he chooses.

> **NASB**
> [T]rue knowledge according to the image of the One. . .
> Colossians 3:10
> [W]ith loud crying and tears to the One able to save from death. Hebrews 5:7
> The One who has the sharp two-edged sword. Revelation 2:12
> But I will warn you whom to fear: fear the One who after he has killed. . .Luke 12:5

Lest those killed should see themselves as "martyrs," all references to martyrs have been removed in new versions.

NEW VERSION		KJV
one	Rev. 2:13	martyr
witnesses	Rev. 17:6	martyrs

(The Greek word is *martus*, meaning martyr.)

The Coming One: Antichrist

New Age matriarch Alice Bailey's chapter, "The Doctrine of the Coming One," has been read by legions of New Agers. In it she states:

> Humanity in all lands today awaits **the Coming One**— no matter what name they may call him. . .Then shall the Coming One appear, his **footsteps hastened** through the valley of the Shadow by **the One** of awful power who stands upon the **mountain top**. . .Let **death** fulfill the purpose of the Coming One.70

A careful re-reading of this quote in the light of scripture reveals the following facts:

the Coming One:	Antichrist ("him, whose **coming** is after the **working** of Satan" 2 Thess. 2:9)
the One:	Satan ("I will sit also upon the **mount**. . ." Isaiah 14:13. . .he was a **murderer** from the beginning. John 8:44)

'The One' is coming in the new versions also.

	NEW VERSIONS	KJV
Matt.11:3, Luke 7:20	Are You the Coming One (NKJV)	Art thou **he** that should come
Mark 1:7	after me One is coming who is mightier than I	There cometh one mightier than I after me.
Luke 3:16	but One is coming who is mightier than I	but one mightier than I cometh
John 4:25	when that One comes	when **he** is come
James 4:12	There is only one Lawgiver and Judge, the One (NIV and NASB)	There is one lawgiver
Matt. 23:8-10	One is your Leader	one is your Master

The Mighty 'One': Lucifer

NIV, NASB et al.		KJV
the Mighty One	Luke 1:49	**he** that is mighty
the Mighty One	Psalm 50:1	the mighty God
the Mighty One	Josh 22:22	the LORD God

God is clearly the mighty one of Israel, the mighty one of Jacob, or the mighty God—never the Mighty One. Its use is a gross perversion of the original bible languages. New versions were preceded in their use of "the Mighty One" by occult literature. Lucifer Publishing Company, which is now called Lucis Trust for public relations reasons, publishes their *Great Invocation* in popular magazines like *Reader's Digest.* It is used to invoke their 'Mighty One'.

> Let the Lord's of Liberation issue forth
> Let the Rider from the Secret Place
> come forth [Revelation 6:2?]
> And coming, save
> Come forth, **O Mighty One**
> Let Light, and Love, and Power, and **Death**
> Fulfill the purpose of **the Coming One.**[71]

Blavatsky called her 'god' Lucifer, 'the Mighty One', in both volumes of her *Secret Doctrine.*[72] Rosicrucian books like *Science of the Soul* do likewise.[73] These are rooted in esoteric Buddhism's "the mighty One" and the Egyptian *Book of the Dead's* "mighty One."[74] The bible usually uses this term to refer to those in opposition to God.

> Cush begat Nimrod: he began to be a mighty one in the earth. . .and the beginning of his kingdom was Babel. Genesis 10:8, 10

Their end is foretold in Joel 3:11 and Jeremiah 46:5-10 where the mighty ones are "beaten down. . .[in] the day of the Lord." Nimrod's tower of Babel, like the feeble 'church' being built by the new versions,

> [H]ad brick for stone and slime they had for mortar. And they said, Go to, let us build a city and a **tower**, whose **top** may reach unto heaven. . .Genesis 11:4

This mighty one's attempt to build was cut short as "the LORD scattered them abroad. . .and they left off to build" (Genesis 11:8). Consequently, esoterics from every civilization have used a tower, with an unfinished *capstone*, to symbolize their sought after 'Mighty One', who will lead a religious and political "ingathering of all the people in the world." New Age books like *The Great Seal* (Price, 1952) and *America's Secret Destiny* (Hieronimos, 1989) trace the history of the top *capstone*, left eye and twoer on the U.S. one-dollar bill, showing it represents the "eye" of "the Mighty One", "the Seventh Avatar" who will come to "the new Temple of Peace." Zechariah 11:17 and II Thess. 2:3,4 unveil this impostor, whose "right eye shall be utterly darkened," leaving only his left eye to peer from the *capstone*, as this "man of sin. . .sitteth in the temple of God, shewing himself that he is God."

New versions not only substitute the "Might One" for the LORD God, in the Old Testament, but the NIV has carved a *capstone* out of the Nebsenti papyrus of the Book of the Dead, and sealed it in five places in their New Testament.

The "household of God" is "built upon the foundation" of "Jesus Christ. . .the chief corner stone" (Eph. 2:20). To the KJv this base is a "precious cornerstone, a sure foundation" (Is. 28:16). The 'New' Babel "builders rejected" this supporting *base* for a floating face.

NIV		KJV
capstone	Matt. 21:42	head of the corner
capstone	Mark 12:10	head of the corner
capstone	Luke 20:17	head of the corner
capstone	Acts 4:11	head of the corner
capstone	I Peter 2:7	head of the corner

Meditation and the One

Since cults and New Agers like to lace their arsenic with scriptures, the adulterated verses in new versions will no doubt find themselves hip to hip with some strange and Godless philosophies. 'The One' in the new versions will certainly be used to perpetuate the idea that the Judeo-Christian God is the same as the god of the New World Religion. New Age 'salesmen' assure the "unlearned and unstable" that "It's in the bible!"

Millions of meditators see new versions as yielding sofas, cradling them and making them quite comfortable as they sit and meditate to 'the One'. *Toward a World Religion for a New Age* tells readers:

> Through meditation man can seek guidance from 'the One' called Lord Maitreya'.[75]

Note how the following New Age groups, such as Transcendental Meditation, the World Instant of Cooperation, the New Group of World Servers, as well as Harvard professors and a host of Hindoos, call on 'the One' in their moments of meditation.

1. "The One Preserver and Power of the Universe "was the object of the World Instant of Cooperation when nearly 900 million participants, including the U.S. Pentagon's Meditation Club, joined this worldwide 'meditation' to 'the One'. It was orchestrated by New Age leader John Price whose work is initiated by his 'spirit guide' "Asher, the Awakened One."[76]

2. 'The One' is invoked on every line of the mantra for the New Group of World Servers. Members, like Notre Dame University's President Theodore Hesburg, are midwifing the coming of the New Age 'Christ'.[77]

3. "[T]he One Being. . .the One Spirit" are represented by the universal mantra OM.[78]

4. "One" is the mantra recommended by Harvard Medical School cardiologist Herbert Benson in his recent book touting the physiological benefits of meditation.

5. TM INITIATION

'The One' is used to conjure the Hindu *devis* in Transcendental Meditation's compulsory initiation ceremony. Initiates kneel in a candle lit room before a swastika marked picture while the initiator chants to 'the One' in Sanscrit.

TM CEREMONY EXCERPTS	THE BIBLE
"the One. . ."	"the wicked one" (I John)
"preceptor of this world"	"god of this world"(2 Cor. 4:4)
"the **eye** of **knowledge** has been **opened** by Him. . .the serpent (bujagindra) ever dwelling in my **heart**" [TM initiators and recent exposes falsely give the translation of *bujagindra* as *Brahman*.]	"the serpent said. . .your **eyes** shall be **opened knowing. . .**" (Genesis 3) "Why hath Satan filled thine **heart**. . .?" (Acts 5)
"And therefore to O most beautiful. . .**Dev**. . .I **bow** down." [repeat 26 times]	"The **devil** said. . .if thou therefore wilt **worship** me. . ." (Luke 4)

The Sanscrit dictionary identifies 'Devi' as "demon" or "the shining **one**." The Hebrew dictionary likewise identifies the "serpent" (*nashach*) as "the shining **one**."[79] Occultists reveal that just as 'Sat' means Satan, so 'Dev' means Devil.[80] *The Serpent Power*, a book written in the 1800's by British scholar Sir John Woodroff calls the specific mantras used by TM, a "garland of letters," each letter summoning a Hindu "demon" (a legion for the price of one). TM Initiators are coached in methods to camouflage the noisome aspects of demonic activity and warned not to allow initiates to meditate more than a few minutes to prevent vomiting. A window is opened and incense burned to dispel offensive odors. The result of all of this conjuring of 'the One' is seen in a recent message channeled from one of 'the legion' of devils.

> [W]e are so close and so One—our legions are with your own. We mingle with you.[81]

The TM *initiation* is just the beginning. 'The One' follows his mantra with a MARK, reveals *The Rays and the Initiations*.

> [L]et him seek **the mark**. . .of the One initiator whose **star** shone forth.[82]

SIX

His Mark & Masquerade

Broadcasting a beacon to be on guard for the gathering clouds which are to escort the end of the world, the book of Revelation gives warning of an unholy triumvirate, "the dragon [Satan]. . .the beast [the Antichrist]. . .and the false prophet," who will govern the globe, mastering mankind (Revelation 16:13-14).

New Age rhetoric is laced with expectations of a one world government that encourages personal freedom in a kind of cozy communalism. A blanket of coercion will cover the earth, and these dreamers alike, as they wake to the despotic control of the antichrist. His reign, as anticipated in the book of Revelation, will not be 'power to the people' but 'over' the people.

> [A]nd power was given him over all kindred, and tongues and nations. Revelation 13:7

The false prophet's shroud, like a dark storm cloud, hides heaven from the earth's inhabitants.

> And he saith unto me, The waters which thou sawest, where the whore sitteth, are peoples, and multitudes, and nations, and tongues. Revelation 17:15

Together they hope to veil the 'dead men's bones' (Matthew 23:27) of their man-made religious and political system—characterized by 'the mark of the beast' and 'the image of the beast'. This section will attempt to unveil this skeleton and its attempted resurrection by examining 'the mark' and 'the image', their roots in history, their branches reaching around the world, crossing cultural and religious barriers, and most importantly their current shoots. These appear blatantly in the New Age Movement and apostate Christianity where visions, Virgins, and new versions are giving voice to these dead men's bones which have no tongue of their own.

The Mark: Christ or Antichrist

> And I looked, and, lo, a Lamb stood on the mount Sion and with him an hundred forty and four thousand, having his Father's name written in their foreheads. Rev. 14:1

This verse, along with Revelation 22:4, reveal that at some point in time, whether symbolically or literally, the Lamb will have "his Father's name" written in his servants' foreheads. Revelation 7:3 and 9:4 attest similarly to God's people being "sealed in their foreheads." In his typical counterfeit counterpoise, we see the deceiver afoot, working through the antichrist. Revelation 13:16 foresees his forgery.

> And he causeth all, both small and great, rich and poor, free and bond, to receive a mark **in** their right hand, or **in** their foreheads: and that no man might buy or sell, save he that had the mark, or the name of the beast, or the number of **his name**. . .and his number is six hundred threescore and six [666].

All new versions make the fatefully frightening addition of three words in Revelation 14:1.

> ". . .the Lamb, standing on Mount Zion, and with him 144,000 who had **his name and** his Father's name written **on** their foreheads." NIV

Will the unwary, reading Revelation 14:1 in a recent version, be persuaded that the bible sanctions and encourages the taking of "his name" before they receive his Father's name? Dr. Carl Sanders, developer of the hypodermically *inserted* Positive Identification Microchip (pim I Sam. 13:21 NKJV), now warns Christian audiences that new versions will deceive many, as they did him, into believing that the forbidden mark is *on*, not *in*, the hand or forehead. Is the U.S. government's top secret laboratory at Los Alamos creating this microchip *and* digitizing the Rockefeller Foundation supported Dead Sea Scrolls because the scrolls prescribe all of the elements necessary to coerse people to conform to the one world political and religious system of the antichrist?[1] With the microdensitometer "You can actually move letters around in the manuscript" allowing manipulation of "the evidence", warns one researcher. The scrolls, created by the esoteric Essenes already call for: 1) confiscation of personal property, 2) two messiahs, one political and one religious (Rev. 19:20), 3) the Sons of Light, "ruled by the angel of light" (II Cor. 11:14), 4) an Arabic Mahdi whose 'Name' and initiation, if rejected, bring death and imprisonment during a 7 year period.[2] The NIV mimics this 'Name' over 80 times and prescribes death for those who will not *bear* it. In the tribulation (and new versions) "his name" is *in* and "the Lord Jesus" is *out*. Will "another Jesus" (II Corinthians 11:4) brand his followers with the mark of the beast, after "his ministers" (II Corinthians 11:15) have prodded them with skewed bible verses? The smoke of Satan's branding iron ascends forever.

> And the smoke of their torment ascendeth up for ever and ever: and they have no rest day nor night, who worship the beast and his image and whosoever receiveth the mark of **his name**. (Revelation 14:11)

NIV, NASB, et al.		KJV
his name and his Father's name written **on** their foreheads	Rev. 14:1	his Father's name written **in** their foreheads
his name	Acts 22:16	the name **of the Lord**
the Name	Lev. 24:11	the name **of the LORD**

NIV, NASB, et al.		KJV
when he blasphemes the **Name**, he must be put to death (NIV)	Lev. 24:16	when he blasphemeth the name **of the LORD,** shall be put to death
I bear **on** my body the **brand** marks of Jesus.	Gal. 6:17	I bear **in** my body the marks of **the Lord** Jesus.
tattoo **upon** the hand the name (LB)	Is. 44:5	subscribe with his hand unto the LORD
your people **bear** your **Name** (NIV)	Dan. 9:19	thy people are **called by** this name
the name which thou hast given me	John 17:11	**those** whom thou hast given me
Name	3 John 1:7, Acts 5:41	name

The number of "his name". . .is 666

There are two modes of communication: 1.) direct and explicit (i.e., the word of God and its doctrines) 2.) indirect and implicit (i.e., symbols and rituals). God uses the first method; Satan uses the second means. The number 666 in the form of a mobius symbol appears on the cover of the *New King James Version* (NKJV), just as it does on the cover of *The Aquarian Conspiracy, the* most popular New Age book. Its meaning is mantled to NKJV readers, a maneuver set in motion by Vera Alder and others who call for the use of such "symbols. . .to conceal certain knowledge from the masses."[3] *Aquarian Conspiracy* fans are privy to the 'conspiracy'.

> What makes it a symbol for people is this strange power to communicate to some and not to others.[4]

Luciferians say it is "recognizable by those who have received certain instructions."[5] Alice Bailey adds:

> [T]he number 666 has to do with. . .the Greater Initiation . . .the initiate is defined as one who has. . .expressed 666.[6]

The Keys of Enoch "instructs the reader to use the numerical sequence 6-6-6 as frequently as possible:"[7]

> 1. [T]o be an "outer and visible sign of an inner and spiritual reality." [8] [The NKJV denies the deity of Christ in Acts 3:13,26, 4:27, 30; Rev. 1:6, Matt. 20:20, 26:64, Gen. 22:8, Mark 14:62 et al.]
> 2. "[T]o invoke Lord Maitreya."[9]
> 3. "[T]o attract higher intelligences from. . .other dimensions."[10]

New Agers heed the call and parade the 666 shaped mobius. The Mobius Group, based in Los Angeles, is a leader in investigating "psychic phenomena." They give much press to the spirits still lingering in Cambridge from Westcott's Ghostly Guild.[11] While New Agers hang 666 over their door, new versions try to push its negative connotations out the back door. A note in the NASB and *Living Bible* nudges readers to believe the number to avoid is not 666, but 616. Their readers are not told that only two insignificant documents, manuscripts *C* and 11 record this error.

The Mark and Image of the Virgin

For thousands of years the mark has been looming in the world's cultural and religious scaffolding, ready to be unleashed at the advent of the antichrist. The 500 million Buddhists worldwide revere effigies of Gautama Buddha and Buddhist 'saints' with a mark on their forehead and on their hand. The 800 million Roman Catholics sport spots on their forehead as a part of their yearly Ash Wednesday service. Daily doses of cow excrement don the foreheads of Hindu Krishna devotees. Surveying the meaning behind this ancient practice may forearm us as to the nature of the religious system of the antichrist. Scholars tell us the forehead mark represents, "the eternal Virgin. . .the One itself." New Agers disclose that this is Lucifer.

> The point-bindu is a standard religious symbol throughout the world. . .bindi—the red **spot** that Hindu women wear on their forehead. It is nothing other than a form of the bindi of esoteric origin. . .and other mystical disciplines. . .[It] is an affirmation that she is Shakti, the feminine power. . .The concept of supreme power as female. . . [arises] from submerged prehistoric mother cults of the earliest people of the subcontinent. The Goddess is the source of all, the universal creator, as **eternal Virgin** (Kumari). . .She is **the One** itself.[12]

Even though most of the world's religious systems are pantheistic, that is, worship 'the One',—the Virgin or Mother Goddess has perennially been the tangible icon through which that nature god has been addressed and venerated. An engraving on a goddess icon from ancient Egypt reads, "I am all that has been, or that is, or that shall be."[13]

The bible opens to expose this accomplice, a talking image, that takes victims by the hand to receive their mark.

> And he had power to give life unto **the image** of the beast, that the image of the beast should both **speak**, and **cause** that as many as would not worship the image of the beast should be killed. And he causeth all, both small and great, rich and poor, free and bond, to receive **a mark** in their right hand, or in their **foreheads**. Revelation 13:15,16

An image of 'the Virgin' appearing in Marienfried, Germany to Barbara Reuss, speaks, calling for the taking of a mark on the forehead. This phantom pronounces to all:

> I am the **Sign** of the living God. I place my sign on the **forehead** of my children.[14]

Just as the esoteric Virgin is the image or outward manifestation of 'the One', so this apparition in Germany calls itself the 'sign of God'. This commonality, among others, identifies this talking entity, not as Mary, but as 'the Virgin', of esotericism. The scriptures identify 'the Sign' as Satan himself.

> Even him whose coming is after the working of **Satan** with all power and **signs** and lying wonders.
> II Thessalonians. 2:9

Lucifer: The Virgin

New Age writers concede that this 'Virgin' is indeed the Great Dragon which Revelation 20:2 reveals to be Satan. Blavatsky states:

> Imprudent are the Christian theologians who have degraded them into Fallen Angels and now call them Satan and his demons. Is he not. . .Sanatsuyala, another name of Mother. . **.the Celestial Virgin**—Mother of the Invisible Universe, also called **the Great Dragon.**[15]

As if we did not know that their Virgin, the Great Dragon, is Satan, Blavatsky proceeds to tell us.

> [T]he Great Magic Agent. . .the Astral Light. . .the Sideral **Virgin**—is that which the church calls **Lucifer.**[16]

Mirjana Dragicevic, one of the six children who reported seeing what now are internationally known 'visions' in Medjugorje Yugoslavia, describes the vision of April 14, 1982. In it, the bible verse, "Satan himself is transformed into an angel of light" (II Corinthians 11:14) was graphically depicted. He transformed himself before Mirjana. Her naive interpretation follows:

> He was ugly, horribly ugly. You cannot imagine how ugly, he almost killed me with his gaze, I almost fainted. . .Then **Satan** went away and Our **Lady** came and said to me:' . . .renew the use of holy water, wear blessed objects and holy objects and put them in your homes.'[17]

This transformation of Satan (or another evil principality and power i.e., Zech. 5:9) into 'the Virgin' is not an isolated incident. The Irish press reports from Mitchelstown, County Cork, Ireland:

> [Twenty thousand] 20,000 pilgrims are said to have visited the town since some children claimed they had seen black blood flowing from a statue of Our **Lady** and an apparition of **the devil** with horns appear behind the statue.[18]

This 'transformation' from a devil to 'the Virgin' was viewed at seven other Irish cities. (Dunkill, Ballinspittle, Mooncorn, Mountcollins, Cartloe, Monasterevin, and Stradbally) Blavatsky confirms the identity of 'the One' who changes form:

> [H]e is the mysterious personage about whom legends are rife in the East, especially among Occultists. It is he who **changes form**, yet remains the same. He is the Nameless **One**. . .who has so **many** names. . .He is the Initiator.[19]

New Versions and Visions

B.F.Westcott, editor of the 'New' Greek text underlying the NIV, NASB and all new versions, agrees with Blavatsky that visions of 'the Virgin' are merely 'God' changing "form." He expresses this in a letter to a cohort from his seance club, written while pursuing apparitions of 'the Virgin' in France.

> As far as I could judge, the idea of La Salette was that of **God revealing himself now**, and not in one **form** but in **many**.[20]

With family friends like Lady Emily Lutyens (who writes in her autobiography of her Luciferian connections with directions to "revive the idea of our Lady" and legalize prostitution) and Westcott's penchant for "the idea of the divine motherhood" and enthusiasm for 'visions', he felt led to write an article.[21] His son notes:

> [O]n his return to England. . .He had fully intended to publish this article but was refrained from doing so by Dr. Lightfoot's advice. The professor feared that the publication might expose the author to charges of

Mariolatry and prejudice his chances of election to a Divinity Professorship at Cambridge.[22]

While pursuing phantoms in France, Westcott was also pouring over documents to find support for the esoteric changes he wanted to make in his 'New' Greek New Testament. From La Salette, he slipped to Milan to mull over the Muratorian Fragment of the N.T.. His view of 'visions' now appears on the pages of all new versions.

NASB et al.		KJV
taking his stand on **visions** he **has seen.**	Col. 2:18	intruding into those **things** which he hath **not seen**

One hundred years ago the reading in today's versions was merely a note in Westcott's *Revised Version* (RV), since only a few manuscripts of bad character omit the word 'not'. The elimination of this highly critical word gives the text the exact opposite meaning intended, adding it to the growing list in which new versions urge the reader to disobey the true word of God. The NASB also adds the word 'visions' which is not in any Greek manuscripts. Further, "taking his stand" is not an accurate translation of *embateuo,* which all interlinear bibles render as the KJV does.

Will this verse, as it stands in new versions, be plucked out of context and replanted in some New Age tome to calcify in the minds of the naive that there is biblical support for these 'angels of light'? (Already, books like *Angels on Assignment*, about Assembly of God Pastor Buck, are urging readers to pursue visions and return to Rome.)

The Image of the Beast?

New Ager Madeline L'Engle's book, *A Cry Like a Bell*, suggests that 'the Virgin' may be the focal point of worldwide ecumenical unity.[23] Almost 100 years ago, religious historian Alexander Hislop concluded that 'the Virgin' would be the "image of the beast" worshipped during the great tribulation.[24] The tremendous power held by the antichrist will produce a psychological climate that will nurture the religion of the false prophet. Social anthropologist, Edmond Leach, concludes that 'Virgin' worship occurs where there is an immense gap between the ruler and the ruled.[25] *Religion and Regime*, a classic in the sociology of religion, states that a society which emphasizes conformity (". . .all both small and great, rich and poor. . .") will lead to a religious emphasis on the female.[26] *Christianity Today* also warns of the "egalitarian social organization" which will emerge with a "nurturing goddess as the cultural image of deity;" a Spring 1994 issue showed an image called 'The Heart of the Beast' being worshipped at a feminist conference by lesbians like the NIV's Virginia Mollenkott.[27] As mentioned earlier, the image of 'the Virgin' is the universal icon of pantheism. Consequently, this goddess could be the yoke pulling pantheists (i.e., Hindoos, animists, Buddhists, Native Americans) and non-pantheists (Muslims, Catholics) to the altar of the false prophet.

Visions of virgins are occurring worldwide and are not the exclusive 'channel' of one religious sect. Recently, just a few miles from Cairo, Egypt, hundreds of thousands of Muslems have traveled to see a "luminous something" hovering in the sky above the Church of the Virgin. The vision, appearing frequently over a three year period, was front page material in the Arab press. The Muslims, joined by the Coptic 'Christian' Church hierarchy, view this as a "messenger from God."

Comments about her appearance varied, but both the press and the huge crowds agreed that "doves of light" were seen flying above her head. This novel addition was necessary to entrap Egyptians familiar with the heathen temple of Hierapolis in Syria and its statue of 'the Virgin Juno', whose head is mounted by a dove. The locals have had this imagery woven into their culture for centuries. Archaeological discoveries of images of Astarte, Cybel, and Isis have the identical dove on their head.[28] This phenomena is based on the Babylonian trinity (Father, Son, and Mother), in which the female replaces the Holy Ghost (the dove).[29]

The "father of lies" and his madame mount the skies to materialize Mary in Medjugorje. To patronize the guys in Cairo, they must revise to Virgin Juno. Soli, a channeled demon, unclouds the phenomenon saying, "However you perceive of us in the spirit dimension, this is how we shall appear."[30]

a virgin or the Virgin?

'The Virgin' is a title which has been used since fallen man sought to construct his own god "and worshipped and served the creature more than the Creator" (Romans 1:25). It likely evolved from God's pronouncement in Genesis 3:15 which foretells of "a virgin" birth. To obscure this origin, the Catholic bible completely crops Christ and adopts 'goddess power'.

CATHOLIC BIBLE	KJV
she shall crush thy head and thou shalt lie in wait for **her** heel[31]	her **seed**; it shall bruise thy head and thou shalt bruise **his** heel

The spokesmen for the recent Yugoslavian apparitions, Fathers Vlasic and Slavko, repeat this false notion and extend the "she" to include 'the Church'.

> [T]he passage, at the beginning of the bible about a Woman being the sign and the salvation by which Satan will be overcome. . .We forget that it is the Woman with her children, and you and I are our Lady's children.[32]

All new versions adopt this Catholic 'holy mother the Church' concept (THE MOTHER OF HARLOTS, Revelation 17:5?), even though all Greek manuscripts identify the church as 'it' here.

NIV, NASB, et al.		KJV
her	Eph. 5:25	it
her	Eph. 5:26	it
her	Eph. 5:27	it

Numerous mythological fables surround 'the Virgin' of the heathen; many counterfeit Christian theology. Mimicking Isaiah 7:14, the Hindu Vedanta scriptures say:

> [I]n the early part of the Kali-Yuga shall be born the son of **the Virgin**.[33]

The title 'the Virgin' has been applied to the goddesses of the Canaanites (Astarte and Ashtoreth), the Babylonians (Rhea or Semiramis), the Egyptians (Isis), the Hindus (Isi, Kanyabava, Trigana), the Romans (mother of Romulus and Remus), and the Greco-Roman goddesses Ceres, Hestis, Vesta, Diana, Artemis, Demeter, and Cybele. For this reason, new versions omit a phrase in Luke 1:28 which speaks of Mary's *unique* position.

NIV, NASB, et al.		KJV
OMIT	Luke 1:28	blessed art thou among women

Clearly, there is a distinction between Mary, the historical mother of Jesus Christ, and this Virgin of the heathen religions. Mary was 'a virgin', as foretold in Isaiah 7:14.

Behold **a virgin** shall conceive and bear a son.

However, the use of the word as a proper name or title, as the capital "V" indicates, implies that this virginity was perpetual. Contrary to the Catholic Council of Chalcedon in A.D.451, which proclaimed Mary's perpetual virginity, the dogma can be rejected based upon the witness of all four gospels. (Matthew 12:46-49, Mark 3:31-34, Luke 8:19-21, and John 2:12), Galatians 1:19, Luke 2:7, and Matthew 1:25, the last of which is omitted in new versions.

NIV, NASB, et al.		KJV
OMIT	Matt. 1:25	firstborn

'The Virgin' of the heathens has found its way into the NIV. The capitalization of the 'V' brings out all sorts of New Age theological possibilities.

NIV		KJV
Virgin	2 Kings 19:21, Isa. 23:12, 37:22, 47:1, Jer. 18:13, 31:4, 31:21, 46:11, Lam. 1:15, 2:13, Amos 5:2	virgin
OMIT	Heb. 1:3	by himself

Alan Schreck's *Catholic and Christian* uses these verses to support 'Mary's Role in God's Plan of Salvation.'[34] He urges all to heed the message given in recent visions.

> God is speaking a prophetic word to the church today through Mary, Christians at least ought to be willing to listen to her message in order to test it. If God does continue to speak to the world through Mary, this could be another sign to Christians of her continuing role in his plan of salvation.[35]

Schreck's comment about Mary's 'role' in God's plan of salvation is a reference to the Catholic church's use of the titles Co-Redeemtrix and Co-Mediatrix. New Ager, Geoffrey Hodson, also speaks of not one but two saviors.

> The divine Messengers sent to save mankind, the Christ, as the son of God and **the** Celestial **Virgin** [Lucifer], [were] sent down from heaven to earth to save perishing humanity.[36]

'New' Greek co-editor F.J.A. Hort shares Westcott's belief that 'the Virgin' is the female personification of the divine principle.

> I have been persuaded for many years that Mary-worship and Jesus-worship have very much in common in their cause and in their results.[37]

Michael Carroll explains the root of their reasoning in his thoroughly researched *The Cult of the Virgin Mary*.

> [T]radition recognizes Mary's. . .role but distinguishes her from Sophia, or Heavenly Wisdom, the female personification of the divine principle, whereas Roman Catholic tradition merges these two concepts and has in the process deified Mary.[38]

William P. Barker, author of *Everyone in the Bible* summarizes:

> Scholars point out that much Mariolatry. . .Mary's supposed immaculate conception by her own parents, her supposed perpetual virginity, her supposed translation bodily into heaven, her supposed appointment as co-redemtrix with Jesus. . .grew out of the devotion to the female cults so extant in the Mediterranean world in the early centuries of Christianity.[39]

Testing the message, given by 'the Virgin', as Schreck requests, is done based upon the word of God. Departures from biblical Christianity are frequent occurrences in the reported appearances. The statements given by 'the Virgin' during her recent daily visits to Yugoslavia are contrasted with verses from the bible.

'Virgin': ". . .search for God within."[40] Mark 7:21,22,23 Jesus said, "For from within, out of the heart of men, proceed evil thoughts, adulteries, fornications, murders, Thefts, covetousness, wickedness, deceit, lasciviousness, an evil eye, blasphemy, pride, foolishness: All these evil things come from within. . ."
'Virgin': ". . .to be stronger than all our difficulties means to be saved. . ."[41] Titus 3:5 "Not by works of righteousness which we have done, but according to his mercy he saved us."

'Virgin': "I have come to bring peace to the world."[42] Luke 12:51/Matthew 10:34 Jesus said, "Suppose ye that I am come to give peace on earth? I tell you, Nay; but rather division." "Think not that I am come to send peace on earth: I came not to send peace, but a sword."
'Virgin': ". . .recite the rosary everyday. . .four hours a day"[43] Matthew 6:7 Jesus said, "When ye pray use not vain repetitions as the heathen do; for they think that they shall be heard for their much speaking."
'Virgin': "I have given myself for you."[44] Luke 22:19 Jesus said, "This is my body, which is given for you."
'Virgin': "Our Lady will knock at our door and the door of the Church."[45] Revelation 3:20 Jesus said, "Behold I stand at the door and knock ."
'Virgin': "Pray to the Mother of Goodness. . .'I offer myself to you by means of your goodness, your love, your grace, save me. . .give me your goodness. Let me gain Heaven by means of it.[46] I accept you as my mother and keep you in my life.'" Acts 4:10-12 "by the name of Jesus Christ . . .Neither is their salvation in any other for there is none other name under Heaven given among men whereby we must be saved."
'Virgin': "Our Lady does not like to talk about sin."[47] John 5:14 Jesus said, "sin no more."

'Virgin': "I must suffer for the salvation of souls."[48] I Peter 4:1 "Christ hath suffered for us in the flesh."
'Virgin': "Jesus comes in the Host."[49] Acts 1:11 "Two men stood by them in white apparel; which also said, Ye men of Galilee, why stand ye gazing up into heaven? this same Jesus which is taken up from you into heaven, shall so come in like manner as ye have seen him go into heaven."
'Virgin': "Pray our Lady's 'PLAN' may go forward."[50] Matthew 6:9 Jesus said, ". . .pray ye. . .thy will be done. . ." [The term 'PLAN' is a New Age buzzword for their agenda]

Carroll, a Princeton scholar, points out that in each of the so-called Marian apparitions, the entity is *never* identified as Mary by the observers. This was the case at Lourdes, Fatima, La Salette, as well as with Catherine Laboure, creator of the popular Marian medals. The observers usually report seeing a "luminous something" which is only later identified as Mary at the prompting of a third party who was not privy to the visions themselves. In some cases, the entity later identifies itself by such names as 'the Angel of Peace', 'the Mother of God' or 'the Immaculate Conception' (meaning *she*, not Jesus, was immaculately conceived). None of these scripturally identifies the speaker as Mary.

The 'light' of Lucifer

NIV, NASB, et al.		KJV
fruit of the light	Eph. 5:9	fruit of the Spirit

Mariolaters and Muslims are now seeing the same "luminous something." This is quite telling since Lucifer is a Latin word meaning 'light bearer', and II Corinthians 11:14 refers to his transformation into an angel of light. There is no word more widely used among New Agers and ancient occultists than 'light'. Benjamin Creme boasts that Maitreya says, "My army of Light. . .shall. . .see Light." He calls his followers to visualize white light during meditation. Elizabeth Claire Prophet talks about 'light from the presence'. New Age magazines report on a group called 'the Light' and 'the Sons of Light'. Having seen a vision of a light is an accompanying feature of New Age consciousness, reports *The Aquarian Conspiracy.*

The Greek *'pneuma'* or Spirit is leading Christians, but the *'phos'* or light is driving the New Age. As Christians, our power for living a life pleasing to God comes from the Holy Spirit. Galatians 5:22 and Ephesians 5:9 enumerate 'the fruit of the Spirit'. Christians are instructed not to 'quench the spirit' that we may bear the fruit of the Spirit. New Agers tell us they are:

> . . .instructed in the development of the Light.[51]

Again, new versions instruct their readers to join ranks with the New Age, calling for the 'fruit of the light', not the fruit of the Spirit. Even the testimony of scripture itself in Galatians 5:22 confirms that it is the 'fruit of the Spirit.'

In occult initiation, the initiate often sees a light which is transformed into an image. Thousands are now seeing this sequence in the most recent apparitions of 'the Virgin'. Viewers describe such visions as being announced with 'a flood of light'. Carroll has observed this phenomena of light preceding apparitions so often, that he has reserved a portion of his book to what he (as a non-believer in the spiritual world) calls, "Hallucinations preceded by Illusions." Spectators of visions of 'the Virgin' report:[52]

> *Zeitoun, Egypt:* "I saw a light."
> *Knock, Ireland:* "a bright light."
> *Fatima, Portugal:* "radiated a brilliant light"
> *La Salette:* "came upon a brilliant light"
> *Banneux, Belgium:* "saw a white light about the size of a human."
> *Hercegovina, Yugoslavia:* "a very bright light"
> *Guadalupe, Mexico:* "saw a brilliant light"

New Ager J.J. Hurtag's candid *Keys of Enoch* boasts that "light pictograms," which will "be able to speak" will be dispensers of knowledge in the New Age, just as they did to civilizations of the ancient Near East.[53] He is referring to the bright light and vision which historically often accompany initiations. Proceus' Commentary on *The Republic of Plato* describes the phenomenon.

> In all the initiations and mysteries, the gods exhibit. . .a formless light. . .sometimes this light is according to a human form.

The accompanying chart shows how lights and visions moved from: 1.) Mystery Babylon to 2.) The Greek world (Plato) to 3.) a few Greek N.T. manuscripts to 4.) the revival of Mystery Babylon by New Agers and apostate Christianity. Westcott's neo-Platonism prompted him to follow those few Greek N.T. manuscripts which exhibit alterations by like-minded Platonists.

MYSTERY BABYLON:

"In a manifestation which one must not reveal. . .there is seen on the wall of the temple a mass of **light** which appears first at a very great distance. It is **transformed**, while unfolding itself, into a visage evidently **divine and supernatural**."[54]

Egypt:

"[S]trange and amazing objects presented themselves. . . sometimes it appeared **bright** and resplendent with **light** and fire. . .sometimes apparitions astonished the trembling spectator."

Wilkenson's *Manner and Customs of Egypt*

Greece

"[B]eing initiated in those mysteries in consequence of this **divine initiator**, we become spectators of entire simple immovable and blessed visions, resident in **light**.

Plato's *Phaedrus*

'New' Greek Editor:

"[A]nd then the truly **initiated** is. . .able to rise above the world of sense and thought. . .inherent communion with a **divine** and supersensuous world."[55]

Westcott's *Religious Thought in the West*

New Age:

"The very highest attainment possible to man on this earth—is to take the Ninth Initiation. . .of **the One Initiator**, sometimes called the Lord of this World. . . **Sanat**. . .the ever **Virgin**."[56]

Geoffrey Hodson

NASB:

"[A] very **bright light** suddenly flashed from heaven. . .but [I] did not understand the voice of **the One** who was speaking to me. . .I could not see because of the brightness of the light."

Acts 22:6-11

To produce this soliloquy in the NASB required the gross mistranslation of five areas of the text. First, their penchant for "bright" and "brightness," paralleling those comments by initiates and Virgin viewers, has no basis in any Greek text. The words are *kikanos*, which means great, and *doxu*, which they translate correctly 170 other places as 'glory'. Again, the neuter 'One' is used where a masculine tense word is called for. Thirdly, the NASB completely removes the three critical words "and were afraid." This distinguishes vision from God from visions of the angel of light. The words "and were afraid" accompany truly heavenly visions throughout the bible. (i.e., Luke 2:9, 24:5, John 6:19, Daniel 8:17, and Revelation 1:17)

Hollywood is preparing its patrons not to be afraid of these 'bright lights' with movies such as *Close Encounters*. Movies like *E.T.* desensitize viewers to the "ugly, horribly ugly" creature described by Mirjana Dragicevic. It seems Sylvania and Satan can produce 'bright lights', but the 'glory of God' is beyond anything special effects artists can produce using 500 watt elliptical reflectors or Fresnel lenses.

Superstition or Religion?

> [T]hey became fools and changed the glory of the uncorruptible God into an image. . .Romans 1:22-25

In direct opposition to the second commandment, "Thou shalt not make unto thee any graven images. . .," new versions are carving a platform to support the idol worship that will fill the globe during the tribulation when they, "worship the image of the beast." (Revelation 13:15)

> [R]epented not of the works of their hands that they should not worship **devils** and **idols**. Revelation 9:20

In the upside down world of recent versions, the apostle Paul's harsh rebuke to the idol worshippers becomes a hearty compliment. Here, as in *many* other places, the *New King James Version* (NKJV) bows down to the idol of a false religion.

NIV, NASB, et al.		KJV
I observe that you are very religious in all respects.	Acts 17:22	I perceive that in all things ye are too superstitious.

The Greek word that is translated 'superstition' contains the root-word for 'devil'! The Greek word for 'religious' (*thresheis* or *sebomai*) occurs no where in the verse. With their NKJV, NIV or NASB in hand (or a Catholic bible which always omits the second commandment in their decalogue addendum), tribulation idolators will feel "very religious" indeed.

Hindoos deny the existence of idols. They assert that their *murti* is merely an expression and an extension of the 'God' immanent in the creation. New versions agree.

NASB		KJV
There is no such thing as an idol.	I Cor. 8:4	an idol is nothing

Bibles which applaud visions and idols are breeding 'Christians' who 'bravo' both. Robert Wise, Reformed pastor and editor of *The Church Divided* tells readers to set up idols, in their hearts (Ezekiel 14:7) or their homes, in his chapter entitled "Praying With Symbols and Images." Sounding exactly like a Hindu defending his *murti*, both Wise and Catholic author Alan Schreck excuse their idolatry citing Westcott's "incarnational principle" which asserts that 'Christ' is now immanent in the creation.

CATHOLIC	APOSTATE CHRISTIANITY
"Again, this is the incarnational principle at work. God works through. . .statues, images. . ."[57] Schreck	"Although the Jewish point of view forbids the making of images of God, it doesn't grasp the whole meaning of the Incarnation. . .Images, symbols. . .all flow together as equal parts of the process by which God and humanity communicate with each other."[58] Wise

The command not to make an image of anything—even "that is in heaven" (Exodus 20:4)—is ignored by 'New' Greek editor B.F.

Westcott. "He could have knelt there for hours," his biographer reports, at a statue of the Pieta.[59] Virgin visions likewise promote the use of such statues. The "horribly ugly"-turned lovely-"Lady" told onlookers in Yugoslavia:

> It is important. . .to have. . .a statue.[60]

These misdirected versions and 'visionaries' are directing people away from God's direct and explicit means of communication—the bible—to the devil's indirect and implicit means of 'corruption'—the mark and the image of the beast.

SEVEN

Mystery Babylon The Great: The Mother of Harlots

Whether a vision or an idol, the image of the beast spoken of in Revelation will not be "blessed visions," as Westcott's master Plato relays. Nor will these idolators be "very religious" partakers of the "fruit of the light" boasting of the "visions he has seen." The 'brightness' of the gold cup in the hand of the harlot will have blinded its viewers from seeing that it was "full of abominations" (Revelation 17:4) which will bar them from entering heaven (Revelation 21:27, 22:15).

Who spawned these abominations? The phantom 'Virgin' of the visions and images materializes before our eyes in Revelation 17:5 revealing her to be the unchaste progenitor THE MOTHER OF HARLOTS AND ABOMINATIONS OF THE EARTH.

The cloak of mystery surrounding the book of Revelation becomes somewhat transparent as each page in the New Age handbook fulfills the prophecies of the bible. For example, "Ecumenical Movement," a massive rally-like meeting sponsored by the National Council of Churches and Auburn Theological Seminary, told participants to reconstruct their image of god to that of goddess and 'Mother'.[1] The Pope, in an address to the bishops, said,

> [P]rogress in Christian worship is necessarily followed by a correct increase in the veneration of the **Mother**. . .All-Holy-**One**. [W]orship of the **Virgin** has deep roots.[2]

The elusive MOTHER OF HARLOTS, who traffics in "the souls of men," is spoken of in Revelation 17 and 18. She is unveiled and embraced with glowing fanfare by the New Age. They are even more candid, admitting 'the Virgin' is the "Mother. . .of Devils. . . Lucifer" Blavatsky writes:

> [T]he Celestial **Virgin** which thus **becomes the Mother of Gods** and **Devils** at one and the same time; for she is the ever-loving beneficent Deity. . .**but** in antiquity and reality **Lucifer** or **Luciferius** is the name. Lucifer is divine and terrestrial Light, 'the Holy Ghost' and **'Satan'** at one and the same time.[3]

The devils, they confess, have chosen the veil of the 'Virgin' and the mantle of 'The Mother' as their masquerade. On a converging course with the New Age, apostate Christianity has applied the Luciferian titles 'Mother of God' and 'Mistress of Devils' to their 'Virgin'. *The Glories of Mary*, by Cardinal St. Alphonse di Liguori, maintains:

> [The Virgin]. . .is even Queen of Hell and **Sovereign Mistress of Devils**. The way of Salvation is open to none otherwise. . .[4] **All power is given to THEE.**[5]

The devil himself removes his mask:

> [A]nd the **devil** said unto him, **'All** this **power**. . .**is delivered unto me**. . .' Luke 4:6

The MOTHER OF HARLOTS' manifesto in Revelation 18:7 declares, "I sit a queen," a *soi-disant* not unfamiliar to those men who portray themselves as women. Today the transvestite church is even called The Church of the Virgin Mother, reports *Modern Utopia*.[6] This serpentine beauty queen is a master of mutation. One version of the Ballinspittle, Ireland 'Virgin' vision recounts to the press:

> I saw the face change [to] a boy. . .a head bathed in light. . .[T]he body beneath became. . .masculine. . .[7]

OMNI magazine's use of the term "sacred androgyny" noises the New Age belief that evolution in consciousness brings about the dissolution of stereotypical gender characteristics.[8] This is rooted in the historic Hindu concept of deity which was carried into some pseudo-Christian sects in the second century.[9] Marcion, author of the mutilated Lord's Prayer used in new versions, was a follower of this fickle feign.

> The Tetrad came down to him from the region which cannot be named in a female form. . .manifesting itself in the form of the Invisible One.[10]

This concord of 'queens', cultists, and so-called Christians is the final flowering of a corrupt tree whose roots have clutched the planet ever since the Babylonian mystery religion heralded the first self-proclaimed "queen of heaven," the mother goddess Ishtar. She spawned the worship of the goddess and became the MOTHER of a stream of harlots which now meander the globe. Her current inroads into the Christian camp were cleared centuries ago. Under the heat of the Mesopotamian sun, the germ began to spread, infecting the Jewish community and bringing God's judgement. The bible records:

> [T]he women knead their dough, to make cakes to the **queen** of heaven. . .that they may provoke me to anger. Jeremiah 7:18

A fifth century B.C. papyrus, found at Hermopolis, Egypt, indicates that the Jews who fled after the destruction of Jerusalem held on to this pagan worship in spite of the judgement it provoked. A thousand years later, the Jewish Collyridians were still offering small cakes—but now to 'Mary', thus beginning the current misassociation between her and the heathen 'Virgin' queen.[11]

As harlots are prone to do, the Babylonian goddess, "lieth in wait at every corner" (Proverbs 7:12). Revelation describes her worldwide inroads, sitting "upon many waters. . .of peoples, and multitudes and nations and tongues." Clericus records that this heathen 'Mother of God' was worshipped by the Persians, the

Syrians, and all the kings of Europe and Asia. Her migration to Egypt is evident in a stone taken from Karnac, now in the British museum. It reads, "The Divine Mother and Lady, Queen of Heaven, Morning Star." These titles were later adopted by the Greeks for the goddess Ceres and by the Romans for Cybele. A *Los Angeles Times* writer advises:

> In addition to their roots in Greek and Roman Mythology, the themes of the Great Mother and the Great Goddess are grounded in Eastern religions.[12]

Erosion—from Egypt to England marks the migrating path of the MOTHER of all false gods and religions. Yet her title tethers her to hell.

> *Egypt*:
> "The Mysterious Mother of the World and Universal Mother" (Isis).
>
> *Hindu*:
> "The Mother of the Universe" (Lakshmi and Saki).[13]
>
> *New Age:*
> "The universal creator as the eternal Virgin. . .the One itself. . .Mother of the Universe also called the Great Dragon. . .The Mother of the Invisible Universe."
>
> *New American Bible:*
> "Mother of the World" (Mary).
>
> *New Greek Editor:*
> B.F. Westcott promoted visions of 'the Virgin' in LaSalette, France. She identified herself as the creator of the world. The vision said, "I have given you six days to labor in. . .I have reserved the seventh day for myself. . .go to mass." (In the mass, 'the Virgin' is invoked silently by the priest approximately every three minutes.)

The title 'Mother of God' is applied to the Chinese Shing Moo and the Hindu Isi, Paramata, Saraswati, Taumatra, Akasa, Devanaki, and Nari-Mariami. The MOTHER makes her way into the 20th century as Rice's *Eastern Definitions* documents with a photograph captioned:

> A Tibetian lama sits in meditation. He uses a rosary as an aid. . .in his pursuit of the Merciful Mother.[14]

Moving to mantle the globe, she moves to Beauraing, Belgium maintaining,:

> I am the Mother of God and Queen of Heaven. . .pray the rosary.

(Its 15th decade begins, "A glorious MYSTERY, the crowning of the queen of heaven.") Two thousand years after the prophet Jeremiah warned against "the queen of heaven," books like *The Apparitions and Shrines of Heaven's Bright Queen* still appear and steer so many to Satan's side.

"May the Force be with you."

Another source for Lucifer's last-days aliases is the book of Daniel. There God reveals that the antichrist will endorse "the God of forces." 'The Force' has been framed for moviegoers and fingered at grocery check-outs in *Readers Digest's* 'Great Invocation' ads, which read:

> Let the Forces of Light bring illumination to mankind.

As the scroll recording his aliases unrolls—the One, the Virgin, the Mother, and the Force—emerge and merge. Lucifer's list looms on lines by both Western occultists and Eastern mystics.

"[T]he Great Magic Agent. . .the Astral Light. . .the Sideral **Virgin**—is that which the church calls **Lucifer**. . .[the] **Force**."[15] Blavatsky	"**The One** whom we adore as the **Mother** is the divine consciousness **Force** that dominates all existence."[16] Sri Aurbindo

New versions skew a true view, giving the OK to those who say, "May the force be with you." These versions leave their readers open to popular New Age books like *The Aquarian Gospel of Jesus the Christ*, which advises, "[E]nter fully into the spirit of the God of Forces" (p. 16).

NIV, NASB et al.		KJV
"the gods of his fathers. . .but instead he will honor a god of fortresses."	Dan. 11:36-39	"Neither shall he regard the God of his fathers. . .But in his estate shall he honor the **God of forces**."

Diana: The Mother, the Queen & the Force

A final forgery in the lineage of Lucifer's pedigree is the designate 'Diana'. Historian Alexander Hislop has identified the "God of forces" as Diana.[17] Revived interest in 'the force' has therefore driven Diana from her dusty tomb to today's tabloids. A subterranean complex situated deep in the heart of Rome "holds a discotheque and bar and is the current favorite among the nocturnal haunts of the *jeuness doree*." This nightclub, called Olimpo is receiving international attention for its "mysterious atmosphere" and "a greater than life-size" figure in which "Diana fixes a victim with her arrow."[18] The New Age movement has served as fairy godmother for Diana. As the goddess of nature, she has been adopted by its 'back-to-nature' wing; as goddess of the moon, she is worshipped by witches. *Los Angeles Times* writer Russell Chandler dispatches:

> The great majority of people who call themselves witches . . .follow the nature oriented polytheistic worship of the Great Mother Goddess whose names include Diana. . .[19]

"Diana was chiefly worshipped by women," and consequently has become the 'patron saint' of the feminist and lesbian arm of the New Age movement.[20] They call her the 'living symbol of God'—just as the apparition in Belgium, who called for a mark, called herself "the Sign of the Living God." The New Age dictum reads:

> She is the **Queen**. . .the chaste Diana. . .[T]he last initiated Father of the church [Origen] died, carrying with him into his grave the secrets of the Pagan temples. . . Diana, **the One Mother of God** having her place in heaven. . .[H]er occult aspects and powers are numberless.[21]

God in his foreknowledge focused 18 scripture verses on Diana and the inroads her image had made into Ephesus and "the world" (Acts 19:24-41). A generation who will "worship the image" of the beast badly needs Paul's rebuke to these Ephesians: "[T]here be no gods which are made with hands" (Acts 19:26). 'New International' versions have dropped Diana, just as she is being picked up by a new international generation in need of undisguised truth.

NIV, NASB et al.		KJV
Artemis	Acts 19:24, 27, 28, 34, 35	Diana

Artemis, the name used in new versions, was an exclusively Greek goddess and not the one Acts 19:27 says, ". . .whom all Asia and the world worshipped." *Harper's Dictionary of Classical Literature and Antiquity* exposes the new version's error revealing that the goddess of Ephesus:

> . . .is no Greek divinity, but Asiatic. This is sufficiently shown by the fact that eunuchs were employed in her worship—a practice quite foreign to the Greek idea.[22]

The Oxford Classical Dictionary explains why the goddess at Ephesus should be called Diana and not Artemis.

> [T]he two cults had quite different origins.

The cult of Diana migrated to Rome where the Aventine temple of Diana had a statue modeled after the Ephesian, not the Greek type.[23]

> The Greek colonists identified her (the Ephesian goddess) with their own Artemis, because she was goddess of the

> moon and power of nature. . .But unlike Artemis, she was not regarded as a virgin, but as a mother. . .[24]

The name Artemis, transliterated directly from the Greek bible into new versions, clearly identified the goddess to Greeks, but *not* to "all Asia and the world" for whom the KJV is intended. The use of the name 'Diana', a dynamic equivalency (translating a word as meant and not as written), shows the breadth of scholarship of the KJV translators. A knowledge of classical mythology was common in 1611 when reading books rather than watching television was the pastime of choice. (New versions use dynamic equivalencies frequently, such as translating 'Jesus' as 'Joshua' in Acts 7:45 and Hebrews 4:8. These, however, shows the naivete of new version editors regarding the prophetic nature of the O.T. references concerning Joshua.)

The Ephesians remained undaunted in their zeal for the 'Mother of God'. Four hundred years after Paul's rebuke these citizens declared 'Mary' the 'Mother of God' at the Council of Ephesus. They were led by: 1) Cyril of Alexandria, Egypt, a follower of 'Sophia' the Mother of God and 2) Egyptian Christians who believed the Trinity consisted of the Father, the Virgin, and the Son.[25] Jesus Christ, speaking to the church at Ephesus, refers to men such as these saying, "[T]hou hast tried them which say they are apostles and are not and hast found them liars."

"I beat my body" (NIV)

> And I saw the woman drunken with the blood of the saints and with the blood of the martyrs of Jesus.
> Revelation 17:6

From the hand of the queen, blood has streamed, says verse six—on a course through the ages to fill river Styx. She beats God's martyrs and treats her followers to floggings too. History traces as the blood races during annual festivals for the bloodthirsty goddesses of Egypt (Isis), Rome (Cybele, Mary) and Ephesus (Diana). Flagellation sects in the Catholic world during the 10th and 14th centuries mirrored the masochism of certain Tibetian, Mongolian and American Indian tribes.

This cultural undertow has begun to overflow as the New Age begins to engage in flagellation. The pages of the best-selling *The Aquarian Conspiracy* promote "shamanistic trances generated by. . .self-flagellation."[26]

Americans pursuing the path of Zen Buddhism have felt the painful blows of the *keisaku* stick inflicted during meditation to the 'Merciful Mother'.[27] Rolfing retreats reportedly sound like "torture chambers" with "screams, shrieks, and murderous screams"—as New Age participants seek "structural integration."[28] Like their effeminate counterparts in the cult of Diana, today's sauna bath devotees have also adopted the practice of "scourging with twigs."[29]

Not only the New Age, but today's major religions stage festivals which gauge the globes misdirected asceticism.

> *Moslems*:
> The Festival of Srinagar parades Shiite Moslems beating their bodies with chains to reenact the martyrdom of their Husain.[30]
>
> *Catholic*:
> The Festival of the Madonna of the Arch near Naples parades self-flagellating *fujenti*. Social scientists observed first aid stations erected for the care of over 25,000.[31]
>
> *Hindu*:
> The Festival of Jugannath in Puri is marked by devotees who fall beneath the carts carrying the idols.[32]

New bible versions have adopted this pagan doctrine that, "[T]hrough self-torture and self-denial one can discipline himself to reach a high state, spiritually."[33]

NIV:	"I beat my body." I Cor. 9:27
Living Bible:	"I punish my body and treat it roughly." I Cor. 9:27
NASB:	"I buffet my body." I Cor. 9:27

None of the Greek words for "beat" (*dero, tupto, proskopto, prosregnumi*, or *rhabdizo*) are in the sentence; nor is the word "punish" (*kolazo, timorea*) or buffet (*kolaphizo*). The word used is "*hupopiazo*". The apostle Paul is saying:

> I keep under [keep down] my body, and bring it into subjection. I Corinthians 9:27 KJV

In other words, he does not allow the "lusts of the flesh" to dominate him. He follows Galatians 5:16; "Walk in the Spirit and ye shall not fulfill the lust of the flesh." The verse uses the word "*doulagogea*" which implies he ruled his flesh rather than allowing it to rule him. This is so far removed from the *Living Bible's* rendition, "treat it roughly" as to be unconscionable.

Having migrated from the barbarians to 'the bible', this behavior has been reported by Bob Larson among Penitents of Colorado, New Mexico, the Philippines and Brazil where, "[T]he bible is their text of choice and symbols include icons and statues."[34] The new version asceticism of Corinthians continues in Colossians:

NIV, NASB, et al.		KJV
self-abasement. . . severe treatment of the body. . .harsh treatment of the body	Col. 2:23	humility. . . neglecting of the body

"Emasculate Themselves" (NIV)

The Galatian believers were troubled by false apostles who Paul wished were cut off from fellowshipping with true believers. His policy of not associating with heretics can also be seen in II John 10. Mutant versions, such as the NIV and the *Jerusalem Bible*, curse their enemies instead.

NIV		KJV
I wish they would go the whole way and emasculate themselves.	Gal. 5:12	I would they were even cut off which trouble you.
J.B.		
I would like to see the knife slip.		
NASB		
Would that those who are troubling you would even mutilate themselves.		

Clearly Paul wished "they," not one of their organs, were cut off. Wishing someone would do themselves bodily harm is not Christian teaching. But it is New Age and ancient occult practice. Carroll writes:

> [T]he *galli*, that is, the priests of the Great Mother, were supposed to work themselves up into a frenzy and castrate themselves. . .[T]his is the one thing that is mentioned by virtually all the classical authorities who discuss the cult of the Great Mother.

Augustine's *City of God* records that the galli were "effeminate [with] relaxed bodies and feminine gates."[35] Evidently sex change operations were not ushered in with the New Age focus on androgyny.

"Mutilate themselves" (NASB)

The NASB renders Galatians 5:12, "Would that those who are troubling you would even mutilate themselves." (The Greek word these versions are 'mutilating' is used again in Acts 27:32 where the soldiers "cut off the ropes." New version translators show their awareness of the true meaning by rendering this "cut" not "mutilate" the ropes.) Here the NASB is giving expression to a practice foreign to Christianity but familiar to the mystery religions. *Fires from Strange Altars* says:

> Self-mutilation including castration was a Babylonian religious virtue.[36]

This is seen in I Kings 18:28 where the prophets of Baal "cut themselves after their manner." Across the globe, "Mayans of all social stations regularly mutilated themselves in gruesome ways," reports *Ancient Empires of the New Age*. The author of this blood bath is not God but the Babylonian mysteries. (These mystery teachings prompted Origen, author of the Greek N.T. manuscripts underlying new versions, to castrate himself.)

God records the end of the harlot's bloodletting saying, he "hath avenged the blood of his servants at her hand" (Revelation 19:2). The blood stained hands of MYSTERY BABYLON, THE MOTHER OF HARLOTS are missing from the new versions, even though "her hands" hide away in *every* Greek N.T. manuscript.

NIV, NASB, et al.	KJV
OMIT	at her hand

New Version Veil

The headwater for all of these "visions," "idols," and "blasphemous names" (The One, the Virgin, The Force, The Mother) issued from the Babylonian mysteries. This system is depicted as a woman in the book of Revelation where her 'Virgin' veil is shed. Her forehead says instead:

> MYSTERY, BABYLON THE GREAT, THE MOTHER OF HARLOTS AND ABOMINATIONS OF THE EARTH Revelation 17:5

The religion of ancient Babylon was called 'the Mysteries'. It appears to be a mirror image of the antichrist's burgeoning One World Religion. To dim the clarity of this likeness, new versions fracture the clear message of her title. They shift the sand, so to speak, removing the key word 'MYSTERY' from her name and forehead. The authors of the minority Greek N.T. text shift the word into the mouth of John, hoping Christians will swallow it—never to be associated with their harlot religious system again. The sand castle, thus constructed, appears in most new versions, hoping not to be washed away by the true "rivers of living water."

As it appears in new versions, "Babylon" becomes, not a religious system, but a geographic location. The flood of recent books and commentators who assign the identity of MYSTERY BABYLON to modern Persia, attests to the power of new versions to alter what the church has accepted as its meaning for almost 2000 years. To buoy up their sinking reconstruction, some versions also eliminate the reference to the trafficking of the harlot in the "souls of men" (Revelation 18:13). Thereby, the religious association with the Babylonian mysteries is again avoided.

NIV, NASB, et al.		**KJV**
"BABYLON"		"MYSTERY BABYLON"
sits, and they	Rev. 17:9,10	sitteth. And there
the great city	Rev. 17:18	that great city
mystically	Rev. 11:8	spiritually

To further hide the identity of this religious system, new versions omit the key word "city" in Revelation 14:8 ("Babylon. . .that great city). Despite attempts by new versions which pretend, "They are seven kings," Revelation 17:9 locates the city which is the center of the last days revival of the Babylonian mystery religion. It is located on "seven mountains," which display her and sustain this faux gem like the prongs of a ring. Geographers, travel agents and even the NAB Catholic bible and official Knights of Columbus, pamphlet #51, agree that this 'city of seven hills' is Rome.

New versions also try to switch the identity of Mystery Babylon from Rome to the Middle East by giving Jerusalem's title "the great city" (Revelation 11:8) to Mystery Babylon and conversely giving Mystery Babylon's 'mystical' title to Jerusalem. The plains of the Middle East are plainly not the city of seven hills.

EIGHT

Seven Hills: Spires of Satan's Church

Popes and Politics

It is within Rome, called the city of seven hills, that the entire Vatican State is now confined.[1]

The Catholic Encyclopedia

According to the book of Revelation, these seven hills will serve as the spires for Satan's church. *What Ever Happened to Heaven*, by Dave Hunt, follows the history of this church where the marriage of Christian terms and pagan ideas takes place. He concluded:

> There seems little doubt that this false abominable last-days religious system called Mystery Babylon (Revelation 17:5) will have its headquarters at the Vatican. The joint histories of the Roman Empire and the Roman Catholic Church provide a fascinating preview of what John in Revelation foretells as yet to come. While its headquarters will be Rome, this false religious system will represent all churches, denominations, cults and religions joined in one.[2]

Religion and politics mix as biblical prophecy points also to the revived Roman Empire as the Antichrist's political base. Some scholars observe that the *Donation of Constantine* set the stage.

> [M]any medieval texts justify papal claims to temporal sovereignty over the Roman Empire by reference to the Donation of Constantine, by which the first 'Christian' emperor, in the 4th century, willed the Empire to the bishop of Rome in gratitude for curing him of leprosy.[3]

This 'donation' has gathered 'interest' down through the centuries. Pope Innocent III and others have tried to 'collect' saying, "[R]oyal power derives from the Pontifical authority." Pope Boniface VIII repeated, "[T]emporal power should be subject to the spiritual."[4] Today many, like U.N. Assistant Secretary General Muller are ready to donate the planet when Rome passes the plate. Muller's book devotes four chapters to Rome's focal place in the 'New World Order'. He remarks:

> One could trace the world's main historic events for the last 2000 years by studying the Pope's visits. I expect the Pope to add a spiritual dimension to the emerging world vision. . .which would make the heart of the world's 4.5 billion people beat as one.
>
> I really wish that someday a book containing the U.N. speeches of the 2 Popes. . .might be published for worldwide distribution. The result would be a kind of Bible for modern times. . .The Holy See has become so close to the U.N.. When I read documents emanating from the Holy See. . .I sometimes have the impression that I'm reading U.N. documents.[5]

The wheel propelling the Pope's political inroads is being oiled by his many patrons and publishing houses. His representatives hold key positions in major organizations working for a One World government. Notre Dame University's President is chairman of Planetary Citizens, Jesuit William F. Ryan is the Pope's proxy at the Club of Rome, while *Pax Christi* retains close ties with Planetary Initiative for the World We Choose.[6] The church's Paulist Press publishes, among their host of New Age books, *Toward a Human*

World Order, promoting the "mark of the beast." While Rome has its eyes on the world, the New Age is setting up its stage in the Pope's vicarage.

The Pope: the New Age Rage

Hypnotized by its hype, New Age dreamers have their glazed eyes fixed on Rome. The *New York Times* and newspapers worldwide ran the full page ad, 'The Christ is Here Now'. Its sponsor, New Age leader Benjamin Creme, says 'Jesus' will be here too, at home in Rome, 'possessing' the Pope.

> In the last 2000 years [Jesus has] worked in the closest relation to the Christ, saving his time and energy where possible and has special work to do with the Christian Church. He [Jesus] is one of the Masters who will very shortly return to outer work in the world TAKING OVER THE THRONE OF ST. PETER IN ROME [emphasis mine]. He will seek to transform the Christian Church, insofar as they are flexible enough to respond correctly to the new reality which the return of Christ and the masters will create.[7]
>
> Benjamin Creme
> *Reappearance of the Christ and the Masters of Wisdom*

New Age watchers have witnessed widespread agreement with Creme's viewpoint.

> Some New Agers will tell you that Jesus is still alive on earth after 2000 years and lives in the Himalayas with the other Masters of Wisdom. Some have recently claimed that Jesus moved to Rome in preparation for the manifestation of Lord Maitreya. He will allegedly take over the Vatican and become future pope.[8]

The blueprint for the New World Order, by Vera Alder, calls for the Pope to take his rightful "position."

> The Head of the Spiritual Cabinet would therefore have to be the most spiritually developed man in the world. . .He

> would occupy the position which could have been that of the Pope all along.[9]

The *New Age Monitor* reported that a rumor was circulating widely that Malachi Martin, a prolific Catholic writer, anticipated signs in the sky regarding the current pope.

> [T]he Pope was expecting a worldwide sign in the skies. . .everybody would see this simultaneously and all would know that Pope John Paul II was to be the New World Leader.[10]

The 'New' Age Catholic Church

The Pope's popularity among New Agers stems from their common mystical and 'Babylonian' bloodlines. The seeds of Hindu occultism grow well on Roman soil which has for centuries cultivated Constantine's crossbreed of Christianity and paganism. A doctoral research project on the profile of a 'New Age channeler' showed:

> Most have been raised Catholic. They were already open to the idea of hearing voices.[11]

As Rome's sway is waxing larger and larger, her sheep's clothing is covering less and less of the wolf's mane. Consequently Roy Livesey of the *New Age Bulletin* reports a shift to the 'East' in the Roman Catholic Church.

> [Rome] is presenting a picture of herself increasingly attractive to New Agers.[12]

The LORD told Ezekiel "great abominations" accompany apostates who lean "with their backs toward the temple of the LORD and their faces toward the east" (Ezekiel 8:16). Tottering toward Eastern mysticism, Pope John Paul II tries to sway souls toward the 'beast'. In his speech *L'Observatore Romano* (*Spiritual Vision of Man*), he calls his 800 million followers to seek:

> India's. . .spiritual vision of man. . .[T]he world does well to attend to this ancient wisdom.[13]

As channelers and the Pope call forth the spirits of paganism, 'spooky stuff' materializes on the pages of the *National Catholic Reporter*'s publications.[14] The following citations from a Winter 1991 issue document Constance Cumby's claim that "[T]his movement. . .is blatant among Roman Catholics."[15] The universal Hindu mantra *OM* is now right at home in R*OM*e. (Ellipses [. . .] usually represent a move to another of this publications 54 pages.)

Occult Techniques: Meditation, Affirmation, Imaging
"**OM** NAMAHA SHIVAYA. . .sanscrit chant [a translation of this from sanscrit is 'I bow down to you, Shiva,' the Hindu Prince of Devils]. . .meditating with a mantra. . .the way of the mantra. . .the Trinity Mantra Chart. . .went to Tibet to study Meditation. . .guided meditation. . .meditation music using nature images. . .the art of centering. . .breathing exercises. . .yoga. . .psychic. . .kything. . .the ancient practice of spiritual presence. . ." "*Affirmation for Personal Power*. . .release the power of the unconscious through affirmation. . ." "*Active Imagination*. . .healing through imagery. . .guided imagery. . .*Beyond Imaging*. . ." "We all have certain powers within us. These powers put everything we need within our reach. . .the divine Child."
Gaia: Hindu and New Age notion that the world is a female goddess of which we are a part.
"*Our Mother Who is in Heaven*. . .guided meditation. . .using feminine imagery of God. . ." "*Gaia's Groove*. . ." "*Earth Mass/ Missa Gaia*. . ." "Some of us have worshipped a Spirit. . .the earth is alive. . . go back to the masters of natural mysticism. . .the Native Americans. . ." "*Kalama: A Sufi Song of Love*. . .an ancient sufi melody created for the Dance of Universal Peace. . .there is no god or self except for the unity which embraces all. . ." "This may be the most important book published in this country right now. . .a massive shift in consciousness as Christians begin to see the Earth as the revelations of God. . . we have often positioned God as separate from, high above and immaterial. . ."

Hard Core Occultism
"[T]he works of. . .Meister Eckhart" "*Enneagram Inventory. . .Enneagrams: The Placement of Attention. . .Naming our Illusions. .*." "Shamanic drumming tradition [witchdoctor]. . .He takes seriously the words of Black Elk, a Lakota Sioux shaman and Catholic catechist, who believes that the beat of the sacred drum is the heartbeat of the universe and the revelation of the mystery of the Great Spirit. . ." "*Exploring the Secret Pathways*: masks, prayer-sticks, medicine circles, altars, paintings and dancing. . ." "RCIA [Rite of Christian Initiation]. . ." "*Magician, Lover*"
Liberalism
["D]escribes homophobia: What it is, how it works and whom it hurts". . .Feminist liberation theology. . .liberation theology. . .What Marx has to offer. . .the weakness of the anti-communist stance."
World Ecumenism
"It did my heart good to see Zen Masters. . .Catholic. . .ex-Jesuits. . .all trying to integrate these elements. . .[R]ooted in the Tibetan tradition. . .spiritual powers are sought through the ancient ways. . ." "Thomas Merton drew deeply from Eastern religious sources, especially Sufism [Moslem]."

The "great abominations" in this 1991 National Catholic Reporter publication represent the devilish debris which descended during a 1986 whirlwind from the East when the Pope called all twelve representatives of the world's religions to Italy. Such moves led Livesey to conclude, "A one-world religion, headed by the Pope, is what Rome seems to have in mind."[16]

The Seven Hills and the Scriptures

According to the century old 'habit' of the Harlot, all travelers on the roads back to Rome are invited in (Proverbs 7)—the Tibetan Buddhist, the Hindu Yogi, the witchdoctor, the occultist and the

Moslem Sufi. Likewise her perennial persecution of biblical Christians also continues. This same issue of the *National Catholic Reporter* 'roasts' Christians with the following fiery darts.

> Perhaps it is sinful to take pleasure in laughing at fundamentalists; but go ahead—risk it.
>
> Fundamentalism is painful. . .how you can cope with and even convert some fundamentalists.
>
> [E]ffective antidote for the fundamentalism of our day
>
> [F]renzied fundamentalists[17]

Leaving sight of the scriptures has left Rome spiritually blind, for few are more "frenzied" than a witch doctor in action or a Sufi whirling dervish. However, Rome's move toward mysticism has always paralleled its 'roasting' of biblical Christians. They have burned and banished bibles from the Majority Greek text, along with their owners, since the 4th century. Standing too close to the fire left that century's scribes with a "seared conscience." So they slipped corrupt *Septuagint* (LXX) readings into the bible to create a 'New' Latin Vulgate. To avoid detection Old Latin Vulgates were cast, owner and all, into the fire.

Modern mystics likewise like *this* 'New' Vulgate and its Septuagint readings rather than the Majority Greek N.T. Text or Hebrew Masoretic O.T. Text of the KJV.

NIV COMMITTEE MEMBER	LUCIFERIAN
"The translators also consulted the more important early versions—the Septuagint. . .the Vulgate. . . The Masoretic O.T. is not to be followed absolutely if a Septuagint reading or other reading is quite likely correct. Earl Kalland	"**Only** the text of the Protestant English bible [KJV] is as usual in disagreement with those of the Septuagint and the Vulgate. . .in the Septuagint [is] the heroine of Pagan fable." Blavatsky

NIV COMMITTEE MEMBER	LUCIFERIAN
"The NIV, in contrast to some other versions, sometimes opted for the LXX [Septuagint] in preference to the MT [Masoretic Text]. " Bruce Waltke "Most of the New Testament citations of the O.T. are from the Septuagint. . .they made primary use of the LXX, even when it disagreed with the Hebrew."[18] Ronald Youngblood	[She goes on to try to prove that Lucifer is the angel for our planet citing the Septuagint rendering of Deut 32:8, 9. "He set the bounds of the people according to the number of the angels." The Hebrew Masoretic and KJV say, "according to the number of children of Israel." The Septuagint's notion, influenced by Origen's gnostic leanings, is being heavily promoted today by fans of Luciferian Rudolf Steiner and David Spangler, contributing editor of *New Age Magazine*. Both say Lucifer is the 'angel of this planet's evolution'.][19]

During the Dark Ages, mysticism fueled ash heaps which turned Rome's seven hills into the Tibetian Himalayas. In the fourteenth century the church of Rome even officially canonized Buddha as a saint. (Centuries later it was discovered that St. Josaphat was from a corrupt translation of Bodhisattva.)[20] This 'mistake' *matched* many others in the 14th century as historians record Rome then, "burned persons who provided the Bible in a language the laity could read for themselves."[21] The *Geneva Bible*, published on the heels of this madness, sent a smoke signal forward. Its note next to Numbers 23:8 ("How shall I curse whom God hath not cursed?") says, "The Pope shall tell thee."[22] Later in the 16th century, the Roman Catholic Church put the Majority Greek New Testament text, then called the *Textus Receptus*, on "The Index" of forbidden books. Now NIV Committee members parrot the Pope's prohibition for the 20th century listener.

> It is now almost universally recognized that the *Textus Receptus* contains so many significant departures from the original manuscripts of the various New Testament books that it cannot be relied on as a basis for translation into other languages.[23] Ronald Youngblood

In place of the *Textus Receptus* the church of Rome offered the Douay version, a 'New Revised' edition of their 'New' Vulgate. Naturally, this is the corrupt version Blavatsky uses throughout her *Secret Doctrine* I and II to support her "Holy Satan" thesis. She remarks:

> In this work the Douay Roman Catholic version is generally followed.[24]

While Blavatsky was promoting Pope Pius IV's version, he was writing his *Syllabis of Errors* which condemned the study of the Protestant bible. Also to further promote Rome's 'version' of the facts, the Pope made the *Vaticanus* (B) manuscript available to a few select non-Catholic textual critics. Spiritualists Westcott and Hort saw in it the same 'kindred spirit' which Blavatsky recognized in Vaticanus' offsprings, the Vulgate and the Douay versions. Westcott and Hort then changed the traditional Majority Greek text until it mirrored the Vaticanus (B). When their grossly altered text finally matched that used by the Catholic church Pope Pius XII [Hitler's friend] said:

> [T]ranslations could be produced in cooperation with separated brethren.[25]

NIV and NASB Outside, Catholic Inside

The Pope's dream has become Christianity's nightmare. Few know that the four wheels driving the current U.B.S. *Greek New Testament*—Aland, Black, Metzger, and Wikgren—were being steered by a fifth wheel—in the driver's seat—Italy's own Carlo M. Martini. His editorship is revealed only on the frontispiece of the edition for translators, lest Protestants panic.

A strong pull toward ultra-liberalism and Rome is very evident in this committee's book, *The Textual Commentary on the Greek New Testament*. It gives a behind the scenes view of their work while admitting, "B.F. Westcott and F.J.A. Hort's. . .edition. . .was taken as the basis for the present United Bible Societies edition." The charge that the new Greek text, and consequently the new versions, are Roman Catholic is confirmed by the church itself, for they have stopped using the *Latin Vulgate* as a basis of translation and now use the Martini, Metzger, Aland, Black, and Wikgren text. Now both Protestant and Catholic versions are based on the same *Vaticanus* minority Greek text. (Nestle's and Bible Societies' texts are now identical.)

NIV (PROTESTANT)	NASB (PROTESTANT)	NAB (CATHOLIC)
"Greek text. . .of the NIV. . .was basically that in the United Bible Societies and Nestle's printed Greek New Testament."[26] Ralph Earle NIV Committee	"The Greek Text used in this book is that of the. . .Nestles. . .and Foreign Bible Society."[27] Introduction NASB	"The text used [was]. . .In general, Nestle-Aland's [. . .and] United Bible Societies."[28] Preface

The Romanization of new versions is no accident. Pope John Paul II's first message to governments and heads of international organization, entitled "To Reach Peace, Teach Peace," dealt with, among other things, *linguistics*. In it he called for the eradication of words and concepts of language which caused "*division.*" Catholic bibles with new version covers (NIV, NASB, et al) have served as tools when placed in Protestant hands to build bridges between denominations which a generation ago felt great *division*. NASB progenitor Phillip Schaff has hewn his tools for just such a job.

> The changes thus far. . .are in the right direction. . .and should contain the germs of a new theology. . .Every age must produce its own theology. . .such a theology will prepare the way for the reunion of Christendom.[29]

Schaff's strong leanings toward Roman Catholic theology led his denomination to "a formal and public indictment for heresy." "[S]harp accusations of Romanism. . .and all manner of doctrinal evils. . .were made against him." Undaunted by his denomination's pressure, he continued to work for the return of all Protestants to the Roman Church. His call for a "Catholic Protestantism, which stands for a new era," echoes from the pages of the new versions.[30]

NEW VERSIONS		KJV
the teachings of the Nicolaitans	Rev. 2:15	the doctrine of the Nicolaitanes, **which thing I hate.**
(*Nico* means 'to conquer'; Webster defines laity as "the people, as distinguished from the clergy; those not of a certain profession." Jesus hates the doctrine which replaces the New Testament priesthood of all believers with a class of clergy or professional scholars who attempt to conquer the common people with their credentials.)		
ceremonially washed	Luke 11:38	washed
votive gifts	Luke 21:5	gifts
a renewal	Col. 3:11	[not in Greek]
festival	Col. 2:16	holyday
OMIT	I Pet. 1:18	by tradition
guardian angel	Acts 12:15	angel
we have no other practice	I Cor. 11:16	We have no such custom [The Greek word is *toioutos*, 'such']

Hundreds and hundreds of other examples of Roman Catholic theology in the new versions could be cited and are explored thoroughly in other books. The Catholic teachings of salvation by works, purgatory, infant baptism, and 'the Virgin' are covered elsewhere in this book. The two major teachings which distinguish Catholicism from biblical Christianity are 1.) the Papacy, 2.) the Roman Catholic sacraments of penance, holy orders, and the 'holy eucharist'. These have been sewn into the new versions by scribes like Schaff and are cultivating a new crop of cross-breed 'Catholic Protestants'.

The Papacy

NEW VERSIONS		KJV
You are Peter, the Rock (NEB)	Matt.16:18	Thou art Peter and upon this rock
Cephas (which translated means Peter)	John 1:42	a stone
And they promptly reported all these instructions to Peter. . .Jesus himself sent out through them from east to west.	Mark 16:20	not in Greek
NEW VERSION EDITOR		
"[T]he reunion of Christendom. . .lies in large part with the pope . . .What if the pope should invite Greeks and Protestants to a fraternal pan-Christian council in Jerusalem, where the mother church held the first council of reconciliation of peace. . .[T]he centre of unification, the honor must be conceded to the. . .Roman communion."[31] Phillip Schaff		
Dean Stanley, Chair of the 'New' Greek Committee calls the pope, "the head of our profession."[32] (He also admires Sakya Muni, a religious prophet of the Hindoos.)		

The Los Angeles Times records the Pope, the false shepherd, calling, "[B]ring the Christian denominations back together again."[33] So the black sheep scurry saying:

> Its time for Protestants to go to the shepherd and say, 'What do we have to do to come home.'[34]
>
> Robert Schuller

> Anglicans are beginning to recognize and welcome a Petrine, universal Primacy in the office of the Bishop of Rome.[35] Archbishop of Canterbury

The Sacrament of Penance

NEW VERSIONS		KJV
confess your sins	James 5:16	confess your faults (Almost all Greek texts have the word for faults here,—not sins.)

The Christian Herald reports:

> Jim Bakker. . .said he had spent the last year. . . confessing to a Catholic priest.[36]

The Sacrament of Holy Orders

NEW VERSIONS		KJV
ministering as a **priest** the gospel of God, that *my* offering of the Gentiles might be acceptable.	Rom. 15:16	ministering the gospel of God that the offering up of the Gentiles might be acceptable. . .
priestly service	Luke 1:23	ministration
lengthen the tassels of their garments	Matt. 23:5	enlarge the borders of their garments

NEW VERSIONS		KJV
OMIT (The 'New' *Greek New Testament* entirely omits verse 14, jumping from 13 to 15.)	Matt. 23:14	Woe unto you, scribes and Pharisees, hypocrites! for ye devour widows houses and for a pretence make long prayer: therefore ye shall receive the greater damnation.

"Here's Johnny"—has become "Here's Father" as priest after priest enter stage left, passing across the semantic bridge on to shows like The 700 Club, 100 Huntley Street, Heritage U.S.A. and Trinity Broadcasting Network. The serpent hopes this high voltage venom of ecumenism will start the requiem for Christendom.

The Sacrament of Holy Eucharist

NEW VERSIONS		KJV
consecrated bread	Matt.12:4 Mark 2:26 Luke 6:4	shew bread
For the bread of God is **that** which comes down out of heaven and gives life to the world.	John 6:33	For the bread of God is **he** which cometh down from heaven and giveth life unto the world.
Unleavened Bread	Matt.26:17	unleavened bread
offered one sacrifice for sins and **took his seat forever** at the right hand of God.	Heb. 10:12	after he had offered **one sacrifice for sins forever,** sat down on the right hand of God
sweet wine	Acts 2:13	New wine (unfermented grape juice)

NEW VERSION EDITOR	
Westcott spoke of the "consecration" of the host.[37] Hort said, "I am a staunch sacerdotalist. . .the sacraments must be the center. [T]he bond of a common divine life derived in Sacraments is the most comprehensive bond possible."[38] Phillip Schaff's son writes, "The doctrine of the real presence Dr. Schaff continued to defend in his later years." Schaff said, "The Lord's Supper is more than a mere commemoration celebration."[39]	

Today Oral Roberts University professor, Howard M. Ervin, joins fellow spiritual 'sight-seers' on a trip to Rome. He comments:

> Pentecostals and sacramentalists share a common world view. In our own experience, we have often observed that many previously nonsacramental Pentecostals/ Charismatics have been, in varying degrees, attracted to sacramental theology as a result of their Pentecostal experience. . .For the sacramentalist the created order is an open one. It is a Spirit/matter continuum [Hindu]. . .[I]s he now unable to turn bread and wine into his body at the Eucharistic feast?[40]

Groups worldwide are being led to an unscriptural view of the Lord's supper "enabling men everywhere to sit down together," boasts Alice Bailey, and share communion with the Antichrist. She writes:

> The great spiritual achievement and evolutionary event of that age will be the communion. . .enabling men everywhere to sit down together in the presence of Christ [Antichrist] and share the bread and wine.[41]

Mankind—from humanists to Hindoos are being prepared for this "evolutionary event." 'Intellectuals' are being set up to believe 'the Eucharist' is a psychological 'quick-fix' in books like Richard Rubenstein's *My Brother Paul.* The author asserts it is "an answer at the deepest level of the psyche to what Freud perceived to be the main barrier to psychological health (killing the father)."[42] In this age of widespread psychological ills, *anything* which promises to remove "*the* main barrier" to mental happiness will be widely received. Pagan cultures worldwide have offered food to idols and then consumed it for 'spiritual power'. The East has long believed that bread 'Consecrated' to Krishna became his real body.

Conclusion: "Come out. . ."

Rome's sand castle cathedrals collapse when closely examined and severely sifted through the screen of God's word. Her bible bonfires sought to sear the screen shut. When 'culture' discouraged such 'live' cremations, she then wove culture's 'fables', like cobweb curtains, across the windows of Satan's seven spired church—screening out the "Sun of righteousness" (Malachi 4:2). "My people," says Jesus Christ, somehow got inside—seduced by the Serpent's Scribes.

> Come out of her, my people, that ye be not partakers of her sins, and that ye receive not of her plagues. Revelation 18:4

PART TWO

The New Christianity

Acrostic algebra reveals the ashy residue on which the NIV and NASV rest. When you shake down the 'Lite' versions like the *New American Standard Version* (NASV) and the *New International Version* (NIV), you find some heresies which are common to both (like their common letters 'N' and 'V', as shown in Step 2.)

The heresies which fill the NASV and NIV are composed of those common to both (N,V) and those unique to each (like the letters A, S, I as shown in Step 3).

When the portions of the true text of the *Authorized Version* (AV) are removed from these other versions, the sheep's clothing comes off and the brand on the hand of the wolf's skin spells—SIN. (Steps 4&5)

Step 1: (NASV-NIV)-AV = X
Step 2: (NASV-~~N~~I~~V~~)-AV = X
Step 3: (ASI+NV)-AV = X
Step 4: ~~A~~SI+N~~V~~-AV = X
Step 5: SIN = X

The leaven has been added
The meal has been digested
The 'New Christians' are coming.

The face of Christianity is changing. 'The Bride' is beginning to look like 'the Whore'. The heavy hand of the scribes, during their 'make-over' of the New Testament, has wrought this transformation. Their pens have traced the fallen features of New Age morality while allowing to waste away the pure words of the water of life. 'Here comes the Bride', —languishing, with a moral health mismatched to her Master's.

Changing God's word to change God's people is a ploy from the past, predating New Testament textual criticism by over 2000 years. The LORD said:

> "I am against the prophets that steal my words. . .and cause my people to err by their lies. . ."
> Jeremiah 23:29-32

The perennial nature of this problem was seen some 600 years later when "the light of the world" revealed the dark and perverse profile of the 'pen pushing' scribes. Jesus said:

> [E]xcept your righteousness shall exceed the righteousness of the scribes. . .ye shall in no case enter into the kingdom of heaven. Matthew 5:20

> The scribes. . .do not ye after their works. Matthew 23:3

Nearly two thousand years after this scathing speech, the scribes still sustain their sinful momentum.

NEW VERSION EDITORS	'NEW' CHRISTIANITY
"[F]ighting and dancing. . .I hope the church of the future will foster."[1] Hort "There was a time when it was usual to draw a sharp line between religious and worldly things. That time has happily gone by."[2] Westcott	"We also like suggestive dancing, movies, and drinking and are trying to enjoy sex for recreational purposes. . .[L]et me say that none of the above has anything whatsoever to do with our salvation."[3]

In the following verses the corrupt countenance of 'the last days' man comes in view, each characteristic, an uncomely canker on the face of the bride.

> This know also that in the last days. . .men shall be **lovers of their own selves, covetous, boasters, proud, blasphemers. . .unholy. . .Without natural affection. . .fierce, despisers of those that are good. . .heady, highminded**, lovers of pleasure. . .
> II Timothy 3:1-4

> Now the spirit speaketh expressly that in the latter times some shall depart from the faith. . .speaking **lies.**
> I Timothy 4:1,2

> Neither repented they of their **murders**, nor of their **sorceries**, nor of their **fornication**. . .and they repented not to give him glory. Revelation 9:21, 16:9-11

But in the new versions, where the old and new man merge, words like these, which purge or even scourge, often submerge. "The prophets that steal. . .words" stubbornly sustain their scheme, hoping 'the Bride' will slip away or stumble down the long aisle. As a light unto her path, the word is the ultimate target. Marrs concludes:

> The New Age Bible will definitely allow for hedonism, based on the belief that no act is sinful.[4]

'Here comes the New Age Bible'—

NINE

Men Shall Be Unholy

TREND ONE

Neither repented they of their. . .FORNICATION.
Revelation 9:21

Abominable Customs

The New Age movement is called, among other things, 'the New Church'. Jean Dixson, a popular seer, anticipates "the foundation of a New Christianity." One New Age group calling itself 'New Christianity', writes in its newsletter, *The Good News*: "Our ministry isn't into sin, guilt, disease, or pain."[1] This group is formulating their own *new* code of ethics. Robert Muller, New Age spokesman, concurs calling for a:

> [N]ew code of behavior which will encompass all races, nations, religions and ideologies. It is the formulation of these new ethics which will be the greatest challenge for the new generation.[2]

Terms like the 'new ethics', 'situation ethics' or the 'new morality' imply that ethics and morals change and can exist outside of the traditional Judeo-Christian Decalogue. Few realize that the word ethics (L. *ethicus*) means only "customs of a nation"; morality (L. *moralis*) means merely "customs, mores." The words themselves are detached from any objective standard of right and wrong. For example, cannibalism and bigamy were considered 'moral' and 'ethical' behaviors among nineteenth century New Guinea bushmen. Abandoning one's tribe and territory, however, was 'immoral', that is, against the group's mores.

God noted that "the customs of the people are vain" (Jeremiah 10:3), and not to be confused with his ordinances.

> Therefore shall ye keep mine ordinance, that ye commit not any one of these abominable customs. . ." [morals or ethics] Leviticus 18:30

The words moral and immoral (according to custom and not according to custom) are an affront to God. They imply that man himself can determine *what* is right and wrong. Eve became the first 'moralist', as she chose to decide *what* is good and what is evil. Rebels, like Eve and Lucifer seek 'the good'. Moralists always claim to adhere to "what is right."

> Ye shall not do after all the things that we do here this day, every man whatsoever is **right** in his own eyes. Deuteronomy 12:8

God spoke these words because the heathen perennially chose their mores over the laws of God. "Taoists maintain morals are relative." The Hindu *Bhagavad Gita* "teaches the supremacy of freedom over morality."[3] Its dialogue between Arjuna and Krishna concludes:

> [T]here can be no absolute moral values because all things are changing, evolving. A particular moral value represents only a particular perspective offered by a particular time at a particular level of evolution.[4]

From the bushmen to the bookmen like Boehm, Blake, Nietzsche, Heidigger and Sartre, man rejects the mandates of God for a man-made morality. A confederacy of educators, carrying Einstein's 'Theory of Relativity' banner, have captured today's students. In a national religious survey, half of the college students polled affirmed that:

> Truth is basically relative; what is right and true for you may not be right and true for me.[5]

The decrees of God have died and man's mores revived in the New Age and new versions as well.

> [M]orality. . .derives from the innermost self, not from mere obedience.[6] *The Aquarian Conspiracy*

> Evil is what you think it is.[7] Shirley MacLaine

> [Is] not based on. . .dualistic concepts of 'good' or 'bad.'[8]
> David Spangler

Moody's Erwin Lutzer concludes:

> The New Age movement [is] promising contact with a religious god who nonetheless doesn't judge anyone.[9]

And so are the new versions.

NIV, NASB, et al.		KJV
but not for the purpose of passing judgement	Rom. 14:1	not to doubtful disputations

Porn

In the battle between man's mores and God's laws, the new versions have opted for the 'popular' morals of the day. They have substituted the relativistic word 'immorality' for the word 'fornication'. The word 'immorality' carries with it no description of what is forbidden. Webster elaborates:

> *Immorality:* State or quality of being immoral
> *Immoral:* Not moral
> *Fornication:* Illicit sexual intercourse on the part of an unmarried person.

The New Testament Greek word is *porneau, porne, pornos, porneia.*

NASB		KJV
OMIT	Rom.1:29	fornication
immorality	I Cor. 5:1	fornication
immorality	I Cor. 6:13	fornication
immorality	I Cor. 6:18	fornication
immorality	2 Cor. 12:21	fornication
immorality	Eph. 5:3	fornication
immorality	Col. 3:5	fornication
immorality	Rev. 2:14	fornication
immorality	Rev. 2:20	fornication
immorality	Rev. 9:21	fornication
immorality	Rev. 14:8	fornication
immorality	Rev. 17:2	fornication
immorality	Rev. 18:3	fornication
immorality	Rev. 18:9	fornication
immorality	Rev. 19:2	fornication
immoral	Heb. 12:16	fornicator
act immorally	I Cor. 10:8	commit fornication
immoral people	I Cor. 5:9	fornicators
immoral people	I Cor. 5:10	fornicators
immoral people	I Cor. 5:11	fornicator
immorality	Gal. 5:19	Adultery, fornication

The NASB calls 'natural', what God calls sin.

natural	James 3:15	sensual
nature	James 5:17	passions

Every young person knows the meaning of the word 'whore'. (Webster's *'whore'*: to have unlawful sexual intercourse; *whoremonger*: lecher; a man given to whoring.)

NASB		KJV
immorality	Eph. 5:5	whoremonger
immoral men	I Tim. 1:10	whoremonger
immoral person	Rev. 21:8	whoremonger
immoral persons	Rev. 22:15	whoremongers

The NASB's non-judgmental translations echo the policy statements of many mainline denominations.

NASB		KJV
homosexual	I Tim. 1:10	them that defile themselves with mankind.

The prediction by Marrs that, "Satan will author an unholy New Age bible, with no restrictions on man's desire to enjoy a licentious lifestyle" is coming true.

Informal polling of university students between 1985 and 1991 with the question posed, "What is immorality?" elicited responses ranging from "pollution" to political issues. The NIV's and NKJV's "sexual immorality" fared no better. To the query "What is sexual immorality?" student response ranged from "one night stands" to various situational scenarios indicative of the highly desensitized and depraved nature of the mores of our current culture. Answers to both questions always evoked responses showing the subjective and relative nature of the word 'moral'. It appears young Americans know Latin etymology and Webster's better than new version editors.

Bibles without objective standards merely reinforce the Values Clarification theories of Louis E. Baths, Merrill Harmon and Sidney B. Simon being used in the elementary schools today. *The Wall Street Journal* notes:

> If parents object to their children. . .engaging in premarital sex, the theory behind Values Clarification makes

> it appropriate for the child to respond, 'But that's just YOUR value judgement. Don't force it on me.'[10]

The harvest from the seeds planted in the sixties (NASB) and seventies (NIV) is ripe and rotting on the vine. A 1990 survey by researchers at Indiana University and Marion County Health department revealed sexual activity is beginning at an earlier age than ever. Dr. Donald P. Orr reported 555 of 677 middle-class students, age 12-14 have engaged in fornication.[11] Another recent survey, done by 8 denominations, polled 1438 'evangelical' teens (those who regularly attend a conservative church). Nearly half had committed fornication; only one-third "declined to brand sex outside of marriage as morally unacceptable." Bibles which omit a clear mandate against, "sexual intercourse on the part of unmarried persons" (Webster's 'fornication') leave parents defenseless in their battle for their children's chastity. An anxious mother called Moody Broadcasting's 'Open Line' program asking Pastor Cole *where* she could find a verse to show her son that pre-marital sex is wrong. He was unable to give one.[12] On a recent 700 Club, the author of *Generation at Risk* was asked why sexually active Christian kids have no sense of guilt. He responded that there was "no absolute standard of scripture" to use and so young people conclude, "If I don't feel bad, it must not be wrong."[13]

The use of the ambiguous word 'immorality' by new versions is more a matter of sales than semantics. "After all, we are in the entertainment business," quips the owner of the NIV, international publishing magnate and purveyor of erotica, Rupert Murdock (*New Age Bulletin*, England, Vol. V, No. 1, p. 2, June 1993) Pressure from mainline denomination, representing large markets, prompts their use of wording which allows the greatest variety of interpretations. The 1991 national committee report from the Presbyterian Church (U.S.A.) represents the reins pulling from religious and 'ethical' markets.

APOSTATE CHRISTIANITY	NEW AGE
"A **reformed** Christian **ethic** of sexuality will not condemn. . .any sexual relationship in which there is genuine equality and mutual respect. What is ruled out. . .are relations in which persons are abused, exploited or violated." Presbyterian Church U.S.A.	"[N]o stigma need be attached to premarital, or extramarital sex or even incest, except where these acts do violence to another."[14] *Ethics in Contemporary Psychic Experience*

Roman Catholics are expressing similar views. Sister Madonna Kolbenschlay said, "[W]omen. . .are in the process of reversing Genesis by validating and freeing their sexuality." Father Matthew Fox in *Original Blessing* writes, "Ours is truly an erotic god."[15]

That morality is really *not* relative is seen in the outrage of the public at the sexual activity of gurus like Swami Muktanada Paramanansa (Gov. Jerry Brown, Marsha Mason and Diana Ross' guru), Maharishi Mahesh Yogi, Rajneesh, Catholic priests and Bishops and fallen evangelical leaders. The secular press has devoted entire books, like the best selling *The Closing of the American Mind*, to bemoan society's substitution of 'values' for 'virtues'. A *Los Angeles Times* writer reflects on the coming cataclysm caused by the rejection of objective standards.

> [R]elative standards of morality breed chaos and ultimately the downfall of society.[16]

TREND TWO

This know also that in the last days. . .men shall be. . UNHOLY. II Timothy 3:2

NIV, NASB et al.		KJV
Then come, follow me	Mark 10:21	and come, **take up the cross** and follow me

The 'New' Christianity has put down their cross to follow Pied Piper preachers who present Christ carrying a credit card instead of a cross. For them life becomes a Supermarket Sweepstakes where the 'Christian Winners', not Christian sinners, scramble for 'position' to pick up all the prosperity and pleasure they can until the trumpet rings. They pick the aisles marked 'Crown' not 'Cross', 'Happy' not 'Holy', 'Easy' not 'Right', 'Now' not 'Later'. The background musak 'ministry' croons:

> Prophesy not unto us right things speak unto us smooth things, prophesy deceits. Isaiah 30:10

But the timing of the tune is off and so is the timing of God's people. The Jews rejected Jesus because they wanted a temporal King 'now', not 'later'. Christians are rejecting the cross now, because they want the crown 'now' not 'later'. They shop the bible for bargains and deals, dodging Hebrews 11:35-40, 13:13-14, Romans 8:17, I Corinthians 4:11-14, II Timothy 2:12, II Corinthians 11:23-27 or Luke 19:17. This chapter will continue to explore how the new versions make better bargains with the conscience.

Crown or Cross?

The temptation to skip the cross and capture the crown was presented to Christ by Satan in the wilderness (Luke 4). Satan pressed for a miracle—manna (verse 3); Jesus offered the word of God instead (verse 4). Satan counter-offered "the world, . . .power. . .and glory" (verses 5 and 6); Jesus called for service and worship toward God (verse 8). The devil demanded fulfillment of scripture promises-NOW (verse 11: Psalm 91:11); Jesus called this tempting God. Today's Christians, in the wilderness of this world, press for miracles. When offered the word instead, they counterclaim 'the world, power and glory' as a fulfillment of scripture promises-NOW. God calls Christians to a life of spiritual sustenance on scriptures, not manna—service and worship, not signs and wonders—and trusting not tempting God.

Satan saved his most subtle scheme for Jesus and often snares super-saints with the same. The evil lay hidden, not in every proposition, but in the timing. Jesus will bring bread miraculously to the rock city of Sela (Petra) and others in the wilderness during the tribulation (Revelation 12:6, Matthew 24:14, Micah 7:14). He will return in the sky (Acts 1:11). And the "kingdoms of this world" will become "the kingdoms of our Lord" (Revelation 11:15). But the cross comes first on Christ's course and Christians are called to "follow."

> If we suffer, we shall also reign with him.
> II Timothy 2:12

Satan snares Christians with the lusts of the flesh ("bread"), the lusts of the eyes ("shewed him") and the pride of life (hey, look at me sky-fly!). His spokesman for the 90's, Luciferian David Spangler offers his New Age bait in place of what Christians so often despise.

> If. . .what Christ represents demands suffering, repentancy and self-negation, then this needs to be seen clearly, in contrast to the New Age which represents love, upliftment of the individual and collective well being.[17]

'Christian' ministries are singing along with Spangler to the New Age musak tune *Easy is Right.*

> You are suffering because you have refused your place in Christ.[18] E.W. Kenyon

They are all following the new version Pied Piper who omitted "longsuffering with joyfulness" from Colossians 1:11.

Adequate or Perfect?

"Be perfect" II Corinthians 13:11

Jesus calls Christians saying, "If any man will come after me, let him deny himself and take up his cross daily and follow me." The Pied Piper merely asks young people to have a "heart," be "mature," get "adequate" grades, "complete" your education, so you will be "fully trained and equipped" for some form of employment. The goal of the New Age and new versions is Spangler's "upliftment of the individual and collective well being." God's goal for Christians is spiritual perfection.

NEW VERSIONS		KJV
men	2 Pet. 1:21	holy men
heart	I Pet.1:22	pure heart
adequate	2 Tim. 3:17	perfect
called	Jude 1:1	sanctified
Campers are equipped, but not necessarily perfect.		
equipping	Eph. 4:12	perfecting
equip you	Heb. 13:21	make you perfect
College students may complete their degree, but are not necessarily blameless or perfect.		
fully trained	Luke 6:40	perfect
complete	2 Cor. 13:11	perfect
completed	Rev. 3:2	perfect
complete	I Thess. 5:23	blameless
complete	Matt. 19:21	perfect
Career *Fortune* 500 managers may get an 'award of excellence', but not of virtue.		
excellence	Phil. 4:8	virtue
Centenarians (100 years old) may be mature, but are not necessarily perfect.		
maturity	Heb. 6:1	perfection
mature	Eph. 4:13	perfect
mature	I Cor. 2:6	perfect

Perfection is truly censored from the new versions. Matthew 5 closes with "Be ye therefore perfect, even as your Father which is in heaven is perfect." New versions omit the preceding verse which would lead to that perfection.

NIV, NASB, et al.	KJV
OMIT	Bless them that curse you, do good to them that hate you, and. . .despitefully use you. Matt. 5:44

P.S. If you can't follow the Pied Piper, at least don't get caught.

if any man is caught in any offense	Gal. 6:1	overtaken in a fault

Alot like Lot?

Lot "sat in the gate"; later "he lingered." Had he adopted the "abundance of idleness" ascribed to the people of Sodom? C.S. Lewis' *Screwtape Letters* warned of Satan's ploy to substitute mental assent for 'menial labor'.

NEW VERSIONS		KJV
We have as our **ambition**. . .to be pleasing	2 Cor. 5:9	We **labor**
If any man **is willing** to do his will	John 7:17	If any man will **do** his will
All who **desire to** live godly	2 Tim.3:12	all that will live godly
confidence	I Tim. 3:13	boldness
Substituting 'talk' for 'walk'?		
reaffirm your love for him	2 Cor. 2:8	confirm your love toward him
encourage	Titus 2:4	teach
gratitude	I Tim. 4:4	thanksgiving
Substituting lucre for labour?		
contributing	Rom.12:13	distributing
Singing 'Easy is Right'?		
seek him	Heb. 11:6	diligently seek him
You shall be holy [magic?]	I Pet. 1:16	be ye holy [do it]

Warren Wiersbe's *Confident Living* magazine warns:

Today there are many Bible translations, versions and paraphrases coming off the press. I am appalled to see how fickle and foolish some Christians are to run out and buy the latest version or paraphrase of the Bible thinking it is some shortcut to a spiritual experience. That isn't so, my friend. The conversion of every sinner is the call of God to holiness.[19]

TREND THREE

This know also, that in the last days perilous times shall come. For men shall be. . .COVETOUS.
II Timothy 3:1,2

$$$ or Righteous

Salvation brings spiritual not material riches. Jesus said to the church in Smyrna.

I know thy. . .poverty (but thou art rich). Revelation 2:9

The following entries can be found safe in the Saint's Savings of Smyrna.

1. rich in faith James. 2:5
2. rich in mercy Ephesians 2:4
3. rich in good works I Timothy 6:18
4. rich toward God Luke 12:21
5. riches of the glory of this mystery. . .which is Christ in you Colossians 1:27
6. riches of his grace Ephesians 1:7, 2:7
7. riches of his goodness Romans 2:4, 9:23
8. riches both of the wisdom and knowledge of God Romans 11:33
9. riches of the full assurance Colossians. 2:2
10. unsearchable riches Ephesians 3:8, 16
11. reproaches of Christ greater riches Hebrews 11:26

But to the Laodiceans Jesus said:

> Because thou sayest, I am rich and increased with goods, and have need of nothing; and knowest not that thou art wretched, and miserable, and poor, and blind and naked: Revelation 3:17, 18

Laying wait for Laodicians today is the same snare. This is a timeless trap, the same one Satan set for Jesus. His bait was 'the world' and the selling price: people's souls. The treacherous King of Sodom tried this trick too, telling Abraham:

> Give me the persons and take the goods to thyself. Genesis 14:21

Lot listened and later "pitched his tent *temporarily* toward Sodom." The tent stakes took root and footers finally clutched four feet down into Sodom's center-city soil. Lot's title deed came with a Compromising Christian Clause: "Beware of practicing your righteousness before men"(NIV). The building code called for closets for Christians, not Sodomites. He began "without the gate," but couldn't wait and took the bait. Once "in the gate," it was too late. He lost his loot, his wife to boot.

Lot's "substance was great," but "fire and brimstone" have a way of changing substance to smoke and spouses to salt. This too will be the lot of the 'New' Christian who lays up his treasures on earth.

The 'New' Christian Codebooks call 'righteousness' into the closet, while parading 'prosperity'. They substitute 'the goods' for 'being good', leaving hands too full to 'take up the cross' and heads too high with a corruptible crown to care about a "crown of righteousness."

NASB, NIV et al		**KJV**
Beware of practicing your righteousness before men	Matt. 6:1	do not your alms before men
wealth	Col. 2:2	riches
wealth and **prosperity** (NIV)	Prov. 8:18	riches and **righteousness**
finds life, **prosperity** (NIV)	Prov. 21:21	findeth life, **righteousness**

NIV		KJV
I know the plans I have for you, declares the LORD, plans to **prosper** you.	Jer. 29:11	For I know the thoughts that I think toward you, saith the LORD, thoughts of **peace**.

Readers can expect even less righteousness in upcoming versions, as Papyrus Bodmer III and other papyrus are used, as recommended by Philip Comfort, NRSV collaborator.[20]

OMIT	Rom. 9:28	in righteousness
OMIT	John 16:10	righteousness
OMIT	John 16:8	righteousness

Herbert M. Wolf, NIV Committee member, admits that the NIV's switch from "righteousness" to "prosperity" is "non-literal." He writes:

> [N]on-literal translations enhance accuracy. . .The word *tsedeqah*—normally rendered 'righteousness' is translated 'prosperity', perhaps understood as the reward of righteous living. . .The abstract quality of 'righteousness' does not **fit.** . .[21]

Perhaps the armour and breastplate of "righteousness does not fit" Mr. Wolf and his pack because they are puffed up and paunchy, because they have devoured souls (Ezekiel 22:25). Furthermore, non-literal translations cannot enhance accuracy when the editor's theology is substituted for the Greek word, as the *Harvard Theological Review* observes is often the case with the NIV.

Paul said that those, like Wolf, who teach that "gain is godliness" are "destitute of the truth." Equating financial prosperity with spirituality is a common characteristic of the 'New' Christianity and the New Age. The Nichiren Shoshu Buddhists have a teaching called *bon no soku adai*, which means, "worldly desires equal enlightenment," or as the new versions put it:

NEW VERSIONS		KJV
godliness **actually** is **a means of** great gain	I Tim. 6:6	godliness **with contentment** is great gain
wisdom brings **success**	Eccles. 10:10	wisdom is profitable **to direct**

Many Christians are trying on Saul's *silver* armour, like David did.

APOSTATE CHRISTIANITY	NEW AGE
	"[He] will eventually acquire riches and wisdom, which in turn lead to his enlightenment."[25] Buddhist
"[Poverty] is a curse that comes on those who either have not served God properly, or who are not following certain laws of God or are temporarily in transit to one of God's destinations."[22] Pat Robertson	[If] we lack anything it is because we have not used our minds in making the right contact with the supermind.[26] . . "You were born to be rich."[27]
"In God's kingdom, you GIVE TO GET."[23] Paul Crouch	"[M]y gift. . .makes possible my greater receiving."[28] Unity
"The Body of Christ is going to end up with all the money because God's will is prosperity."[24] Gloria Copeland	"[T]he more enlightened a person is, the more money and success will naturally occur in his life."[29] New Age

'Open' Says Me

God will open the windows of heaven and supply all of our needs, but greeds must be met by manipulation, using methods of magic such as the power of the mind or the spoken word. Both methods have infiltrated the 'New' covetous church. The *Occult Encyclopedia* says:

> It has been said that religion consists of an appeal to the gods, whereas magic is the attempt to force their compliance.[30]

Christians are copying the incantation formula of occultists like Tara Center's Mary Bailey.

Pat Robertson	Kenneth Hagin	Mary Bailey
"We are. . .to **command** the money to come to us."[31]	"You are not **demanding** anything of the Father. . .You're **demanding** of the Devil."[32]	"Then do we have a right to ask, to invoke, to **demand** money."[33]

All new versions arm their readers with enough ammunition to hijack heaven. Marrs saw the shakedown coming:

> [T]he belief that all men can unlock magical forces in their minds to perform miracles will be among the doctrines included in the New Age Bible.[34]

Now that new versions have replaced 'faith' with 'faithfulness' as a means of salvation (See Chapter 15), 'faith' can have a new meaning. It is no longer 'faith in God', but 'faith for things'. B.F. Westcott's years of association with the esoteric world led him to call "faith". . .a "power" we can "use."[35] In this form of magic, the quantity of faith, as opposed to the object of faith, is emphasized. New versions foster the phoney faith teachers which flood the media.

NIV, NASB, et al.		KJV
because of the littleness of your faith	Matt. 17:20	Because of your unbelief

The size of their faith was not the issue since the verse closes with ". . .If ye have faith as a grain of mustard seed. . .nothing shall be impossible to you." However, a big 'gimme' requires a big gun to "force" compliance. This 'gun powder' faith power is being promoted in every sector of the culture. Burger King passes out crowns whose cartoon characters call kids to use the "power" of "imagination" to get what they want. Unwary parents, who would not think of using what occultists call "a wishing cap" or "Fortunatus cap", crown their kids with the same. Even the man in the pulpit sounds like the message on the pages of the *Occult Encyclopedia.*

> **APOSTATE CHRISTIANITY**
> Symbols and images are all means by which communication occurs between the spiritual and nonspiritual realms. . .visualization prayers can be so powerful. . .Any form of active imagination is to experience the inner world. . .We can help people visualize and use their imagination. . .Many times there is no exact chapter or verse to describe it.[36]
>
> Robert Wise *The Church Divided*

The "verse to describe" what this and some other pastors are preaching is on page 551 of *The Occult Encyclopedia* in their tutorial on 'magic'.

> ***THE OCCULT ENCYCLOPEDIA***
> Of this we may rest assured that through full and powerful imagination only can we bring the spirit into an image. . .Through faith the imagination is invigorated and complete, for it really happens that every doubt mars its perfection. Faith must strengthen the imagination, for faith establishes the will.[37]

With the cooperation of the NKJV and other new versions, Christians 'conjure up' instead of 'cast down' imaginations.

NIV		KJV
We demolish arguments.	2 Cor. 10:5	Casting down imaginations.

The belief that one's thoughts and words can effect external reality is based on an occult technique called 'sympathetic magic'. "There is a link between sorcery and pantheism," notes one author.[38] If all is One, then speaking or thinking naturally affect the rest of reality, rather like a wave set up by a tossed stone. Certain circles of Christianity have adopted this monistic world view to support their methods.

APOSTATE CHRISTIANITY	HINDUISM
"God is no longer boxed in by the arbitrary Spirit/matter categories of an outmoded physics. . .[T]he created order is an open one. It is a Spirit/matter continuum."[39] *Conversion/Initiation and the Baptism in the Holy Ghost*	"Matter is not a contradiction of spiritual consciousness; it is simply the lowest expression of it."[40]

All this patter about spirit/matter continuums conceals the real trigger fingers which set the 'magic in motion'. They are the "spirits of devils, working miracles" (Revelation 16:14). The "wishing caps" for kids and corruptible crowns for carnal Christians are a dress rehearsal for the forthcoming false prophet who fulfills the fantasy of every spiritual power monger "by means of those miracles which he had power to do. . ." (Revelation 13:14). (The NASB's false prophet performs no miracles, merely some signs. New versions focus on the flamboyant rather than the spiritual work which Christ did often calling his 'mighty works' 'miracles'. So when the false prophet comes with 'miracles', people will say "This is the work of God!")

The Country Club or the Cross

New Agers say fundamentalists have the "virus of separation."[41] So 'society' Sunday schools immunized weekly with sermon serum: "Should a Christian own a BMW?" New versions have parked inside 'the Club' not outside 'the camp' (Hebrews 13:13). They read like a Christian Country Club Membership Check List.

	NEW VERSIONS		KJV
x	boast	Heb. 3:6	rejoicing
x	keep aloof	2 Thess. 3:6	withdraw yourselves
x	proper clothing	I Tim. 2:9	modest
x	propriety	I Tim. 2:15	sobriety
x	respectable	I Tim. 3:2	of good behavior
x	be dignified	I Tim. 3:11	be grave
x	dignity	I Tim. 3:4	gravity
x	dignified	Titus 2:7	gravity
x	dignified	Titus 2:2	grave
x	Deacons must be men of dignity	I Tim. 3:8	Likewise must the deacons be grave.
x	more important	Phil. 2:3	better
x	furthering the administration	I Tim. 1:4	godly edifying
x	without honor	I Cor. 4:10	despised
x	poorly clothed	I Cor. 4:11	naked
x	had all things in common	Acts 2:44	had all things common
x	Let no one disregard you	Titus 2:15	Let no man despise thee
x	**Again 'righteousness' is rejected; a respectable and sober funeral parlor director will be 'adequate'.**		
x	respectable	Luke 5:32	righteous
x	soberminded	I Cor. 15:34	righteousness

Preppie or Peculiar? Pick one. For example, apparel representing modest and godly moderation, not models and glossy magazines, has a price tag which reads: PER$ECUTION. A lifestyle driven by verses not vogue, will brand one as "peculiar" (NERD, in the vernacular). Unwilling to bear "his reproach," the NIV's Edwin Palmer pushes the "peculiar people" of Titus 2:14 and I Peter 2:9 into the closet—already crowded with the 'righteous' and 'the perfect'. Palmer writes:

> . . .a peculiar people. Today that means odd. It should be. . .42

It meant odd when Peter and Paul wrote it and when Moses wrote it 4000 years earlier.

> Ye shall be a peculiar treasure unto me above all people. Exodus 19:5

Webster's says 'odd' means "unusual," and 'peculiar people' means:

> different from the usual or norm. Jehovah's own people; the people of Israel; —used of themselves by many Christian bodies.

The Root of All Evil

At the root of all the rhetoric about the need for new versions lies the true cause—covetousness. "The love of money is the root of all evil." Some "destroy souls to get dishonest gain" (Ezekiel 22:27). Are there ministries which promote the new versions because they, in turn, pack their treasuries?

ROMANS 12:8	KJV
contributing. . .give generously (NIV)	giveth. . .with simplicity
gives,. . .do so generously (NAB)	
be generous (LB)	
do it generously (TEV)	
give with liberality (NASB)	
gives, with liberality (NKJV)	
gives, with liberality (J.W. Translation)	
ROMANS 12:13	
contributing (NASB et al.)	distributing

> The word of God is not bound. II Timothy 2:9

The KJV is the only version not bound by a copyright. No author or publisher receives a royalty because God is the author.

However, "God is not the author of confusion" (I Corinthians 14:33) or of "commercial ventures." The latter term was used to describe the ASV (NASB, *Living Bible*), RV (RSV) and 'New' Greek Text by Philip Schaff the chairman of their American Committee. His autobiography exposes the sordid details of "intense fighting" and "battles" over the profits to ensue. God did not author these versions, as Schaff's book reveals. He admits the translation moved to "publisher's control mid-stream"; each verse was "subject to approval of the University presses" who had "assumed all the expenses of the enterprise. . .$100,000." He states further:

> [P]roperty and commercial rights were the bone of contention. . .[I] fought with the New Testament Company for three hours for the American rights. . .The syndics of the University presses. . .agreed to ratify them on the condition that the American Committee purchase the copyright of the revision for. . .5000 pounds [several million American dollars today]. . .[I]n return for the 5000 pounds the American Committee would then at all events obtain complete command of the American market [$$$]. . .The battle over commercial rights was so great that. . . the University presses had prohibited the British companies from sending any more material to the U.S.. . .After intense fighting, it was agreed that the American Committee could not release their version for 14 years.[43]

The autobiography of J.B. Phillips [*NASB Interlinear Greek-English New Testament* Forward, *J.B. Phillips Translation*] likewise lays bare his beliefs (about his billfold). He not only expects to receive royalties from the sale of these versions but those who use "extended quotes. . .must expect to pay a proper copyright fee."[44] Dr. Frank Logsdon, a force behind the NASB, says of his partner, Dewey Lockman, "[H]e did it for money." Is it any wonder new version editors twist verses which warn of seeking wealth?

NIV, NASB, et al.		**KJV**
Nobody should seek his own good.	I Cor. 10:24	Let no man seek his own. . .wealth
the love of money is **a** root of all **kinds of** evil	I Tim. 6:10	For the love of money is **the** root of **all** evil

TREND FOUR

This know also that in the last days. . .men shall be. . .FIERCE II Timothy 3:2

The hardhearted fierceness which will characterize the "last days" man is fed by the new versions.

NEW VERSIONS		KJV
OMIT	Matt. 5:44	do good to them that hate you
OMIT	Mark 11:26	But if ye do not forgive, neither will your Father which is in heaven forgive your trespasses

The beheading of Christians during the tribulation receives no censure from them in the following verses.

Neither repented they of their murders. Revelation 9:21

NEW VERSIONS		KJV
OMIT	Gal. 5:21	murders
Don't extort money	Luke 3:14	Do violence to no man
haters of good	2 Tim. 3:3	despisers of **those that are** good
loves what is good	Titus 1:8	a lover of good **men**

These martyrs will be beheaded by the hands of:

MYSTERY BABYLON THE GREAT, THE MOTHER OF HARLOTS AND ABOMINATIONS OF THE EARTH **drunken** with the blood of the saints. . .[T]he inhabitants of the earth have been made **drunk** with the wine of her fornication. Revelation 17:2,5,6

The inflamed feelings which shadow such escapades mark the fierce tribulation tyrants as "drunken." The dispassionate and calm reason which characterizes sobriety is gone. So the word 'sober' is also gone from the new version. They deny their reader the two-fold meaning of the word by divorcing it from its Latin root (*se*. means apart; *ebrius* means drunken). Being "apart from drunkenness" is a characteristic missing from the WHORE, the "inhabitants of the earth," and the new versions.

NEW VERSIONS		KJV
discreetly	I Tim. 2:9	sobriety
sensible	Titus 1:8	sober
temperate	Titus 2:2	sober
self-restraint	I Tim. 2:15	sobriety
prudent	I Tim. 3:2	sober

The "discreet," "sensible" and "temperate" use of alcohol is accepted by society. A 1991 survey showed that 50% of all high school students used alcohol regularly, a marked rise in consumption in this age group.

TREND FIVE

Now the Spirit speaketh expressly, that in the latter times some shall depart from the faith. . .SPEAKING LIES I Timothy 4:2

[T]hey received not the love of the truth. . .
II Thessalonians 2:10

A prominent Christian psychologist said that people tell, on the average, 100 lies per day. . .not a good habit since,

All liars, shall have their part in the lake which burneth with fire and brimstone... Revelation 21:8

The word 'honesty' is not a part of the New Age vocabulary. They believe:

> [T]ruth is intensely personal and entirely subjective. . .It is the apex of love to allow others to have their own truth. . .[A]nything can be true for the individual but nothing can be true for everyone.[45]

New Age

"[T]he many sided Diamond of Truth . . ."[46] — Vera Alder

"[T]he end sanctifies the means."[47] — Jesuits

"It doesn't matter if you lie teaching people."[48]
Bob Kropinchi, Former T.M. Instructor

"A lie told in the name of evolution is truth."
Maharishi Mahesh Yogi

"If you tell a lie to make a person better then that is not a sin. . .Even God tells lies very often."[49]
Moon, "Heavenly Deception"

The KJV calls for 'honesty' ten times in the New Testament, the NIV and NASB only once. Do you think the KJV might produce honest Christians and the other versions might not?

NEW VERSIONS		KJV
OMIT	Rom. 13:9	Thou shalt not bear false witness
honorable	2 Cor. 8:21	honest
honorable	Phil. 4:8	honest
excellent	I Pet. 2:12	honest
dignity	I Tim. 2:2	honesty
shame	2 Cor. 4:2	dishonesty
adulterating	2 Cor. 4:2	deceitfully
error	I Thess. 2:3	deceit
false	Rev. 2:2	liars

The NIV's penchant for personal interpretation rather than translation is seen in Psalm 40:4 and Amos 2:4 where the Hebrew word for lies, *kazab,* is left untranslated. The KJV does not lie.

> For he said, Surely they are **my people**, children that will not lie: so he was their Saviour. Isaiah 63:8

NIV Positive?

The NIV aided the AIDS epidemic when their editors and literary consultants silenced all of God's warnings against the means of transmission of the HIV virus—sodomy. (Webster's sodomy: copulation between members of the same sex or with animals) The NIV's Dr. Virginia Mollenkott jabs, "My lesbianism has always been a part of me." (Episcopal, *Witness*, June, 1991) Her pro-homosexual book, *Is the Homosexual My Neighbor?* echos her NIV's assertion that the bible censures only criminal offences like "prostitution" and "violent gang rape," not "sincere homosexuals. . .drawn to someone of the same sex."

NIV, NASB et al.		KJV
male prostitutes nor homosexual offenders	I Cor. 6:9	effeminite
shrine prostitutes	Deut. 23:17, I Kings 15:12, 22:46; 2 Kings 23:7	sodomites

The deadly virus runs from the pens of the NIV scribes—signing the obituary of millions worldwide who practice sodomy. Immune to their cries, the NIV lies. They focus instead on a sin already dead—shrine prostitution. Archaic.

There will always be buyers for the new 'no righteousness' bibles—babes in Christ who want to be saved, not holy—and some who want to be holy but protest the purging which precedes it. Add to them the senior scribes, stuck in spiritual adolescence, wanting to be god and hoping God doesn't mind. Coming next in line are the carnal Christians who would like a corruptible crown NOW, not a 'crown of righteousness' LATER. Last in line are the "last days" liars who aren't in line to buy a bible, but to rob the store.

TEN

Self-Esteem Dream

TREND SIX

For men shall be lovers of their own selves. . . boasters, PROUD. . .II Timothy 3:2

Men who are "lovers of their own self" feed on flattery. So the fare offered by the false prophet and antichrist is a smorgasbord of honeyed words. Once swallowed, Daniel said, such would eat men's souls.

> And such as do wickedly against the covenant shall he corrupt by flatteries. Daniel 11:32

The MOTHER OF HARLOTS plays car hop and serves their bluff, buttered up.

> [A]n harlot. . .with her much fair speech she caused him to yield, with the flattering of her lips. Proverbs 7:10-21

So she writes the recipe for the 'New' religion. It calls for just a dab of Christ's deity but extra self-esteem.

There is a heated debate today in the church over the topic of self-esteem. Behind some pulpits posture proponents of an ego matched only by the ten foot tall giant Goliath, clad in *amour-prope* (self-love). Other sermons sell a seven foot Saul-sized self-assurance. In their shadow stands simple shepherds like David, destroying any devotion to self. Why the disparity? All claim 'the bible' as the basis of their beliefs. For instance, one supporter of self-esteem submits:

> Our attempt to defend self-esteem as a viable Christian belief is not an attempt to compromise the biblical data in order to pacify Christian psychologists. Rather, it is an earnest effort to be fair to all that the Bible says about ourselves. [T]here are many verses that affirm man's intrinsic value and how he ought to love himself. . . Scripture maintains that man is neither completely good nor entirely evil.[1]

Conversely Dave Hunt contends:

> The Bible never urges self-acceptance, self-love, self-confidence, self-esteem nor any of the other selfisms that are so popular today. . .the seductive gospel of self-esteem is now preached by prominent pastors.[2]

Expressions like "the Bible says. . .There are many verses. . .Scripture maintains," used by both sides of the issue, show the root of the dispute. It is evident from the writings of proponents on both sides that their view directly reflects that of their bible version. Those who look up to man, spying from the serpent's lowly point of view, usually cite the NIV or NASB. These provide ample armour to build Saul or Goliath size egos. Others, using the KJV, seem to scan a smaller man, as if from God's sky-high vantage point.

"For men shall be. . .proud"

The 'New' version of man is being held up with the bones from culture's graveyard. Ancient Greek mythology says Zeus sent Hermes with 'self-esteem'. "Hermes was the great original prophet of idolatry," writes Hislop.[3] Today, "Humanism is a sophisticated form of idolatry," adds another author.[4] So Hermes sent Westcott and other prophets of pride, like Robert Schuller, author of *Self-Esteem: The New Reformation,* to sustain this idol called 'self'. Schuller tells his congregation:

> Believe in the God who believes in you.

This god must be Zeus, not the God of the bible. Yet Schuller advises:

> Do not fear pride. . .God's almost impossible task is to keep us believing every hour of the day how great we are.[5]

The new versions, with help from Westcott's Hermes Club, put pride on a pedestal. They play pride's praises to the 1966 hit parade tune *They'll Know We Are Christians*; we "save each man's pride."

> God resisteth the proud James 4:6

> [B]e not proud Jeremiah 13:15

> Pride goeth before destruction Proverbs 16:18

NIV, NASV, et al.		KJV
be proud	2 Cor.1:14	your rejoicing
be proud	2 Cor. 5:12	glory on our behalf
our proud confidence	2 Cor. 1:12	rejoicing
Great is my confidence in you	2 Cor. 7:4	boldness of speech toward you
take pride in	James 1:10	—(no Greek)
proud confidence (NASB)	Phil 1:26	your rejoicing
ought to take pride	James 1:9	rejoice
he can take pride	Gal. 6:4	shall he have rejoicing
take great pride	2 Cor. 7:4	great is my glorying

The word pride or proud, *huperephanos*, occurs no where in any of these verses. The word in all Greek MS is *kauchaomai*. Bultman says it, "can have the. . .sense of verbs like "to rejoice."

Like *alazoneia*, it can mean "extraordinary expression of joy," says Peterson.[6] It always means, "rejoice (*kauchaomai*) in Christ Jesus, and have no confidence in the flesh."

Author of *Inside the New Age Nightmare* observes, "The New Age is obsessed with self-empowerment."[7] The concept of self-control "permeates Buddhist writings," notes Lola Davis.[8] Yet Paul quizzed the Galatians: "[H]aving begun in the spirit, are ye now made perfect by the flesh?" Which is to empower a Christian, the Spirit or self? Paul pointed these Galatians to "the fruit of the Spirit," not 'the Self'. Yet dozens of times, new versions confuse the root with "fruit," substituting "self-control," or "self-restraint" for virtues which are solely the fruit of the Spirit (I Timothy 2:15, Acts 24:25, I Corinthians 7:5, I Corinthians 9:25, Galatians 5:23, II Timothy 3:3, and Peter 1:3). The Greek words here, *sophrosune*, *egkrateia*, and *akrates* in no sense stir the spattering of the word 'self' which spots so many new version pages.

The new versions' campaign for self-esteem extends to their almost total censorship of pride's opposite—meekness. Its 31 occurrences in the KJV shrink to 3 or 4 in new versions. It has been completely omitted as one of the 9 fruit of the Spirit. Webster offers 'humble' as the synonym of meekness; then he defines humble as "not proud." The new version's substitute word is defined as "wellborn, Honorable,. . .refined, from the Latin *gentiles* meaning noble, of high birth."

"For men shall be lovers of their own selves"

'Self' stands first in the lines of new versions.

NASB et al.		KJV
not *just* please ourselves	Rom. 15:1	not to please ourselves
let not your adornment be *merely* external	I Pet.3:3	Whose adorning let it not be that outward adorning.

(Both italic words are not in any Greek text; their use causes the phrase to give the exact opposite meaning of the Greek.)

Imitation or New Creation?

The plastic saints have moved from the dashboard to the driver's seat. They "have been saved" at baptism and now "are being saved" by "faithfulness" and "obedience." They are "very religious in all respects" but have never given up the driver's seat to God, or read his road map, the bible. If these "wandering" cars don't stop for directions, they will be eternally lost.

These wayfarers were deceived by billboards on the broad way, painted by con artists like Peale who publicize "the innate goodness" of man.[9] God's road map warns instead that the *antahkarana* bridge is out (the New Age bridge leading to the divinity of man).[10] God's 'guidepost' reads, "GOOD-GOD=0".

> There is none good but one, that is God. Mark 10:18

Trying to be "**like** the most High" was Lucifer's downfall. God said, "I am God and there is none **like** me" (Isaiah 46:9). In spite of this, followers of Hinduism have a "devotion to acquiring Godlike qualities."[11] Gurus like Dr. Galyean, recipient of numerous federally funded grants, tell students "the whole purpose of human life is to reown the Godlikeness within us." The author of *Toward a World Religion for the New Age* observed that the occult theme wherein man "has potential to express many God-like qualities" is being "emphasized in Christianity" of late.[12] New versions have supported this and salute the substitution of a dashboard 'likeness'.

NIV, NASB, et al.		KJV
like newborn babes	I Pet. 2:2	as newborn babes
put on the new self which **in the likeness of** God has been created in righteousness and holiness	Eph. 4:24	put on the new man which after God is created in righteousness and **true** holiness.

(The words "as" and "like" are not interchangeable. e.g., "As a surgeon, I believe you need an operation." "John carves the turkey like a surgeon, maybe he could perform it and save us some money.")

Satan himself is "transformed into an angel of light." So God warns us to expect Satan's ministers to be imitators of "ministers of righteousness" (II Cor 11:15). Among them are the Buddhists who "set a high value on imitating the behavior of the highest" and mystics like the U.N.'s Dag Hammerskjold and Robert Muller who both read between the lines of Thomas a Kempis' *The Imitation of Christ.*[13] Luciferian David Spangler prefers 'Christians' who are an imitation rather than a new creation.

> [O]rthodox Christianity has a mystical side that to the best of its ability has taught the imitation of Christ.[14]

Imitation bibles produce imitation Christians. The dictionary destroys any notion that imitations are anything but an "artificial likeness."

NIV, NASB, et al.		KJV
Be imitators	I Cor. 11:1	followers of me
Be imitators of God	Eph.5:1	followers of God

TREND SEVEN

For men shall be. . .BLASPHEMERS II Timothy 3:2

Having swallowed the psychology of self-esteem whets the appetite for an epicurean ego. Books like psychologist Eric Fromm's *Ye Shall Be As Gods* are the next course. No man has ever resisted a taste of the temptation to be his own God.

NASB		KJV
YOU ARE GODS	John 10:34	Ye are gods
around the throne were twenty four thrones	Rev. 4:4	around about the throne were four and twenty seats
Like God did God make man. (LB)	Gen. 1:27	in the image of God

These bites of the New Age bill of fare leave 'Christians' belching the New Age blasphemy. Books like Paul Billheimer's *Destined For the Throne* see Christians as an "extension of the Godhead. . .elevated to the most sublime height possible short of becoming members of the Trinity itself."[15]

APOSTATE CHRISTIANITY	NEW AGE AND CULTS
"I AM A LITTLE GOD." Paul Crouch "I am an exact duplicate of God." Casey Treat	"WE SHALL THEN BE GOD. . .you are setting out a training to become creator—to become God."[16] Herbert W. Armstrong
"I'm God. . ." Fred Price	"I am God. . .Everyone is God."[17] Shirley MacLaine
"You are all God. . .you don't have a God living in you. You are one. Don't be disturbed when people accuse you of thinking you're God."[18] Kenneth Copeland	"You are God. . .Every individual is, in his true nature, the impersonal God."[19] Maharishi
"You are. . .a God kind of creature."[20] Robert Tilton	"[Y]ou are God."[21] Krishnamurti

The two-fold meaning of the word 'blasphemy', as given by Webster, includes not only slander against God, but "acts of claiming the attributes or prerogatives of deity." John 10:33 repeats, "For a good work we stone thee not; but for blasphemy; and because that thou, being a man, makest thyself God." This is the chief sin of New Age philosophy yet new versions hide this critical aspect of the word.

NIV, NASB, et al.		KJV
slander	Col. 3:8	blasphemy
slander	Mark 7:22	blasphemy
slanders	Matt. 15:19	blasphemies
dishonored	Titus 2:5	blasphemed
revilers	2 Tim. 3:2	blasphemers

The Antichrist's "divine nature" Defended

The antichrist's ability to receive worship hinges upon the belief by the masses that man can be divine. New Age writers are fervently feeding their flocks this fodder.

New Age

We are all 100% divine.[22] Maharishi

We need a World Religion. . .based on Divine Essence in each person. Peace can only come when we recognize the divinity in each person.[23] Lola Davis

All men are innate divinity.[24] Annie Besant

The knowingness of our divinity is the highest intelligence. . .You know you are divine. But you must continually remember your Divinity. . .we had all forgotten we were each Divine.[25] Shirley MacLaine

The ancient Monophysites believed that Jesus had a "deified human nature."[26] This idea led men like Athanasius of Alexandria to say, "He became man that we might become divine."[27] New versions fall back into what the Greeks called *apotheosis*—a belief in the divinity of man. The KJV, on the other hand, presents the Trinity as distinct from man in both identity and nature.

NIV, NASB, et al.		KJV
divine **nature**	Rom.1:20	The Godhead
the divine being	Acts 17:29	the Godhead

Now 'Christian' and cultic blasphemies bear a strong resemblance.

NEW AGE	APOSTATE CHRISTIANITY
"[T]he Christ **nature** is in every **human being**"[28] Alice Bailey "In his real **nature** man is **divine**."[29] Maharishi "This is the purpose for which you and I are here—to bring the soul to a clear realization of its own **divine nature**."[30] Gopi Krishna	"[T]he revelation of the Divine in man realized in and through Christ. . .Man is divine. . .Every type of essential human excellence coexists in Christ. . . humanity has been raised in the Son of Man to the right hand of God."[31] Westcott "I was born of God and so I became a human-divine being."[32] Kenneth Hagin

All of this blasphemy got a boost from new version editors, like Westcott, who said Psalm 8:5 helps "man recognize his divine affinity."

NIV, NASB, et al.		KJV
Yet Thou hast made him a little lower than **God**.	Ps. 8:5	For thou hast made him a little lower than the **angels**.
Thou hast made him **for a little while** lower than the angels.	Heb. 2:7	Thou madest him a little lower than the angels.

TREND EIGHT

and they repented not to GIVE HIM GLORY
Revelation 16:9

In man's mad march for glory he has gained no ground. The terrors of the tribulation find his footing firmly fastened to the same spot. His pace has done little more than pound out a grave-size sepulcher in the sod. In the tribulation, ". . .they repented not to give him glory." They have not budged since the beginning.

> [W]hen they knew God, they glorified him not. . .and worshipped and served the creature more than the creator. . . Romans 1:21, 25

Martin Luther observed what he called, the "theology of glory," in his day. Evidently, this sin has always had advocates stomping around in theological circles. Today Robert Schuller parades around his pulpit preaching what Hunt's *Beyond Seduction* calls, "a man centered theology to replace the traditional God-centered theology." Schuller states:

> Every person's deepest need—one's spiritual hunger for glory.[33]

Moody's *Agony of Deceit* cites seven signs of a false prophet; one symptom listed is "They are man-centered."[34] According to Donald Barnhouse:

> If you exalt man in any way God is thereby debased. But if you exalt God, as He should be, man thereby takes his true position of utter nothingness.[35]

In the process of building a pedestal for man, the new versions have not only chiseled away at Christ and jig-sawed around Jesus' name, but have routed out references to God.

NIV, NASB, et al.		KJV
He shall wipe away	Rev. 21:4	God shall wipe away all tears
I have come to do thy will	Heb. 10:9	I come to do thy will, O God
He who was revealed	I Tim. 3:16	God was manifest
But when He (NASB)	Gal. 1:15	But when it pleased God
He is not	Matt. 22:32	God is not
the head (NASB)	Col. 2:19	the Head
His Kingdom	Matt. 6:33	The Kingdom of God

Man's New Age 'divine' spirit has replaced 'God'.

NIV, NASB, et al.		KJV
A man like this in whom is a divine spirit?	Gen. 41:38	a man in whom the Spirit of God is?
But what is the divine response (NASB)	Rom. 11:4	What saith the answer of God
her divine majesty	Acts 19:27	her magnificence
a divine being	I Sam. 28:13	gods

Thousands of years ago the prophet Jeremiah pointed out the by-product of pride in God's own people.

> Wherefore say my people, We are lords, we will come no more unto thee. Jeremiah 2:31

This parade of personal power, pushing God to the side, presses from new version editors, to the pages of their version, to the pulpits, and finally to the people. First we hear Westcott:

> [T]he knowledge of Christ,. . .has its analogues in human power. . .the Son of Man gives the measure of the capacity of humanity. . .Nothing implies that the knowledge of the Lord was supernatural.[36]

NIV, NASB, et al.		KJV
the weapons of our warfare are not of the flesh but divinely powerful	2 Cor. 10:4	For the weapons of our warfare are not carnal but mighty through God
This man is the divine power known as the Great Power. (NIV)	Acts 8:10	This man is the great power of God.

Finally the radio waves echo the esoteric 'divine' powers of man as Kenneth Copeland resounds the spiritual static of centuries past.

> They mistakenly believe that Jesus was able to work wonders. . .because he had divine powers that we do not have.[37]

Man's 'divine' powers preclude the need for God as new versions either omit 'God' entirely or show man 'helping him along'.

NEW VERSIONS		KJV
as he hath prospered	I Cor. 16:2	as God hath prospered him
we might become the righteousness of God	2 Cor. 5:21	we might be made the righteousness of God **in him**
the families of the earth shall bless themselves (RV)	Gen. 12:3	in thee shall all families of the earth be blessed
To your descendants I will give this land	Gen. 12:7	Unto thy seed will I give this land.
(Gal. 3:16 identifies the correct version saying, "He saith not, And to seeds, as of many; but as of one, And to thy seed which is Christ.)		
with the help of the LORD I have brought forth a man	Gen. 4:1	I have gotten a man from the LORD
Jesus answered. . . We must work	John 9:4	Jesus answered. . .I must work
was manifested in us.	I John 4:9	the love of God toward us.
strength which God supplies	1 Pet. 4:11	ability which God giveth
(New versions seem to reduce God's role here; ability includes, "physical, moral, intellectual capacity; skill or competence"; they limit his input to 'strength'.)		
TEV		**KJV**
What my Father has given me is greater than everything	John 10:29	My Father, which gave them me, is greater than all.
(The new version, *Good News For Modern Man*, tells man that *he* not *God*, "is greater than everything." The NIV and NASB concur in their footnotes.)		

NIV, NASB, et al.		KJV
all its glory like the flower of grass	I Pet. 1:24	all the glory of man as the flower of grass.
(Having grafted God's glory on to man, new versions must now keep under wraps the verse which windows the withering of man's glory.)		

They "esteemed him not" (Isaiah 53:3)

Self-esteem comes from a reservoir of esteem stolen from God. Before men can "claim the attributes of God" (blasphemy), they must rob God of his glory (blasphemy). Once God is stripped of his glory, what remains is the amoral and impersonal god of Hinduism who gives "instructions," then capriciously punishes and humiliates man. The wise God of scripture "commands," because he cares and is "grieved" when for purposes of growth, he must chasten his children. New versions present a god whose despoiled character matches the New Age version of God.

God is a consuming fire. Hebrews 12:29

NIV, NASB, et al.		KJV
instruct	Matt. 10:5	commanded
precepts	Mark 7:7	commandments
God said	Matt.15:4	God commanded
respect	Matt. 21:37	reverence
instructed	Mark 6:8	commanded
prescribe	I Tim. 4:11	command
reverence	I Pet.3:15	fear
greatness	Luke 9:43	mighty power
shall shepherd	Matt. 2:6	shall rule

"The Lord is great." Psalm 99:2

NIV, NASB, et al.		KJV
news	Matt.4:24,9:26	his fame
God	I Tim.1:17	wise God
our God	Rev. 19:1	the Lord, our God

"God is love." I John 4:8

OMIT	Titus 1:4	mercy
I was angry	Heb. 3:10	grieved
punished	2 Cor. 6:9	chastened
discipline and instruction of the Lord	Eph. 6:4	nurture and admonition
God may humiliate me	2 Cor. 12:21	humble
stop clinging to me	John 20:17	Touch me not
thorn bush	Acts 7:30, 35	bush

TREND NINE

And they REPENTED NOT. . .Revelation 16:9

"The logic of God loving us is that we must be lovable," says one supporter of the self-esteem dream.[38] Only when we are in lullaby land or on the lines of the latest version does the likeness of a lovable man appear. Verses which mar Narcissus' vision of himself are missing. "Lovable" people, after all, when visited by their creator, do not strike him, accuse him, or constrain him.

NIV, NASB,et al.		KJV
OMIT	Luke 22:64	they struck him on the face

NIV, NASB,et al.		KJV
OMIT	Luke 11:54	that they might accuse him
OMIT	Luke 22:68	nor let me go

The champions of self-esteem state, "A healthy self-image is seeing yourself as God sees you."[39] But glaring back from God's looking glass, the bible, is a "disobedient," "wicked," "vile," "envious," "superstitious," "weak," "ignorant," "transgressor." When Job saw himself, "as God sees" him, he said, "I abhor myself and repent in dust and ashes." New versions substitute dark sunglasses for looking-glasses. In them man at his worst is "unimpressive" and "humble." No wonder the Job of the new versions merely "retracts."

NIV, NASB, et al.		KJV
the wrath of God is coming	Col.3:6	the wrath of God cometh **on the children of disobedience**
old self which is being corrupted	Eph. 4:22	The old man which is corrupt
OMIT	Mark 15:28	And the scripture was fulfilled which saith, "And he was numbered with the **transgressors**."
The whole world lies (in the power of the evil one).	I John 5:19	the whole world lieth in wickedness
Friend	Luke 5:20	Man
you are very religious in all respects	Acts 17:22	ye are too superstitious
OMIT	Matt.15:8	This people draweth nigh unto me with their mouth
unimpressive	2 Cor. 10:10	weak
our humble state	Phil 3:21	our vile body

NIV, NASB, et al.		KJV
He jealously desires the Spirit which He has made to dwell in us.	James 4:5	The spirit that dwelleth in us lusteth to envy.
unaware	I Cor. 10:1	ignorant
unaware	I Cor. 12:1	ignorant
unaware	2 Cor. 1:8	ignorant
But if anyone does not recognize this, he is not recognized	I Cor. 14:38	But if any man be ignorant, let him be ignorant
Professing to be wise	Rom. 1:22	Professing **themselves** to be wise
woe to the earth	Rev. 12:12	Woe to the inhabiters of the earth

New versions shatter the only mirror betraying man's seared conscience. Consequently 'Christians' can conclude with Starhawk, the New Age's most outspoken witch, "There is nothing to be saved from." Her haughty hammer vibrates from the pages of new version verses, while the KJV hums a humble hymn.

NEW VERSIONS		KJV
My conscience is clear (NIV, NASB)	I Cor. 4:4	For I know nothing by myself
I retract (NASB)	Job 42:6	I abhor myself and repent in dust and ashes.
We have been approved by God	I Thess. 2:4	We were allowed of God
OMIT	Luke 9:55,56	Ye know not what manner of spirit ye are of. For the Son of man is not come to destroy men's lives but to save them.

NEW VERSIONS		KJV
OMIT	Matt. 18:11	For the Son of man is come to save that which was lost.
(As usual the NIV and NASB's footnote, 'Some manuscripts have. . .' is spurious since there are four times as many manuscripts which have the verse than the few that omit it.)		

Fifty years ago the Fuerher and his friend Kittel coined the term,"Positive Christianity." Today major denominations have become comrades in the common cause to jilt guilt and sin for a gilded self. Schuller summarizes saying, "I believe that the responsibility of this age is to positivize religion."[40] With the help of the new versions, pulpiteers can see the world like pagan goddess worshipper Margot Adler.

NEW AGE	APOSTATE CHRISTIANITY
"Fundamentalists. . .see this world as sinful."[41] Adler	"Fundamentalists. . .deal constantly with words like sin."[42] Schuller

"New Age leaders. . .possess a common hostility toward the Christian belief that Jesus Christ died on the cross for **our sins**," writes Marrs.[43] This hostile pressure from the humanistic and 'religious' poles of the culture has squeezed **our sins** from the sentences in new versions. When Schuller says, "positivize the words," new versions comply.[44]

NEW VERSIONS		KJV
the body of the flesh	Col. 2:11	the **sins** of the flesh
If He would render Himself as a guilt offering	Isa. 53:10	**When** thou shalt make his soul an offering **for sin**
take away sins	I John 3:5	**our** sins
committed in ignorance	Heb. 9:7	not in Greek

NEW VERSIONS		KJV
woe unto the world because of stumbling blocks	Matt. 18:7	woe unto the world because of **offences**
He had made purification of sins	Heb. 1:3	by himself purged **our** sins
Christ hath suffered	I Pet. 4:1	Christ hath suffered **for us**
has been sacrificed	I Cor. 5:7	is sacrificed **for us**
This is my body [words probably not in the original writing] *NASB Interlinear Greek-English*	Luke 22:19-20	This is my body **which is given for you**; this do in remembrance of me. Likewise also the cup after supper, saying, This cup is the new testament in my blood, which is shed **for you**.
This lengthy statement is in all Greek MS, even early ones like P75. It is out in only one 5th-6th century manuscript (D). The Nestle's text used for the NASB Greek follows manuscript D alone numerous times.		

Like the Pharisees of old, new version editors have "rejected the council of God against them" (even rejecting that verse).

NIV, NASB, et al.		KJV
rejected God's purpose **for** themselves	Luke 7:30	rejected the counsel of God **against** themselves

With a push from the increasing sales of new versions, books like *God Calling*, claiming the divinity of man, pop up on the top ten Christian Bestseller's List.

Move over—The New Christians are coming.

ELEVEN

King James for Kids

TREND TEN

In the last days. . .men shall be HEADY, HIGHMINDED II Timothy 3:4

At the intersection of Bible Boulevard, Madi$on Avenue and Wall $treet, there are many crooked turns of the truth. Advertising campaigns create a cloud of confusion, calling the KJV "obscure, confusing and sometimes incomprehensible," while they crown the NIV's "clarity and ease of reading" and the NASB's "contemporary English." Christians are coerced by full color ads written to color the plain facts by advertising, not English majors.

The Flesch-Kincaid research company's Grade Level Indicator betrays the strictly black and white nature of the issue showing the new version's true colors. The KJV ranks easier in 23 out of 26 comparisons. (Their formula is: (.39 x average number of words per sentence) + (11.8 x average number of syllables per word) - (15.59) = grade level. The first chapter of the first and last books of both the Old and New Testaments were compared. (All complete sentences, whether terminating in a period, colon, or semi-colon, and all incomplete phrases ending in a period, were calculated as 'sentences'.)

	KJV Grade Level	NIV Grade Level	NASB Grade Level	TEV Grade Level	NKJV Grade Level
Gen. 1	4.4	5.1	4.7	5.1	5.2
Mal. 1	4.6	4.8	5.1	5.4	4.6
Matt. 1	6.7	16.4	6.8	11.8	10.3
Rev. 1	7.5	7.1	7.7	6.4	7.7
Grade Level Average	5.8	8.4	6.1	7.2	6.9

To extend the inquiry, one each of the three book-types (Gospel, Pauline epistle, General epistle) were surveyed. The resulting data confirms the readability of the KJV.

	KJV	NIV	NASB	Good News (TEV)	NKJV
John 1:1-21	3.6	3.6	4.2	5.9	3.9
Gal. 1:1-21	8.6	9.8	10.4	6.7	8.9
Jas. 1:1-21	5.7	6.5	7.0	6.0	6.4

Why is the KJV easier to read? The KJV uses one or two syllable words while new versions substitute complex multi-syllable words and phrases. Their "heady, high-minded" vocabulary hides the hope of salvation from simple saints and sinners.

> Seeing then that we have such hope, we use great plainness of speech. (KJV) II Cor. 3:12

The NASB substitutes "lividness of speech" here and carries this confusing and condescending vocabulary from cover to cover. Children and church members need to change to the KJV for "clarity." An extensive list is given because Christians have been so extensively brainwashed to 'believe a lie'.

NASB vs. KJV

	HARD WORD (NASB)	EASY WORD (KJV)
Matt.1:11, 1:17	deportation	carried away
Matt.1:20	considered	thought
Matt.2:1, 2:7	magi	wise men
Mark. 2:21	unshrunk	new
Matt. 2:16	environs	coasts
Luke 3:17, Matt. 3:12	winnowing fork	fan
Luke 11:33, Matt. 5:15, Mark 4:21	peck-measure	bushel
Matt. 5:19	annuls	break
Matt. 5:21	murder	kill
Luke 5:29, Matt. 8:11	recline at the table	sat
Matt. 8:32	begone	go
Matt. 9:13, 12:7	compassion	mercy
Matt. 9:17	wineskins	bottles
Matt. 9:18	synagogue official	certain ruler
Mark 5:25, Matt. 9:20	hemorrhage	issue of blood
Matt. 9:20, 14:36	fringe	hem
Matt. 9:38	beseech	pray
Matt. 10:1	summoned	called
Matt. 10:10	tunics	coats
Matt. 10:16	shrewd	wise
Matt. 11:26	well pleasing	good
Matt. 13:46	value	price
Matt. 14:24	but the boat was already many stadia away	was now in the midst of the sea
[But in Mark 6:47, NASB uses "midst of the sea" and in John 7:14 they use "midst of the feast."]		
Matt. 14:24	battered	tossed

	HARD WORD (NASB)	EASY WORD (KJV)
Matt. 15:6	invalidated	made
Matt.15:17	eliminated	cast out
Matt. 16:27	recompense	reward
Matt.17:24	two-drachma tax	tribute money
Matt.17:27	stater	piece of money
Matt.18:32	entreated	desiredst
Matt. 20:15	generous	good
Matt. 20:2	denarius	penny
Matt. 21:15	indignant	displeased
Matt. 22:38	foremost	first
Matt. 23:37	were unwilling	would not
Matt. 24:2	torn down	thrown down (implies violence)
Matt. 25:2	prudent	wise
Matt. 25:10	make the purchase	buy
Matt. 26:4	stealth	subtilty
Matt. 26:7, Luke 7:37	vial	box
Matt. 26:46	arise	rise
Matt. 26:50	seized	took
Matt. 26:58	entered	went
Matt. 26:59	in order that they might	to
Matt. 27:27	Praetorium	common hall
Matt. 27:27	whole Roman cohort	band of soldiers
Mark 15:16	whole Roman cohort	band
Matt. 27:65	know how	can
Mark 1:12	impelled	driveth
Mark 1:14	custody	prison
Mark 4:37	gale	storm
Mark 4:38	stern	hinder part of the ship
Mark 5:4	subdue	tame
Mark 5:5	gashing	cutting
Mark 6:8	mere	only
Mark 6:53	moored	drew
Mark 8:36	forfeit	lose
Mark 12:28	foremost	first
Mark 13:9	flogged	beaten
Mark 14:1	stealth	craft
Mark 14:3	vial	box
Mark 14:3, 14:18	reclining	sat

	HARD WORD (NASB)	EASY WORD (KJV)
Luke 1:22	mute	speechless
Mark 15:16	palace	hall
Mark 15:18	acclaim	salute
Luke 3:5	ravine	valley
Luke 6:17	descended	came down
Luke 5:5	bidding	word
Luke 6:22	ostracize	separate you from their company
Luke 6:48	torrent burst	stream beat
Luke 6:49	collapsed	fell
Luke 7:2	highly regarded	dear
Luke 7:32	sang a dirge	have mourned
Luke 8:15	perseverance	patience
Luke 8:31	the abyss	the deep
Luke 8:33	rushed	ran
Luke 9:39	seizes	taketh
Luke 9:42	dashed him to the ground	threw him
Luke 9:45	concealed	hid
Luke 10:2	plentiful	great
Luke 10:2	beseech	pray
Luke 10:20	recorded	written
Luke 10:21	well-pleasing	good
Luke 11:21	undisturbed	in peace
Luke 11:28	observe it	keep it
Luke 23:45	being obscured	darkened
(This has other implications. It states that the sun was darkened by being obscured, implying the natural phenomenon of an eclipse rather than a supernatural move of God.)		
Luke 18:40	questioned	asked
John 6:60	difficult	hard
John 7:6	opportune	ready
John 10:23	portico	porch
John 10:24	suspense	doubt
John 11:17	tomb	grave
John 11:57	seize	take
John 11:39	stench	stinketh
John 12:45	beholds	seeth
John 12:40	perceive	understand
John 13:12	reclined	set down

	HARD WORD (NASB)	EASY WORD (KJV)
John 13:23	reclining	leaning
John 14:27	fearful	afraid
John 16:8	concerning	of
John 16:19	deliberating	inquire
John 16:25	figurative language	proverbs
John 16:26	on your behalf	for you
John 17:4	accomplished	finished
John 17:8	understood	known
John 17:9	I ask on their behalf	I pray for them
John 18:1	ravine	brook
John 18:3, 18:12	Roman cohort	a band
John 18:28, 18:33, 19:9	Praetorium	hall of judgement
John 19:2	arrayed	put on
John 19:20	inscription	title
John 19:23	tunic	coat
John 21:7	stripped for work	naked
John 16:16, 16:19	behold	see
John 16:19	are you deliberating	do you inquire
John 18:12	arrested	took
John 18:14	on behalf of	for
Acts 1:7	epochs	seasons
Acts 1:7	fixed	put
Acts 1:16	arrested	took
Acts 2:22	attested	approved
Acts 2:26	exulted	was glad
Acts 2:26	abide	rest
Acts 3:11, 5:12	portico	porch
Acts 3:12	piety	holiness
Acts 5:40	flogged	beaten
Acts 7:13	disclosed	made known
Acts 8:20	silver	money
Acts 10:1	cohort	band
Acts 10:5	dispatch	send

	HARD WORD (NASB)	EASY WORD (KJV)
Acts 10:30	garments	clothing
Acts 11:6	gaze	eyes
Acts 11:23	rejoiced	glad
Acts 11:24, 11:26	considerable numbers	much people
Acts 12:5	fervently	without ceasing
Acts 12:8	cloak	garment
Acts 12:19	to execution	put to death
Acts 12:21	rostrum	throne
Acts 13:7, 13:8, 13:12	proconsul	deputy of the country
Acts 13:7	summoned	called for
Acts 13:9	fixed his gaze	set his eyes
Acts 13:17	uplifted	high
Acts 13:28	no ground	cause
Acts 13:43	were urging	persuaded
(Persuaded implies a consumption and success from urging; urging itself does not indicate the results.)		
Acts 13:46	repudiate	put it from you
Acts 13:50	prominence	honourable
Acts 13:50	instigated	raised
Acts 14:2	embittered	made their minds evil
Acts 14:17	satisfying	filling
Acts 15:5	observe	keep
Acts 16:40	encouraged	comforted
Acts 19:15	recognize	know
Acts 27:18	jettison the cargo	lightened the ship
Acts 27:17	aground on the shallows of Syrtis	fall into the quicksands
Rom. 1:18	suppress	hold
Rom. 1:30	arrogant	proud
Rom. 1:30	insolent	despiteful
Rom. 5:2	exult	rejoice
Rom. 5:11	exult	joy
Rom. 9:29	posterity	seed
Rom. 12:8	liberality	simplicity
Rom. 16:18	unsuspecting	simple
2 Cor. 1:17	vacillating	minded
2 Cor. 4:3	veiled	hid
2 Cor. 11:32	the ethnarch	the governor

	HARD WORD (NASB)	EASY WORD (KJV)
Gal. 1:14	contemporaries	equals
Gal. 5:20	enmities	hatred
Eph. 5:12	disgraceful	a shame
Phil. 1:9	discernment	judgment
Phil. 1:13	praetorian guard	palace
Phil. 4:9	practice	do
Phil. 4:11	circumstances	state
Col. 1:13	domain of darkness	power of darkness
(New versions divest the culture of our literary spiritual heritage ; e.g., Tolstoy's famous play, *The Power of Darkness*, was titled after the KJV phrase here.)		
Col. 1:23	steadfast	settled
Col. 1:28	admonishing	warning
Col. 2:4	argument	words
Col. 2:13	transgressions	sins
Col. 3:21	do not exasperate	provoke
Col. 4:6	respond	answer
I Thess. 2:2	amid	with
I Thess. 2:17	having been bereft of you	being taken from you
I Thess. 2:18	thwarted	hindered
I Thess. 5:1	epochs	seasons
I Thess. 5:14	admonish	warn
2 Thess.2:3	apostasy	falling away
2 Thess. 2:3	lawlessness	sin
2 Thess. 3:2	perverse	unreasonable
2 Thess. 3:6	aloof	withdraw
I Tim.1:15	foremost of all	chief
I Tim. 2:8	dissensions	doubting
I Tim.2:9	discreetly	sobriety
I Tim. 3:2	prudent	sober
I Tim.3:2	respectable	of good behavior
I Tim. 3:3	pugnacious	striker
I Tim. 3:3	uncontentious	not a brawler
I Tim.3:8	sordid	filthy
I Tim. 5:12	previous pledge	first faith
I Tim. 6:3	advocates	teach
I Tim.6:4	conceited	proud
I Tim. 6:10	a pang	sorrows
2 Tim. 3:2	arrogant	proud
Titus 1:6	dissipation	riot
Titus 1:7	sordid	filthy

	HARD WORD (NASB)	EASY WORD (KJV)
Titus 3:2	to malign no one	to speak evil of no man
Titus 3:2	uncontentious	to be no brawlers
Titus 3:10	factious	heretick
Phil. 2:1	consolation	comfort
Phil. 2:30	deficient	lack
Heb. 2:17	propitiation	reconciliation
Heb. 5:10	designated	called
Heb. 7:2	apportioned	gave
Heb. 12:1	encumbrance	weight
James 1:2	encounter	fall into
James 1:11	in the midst	in his ways
James 5:11	blessed	happy
I Pet.4:4	dissipation	riot
I John 5:10	borne	gave
Rev.1:3	heed	keep
Rev. 1:9	perseverance	patience
Rev. 2:2	perseverance	patience
Rev. 2:3	perseverance	patience
Rev. 3:10	perseverance	patience
Rev. 2:23	pestilence	death
Rev. 4:1	standing	was
Rev. 5:11	myriads of myriads	10,000 x 10,000
Rev. 6:8	ashen	pale
Rev. 6:8	famine	hunger
Rev. 6:8	pestilence	death
Rev. 7:15	spread His tabernacle over	dwell among
Rev. 9:11	abyss	pit
Rev. 11:7	abyss	pit
Rev. 11:9	laid in a tomb	put in graves
(It refers to the two witnesses, so graves plural are needed.)		
Rev. 11:11	who *were beholding* them	saw
Rev. 12:3	diadems	crowns
Rev. 13:1	diadems	crowns
Rev. 13:5	arrogant words	great things
Rev. 13:10	perseverance	patience
Rev. 16:9	fierce	great
Rev. 16:21	severe	great
Rev. 17:1	harlot	whore
Rev. 17:8	abyss	bottomless pit
Rev. 17:16	harlot	whore

	HARD WORD (NASB)	EASY WORD (KJV)
Rev.18:1	illumined	lightened
Rev. 18:2	prison of every. . . bird	cage
Rev. 18:7	mourning	sorrow
Rev. 18:8	pestilence	death
Rev. 18:11, 18:12	cargoes	merchandise
Rev. 19:12	diadem	crown
Rev. 19:20	seized	taken
Rev. 20:1, 20:3	abyss	bottomless pit
Rev. 21:8	cowardly	fearful
Rev. 22:7	heeds	keepeth

Scriptures to Memorize, But What Size?

> Thy word have I hid in mine heart, that I might not sin against thee. Psalm 119:11

The memorization of scripture, which is the "sword of the Spirit," is a necessary self-defense against sin. Simple sentence structure and single syllable words certainly simplify this task. Satan strives to stop this safeguard against sin, so new versions keep the "sword" wrapped in a sheath of words. They consistently use twice the number of words and syllables as the KJV, to say the same thing.

> For I testify unto every man that heareth the words of the prophecy of this book, If any man shall add unto these things, God shall **add** unto him the plagues that are written in this book: Revelation 22:18

NASB	Syllables		KJV	Syllables
Keep watching and praying	6	Matt. 26:41	Watch and pray	3
in order that they might	6	Matt. 26:59	to	1

NASB	Syllables		KJV	Syllables
you are looking for	5	Matt. 28:5	seek	1
who he was	3	Mark 1:34	him	1
am willing	3	Mark 1:41	will	1
speak that way? He is blaspheming	8	Mark 2:7	speak blasphem-ies	4
Rise and come forward	5	Mark 3:3	Stand forth	2
Be on the alert	5	Mark 13:37	Watch	1
Keep watch	2	Mark 14:34	watch	1
he began to weep	5	Mark 14:72	he wept	2
astonishment had gripped them	7	Mark 16:8	were amazed	3
continued to grow	5	Luke 1:80	grew	1
downtrodden	3	Luke 4:18	bruised	1
seized with astonishment	6	Luke 5:26	amazed	2
what they were thinking	5	Luke 6:8	their thoughts	2
it was he who	4	Luke 7:5	he hath	2
one who is more	4	Luke 7:26	much more	2

NASB	Syllables		KJV	Syllables
burst his fetters	4	Luke 8:29	break the bands	3
became frightened	4	Luke 8:35	were afraid	3
Who is the one who touched me?	7	Luke 8:45	Who touched me?	3
Do not be afraid any longer	9	Luke 8:50	Fear not	2
was saying	3	Luke 9:23	said	1
those in it who are	5	Luke 10:9	the	1
be on your guard	6	Luke 12:15	beware of	3
am not strong enough to	6	Luke 16:3	cannot	2
Give me legal protection from my opponent	12	Luke 18:3	avenge	2
bring about justice	5	Luke 18:7	avenge	2
in the passage about the	7	Luke 20:37	at	1
they began to come up to Him, and say	10	John 19:3	said	1

NASB	Syllables		KJV	Syllables
to give Him blows in the face	7	John 19:3	they smote him	3
no question	3	John 16:23	nothing	2
And they began to come up to Him and say	11	John 19:3	said	1
stripped for work	3	John 21:7	naked	2
with a view to	4	Eph. 1:14	until	2
seasoned, as it were, with salt	7	Col. 4:6	seasoned with salt	4
are trying to deceive	6	I John 2:26	seduce	2
rising of the sun	5	Rev. 7:2	east	1
spread his tabernacle over	8	Rev. 7:15	dwell	1
	214 **Total** Syllables		72 **Total** Syllables	

The sentence structure of the new versions can only be called a labyrinth.

NASB		KJV
Question those who have heard what I spoke to them (10 words/11 syllables)	John 18:21	Ask them which heard me. (5 words/5 syllables)
Do not be afraid any longer but go on speaking (10 words/14 syllables)	Acts 18:9	Be not afraid but speak (5 words/6 syllables)
you do not have any fish do you? (8 words/9 syllables)	John 21:5	have ye any meat (4 words/ 5 syllables)
the prayer offered in faith will restore the one who is sick (12 words/14 syllables)	James 5:15	the prayer of faith shall save the sick (8 words/ 8 syllables)
flashes of lightning and sounds and peals of thunder (9 words/12 syllables)	Rev. 4:5	lightnings, and thunderings, and voices (5 words/9 syllables)
angels who had seven plagues which are the last (9 words/11 syllables)	Rev. 15:1	angels having the seven last plagues (6 words/ 9 syllables)
Total: 58 words/ 71 syllables		**Total:** 33 words 42 syllables

NKJV vs. KJV

Only a multi-million dollar marketing campaign could capture unsuspecting customers for the *New King James Version* camp. An actual collation of its text proves it *more difficult*, not "clearer", as claimed. Second grade students can define *all* of the following sample KJV words, but *none* of their corresponding NKJV substitutes.

	HARD WORD (NKJV)	EASY WORD (KJV)
Amos 5:21	savor	smell
2 Cor. 5:2	habitation	house
Eccl. 2:3	gratify	give
Is. 28:1,4	verdant	fat
Is. 34:6	overflowing	fat
Is. 13:12	mortal	man
Deut. 28:50	elderly	old
Judges 19:29	limb	bones
Ps. 43:1	Vindicate	Judge
Rom. 14:13	resolve	judge
Josh. 22:24	descendants	children
Heb. 7:8	mortal men	men that die
John 6:7	denarii	pennyworth
Acts 17:22	the Areopagus	Marrs Hill
Ez. 31:4	rivulets	little rivers
Joel 1:2	elders	old men
N.T.	hades	hell
I Kings 10:28	Keva	linen yarns
I Sam. 13:21	pim	file
John 18:28	Praetorium	judgement hall
Eccl. 4:4	skillful	right
Rom. 13:1	governing authorities	higher powers
Gal. 5:4	estranged	no effect
Is. 2:16	sloops	pictures
Phil. 1:16	the former. . .the latter	the one. . .the other
Lam. 5:3	waif	fatherless
I Sam. 10:19	clans	thousands
Eccl. 5:1	Walk prudently	Keep thy foot
Luke 16:8	shrewdly	wisely
Jude 1:22	distinction	difference
Acts 17:5	were not persuaded	believed not
Ezra 6:1	archives	house of rolls
Acts 27:17	Syrtis Sands	quicksand
Ps. 139:23	anxieties	thoughts
Neh. 3:7	residence	throne
Obad. 1:12	captivity	stranger
2 Cor. 11:5	eminent	chiefest

	HARD WORD (NKJV)	EASY WORD (KJV)
Job 2:10	adversity	evil
I Sam. 16:14	distressing	evil
Jer. 19:3	catastrophe	evil
2 Kings 22:16	calamity	evil
Eccl. 12:1	difficult	evil
Eccl. 8:5	harmful	evil
Ezek. 5:16	terrible	evil
Ezek. 5:17	wild	evil
2 Sam. 17:14	disaster	evil
I Kings 17:20	tragedy	evil
Prov. 16:4	doom	evil
Jer. 44:17	trouble	evil
Amos 9:4	harm	evil

	NKJV	KJV
I Cor. 3:3	behaving like mere men (6)	walk as men (3)
2 Cor. 11:29	do not burn with indignation (8)	burn not (2)
Ps. 40:9	I have proclaimed the good news of (8)	I have preached (3)
I Cor. 11:10	a symbol of authority (8)	power (2)
I Sam. 25:12	on their heels (4)	their way (2)
	34 syllables	12 syllables

NIV vs. KJV

The advertised "readability" of the NIV is also a ruse. A mind trying to meditate or memorize the word becomes entangled in a maze of multi-syllabic 'cerebral' sounding sentences.

	NIV	KJV
Exod. 32:6, I Cor. 10:7	indulge in revelry (6)	rose up to play (4)
Lev. 14:2, 57	regulations for infectious skin diseases and mildew (15)	law of leprosy (5)
Lev. 11:30	skink (1)	snail (1)
2 Chron. 2:2	conscripted (3)	told (1)
Rom. 1:28	think it worthwhile (4)	like (1)
Eph.4:16	supporting ligament (6)	joint (1)
Luke 10:35	reimburse (3)	repay (2)
Luke 11:26	final condition (5)	last state (2)
Total Syllables	43	17

So the reader will not think 'select' verses are presented, a thorough comparison of one book, Hebrews, follows. The NIV's vocabulary evades young and old alike.

	NIV	KJV
Heb.1:2	universe (3)	worlds (1)
Heb. 1:3	radiance (3)	brightness (2)
Heb. 1:3	representation (5)	image (2)
Heb. 1:3	sustaining (3)	upholding (3)
Heb. 1:3	provided purification (8)	purged (1)
Heb. 1:4	superior to (5)	better than (3)
Heb. 2:3	announced (2)	spoken (2)
Heb. 2:10	exists (2)	are (1)
Heb. 4:2	combine (2)	mixed (1)
Heb. 4:15	sympathize (3)	be touched (2)
Heb. 5:7	his reverent submission (7)	he feared (2)
Heb. 5:10	designated (4)	called (1)
Heb. 5:13	not acquainted (4)	unskillful (3)
Heb. 6:6	subjecting him to (5)	put him to (3)
Heb. 7:16	indestructible (5)	endless (2)
Heb. 8:13	obsolete (3)	old (1)
Heb. 10:26	deliberately (5)	wilfully (3)
Heb. 10:27	expectation (4)	looking for (3)
Heb. 11:5	experience death (5)	see death (2)
Heb. 11:22	exodus (3)	departing (3)
Total:	81 syllables	41 syllables

World Class Bible

God wrote a world-class book, not a nineteen-nineties novelty. The language of the KJV was carried from continent to continent for 400 years as the British Empire colonized the globe. The British presence, power, and cultural pull on the Near, Far and Middle East, Africa, India, Australia, Europe, Canada, Russia, etc. has carried Anglistics to centuries of students. (*All* International students I have encountered speak British-English, not American-English.)

The one in 8,000 words in the KJV, which are unfamiliar, at first glance, to dictionary shy Americans are actually simpler and more accurate than their new substitutes. A 'stomacher' for example (Is. 3:24) is *not* a belt, as new versions indicate, but a chest ornament. (It seems the only 'simpler' words in new versions are incorrect or from a corrupt Greek text.) New versions not only do not improve the KJV's 'sackbut' (Daniel 3:7), calling it a 'trigon', but in the same sentence change the KJV's simple 'harp' to a 'zither'.

The KJV's unfamiliar words can be handled easily in one of four ways.

1. Use a dictionary. For very specific and correct definitions use the *Oxford Unabridged, The Glossary of the Cambridge Interleavened Bible* or *The American Dictionary of the English Language*, Noah Webster.

2. Use the bible's self-contained dictionary—the context of one or more of the word's occurrences.

3. See I Samuel 9:1-11 which shows **God's** method of dealing with outmoded words. He defines them while still retaining them.

4. Realize that the 'Thee's and thou's' are not 1611 English, but bible language. At the time of the translation, these singular forms had already been replaced in conversation by 'you'. The glaring difference between the style of the KJV's preface and text reveals that, "Its style is that of the Hebrew and New Testament Greek."[1] Replacing thee, thou, thy and ye with you and your does not convey the significant spiritual distinction between

the singular (thee, thou, thy) and the plural, ye. (eg. Matthew 16:13-20)

The KJV for Kids

The young children ask bread and no man breaketh it unto them. Lamentations 4:4

A news flash reported, "Middle-class youth vandalize suburban Cleveland home, spray-painting obscenities and the word 'LUCIFER' across its entire exterior." This generation of scripture starved students are easily seized by Satan. Slick substitutes, like *The Living Bible* or *Good News for Modern Man*, sweep Satan from Isaiah 14 and slip in enough salty language to send chills down a mother's spine.

NEW VERSION		KJV
"May you and your money go to hell" (*Good News for Modern Man*)	Acts 8:20	"Thy money perish with thee"
"you illegitimate bastard" (*The Living Bible*)	John 9:34	"thou wast altogether born in sins"
"You son of a bitch" (*The Living Bible*)	I Sam.20:30	"Thou son of the perverse rebellious woman."

Satan gets off scot-free in Isaiah while Jesus Christ gets a bum rap in Zechariah.

LIVING BIBLE		KJV
And if someone asks, 'Then what are these scars on your chest and your back? he will say, 'I got into a brawl at the home of a friend'. (Taylor's footnote says, "self-inflicted cuts. . .this is not a passage referring to Christ.")	Zech. 13:6	And one shall say unto him, What are these wounds in thine hands? Then he shall answer, Those with which I was wounded in the house of my friends.

Grade: C in English

T.S. Eliot, famous American writer, described one new version as an 'example of the decadence of the English language in the middle of the twentieth century.' One new version editor parades his problem with proper English, saying:

> It is much more clear than the KJV.[2]

Anyone who would say "more clear" instead of "clearer" can be counted on to continue this 'C-' English in countless new version verses. Countering this is the KJV, selected recently by the ivy league scholars in their *Norton Anthology of Literature,* as one of the finest samples of writing style in existence. If your little one brings home a 'C' in English, perhaps he just picked up one of the redundant pronouns, dangling prepositions or poorly edited sentences in his 'easy-to-read' version.

NEW VERSION	
You people judge	John 8:15
You *people* see	John 4:48, 4:20
For He Himself is our peace	Eph. 2:14
I have sent them Myself.	Acts 10:20
He made Himself out to be the Son of God.	John 19:7
not be delivered up	John 18:36
those who had come off victorious from the beast	Rev. 15:2
make yourself out to be God	John 10:33
cast a net in the sea	Mark 1:16
Let us go somewhere else to the towns nearby in order that I may preach there also for that is what I came out for.	Mark 1:38
Take Him yourselves.	John 18:31
but if it is of God, you will not be able to overthrow them.	Acts 5:39

NEW VERSION	
I am the way, and the truth and the life.	John 14:6
if each of you does not forgive his brother from your heart	Matt. 18:35
it remains by itself alone	John 12:24

For New Version Kids, the "maker" of the world (Hebrews 11:10) becomes its "architect." David didn't kill Goliath, "Elhanan the son of Jaare-oregin, a Bethlehemite killed Goliath" (II Samuel 21:19). (KJV clarifies that Elhanan slew Goliath's brother in I Chron 20:5-8.) The dramatic parting of the Red Sea becomes a story about some sox that became 'soakers' wading through the 'sea of reeds'. New versions obscure simple geography, as Ethiopia becomes Cush, Syria becomes Aram and the valley of the sons of Hinnon is transliterated as the Valley of Ben Hennon.

NIV editor Larry Walker admits further that, "[S]ome Bible characters appear to have disappeared from the text."[3] Is it any wonder since Westcott said, "David is not a chronological. . .person."[4] These omissions have an advantage—less bible to memorize.

> And these words, which I command thee this day shall be in thine heart: And thou shalt teach them diligently unto thy children, and shalt talk of them when thou sittest in thine house and when thou walkest by the way, and when thou liest down and when thou risest up. Deut. 6:6,7

"Talk of them" implies that parents are to impart scripture, which they have memorized, to their children—an impossible task if a new version is needed each year (100 versions since 1881) or even for each generation. The bible speaks of Lois who learned the scriptures and taught them to her daughter Eunice who was thereby able to teach them to Timothy, of whom Paul wrote:

> [F]rom a child thou hast known the holy scriptures.
> II Timothy 3:15

The generation *gap* created by new versions is just what the devil ordered. New Agers agree saying, "[I]t takes a generation or more. . .to escape the old ways." Mystic Robert Muller wrote:

> Give me your children and I will give you the world.

Sounds familiar. Satan and the King of Sodom said the same (Exodus 10:11). The generation which will "worship the Dragon" (Revelation 13:4) will have fallen through the gap which in eternity becomes "a great gulf fixed" (Luke 16:26). This lost generation is not irreligious—merely worshipping the wrong 'Christ', in the wrong church, with the wrong beliefs—all learned from the wrong book.

TREND ELEVEN

In the last days. . .men shall be. . .WITHOUT NATURAL AFFECTION. II Timothy 3:3

Before Satan can break into a child's soul, he must first break through the fortress of the family structure. In these last days he finds father's hearts a frail target. As Paul said, "Men shall be lovers of their own selves." The lost mortar of "natural affection" leaves the family fortress leaning like the hovels housing cultures worldwide, where children are valued only as chattels and wives as workers.

The culture which produced Plato's 'women are slaves' philosophy also altered the then radical New Testament documents in verses which show that Christ came to "preach deliverance to the captives" (Luke 4). New versions dig up these corrupted Greek manuscripts from centuries past and try to shackle a society freed from such Satanic sentiments. The whip cracks over women in the words of new versions, as their editors have fallen prey to the Egyptian taskmasters.

Hindoos burned their widows (*suttee*) and bartered their daughters until the British brought their KJV's and broke the tradition.

NEW VERSIONS		KJV
If any **woman** who is a believer has dependent widows let **her** assist them.	I Tim. 5:16	If any **man or woman** that believeth have widows, let **them** relieve them.
free **men** and slaves	Rev. 13:16	free and bond

The New Age Society of KRISHNA Consciousness has resuscitated those ancient Hindu widows for work saying women are, "worthy of only serving men."[5] The handful of Greek texts used by new versions agree, substituting *ergo*, to work, for *ouros*, to guard or keep in Titus 2:5. New version Marthas will polish while Majority Text Marys will 'pray'.

workers at home (NASB)	Titus 2:5	keepers at home
busy at home (NIV)		
keep house (The word in Timothy is not 'keeper' *ouros*, but 'guide' *oikod*.	I Tim.5:14	guide the house

The NIV uses some very 'original' Greek in Hebrews 11:11. The words in bold are not found in *any* Greek manuscripts.

NIV	KJV
By faith **Abraham even though he was past age**—and Sara herself was barren—**was enabled to become a father because he** considered him faithful who had made the promise	Through faith also Sara herself received strength to conceive seed, and was delivered of a child when she was past age, because she judged him faithful who had promised.

Hiding under the bedcovers embroidered by the scribe of manuscript 'B', are the "last days men"—"lovers of pleasure."

NEW VERSIONS		KJV
1. You adulteresses (NASB) unfaithful wife (LB)	James 4:4	Ye **adulterers and** adulteresses
2. wicked women (New Scofield)	p. 314	Children of Belial
3. [[The earliest and most reliable manuscripts and other ancient witnesses do not have John 7:53-8:11]] notes the NIV et al.	John 7:53-8:11	These twelve verses show Christ revealing the adulterers among the "scribes" and forgiving the adulterous woman. Von Soden reveals "in the great majority of the manuscripts it stands in the text."[6] One Princeton scholar adds, "The notes printed in the modern versions are completely misleading."[7]
4. OMIT	Luke 16:14, Rom. 1:29, Eph. 5:3, Col. 3:5, 2 Tim. 3:2, Ps. 10:3, 119:36, Jer. 22:17, 6:13, 8:10, Ezek. 18:21, Prov. 28:16, Isa. 57:17	The commandments against covetousness include, 'Thou shalt not covet thy neighbors wife'. New versions omit this form of covetousness.
5. passion	Col. 3:5	inordinate affection (passion with one's wife is allowed).
6. OMIT	Matt. 19:29	wife

Liberals crying for a bible which 'liberates' women would do well to look back to the KJV.

NEW VERSIONS		KJV
O men	Luke 12:28	O ye
O men	Matt. 6:30	O ye
spiritual men	I Cor. 3:1	spiritual
adoption as sons	Eph. 1:5	adoption of children
purchased for God with thy blood, *men* from every tribe.	Rev. 5:9	redeemed us to God by thy blood out of every kindred
sons	Luke 20:34	children
sons	Luke 20:36	children
sons of light	John 12:36	children
sons	Acts 7:23	children
sons	Acts 7:37	children
sons	Acts 9:15	children
sons	Acts 10:36	children
son	Acts 13:10	child
sons	Eph. 2:2	children
sons	Eph. 5:6	children
sons	I Thess. 5:5	children
sons	Heb. 12:5	children
sons	Rev. 7:4	children
sons	Matt. 12:27	children
sons	Matt. 17:26	children
sons of the kingdom	Matt. 8:12	children of the kingdom
sons of the kingdom	Matt. 13:38	children of the kingdom
his faith	Rom. 12:6	faith
boy	Isa. 11:6	child
boys	Matt. 2:16	children
two men	Matt. 24:40	two
blind men	Matt. 23:17	blind
free men	Rev. 13:16	free
such men	2 Tim. 3:5	such
men who	I Tim. 4:3	them which
he shall be saved	Matt. 24:13	shall be saved
foolish men	Luke 24:25	fools

"While they promise them liberty, they themselves are the servants of corruption." II Peter 2:19

TWELVE

Finally: They Worshipped Devils

TREND TWELVE

Yet repented not. . .that they should not WORSHIP DEVILS Revelation 9:20

How do Devils become Gods?

Perhaps an untold scene from C.S. Lewis's *Screwtape Letters* might view the devils venting their envy, triggered by the acquittal fellow fallen angel Lucifer has received at the hands of the New Age and liberal theologians. Straining one's ears, we might hear:

> "Vindication! Devil is such a demeaning title, after all.
> We wanted to be '. . .like the most High,' too."

No sooner said than done and aided by the willing fountain pen of Mme. Blavatsky. Driven, as she acknowledges, by spirit entity, Koot Hoomi Lal Sing, she recommends a switch from the title 'devils' to 'demons'.

> [T]he Church is wrong in calling them Devils. . .[T]he word demon however, as in the case of Socrates, and in the spirit of the meaning given to it by the whole of antiquity, stand[s] for the Guardian Spirit or Angel not a Devil of Satanic descent as Theology would have it. . . Demons is a very loose word to use, as it applies to. . . minor Gods;. . .there are no devils.[1]

The last line, ". . .there are no devils," is unfortunately true of the NKJV and other recent bible versions. Marching hand-in-hand with the New Age they have eliminated all references to 'devils' and replaced them with 'demons'.

NIV, NASB, et al.	KJV
demon	devil

Even Webster would revoke their 'semantic license' as the dictionary distinguishes sharply between the two terms.

> demon: 1. A tutelary divinity; a demon. 2. . . .neut. of *daimonios* of a divinity
>
> devil: 1. In Jewish and Christian theology, the personal supreme spirit of evil and unrighteousness. 2. A lesser evil or malignant spirit. . .[2]

New Age books document that 'demon' is a word wrapped with positive connotations both currently and historically.

> *The Metaphysical Bible Dictionary*
> demon: a superior power
> devil: all thoughts. . .that fight against the truth.

The KJV's evil spirits have become 'gods' in new versions, according to the New Age consensus.

> *The Theosophical Dictionary:* demon: In the. . .ancient classics. . .it has a meaning identical with that of 'god', 'angel' or 'genius'.

> *The Encyclopedia of Occultism & Parapsychology:* demon: s.v Guiding Spirits. Socrates said, "[A] voice has been heard by me throughout my life. . .I call it a God or a daemon."[3]

Clutching to an aura of intellectuality, New Agers attempt to sway their audiences with quotes, such as the following in which Plutarch explains Socrates' elevated view of demons.

> Everyone has a demon, a god, or a spirit that swims above and touches the extremest part of man's head. . .the more intelligent, who know it to be without, call it a Daemon.
>
> Socrates. . .taught that he had a daemon, a spiritual something that put him on the road to wisdom. The Greeks meant by the word Demon, a demigod.[4]

All of the world's religions, except biblical Christianity and Judaism, believe that those entities which the bible calls evil spirits are demigods, worthy of veneration or placation. In the West, New Agers are told that Nathaniel Hawthorne, "ascribe[s] some measure of importance and success to his prompt obedience to the wise Daemon's direction."[5] Eastward, Buddhists tell of "good demons," *mosri sho shu* and mischievous demons, *nushi sho shu.* Both the New Age and Webster's have adopted definitions which reflect this worldwide consensus. By switching to the globally acceptable 'demons', new 'International' versions follow their admitted philosophy of choosing words which "allow each reader to decide for himself" what a verse means.[6] God, however, has already decided.

N.T. Greek dabblers may jump to the floor with reference to the Greek's use of both *diabolos* and *daemonium* to refer to Satan and the devils, respectively. Any objection to translating two different Greek words as one English word fails disastrously since new version editors themselves translate two different Hebrew words, *shed* and *sair,* as one word 'demon'. Scholars who live in glass houses should refrain from throwing 'original language' stones, particularly when their house of cards appears to have been designed by a New Age architect.

TREND THIRTEEN

Men shall be DESPISERS OF THOSE THAT ARE GOOD.
II Timothy 3:3

"Servants. . .From the Heart" (KJV) or "Slaves" (NIV, NASB)?

Billy Graham called attention to the sharp distinction between servants and slaves during his 1988 Denver Crusade, pronouncing, "You are either servants of God or slaves of Satan." Three hundred years earlier John Bunyan's *Pilgrim's Progress* painted graphic word-pictures allegorizing Satan's tyrannical dominion.

> It came burning hot into my mind, whatever he said and however he flattered, when he got me to his house, he would sell me for a slave.

Webster presents the disparate imagery of 'servants' and 'slaves'.

> Slave: . . .a person held in bondage, a thrall. One who has lost control of himself, freedom of action. A drudge.
>
> Servant: . . .one who exerts himself for the benefit of another master. . .as a public servant, an official of a government.7

The images of cruel bondage, generated by the word 'slave', are alien to our 'sonship' motivation expressed in Ephesians 6:6.

> . . .but as servants of Christ, doing the will of God from the heart.

The difference between the two words has not only been well-marked by Graham, Bunyan, and Webster, but by New Age writers. The prevailing term among New Agers to describe Christians is 'slave'. Scanning the examples to follow reveals the broad range of strange philosophies which have embraced this deprecating term regarding Christians.

"Slaves of Christ" (Ephesians 6:6 NASB, NIV)

Confiscated and turned over to the police in Orange, California as part of an investigation into Satanic group crime and ritual killing, this bizarre note calls Christians the "Slaves of Christ" just like the new versions.

> All the god believers will all become the slaves of their new master. Since they are slaves, then Kryst [sic] is the King of Slaves—the shackles [sic] and chains are tight on the torn hands of the bearded faggot who long ago preached. . .Kryst's [sic] destiny awaits him in the cold steel which will behead him in front of all his quivering followers—all who have done good in his name. Satan sits on the throne of God—he raises his blood-sprayed sword and proclaims himself the new ruler of the universe.[8]

The book of Revelation corrects the erring conclusions of this bitter harangue and shows Christians as Webster's "servants. . .public servants, officials of government."

> ". . .and we shall reign on the earth." Revelation 5:10
> ". . .and they lived and reigned with Christ a thousand years." Revelation 20:4
> ". . .and they shall reign for ever and ever." Revelation 22:5

Satanists across the country concoct their brew with the same rigid vocabulary. Read over the nation's airwaves was a letter from a Satanist; the recipient, Bob Larson, noted its characteristic points: it was signed in blood and referred to Christians as slaves, not once but twice.

The July 20, 1986 edition of the San Antonio, *Texas Express News* echoes:

> A midnight raid by deputies caught eleven teens suspected of conducting Satanic rituals. . .Sheriff Copleland found **anti-Christian** graffiti and profanity scrawled on the ruins of the bath-house. . .They also found charred bones

> of animals. . .[which] had apparently been sacrificed. There was a concrete slab used as an altar. . a staircase led to two small rooms under the alter called 'slave quarters'.

Bible versions that switch to "anti-Christian" terms, as the article calls them, can hardly be considered an improvement. Being in concord with the hatchers of heresy is a chilling place to be. The New Agers also see Christ's church as:

> . . .bigoted and cruel to all who do not choose to be its slaves.[9]

New Age leaders say Adam was a "slave" before he ate from the Tree of Life.[10] He was then "emancipated" just like Lucifer, who ". . .preferred free will to passive slavery."[11] Another New Age author writes:

> [D]ogmas have made weaklings and slaves of men. . . Justification by faith and vicarious atonement were taught as gospel truth and man became a greater slave than before.[12]

Those last words sound strikingly similar to the new versions.

> But now having been freed from sin and enslaved to God. . .
> NASB Romans 6:22

How sharply this notion contrasts with John 8:32,36:

> Ye shall know the truth and the truth shall make you free. If the Son therefore shall make you free, ye shall be free indeed. KJV

Demoted or Promoted?

The "anti-Christian" graffiti has been grafted on to the new versions. A rapid review follows the dozens of 'demotions' Christians receive at the hands of the new translations.

NASB		KJV
slaves	John 13:16	servants
slaves	John 15:15	servants
slave/master	John 15:20	servant/lord
slave	John 18:10	servant
slave-girl	John 18:17, Acts 16:16	damsel
slave	Mark 10:44	servant
slave	Luke 12:37	servant
slave	Luke 12:43	servant
slave	Luke 12:46	servant
slave	Luke 12:47	servant
slave	Luke 15:22	servant
slave	Luke 7:2	servant
slave	Luke 7:10	servant
slave	Luke 19:13	servant
slave	Luke 19:15	servant
slave	Luke 20:10	servant
bondslave	Luke 1:38	handmaid
slaves	John 18:26	servant
bond slave	Acts 2:18	servant
bond servant	Rom. 1:1	servant
slaves	Rom. 6:17, 19	servants
servant	Rom. 15:8	minister
slave	I Cor. 7:21	servant
slave	I Cor. 7:22	servant
servants	2 Cor. 3:6	ministers
servants	2 Cor. 11:15	ministers
(The use of the word servant here obscures the fact that Satan has "ministers.")		
bond-servant	Gal. 1:10	servant
bond-servant	Phil. 1:1	servant
slaves	Eph. 6:5	servant
slaves	Eph. 6:6	servants
slaves	Eph. 6:8	bond
slaves	Col. 3:22	servants
slaves	Col. 4:1	servants
bondslaves	Col. 4:12	servants
servant	Col. 4:7	minister

NASB		KJV
slaves	2 Pet. 2:9	servant
slaves	I Tim. 6:1	servant
bondservant	2 Tim. 2:24	servant
slaves	Philem.1:16	servant
bondslave	I Pet. 2:16	servant
bondservant	Titus 1:1	servant
bondservant	James 1:1	servant
bond servant	Jude 1:1	servant
bond servant	Rev. 1:1	servant
slave	Rev. 6:15	bondman
bond-servant	Rev. 7:3	servant
bond-servant	Rev. 15:3	servant
bond servant	Rev. 19:5	servant
bond servant	Rev. 22:3	servant

Double Minded?

Lack of uniformity in the way new versions translate Hebrew and Greek words, rendered as "servant" in the KJV, testifies to the insecure foundation on which their choice of words lies. They translate the Hebrew *ebed* as both 'slaves' and 'servants'. The Greek *pais* is inconsistently rendered as both 'slaves' and servants. *Doulos*, the word most often translated 'slaves' by the recent version, becomes 'servants' by those same pens in Revelation 10. Schizophrenia in scholarship strikes again as 'sundoulos' is translated as 'servants' and 'slaves'. When in doubt, as Paul admonishes us, "Abstain from all appearance of evil. . ." (I Thessalonians 5:22).

PART THREE

Another Gospel and Another God

Initiated or In Christ

Striving or Saved

Gospels & Gods

New Age or New Earth

Interment or Judgement

THIRTEEN

Another Gospel

. . .[I]f he that cometh preacheth. . .another gospel
II Cor 11:4

NIV, NASB	KJV
Children, how hard it is to enter the kingdom of God.	Children, how hard it is for them that trust in riches to enter into the kingdom of God. Mark 10:24
difficult is the way (NKJV)	narrow is the way Matt. 7:14

The Coming World Religion, taking a chapter from the New Age movement and one from apostate Christianity, constructs a course like a Chinese puzzle to the "kingdom of God." The expedition proposed by new versions is "hard," as evidenced by the aforementioned verse. Traveling their thorny trail, the signposts read as follows:

I. Initiation

II. Process

- A. Works
- B. Reincarnation
- C. Cycles/Ages

III. Perfection: Christ Consciousness

Ignoring the word of God, which shows us *the* way, and following some New Age atlas, many turn down these blind alleys looking for avenues of spiritual advancement. The street signs leading to salvation have been switched in recent bibles. They now map out a migration away from the New Jerusalem.

	NEW VERSIONS	NEW AGE	KJV
WHEN	have been (baptized/ initiated)	have been (baptized/ initiated)	are saved
	are being	are being	are saved
HOW	obey	obey	believe
	faithfulness	faithfulness	faith
WHAT	**a** gospel	a gospel	**the** gospel
	a message	a message	his word
WHO	**a** God	a God	**the** God
	a son	a son	**the** Son
	a Savior	a Savior	**the** Saviour
	a spirit	a spirit	**the** Spirit
WHERE	**an** age	an age	**the** world

New Version Editors Reject Scriptural Salvation

> Woe unto you scribes. . .hypocrites. For ye shut up the kingdom of heaven against men: for ye neither go in yourselves, neither suffer ye them that are entering to go in. Woe unto you scribes. . .Matthew 23:13, 14

These alterations exist because many of the new version editors are openly antagonistic to the gospel of faith in Christ. Their route of salvation runs the gamut from the unreasonable Reformed and Romish view to the repellent notion of a 'Ransom to Satan'. The following citations from their other writings convey the verbal villainy woven into their versions.

 **Edwin Palmer: NIV**

He was the "coordinator of all work on the NIV" and

"selected all of the personnel of the initial translation committee."[1] He also edited the *NIV Study Bible* which Zondervan says includes the "liberal position."[2] His scandalous and sacrilegious statement will stun and shock the reader. In one of his books he quotes a verse of his own translation, then says:

> [T]his [his own translation] shows the great error that is so prevalent today in some orthodox Protestant circles, namely that regeneration depends upon faith. . .and that in order to be born again man must first accept Jesus as his Savior.[3]

If he denies "faith" and each individual's responsibility to "accept Jesus as his Savior," what does he offer in its place?

NIV	KJV
By standing firm you will save yourself.	In your patience possess ye your souls. Luke 21:19

He is not alone in his views. Another 'liberal' new version editor comments regarding this switch in Luke 21:19:

> [O]f all of the changes in the RV, that in Luke 21:19 is the one to which I look with most hope. We think of our souls as something to complete. . .[4]

Palmer devoted an entire chapter in his book, *The Five Points of Calvinism* , to disprove the idea that "man still has the ability to ask God's help for salvation."[5] His "Five Points" form a Satanic pentagram. His book is so irrational that he is periodically forced to interrupt himself with comments like, ". . .as contradictory as that may seem." In defense of the obviously unscriptural character of his chapters, he quips, "The lack of a [scripture] text does not destroy their character."[6] He whittles away at John 3:16 and concludes that the view "that Christ loved the whole world equally and gave himself up for the world" is wrong.[7]

Even the spiritual elitism of gnosticism and the New Age allows that 'cosmic consciousness' is available to everyone following their 'evolution of consciousness' in numerous reincarnations; Palmer, however, is not so inclusive. He says, "God intends that salvation shall be for only a few. . ."[8] Sounding like one of the Jehovah Witness 144,000 he says, "God chose only a certain number to be saved." "For God so loved the world" becomes "only those whom he loved. . .would be saved. . .If God loves us, we are called."[9] Calvinist NASB editors likewise distort the clear responsibility of man in Hebrews. 8:9 and present a cruel and fickle God.

NASB	KJV
For they did not continue in my covenant and I did not care for them.	**Because** they continued not in my covenant, and I regarded them not.

Palmer's chapter on the 'Elect' elite is reflected in his translation of I Thessalonians 1:4, "he has chosen you." He admits his change "suggests the opposite of" the KJV's "your election of God." In his system, God elects a few 'winners'. In Christianity, God calls *all* sinners, but few elect to respond. Palmer denies that man should respond, and like psychologist B.F. Skinner, author of *Beyond Freedom and Dignity*, Palmer believes, "Man is entirely passive." He points to his alteration of John 1:13 asserting that it 'proves' man has no free will.[10]

His 'elite' were serenaded by the heavenly host in Luke 2:14 in the NIV and NASB. However, in the KJV the good will of God was extended to all men, not his favorite 'God-pleasing' elect.

NASB	NIV	KJV
Glory to God in the highest, and on earth, peace among men with whom He is pleased.	Glory to God in the highest, and on earth peace to men in whom his favor rests.	Glory to God in the highest and on earth peace, good will toward men.

Here, the new versions follow manuscripts Aleph, B, C and D. Their Greek differs from the overwhelming majority of manuscripts by one letter, 's'. The former has the genitive *eudokios*, while the latter has the nominative *eudokia*. Watch out for the letter 's'—sin, Satan, Sodom, Saul (had to be changed to Paul). The added 's' here is the hiss of the serpent. The KJV and the Majority text reading of *eudokia* is attested by not only *most* MSS but also by the oldest witnesses.

> *2nd Century:* Syriac Version and Irenaeus
> *3rd Century:* Coptic Version and the Apostolic Constitution
> *4th Century:* Eusebius, Aphraates, Titus, Didymus, Gregory, Cyril, Epiphanus, Ephraem, Philo, Chrysostom.

It is also attested to by the old Armenian, Georgian, Ethiopic, Slavonic, and Arabic Versions, as well as every known lectionary in the world. In their passion to give space to Satan's sermon, they follow four corrupt fourth and fifth century MSS while ignoring a total of 53 ancient witnesses including 16 belonging to the second, third and fourth centuries and 37 from the fifth, sixth, seventh and eighth centuries.[11]

Although the advertisements for the NIV boast that it was translated by a committee of 100 scholars, Palmer's hand picked CBT (Committee on Bible Translation) "would choose a translation other than that of the initial or intermediate or general editorial committees." Therefore Palmer and his cronies could ignore all three intermediate committees and make their own translation.[12] This is evident in verses such as Romans 1:28 where a concept from Palmer's chapter entitled "Total Depravity" finds its way. He admits his purposeful switch saying, "Paul was not speaking of the reprobate but the depraved."[13] (Isn't that the word Kittel used to incite the Nazi's to kill the Jews? See chapter 42.) His power and influence can also be seen in the Commonwealth edition of the NIV in which "Edwin Palmer. . .agreed with many of the changes himself to save time."[14] (The Greek *Textus Receptus* is often ignored by critics who insist Erasmus hurried it along to save time.) Palmer's Calvinism did not rest with his influence in the NIV. The *New King James* Committee boasts seven members who subscribe to Palmer's elite 'Elect' and damned 'depraved' classes.

J.B. Phillips: *NASB-Greek-English Interlinear* Preface, *J.B. Phillips Translation* et al.

Phillips believes that even those who doubt the existence of

God are saved, even though they have never received Jesus Christ as their Saviour. He contends:

> Those who give themselves in love to others did in fact 'know God', however loudly they might protest their agnosticism.[15]

☑ B.F. Westcott: The 'New' Greek Text

He subscribes to "only a social interpretation of the Gospel." Commenting on I John 2:2 which reads, "[H]e is the propitiation for our sins," Westcott says, this verse is "foreign to the language of the New Testament." He has "great difficulty with the notion of sacrifice and vicarious punishment." He sees, "man paying this debt." And notes, "Some by diligent obedience have been raised to the loftiest places in the celestial hierarchy." He supports the removal of "through his blood" in Col 1:14 since he feels, "the redemptive efficacy of Christ's work is to be found in his whole life." Consequently, he writes, "The redemptive work of Christ was complete in his last discourses." He admits however, "No doubt many do not agree with me."[16]

☑ F.J.A. Hort: The 'New' Greek Text

He also "pleaded for the social interpretation of the gospel." He looked to the day when, "the crude individualism of common notions of salvation is corrected, as expressed in 'too purely personal Evangelical hymns.'" Hort mockingly calls Evangelical Christianity, the "easy belief." "Without any act of ours, we are children of the Great and Gracious Heavenly Father," he says. "Christ's bearing our sins. . .[is] an almost universal heresy." Of the bible Hort contends:

> There is no direct reference to the idea of purchase or ransom. . .or to the idea of sacrificial atonement. . .[The] lamb without blemish [is] the passover lamb and not the lamb of God. [He admits], [O]bjections might be taken to his views, especially on the doctrine of the Atonement. . .**if it existed.** [emphasis mine]

Its only merit for him was the Platonic "acting out of and manifestation of some eternal principle. . .not a substitute which makes all other sacrifices useless. . ."

> I confess I have no repugnance to the primitive doctrine of a ransom paid to Satan. I can see no other possible form in which the doctrine of a ransom is at all tenable; anything is better than the doctrine of a ransom to the father.[17]

Hort evidently went to one too many Ghostly Guild meetings. Dr. Louis Talbot comments, "Some. . .including Origen. . .conceived that the ransom was given to Satan. . .this mythological tale had a strong appeal. . .but not to anyone who believes God's word."[18]

Made in the image of their creators, the new versions mirror clearly these editor's marred views of salvation, reflecting each and every movement along the metaphysical maze of their minds. The typical journey begins with 'initiation' and the new versions have all the semantic signposts.

FOURTEEN

Initiated or 'In Christ'?

Our spiritual sustenance comes from a daily diet of the word of God. The serpent told Eve to put that aside; he would feed her with just one gulp. So throughout the centuries his scribes have offered a magic carpet ride to spontaneous spirituality. The serpent's rap was:

> it was pleasant to the eyes. . .to make one wise. Genesis 3:6

Eating the fruit or participating in a ceremony is a ritual/magic act which feeds the flesh while it pretends to feed the spirit. The split second spirituality and sense pleasing trappings of initiation rites—whether they be those of Sacramentalists with their infant christening caps and gowns or Satanists in their infidel-costumed cape and garb—are reminiscent of Eve. The rap of her lip-service religion will levitate the unwary into the kingdom of the king of the bottomless pit (Rev 9:11).

The word initiation generates bizarre visions of occult ceremonies such as those described in *Supernatural Powers and the Occult* or *Religious Movements in Contemporary America*. One can only become a witch or Satanist by being 'initiated' into an existing group. Few but the fringes of society are likely to acquiesce to this door to the chambers of death. So the snake has changed his skin to seduce the other strata of society. Now yuppies are 'initiated' by the auditorium full while attending seminars held by Werner Erhard or Lynn Andrews. The flower children became Rajneesh's '*sanyassin* initiates', while businessmen were 'initiated' into TM. Middle America minds the 'Masonic Keys of Knowledge and Initiation'. Housewives, haunting the pages of women's magazines for advice, light upon Rosicrucian ads offering their brand of 'initiation'. The idea of initiation was implanted in a generation of children as they watched the Star War's initiation of Luke Skywalker by the Jedi Knights. Saturday cartoons will cultivate the seed. All of these cultural indoctrinations to the concept of initiation are setting the stage for the final initiation—the mark of the beast. Constance Cumby believes:

> Initiation is considered by them to be the heart and core of the planned New World Religion.[19]

Bookstore shelves become the altars of the new religion offering unwary victims, dabblers and dervishes, books such as *Initiation of the World, Initiation: Human and Solar, Initiation, Eternity, and the Passing Moment, The Rays and the Initiations,* and *The Supreme Initiation of the Blessed Virgin.* Your letter carrier can channel "The Initiator," a newsletter of the group 'Planetary Initiative for the World We Choose'. Members like Norman Cousins and the late Buckminster Fuller offer instantaneous initiation into the new age in the privacy of your own home.

Lucifer: The One Initiator

Converted New Age leader Randall N. Baer, in his book *Inside the New Age Nightmare,* reveals the stowaway behind this wave of initiations.

> Initiations are all the rage. . .There are innumerable varieties of initiation within the spectrum of N.A. activities, all invoke a direct interlinking of the individual with demon power.[20]

The sea serpent behind the swell shows as Steiner says:

> Let us. . .take the first step on the path of Initiation. . .it is really Lucifer who acts as his lightbearer.[21]

Reflections on the Christ reveals these red herring initiation ceremonies harbor deep dark waters which will "drown men in destruction" (I Timothy 6:9). In it Spangler says:

> Luciferic initiation. . .is an invitation into the New Age. The true light of Lucifer cannot be seen through sorrow [New version manuscript *The Shepherd of Hermes* agrees; see chapter 40] The true light of this great being can only be recognized when one's own eyes can see with the light of Christ. Lucifer works within each of us to bring us to wholeness. . .[It is] the Luciferic initiation. . .through which the individual must pass if he is to come fully into the presence. . .[22]

Baptism by the Beast

The word 'initiation' rends the air like the wail of a wolf; it is clearly not a Christian term. Consequently 'the Counterfeiter' must camouflage his wolf in the wool of a sheep, with words like 'Christian Initiation' or 'Baptism/Initiation'. *Toward a Religion for the New Age* explains why:

> Because religion is such an important part of daily life, if a new religion did not integrate at least some familiar ritual and practice it probably would not be accepted by the majority. But if familiar elements were included in the synthesis, acceptance and easy transition into the new religion could be promoted.[23]

Occult writings, that might incite the worship of the Beast, are commonly imagined to be uncanny and unclouded evil. Consequently, the charge that the new versions of the bible are 'leavened' with occult philosophy seems unbelievable. However, the black-hearted books of the occult world *usually* beat inside the cover of a Christianized corpse. As Jesus said, ". . .insomuch that if it were possible they shall deceive the very elect (Matthew 24:24). This lengthy excerpt from Bailey's New Age book, *The Reappearance of the Christ* shows how they graft Christian concepts on to their Frankenstein, hoping to infuse life into their dead deception. Note the role Baptism/Initiation will play in the new world religion.

> As *Nourisher of the Little Ones*, we are dealing with an aspect of Christ's work which involves the stimulation of the consciousness of His disciples as they prepare to undergo **initiation** or to enter into deeper phases of spiritual awareness. The result of His work in the Triangle with the masses of men will be the presentation of the first initiation—the Birth of the Christ in the cave of the Heart—as the **basic ceremony** in the **new world religion**. By means of this ceremony, the masses of men in all lands will be enabled to register consciously the "birth of the Christ" in the heart, and the "being born again" to which He Himself referred (John III.3) when here on Earth before. *This new birth is what esotericists mean when they speak of the first initiation.* It will not, in the future, be the experience of the occasional disciple but the general experience of countless thousands towards the close of the Aquarian Age. The **purifying waters of the Baptism Initiation** (the second initiation) will submerge hundreds of aspirants in many lands, and these two initiations (which are preparatory to true service, and the third initiation of the Transfiguration) will set the seal on Christ's mission as the Agent of the great spiritual Triangle which He represents.
>
> The major work of Christ, however, as far as the disciples and the definitely spiritually-minded people of the world are concerned, plus the hundreds of thousands of advanced humanity, is so to "nourish" their spiritual consciousness and life that they will be enabled to take the third and fourth initiations—those of the Transfiguration and the Renunciation (or Crucifixion).
>
> As esotericists know, the term "little ones" refers to those disciples who are "babes in Christ" (as The New Testament terms it) and who have taken the first two initiations of the Birth and the Baptism. They are aware of the spiritual aspiration which is indicative of the Christ life in their hearts, and they have subjected themselves to the processes of purification which culminate in the

> baptismal waters. Christ must prepare these aspirants for the higher initiations and so nourish and aid them that they can stand before the **One Initiator** and become pillars in the Temple of God (i.e., agents of the spiritual Hierarchy and, therefore, active, working disciples).[24]

"Lucifer is the 'One Initiator' whose star shines forth," writes Bailey in her *Rays and Initiations*. Sanat (a scramble for Satan) is also called the "One Initiator" in New Age circles. Hence their baptismal Jordan is the lake of fire. Adrift in the same boat, Bailey and the 'bogus brethren' baptize for "purification" (i.e., the remission of sins) not, as the bible clearly commends, as "the answer **of** a good conscience toward God" (I Peter 3:21).

This is the clearest verse in the bible distinguishing the role of Christian baptism from 'esoteric' baptism. As such, it has been altered in new versions to match the new age, making baptism efficacious not symbolic. A single word hinges which way one swings in the debate. The KJV says "of" but many new versions say, "for a good conscience." In the debate as to whether the genitive is regarded as subjective or objective, these editors swing to Satan's side. Those subscribing to regenerative baptism cite the new translations to support their view.[25]

(Bailey also mentioned the "little ones"; today Benjamin Creme, channeling Maitreya, says, "I am the Initiator of the little one."[26] Are the apostates baptizing babies for the beast?)

Christian (?) Initiation

> Once the whole world falls under the iron rule of the antichrist, all of humanity must undergo the Initiation that leads to the Mark.[27]

"Mass planetary initiations" will take place in "revitalized Christian Churches," insists Benjamin Creme.[28] Bailey's *Externalization of the Hierarchy* reveals that the masses will be "softened up" and "indoctrinated" to accept the idea of initiation before the "final pledge." The softening up includes changes in the new versions and 'initiation' for 'Christians'. (They have even changed "first faith" to "previous pledge" in I Timothy 5:12 to present the first in the series of occult initiations. Every Greek text says "first faith.")

The frontispiece frames the most frightening face you've ever seen—a photograph of author Rudolph Steiner, Satan's staunchest apologist. His book *Esoteric Christianity* heralds a chapter entitled "Christian Initiation" insisting:

> Christianity must bring mankind to an acceptance of some of the ancient principles of initiation.[29]

The defectors defer to the devil's desires as evidenced by the following newspaper notice:

> The Rite of **Christian Initiation** (RCIA), a process of bringing new people into the [Catholic] faith, will begin Tuesday September 3 at 7:30p.m. in room seven of the lower church hall.

Apostasy knows no denominational boundaries. Howard M. Ervin, professor at Oral Roberts University, makes remarks in his book, *Conversion-Initiation and the Baptism in the Holy Ghost,* which sound sinisterly close to Mme. Blavatsky's:

APOSTATE CHRISTIANITY	LUCIFERIAN
"[The] initiatory role of water baptism [is]. . .Christian Initiation . . .[A]part from the water rite, the metaphors have little meaning. . .the ceremony is substantively more than symbolic, it is sacramental. . .[The] perception that Pentecostals and sacramentalists share a common world view is correct. The baptism in/filling with/gift of the Holy Spirit is therefore subsequent to conversion and initiation. The NIV captures the nuance correctly, 'it [baptism] saves you. . .'"[30] Ervin	"After the usual baptism by purification of water. . .[the] baptismal font, upon entering from which the neophyte was 'born again' and became an adept. . .In the cycle of Initiation which was very long, water represented the initial lower steps toward purification. . .there is another baptism of the Spirit of Holy Light." [The NIV changes 'Spirit' to 'light' in Eph. 5:9.][31] Blavatsky

Non-charismatics have also lapsed into listening to Lucifer's line. James D.G. Dunn's anti-Charismatic book, *Baptism in the Holy Spirit,* appropriated annals of New Age terms, repeatedly referring to 'initiation'. Contrary to true Christianity, he contends:

> [T]he N.T. nowhere speaks of conversion as receiving Christ. . .Baptism is the act of faith. . .a specific moment in the ritual of initiation prior to immersion. . .the rite of initiation. . .the rite of water baptism not only symbolizes burial with Christ but. . .helps in some way effect it.[32]

"Sadly the New Age movement has infiltrated many of our Christian denominations with this pagan concept," observes Constance Cumby.[33] Marrs agrees stating, "False prophets and false teachers will seduce people's minds and initiate them into the Mystery of Iniquity." [34]

> Satan wants humans to encounter him and think that they are in touch with the living God. . .his most subtle deception [is] the duplication of religious experience. . .[T]hose who refuse to be initiated into Satan's kingdom. . .will be eliminated.[35]
>
> Erwin Lutzer Pastor, Moody Church

The Church of Cain

> The required theological reconstruction is proceeding in a number of quarters.[36]
>
> Southeastern Baptist Theological Seminary

Clement, the second century core of the new versions, contrived a system in which "baptism is decidedly more prominent than redemption by the blood of Christ," since he had been "initiated by the laver of illumination into the true mysteries." His formula for salvation became fixed in print at the Council of Constantinople and later by the Council of Trent. The foundation, "One baptism for the remission of sins, "was framed on a fault line extending back to Cain, the father of false creeds. New version editors have built their churches and versions on this volcanic rock. Westcott writes of "initiation in the Mysteries. . .deep in mystic rites. . .purified with holiest water. . ." Elsewhere he says,

> The remission of sins has always been connected with Baptism, the sacrament of incorporation. . .[We are] placed in relation to God by Baptism.[37]

Philip Schaff, at the hub of the 'New' Greek and ASV, was tried for heresy by his denomination for his belief in baptism/initiation regeneration. From his hub, spokes like the *Living Bible* and NASV moved this creed into the next century. Hort peddled the same heresy:

> I am a staunch sacerdotalist. . .Paul connected the state [salvation] with a **past completed** act [baptism] by which it was formerly taken possession of.[38]

See this *"past completed"* action of baptism in the NASV, NIV and all new versions. Their verbs are mistranslated, as even the preface of the *NASB Interlinear Greek-English New Testament.* admits:

> The Authorized Version is idiomatically correct. . .[39]

Christians "are saved" (present tense) when they receive Jesus as Saviour. The new versions present the baptism/initiation views as intended by their editors, a past completed act that does not necessarily follow into the present.

NEW VERSIONS		KJV
has been baptized	Mark 16:16	is baptized
have been saved	Eph. 2:8	are saved
have been sanctified	I Cor. 1:2	are sanctified
have been raised	Col. 3:1	be risen
have come to know him	I John 2:3	know him
have been born again	I Pet. 1:23	being born again
have been made complete	Col. 2:10	are
have died	Col. 2:20	be dead
have died	Col. 3:3	are dead
died	2 Tim. 2:11	be dead
were called	I Tim. 6:12	art also called

NEW VERSIONS		KJV
were washed were sanctified were justified	I Cor.6:11	are washed are sanctified are justified
were enriched	I Cor. 1:5	are enriched

Sounding like the scribes in the synagogue who "laughed him to scorn" (Mark 5:40), Calvin Linton, NIV Committee member refers to those who disagree with the alterations in the new versions as "uninitiated" and "amusingly uninformed."[40]

> The just upright man is laughed to scorn. Job 12:4

Hort and the new version editors who, "have been saved" at baptism, have a spokesman today in Alan Schreck, author of *Catholic and Christian.*

> Evangelical Protestants will sometimes ask a Catholic acquaintance, 'Have you been saved?'. . .[T]he question seems to suggest that a person's salvation is a once-and-for-all event that happens in a single moment, rather than a process. . .I believe that a Catholic can adequately answer the question. The Catholic can say that, 'I have been saved [Catholic baptism]; I am being saved' [works, obedience, perseverance].[41]

The new versions echo Schreck saying, "have been saved" (Eph 2:8) and "are being saved" (I Cor 1:18 et al.). In both of these verses the KJV says "are saved," which clearly describes the once-and-for-all event that occurs when Jesus Christ is received as Saviour. One can only ask, are the new versions Catholic or Christian? Notice how the new versions present the process theology of the New Age and apostate Christianity where initiation commences an incessant course conveying one to salvation.

NEW VERSIONS		KJV
Are there few who are being saved?	Luke 13:23	be saved
are being saved?	2 Cor. 2:15	are saved
those who are perishing foolishness, but to us who are being saved	I Cor. 1:18	are saved
darkness is passing away	I John 2:8	is past
are turning to God	Acts 15:19	turned
your brother was dead and *has begun to live*	Luke 15:32	is alive
is being renewed	Col. 3:10	is renewed
were being saved	Acts 2:47	should be saved
are perishing	2 Cor. 4:3	are lost

Dean Burgon, noted Greek scholar, comments on the "are being saved" and "have been saved" rendition of the Greek verbs.

> [T]he schoolboy method of translation is therein exhibited in constant operation throughout. . .We are never permitted to believe that we are in the company of Scholars. . .the idiomatic rendering of a Greek author into English is a higher achievement by far. . .[E]xamples of their inconsistency. . .reduces the whole matter to a question of Taste. . .[T]he vast number of cases in which they have forsaken their own rule shows that it could not be followed without changing the meaning of the original. . .They virtually admit that they have been all along unjustly forcing on an independent language an alien yoke.[42]

Foster of the NIV and NKJV committees agrees, admitting, "This in itself results in an unnatural straining of the tenses of the English."[43] However, the doctrinal bend of the translator tends toward a progressive kind of salvation and this is reflected in their new versions. As one says, "[T]he work of a life is to realize this idea [Plato]. . .aorist in contrast with the present." Or as channeled entity Lazaris phrases it: "[T]hat is the human condition: to be saving itself."[44]

New versions also present a progressive, tentative salvation in the following verses.

NIV or NASB et al.		KJV
repentance. . .*leading* to salvation (leading is not in any Greek)	2 Cor. 7:10 Acts 11:18	repentance to salvation
and a large number who believed turned to the Lord	Acts 11:21	a great number believed and turned unto the Lord.
return [to your baptismal faith]	Acts 28:27, 3:19	be converted [for the first time]
remember that you were at that time separated from Christ [like the Prodigal son]	Eph. 2:12	without Christ [Period]
new things have come	2 Cor. 5:17	all things are become new
And you were dead in your trespasses and sins	Eph. 2:1	and you hath he quickened, who were dead in trespasses and sins
he freely bestowed upon us in the Beloved	Eph. 1:6	he hath made us accepted in the beloved

Cults of Cain

Alan Schreck and the new versions are "falling away" toward a course already charted by the cults. F. Aster Barnwell's bizarre book, *The Meaning of Christ for a New Age* presents the view that, "[S]alvation is not an event but a lifelong process."[45] Herbert W. Armstrong teaches, "[T]he born again experience is a process, not an instantly imputed act."[46] In his pamphlet 'Why were you born?' he says:

> Salvation is a process! . . .He tries to deceive you into thinking all there is to it is just accepting Christ with no works and presto chango, you are pronounced saved.?[47]

Scientology has a "process for breaking through the engram." *Est* has a 'Truth Process/Danger Process.'[48] The Rosicrucians write of the process of "the becoming of the Son of God. . .[as] you are becoming a Son of God."[49] Unity says, "In man a wonderful being is in process. . .This being is spiritual man who will be equal with God."[50] Last but not least, England and Canada host the Process Church where Jehovah, Satan and Lucifer are the three gods worshipped.

Process Theology

> And in **process** of time it came to pass that Cain brought of the fruit of the ground an offering unto the Lord. . .But unto Cain and to his offering he had not respect.
>
> Genesis 4:3,5

Norman Geisler calls Cain's 'Process Theology', "the major movement in contemporary theology." Norman Pittinger, Shubert Ogden and Nelson Pike are among its advocates. Elliot Miller observes:

> Process theology, currently in vogue among liberal Protestant theologians has affinities with New Age thinking. This theology is now making inroads into evangelical circles especially among those who do not hold the complete inerrancy of scripture.[51]

Liberals like M. Scott Peck believe, "Spiritual development is a process of ascension just like physical evolution." The pulse of this present parody pounds from the pages of books like *New Directions in New Testament Study*. The author uses the word 'initiation' for 'baptism' and quotes New Age shaman Mircea Eliade's perspective.

> [B]aptism by Paul [is] a rite of initiation. . .a genuine starting, for salvation is presented as a process.[52]

Process Theology's Past

The Hindu deity *Kali* is called the "goddess of becoming, of evolution." Plato spoke of the world as "that which is always becoming."[53] Aristotle believed that the world and the individual "were being" redeemed through a process. From this background Clement and Origen viewed "salvation as an educational process."[54] They introduced this concept in I Peter 2:2, among other places, by adding "to salvation" to their Greek N.T. manuscripts. As a result, the new versions read:

NASB		KJV
You may grow in respect to salvation	I Pet. 2:2	ye may grow thereby

Of course we "grow in grace and in the knowledge of our Lord and Saviour Jesus Christ" (II Peter 3:18) and grow in "faith" (II Thessalonians 1:3); but Christians do not grow "to salvation." New versions follow Aleph, B, and P72 here, ignoring the vast majority of MS which agree with the KJV. If P72 (now held by the Vatican) is to be taken as a reliable witness, then its apocryphal additions such as 'the Nativity of Mary', 'the Eleventh Ode of Solomon', Melito's Homily on the Passover, and the 'Apology of Phileas' should be tacked on the end of the NASB.

Hegel haunted the nineteenth century with the heresy "History is God in process." Schlegel shadowed with his saying, "[M]an is progressively becoming God." Author of *The Occult Establishment* observes the possessing of society by this specter.

> [P]rogress is found as the cardinal point in all mystical texts. . .and relates to the mystical ascent toward God. The doctrine of spiritual progress was resurrected by the prophets of the nineteenth century occult revival.[55]

Some serve up Satan's story straight, while new version editors spruce it up with surplice and scapular.

NEW AGE	NEW VERSION EDITOR
"Neither the form of man. . . has ever been created. . .it commenced becoming. . . Matter is the vehicle of becoming. . .Nature was a perpetual becoming." Blavatsky "The evolutionary process is part of a spiritual plan for the redemption of the human race."[56] *Metaphysical Bible Dictionary*	A Christian never "is" but always "is becoming." "The universe develops in successive stages. . .each man is. . .a new power in the evolution of the race."[57] Westcott

Cain at the Crossroads

Mainstream America was introduced to the real 'creator' of process theology in the highly popular television series, *The Power of Myth.* In it, Joseph Campbell reveals:

> The Being of all being is the serpent father. . .creator of everlasting becoming.[58]

The serpent still swings from the tree of knowledge as the schools provide support for his subtle scheme to the tender branches of society. President Gerald Ford's education consultant boasted, "The psychology of becoming has to be smuggled into our schools." College humanities classes indoctrinated a generation of teachers with Mortimer Adler's *On Becoming a Person*, Alfred Whitehead's *Process and Reality* and Teilhard de Charden's 'evolution of consciousness'. Science classes concur with Einstein's 'Theory of Relativity' and the more recent General Systems Theory. Perhaps most instrumental was Darwin's *Origin of the Species,* which few know is subtitled: *The Preservation of the Favored Races in the Struggle for Life.* Darwin opens with this Root-race rhetoric and closes the last page with a line which today entwines the New Age *and* the new versions.

> [You] are being evolved.[59]

FIFTEEN

Striving or Saved?

But to him that worketh not but believeth on him that justifieth the ungodly, his faith is counted for righteousness. Romans 4:5

Worketh not, but believeth. . ." is a manifesto which marks a MAJOR distinction between Christianity and those religionists who take the first step of initiation/or baptism and then spend the remainder of their lives *laboring* on the ladder, hoping each 'good work' will lift them closer to God's blue vaulted landing. Clouds of unbelief conceal from their view the Son of God descending Jacob's ladder to reach mankind. Jesus said, he that "climbeth up some other way, the same is a thief. . ." (John 10:1). Robbers in the West like Aristotle, and later Aquinas attempted the ascent, erecting a staircase for scholars. The East has its highwayman, the Hindu, who, "considers himself alone to be responsible for his salvation," a feat similar to scaling the Himalayas.[60] Buddhists boost themselves up the steep bank traveling their 'Eightfold Path': (1) right views (2) aspiration (3) speech (4) conduct (5) livelihood (6) endeavor (7) mindfulness (8) meditation. Airports full of American Krishnas coax passersby, "Salvation must be earned by performing a series of works." Mediums like Edgar Cayce agree saying, "Salvation is something man does on his own. It is not a work of God. . ."[61] New Age leader David Spangler chimes, "Man is his own salvation."[62] His sentiments voice the opinion of the movement as a whole says Constance Cumby.

> The movement teaches that man is saved by initiation and works rather than through the grace of God and faith in the sacrifice of Jesus Christ.[63]

A new world religion springing from a world already weighed down with a works-based salvation will adapt to this status quo. So the new versions are modified to match their mentor—Martha, not Mary. (Their changes are usually based on the 'Ghostly Guild's Greek 1% Text so manuscript evidence will not be cited for each change.) Observe the trend in the following eight instances.

> Martha was cumbered about much serving. . .Jesus answered and said unto her, Martha, Martha thou art careful and troubled about many things: But one thing is needful and Mary hath chosen that. . .Luke 10:40-42

(1) "One thing" is changed to "a few things" in the NASB, in spite of the fact that the oldest papyri, P75 and P45, as well as the great majority of manuscripts, say "one thing." Embarrassed scholars are now doing an about face.

(2) Regarding the 'one thing' that was needful, that is, listening to Christ's words, the new versions omit or obscure references to bible teaching, studying or meditation.

NEW VERSIONS		**KJV**
man shall not live on bread alone	Luke 4:4	That man shall not live by bread alone, **but by every word of God**.
long for the pure spiritual milk	I Peter 2:2	desire the sincere milk **of the word**
take pains with [ouch]	I Tim. 4:15	meditate upon

NEW VERSIONS		KJV
Be diligent [with what?] to present yourself	2 Tim. 2:15	Study to shew thyself approved
shepherd the church	Acts 20:28	Feed the church
be their shepherd	Rev. 7:17	feed them
tending	Luke 17:7	feeding
Tend my lambs	John 21:15	Feed my lambs
Shepherd my sheep	John 21:16	Feed my sheep
Tend my sheep	John 21:17	Feed my sheep
The word of God is. . .active	Heb. 4:12	The word of God is. . .powerful

(3) Watch Martha keep busy with the following 'few things'.

NEW VERSIONS	KJV
God keeps him busy NKJV	God answereth him Eccles. 5:20
be willing to do menial work NASB (f)	condescend to men of low estate Rom. 12:16

(4) The new versions substitute "a form of godliness" for the 'one needful thing', faith and its simplicity.

NASB, NIV et al.	KJV
purity of devotion to Christ	the simplicity that is in Christ 2 Cor. 11:3
sincerity of heart	singleness of heart Acts 2:46
sincerity of heart	singleness of heart Col. 3:22
sincerity of your heart	singleness of your heart Eph. 6:5
If your eye is clear	thine eye be single Matt. 6:22

Salvation is simple.[64]

•It's as simple as calling to the Lord.

For whosoever shall call upon the name of the Lord shall be saved. Romans 10:13

•It's as simple as coming when called.

Come unto me, all ye that labour and are heavy laden, and I will give you rest. Matthew 11:28

•It's as simple as entering a door.

I am the door: by me if any man enter in, he shall be saved. John 10:9

•It's as simple as receiving a gift.

For the wages of sin is death: but the gift of God is eternal life through Jesus Christ our Lord. Romans 6:23

•It's as simple as believing God.

Verily, verily, I say unto you, He that believeth on me hath everlasting life. John 6:47

(5) "For by grace are ye saved through faith: and that not of yourselves: it is the gift of God: not of works, lest any man should boast" (Ephesians 2:8,9). Verses critical to an understanding of this concept are omitted from the new version.

NIV, NASB, et al.	KJV
OMIT	But if it be of works then it is no more grace: otherwise work is no more work Rom. 11:6
OMIT	grace Col. 3:16, Gen. 6:8
OMIT	Verily I say unto you, It shall be more tolerable for Sodom and Gomorrah in the day of judgment than for that city." Mark 6:11 (Not receiving Jesus Christ is a greater sin than sodomy etc.. Consequently those with 'good works' but without faith in Christ will be judged more harshly than the Sodomites. This verse is in the majority of Greek MSS.

(6)The word 'deeds' is added with no Greek basis. The "evil heart of unbelief" in Hebrews 3:12 is also scrambled in the new versions, obscuring God's definition of evil and good.

NASB	KJV
Those who do good *deeds* to a resurrection of life; those who commit evil *deeds* to a resurrection of judgement.	they that have done good, unto the resurrection of life; and they that have done evil, unto the resurrection of damnation. John 5:29

(7) Just so you won't miss it—

NASB	KJV
DEEDS	deeds Rom. 2:6

(8) New versions substitute will-power for the power of the indwelling spirit.

NIV, NASB et al.		KJV
began devoting himself	Acts 18:5	was pressed in spirit
in purity	I Tim. 4:12	in spirit

Believe or Obey?

Assertions like "I am your brain," from cult leader and demigod Reverend Moon, are a reminder of the obedience demanded by coercive cults, czars, Caesars and the coming antichrist, in their craving for control. Consequently, groups like the Mormans include in their *Articles of Faith* a mandate for obedience:

> [A]ll mankind may be saved by obedience to the laws and ordinance. Article 3

Former head of the Jehovah Witness Watchtower and Tract Society, Charles Taze Russell writes in his *Studies in Scripture* (Vol. 1, p. 158):

> [E]ach for himself [must] prove by obedience or disobedience their worthiness of life eternal.

The Jehovah Witness Bible consequently substitutes the word 'disobedience' for 'unbelief' and 'obey' for 'believe'. Is there a typographical error in the new versions, which also make these substitutions? Or is the error on their covers, which say 'Holy Bible' instead of *Jehovah Witness Bible*?

NASB (NIV et al).		**KJV**
obey (NASB)	John 3:36	believeth
disobedience	Rom. 11:32	unbelief
disobedient	Heb. 3:18	believed not
disobedience	Heb. 4:6	unbelief
disobedience	Heb. 4:11	unbelief
disobedient (NASB)	Rom. 15:31	do not believe

Scholar Rudolf Bultmann reminds Greek-o-philes that "faith is obedience" and the KJV consequently renders the word *apeitheo* as a 'dynamic equivalent' within the context of Christianity, not Platonism.[65] Even the NIV and NASB render *apeitheo* as 'unbelief' in Acts 14:2, conceding the appropriateness of this translation.

A salvation based on obedience allows an act of 'disobedience' to disannul that salvation. Much study of the new versions leaves Christian leaders spouting:

> The durability of his justifying grace is on the basis of obedience to God. A person can lose his salvation through neglect or disobedience.[66]

Jimmy Swaggart penned the previous statement before he 'disobeyed' and discovered that his fallen state did not void his sonship. He perhaps garnered his view from the new versions in the following verses.

NIV, NASB, et al.	KJV
lest anyone fall through following the same example of **disobedience**	lest any man fall after the same example of **unbelief** Heb. 4:11
failed to enter because of **disobedience**	entered not in because of **unbelief** Heb. 4:6

Other verses lead new version readers to think salvation is dependent upon perseverance, endurance, or steadfastness.

NEW VERSIONS		KJV
persevere [work]	Rom. 5:4 2 Cor. 12:12, 6:4	patience [wait]
endurance endurance	Heb. 10:36 2 Cor. 6:4	patience patience
steadfast [don't mess up]	Col. 1:23	settled [resting]
if we endure [if we made it]	2Tim. 2:12	suffer [if we suffer]
to remain true [don't mess up]	Acts 11:23	cleave unto [rely on him]
are protected by the power of God [Is God a body guard?]	I Peter 1:5	are kept [God keeps you]
confidence of our hope [I 'hope' I make it!]	Heb. 10:23	profession of our faith

Faith or Faithfulness

> Justification by faith [and] salvation by faith are a hideous nightmare and have no place in the CODE OF MANHOOD OF THE NEW AGE.67

A branch of Buddhism called *Hinayana*, popular in Cambodia, Thailand, Burma and Sri Lanka, has as one of its tenets:

"Salvation is achieved through self-discipline [faithfulness] not faith. . ."[68] Christians, on the other hand, are "justified by faith."

Jesus Christ is called "Faithful and True" (Revelation 19:11). Because he is faithful, we can have faith. Our faith (*pistis*) brings faithfulness (*pistos*). The two words are clearly different in meaning in both Greek and English. Yet all new versions, in their attempt to present a 'works' based salvation mistranslate *pistis* as 'faithfulness' in the following verses.

NIV, NASB, et al.		KJV
faithfulness	Matt.23:23	faith
faithfulness	Gal.5:22	faith

A noted dissenting new version editor points out this error in these new versions:

> [I]t is scarcely right to put *'pistis'* and *'pistos'* in direct parallelism. The word 'faithfulness' as it would be understood by most English readers would not, as far as I can judge, convey the idea of *pistis*. . .[There is a] difference between faith and faithfulness.[69]

New version editors know that *pistis* means 'faith' because they translate it as such elsewhere. As usual, their mistranslations are not wholesale, just enough to leaven the loaf. To further dismantle 'faith', the new versions, based on less than 1% of the Greek manuscripts, completely eliminate 'faith' from Acts 6:8 where Stephen is "full of faith."

New versions goad the 'falling away' as they give expression to New Age philosophies. Their New Age bywords act as battering rams in this declination. For example, in a June 6, 1990 *Focus on the Family* series on the 'fruit of the spirit' (Galatians 5:22) guest Joanne Wallace, in an otherwise accurate presentation, described 'faithfulness' (NKJV, NIV, NASB Galatians 5:22) as "paying your bills on time and canceling appointments when you can't make them." This is a far cry from the 'faith' (KJV Galatians 5:22) "which was once delivered unto the saints" (Jude 3). New versions produce pulpiteers like Kenneth Copeland, who pronounce, "The Bible commands ministers to be faithful not correct."[70] New versions prod people along the same path, ending with the same plunge (Revelation 20:15) awaiting New Age California State Assemblyman John Vasconcallos.

> The issue is always whether or not we believe that we humans are inherently good. . .our new-found faithful sense of ourselves. . .our individual self-esteem.[71]

The following are a few of the flood of new version verses which choke the voice of faith. Of course, *the* two key verses opening the door to an understanding of faith are mistranslated.

Verse 1

Received ye the Spirit by the works of the law, or by the hearing of faith? Galatians 3:2 KJV

To cloud the readers comprehension of Galatians 3:2 and 5, two of the most critical verses distinguishing faith from works, the NIV editors feign a lack of understanding of Greek and English grammar. They translate the simple Greek noun "works" into a complex verbal noun "observing"; then they reverse both the position and grammatical function of both "hearing" and "faith."

Verse 2

Now faith is the substance of things hoped for, the evidence of things not seen. Hebrews 11:1 KJV

In the above verse, the NIV and TEV change two Greek nouns to adjectives! The NASB mistranslates the noun "substance."

Verse 3

Isaiah said this **because** he saw Jesus' glory. NIV	These things said Esaias when he saw his glory. . . KJV John 12:41

The majority of Greek MS read 'when', which points to faith.

SIXTEEN

Gospels and Gods of the New Age

"The Father sent **the** Son to be **the** Saviour of **the** world." (I John 4:14) In the New Age however, "**a** God, one of many, sends **a** son, or avatar, with **a** message, to be **a** Savior, for each age. Once again the new versions line up with "the goats on the left."

NIV, NASB, et al.	KJV
a gospel	**the** gospel
a message	**the** words
a God	**the** God
a son	**the** Son
a Savior	**the** Saviour
an age	**the** world

To appeal to a broader market, new versions repeatedly spell out the One World Religion of the coming false prophet. A New Age spokesman could justly say, "You took the words right out of my mouth!" when reviewing the following charts of new version verses.

A Gospel	The Gospel
NASB, et al.	**KJV**
You have words of eternal life	Thou hast **the** words of eternal life John 6:68
NEW VERSION EDITOR	
"[It is] significant that the original only gives 'words' without the definite article. . .The religions of the world surrender to a supreme King. . .and are not far from the Kingdom. . ."[72]	New versions add articles in many, many other places, but refrain from doing this when it crosses their doctrinal biases.
NIV, NASB, et al.	**KJV**
an eternal gospel	**the** everlasting gospel Rev. 14:6
gospel	glorious gospel 2 Cor. 4:4
in truth	**the** truth 2 John 1:1
a common faith	**the** common faith Titus 1:4
a door of faith	**the** door of faith Acts 14:27
a baptism of repentance	**the** baptism of repentance Mark 1:4
good news	**the** gospel Heb. 4:2
my house shall be called **a** house of prayer	. . .**the** house of prayer Matt.21:13
the temple	the temple **of God** Matt. 21:12
NEW AGE	**CHRISTIANITY**
•"[F]undamentalist Christians. . .believe that Christianity is the only religion. . .These are very primitive ideas."[73] Bhagwan Rajneesh •"God works in many ways through many faiths."[74] Alice Bailey	•"He is not *a* way, he is *the* way." Jerry Falwell Jan. 10, 1980 Old Time Gospel Hour (The NKJV, however has 'truth' not 'the truth' in III John 1:1.)
•"[If] you think you have the only way then your God is too limited."[75] *The Eternal Dance*	•Jesus said, I am the way, the truth and the life: no man cometh unto the Father but by me.

A Message	The Word
NIV, NASB, et al	**KJV**
Man shall not live on bread alone. [OMIT]	That man shall not live by bread alone, **but by every word of God**. Luke 4:4
the word of God's message	the word of God I Thess 2:13
[OMIT]	that **word** Acts 10:37
a message	words Acts 10:22
the whole message	all the **words** Acts 5:20
the message	the **word** Acts 4:4
the sayings	the **words** John 10:21, 12:48
your bidding	thy **word** Luke 5:5
some statement	his **words** Luke 20:20
message	word Luke 4:32
a word	**the** word I Peter 3:1
the utterances of God	the oracles of God I Peter 4:11
words of eternal life	**the** words of eternal life John 6:68
Every scripture inspired by God (GNB)	All scripture is given by inspiration of God. II Timothy 3:16
NEW VERSION EDITORS	**CHRISTIANITY**
Calvin Linton: NIV The bible is "God's message" and not his words, contends Linton. He believes the bible is "the wrong side" of a beautiful embroidery. The picture is still there, but knotted, blurry—not beautiful, not perfect. He calls Christians "amusingly uninformed," who "presume the Holy Spirit dictated the actual **words** of the text of the original writers."[76]	For verily I say unto you, Till heaven and earth pass, one jot or one tittle shall in no wise pass from the law." Matthew 5:18 (A 'jot' is the smallest letter and a tittle is the smallest ornament placed on a letter.)

NEW VERSION EDITORS	CHRISTIANITY
Notes that there are "**mistakes** in transmission."[77] Burton Goddard: NIV	Thy word is very **pure**. Ps. 119:140
The bible is the "**words of men**," a "literary production."[78] Ronald Youngblood: NIV	The **word of the Lord** endureth forever. I Peter 1:25
"I felt bound to abandon the **God**-dictated-**every-word**-from-cover-to-cover attitude."[79] J.B. Phillips	**Every word of God** is pure. Proverbs 30:5
"Every member of the Panel was conscious that some of its decisions were in no sense certain."[80] NEB Committee	The words of the Lord are **pure** words. Psalm 12:6
"It is not surprising that [one] should be startled when they are told abruptly how many points of contact in form or substance our scriptures have with other writing, how **fragmentary** they are, how intensely **human**. We are coming to know the blessings which the withdrawal of old opinions discloses. . ."[81] B.F. Westcott	The **word of the Lord** endureth **forever**. And this is the word which by the gospel is preached unto you. I Peter 1:25
He expressed ". . .doubts about infallibility" saying, "I am also glad that you take the same provisional ground as to infallibility that I do. . ."[82] F.J.A. Hort	

A God	The God
NEW AGE	**CHRISTIANITY**
Hindu: "God has an unlimited variety of names."[83] International Society for Krishna Consciousness	[M]ake no mention of the name of other gods, neither let it be heard out of thy mouth. Exodus 23:13
Buddhist: The Nichiren Shoshu Buddhists pray to a large black box containing a scroll with the many names of the Buddhas in the *Lotus Sutra*.	Neither is there salvation in any other: for there is none other name under heaven given among men whereby we must be saved. Acts 4:12
Muslims: Mohammed listed 99 names of Allah in his *Koran*; Muslims use prayer beads reciting these names. *New Age:* "We consider our work to be spiritual in that it is based on the fact of the one God, known by many different names."[84] Theosophist Mary Bailey "[T]he major and minor deities are mentioned under various names in all bibles."[85] Vera Alder	Wherefore God also hath highly exalted him and given him a name which is above every name. That at the name of Jesus every knee should bow. Phil. 2:9, 10 For whosoever shall call upon the name of the Lord shall be saved. Romans 10:13 [C]all upon the name of Jesus Christ our Lord. I Cor. 1:2
NIV, NASB, et al.	**KJV**
a son of the **gods**	**the** Son of **God** Daniel 3:25
a living God (NASB)	**the** living God Acts 14:15
a living and true God (NASB)	**the** living and true God I Thess. 1:9
knowing that both their Master and yours is in heaven	knowing that your Master also is in heaven. Eph.6:9
worthy of the God who calls you	worthy of God, who hath called you I Thess. 2:12
you believe that God is one	there is one God James 2:19

NEW AGE
"Each [man] is **a** God within himself."[86] Elwood Babbitt "[I]n the temple within. . .is **a** God held bound there struggling for freedom and the Light."[87] Swineburn Clymer
APOSTATE CHRISTIANITY
"It's narrow or unloving when we insist that Jesus is the only way."[88] Campus Pastor, University of Wisconsin

A Son	The Son
NIV, NASB, et al.	**KJV**
among the lampstands was someone like **a son** of man.	in the midst of the seven candlesticks one like unto **the Son** of man.Rev. 1:13
sitting on a cloud was one like **a son** of man	upon the cloud one sat like unto **the Son** of man Rev. 14:14
Holy One of God	Christ, the Son of the Living God John 6:69
a son (f)	**the Son** of God Matt. 27:54
a son of God (f)	**the Son** of God Mark 15:39
a son of the gods	**the Son** of God Dan.3:25
OMIT (f)	**the Son** of God Mark 1:1
a beloved son	one son, his well beloved Mark 12:6
You, Son of God	Jesus, thou Son of God Matt.8:29
Do you believe in the Son of Man?	Dost thou believe on the Son of God? John 9:35

NIV, NASB, et al.	KJV
He will judge the world in righteousness through **a** man. . .(RV)	he will judge the world in righteousness by that man. . .Acts 17:31
who needs **a** physician	. . .need of **the** physician Mark 2:17
an angel of God	the angel of the Lord [Jesus Christ] Acts 27:23, 12:23
NEW AGE	**CHRISTIANITY**
"In the New Age scheme of things, Jesus is **not the** Son of God, but another enlightened, reincarnated Spirit."[89] Texe Marrs "**a** divine son of God has come forth and under many different names"[90] Alice Bailey "**a** god man is called an avatar. This event takes place once for each age."[91]	"Jesus was not called "a son of God" but THE Son of God. The singular usage puts to shame the doctrine of the New Age that we are equally divine with Jesus."[92] Joseph Carr
"The Nazarene. . .nowhere claimed to be the only son of God. . .**a** son not **the** Son of God."[93] *Science of the Soul* "According to Urantia, Jesus is **a** son of God. . .merely number 611,121 in the evolving scheme of Creator Sons."[94] The Urantia Book "There can be no Son of God."[95] Buddhism	

APOSTATE CHRISTIANITY	
"It was hard not to pray to Apollo. . .addressing Christ *sub specie Appollinis.*"[96] C.S. Lewis (Rev. 9:11 says Appollinis is the Angel of the bottomless pit.)	
NEW VERSION EDITOR	
Foster of the NIV and NKJV committee admits that the translation "a son" "weakens the presentation of Christ."	

A Savior	The Saviour
NIV, NASB et al.	**KJV**
"wait for **a** Savior	"look for **the** Saviour" Phil. 3:20
OMIT (LB)	having salvation Zech. 9:9
NEW AGE	**GREEK SCHOLARS**
Talks with Christ and His Teachers by Elwood Babbitt reports an entity calling itself Jesus Christ, appeared and said, "I am **not the** Savior; For each man is **a** Savior within himself."[97]	"[A] vicious system of rendering the Greek article is attended by consequences of a serious nature."[100]
"Spiritualism accepts him as one of many Savior Christs. . .**a** world Savior but **not the** only name given."[98] Josh McDowell "[The] Messiah promised in each religion The Lord Maitreya, Krishna, the Iman Mahdi, The Christ [is] the same Divine Principle called by several names."[99] Lola Davis	Webster's even distinguishes sharply between savior and Saviour. *savior*: One who saves or delivers. *Saviour*: Jesus Christ, the Redeemer.

NEW AGE
"Ramakrishna. . .considers God to be manifest in various ways and various forms. . .as the Divine Mother, as Krishna, as Jesus."[101] David L. Johnson
NEW VERSIONS EDITOR
"[Virgin apparitions are] God revealing himself now and not in one form but in many . . .the manifold comings of Christ. . .The Word has different forms, manifesting Himself to each as it is expedient for him."[102] B.F. Westcott Unitarian committee member G. Vance Smith strongly supported the switch from "the" to "a" stating that "the" "misrepresents" his beliefs.
APOSTATE CHRISTIANITY
"The Christ has taken many forms and has been known by different names."[103] Rodney Romney, Baptist Minister "Humans are to become saviors."[104] Calvin College's *Earthkeeping*

Greek: Arbitrary or Aleph Again

There is no indefinite article in Greek, consequently those with a meager background in Greek will comment that the word 'the' does not appear. However, there are hundreds of times when all new versions arbitrarily add 'the' and hundreds of times when they leave it untranslated. For example, in Matthew 12:28 they add one 'the' and drop another 'the'. (See Middleton's *On the Doctrine of the Greek Article*). If the new versions were consistent in their insertion of "a" where no definite article exists, they would, like the Jehovah Witness Bible, translate John 1:1,2 as "the Word was a god."

In the upcoming verses the article is not in question. For these verses the KJV habitually follows the majority of manuscripts and the earliest witnesses. For example, in John 9:35, the KJV's "Son of God" was cited in Tatian's Diatessaron (A.D.180), whereas the new version's "son of man" comes from the later fourth century MSS, Aleph and B. Again, Acts 8:37, which records the salvation of the eunuch, was cited by Irenaeus, Cyprian, and the Old Latin up to 200 years before the dissenting Aleph and B MSS.

The following charts continue to show how 'the beasts' bloodless bibles hide the keys to God's kingdom—leaving souls out in the cold kingdom of the coming "king of nations."

Antichrist	Lord Jesus
"That if thou shalt confess with thy mouth the **Lord** Jesus and shall believe in thine heart that God hath raised him from the dead, thou shalt be saved." (Rom. 10:9) The thief on the cross did it, Paul did it and the Ethiopian eunuch did it—but not in the new versions.	
NIV, NASB	**KJV**
Do you believe on the **son of Man**?	Dost thou believe on the **Son of God**? John 9:35
	Paul:
[omitted]	**Lord**, what wilt thou have me to do? And the Lord said unto him. . .Acts 9:6
	The eunuch:
[omitted]	And Philip said If thou believest with all thine heart, thou mayest. And he answered and said, **I believe that Jesus Christ is the Son of God.** Acts 8:37

NIV, NASB	KJV
	The Thief:
Jesus, remember me?	Jesus, **Lord** remember me. Luke 23:42
NEW AGE	
"The Nazarene did not say: "If you have faith **in me**. . .he made a clear statement; one indicating that the faith must be in ourselves."[105] Rosicrucian	
NIV, NASB, et al.	**KJV**
who believes	little ones that believe **in me** Mark 9:42
whosoever believes	whosoever believeth **in him** John 3:15
he who believes has everlasting life	He that believeth **on me** hath everlasting life John 6:47
calling on His name	calling on the name **of the Lord** Acts 22:16
gospel	gospel **of Christ** Rom. 1:16, I Cor. 9:18
Neither is circumcision anything	**For in Christ Jesus** neither circumcision availeth any thing Gal.6:15
the blessing of Christ	the blessing of **the gospel** of Christ. Rom. 15:29
In Him	In whom **ye also trusted** Eph. 1:13
also have obtained an inheritance	**In whom** also we have obtained an inheritance Eph.1:11

The Beast	The Blood
NIV, NASB, et al.	**KJV**
in whom we have redemption	in whom we have redemption **through his blood** Col. 1:14
faith	through faith **in his blood** Rom. 3:25
innocent blood	**the** innocent blood Matt.27:4 (Jesus is the only one with innocent blood.)
freed us from our sins	**washed** us from our sins Rev. 1:5
cup which is poured	**blood** which is shed Luke 22:20
NEW AGE	
"The erroneous doctrine concerning the blood sacrifice of Jesus."[106] Elizabeth Claire Prophet	
"Blood Sacrifice. . .a picture of the Christ impossible for the majority of thinking people."[107] Benjamin Creme	
"Patience and perseverance matter more than the blood of crucifixion." Buddhist Church of America (pamphlet)	
"[A] God that takes delight in sacrifice, in blood. . .is not my Father God."[108] *Aquarian Gospel of Jesus the Christ*	
NIV, NASB, et al.	**KJV**
that which is lacking in Christ's afflictions	the afflictions of Christ in my flesh Col. 1:24
APOSTATE CHRISTIANITY	**CHRISTIANITY**
"When his blood was poured out it did not atone."[109] Kenneth Copeland	"Redemption is through his blood." Dave Hunt

New Age Avatar	Suffering Saviour
NIV, NASB, et al.	**KJV**
This is my body which is for you.	This is my body which is **broken** for you. I Cor. 11:24
Christ also died.	Christ also hath once **suffered**. I Pet.3:18
carried away our diseases	bare our sicknesses Matt.8:17
to the redemption of God's (own) possession	the redemption of the **purchased** possession. Eph. 1:14
nailed it to the cross	nailing it to **his** cross. Col. 2:14
NEW VERSION EDITORS	
"This cannot possibly mean the sufferings of Christ."[110] F.J.A. Hort	
"I can no longer worship in a theological context that depicts God as an abusive parent and Jesus as the obedient trusting child."[110] Mollenkott	
NEW AGE	
"Christ never suffered" How could suffering be associated with the One."[111] Maharishi Mahesh Yogi	
"[T]he moral sense of the Western World has been blunted by a theology which teaches vicarious atonement of sin through Christ the Son of God."[112]	
"I don't like Christianity's emphasis on the cross. . .its so morbid."[113] Disciple of Sai Baba	

NEW AGE
"What is needed in Buddhism is enlightenment, neither crucifixion nor resurrection."[114] D.T. Suzuki

God in All	God in Christians
NIV, NASB, et al.	**KJV**
God and Father of all who is over all and through all and **in all.**	One God and Father of all who is above all and through all and in **you** all. Eph. 4:6 (Eph. 1:1 is written "to the saints. . .to the faithful."
The grace of the Lord Jesus be with **all**. (NASB)	The grace of our Lord Jesus Christ be with **you** all. Rev. 22:21 (Rev. 1:1 says it was written to his servants.)
NEW AGE	
"Each morning I center myself to touch the God light I believe is **in all** of us."[115] Oprah Winfrey	
"Theosophy's purpose is "the nucleus of the Universal Brotherhood of Humanity."[116]	
"Think what a difference it would make if the majority of mankind, including decision makers, believed the teaching of a World Religion for the New Age that **all** people are brothers because they are children of God."[117] Lola Davis	

NEW AGE	
"Let us drop our. . .religious differences and think in terms of one family."[118] Foster Bailey	
MUSLIM	**KJV**
"**All** men are children of God."[119]	"For ye are all the children of God **by faith in Christ Jesus**. Gal. 3:26
CULTS	
"**All** men and women are sons of God."[120] Edgar Cayce	
"God says. . .every person is his child.[121] Emile Cady	
APOSTATE CHRISTIANITY	
"Every man is my brother."[122] Pope Paul VI 1971	

Antichrist: King of Nations	Christ: King of Saints
NASB, NIV et al.	**KJV**
King of the **nations**	King of **saints** Rev.15:3
(Greek texts vary here. Westcott-Hort has *aeon*, Nestle-NASB has *ethos* (which they translate as 'pagans' elsewhere!), the *Textus Receptus* has *hagios*, translated elsewhere as 'holy'! Three different Greek words, as diverse as 'pagan nations' and 'holy saints' fractures the freshman fantasy of *the* original Greek.)	
And the nations shall walk by its light	And the nations of them **which are saved** shall walk in the light of it (Rev.21:24)

NEW AGE	
"None are saved. None are lost. . .[S]aved and lost are meaningless" terms.[123] David Spangler	
NEW VERSION EDITOR	**CHRISTIANITY**
"[T]he universal fatherhood of God. . .a brotherhood of men, but also a brotherhood of nations. . .[is] the destiny of mankind."[124] B.F.Westcott	"We have one Father, even God." Jesus said. . ."Ye are of your father the devil" John 8:41-44
NEW WORLD ORDER	
"World government will not be imposed on mankind but will be the result of the manifested brotherhood."[125] Benjamin Creme	
"We must be grateful to anyone who gives the work of the U.N. a spiritual interpretation. Prophets and philosophers have all perceived the fundamental unity and brotherhood of humans, but for the first time such a community is now truly being born."[126] Former U.N. Asst. Sec. General Robert Muller	

Universalism	Christianity
LIVING BIBLE	**KJV**
Christ. . .was accepted by men everywhere.(LB)	preached unto the Gentiles. I Tim.3:16
CULTS	
"Even the unbelieving heathen are redeemed."[127] Mormon *Articles of Faith*	"He was despised and rejected of men." Isa. 53:3

APOSTATE CHRISTIANTIY	
"Redemption embraces the totality of creation."[128] Theodore M. Hesburg, Notre Dame	
NEW VERSION EDITOR	
"The fruit of his work is universal. . .the redemption of the world. . .the ascension shows the oneness of their common destination." B.F. Westcott Westcott and others believe that the gospel is 'telling people that they **are** saved'. He said, "The **proclamation** of the union [of God and the world] is the message of the gospel. . .the Gospel **proclaims** that we **are** members of one another."[129]	
NASB	**KJV**
proclaiming	preaching Matt.4:23 Luke 9:2 Acts 8:5, 10:37, 13:5, 13:24, 13:38 et al.
Jesus Christ has set you free	Jesus Christ hath made me free Rom. 8:2; see Gal. 5:1

The Broadway: The Way or the way

[H]e led them forth by the right way. Psalm 107:7

Intervarsity Press editor James W. Sire observes:

I have long had a theory that the far-out, weird, and strange writers who make themselves out to be god—or the God—capitalize every other word or so. Manuscripts I have received as an editor. . .bear this out.[130]

Author, Dr. Louis Talbot, also noticed that occultists' words are "always spelled with a capital."[131] In New Age monism, everything is God—so everything becomes a 'proper noun or adjective'. New Age literature is peppered liberally with capitalized words such as Truth, Love, Man, Power. New versions capitalize dozens of words, not capitalized in the *Authorized Version,* such as Great Power (Acts 8:10), Law (Gal 2:16, Matthew 5:17, Luke 16:17), the Name (III John 1:7), the Beginning (Revelation 3:14), Great (Matthew 5:35), Man (Mark 2:28, Luke 6:5, Luke 9:58 et al), Unleavened Bread (Matthew 26:17, Mark 14:1), and Benefactors (Luke 22:25). Webster notes that, "Abstract ideas or inanimate objects "are capitalized only when personified." As a result, the "Beginning" (for Arians) and the "Unleavened Bread" (for Sacramentalists) become Jesus Christ, when the text intends no such interpretation.

The capitalization of the term the 'Way' is blatantly New Age.

NIV, NASB, et al.		KJV
the Way	Acts 9:2, 19:9, 19:23, 22:4, 24:14, 24:22	the way

With unity as its aim,
the New Religion needs a name.
Since Satan's game is the same,
Members-to-be all agree.

World Religions

***Buddhism*:**

- The mark on the forehead of Buddha is called "the lotus of the true Way."
- Buddhism itself is called 'the Way'.[132]
- Buddhism is split into two schools, one is called "the Way."[133]

***Shintoism*:**

- This popular religion in Japan comes from the word Shinto which means "The Way of the gods." They worship a sun goddess, the ruler of heaven.

Taoisms:

- The religion of China is Taoism, which is Chinese for 'The Way'.
- Its bible is called *Tao Te Ching*, "The Way and its Power." The first line says, "The Way that can be told is not the Absolute Way. The names that can be named are not the absolute Names."[134] (Of course, new versions capitalize 'Name' in 3 John 1:7)

Islam:

- Moslem mystics call their Sufi branch, "a search for the Way, a Way that is. . .seeking divine ecstasy."[135]

Hinduism:

- Hinduism is officially defined as "The Way of the majority of people in India, a Way.""[136]

Gnosticism:

- Ancient Gnosticism's "Path of Initiation" was called 'the Way'.[137]

New Age

1. Alice Bailey: "In an ancient book on numbers, the initiate is defined as one who has experienced and expressed 666. . .and has there found himself upon the Way. . .the radiant Way, the lightest Way which leads from one great experience of divinity in man to another."[138]

2. The author of *Toward a World Religion for a New Age* says, "Jesus said He was the Way. . .[there are] a variety of approaches to the Way [She goes on to list numerous occult groups.]

3. Corinne Helene's *New Age Bible Interpretation* says, "The deeper truths of the Christian Initiations are received directly by man himself; the spiritual force reaches him direct from the Sun, for the Christ has opened the Way. The early Christians were followers and demonstrators of the Way, the Path of the Solar Mysteries."[139]

4. Guru Da Free John's *Dawn Horse Testament* says "The Way that I teach is the Way based on the 7th stage wisdom."[140]

5. Luciferian Anna Kingsford's book extolling the virtues of worshipping the devil is called *The Perfect Way.* Also popular among New Ager is *The Way of the Shaman.*

6. Cults like ECK say, "The ECK therefore is the Way."[141]

7. The cult called 'The Way' headed by Victor Paul Weirwille boasts 200,000 members in 62 countries. Its motto is 'One God'. Spokesmen say, "God dying on a cross. . .is an image that binds man into continuous slavery."[142]

8. Apostate Christians like Baptist Pastor Rodney Romney agree saying, "Each of us must find our own way to the Way. . .Jesus cults, stopping short of the Way by worshipping the Way-Shower."[143]

9. *The Living Bible* is published in an edition called *The Way.*

10. Rosicrucian manual, *Science of the Soul* summarizes the difference between 'the Way' of the occultist and 'the way' of Christianity.

Those seeking for the spiritual knowledge of the **Initiates** must come as children willing to **obey**. . . those who have gone **the Way** before. It is a favorite precept of those who are at heart dishonest and who would shift to others. . .the payment of their debts to God. . . These believe that "God so loved the world that he sent **his own Son** that their sins might be paid" for them. We would substitute this. The world is in need of those-many of them, who are so imbued with **faith in the New Age** [not in Christ] pointing out. . .**the Law**. [New versions capitalizes 'the Law' in Galatians, Matthew

> and Luke.] We need leaders. . .who are seeking **the Way** to life.[144]

He and the new versions agree on—1)"obey," 2)"The Law," 3)"The Way," 4)"faith" (but not 'in him'), and 5)"a son" (that is not his "only begotten Son").

Why the consensus? Led astray by the 'Way', the New Age is following "the broad**way** that leadeth to destruction and many there be which go in thereat." "[T]hat way which they call heresy." (Acts 24:14) "leadeth unto life and few there be that find it." (Matt. 7:14) They have "gone the **way** of Cain." (Jude 11)

Even though God warned his people, "Learn not the **way** of the heathen," (Jer. 10:2) new version editors "have forsaken the right **way** and are gone astray following the **way** of Balaam. . .who loved the wages [$] of unrighteousness." (II Pet. 2:15) The gods, gospels and 'good' books are cunningly crafted perversions of God's true way.

The Plan: *perversion*
The Procedure: *subtlety*
The Perpetrator: *child of the devil*

O full of all **subtlety**
. . .thou child of the devil
. . .wilt thou not cease
to **pervert** the right **ways**
of the Lord.
Acts 13:10

SEVENTEEN

The New Earth or a New Age?

[T]he earth also and the works that are therein shall be burned up. Seeing then that all these things shall be dissolved. . .the elements shall melt with fervent heat? Nevertheless we according to his promise look for new heavens and a new earth. II Peter 3:11-13

Genesis 1 marked the beginning of earth's time. The hands of humanity sweep across the face of the earth hastening a halt to creation's clock. Mankind's sin has seeded the planet with land mines making its terrain a time bomb. Revelation 20:11 reveals earth's explosive end. A contrary scenario is presented by the other religions of the world. They present a cyclical view of life in which reincarnation of the individual and evolution of the species provides the needed 'time' for their works-based salvation to bear fruit. Confucius confuses many saying, "The process of change is cyclical."[145] Buddhism teaches that time progresses in a series of cycles.[146] Hinduism's god Vishnu commences each cycle and Shiva closes it. The Mayans will mark the end of their recent "great cycle" in A.D.2012. Tracing this twisted pattern, Luciferian

Rudolf Steiner repeats, "[T]he earth goes through evolutionary cycles."[147]

The new versions rehearse this cyclical view of time in the ears of listeners and also revise the verses which speak of the creation and subsequent destruction of the world. Concepts held by the author of the 'New' Greek text commenced this most recent caravan to the East. Westcott traces the tracks of the 'lost' travelers, once again.

NEW VERSION EDITOR	**NEW AGE AND LUCIFERIAN**
"[E]ach new element returns to its source. . .as the **great cycle** finds fulfillment."	"[A]ll shall be absorbed at the end of the **great cycle**."[148] Blavatsky
"So things come into existence and then are **dissolved** as the great **cycle** [proceeds]."	"Kalpas alternate in **dissolution** and creation. The great **cycle** or kalpa is of 420,000 years."[149]
"All things come from God and go to God. . .From God to God. . .Worlds grow out of worlds directs the cyclic periods."[150] B.F. Westcott	"Brahman. . .sends the world out from himself. But he brings it back to himself. The process is one of involution and evolution."[151]

"Age to Age": Attune to Apostasy

In turning to the cyclical theory of time, the New Age has also adopted the astrological idea of shorter ages which make up the longer cycles. Their imaginary astrological cycle is 25,000 years long and is divided into ages of about 2000 years each. Since the sun is a type of Christ, God set the autumnal equinox at the time of Christ's birth in September and the vernal equinox in March during his death and resurrection. But mankind "did not like to retain God in their knowledge," "changed the truth of God into a lie" and became "vain in their imaginations" (Romans 1:19-28). So the Chaldeans, with their observatory in the tower of Babel, invented 'imaginary' zodiacal boundaries in the sky in relation to the equinox to make a celestial calender for their system of ages and astrology.

These "observers of times," *anan*, were condemned in the bible in II Chronicles 33:6, Deuteronomy 18:10, 11, II Kings 21:6 and Leviticus 19:26. The NKJV, NIV and NASB have completely removed this warning. Most versions pretend *anan* is *kashshaph* and render it as 'sorcery'. They translate both *anan* and *kashshaph* as 'sorcery', hiding the distinction God has made between these two Hebrew words. *Anan* literally means 'observing the heavens', which is a distinct form of enchantment (Jer 27:9).

Ancient Babylon adopted astrology from the Chaldeans. So MYSTERY BABYLON, the religious system of the end times, which "sitteth upon many waters," has carried astrology's ages around the world. The Aztecs believed they were living in the 'fifth age'. The Hindoos think we are now living in the kali-yuga or 'black' age. The Bahai's are waiting for their 'golden age'. New Agers, watching the zodiac move out of Pisces into Aquarius, anticipate the 'New' Age. Today, the 60's hit "Age of Aquarius" blares in the background while readers browse books like *The Aquarian Gospel of Jesus the Christ, The Aquarian Conspiracy, Finding Your Place in the Golden Age,* or *Discipleship in the New Age.* Even cults like the Jehovah Witnesses are waiting for their 'Kingdom Age'. Mary Baker Eddy's followers think she is the "voice of Truth to this age."[152]

Beyond the rim of 'religious' circles, secular thinkers scan the horizon for a new age. The Humanist Manifesto II says, "[W]e stand at the door of a new age."[153] Former U.N. Assistant Secretary General Robert Muller translates New Age philosophy into Antichrist's politics:

> We are now entering a new age. . .we must pass from the national age to the planetary age.[154]

New *Age* Versions

The real religion of America is astrology, if the study of Northern Illinois University is correct, indicating that 70% of Americans read their horoscope. The children are following, as Gallop's pole showed 60% of them also believed in astrology. If 'ages' are standard in the religion of today's internationals and Americans, be assured that the *New International Version* , *New*

American Standard and the *New King James* are attuned to the religion of the age. So dozens of times they substitute 'ages' for 'world', reinforcing the ideas of the 'New' age movement.

NIV, NASB et al.		KJV
either in this **age** or in the age to come	Matt.12:32	neither in this world, neither in the world to come
not only in this **age** but in the one to come	Eph. 1:21	not only in this world, but also in that which is to come
in the present **age**	Titus 2:12	in this present world
this present evil **age**	Gal.1:4	this present evil world
the **age** to come	Mark 10:30	the world to come
the **age** to come	Luke 18:30	in the world to come
the **age** to come	Luke 20:35	obtain that world
King of the **ages**	Rev. 15:3	King of saints

Why do the new versions render Hebrews 6:5, "the **powers** of the **age** to come" instead of "the world to come." Could the evolutionary philosophy of new version editors have influenced them? One writes:

> We know also that more of the total **powers** of humanity and more of the fulness of the individual man are brought from **age to age**.[155]

Luciferian, H.P. Blavatsky said, "Both Jesus and St. John the Baptist preached the end of the Age. . .So little did the *uninitiated Christians* understand that they accepted the words of Jesus literally and firmly believed he meant the end of the world." (*Isis*, Vol. II, p. 144) Her initiate Alice Bailey therefore concluded that Matthew 28:20 should read, "Lo, I am with you all the days, even unto the end of the age." (*Reappearance*, p. 38) Today, the new version 'initiates' and the "uninitiated Christians" still present these opposite world views.

NIV, NASB et al.	KJV
[L]o, I am with you always even to the end of the age.	[L]o, I am with you alway, even unto the end of the world. Amen. Matt. 28:20

In the beginning

A cyclical view of time precludes any singular beginning of the world. So Buddha says, "No origin can be perceived." Corresponding to this, the new versions have no 'beginning of the world' but present instead a series of 'ages'.

NIV, NASB et al.		KJV
for ages	Eph. 3:9	from the beginning of the world
long ages ago	Titus 1:2	the world began
for long ages past	Rom. 16:25	since the world began
from old or for ages	Acts 15:18	from the beginning of the world
from of old or of long ago	Luke 1:70	since the world began
from ancient time or long ago	Acts 3:21	since the world began
from all eternity	2 Tim. 1:9	before the world began
Since the beginning of time	John 9:32	Since the world began
a (second, third, fourth, fifth) day	Gen. 1	the (second, third, fourth, fifth) day
the city. . .whose architect and builder is God	Heb. 11:10	builder and maker*

*(Architects design cities, builders build them, but God makes the raw material.)

In place of "In the beginning God created the heaven and the earth" (Genesis 1:1), one new version begins with "By periods God created," showing the author's belief in progressive ages. 'New' Greek editor B.F. Westcott writes, "No one now. . .holds that the first three chapters of Genesis give a literal history. . .I could never understand how anyone reading them with open eyes could think they did."[156] Another new version editor says, "No such state as Eden ever existed. . .it is a treat to read Darwin."[157] Perhaps these editors chose the Vaticanus B manuscript because it omits Genesis 1:1 to Genesis 46:28. Listen as the 'End Times Trio' rehearses their harmony.

APOSTATE CHRISTIANITY	APOSTATE BIBLE	NEW AGE
"Genesis is a Myth."[158] Pope John Paul II's emissary	"Once upon a time" Gen.1:1 TEV	"The whole Genesis record is an allegory."[159] Charles Filmore

The End

In the new bibles, the world doesn't end, the age simply ends and another begins. If the world ends, the sinner has nothing to stand on; if the age ends, he merely changes his calendar. Consequently, verses such as I Corinthians 8:13, "while the world standeth," are omitted entirely in the new versions.

NIV, NASB, et al.		KJV
end of the age	Matt.24:3	end of the world
lo, I am with you always even to the end of the age	Matt.28:20	end of the world
end of the age	Matt.13:39	end of the world
end of the age	Matt.13:40	end of this world
end of the age	Matt. 13:49	at the end of the world
end of the age	Dan. 12:13	end of the days
this age	I Cor. 3:18	this world

NIV, NASB, et al.		KJV
ends of the ages	I Cor. 10:11	ends of the world
consummation of the ages	Heb. 9:26	in the end of the world
is passing [entropy?] (NKJV)	I John 2:17	passeth away [judgement]
an hour is coming	John 4:21	the hour cometh

Since the destruction of the earth is a result of God's judgement, those verses describing the severity of that judgement are 'softened up' or omitted. As one noted Greek scholar observed:

> [There is a] fidgety anxiety manifested throughout. . .to explain away or at least evacuate expressions which have to do with eternity.[160]

NIV, NASB, et al.		KJV
[OMIT]	Mark 9:44	Where their worm dieth not and the fire is not quenched.
[OMIT]	Mark 9:46	Where their worm dieth not and the fire is not quenched.
[OMIT]	Mark 6:11	the day of judgement
day of their wrath	Rev. 6:17	day of his wrath
dealing out retribution	2 Thess. 1:8	taking vengeance
righteous acts have been revealed	Rev. 15:4	thy judgements are made manifest
shall be liable to the court.	Matt.5:21	shall be in danger of the judgement
guilty before the supreme court	Matt.5:22	shall be in danger of the council

NIV, NASB, et al.		KJV
scatter him like dust	Matt.21:44 Luke 20:18	grind him to powder
sentence of hell	Matt. 23:33	damnation of hell
Hades	Luke 10:15, 16:23	hell
a great tribulation	Matt. 24:21	great tribulation
judgement	Heb. 9:27	the judgement
eternal sin	Mark 3:29	eternal damnation
the fear of the Lord	2 Cor. 5:11	the terror of the Lord
[OMIT]	Luke 17:36	Two men shall be in the field, the one shall be taken and the other left.
[OMIT]	Luke 21:35	for as a snare
[OMIT]	Rom. 8:1	who walk not after the flesh, but after the Spirit

NEW AGE	
"God. . .will allow you to be and do anything you wish and hold you judgeless. God has never judged anyone."[161] Ramtha	
NIV	**KJV**
"The earth and everything in it will be laid bare."	The earth also and the works that are therein shall be burned up. 2 Pet. 3:10
The majority of MSS say "Burned up." The NIV footnote is false, once again, saying, "Some MSS say "burned up."	

NIV	KJV
The NASB Greek-English Interlinear contradicts the NIV's note saying, "Some ancient mss read "discovered."	
NEW VERSION EDITORS	
"[T]he second death is probably a combination of the Deluge and Sodom. . .it stands between the Garden of Eden and the Manna. . .[F]inite sin cannot deserve infinite punishment."[162] F.J.A. Hort "[T]he wrath to come" refers to "unbelieving Israel."[163] B.F. Westcott	

Greek Speak

The new versions translate *aeon* as 'world' dozens of places where the context would not allow the strange intrusion of 'ages'. Translating the word *aeon* as age is New Age and pagan. One witchcraft newspaper advertises a book entitled *Traditional Magicks for a New Aeon.* The definitive analysis, done by the Greek language scholar Hermann Sasse, says that pagans such as Plato and the Gnostics defined aeon as "timeless" but:

> [T]his understanding is contrary to the biblical doctrine of time and eternity. The idea of eternal recurrence cannot be united with the understanding of the creation and end of the world as an absolute beginning and absolute conclusion. The biblical view. . .stands in antithesis to the pantheistic and astrological doctrine of recurrence.[164]

Although the pagan Plato used *aeon* to mean "timeless," Aeschylus in his *Septum Contra Thebas* uses it to mean 'world'. So evidently at the time of Christ, its meaning was adjusted to the cosmology of the user, just as it is now. One new version editor admits the change to 'ages' in the new version reflects his New Age theory of 'ages'.

> [T]here is something strangely grand in this concept of aeons of human life. Some perhaps are even led to pause on the wonderful phrase in Eph 3:21. . .'the ages of the ages' . .and reflect on the vision so open of a vast aeon of which the elements are aeons unfolding, as it were, stage after stage, the manifold powers of one life fulfilled in many ways, each aeon the child of that which has gone before.[165]

Apostasy Abstract

A traveler on the semantic bridge to the New Age, Dr. Rodney Romney, a prominent Seattle Baptist minister, uses new version jargon to lead his listeners, not across the stormy waters but directly into the lake of fire. He prods:

> Most students of the spiritual **realm** agree that we are entering today into a New **Age** of **Light** on this planet.[166] [emphasis mine]

Like a good Baptist, he has obviously been reading his bible, but not *the* bible.

NIV, NASB, et al.		KJV
My kingdom is not of this **realm**. NASB	John 18:36	My kingdom is not of this world
not only in this **age** but in the one to come.	Eph. 1:21	not only in this world but also in that which is to come
fruit of the **light**	Eph. 5:9	fruit of the Spirit

EIGHTEEN

Judgement or Interment?

"God is love." I John 4:8

"God is a consuming fire." Hebrews 12:29

"Behold therefore the goodness and severity of God." Romans 11:22

These two attributes of God are shown most clearly at the cross. God's justice required judgement for our sins. "Cursed is everyone that continueth not in all things which are written in the book of the law to do them." (Galatians 3:10) Yet God's love moved him to take that punishment due each of us. "Christ hath redeemed us from the curse of the law, being made a curse for us: for it is written, Cursed is everyone that hangeth on a tree." (Galatians 3:13)

A place of "everlasting fire" exists and was spoken of by Jesus. He lovingly forewarned of his final words to those who reject his free gift of salvation and remain under the curse.

"Depart from me, ye cursed, into everlasting fire, prepared for the devil and his angels." Matthew 25:41

As seen in the above scriptures, hell was not created for man, but ". . .hell hath enlarged herself" (Isaiah 5:14) to accommodate those of mankind who reject the love of God. The existence of hell does not diminish the love or loveliness of God. It speaks only of the rabid villainy of creatures—Satan, his angels, and mankind, who as Matthew records, could "spit in his face" (Matthew 26:67), the face of their creator. Often the unwillingness of man to face his own culpability and sinfulness prompts him to saddle God with the burden of blame for the existence of hell. Truthfully, hell pronounces the malfeasance of the creatures, not of the creator. The doctrine of hell is an affront to proud mankind.

Hell's presentation in the bible can hardly be extinguished, but recent versions have diluted it by submerging the reader in a welter of words, substituting 'death', 'grave', 'sheol', 'hades' and 'the depths' for the word, 'hell'. Using five additional ambiguous words fractures the impact. The shatterment flies in the face of clarity, obscuring God's warning. Descending progressively downward from "death," to the "grave," then to "sheol" or "hades," then "the depths," and finally to "hell," the NIV offers a station, waiting to prove the afterlife theory of every philosophy and cult afloat.

Hell or Death

Agnostics, atheists, humanists, Jehovah Witnesses and a variety of cults believe eternal death, not hell, lies beyond the last breath. Again, Blavatsky dictates and the NIV and its editors comply—replacing the word 'hell' with 'death'.

LUCIFERIAN	NIV EDITOR
"Whenever the word 'hell' occurs in the **translation**. . . it is unfortunate. . .in the original text it **stands**. . . **death**. . .Hell and its sovereign are both inventions of Christianity."[1] Blavatsky	"In the face of these theological differences, a number of modern **translations** simply do not translate the word. . . [Hell] may well **stand** for eternal **death**."[2] R. Laird Harris

NIV		KJV
death	Deut. 32:22	hell
death	Job 26:6	hell
death	Prov. 23:14	hell
death	Prov. 27:20	hell
death	Isa. 28:18	hell
death	Isa. 57:9	hell

The Hebrew words for death, *muth* or *maveth* appear in none of these verses. Yet NIV editors admit that 'translating' takes a back seat to their own peculiar personal theology which is identical to that of many cults.

	NIV EDITOR
	"The committee did not feel absolutely bound to the Hebrew text. . .The other Canannite deity, mot (death). . .is personified. . ."[3] Larry Walker
ARMSTRONGISM	**NIV EDITOR**
"The concept of hell is part and parcel of folklore. . .as a place of **punishment**. . . When a human being dies he is **dead**."[4]	"Regarding further **punishment** after their **death**, the text is silent."[5] R. Laird Harris
JEHOVAH WITNESS	
"The doctrine of a burning hell. . .after **death cannot** be true. A dead person is unconscious, inactive. The **soul** is **dead**."[6]	"[D]eath for the wicked may actually speak of **spiritual death**. . .[T]he grave and **death** may well stand for eternal death,"[5] R. Laird Harris

Hell or the Grave

The NIV has again erected a shaky fire escape on the foundation of their faulty theology.

NIV		KJV
grave	Job 11:8	hell
grave	2 Sam. 22:6	hell
grave	Ps. 18:5	hell
grave	Ps. 55:15	hell
grave	Ps. 116:3	hell
grave	Ps. 55:15	hell
grave	Prov. 7:27	hell
grave	Ps. 16:10	hell
grave	Ps. 86:13	hell
grave	Ps. 9:17	hell
grave	Prov. 15:24	hell
grave	Isa. 5:14	hell
grave	Isa. 14:15	hell
grave	Isa. 28:15	hell
grave	Ezek. 31:16	hell
grave	Ezek. 31:17	hell
grave	Ezek. 32:21	hell
grave	Ezek. 32:27	hell
grave	Jon. 2:2	hell
grave	Hab. 2:5	hell
grave	Acts 2:27	hell
grave	Acts 2:31	hell
depths	Ps. 139:8	hell
depths	Matt. 11:23	hell
depths	Luke 10:15	hell

JEHOVAH WITNESSES	NIV EDITOR
"[Hell] applies to the common **grave** of all mankind. . .The words contain no thought of or hint of pain."[7] *New World Translation* appendix	"The NIV translators. . . came to a decision regarding the meaning of the word [hell]. . .the meaning grave fits. . .The translation grave is the most appropriate one. The terms [hell and grave] are synonymous. . .no more than darkness, dissolution, and dust of the tomb. . .to lie in the dust. . .decay or perish in the **grave**."[8] R. Laird Harris

Hell or *Hades* and *Sheol*

NIV editor R. Laird Harris concedes regarding hell:

> Its translation brings up a number of theological. . . matters. [T]here is discussion as to what it means. . .a number of modern versions simply do not translate the word. . .They. . .leave each reader to decide for himself. . .[9]

Consequently the NASB, and frequently the NKJV, join the Jehovah Witness *New World Bible* and leave the Hebrew *Sheol* untranslated. The NIV and NKJV join them both in not translating the Greek *hades*.

NIV, NASB, NKJV, Jehovah Witness *New World Translation*		KJV
hades	Matt. 11:23	hell
hades	Matt. 16:18	hell
hades	Luke 10:15	hell
hades	Luke 16:23	hell
hades	Acts 2:27	hell
hades	Acts 2:31	hell
hades	Rev. 1:18	hell
hades	Rev. 6:8	hell
hades	Rev. 20:13	hell
hades (NIV 5 times)	Rev. 20:14	hell

NASB & JEHOVAH WITNESS TRANSLATION		KJV
Sheol	entire O.T. (67 times)	hell

Historical *Hades*

A 'Revised' and 'Amplified' version of hell has been 'Standard' and quite 'International' since the Assyrio-Chaldean culture. The new 'Version' of the facts is not so 'New', but represents an historically heathen picture of the afterlife. The Assyrian culture introduced the idea of *hades* as an intermediate state. They called it the Elysian or Happy Fields and described it as having 'silver skies', 'resplendent courts'—'an abode of blessedness'. Their female goddess Ishtar descended into Hades seeking Tammuz and found it a place of gates and shadows.

Such "cunningly devised fables" abound in world literature. The Egyptian Hades was called 'Amenti', a place of dreamless sleep. Inhabitants did not remain long in this 'Land of Bliss', but moved quickly to Amk, the exit gate. Scandinavian mythology tells of Frigga's son, Bal-dur, who found himself upon death, in *hades*, seated on a stone, reading. In Greek mythology's *Prometheus*, Hercules, the Sun god descends into *Hades'* cave of Initiation. Aeschylus wrote that this 'Meadow of Hades' was the place where both good and evil people were purified by doing good works.

New Age *'Hades'*

Thanks to the new bible versions, New Age chieftains like Lola Davis can now say:

> We now know that there is no 'down there' where there is a tangible hell.[10]

New Agers cling to the 'new version' of hades as a second chance.

> Through the soul in Hades, having awakened to its unfortunate state, desires a change, it can attain such a change through reincarnation.[11]

New Agers join ranks with the NIV, NASB, NKJV and Jehovah Witnesses in replacing the 'torments of hell' with, as Blavatsky called them, the "seven mansions of Hades." She defines the 'new version' of hell as follows:

> Hades was quite a different place from our region of eternal damnation and might be termed rather an intermediate state of purification.[12]

When new versions do not translate *hades,* because they want to "leave each reader to decide for themselves" what is meant, they give consent to the fraudulent fables of the New Age. Bible verses on 'hades' now give voice to the unicorn, a popular New Age symbol of Amduscias, the grand duke of Hades. He represents:

> [T]he seventh division of Avichi of the Astral world. . . [It] is the only hell that exists. . .not eternal. [I]t is a purgatorial state.[13]

New Version Editors, Purgatory, *'Hades'* and Hell

The open door to hades in new versions merely vents the views of their editors. 'New' Greek editor F.J.A. Hort called purgatory, "a great and important truth."[14] His American counterpart Philip Schaff believed in an "extension of the period of grace for non-Christians beyond the limits of the grave."[15] NIV editors believe men merely lie in the grave. Other N.T. 'editors' believe as follows.

N.T. EDITION	EDITOR	BELIEF
Aleph & *B* Manuscripts	Origen	Hell is 'figurative'. The devil and fallen angels will exit hell and return to heaven.[16]
'New' Greek N.T., A.S.V. (NASB and *Living Bible*)	Schaff	He protested, "against a gross materialistic theory of hell" and points his audience to "the greatest of divines. . . Origen."[17]
'New' Greek N.T.	Hort	Hell is "figurative."[18]
J.B. Phillips Translation	Phillips	Does hell exist? Phillips says, "I seriously doubt this."[19]
'New' Greek N.T.	Westcott	Hell is "not the place of punishment of the guilty" but Hades is "the common abode of departed spirits."[20]

Despite the fact that Jesus said he would "prepare a **place** for" those who were not going to "a **place** of torment" (Luke 16:28), Westcott said each was "a state and *not* a place."[21] Again, new version editors merge minds with the cults.

Buddhism: *hell*: "condition of feeling and emotion not loci."[22]
Unity: *hell*: "a state of consciousness. . .a state of mind."[23]
Mind Science: *hell*: "mental states."[24]

Everlasting: Lasting Forever

Liberal scholars and cults disagree with conservatives regarding the length of punishment for the lost. So as one scholar notes, "[I]n view of the present controversy about the distinction between. . .eternal and everlasting" punishment, new versions have replaced the highly explicit word 'everlasting' with the non-descriptive word 'eternal'.[25] Everlasting is "objected to by the unbelieving schools," the scholar notes, and is typified by 'New' Greek editor B.F. Westcott who finds everlasting punishment (Matthew 25:46) "wholly inconceivable."[26]

MORMONISM	NEW VERSION EDITOR
"[P]unishment. . .may endure for one hour, one week, or one year, or an age."[27] *The Plan of Salvation*	"We have no sure knowledge respecting the duration of future punishment, and the word eternal has a far higher meaning."[28] F.J.A. Hort
ARMSTRONGISM	
"Everlasting" means age ending. "The translation everlasting is misleading, since the fire itself will not burn forever."[29]	
UNITY	
"There is no warrant for the belief that God sends men to everlasting punishment."[30] Charles Filmore	

The NASB has entirely omitted "everlasting punishment" from the New Testament. The NIV has also dropped all references to "everlasting punishment" for man. The NIV editor's theory that the lost are destroyed and left to rot in their graves pops up in the NIV's use of "everlasting" destruction in II Thessalonians 1:9.

NEW VERSIONS		KJV
eternal fire	Matt. 18:8	everlasting fire
eternal fire	Matt. 25:41	everlasting fire
eternal punishment	Matt. 25:46	everlasting punishment
eternal dwellings	Luke 16:9	everlasting habitations
eternal destruction	2 Thess. 1:9	everlasting destruction
eternal bonds	Jude 1:6	everlasting chains

PART FOUR

Christ or Antichrist

NINETEEN

Antichrist Is Here: Denying the Deity of Christ

All of the spiritual sabre-rattling in Satan's scuffle for supremacy was summarized succinctly by Erwin Lutzer when he said, "The final conflict will come down to 'Who is God?'"[1] Jesus Christ, who is God "manifest in the flesh" (I Timothy 3:16) must be diminished in the eyes of his subjects before the devil dares depose him. Who could curtail him? — a mugger, a marauding maniac, or a mass murderer like Mao or Mussilini. Too blatant.

When Satan wanted to unmiter the master, he conscripted Christ's veteran sparring partners—the scribes. Their method: *subtlety.*

> [T]he scribes. . .consulted that they might take Jesus by subtilty and kill him. Matthew 26:3,4

> [T]he scribes sought how they might take him by craft and put him to death. Mark 14:1

> [T]he scribes. . .sought how they might destroy him. Mark 11:18

> [T]he scribes the same hour sought to lay hands on him.
> Luke 20:19

Because he was "rejected of the. . .scribes," (Mark 8:31) Comfort reports:

> [T]he early manuscripts exhibit some very significant differences. . .pertaining to the title of the Lord Jesus. . . [M]ost scribes felt free to express their individuality. . . [regarding] divine titles.[2]

New versions rely on these one or two dissenting manuscripts and disregard the vast majority.

I COR. 5:4,5	EVIDENCE
Lord (NIV)	P46 & B
Lord Jesus (NASB)	Aleph
Lord Jesus Christ (KJV)	Majority

A Princeton scholar concludes:

> Very probably it represents an attempt on the part of some scribes to lower Christ's claim to deity.[3]

We are warned, "Beware of the scribes which desire. . .the highest seats in the synagogues." (Luke 20:46) Evidently from that elevated vantage point 'JESUS' is diminished, as are all of his titles in the new versions.

NIV, NASB et al.		KJV
Jesus	Luke 2:21	JESUS
Jesus	Matt.1:25	JESUS
Jesus	Luke 1:31	JESUS

Moslems have perennially complained, "They deified the messenger!"[4] New Agers like Alice Bailey protest that in Christianity there is, "over emphasis laid upon his divinity."[5] New versions are marching in step with Satan and the soldiers of the New World

Religion. To stay in stride, "They stripped him" (Matthew 27:28) of his divine titles, tearing him down one step with each title.

NIV, NASB, et al.		KJV
Teacher	Matt. 19:16	Good Master
master	e.g., Matt. 25:21	thy Lord
he	e.g., Matt. 12:25	Jesus
Jesus	e.g., Luke 2:21	JESUS
Jesus	e.g., 2 Cor. 4:10	Lord Jesus
Jesus	e.g., Acts 19:4	Christ Jesus
Christ	e.g., 2 Cor. 5:18	Jesus Christ
the Christ	e.g., Acts 5:42	Jesus Christ
the Lord	e.g., I Cor. 16:22	the Lord Jesus Christ
Lord Jesus	e.g., 2 Cor. 11:31	Lord Jesus Christ
Jesus Christ	e.g., 2 John 1:3	The Lord Jesus Christ

Jesus said he was not bruised by bandits, but by the brethren (Zechariah 13:6). "I was wounded in the house of my friends." Among new version editors, such a 'friend' "struck Jesus with the palm of his hand" (John 18:22) over 100 times as it couched the pelts of his pen.

Before "they struck him on the face". . ."they had blindfolded him" (Luke 22:64). Likewise, the frontal assault of these 'friends' attempts to leave Christians groping in the dark world of 'Greek-speak'. D.A. Carson is first in line.

> I suppose that no doctrine is more repeatedly thought to be under attack in the non-Byzantine tradition [new versions] than the doctrine of the deity of Christ. To prove [this wrong]. . .in detail would presuppose in the reader a fair degree of competence in the Greek, so I shall pass up the opportunity.[6]

He throws the pass, because he has no chance of scoring with a discussion of 'the Greek'. Catching his pass and scoring points which will touch down into the hearts of believers is simple. To summarize: (1) New version's abbreviated and altered titles come from less than 1% of the manuscript evidence, usually less than a handful. (2) KJV titles come from the Majority Text, represented in many cases by as many as 600 manuscripts, a listing which would fill the page.[7] Note the following examples.

LESS THAN 1% OF MS		MAJORITY TEXT
Lord (i.e., Aleph, B, A)	I Cor. 16:22	Lord Jesus Christ (Majority Text)
Lord Jesus (i.e., B, A)	I Cor. 5:4	Lord Jesus Christ (Majority text, Aleph, and P46, earlier than B and A)
Jesus Christ (i.e., B, A)	2 John 1:3	Lord Jesus Christ (Majority text and Aleph)

Those manuscripts which characteristically lower Christ's claim are those Alexandrian MS: Aleph, B, P75 et al, which came under the spell of the masters of subtlety, the Egyptian magicians, Clement and Origen. Their wand waved away words which attested to Christ's deity. A few strokes here and there changed a portrait into a caricature. On the defaced canvas of Aleph and B, the editors of the 'New' Greek text saw a disfigured deity. "[H]is visage was so marred" (Isaiah 52:14) it matched their distorted views.

"Christ was and is perfectly man." "He never spoke directly of himself as God." "He does not expressly affirm the identification of the Word with Jesus Christ."[8] B.F. Westcott	"[T]he divine anointing or Christhood. . .the prophet, the people. . . and the dimly seen Head. . .are all partakers of the divine anointing and messiahship."[9] F.J.A. Hort

Under the century old spell of the Westcott and Hort Greek Text, NIV editor Edwin Palmer comes to his chilling theological conclusion!:

> [There are] few clear and decisive texts that declare that Jesus is God.[10]

Palmer should qualify his statement noting, "*In the new versions*, there are few clear and decisive texts that declare Jesus is God."

NIV, NASB, et al.	KJV
We know love by this, that he laid down his life for us.	Hereby perceive we the love of God because he laid down his life for us. I John 3:16
our only Master and Lord, Jesus Christ	the only Lord God, and our Lord Jesus Christ Jude 1:4
We should not test the Lord, as some of them did and were killed by snakes.	Neither let us tempt Christ, as some of them also tempted and were destroyed of serpents. I Cor. 10:9
God's judgement seat. . .For we will all stand before God's judgment seat.	judgment seat of Christ. . . So then every one of us shall give account of himself to God. [Christ is God.] Rom. 14:10,12
to seat one of his descendents upon his throne	he would raise up Christ to sit on his throne. Acts 2:30
OMIT [Their omission in verse 11, breaks the connection between the "Alpha and Omega" of verse 8, who is the eternal God, and "the Son of man. . .[who] was dead; and behold I am alive for evermore" in verses 13 and 18. Hort says, "The speaker cannot be our Lord."[11]]	I am Alpha and Omega. Rev. 1:11 [As the chapter is written in the KJV, it is the best defense of the deity of Christ that can be shown to a Jehovah Witness. They believe that the Alpha and Omega is God, but their version agrees with the new versions which obscure the deity of Christ.]
saved from the wrath of God through Him	saved from wrath through him [He is God!] Rom. 5:9

Blavatsky echoes Palmer:

> [T]here is not a word in so-called sacred scriptures to show that Jesus was actually regarded as God by his disciples. Neither before nor after his death did they pay him divine honours. . .there is not a single act of adoration recorded on their part. . .[12]

Palmer and Blavatsky are facing a plastic dashboard Jesus, driven by the vehicle of the new versions. Picking up passengers as they pass by, the new versions have prompted Kenneth Copeland to conclude:

> He never made the assertion that He was the most High God. . .He didn't *claim* to be God when He lived on earth. . .Search the Gospels for yourself. If you do, you will find what I say is true.[13]

The book *Agony of Deceit* chronicles the down swing of many ministries, including Copeland's. In response to Copeland's comment, the authors cite Philippians 2:5-7 in the KJV. They could not use another version here because *all* other versions *deny* Christ's deity in this verse. The NKJV, here as well as in other places, denies Christ's deity also.

NIV, NASB, et al.	KJV
did not consider equality with God something to be grasped.	thought it not robbery to be equal with God.

The spiritual nature of this battle became all too apparent when I was showing this verse to a 'Christian' linguistics major. She could not see that the KJV and the new versions expressed diametrically *opposite* views here.

"Worship him"

God's two signal lights—"Thou shalt worship the Lord thy God and him only. . ." (Matthew 4:10) and "[L]et all the angels of

God worship him (Hebrews 1:6) clearly reveal the deity of Jesus Christ. In recognition of this, there are twelve instances in the New Testament in which Jesus is worshipped. The NASB seizes seven of these for omission or subterfuge.

NASB		KJV
OMIT	Luke 24:52	They worshipped him.
Manuscript Evidence: [O]mitted in D only (5th and 6th century). Metzger admits that ". . .special theological interests on the part of scribes may account for their deletion. . ."[14]		*Manuscript Evidence:* Included in P75, Aleph, B, C (2nd and 5th Century), K, L, W, X, Delta, Psi, Pi, 063, f1, f13, 28, 33, 565, 892, 1009, 1010, 1071, 1079, 1195, 1216, 1230, 1241, 1242, 1365, 1546, 16, 46, 2148, 2174.

"They that worship him must worship him in spirit. . ." (John 4:24) yet the NASB substitutes 'bow,' a position of the body, for "worship," an attitude of the spirit, in the following verses.

NASB		KJV
bowed down	Matt. 9:18	worshipped him
bowed down	Matt. 8:2	worshipped him
bow down	Matt. 15:25	worshipped him
bowing down	Matt. 20:20	worshipping him
falling down prostrate	Matt.18:26	worshipped him
bowed down	Mark 5:6	worshipped him

The meaning of the word *proskun* returns to their lapsed memories in Revelation.

	NASB
Rev. 13:4	worshipped the beast
Rev. 13:4	worshipped the dragon
Rev. 9:20	worship demons

The real words for 'bow' is *kampto, klino*, or *tithemi*. The latter is used only in a mocking manner by Christ's executioners.

> And they smote him on the head with a reed and did spit upon him, and bowing. . .Mark 15:19 KJV

Everyone has observed the Japanese and others from the East exchange bows, just as Westerners offer a hand shake. The general public sees this as a cultural gesture of greeting. Well-read New Agers know the motive is religious, not cultural. It stems from the Eastern belief that 'a god' resides in everyone. It is to this 'god' that the bow is addressed. Their 'god' or 'Christ Consciousness', thought to be in everyone, is respected and honored but not worshipped. This 'Christ consciousness' "is a universal force to be experienced (instead of worshipped as a deity)," observes Bob Larson.[15] "New Agers say that Jesus wanted us to become his equals, not to worship him," comments the editor of the *Christian Research Journal*.[16] It is within this cultural milieu that the new version's "bowing" to Jesus will be viewed.

Those who breeze through the bible do not detect the doctrinal blows buried in linguistic landmines by new version editors. As Jesus said, "The children of this world are in their generation wiser than the children of light." (Luke 16:8) Vance Smith, Unitarian member of the 'New' Greek Committee applauds the *purposeful* alteration of words and verses to deny the deity of Christ. He comments:

> The only instance in the N.T. in which religious worship or adoration of Christ was apparently implied has been altered by the Revision: 'at the name of Jesus every knee should bow.' (Phil 2:10) is now to be read 'in the name' . . .as it is well understood that the N.T. contains neither precept nor example which really sanctions the religious worship of Jesus Christ.[17]

Christ's 'friends', Palmer and Smith voice Blavatsky's battle cry as they board the Trojan horse. Their 'bibles' follow this first round of 'shots' with a barrage of fire against Christ himself.

TWENTY

Test 1 for Antichrist

Is Jesus the Christ?

mong the scribes who "love the uppermost seats" are the "seats of the scornful" where new version editors look down in contempt saying:

NIV, NASB et al.		KJV
[T]his is not the Christ, is it?	John 4:29	[I]s not this the Christ?
Jesus	Acts 19:4	Christ Jesus
Jesus	I Cor. 9:1	Jesus Christ
Jesus	I John 1:7	Jesus Christ
Jesus	Rev. 1:9	Jesus Christ
Jesus	Rev. 12:17	Jesus Christ
Jesus	Heb. 3:1	Christ Jesus
Jesus	Acts 9:20	Christ
OMIT (L.B.)	John 6:69	Thou art that Christ

The title Lord Jesus Christ capsulizes the New Testament theme of "God, our Saviour" (Jude 25). Consequently, when asked, "What must I do to be saved?" the apostles responded, "Believe on the Lord Jesus Christ and thou shalt be saved. . ." (Acts 16:31). Christ said, "I am the door" but the devil dares 'not open the house of his prisoners' (Is 14:17) so he darkens 'the door' in the new versions. His shadow falls over the word 'Christ'.

NIV, NASB, et al.		KJV
Lord Jesus	Acts 15:11	Lord Jesus Christ
Lord Jesus	Acts 16:31	Lord Jesus Christ
OMIT	Rom. 1:3	Jesus Christ our Lord
Lord Jesus	2 Cor. 11:31	Lord Jesus Christ
Jesus our Lord	I Thess. 3:11	Jesus Christ our Lord
our Lord Jesus	2 Thess. 1:8	our Lord Jesus Christ
our Lord Jesus	2 Thess. 1:12	our Lord Jesus Christ
our Lord Jesus	I Cor. 5:4	our Lord Jesus Christ
OMIT (L.B.)	Eph. 3:14	our Lord Jesus Christ

Evidently they are "ashamed of the gospel of Christ," for they also omit "of Christ" in this very verse.

the gospel	Rom. 1:16	the gospel of Christ

> Who is a liar but he that denieth that Jesus is the Christ? He is antichrist. . .I John 2:22

The palms of the scribes start to sweat under the white-hot light of the apostle John's lie detector test. Suddenly their "chief seats" become the 'hot seat' as they hear John's verdict: "liar. . .antichrist." The apostle John's close point of view discloses the nucleus of the New Testament—Jesus is the Christ.

> But these are written that ye might believe that Jesus is the Christ, the Son of God; and that believing ye might have life through his name. John 20:31

The ultimate campaign against Jesus is to deny that he is the Christ. The editor of the *Christian Research Journal* observes:

> For scholars agree that it was exactly this error, (separating the man Jesus from the divine Christ), as promulgated by early Gnostics that the apostle John was

indicating when he coined the term antichrist. (I John 2:18-23)[18]

John judged, "[N]ow are there many antichrists" (I John 2:18). He calls the Antichrist's accomplices 'antichrists' also. As accessories to the crime, new version editors alter I John 2:22 so that it appears this is a 'one man job'.

NIV, NASB et al.
[W]ho is **the** liar but *the one* who denies that Jesus is the Christ? This is **the** antichrist *the one* who denies the Father and the Son.

[T]he one came from 'the gang', not the Greek. *'T-h-e'* is introduced, three bullets they often leave in their gun, unless needed to dismantle some doctrine.

"Whom say ye that I am?" asked Jesus. Peter replied, "Thou art the Christ." Jesus responded, "Blessed art thou Simon Barjona: for flesh and blood hath not revealed it unto thee, but my Father which is in heaven" (Matthew 16:17). Only the inspiration of God brings to light that Jesus is the Christ. New versions all too often leave the reader in the dark and unblessed.

NIV, NASB, et al.		KJV
I can do everything through **him** who gives me strength.	Phil. 4:13	I can do all things through **Christ** which strengtheneth me.

The stark decor of each New Age Self-Realization Fellowship makes the membership, some 500,000 world wide, focus on their 'picture gallery', a line up of likenesses of Krishna, Buddha, Christ, Yogananda, their founder, and a handful of others who, in their view, contributed equally to the religious strength of their time and nation. A framed NIV scripture plaque, with its fill-in-the-blank deity, would finish their artful facade of fraud.

Another Jesus

The scriptures signpost a perverse pair on this warpath: "another Jesus" and "false Christs."

> For if he that cometh preacheth another Jesus. . .
> 2 Cor.11:4
>
> [T]here shall arise false Christs. Matt.24:24

The dividing of Jesus Christ into "another Jesus" and a "false Christ" is like splitting the hydrogen atom—it becomes a hydrogen bomb. The New Age/new version war of words now escalates from an armchair war of attrition, a falling away, to an atomic war.

Who is this other Jesus that appears when new versions say 'Jesus' instead of 'Jesus Christ'?

HINDU

"Jesus is the son and Krsna is the Father."

ISLAM

Jesus (Isa) is a prophet, a *nabis* or 'messenger of god'.

CULTS

Jehovah Witnesses: Jesus is the archangel Michael.
Mormon: Jesus is the brother of Lucifer.
Edgar Cayce: Jesus is the reincarnation of Adam.
Unification Church: 'Jesus' appeared to Moon telling him to start the Unification Church.

NEW AGE

Channeled Books:

1. *A Course in Miracles* was channeled to Helen Schucman by an entity calling itself 'Jesus'.
2. *The Jesus Letters* by Jane Palzere and Anna Brown was channeled from 'Jesus'.
3. *The Aquarian Gospel of Jesus the Christ* was channeled to Levi Dowling by 'Jesus'.

Channelers:

1. The Aetherius Society (U.F.O.s)is receiving messages from "Master Jesus" (Aetherius is Venus, which is Lucifer's planet.)

2. Elizabeth Claire Prophet channels 'Jesus' along with Buddha and Merlin the Magician.

Satanism:

1. Kurt Koch reports hearing demons say "I am the unholy Jesus, the Jesus of Satan.[19]
2. Johanna Michaelson, author of *Beautiful Side of Evil*, spoke with a demon calling itself 'Jesus'.

False Christs

Satan assaults the throne from two vantage points. First, he denies Jesus' claim to Godhood. If that fails, he denies the uniqueness of Christ's claim saying that there are many 'Christs'. Texe Marrs warns, "New Age leaders believe and will spread the apostasy that Jesus is neither Christ nor God."[20] New version editors become "New Age leaders" by his definition. Does this new version editor also become a Luciferian leader because of his continuous concurrence with Blavatsky, her creed and her 'Christ'?

NEW VERSION EDITOR	LUCIFERIAN
"The Son of man was not necessarily identified with the Christ." "It is not said that Jesus glorified not himself, but the Christ. He never speaks directly of himself as God."[21] Westcott	"In the idea of Christians Christ is but another name for Jesus. . .The Christ with the Gnostics mean the Impersonal Principle. . .not Jesus. . .Jesus, the-Christ-God is a myth."[22] Blavatsky

Jesus' warning in Mark 13:5,6 against this false 'Christ' is omitted in the new versions.

NIV, NASB, et al.	KJV
Watch out that no one deceives you. Many will come in my name, claiming, 'I am *he*' and will deceive many. [The word 'he' does not appear in any Greek MS either.]	Take heed lest any man deceive you: For many shall come in my name, saying, I am *Christ* and shall deceive many.

With this warning removed, the many deceivers in the cults and the New Age movement are free to commit 'Christ' to their cause. Foster Bailey believes,

> The word Christ is a name in the hierarchy. . .He is not at all limited to Christianity.

NEW AGE	CULTS
"The revelation of the Christ is not limited to Jesus of Nazareth."[23] *The Esoteric Basis of Christianity*	"Jesus is the human man and Christ is the divine idea. Hence the duality of Jesus the Christ."[24] Christian Science, *Science and Divine Health*
"Christ. . .used for some three years the human body of Jesus."[25] *Esoteric Christianity*	"Jesus was only one manifestation of Christ; there were many others."[26] Edgar Cayce

The many false Christs foretold by Jesus can be seen in the *avatar* system of Hinduism and Buddhism. It has been imported to the Western world through popular New Age books like, *Diagrams for Living: The Bible Unveiled*, which states:

> The Christ is not Jesus. In the history of all races the Cosmic Christ has incarnated in. . .Buddha, Moses, Elijah and in many other leaders; in this New Age the Cosmic Christ will come.[27]

Mohammed, Confucius, Krishna, each a *bodhisattva* or *Imman Mahdi*, a so-called Christ, are Satan's stepping stone to the throne. So that he finally, "sitteth in the temple of God, shewing himself that he is God" (II Thessalonians 2:4). Books like, Alice Bailey's *The Reappearance of the Christ*, Benjamin Creme's *The Reappearance of the Christ and the Masters of Wisdom* and David Spangler's, *Reflections On The Christ*, are preparing minds for the replacement of 'Jesus', their Piscean Age 'Christ', by the new 'Christ' of the Aquarian Age. Note how the new versions confirm the view that Jesus was 'Christ' for the Piscean 'age' only.

NIV, NASB, et al.	NEW AGE
I am with you always even to the end of the age.	"Christ in all ages. Jesus in only one."[28] *Edgar Cayce on Reincarnation*

NIV, NASB		KJV
Let this Christ	Mark 15:32	Let Christ
[The word *this* is in no Greek MSS.]		

'Christ' takes center stage in the new versions as Satan attempts to move the true God, Jesus Christ into the wings. Their rendition of Matthew 23:10 sets the tone for the Antichrist's take-over.

One is your Leader, that is Christ. NASB

NIV, NASB, et al.		KJV
Christ	2 Cor. 5:18	Jesus Christ
OMIT	Acts 4:24	Thou art God
word of Christ	Rom. 10:17	word of God
the peace of Christ	Col. 3:15	the peace of God
Christ as Lord	I Pet. 3:15	the Lord God

The Antichrist

The words of Revelation 6 allow us to witness from the wings that warrior, number 666. This invading 'impersonator' is the Antichrist, not Christ, as postmillennial marginal notes masquerade. In addition, new versions dramatically alter the prophecy of Daniel, making it a script which rehearses an applauded entrance of the Antichrist. By adding several words, not in the Hebrew, to Daniel 9:27, they add a second performer to the stage, thereby giving the impression that the ruler who makes a covenant "with many" for one week is the Messiah 'the Christ' of verse 26 not the Antichrist who commits the "abomination of desolation" of verse 27. (See NASB particularly.) By presenting this first white horse rider as 'the Christ', new versions are echoing exactly a popular Hindu story well circulated among New Agers:

> The Lord Vishnu will appear as Kalki at the end of the age of strife riding a white horse and holding a sword blazing like a comet to punish evildoers and to establish a golden age.

Another New Age book boasts:

> The Lord Buddha. . .entered the region of demons. . .[and] is described as riding on a white horse (The Coming Avatar to appear at the end of the present dark age. . .) holding a bow and wearing a crown.[29]

Christians will bear the brunt of this bow when seen as the "evildoers" of the New Age. Westcott agrees with the Hindu saga saying, "[T]he return of Christ appears to be placed after the conquest of his enemies."[30] The *Living Bible* also sets the stage for the worship of the Antichrist when he "sitteth in the temple of God shewing that he is God."

LIVING BIBLE	**KJV**
The one you are looking for will come suddenly to his temple.	[T]he Lord, whom ye seek, shall suddenly come to his temple. Mal.3:1

This merger of Antichrist and Christ (Revelation 6, Daniel 9) and Satan and Christ (Isaiah 14) in the notes and text of new versions represents a trend in liberal scholarship as seen in the following books by 'Christians'.

"Christ must be reconceived and not bound to the historical Jesus."[31] *Christ in a Pluralistic Age*	"[T]he radical suggestion: Antichrist is the completion of Christ. . .[T]he full meaning is not to be found in the historical Jesus, . . . but rather in the paradoxical combination of Christ and Antichrist."[32] *New Dimensions in New Testament Study*

Not to be left out, new version editors league once again with the Luciferians, in their open-ended ideas about 'Christ'.

NEW VERSION EDITOR	LUCIFERIANS
"The belief is 'in Christ' not in any propositions about Christ."[33] Westcott	Lucifer told Spangler, "Am I God? Am I Christ. . .I am." "Christ is the same force as Lucifer," concludes Spangler. Blavatsky agrees, "Lucifer or Christ [is] the bright and Morning star." The Hindu's 'Christ' Krishna agrees saying, "I am the prince of demons."[34]

The source of these New Age 'propositions' about 'Christ' is described by Texe Marrs:

> Satan is using demons to promote the New Age gospel to soften up humanity for the arrival of the Antichrist whom millions will believe is Christ because of the propaganda now being spread by these lying spirits.[35]

The new versions paint the Antichrist into the picture and paint Jesus out in spite of God's command:

> [A]t the name of Jesus every knee should bow
> Philippians 2:10

NASB (NIV et al.).		KJV
You, Son of God	Matt.8:29	Jesus, Thou Son of God
He	Luke 24:36	Jesus
He	Matt. 4:18	Jesus
He	Mark 2:15	Jesus
Him	Mark 10:52	Jesus
knowing their thoughts	Matt.12:25	Jesus knew their thoughts

T-H-E Christ: Antichrist

Bob Larson's lifelong familiarity with the cults and the New Age prompted this warning:

> By using the definite article (the) when referring to Christ, mind sciences distinguish between Jesus the man and the divine idea of Christ-realization attainable by men.[36]

Liberty University's past Dean, Norman Geisler, warns of the *Infiltration of the New Age*, documenting their use of the term 'the Christ' 28 times in his brief 22 page 'Summary of New Age Beliefs' (pp. 107-128).

Real references to Jesus as 'the Christ' are rare; however the NKJV and new versions literally paint their pages with this pawn.

NIV, NASB, et al.		KJV
the Christ	Matt.2:4	Christ
the Christ	Matt. 22:42	Christ
the Christ	Matt. 24:5	Christ
the Christ	Matt. 24:23	Christ
the Christ	Mark 12:35	Christ
the Christ	Luke 4:41	Christ
the Christ	Luke 20:41	Christ
the Christ	Luke 23:39	Christ
the Christ	Luke 23:35	Christ
the Christ	Luke 24:26	Christ
the Christ	Luke 24:46	Christ
the Christ	John 1:25	Christ
the Christ may come	John 7:27	Christ cometh
the Christ	John 7:31	Christ
the Christ	John 7:26	very Christ
the Christ	Matt. 1:17	Christ
The Christ is to remain forever	John 12:34	Christ abideth forever
preaching Jesus as the Christ	Acts 5:42	preach Jesus Christ
is the Christ	Acts 9:22	this is very Christ
proof of the Christ who speaks in me	2 Cor. 13:3	a proof of Christ speaking in me

NIV, NASB, et al.		KJV
the Christ	Acts 26:23	Christ
the Christ	Acts 8:5	Christ
the Christ	Acts 18:28	Christ
the Christ. . .the Christ	Acts 17:3	Christ. . .Christ
the Christ	Acts 3:20	Christ
His Christ	Acts 3:18	Christ
the Christ	Heb. 6:1	Christ

The following verses will be ripe for picking from the serpent's tree to force feed the starving souls following 'the Christ'. The KJV clearly presents the past tense visit of Jesus Christ. The new version have 'the Christ' to come.

NIV, NASB et al.	KJV
the Christ, according to the flesh	Christ came, who is over all. Rom. 9:5
the resurrection of the Christ	the resurrection of Christ Acts 2:31
the Christ should suffer and rise again from the dead. [The last two verses will no doubt be used to fulfill Rev. 13:3, "And I saw one of his heads as it were wounded to death; and his deadly wound was healed: and all the world wondered after the beast."]	it behoved Christ to suffer and to rise from the dead. Luke 24:46

The bad fruit from the new versions is already appearing.

NIV, NASB, et al.	NEW AGE
"Surely the Christ is not going to come from Galilee, is He?" John 7:41	"[F]or the man child who was to rule all nations with a rod of iron is surely not the meek son of God, Jesus."[37] Blavatsky

NIV, NASB, et al.	NEW AGE
"[H]ere is the Christ." Mark 13:21 Matt. 24:23	"The Christ is now here" Tara Center full page ad in *USA Today, Reader's Digest, New York Times*, et al., promoting the 'Christ' of the Aquarian Age.
"I am the Christ." Matt. 24:5	"I am the Christ." 1. "I am the Christ. . ." was chanted by 875 million participants from 100 countries during the New Age World Healing Meditation. The U.S. Pentagon's Meditation Room participated. 2. *The Metaphysical Bible Dictionary* and *Christian Healing*, books by Unity's Charles Filmore call for the use of the words, "I am the Christ" as a meditation technique.[38]

Christ is "Each of us"

By separating 'Jesus' from 'Christ', new versions allow the definition of Christ to expand to include "each of us." New version editors and New Agers climb on board together, clamoring to be little 'Christs'.

NEW AGE	NEW VERSION EDITOR
"Each of us is the Christ. . . the true spiritual self. . .the anointed son of God."[39] Filmore	"Each Christian is in due measure himself a Christ. . .Christians are in a true sense Christs, anointed ones."[40] Westcott

Can the Luciferians be far behind?

> [F]or Christ. . .is no man but the DIVINE PRINCIPLE in every human being.[41] Blavatsky

> We learn to. . .be Christs ourselves.[42] Spangler

Separating 'Jesus' from 'Christ' serves another purpose in the heart of new version editors. Westcott and others believe 'Christ' now is 'the church'. Denying his bodily resurrection he says:

> The Resurrection of Christ [is only] the church, which is Christ's body. . .through this each believer comes nigh to God. . .he that is in you [I John 4:4 means] that is in the Christian Society.[43]

'Christian' publications like *Restoration Magazine* and cults like the *Church of the Living Word*, "Rob Christ of his personhood by claiming he is now embodied in the church. . ."[44]

> Here we have the roots of another popular but very serious error: the teaching that Christ is the Church.[45]

This theme is not limited to small fringe organizations. Many large mainline Protestant denominations believe membership in their church is equivalent to receiving Christ, since they believe the members 'are Christ'. Even the *Dogmatic Constitution* "Lumen Gentuim," no. 14 from the Second Vatican Council says, the Roman Catholic Church is 'Christ'.

> For Christ, made present to us in His Body, which is the Church, is the one Mediator and the unique Way of salvation.[46]

"Who is a liar," says the apostle John, but he who claims to be Christ. "Jesus is the Christ," not Buddha, a church, "each of us" nor the coming Antichrist.

TWENTY - ONE

Antichrist: The World Teacher

The antichrist hides, not only under the cover of 'Christ' but a second title—'Teacher'. Roy Livesey, author and publisher of *New Age Bulletin* in England explains what New Agers believe:

> Christ, however doesn't refer to the Lord Jesus Christ but to the World Teacher.[47]

Other books like Harriet and F. Homer Curtiss' *Coming World Changes* also connect the anticipated new 'Christ' with the title "long expected Great Teacher."[48] Alice Bailey describes the 'Emergence of the World Teacher' of the New Age:

> In June 1945 at the time of the full moon, He. . .took over [from Jesus] as the Teacher during the Aquarian Solar Cycle. He is the first of the Great World Teachers to cover two zodiacal cycles. This inflow of aquarian energy is one of the factors which will enable the Christ to complete his task as world Savior and world Teacher. . . [and] the Teacher of the Aquarian Age. . .It is as World Teacher that he will work. . .not Christian Teacher.[49]

If the world wants a 'Teacher' and not a 'Lord and Master', the new versions are willing to accommodate, again following their habit of knocking each title of Jesus down one notch.

NIV, NASB, et al.		KJV
teacher (good is omitted in the 1% MSS)	Matt.19:16	Good Master
Teacher	Matt.8:19	Master
teacher	Matt.17:24	master
Teacher	Matt.23:8	Master
Teacher	Mark 4:38	Master
Teacher	Mark 5:35	Master
Teacher	Mark 13:1	Master
Teacher	Mark 14:14	Master
Teacher	Luke 3:12	Master
Teacher	Luke 8:49	Master
Teacher	Luke 11:45	Master
Teacher	Luke 12:13	Master
Teacher	Luke 18:18	Master
Teacher	Luke 19:39	Master
Teacher	Luke 20:21	Master
Teacher	Luke 20:28	Master
Teacher	Luke 20:39	Master
Teacher	Luke 21:7	Master
Teacher	Luke 22:11	Master
Rabbi	John 4:31	Master
Rabbi	John 11:8	Master
Teacher	John 11:28	Master
Teacher	John 20:16	Master
Rabbi	Mark 11:21	Master
Rabbi	Mark 14:45	master
Good Teacher Teacher	Mark 10:17 Mark 10:35	Good Master Master
you call me. . . teacher	John 13:13	Ye call me. . . Master

These changes in the new versions accommodate several aspects of the agenda of the New World Order. (1) They clear the footpath of 'sectarian' Christian vocabulary. (2) They emphasize those titles ascribed to the Antichrist—'Christ' and 'Teacher'. (3)

They accommodate the 'historical' Jesus in a manner that is acceptable to all of the religions of the world, i.e., He is Jesus, one of a series of 'Teachers'.

As early as the second century, sects like the Essenes rejected Jesus Christ as 'Lord' but acquiesced to the title Jesus, 'Teacher of Righteousness'. The Dead Sea Scrolls promote this "right-teacher" who comes right "before the final era. . .to usher in the Golden Age." Since the nineteenth century, the title 'teacher' has been the appellative of choice among liberals and esoterics, when referring to Jesus or any of the world's 'avatars'. Even Blavatsky will say, "Jesus [was] a teacher of the most sublime code of ethics."[50] Bailey parades Jesus among her troop of teachers as an unnamed 'lesser teacher'.

> All the Cyclic Teachers have mastered life for themselves in the three worlds of human evolution. The first such Teacher. . .[was] Hercules. . .Later the great Teacher, Yass. . .Between the times of these two teachers, the Buddha and the Christ, lesser teachers appeared.[51]

Modern New Age churches tally these 'Teachers' as well:

> At Collegians we acknowledge the World Teacher who has appeared as Jesus the Christ, also known variously as the Lord Maitreya and the Bodhisattva as well as other appearances of the Christ through such personalities as Melchizedek, Krishna, and Mithra.[52]

The New Age group 'Holy Order of MANS' professes, "Jesus was a great teacher, but only one of several great avatars. . . Christ is not eternal God but merely a great teacher."[53] Authors of *Ancient Empires of the New Age* summarize:

> Neo-pagans are more than willing to ascribe the title Teacher. . .to Jesus. . .but utterly refuse to consider claims that Christ Himself made that he was God.[54]

Like good pagans, new version editors change the honorific "Good Master" of Matthew 19:16 to the egalitarian term 'teacher' to keep up with the 'times'. NIV's Edwin Palmer bends to *today's* breeze saying:

> Forty-six times the KJV used the term 'master' when for today's reader it should use the term teacher.[55]

Hort agreed, not seeing Jesus as Lord *'Adon'*, "but as the Aramaic *Mar* sometimes applied to teachers by their disciples." (Note his use of the *plural* 'teachers'.)[56] Both neo-pagans and their 'Christian' mouthpieces have fallen in with the wrong 'gang', as Alice Bailey reveals:

> [T]his group is a channel for the activities of the Christ, the World Teacher.[57]

The NIV's rendition of Matthew 23:10 makes it all too clear that Bailey and the boys on the NIV committee are on the same 'channel'.

> You have one Teacher, the Christ. NIV

Acting as a channel for the Antichrist calls for demonic activity. Another researcher comes to the same conclusion.

> Reading the reports of mystics, demonstrates three aspects that seem to indicate demonic activity. . .[M]ost of the entities encountered. . .tell us that Jesus was a great teacher, one of many Christs.[58]

One of many:

NIV		KJV
a stone	I Pet. 2:6	a chief corner stone

What Time Is It?

> The warfare for man's soul involves a series of battles over doctrine.[59]

When at sword's point, our stronghold of safety in this spiritual struggle is the shelter of our "spiritual house," resting on the "chief corner stone" and sealed at every seam with the cement of sound doctrine (I Peter 2:5). Because biblical doctrines bind the body of Christ, the enemy is bound to bring its battering ram against this bulwark. New Ager Alice Bailey calls for:

> [T]he elimination of doctrine [so] the New World Religion can give its 'teachings'.[60]

The 'Teachers' or Avatars of the New Age bring with them a series of 'teachings'. Nichiren Shoshu, a Buddhist group, clearly distinguishes in their writings between "the burden of doctrine" and their "teachings." Their founder, "wanted the Buddhist teaching but cut out. . .doctrine," remarks one follower.[61] The word 'teaching' pervades those world religions which the New Age has adopted as its own. *Theravada*, the 'teaching' of the elders and *dharma*, the 'teaching' are terms central to Hinduism and Buddhism.

Alice Bailey's 'declaration of war' calls for the "elimination of doctrine," our only defense, in exchange for her 'teaching'. Like Elijah, the new version editors hand over their swords to the new Jezebel.

NIV, NASB, et al.		KJV
teaching	Matt. 7:28	doctrine
teaching	Matt. 15:9	doctrine
teaching	Matt. 16:12	doctrine
teaching	Matt. 22:33	doctrine
teaching	Mark 1:22	doctrine
teaching	Mark 1:27	doctrine
teaching	Mark 4:2	doctrine
teaching	Mark 7:7	doctrine
teaching	Mark 11:18	doctrine
teaching	Mark 12:38	doctrine
teaching	Luke 4:32	doctrine
teaching	John 7:16	doctrine
teaching	John 7:17	doctrine
teaching	John 18:19	doctrine
teaching	Acts 2:42	doctrine
teaching	Acts 5:28	doctrine
teaching	Acts 13:12	doctrine
teaching	Acts 17:19	doctrine
teaching	Rom.6:17	doctrine
teaching	Rom. 16:17	doctrine

NIV, NASB, et al.		KJV
teaching	I Cor.14:6	doctrine
teaching	I Cor. 14:26	doctrine
teaching	I Tim.1:10	doctrine
teaching	I Tim. 4:13	doctrine
teaching	I Tim.4:16	doctrine
teaching	I Tim.5:17	doctrine
teaching	2 Tim.3:10	doctrine
teaching	2 Tim.3:16	doctrine
teaching	2 John 1:9	doctrine
teaching	Rev. 2:14, 15, 24	doctrine

The Apostle Paul foresaw this drift toward 'teachings' and disdain for doctrine:

> For the time will come when they will not endure sound **doctrine; but** after their own lusts shall they heap to themselves **teachers**. . .II Timothy 4:3

He knew that as mortar, 'teachings' were tenuous, as Webster writes, merely, "that which is taught." But doctrine is tenacious, "accepted as authoritative. . .dogmas that are true and beyond dispute." Religious historian David L. Johnson observes, "Doctrine specifically states that which is of ultimate concern."[62] Another scholar sees the distinction between 'doctrine' and 'teaching' as a tactic in our defense.

> Our plan of action requires. . .sound doctrine. [I]t is the formal basis of our opinions and beliefs. If we do not maintain good doctrine then all manner of bad teaching can creep into the church.[63]

The word 'doctrine' has a particularly 'Christian' tone, since Christianity is perhaps the only world religion that is dogmatic, not allowing for the truthfulness of any other religion. It is in that sense that Karl Rengstorf, renowned Greek scholar and author of the definitive treatise on the Greek words *didaskalia* or *didache,* points to their translation in the English New Testament as the word 'doctrine' since it:

> [D]enotes the essential difference between Christian proclamation and the various movements which threaten the community.[64]

The menace Rengstorf mentions materializes in *Messages from Maitreya* channeled by Benjamin Creme:

> My Plan is that my Teaching should precede my presence . . .My Plan is to release into the world a certain Teaching.[65]

Alder says, "We can never have the New Age without *our sacred Teaching*" or as Maitreya mentions, "a *certain* Teaching."[66] This 'teaching' is summarized by Edwin Lutzer.

> [D]octrine is not important [in the New Age]. What is important is religious experience.[67]

New Agers like Marilyn Ferguson in her book *Aquarian Conspiracy*, boasts:

> [D]octrine is losing its authority. . .Doctrine. . .is second hand experience. Knowing is. . .the transmission of knowledge through direct experience.[68]

She, along with Hindu Ramakrishna, teaches, "[R]eligion does not really deal with doctrines. . .Religion is experience."[69]

The replacement of doctrine by experience, as a validator of truth, has wedged its way into the church. *War on the Saints* by Jessie Penn-Lewis describes the spiritual deception which ensues when contact with God is sought through sense experiences rather than scripture. It is *must* reading in today's spiritual climate when the winds of deception try to sway every believer.

> The evil spirits as teachers get men to receive their teachings. . .by giving spiritual revelation to those who accept everything supernatural as from God. . .The aim of the wicked spirit is to displace the Word of God as the rock-ground of life. . .Their aim is to move the man by feelings. . .Believers too often look upon a communion with God as a thing of sense and not of spirit. [W]hen the

believer is yearning for the *SENSE* of God's presence. . . the subtle foe approaches. The counterfeit presence of God is given by the deceiving spirits working upon the physical frame. . .upon the senses. . .they set the mind on bodily sensations. . .the believer is occupied with the sense experience. His support is now within upon his experience rather than upon. . .the written word. Through this secret confidence that God has specially spoken to him the man becomes unteachable. . .Some of the suggestions made to the believer by deceiving spirits may be: (1) You are a special instrument of God, working to feed self-love. (2) You are more advanced than others, working to blind the soul to sober knowledge of itself.[70]

TWENTY - TWO

King of Kings & Lord of Lords

Lord Jesus Christ

God hath made that same Jesus whom ye have crucified both Lord and Christ. Acts 2:36

New version banditry not only carries away the title of 'Christ' from Jesus, it also lifts the word 'Lord' from their leaves. One researcher observes:

The Christians weren't thrown to the lions for believing in Jesus. One more god could easily be added to the Pantheon. But for believing Jesus is Lord (over Caesar). . .[71]

So the new versions take the 'bite' out of Christianity by removing the 'objectionable' 'Lord' from his title. *U.S. News and World Report* records the recent roar from the ecumenical and liberal 'lions' who put pressure on new versions to drop the word 'Lord'.[72] These 'cowardly lions' flinch at being "reproached for the name" (I Peter 4:14), 'hated of all men for my name' (Matthew 10:22) or 'persecuted. . .that the name of our Lord Jesus Christ may be glorified' (II Thessalonians 1:4, 12). The title is so hated, it brings death, yet so powerful, it brings eternal life. "If thou shalt confess with thy mouth the Lord Jesus. . .thou shalt be saved." Yet—

> Certain men crept in unawares. . .ungodly men. . .denying the only Lord God and our Lord Jesus Christ. Jude 4

NIV, NASB et al.		KJV
Jesus Christ	2 John 1:3	the Lord Jesus Christ
Christ Jesus	2 Tim. 4:1	the Lord Jesus Christ
Rabboni,. . .Him	Mark 10:51, 52	Lord. . .Jesus
Jesus	2 Cor. 4:10	the Lord Jesus
OMIT	I Cor. 15:47	the Lord
OMIT	Luke 23:42	Lord
master	Matt. 25:21	thy Lord
master	Matt. 24:45	lord
master	Matt. 25:18	lord
master	Luke 12:45	lord
master	Luke 12:46	lord
master	Luke 12:47	lord

> No man can say that Jesus is the Lord but by the Holy Ghost. I Corinthians 12:3

In the latter instances, 'master' is substituted for 'lord', even though the Greek *kurios* is translated as lord elsewhere in the new versions. Hence their switch here is arbitrary and just another in a series of attempts to demote Jesus Christ. In the former, the vast majority of Greek manuscripts attest to the title 'Lord' rather than the shortened titles of the 'new' Greek and 'new' versions. The NIV footnote concedes, "[M]any MSS say Lord." The handful of MS which omit this were altered to accommodate Marcion's *Antithesis* and other Gnostic writings which contended that the Law and the Gospels were at variance and could not have both come from 'the Lord' of the Old Testament. The apostle Peter pronounces "swift destruction" for these teachers and others who omit 'Lord' from their description of Jesus Christ.

[T]here shall be false teachers among you, who privily shall bring in damnable heresies even denying the Lord. . .
II Peter 2:1

Such judgement ensues because the word Lord, used in conjunction with Jesus Christ, points to his eternal deity and preexistence. It is *the* word that connects Jesus Christ with the LORD of the Old Testament. Jesus is "the image of the invisible God" (Col. 1:15) and the "express image of his person" (Hebrews 1:3). It is also the word which reveals the triune nature of God, since JEHOVAH, Jesus Christ and the Holy Spirit alone are given this title.

The LORD be my God. Genesis 28:21

When the new versions do use 'Lord', it appears they like to use it alone, a ploy which makes their bible a more 'International' document.

NIV, NASB, et al.		KJV
Lord	Acts 4:24	Lord, thou art God
Lord	Acts 7:59	God
Lord	Acts 8:22	God
The Lord	Col. 3:22	God
The Lord of the earth	Rev. 11:4	God
The Lord	Acts 19:10	The Lord Jesus
The Lord	I Cor. 16:22	Lord Jesus Christ
The Lord	2 Thess. 2:2	Christ
The Lord	2 Tim.2:19	Christ
The Lord	I Cor. 10:9	Christ

The Hindoos use 'Lord' to mean *'Ishvara'*, that is, God in his personal manifestation. Consequently when Beattle George Harrison serenaded Krishna, he sang, *My Sweet Lord.* Even cults like Unification Church adopt this title. (i.e., Moon calls himself 'Lord of the Second Advent' and his son 'Lord Hering'.[73])

New Agers await the 'One' variously called, Lord Maitreya, the Aquarian 'Christ' and World Teacher. Summonsing him, the NIV and NKJV harmonize with 'Come, O Lord' and 'Oh Lord, come' (I Cor 16:22). A noted scholar warns that this "represents a widely different notion than the KJV's Aramaic *Maranath* which means "The Lord has come."[74] Noted Greek scholar, K.G. Ruhn says:

> The early Church always takes it this way [KJV]. . . [M]odern expositors usually modify it [NIV, NASB]. . . [T]o the best of my knowledge there is not a single instance in all Aram. Hence to construe the perf. . .as 'our Lord comes' in the future tense is hardly possible.[75]

TWENTY - THREE

Test 2 for Antichrist:
Is Jesus the Son of God?

John records the violent reaction of the scribes of old when Jesus said he was *the* 'Son of God'.

> [T]he Jews sought the more to kill him, because he. . . said also that God was his Father, making himself equal with God. John 5:18

Mohammed, marshall of the Middle Eastern men at arms, said menacingly in his *Surah* IV, 171, "Far be it from Him that he should have a son." "The Son of God is not Jesus but our combined Christ Consciousnesses," figures one famous New Ager.[76] Since *the* 'Son of God' does not fit the frame of this fetish god of the New World Religion, the new versions will chisel away until he does. As the chips fall, the image of the Antichrist appears once again.

> He is antichrist that denieth the Father and the Son. . . whosoever denieth the Son, the same hath not the Father. I John 2:22,23

NIV, NASB, et al.		KJV
an heir through God	Gal. 4:7	an heir of God **through Christ**
God, who created all things	Eph. 3:9	God who created all things **by Jesus Christ**
the Father	Eph. 3:14	the Father **of our Lord Jesus Christ**
Grace to you and peace from God our Father	Col. 1:2	Grace be unto you and peace from God our Father **and the Lord Jesus Christ**
Son of Man	John 9:35	Son of God
(NASB footnote: "Many MSS do not have the Son of God." NIV footnote: "Some MSS do not have the Son of God." Note the contradiction.)	Mark 1:1	Son of God (Only a handful of corrupt MSS omit this; even B has it says one Princeton scholar. "[T]he texts of Papyrus 75 and Aleph were the handiwork of heretics who for some reason were reluctant to acknowledge Jesus as the Son of God.")[77]
the Son	John 3:17	his Son
Holy One of God (This is a derogatory term used only by devils in Mark 1:24 and Luke 4:34.)	John 6:69	**Christ the Son** of the Living God
My Chosen One (This is a derogatory term used toward Jesus in Luke 23:35.) The Nag-Hammadi papyri reveals Gnostics	Luke 9:35	beloved **Son**

NIV, NASB, et al.		KJV
regarded 'the Son of God' as a mystic name which should not be pronounced except by the initiated; consequently they introduced substitutes like 'My Chosen One' or 'the Living One' from the Gospel of Thomas, a document now very popular among New Agers.		
the Father	Matt.24:36	my Father
OMIT	Acts 8:37	I believe that Jesus Christ is the Son of God.
servant	Acts 3:13	Son
servant	Acts 3:26	Son
holy servant Jesus (They use son for *paida* in John 4:51 in reference to the centurion's son.) This puts Jesus on the same level as the NIV's "Paul, a servant," "James, a servant," "Simon Peter, a servant," "Jude, a servant," and "Moses the servant."	Acts 4:27, 30	holy **child** Jesus
his father and his mother (RV)	Luke 2:33	Joseph and his mother
OMIT	Matt.1:25	her firstborn son
a young woman *Good News for Modern Man*	Isa. 7:14	a virgin shall conceive

The Only Begotten Son

If, "He is antichrist. . .that denieth the Son," surely the Jehovah Witnesses and new version editors, who have discharged 'the Son' from John 1:18, are arch-antichrists. Recent printings of the NIV do likewise.

J.W. TRANSLATION	**NASB**	**KJV**
the only begotten god	the only begotten God	the only begotten Son

Christians have held tenaciously to the doctrine that Christ is God and co-eternal with the Father. The term 'begotten', in reference to Christ, is introduced and interpreted in John 1:14.

> [T]he Word was made flesh and dwelt among us (and we beheld his glory, the glory as of the only begotten of the Father. . .John 1:14

From this we gather that "begotten" is used in reference to the body of "flesh" "beheld" by mankind. Gabriel said to Mary (Luke 1:35):

> The Holy Ghost shall come upon thee and the power of the Highest shall overshadow thee: **therefore** also that holy thing which shall be born of thee, shall be called the Son of God.

Regrettably, John 1:18 was ripped from its context and fed to the wolves of history past. It was chewed by the Gnostics, along with the "begotten Gods" of Oriental and Greek mythology, until its unrecognizable form was spewed from the mouth of Valentinus, an Egyptian Gnostic. From his "unbegotten God" came a series of aeons or 'begotten' Gods. (i.e., Sophia, Demiurge, Logos, Monogenes, Zoe, Ecclesia, Christ, each begotten by the previous, for a total of 30)

> From the father as Supreme God there proceeds a number of beings. . .a family of gods.[78]

The Valentian Gnostics named one of these Gods, The Beginning or the *Nous* (from Plato), the Only Begotten.

> Something named the Beginning. . .was the first thing God created. . .a god, but inferior to the Father.[79]

Consequently the NASB's 'begotten God' (John 1:18) becomes 'The Beginning' in their rendition of Revelation 3:14.

NASB	KJV
The Amen, the faithful and true Witness, the Beginning of the creation of God, say this. . .	These things saith the Amen, the faithful and true witness, the beginning of the creation of God.

The KJV clearly states that Jesus Christ is the source of the creation. The NASB, however, by capitalizing the word 'Beginning', changes it from an event to a person with a proper name. Their rationale is best expressed by Hort who believed, "The words might no doubt bear the Arian meaning of [Jesus as] the first created thing."[80]

The Encyclopedia of Religion and Ethics calls John's gospel, "an underlying polemic against the Gnostic teaching."[81] Consequently, history records Valentinus' attempt to deaden John's blow by changing "begotten Son" to "begotten God" (see Theodotus' *Excerpts from Theodotus*). The compass of Valentinus' touched precisely the territory and term of the production of new version papyri 72 and 66, as evidenced by their adoption of his "begotten God." This notion would easily nest in a region ripe with Clement's contentions. (i.e., "The Son is a creature" and "God is a Being. . . beyond even the One and the Monad."[82])

The conflict continued into the fourth century as Arius, a student of Origen's, crusaded for Jesus as "the begotten God," only to be met by campaigning Christians like Athanasius, Hilary, and Ambrose armed with "the only begotten Son" in their canon's mouth. (See *Arian Candidus*, *Epiph* 73.) Arius believed that Jesus was "created by God before the foundation of the world," as 'a God'. The public popularity of this 'Ariansim' prompted Eusebius, a semi-Arian to add, "firstborn of all creatures, begotten of the Father before all ages," to Constantine's church creed in A.D.325. The further swell of Arianism by A.D.330 prompted Constantine to replace semi-Arian Eusebius of Caesarea with Arian Eusebius of Nicodemia. He also exiled Athanasius in A.D.335, since he was the most outspoken proponent of "the only begotten Son." It is in this climate that Constantine requested the production of manuscripts B and Aleph. Their use of "only begotten God" in John 1:18 was no doubt a political expedient.[83]

The term "the only begotten Son" is seen in the vast majority of MSS and is witnessed to by the earliest extant record of John 1:18, Tertullian in A.D.180. Even Alan Wikgren of the *UBS Greek New Testament* committee admits:

> It is doubtful that the author would have written 'begotten God' which may be a primitive, transcriptual error in the Alexandrian tradition.[84]

However the critical apparatus of the *UBS Greek New Testament* cites, P66, P75, Aleph, B, C and L, as well as Valentinians, Theodotus, Clement, Origen and Arius, as support for their use of "begotten God," in spite of the doctrinal bias of these witnesses. This bias is shared by new version editors who add a kind of semi-Arianism to their already long list of heresies.

NEW VERSION EDITORS	
"From all eternity the father begat the Son. But it is remarkable that the bible does not say that the Holy Spirit was begotten by the Father. . ."[85] Palmer "It is impossible to suppose that two beings distinct in essence could be equal in power. We find ourselves met by difficulty which belongs to the idea of begetting. . .If we keep both [Arianism and Sabellianism] before us we may hope to attain. . .to that knowledge of the truth."[87] Westcott	"Christ [is] the divine-human personably. [T]he dwelling of God in Him is the only satisfactory solution of the problem of his amazing character."[86] Schaff

As can be expected this 'created God' appears in a number of other new version verses.

NEW VERSION	KJV
whose **origins** are from old, from ancient times NIV	whose goings forth have been from of old from everlasting. Mic. 5:2
For he who sanctifies and those who are sanctified are all of one **origin** (or all from one Father).	For both he that sanctifieth and they who are sanctified are all one. Heb.2:11

Regarding the following verse Bruce Metzger, member of the *UBS Greek New Testament* committee, warns, "This is the verse the Jehovah Witnesses (along with Arians of every age) appeal to most frequently to confirm their view that Jesus Christ was a created being."[88]

NEW VERSIONS	KJV
The Lord formed me in the beginning before he made anything else. *Living Bible*	The LORD possessed me in the beginning of his way, before his works of old. Proverbs 8:22
Jehovah himself produced [created in footnote] me as the beginning of his ways, the earliest of his achievements of long ago. *New World Translation* (J.W.)	[Verse 1 of chapter 8 identifies "wisdom" as the object possessed; this is a far cry from 'a created God'.]
The LORD brought me forth as the first of his works, before his deeds of old. NIV	

NIV committee member Larry Walker boasts, "The majority of other new translations also express the new idea in the text, using 'created', 'formed' or 'begot' (cf. JB, NAB, RSV, TEV, LB, NEB)."[89] The NAB's note points to "Wisdom. . .a divine being. . .that plurality of divine persons."[90]

Wisdom is not a divine being, except to Gnostics, who include Sophia (Wisdom) among the begotten Gods.

NEW VERSIONS		KJV
begotten from the Father	John 1:14	begotten of the Father
the first-born of all creation	Col. 1:15	the first born of every creature
first-born	Rev. 1:5	begotten
firstborn	Heb. 1:6	firstbegotten
He is the. . .exact representation of His nature	Heb. 1:3	express image of his person
Christ. . .was foreknown	I Pet. 1:19,20	Christ. . .was foreordained
He has explained Him	John 1:18	he hath declared him.

Today's cults carry this foray forward, using new version verses as fuel. *Good News for Modern Man* (TEV) provides aid to the enemy in John 1:1.

TEV	KJV
Before the world was created, the Word already existed.	In the beginning was the Word.

Children of God
"He, Jesus was a creation of God. Oh, this is exactly according to scripture! Can you think of a verse on it?"[91]

Jehovah Witnesses
"Jesus, the Christ, a created individual, is the second greatest personage of the universe. . ."[92]

Make Sure of All Things

"He was a god, but not the Almighty God. . ."[93]

Let God be True

"Jesus Christ, who did have a beginning. . ."[94]

Let God Be True

The Way
"Jesus Christ was not literally with God in the beginning."[95] Victor Paul Wierwelle

Astara
"Jesus. . .begotten before the beginning of our time and age."[96]

Not only the Cults, but confused 'Christians' are parroting the pages of these perverse versions. Kenneth Copeland says:

> Jesus is no longer the only begotten Son of God. . .God begets gods. . .[therefore] You are all little gods.[97]

Monogenes: Only Begotten

The controversy quickly becomes a travesty. While there are a few MS to support the only begotten "God" of the NASB, there are *none* to support the dismissal of "begotten" seen in other new versions. The Greek word preceding 'Son' or 'God' is always *monogenes*, a two part word in which *mono* means 'only' or 'one' and *genes* means 'begotten', 'born', 'come forth'. Buchsel, in his definitive treatise on the meaning of the word '*monogenes*' said, "It means only-begotten." All interlinear Greek-English New Testaments translate it as such.[98] However, most new versions do not translate *genes*, the second part of the word. The NIV and other versions leave it untranslated in John 1:14, 18, 3:16, 3:18, Hebrews 1:6, 11:17 and I John 4:19. Hence we see "only Son" (*Living Bible*), "one and only Son" (NIV) and "unique Son" (RV).

NEW VERSIONS	KJV
only Son (LB) one and only Son (NIV) unique Son (RV)	only begotten Son

This departure from the Greek displays once again that these new version editors have disappeared behind the door marked 'New Age'. The word 'only begotten' emphasizes too strongly the distinction between Jesus Christ, the begotten Son, and believers who are adopted sons. "Only begotten" also flattens any New Age assertion that Jesus is one in a long line of avatars.

The 'censored' versions stand ready to support those unscriptural schemers who subscribe to a Son who was not 'begotten'.

> [H]e, Jesus, is the unique Son of God. . .but there have been lots of others like him. . .he was a guide and I can be just like him.[99] New Ager

> The only Son, Jesus is mankind's Savior. The second advent of Jesus is in Korea.[100] Reverend Moon

> The Spirit of Eternity is One. . .God the Mother is omniscient. . .[T]he only Son is Christ, and Christ is Love.[101] *The Aquarian Gospel of Jesus the Christ.*

Behind the New Age door lies the defense given by new version editors. The door opens to a crypt. Beneath centuries of sod new version advocates disentomb ancient occult documents and eulogize:

> [T]he lexical evidence. . .points to the rendering in modern versions. . .as the word was used in documents approximately contemporary with the N.T., it did not have the meaning 'only begotten'.[102]

The dirge includes, *The Magical Papyri, Pseudo-Philo, Tobit,* and Blavatsky's favorite the blasphemous Gnostic *Orphic Hymns. These* and other esoteric documents are listed in "The One and Only Son" an essay by Richard Longenecker, NIV committee member. He points particularly to a citation from Clement regarding 'the Phoenix'. (It is an ancient occult symbol, used like the Egyptian myth of Horus, to promote the myth that Christ's resurrection was only one of many. This theme is popular in Blavatsky's books and has been promoted recently in the TV mini-series *The Power of Myth,* adapted from Joseph Campbell's book *Hero with a Thousand Faces.*) Longenecker joins the skeptics saying:

> [T]he Phoenix, that mysterious bird of the East, as *monogenes*. .it makes for itself a coffin of frankincense and myrrh. . .then dies. . .as the flesh rots, a certain worm is engendered which is neutered from the moisture of the dead creature and puts forth wings and. . .flees to the altar of the Sun. . .It is in the light of this conceptual background that the title as applied to Jesus must be seen.[103]

Longenecker's panoramic view of "*monogenes*" is called "the broad way." It leads him to believe '*monogenes*' is "an adjective stressing quality rather than derivation or descent." (As Mohammed said, "Far be it from him that he should have a son.") He rails the KJV for translating the word literally, "because it leaves open the possibility of an etymological emphasis on *genes* (the idea of generation)."[104] Longenecker is merely repeating what Luciferian H.P. Blavatsky said 100 years ago, "Neither was he physically begotten."[105]

Blavatsky directs the following distorted duet. The jarring tone of 'Christians' harmonizing with cultists is confounding. (Recall Palmer hand picked the members of the NIV committee and had the final say on all translations.)

NIV EDITORS	MORMON DOCTRINE
"The Holy Spirit did not beget the Son."[106] Edwin Palmer NIV Committee Executive Secretary	"He [the Son] was not begotten by the Holy Spirit. . ."[107] Brigham Young
"Son of God. . .denote[s] Jesus' **unique** relationship to God and his response of loving **obedience** to the Father's will."[108] Richard Longenecker NIV Committee	"By **obedience** and devotion He attained to the pinnacle. . .He is greater than all others by reason of his **unique** status."[109] *Mormon Doctrine, Doctrine and Covenants*

The Rank of 'Christ Consciousness'

The NIV editors join the cults, the Luciferians, the Moslems and the bulk of lost humanity when they deny that Jesus was God's 'begotten' Son. To Longenecker, Jesus was "chosen" to receive the title 'Son of God' because he earned it through "obedience." He says, that Jesus,

> . . .exemplified in his life an unparalleled obedience. . . [H]e has the greatest right to the title. . .God's Son *par excellence*.[110]

The King James Version Debate by D.A. Carson, defends the new version's dismissal of "begotten," saying that Jesus is "the son. . .because He always does what is pleasing in the Father's sight."[111]

Both Longenecker and Carson are expressing a view similar to that held by the early Adoptionists, Dynamic Monarchists or Ebionites. They believed "Jesus was a man specially chosen by God."[112] Today many see Jesus as a mentor and not as Master.

NIV EDITOR	NEW AGE
"Thus in the synoptic Gospels sonship is attributed to Jesus and the believer in a manner that is primarily **functional**, with that of Jesus being set off from others by the addition of the adjective. . .best-loved."[113] Richard Longenecker	"This is a special unique Son. . .He is unique in several ways. . .They are related to his assigned role and **function**."[114] Lola Davis, *Toward a World Religion for the New Age* "In the New Testament this self is represented by the Christ, the only begotten [best loved] Son of God. Man in his true self, therefore, is a son of God. . .The difference between Him and us is not one of inherent spiritual capacity but of a difference in demonstration."[115] *What Unity Teaches* Elizabeth S. Turner

Longenecker's hammer that Jesus earned the "right to the title" through "obedience" strikes a New Age note. It rings like New Age rhetoric regarding a spiritual hierarchy of ranks of merit. This hierarchy is pervasive in New Age and Eastern writings. The Sufis have a ranking system called *awliya*. Buddhism has 31 planes of existence. Luciferian Rudolf Steiner wrote *The Spiritual Hierarchies* (1909) to condition his generation with this ranking system. Today the Sherman Oaks Woman's Club sponsors 'Merlin and the Spiritual Hierarchy' for monthly channeling sessions. This system of ranks permeates New Age literature.

> Christ then is a glorious Being belonging to the great spiritual hierarchy.[116] Anne Beseant

> [M]ore and more intelligent men and women are coming into touch with the emerging ideas of the Hierarchy.[117]
> Alice Bailey

This ranking system has little regard for Jesus (whom they distinguish from 'Christ'). Cumby observes:

> The New Age has a hierarchy of masters. Jesus is on the lowest **rank**, he reports to the Venetian Master.[118]

Carr elaborates,

> [T]hose who de-Christify Jesus only give him the **rank** of a 4th degree initiate.[119]

The new versions once again take up the cause of the Luciferians and the New Age.

NEW VERSIONS	KJV
He. . .has a higher **rank** than I. NASB (The NASB translates this word as 'before' in 30 places.)	he. . .is preferred before me. John 1:30

NEW VERSIONS	KJV
Only to Christ he said—you are a priest forever with the **rank** of Melchizedek *Living Bible*	Thou art a priest forever after the order of Melchisedec. Heb. 7:17
LUCIFERIAN	
"Jesus was considered only in the light of a high priest like Melchesidek—another avatar."[120] Blavatsky	

As a consequence Moody Broadcasting's Donald Cole misdefined "begotten" for a caller. He used the words "rank" and "hierarchy"—saying Jesus was of a higher rank than we are. One critic of the New Age notes:

> Most New Agers believe that Christ is not a man but an **office** or spiritual state of higher consciousness.[121]

Bob Larson points out that Christ "refers to Jesus not an office."[122] The new versions and their editors fit the label 'New Age' once again. "It is commonly supposed," writes Westcott, that Hebrews 1:8 defends the deity of Christ, whereas it is merely a "description" of his "office."

NEW VERSION EDITOR	NEW AGE
"One, truly man, fulfilled a divine **office**, that [is] Jesus."[123] B.F. Westcott	"In the esoteric tradition, the Christ is not the name of an individual but of an **office** in the hierarchy."[124] *The Aquarian Gospel of Jesus the Christ*

In their view, "He perfected himself through various spiritual disciplines until he was a suitable habitation for 'the Christ' consciousness."[125] Since Christ is not a person, in the New Age paradigm, new versions change 'a person' into a 'thing' in the following verses.

NEW AGE	NEW VERSIONS	KJV
"Born-again Christianity emphasizes the personality of Jesus; what I call Christian Yoga sees Christ as a consciousness."[126] *Yoga Journal*	something greater than the temple is here	one greater than the temple Matt.12:6
"Jesus was an historical person, but the Christ is an eternal transpersonal condition."[127] *A Course in Miracles*	something greater than Jonah	a greater than Jonas Matt.12:41
"Many believe that either you accept Jesus as your personal savior or you will go to hell. This limits the experience of the Christ Consciousness to only one man."[128] *The Eternal Dance*	something greater than Solomon is here	a greater than Solomon is here Matt.12:42
	something greater than Solomon is here	a greater than Solomon is here. Luke 11:31

The ancient Adoptionists believed that 'the Christ Consciousness' entered Jesus at baptism (and hence the use of baptism in esoteric circles). Now New Agers espouse the same doctrine. *The Aquarian Gospel of Jesus the Christ* voices a line like Longnecker's.

> Jesus won his sonship by a strenuous life. . .Jesus was not always the Christ. . .we have a record of the event of his Christening or receiving the degree Christ.[129]

The writings of new version editors are crawling with quotes in concert with 'the crazies'.

NEW VERSION EDITOR	LUCIFERIAN
"We realize the perfect **humanity** of Christ. . .at this crisis [baptism] first became 'conscious' as a man of a **power** of the spirit within him."[130] B.F. Westcott	"Christ, who was **human** until receiving the Christ Essence at his Jordan baptism."[131] Anthroposophy "This saving **power**, the Christos, entered into the man Jesus, the **human** vehicle, at the moment of his baptism."[132] *Hidden Wisdom in the Holy Bible*

Sadly, "the legion" of quotes is heard by more than the "herd of swine," as 'Christians' go "rushing" to Jordan for a New Age christening.

APOSTATE CHRISTIANITY	LUCIFERIAN
"[H]e only **became** Messiah and **Son** at Jordan. . .as Jesus entered the new age and covenant by being baptized in the Spirit in Jordan."[133] James D.G. Dunn *Baptism in the Holy Ghost*	"Jesus had **become** the **Son** of God the moment of his initiation by water."[134] Blavatsky

The ancient popularity of the theory that 'the Christ' entered Jesus at Baptism and left before his crucifixion is seen in alterations to manuscripts like Aleph and B. Indications of his spirituality or deity, before his baptism or while on the cross, are removed.

NEW VERSIONS	KJV
and the **Child** grew and became strong	and the child grew and waxed strong **in spirit** Luke 2:40
Jesus, remember me	Jesus, **Lord** remember me Luke 23:42

The NASB capitalizes 'Child' nearly a dozen times, keeping pace with the veneration of Mother-Child imagery seen in India (Indrani and the Child), China (Shingmo and the Child) and Europe, Russia and Central and South America (Madonna and Child). Sophisticated New Agers, who would disdain such external pageantry, instead burn incense to the idol 'inside'. Two New Age writers express what the NASB's Christ 'Child' means to thousands of New Agers.

> [A]t the very center of our being there is the. . .Christ Child. . .This Christ or perfect-man idea. . .is the true spiritual higher-self of every individual.[135]
>
> Charles Filmore

> [P]eople experience the birth of the Christ Child within their hearts as they give themselves in surrender at last to the New Age.[136] Vera Alder

TWENTY - FOUR

Test 3 for Antichrist:

Has Jesus Christ Come in the Flesh?

NIV, NASB, et al.	KJV
every spirit that does not acknowledge Jesus is not from God	And every spirit that confesseth not that Jesus **Christ is come in the flesh** is not of God: I John 4:3

Bruce Metzger, author of the *Reader's Digest New Testament*, as well as co-editor of the *UBS Greek New Testament*, picked the wrong verse to help create a slimline bible. By omitting "Christ" and "is come in the flesh," new versions are *not* confessing that "Jesus Christ is come in the flesh"; as John says, "this is that spirit of antichrist." Readers, who subscribe to these "deceivers," may have full bookshelves instead of a "full reward."

> For many **deceivers** are entered into the world, who confess not that Jesus **Christ** is **come in the flesh**. This is a **deceiver** and an **antichrist**.

Look to yourselves that we **lose not** those things which we have wrought, but that we receive a full reward.

Whosoever transgresseth and abideth not in the **doctrine of Christ**, hath not God. . .

If there come any unto you and bring not this doctrine, **receive** him not into your house. II John 1:7-11

The previous documentation clearly shows that the new versions 'cross out' Christ over one dozen times. In addition, they blue-pencil, "Christ" has "come in the flesh." Since the apostle John warns that we are not to be receivers of "deceivers," new versions go into a heap, not "into your house."

To compound their crime, the new versions also deny that "God" has "come in the flesh" in I Timothy 3:16. The *Westminster Confession of Faith* cites I Timothy 3:16 as *the* verse attesting most strongly to the deity of Christ (Section 8, par. 2).

NIV, NASB, et al.	KJV
And by common confession great is the mystery of godliness: He who was revealed in the flesh. NASB	And without controversy great is the mystery of godliness: **God** was manifest in the flesh, I Tim. 3:16
He appeared in a body. NIV	
He was made manifest in the flesh. *New World Translation* (J.W.)	
The One who shewed himself as a human being. *Phillip's Translation*	

1. Of the 300 Greek manuscripts containing I Timothy 3:16, only five late manuscripts (9th, 12th and 13th century) omit "God." The uncials, Aleph and especially A and C, have been altered here so that *either* "God" or "who" can be deduced.

2. The earliest witnesses support the inclusion of "God": Dionysius of Alexandria A.D. 265, Gregory of Nyssa A.D. 394, and Didymus A.D. 398. In addition, Ignatious A.D. 110, Barnabas and

Hippolytus A.D. 235, and Diodorus of Tarsus A.D. 370 allude to the inclusion of "God." Of writers before A.D. 400, Origen, the exiled heretic, stands alone in omitting "God".

3. Versions used around the world, such as the Italian *Diodati*, the French *Osterwald*, the Spanish *Valera*, the Portuguese *Almeida* and Luther's German Bible, all attest to "God was manifest in the flesh."

4. The overwhelming majority of manuscripts say, "God." The NIV and NASB footnote stating, "some later mss read God," should read "some later mss read who." Those few copies that have "who" in place of "God," do not have a complete sentence. There is no subject without "God." In addition, a neuter noun "mystery" cannot be followed by the masculine pronoun "who." To avoid having a clause with no subject, the NIV and J.W. bible arbitrarily drop the word "who" and invent a new word,"He." The NASB retains "who" and adds "He." By making these additions and subtractions, the new versions, in I Timothy 3:16, follows no Greek manuscripts at all, not even the five late uncials.

5. The omission of 'God' in the new versions is based on its deletion in 1881 by the Westcott and Hort revision which Metzger says, "was taken as the basis for the present United Bible Societies' edition."[137] Its omission resulted from the doctrinal stance of the 1881 committee, not from any overwhelming manuscript evidence. Of the committee's two Unitarian members, Smith and Thayer, the former reveals *why* the revisors dropped 'God'.

> The old reading ["God"] has been pronounced untenable by the revisors. . .a reading that was the natural result of the growing tendency in early Christian times to look upon the humble Teacher as the incarnate word and therefore as God manifest in the flesh.[138]

It was simple for the Unitarians of the 1881 committee to find a manuscript or two to support their denial of the deity of Christ. The Arians of the fourth century, became the Nestorians of the fifth century. These were followed later by the Socinians of the sixteenth century and the Jehovah Witnesses of today. Dr. George Bishop summarizes:

> '[H]e who was manifest in the flesh' [is] the precise rendering for which all the Unitarians have been contending for the last 1800 years.[139]

Other new version verses reinforce their denial that Jesus Christ was God "manifest in the flesh."

NEW VERSIONS		KJV
representation of his nature	Heb. 1:3	image of his person

TWENTY - FIVE

Resurrection or Reincarnation?

> [H]ow say some among you that there is no resurrection of the dead?. . .And if Christ be not raised, your faith is in vain; ye are yet in your sins. I Corinthians 15:12,17

For the NIV's Longenecker, "the flesh" of the Phoenix "rots." "[I]n the light of this conceptual background," can Jesus have a bodily resurrection? Eastern religions, the New Age and their pet bird, the Phoenix, allow for an afterlife of the soul or spirit, but not a bodily resurrection. Roper and Gallup poles show that between 22 and 44% of Americans agree and therefore hold to the doctrine of reincarnation.

The bible is a barrier to this belief because of the verses testifying to the bodily appearances of Jesus Christ after his death. However, efforts to evade this reality are in evidence in New Age writing and new versions as well. One observer summarizes the New Age view of the resurrection:

> The typical New Age response to Christian claims might be that it was not a real physical body but rather a phantasmic ethereal body that was seen. . .Of course the

argument crumbles in the face of Thomas' testimony. Doubting Thomas wanted to feel the wounds in Jesus' body—how can one feel wounds on a phantom?[140]

The new versions try to de-materialize Jesus by dissolving the verses pointing to his bodily resurrection.

NASB	KJV
[words probably not in the original writings] This is omitted in the *NASB Greek-English Interlinear* with a note, "Many manuscripts do not contain this verse." This is a lie on the part of these editors, since only one manuscript, D, omits this. It is in every known MS including the earliest, P75, Aleph and B.	And when he had thus spoken, he shewed them his hands and his feet. Luke 24:40
NASB Greek-English Interlinear [Probably not in the original writings]. Again, a lie. This is in every known manuscript except one, D. It is in P75, Aleph and B, as well.	He is not here, but is risen. Luke 24:6
[words probably not in the original writings] Again, this verse is in every known manuscript except D. It is in P75, Aleph and B also.	Then arose Peter, and ran unto the sepulchre; and stooping down, he beheld the linen clothes laid by themselves and departed wondering in himself at that which was come to pass. Luke 24:12
Omitted by *Nestle's Greek*	The Son of man must be delivered into the hands of sinful men, and be crucified, and the third day rise again. Luke 24:7

NASB	KJV
New versions do not translate the Greek word *tekmerion*, 'infallible proofs', but pretend it is *elegcho* which they translate as "conceit" elsewhere.	To whom also he shewed himself alive after his passion by many infallible proofs. Acts 1:3
OMIT (The only manuscript in the world which omits this is D. It is in Aleph, B, 18 uncials and all known cursives and versions.	and saith unto them, 'Peace be unto you.' Luke 24:36, 51-52
NIV and NASB notes relay Nestle's double bracket identification [[are known not to be a part of the original text]][141]	Now when Jesus was risen early the first day of the week, he appeared first to Mary Magdalene. . . After that he appeared unto the eleven. Mark 16:9, 12, 14, 19
he should be the first to proclaim light	he should be the first that should rise from the dead. Acts 26:23
the third day I shall reach my goal	the third day I shall be perfected. Luke 13:32

The brackets and footnotes are subtle artillery, but have resulted in what Norman L. Geisler calls *The Battle for the Resurrection.* His book and others become necessary since new versions question almost every appearance of Jesus after his resurrection. As a result of the new omissions "evangelical scholars" and the cults are beginning to agree.

"EVANGELICAL SCHOLARS"	JEHOVAH WITNESSES
"Norman Geisler finds even a few evangelical scholars asserting that Jesus' resurrection body was merely spiritual. . .the concluding chapter encourages the church to spot and prevent theological drifts away from the true faith."[142]	"Christ's body was not raised in flesh but with a spiritual body."[143]

The drift originated with the excision of many of these passages in the second century by Marcion. Only manuscript D records his mutilated 'version'. Luciferians, like Blavatsky, look to such corrupted manuscripts to support their phantom 'Jesus'. She writes:

> The author of the fourth gospel, himself an Alexandrian Gnostic, describes Jesus as what would be termed a materialized divine spirit.[144]

The resurrection of this heresy by new version editors is a reflection of their harmony with history's heretics. These apostates hammer on the same anvil as the scoffers; both believe bodily resurrection is out. Their rhetoric again sounds like a stereo recording.

NEW VERSION EDITOR	CULTS
"Socrates [said]. . .'such as have **purified** themselves by philosophy live wholly without bodies for the future',. . .the words are surely memorable. . ." Westcott	"Eventually you will be able to have **purified** your mind and body. . .to such a degree that you will be able to quicken it to spiritual expression as did Jesus the Christ."[145] Unity

NEW VERSION EDITOR	CULTS
"[H]is [Christ's] **flesh** would be removed. . .through earthly dissolution." Westcott	"Christ's body disappeared. Christ was raised as a divine spirit."[146] Herbert W. Armstrong
"The Resurrection seems to me to be the image of man unfallen to a **higher** life. . . not future but present: . . . not I shall be hereafter but **I AM**."[147] Westcott	"Resurrection is spiritualization of thought."[148] Christian Science "Man becomes a spirit after death. . .to higher and **higher** heavens."[149] Spiritualists "You are **I AM** and **not flesh and blood**. . .born of Spirit."[150] Unity

If the cults forfeit "the flesh" and bones, new versions perform the necessary surgery.

NIV, NASB, et al.	KJV
For we are members of his body	For we are members of his body, **of his flesh, and of his bones**. Eph. 5:30

NIV stylist Virginia Mollenkott even expresses the New Age teaching of reincarnation and the transmigration of souls from one body to another. She states in *Sensuous Spirituality* (p. 16),

> Perhaps my Self has been on earth before in other **bodies**, perhaps not.

TWENTY - SIX

The Ascended Christ or Antichrist?

The Absent Ascension

As the new versions accelerate into the arms of the Antichrist, they by-pass the ascension of Christ, omitting almost every mention of it.

NEW VERSIONS		KJV
omits last phrase	John 16:16	A little while and ye shall not see me: and again, a little while, and ye shall see me, **because I go to the Father**. [This is in all uncials including A and I, both 4th century, every known cursive, Nonnas 3rd century and Chrysostom and Cyril 4th century and all versions.]

NEW VERSIONS		KJV
He parted from them. (omits last section)	Luke 24:51, 52	he was parted from them **and carried up into heaven. And they worshipped him.**
[[double brackets]] means "are known not to be part of the original text."	Mark 16:9-20	So then after the Lord had spoken unto them, he was received up into heaven and sat on the right hand of God.
He was. . .taken. . .in glory	I Tim. 3:16	God was. . .received. . . into glory.
OMIT	John 3:13	the Son of man which is in heaven

Acting as fairy godmother, new versions forward the frail fantasy of New Age books like *The Mystical Life of Jesus* whose author says:

> [T]here is nothing in the original account of it to warrant the belief that Jesus arose physically or in his physical body in a cloud into the heavens. . .[He must be using a new version] Jesus retired to the monastery at Carmel. He lived for many years and carried on secret missions with his apostles.[151]

Such New Age fiction is fostered by the NASB's rendition, "He parted from them," which omits the remaining, "and was carried up into heaven." It lends a hand to such legends as a visit by Jesus to India as Krishna or Saint Issa, time spent with the Essenes as the 'Teacher of Righteousness', or even the Mormon myth of his visit to the American Indians.

New Agers often deny his death, as well. Alice Bailey writes of the life of Christ, "prior to his disappearance." She and the NASB agree, "He never left. . .he apparently departed."[152]

NASB	KJV
speaking of his departure	spake of his decease Luke 9:31

Those who admit that he died, deny that he is still in his resurrected body.

> Jesus had never left the earth,. . .while Jesus had had a resurrected body, he had to forfeit that body because he had not earned the right to keep it for the reason that Jesus was only a fourth level initiate. . .whereas Gautama Buddha was a sixth level initiate. However Maitreya himself was a seventh level initiate. . .[153]

The NASB consorts and concurs again.

NASB		KJV
has been raised	I Cor.15:16,17	be. . .raised
has been raised	I Cor. 15:20	is. . .risen

The Second Coming

His ascension is critical, not only as an attestation to his deity, but because it portrays the mode of his second coming.

> [T]his same Jesus, which is taken up from you into heaven, shall so come in like manner as ye have seen him go into heaven. Acts 1:11

This verse gives two important clues which distinguish the coming Antichrist from the coming King. (1) We are to look for the "same Jesus." (2) He will return "in like manner as ye have seen him go." New versions become silent supporters in service of the walk-on false Christ spoken of by Jesus.

> For there shall arise false Christs. . .wherefore if they shall say unto you, Behold he is in the desert; go not forth: behold, he is in the secret chambers; believe it not.

> For as the lightning cometh out of the east and shineth even unto the west; so shall also the coming of the Son of man be. Matthew 24:24-28

In spite of Christ's warning, New Agers pronounce,"The Masters of Wisdom. . .have remained largely in the remote desert." The NASB's 'walk on' Messiah is seen in *USA Today's* full page ad entitled, "The Christ is in the World."[154] His promoters pronounce:

> The Christ cannot return because he has always been here upon Earth. . .securely concealed. . .He has guided the affairs of the Spiritual Hierarchy.[155] Alice Bailey

> The Christ is a reincarnation of the Christ spirit in an occult master who has lived in the Himalayas for the past 2000 years.[156] Benjamin Creme

The liberals and the cults have always had a 'Christ' who returned some way other than in the clouds. So the new versions fit their 'fashionings' as well.

1. Jehovah Witnesses say he returned 'spiritually' in 1914.
2. Reverend Moon said the second coming was 'his' flight on a DC-10.
3. Westcott wrote of the "many comings of Christ in the social forces."
4. Liberals say he comes, at baptism or as the church.

Although the liberals, cults, and New Agers seem reluctant to concede Christ's ascension, they revel in reading about Ramtha, a channeled entity who boasts, "I did not die; I ascended. . .for I learned to harness the power of my mind and to take my body with me."[157] While Ramtha bewitches television talk show audiences with his 'ascension' claims, the kiddies are being mesmerized by E.T. whose death, resurrection and ascension portray a crass caricature of Christ's. Young and old see Christ fading from the pages of the bible, while counterfeit characters are created in exchange. God calls them idols.

Misrepresented Manuscript Evidence

An overview of the textual evidence for the inclusion of these ascension verses will shock the average reader. The NIV says of Mark's witness, following a bold black line separating Mark 16:9-20 from the rest of Mark:

> The most reliable early manuscripts and other ancient witnesses do not have Mark 16:9-20.

A more deceptive statement cannot be imagined. The facts follow.

	OMIT: MARK 16:9-20	INCLUDE: MARK 16:9-20
EARLY WITNESSES		
1st Century	None	Papias
2nd Century	Ammonius Saccus	Justin Martyr Irenaeus Tertullian Tatian's *Diatessaron*
3rd Century	Clement Origen Coptic (Egyptian)	Hippolytus Council of Carthage Vincentius Sahidic Version *Acts Pilati*
MANUSCRIPTS		
4th-15th Century	1 cursive 2 uncials (These include Aleph, B and one 12th century cursive; actually B left a long space indicating its parent contained the verse.)	600 cursives 18 uncials

Bruce Metzger, co-editor of the UBS 3rd edition and author of its companion *A Textual Commentary on the Greek New Testament* says:

> The traditional ending of Mark, so familiar through the AV and other translations of the *Textus Receptus* is present in the vast number of witnesses. . .[158]

The only "witnesses" who exclude it are the Alexandria, Egypt line, initiated by Ammonius Saccas, who was cited by Mme. Blavatsky as the 'founder' of her Luciferian Theosophy. As early as A.D.180 Irenaeus wrote of the Docetic heretics who used this corrupt and shortened Gospel of Mark because they believed that the complete gospel emphasized the *bodily* resurrection of Christ too much.

The author of the most intensely researched volume on the subject, *The Last Twelve Verses of the Gospel of Mark: Vindicated Against Recent Critical Objections*, comments regarding notes, black line and brackets in new versions:

> [These are] not for learned readers certainly. . .[S]cholars know something more about the matter. Can it then be right still to insinuate unto unlearned minds distrust?[159]

Likewise overwhelming is the textual evidence for the inclusion of "he was parted from them and carried up into heaven. And they worshipped him" (Luke 24:51,52).

OMIT: LUKE 24:51, 52	INCLUDE: LUKE 24:51, 52
Aleph, D (Actually Aleph only omits "carried up into heaven")	P75, (earlier than Aleph or D), Aleph^{c}, A, B, C, K, L, W, X, Delta, Pi, Psi, 063, f1, f13, 28, 33, 565, 700, 892, 1009, 1010, 1071, 1079, 1716, 1230, 1241, 1242, 1253, 1344, 1365, 1546, 1646, 2148, 2174. It is also in Tatian's 2nd century *Diatessaron*. Additionally, Luke's opening statement in Acts says he included the ascension in his Gospel.

Here the NASB omits 'and was carried up into heaven' based on the two manuscripts on the left. Their note excuses this omission stating, "Some mss add, and was carried up into heaven." In fact, it should say, "most mss add." The NASB follows Hort's Greek text here, however. He, like Alice Bailey, calls Luke 24, merely "a separation from the disciples at the close of a Gospel."[160] The NASB omits "And they worshipped him" based on manuscript D alone!

The Holy Spirit included the record of Christ's ascension in two Gospels, Luke and Mark, because, as Jesus said, "in the mouth of two or three witnesses every word may be established." (Matthew 18:16) As scholars know, "Basing opinions on a single verse—i.e., proof texting—frequently leads to error."[161] Even KJV opponents admit that this is the case. Carson concedes:

> [W]ould that not place the doctrine in jeopardy. . .Yes, I suppose it would.[162]

TWENTY - SEVEN

The Final Blow

[W]ho convinceth me of sin?

Christ's question is answered in Psalm 39:8-10—the foolish.

[M]ake me not the reproach of the foolish. I was dumb, I opened not my mouth, because thou didst it. Remove thy stroke away from me: I am consumed by the blow of thine hand.

Only the foolish reproach him, yet no one can convict him of sin. Who accuses Jesus Christ of sin?

[S]cribes stood and vehemently accused him. Luke 23:10

The new version scribes strike a final blow by charging Jesus with "sin." Their 'frame-up' takes the form of an omission from Matthew 5:22.

NIV, NASB, et al.	KJV
Anyone who is angry with his brother will be subject to judgement.	That whosoever is angry with his brother **without a cause** shall be in danger of judgment.

The accusers advance quickly to the occasion when Jesus angrily overthrew the tables of the money changers (John 2:15). They point also to the time the religious leaders rebuked Jesus for healing on the Sabbath and he had looked round about on them with anger (Mark 3:5). The footnote in one reference bible begins:

> According to some this would prove that Christ was not sanctified and that he had the 'old man' in him. . .[163]

The clause, "without a cause," is in the vast majority of manuscripts and is witnessed to as early as A.D.150 by Tatian and A.D.150 by Irenaeus. Westcott, however, omitted the clause because he believed Christ had sinned.[164] So the 'weak' Jesus, appearing in movie theaters in *Jesus Christ Superstar* and *The Last Temptation of Christ*, appears in the new version, as well.

NIV, NASB, et al..		KJV
he himself is subject to weakness	Heb.5:2	he himself also is compassed with infirmity.

The Nazarene

J.I. Packer warns Christians to watch for "any fragmenting of the seamless robe of scriptural testimony to Jesus' person and place."[165] Occultists have perennially used the title '*The* Nazarene' or 'Jesus the Nazarene' to place him in a limiting context. Representative is the Rosicrucian book *Science of the Soul* which uses the title dozens of times.

> Jesus the Nazarene was the man of flesh and sorrow. While Christ or the Christ is the divine Spark having attained Conscious Individualization as a result of Cosmic Illumination. . .[T]he Nazarene [is] the Initiate of the Essenes.[166]

In the New Testament, the term is never used except by an "accuser of the brethren" who calls Paul "a pestilent fellow. . .a ringleader of the sect of the Nazarenes." (Acts 24:5) Acting like Satan's 'second' in this duel of words, new versions call Jesus 'the Nazarene' a dozen times; it is a blow to the ears of anyone familiar with the use of this term as a 'weapon' by New Age writers. (The inconsistent translation of the word 'the' by new versions (e.g., Acts 26:9) further points to their complicity.)

NASB et al.		KJV
Jesus Christ the Nazarene	Acts 4:10	Jesus Christ of Nazareth
this Nazarene, Jesus	Acts 6:14	Jesus of Nazareth
JESUS THE NAZARENE	John 19:19	JESUS OF NAZARETH

The Straw Man

The reader, at this point, may wonder what response new version advocates give when presented with evidence, such as the preceding over 100 instances in which the deity of Christ is avoided. D.A. Carson, a most forward new version advocate, responded in his book and elsewhere:

> This theory is being presented in popular literature to pastors and laymen everywhere, many of whom have never read a rebuttal at the same level and who are not equipped to do the more advanced work that demonstrates the theory to be false. The KJV translators obscured the N.T. witness to that truth [the deity of Christ]. . .[I]f we compare all of the verses of the new testament that can be translated in such a way that they directly call Jesus God, we would find that the KJV missed half of them.[167]

He proceeds to give, as "advanced work," a small chart from the promotional brochures used to 'advance' the sale of new versions. It quickly becomes apparent that he must mean—'advanced' con artistry not 'advanced' scholarship. The chart is composed of only eight verses, which he calls, "all the verses of the New Testament that can be translated in such a way that they directly call Jesus, 'God'." (He must be using a new version.) Books such as *Nave's Topical Bible* or Lockyer's classic *All the Doctrines of the Bible* do not even mention five of these verses under the heading 'Deity of Christ'. However, these books do cite many of the verses covered in this book which are omitted by new versions.

The following is an abridgement of the trumped-up chart used by new version publishers and Carson.[168]

VERSES THAT IDENTIFY JESUS AS GOD

	John 1:1	John 1:18	John 20:28	Rom. 9:5	2Thess. 1:12	Titus 2:13	Heb. 1:8	2Pet. 1:1
KJV	Yes	No	Yes	Yes	No	No	Yes	No
NIV	Yes	Yes	Yes	Yes	No	Yes	Yes	Yes
NAS	Yes	Yes	Yes	Yes	No	Yes	Yes	Yes

The KJV's four out of eight verses marked 'No', to which Carson points to support his claim that "the KJV missed half" of the verses on Christ's deity, prove to be straw men which fall with a touch of scholarly inspection. The KJV expresses the deity of Christ in **all** eight.

1. John 1:18: a "begotten God" or "begotten Son" was covered in chapter 23. John 5:17-26 proves the KJV title "Son" makes Jesus Christ "equal with God."

2. II Thessalonians 1:12: **All** versions read "our God and the Lord Jesus Christ." The originator of the chart thinks a comma should be added. The title 'Lord', omitted 12 times in new versions, proves his deity. (see chapter 22)

3. Titus 2:13: **All** Greek texts have the wording of the KJV, "God and our Saviour Jesus Christ." None render it as the new versions do.

4. II Peter 1:1: Lewis Foster, NIV and NKJV committee member, reveals *why* new version editors insert Christ's deity in Peter and Titus, yet removed it nearly 100 other places.

> Some would point out that in passages in Titus and II Peter, the expression of the deity of Christ has been strengthened by renderings even in liberal translations. What many do not realize is that even here the strong affirmation of deity is used to serve a purpose. The liberal translator ordinarily denies that Paul wrote Titus or that Peter wrote II Peter. He points to the very language deifying Jesus as an indication of the later date of these epistles when Paul and Peter could not have written them.[169]

5. The expression "God and our Saviour Jesus Christ" in Titus 2:13 and II Peter 1:1 follows the same grammatical construction used to express the deity of the Father in Galatians 1:4, I Thessalonians 1:3 and Philippians 4:20—"God and our Father." II Thessalonians 1:12, Titus 2:13, and II Peter 1:1 are called *hendiadies,* from the Greek *hen dia dyoin,* 'one by two'. Grammatically it is the "expression of an idea by two nouns connected by *and,* instead of by a noun and an adjunct. It would be like introducing one's spouse as "my wife and best friend."

6. In addition to the 100 or so verses which deny the deity of Christ, new versions add words to Jude 25 to give the impression that Jesus is not God.

NIV, NASB, et al.	KJV
God our Savior. . .through Jesus Christ our Lord.	God our Saviour [Our Saviour is Jesus; therefore Jesus is God.]

Standing Room Only

This section was crowded with quotes showing new versions and their editors couched cozily with cultists and New Agers. *Understanding the Cults* by Josh McDowell clears up the reason for their concurrence.

> The Jesus of the cults is always someone less than the Bible's eternal God.[170]

After seeing the blows the scribes bring to this "eternal God," it is no wonder they conclude in John 4:12:

> You are not greater than our father Jacob, are you? NIV, NASB et al.

The scribes suddenly switch from "scornful" seats to "Satan's seat." The Old Testament reveals that the "depths of Satan," the most depraved of his acts, involves getting pleasure from watching others suffer (Ezekiel 32:31). His alliance is with those, like the audience in the Roman Coliseum, who gawked as God's people were liquidated by the lions. The deep-seated degeneration of the scribes is seen in Matthew 27:33-44, where they are seen "sitting down," glaring from the grandstand at Christ. "They watched him" in agony and anguish on the torture tree. The scribes moved from their "uppermost seats" to the top seats in Satan's stadium of sadism.

Soon the scene will shift as their seats pass out of sight and they must "stand before God" —seated on his throne.

> And I saw a great white throne, and him that sat on it from whose face the earth and the heaven fled away; and there was found no place for them. And I saw the dead small and great, **stand** before God. . .Revelation 20:11, 12

TWENTY - EIGHT

The Godhead's Gone:

The Father, the Word and the Holy Ghost

My Name JEHOVAH

The attack on the deity of Jesus Christ is accompanied by an equal assault on the other two persons of the Godhead: the Father (JEHOVAH) and the Holy Ghost.

> [I]n the latter days ye shall consider it perfectly. I have not sent these prophets. . .which think to cause my people to forget my name. Jeremiah 23:20-27

New Agers say, "[Y]our Jehovah. . .we will never accept him."[1] So NIV editor Kenneth L. Barker bows to their bidding saying, "It is unfortunate that the name was translated. . .Jehovah."[2] The NKJV and most new versions, in deference to world ecumenism and courting a world market (e.g., *The New 'International' Version*) have removed any trace of the name JEHOVAH and have replaced it with a title, "the Lord".

NIV, NASB	KJV
Lord	JEHOVAH

The identity of the God we worship is of paramount importance. In this fallen world, speaking of one's Lord can have multiple meanings. In I Corinthians 8:5, Paul writes regarding the heathen pantheon.

> For though there be that are called gods, whether in heaven or in earth, (as there be gods many and **lords many**,) But to us there is but one God. . .

Hindoos worship Lord Shiva, Lord Krishna, and Lord Narayana. Closer to home, the rock group Venom extols 'Lord Satan'. Although Christians know that there is "One Lord" (Ephesians 4:5) yet, "some have not the knowledge of God" (I Corinthians 15:34). In exclusively using the term "the Lord," new versions have created a generic religious document. Since only the title is given, anyone of any religion can 'plug in' the name of their lord. This generic 'Lord' often replaces the Lord Jesus Christ in the New Testament as well.

NIV, NASB, et al.		**KJV**
the Lord	Acts 19:10	the Lord Jesus
the Lord	I Cor. 16:22	the Lord Jesus Christ
my name Lord	Ex. 6:3	my **name** JEHOVAH
. . .Lord. . .	Ps. 83:18	That men may know that thou whose **name** alone is JEHOVAH, art the most high over all the earth.

The name JEHOVAH comes from the Hebrew Tetragrammaton, JHVH, which appears thousands of times in the Old Testament. It is rendered "LORD" most of the time, because the Hebrews feared profaning the name of God and violating the Third Commandment. There are seven instances (two above, five following) when the context mandates "JHVH" be expressed explicitly as the name "JEHOVAH".

NIV, NASB, et al.		KJV
. . .the LORD	Gen. 22:14	called the **name** of that place Jehovah-jireh
. . .the LORD	Ex. 17:15	called the **name** of it Jehovah-nissi
. . .the LORD	Judg. 6:24	called it Jehovah-shalom

The final two cases involve the use of two words which can not be rendered "Lord Lord" and be true to the existence of two *different* words in the originals.

NIV		KJV
. . .the LORD the LORD. . .	Isa. 12:2	for the LORD JEHOVAH is my strength and my song
. . .the LORD the LORD. . .	Isa. 26:4	for in the LORD JEHOVAH is everlasting strength
(The NASB translates JHVH as God here even though they translated it as LORD elsewhere!)		

Hebrew or Greek Old Testament?

The use of the word JEHOVAH by the KJV is based on the Hebrew Masoretic text since, "unto them were committed the oracles of God." (Romans 3:2) The Greek Old Testament, on which new versions base their use of the title "the Lord" (*kyrios*), is now questioned since the discovery of papyrus number 266 now kept by the Societe Royale de Papyrologie du Caire. It retains the use of the Tetragrammaton even within the context of a Greek version. All well respected Greek-English lexicons state emphatically that the use of these two Greek words by the Greek manuscripts is wrong and is used in place of the correct rendering, "JEHOVAH".[3] The preface to both the NASB and NIV have sheepish admissions of their malfeasance regarding the accurate translation of these verses. The

KJV is also the only bible that always distinguishes between the Hebrew *Adonai* and *JHVH* , using 'Lord' for the former and 'LORD' for the latter.

Nameless God of the New Age

ANTISEMITISM

Internationalists and humanists have always protested what appears to be ethnocentricity in the Old Testament. JEHOVAH is the name of the Jewish national God. More specifically, the name was used predominantly when God was speaking to the descendants of Abraham, Isaac and Jacob in fulfillment of the promises and covenants God had made earlier. Why, they ask, would God select one small group, the Hebrews, with which to have his exclusive dealings. Surely, they claim, the gods of other nations are simply culturally modified manifestations of the same God. Consequently, anthropologists speak of JEHOVAH as a 'tribal god'. The anti-Semitism seen elsewhere in the Greek Old Testament (LXX) rears its ugly head again in these new 'international' versions. Globalists regard the State of Israel as ultranationalist, a position not in keeping with their plans. A version made to be sold to a broad world market could not honor Israel's JEHOVAH God.

PANTHEISM

Replacing "JEHOVAH" with "The Lord" fits perfectly into the pantheistic picture the New Age is trying to paint. The personal name, JEHOVAH, speaks too clearly of the external God of Christianity and so opposes their *Metaphysical Bible Dictionary's* 'I am God' philosophy.

> The Hebrew Jehovah. . .means external ruler. Bible students say that Jehovah means, '. . .the self-existent One'. . .[W]e should read "I am." It makes a great deal of difference whether we think "I am" self-existence is within or. . .master without.[4]

The nameless god of the New Age, has edged JEHOVAH off the page. Blavatsky writes:

> [T]he spirit calling itself Jehovah [is not]. . .the One who is in reality. . .nameless.

CUNNINGLY DEVISED FABLES

JEHOVAH is unacceptable to the New Age because, "The Gnostics. . .Brahmanism. . .and Buddhism taught that the Old Testament was a revelation of an inferior, a subordinate deity."[5] The "cunningly devised fables" (2 Pet. 1:16) taught to New Agers include the following:

1. The Hindu *Vedas* contain a mythological narrative recounting a cruel god (JEHOVAH), whose wife Tara, representing mankind, is kidnapped, enlightened and initiated into the mysteries by the Ushanas of the planet Venus (Lucifer).

2. That story was re-cast by the Ophite Gnostics who taught that the Celestial Virgin created Ilda-Booth (JEHOVAH), who in turn clumsily created the world. (The title 'The Mother of God' is rooted here.) *She* came to the rescue by sending the serpent.

3. The Gnostic Nazarenes had a fable in which Ferho created Fetahil (JEHOVAH).

4. The Jewish Kabalists and Hillel placed the imaginary Ain Suph as the creator of JEHOVAH.

The final encore for the dethronement of JEHOVAH can be seen in the fiction penned by the New Age.

> The appellation Sa'tan, in Hebrew Satan, an Adversary. . . belongs by right to the first and cruelest adversary of all the other Gods—Jehovah; not to the Serpent, which spoke only words of sympathy and wisdom. . .It is the Lord God, evidently who was the real cause of all the mischief. . .The serpent, moreover, is not Satan, but the bright angel, one of the Elohim clothed in radiance and glory who—promising the woman if they ate of the forbidden fruit, 'Ye shall not surely die'—kept his promise and made

> man immortal in his incorruptible nature. . .; thus showing that the Bright Angel Lucifer is the light and giver of immortality, and as 'Enlightener'. . .in the original Hebrew. . .it becomes easy to see that Jehovah and Satan are one and the same in every particular.[6]

As a sequel to these delusions, the New Age blasphemously calls JEHOVAH, "the Great Deceiver," "Cain," "bisexual," as well as "Baal," "Pan," and "Moloch."[7] No wonder he had to be removed from the new versions and severed from the glowing tributes rightly due him—just as Lucifer's name was removed from the caustic accusations which are his due.

If someone were to pose the query, "Who is JEHOVAH?" or "Who is Lucifer?" the upcoming generation of Christians will have no biblical basis for their answer. Instead they will be compelled to rely on the distorted images presented in secular sources.

The Trinity

When the Hebrew *shema* declares, "Hear, O Israel, the LORD our God is one LORD:" (Deuteronomy 6:4), it signifies that JEHOVAH our *Elohim* [Gods] is one [*echad*] JEHOVAH.'

Elohim is a plural noun. The word "one" (*echad*) also allows plurality, as seen in Genesis 2:24, Exodus 36:13, or II Samuel 2:25. Other Old Testament references to God are also plural. (e.g., Psalm 149:2 'maker', Eccl. 12:1 'creator', Isaiah 54:5 'husband', Genesis 3:22, 1:26, 11:7, Isaiah 6:8 'us')

Yet Elohim [Gods] says, "I AM THAT I AM" (Exodus 3:14)—One God. This Trinity is expressed in Isaiah 48:12-16.[8]

> Hearken unto me, O Jacob and Israel, my called; I am he; I am the first, I also am the last. Mine hand also hath laid the foundation of the earth. . .from the time that it was, there am I: and now the Lord GOD, and his Spirit, hath sent me.

New versions not only sabotage this key Old Testament verse, but further clear Satan's path to the throne by dissolving four of *the* most significant New Testament verses on the Trinity.

NIV, NASB, et al.		KJV
divine nature	Rom. 1:20	Godhead
Deity	Col.2:9	Godhead
divine being	Acts 17:29	Godhead
OMIT	I John 5:7,8	For there are three that bear record in heaven, the Father, the Word, and the Holy Ghost: and these three are one.

Scribes who seize such scriptures escort this 'divine being' to the throne—left vacant as they omit the Godhead: Father, Son and Holy Ghost. The dark shadow of this 'being' keeps those following him from seeing that these doctrinal gaps are his traps. (Tripped up as the Trinity is taken from its place are 'Christians' like John. He tried to convert a Jehovah Witness to Christianity, but could *not* prove the Trinity to them. The trap took him instead, as *they* then converted *him*.[9])

The verse (I John 5:7+8), omitted by new versions, is called "the famous Trinitarian proof text" (Zondervan's *Words About the Word*).[10] Now that *the proof* has been removed, the spoof can proceed. The verse was omitted 100 years ago by Westcott and Hort's 'New' Greek New Testament. The J.W's of that day saw in this 'New' Greek, a text to "promote the doctrine of the Watchtower."[11] To this day their *New World Translation* begins:

> [A] modern language translation of the Westcott-Hort Greek text.[12]

With this Greek text, J.W's and cultists of every creed can claim:

JEHOVAH WITNESSES	THE WAY INTERNATIONAL
"There is no authority in the Word of God for the doctrine of the Trinity of the Godhead."[13] Charles Taze Russell	"If the Bible had taught that there is a Christian Trinity, I would have happily accepted it."[14] Victor Paul Wierwille

Now that new versions, like the NIV and NASB, use the Westcott-Hort 'New' Greek Text, Christians sound like cultists.

CULTS	APOSTATE CHRISTIANITY
"This cannot rationally be construed to mean that the Father, the Son, and the Holy Ghost are one in substance and in person. There are three Gods. . . united in **purpose**."[15] *Mormon Doctrine*	"Many people conclude that the Father, the Son and the Holy Spirit are all one. You can think of God. . .as 3 different persons. . .their oneness pertaining strictly to their being one in **purpose**."[16] Jimmy Swaggart

Spiritualists (the term ascribed to Westcott by his son) believe, "The doctrine of the Trinity seems to have no adherents in advanced circles of the spirit world."[17] Hort's hostility to I John 5:7+8 haunts his writings. "It could be gotten rid of. . ," he stabs.[18]

Today one NIV editor admits, "It is the strongest statement in the KJV on the Trinity."[19] So out it goes from the NIV; its omission is masked to readers because the NIV steals some of verse 8 and calls it verse 7. The NASB's slight of hand instead slipped out some of verse 6 and calls it 7. For 100 years the 'Master Magician' has mesmerized his 'captive' audience with this type of legerdemain. His hex always sounds EXACTLY the same.

LUCIFERIAN	NIV EDITOR
"This verse. . .is now known to be spurious. It is not to be found in any Greek manuscript save one. . .In the first and second editions of Erasmus, printed in 1516 and 1519, this allusion to these three heavenly witnesses is omitted; and the text is not contained in any Greek manuscript which was written earlier than the fifteenth century."[20] Blavatsky 1880's	"There can be no doubt today that the words are not a part of the original text of I John. . .it has no basis in the Greek text. . . Erasmus did not leave it in his first edition of the Greek New Testament (1516) or his second (1519). . .The passage is found in the text of one other manuscript (fifteenth century)."[21] Ralph Earle 1980's

	UBS/NESTLE GREEK EDITOR
	"That these words are spurious. . .is certain. The passage is absent from every known Greek manuscript except four. . ."[22] Bruce Metzger

With words, they hope to wave the wizard's wand and levitate these weighty lines from the bible. Just as the missing hare from the hat hides up someone's sleeve, so the omission of this verse from many Greek manuscripts is an error by scribes—naive or deceived. 1.) The *naive* fell prey as their eyes went astray (a *homotoleleuton*), skipping from the "three that bear witness" in verse 7 to the "three that bear witness" in verse 8. These verses which reiterate, separate the lines which scribes failed to translate—a very common scribal error. 2.) The *deceived* determined that the verse was an addition, by members of a sedition, such as the Monarchists, Modalists, Noetists, Patripassians or Sabellians—all five run, like the Unitarian, in a direction, which sees God as only *one* person.

However 'the Magician' can't keep the rabbit hidden for long. The testimony of early writers, the great mass of Old Latin and Vulgate manuscripts, the necessities of Greek syntax and the cry of the priesthood of believers, all mandate its inclusion in the text.

1.) Early evidence includes:

Versions: Old Syriac A.D.170, Old Latin A.D.200, Vulgate: 4th and 5th century, Italic: 4th and 5th century. ***Writers***: Tatian A.D.150, Tertullian A.D.200, Cyprian A.D.225, Athanasius A.D.350, Pricillian A.D.350, Vadmarium A.D.380, Cassian A.D.435, Jerome A.D.450, Cassiadorius A.D.480, Vigilius A.D.484, Victor-Vita A.D.489, Fulgentius A.D.533, PS Athanasius A.D.550. ***Writings***: *Liber Apologeticus* A.D.350, Council of Carthage A.D.415.

The fourth century manuscripts, Aleph and B, which are used to discredit the verses, are no earlier than documents, such as the *Liber Apologeticus* (4th century) which contain them. Even 'New' Greek editor Bruce Metzger admits:

> [It] was quoted by Latin Fathers in North Africa and Italy as part of the Epistle and from the sixth century onward it is found more and more frequently in manuscripts of the Old Latin and Vulgate.[23]

Another 'New' Greek editor, Kurt Aland, concedes:

> Theoretically the original reading can be hidden in a single manuscript thus standing alone against the rest of the tradition.[24]

Author of *Harvard Theological Review's*, "Introduction to the Manuscripts of the New Testament" and Oxford University's *The Greek New Testament*, R.V.G. Taskier agrees saying:

> The possibility must be left open that in some cases the true reading may have been preserved in only a few witnesses or even in a single relatively late witness.[25]

2.) The sentence structure as it stands in the Nestle/UBS Greek is wrong.

> The masculine article, numeral, and participle HOI TREIS MARTUROUNTES, are made to agree directly with the three neuters, an insuperable and very bald grammatical difficulty. If the disputed words are allowed to remain, they agree with two masculines and one neuter noun HO PATER, HO LOGOS, KAI TO HAGION PNEUMA and, according to the rule of syntax, the masculine among the group control the gender over a neuter connected to them. Then the occurrence of the masculines TREIS MARTUROUNTES in verse 8 agreeing with the neuters PNEUMA, HADOR, and HAIMA may be accounted for by the power of attraction, well known in Greek syntax.[26]

(Detractors excuse the difficulty asserting that 'personalization' caused a gender change. This did not occur in verse 6, so there is no basis for stating that it occurs in verse 8.)

The *real* reason for the omission of the Trinity: the Father, the Word, and the Holy Ghost in I John 5:7+8 becomes apparent in a verse which follows it.

> This is the true God. . .I John 5:20

The Holy Spirit or the Spirit of the New Age

The third person of the Godhead, the Holy Spirit, has had his 'Holy' identity transformed, just as the Father and the Son have—all to meet the demands of a One World Religion that worships "a new god." New Age writer Vera Alder identifies with 'the Spirit' of the New Age.

> Let us steer our lives by the light of the Spirit.[27]

The author of *The Aquarian Gospel* says: "[M]en of this new age. . .message bearer of the Spirit age. . .take up our pen and write."[28] Unitarian editor of the 'New' Greek Text, Vance Smith heeds the call and urges new versions to replace the 'Holy Ghost' with 'the Spirit'.[29] The changes arise from 'ecumenical' pressures not from Greek manuscript evidence.

NIV, NASB, et al.		KJV
1. the Spirit	Acts 8:18	the Holy Ghost
(The earliest papyri (P45 and 74) say "Holy Ghost.")		
2. the Spirit	Rom. 15:19	the Spirit of God
(The earliest papyri (2nd century P46), Aleph, Nestle's 26th edition, and the Majority Greek Text agree on the reading, "the Spirit of God." New versions follow *one* 4th century manuscripts, B.)		
3. the Spirit	John 7:39	the Holy Ghost
(The original writing on the oldest papyri (P66) says, "the Holy Ghost.")		
4. the Spirit	Acts 6:3	the Holy Ghost

NIV, NASB, et al.		KJV
5. the Spirit	I Cor. 2:13	the Holy Ghost
6. the Spirit	Matt. 12:31	the Holy Ghost
7. a spirit	Rom. 8:15	the Spirit

Job's rebuke to those who were moved, not by the Holy Spirit of God (Galatians 3:5), but by their human 'spirit' (I Corinthians 2:11) or an unclean 'spirit' bears repeating to those following 'the Spirit of the New Age'.

> [W]hose spirit came from thee? Job 26:4

The New Age 'Spirit' received by many today is promoted by other changes in the new versions. The controversy regarding *when* the believer receives the Holy Ghost is fueled by these changes.

NEW VERSIONS		KJV
[Y]ou will be baptized with the Holy Spirit. If God therefore gave them the same gift as He gave to us also **after** believing in the Lord Jesus Christ.	Acts 11:17	[Y]e shall be baptized with the Holy Ghost. Forasmuch then as God gave them the like gift as he did unto us **who** believed on the Lord Jesus Christ.
Did you receive the Holy Spirit **when** you believed? They answered, '**No**. . .	Acts 19:2	Have ye received the Holy Ghost **since** ye believed? And they said unto him, We have not so much as heard whether there be any Holy Ghost.

Unholy 'spirits' do arise,
among new versions' many lies.
Its no surprise,
we shall advise.
The chapters yet will show their ties.
A Ghostly Guild—their enterprise,
where scribes and 'spooks' can socialize.
Their doctrines often sympathize,
so bible terms they must revise,
'til Satan's plans materialize.

The Men and the Manuscripts

PART ONE

The Men

6000 years ago, or so, the serpent
brought a world of woe,
So on "thy belly thou shalt go,"
a creature cursed and now God's foe.
Now limbless, with no arms to fight,
he charms the Serpent's Scribes to write.

TWENTY - NINE

The Serpent's Scribes

> [T]he scribes. . .feign themselves just men that they might take hold of his words. Luke 20:19-20

"Beware of the Scribes" (Luke 20:46)

Jesus split the curtains on the boundaries of time when asked, "What shall be the sign of. . .the end of the world?" He answered by spotlighting the villain in this last days play, saying:

> Take heed that no man deceive you. Matthew 24:4

Deceivers, striking spiritual death blows, pose *the* most diabolical danger in these last days. In the actor's arena are the scribes, playing the part of "just men." Their company will be 'staging' a morality play for an audience of apostasy. Jesus, however, warns that the true 'plot' is deception. "Ye serpents, ye generation of vipers," was his greeting to the scribes. At this moment the actors are in full costume, disguising "themselves as the apostles of Christ." Kurt Koch writes, "It is one of Satan's specialties to hide under a Christian disguise."[1] But what does a 'Christian disguise' look like? Their writing is *full* of ecclesiastical properties to set the stage for deception. With "whitewashed" words "the scribes. . .indeed appear beautiful outward." (Matthew 23:27) The impersonators "draw nigh unto God with their lips" (omitted in new versions) and "by good words and fair speeches deceive the hearts of the simple." Their repertoire includes the needed repartee, calling "Jesus, the Son of God" or "the Holy One of God," following the devil's script in Matthew 8:29 and Mark 1:23, 24. The worm pops in and out of the apple they offer; we catch a glimpse of it often enough to keep from biting the bait. This book goes backstage behind their dressing room doors, where the real drama's scenery changes from a 'spook' house to a 'crazy' house to a courthouse for murder and heresy.

"Professing themselves to be wise" is also part of their script. "The scribes. . .began to reason" (Luke 5:21) and continue today in the world's longest running play. When Pharaoh, a type of Satan, wanted to mimic the miracles of Moses, he called "the wise men." However, wisdom is not a prerequisite to spirituality; in fact, it gave rise to the devil's demise. True wisdom is beyond the range of the subtle sage (See Appendix C). Jesus said:

> I thank thee, O Father, Lord of heaven and earth, that thou hast hid these things from the wise and prudent, and hast revealed them unto babes: even so Father; for so it seemed good in thy sight. Luke 10:21

Of the Old Testament scribes, God said, "They that handle the law knew me not." Of the new scribes a Dallas Theological Seminary professor repeats, "[C]ommitment has not been shown by many."[2] Lewis Sperry Chafer writes:

> Such religious leaders may be highly educated. . .but if they are not born again their judgment in spiritual matters is worthless and misleading.[3]

An intellectual knowledge of the bible is so distant and far removed from knowing 'him', that Paul shouts across the chasm:

> Where is the scribe?. . .hath not God made foolish the wisdom of this world? I Corinthians 1:20

Some Scribes: Saved Yet Sinning

"All we want is a few good men." This is the slogan of the Marines and the myth merchants of our day. Madison Avenue knows packaging serves as a magnifying glass around the product, exaggerating its value. As Marshall McLuan said, "The medium is the message." Satan capitalizes on Christians whose clean image can be used to sell his soft soap. The scribes who "make clean the outside of the cup" are perfect candidates. Some of the scribes who have served as editors on new versions are saved but sinning Christians for whom the "lusts of the mind" and the "pride of life" have given place to the devil. "Why hath Satan filled thine heart?" were words spoken to a Christian (Ananias) not a Satanist. Moved by the "spirit that now worketh in the children of disobedience," such new version editors join those who, according to Lola Davis, are "*unconsciously* preparing mankind for a World Religion that is compatible with the New Age."[4] [emphasis mine] The Old Testament scribes who "steal my words" rose from "among my people" (Jeremiah 5 and 15). Once again the plunder of God's people will be an 'inside job' as thieves "enter in among you" (Acts 20:30). We are to "watch" for these wolves, not dog their footsteps.

The scribes have "enlarged the borders of their garments" for so long, they are beginning to look like *swamis*. The church has joined the New Age in adopting the Hindu system called *guruvada*, in which, "knowledge by the teacher is exempt from critical analysis."[5] "How better to delude one's followers than to persuade them that they dare not think for themselves," warns Dave Hunt.[6] To "outwardly appear righteous unto men," the scribes today hide their saffron robe under a serge suit. Hunt cautions further:

> It was never God's intent that an elite corps of specialists would be the sole proprietor of biblical truth. . .The saints to whom this faith has been delivered to guard and disseminate are not a special class. . .Uncritical acceptance of whatever Christian leaders teach. . .is the seeds of apostasy.[7]

The sin which "so easily besets us" all does not put these scribes in some category of global iniquity and those of us not so tempted in a sphere of insular virtue. Misdeed and remorse can be the daily diet of Christians who will swallow their pride. (Three key men, grass roots participants in the NKJV and CEV, are now alerting fellow scholars and church members of the problems in those versions, as noted in this book.)

Other new version editors admit that their versions, like sponges, have absorbed the beliefs of the men who have pored over them. Calvin Linton of the NIV Committee, "hazards that the translators own interpretation may color the text or even misrepresent it." Lewis Foster of the NKJV and NIV Committees also concedes:

> Each person has his own beliefs. These are bound to influence his judgement to some degree. If a person claims to be entirely unbiased, he is either fooling himself or trying to fool others. Neither the ancient scribes nor the modern translator can make decisions without being influenced by their beliefs. . .the objectivity of man has its limitations. . .No matter how accomplished the individual may be, he has his blind spots and particular views. . .Study the translators as well as their translations. . .a change may be better understood by knowing the position of the translator. . .whether they are based upon. . .a shift in the theological beliefs of the translator.[8]

Another NIV editor, Ronald Youngblood adds:

> It may be true at times that the NIV translators have been guilty of reading something into the text.[9]

The NIV's Concordance editor also observes:

> Translations do evidence the theological convictions of their translators. . .It is complex because of individuals who favor one Bible over another for theological reasons and publishers who promote one version over another at least partly for economic reasons.[10]

These men are merely mirroring the conclusions of other scholars.

> Some modern translations tend toward the heretical by virtue of the force of the presuppositions that govern the translation.[11] D.A. Carson

> [T]hey desired to make Holy Scriptures witness to their own peculiar beliefs.[12] John Burgon

"Woe Unto You Scribes" (Matthew 23:14)

For many other new version editors, pride has made them slaves to the "king over all the children of pride" (Job 41:34). Carr writes:

> One must keep in mind that scholars are not perfect and scholarly opinion changes often. . .Sometimes the adamant refusal to budge from the previous position is due to a need to maintain reputation.[13]

Chapter 32 gives a view into the woes which befall God's unrepentant foes. This the bible did foresee, but not in 'their' version of the story.

NIV		KJV
OMIT	Matt.23:14	Woe unto you scribes. . . hypocrites!. . .ye shall receive the greater damnation.

Jehoiakim's pen knife cut the word of God (Jer. 36), so God took "his part out of the book of life" (Rev. 22:19) in the genealogy in Matthew 1:11. (Josias was Jechonias' grandfather.) New version editors, who use their 'pen' knife to whittle away at the written word, are like "the scribes" who "came with swords" to seize the living Word. Jesus said, "All they who take the sword shall perish with the sword." Goliath's head was severed by his own sword—in little David's hand. Today's heady 'giant' editors will likewise be stalled by their own statements—documented in this book. "The lips of a fool will swallow up himself." (Ecclesiastes 10:12)

The use of New Age words is one of the 10 warning signs of the New Age, according to *The Infiltration of the New Age.* Scholars worldwide, working in the field of philosophy, have regarded the use of a particular vocabulary term, as an indication of the adoption of the philosophy of the group or person initiating that term. The *Encyclopedia of Religion and Ethics, the* definitive work on comparative religions, uses this method. The adoption of New Age terms and philosophies by new versions editors is compounded by those, "who couple terminology with doubtful practices that have their origin in Eastern mysticism or Western occultism." Dave Hunt sees this as "conclusive evidence of involvement or guilt."[14] Investigation into the lives of the scribes uncovers not only a mystical mind-set but occult practices. The first prod finds the new version squad seancing Hermes, 'The Sacred Scribe of the Gods'.

> For there is nothing covered that shall not be revealed; neither hid that shall not be known. Luke 12:2

THIRTY

The Necromancers

A cannon ball, in the form of a *new* and altered Greek New Testament text, was catapulted in the 1880's by two pirates, Brooke Foss Westcott and Fenton John Anthony Hort; it carries its doctrinal deathblow into the laps of unsuspecting Christians holding translations of this text. These new versions exhibit deep trenches in the text as a result of this barrage. Clefts in the content include the ascension, the deity of Christ, the Trinity, the virgin birth, New Testament salvations (e.g., Paul, the Ethiopian eunuch, the thief on the cross) and an army of other victims. These two swashbucklers approached the written word with a sword much like the soldier who pierced the side of the living Word. The sound of a 'New World Religion' echoes back from these sounding boards framed with the theories and philosophies of Westcott and Hort. The body of standard Christian reference works affirm their pivotal and powerful role in this war of words. Scanning the major works will document the singularity and paramountcy of their role.

John R. Kohlenberger, spokesperson for Zondervan, (publisher of the NASB, *Living Bible*, *Amplified Bible*, NIV, and RSV) is author of a *Hebrew/NIV Interlinear,* as well as, *Words about the Word: A Guide to Choosing and Using Your Bible*. He discloses:

> Westcott and Hort. . .all subsequent versions from the Revised Version (1881) to those of the present. . .have

> adopted their basic approach. . .[and] accepted the Westcott and Hort [Greek] text.[1]

He goes on to salute Westcott's, *A General Survey of the History of the Canon of the New Testament*, saying,"This century old classic remains a standard."[2] Christians may not return the salute, but ask *why* the work of esoterics are "standards" and "classics" for the body of Christ.

Baker Book House, publisher of half-a-dozen modern translations, also prints a bible selection guide entitled, *The King James Version Debate.* Author D.A. Carson admits:

> [T]he theories of Westcott and Hort. . .[are] almost universally accepted today. . .It is on this basis that Bible translators since 1881 have, as compared with the *King James Version*, left out some things and added a few others. Subsequent textual critical work accepted the theories of Westcott and Hort. The vast majority of evangelical scholars. . .hold that the basic textual theories of Westcott and Hort were right and the church stands greatly in their debt.[3]

The error of their textual theories and their recent abandonment by many scholars, in spite of Carson's last comment, will be discussed in a later section. In spite of this increasing elbowroom, their revised Greek text is still almost a mirror image of that used to translate the NIV, NASB, and all other new versions. Dr. E.F. Hills, Princeton and Harvard scholar, impresses, the "*New International Version*. . .follows the critical Westcott and Hort text."[4] Philip W. Comfort's recent *Early Manuscripts and Modern Translations of the New Testament* concedes:

> But textual critics have not been able to advance beyond Hort in formalizing a theory. . .this has troubled certain textual scholars. . .[5]

Even abbreviated histories of the canon, in reference works like *Halley's Bible Handbook* and *Young's Concordance* observe, "For the English speaking world the work of B.F. Westcott has proved of abiding worth."[6] "The New Testament Westcott and Hort

Greek texts, which, in the main, are the exact original Bible words. . ."[7] J. H. Greenlee's *Introduction to New Testament Textual Criticism* (Grand Rapids, Michigan: Wm. B. Erdmanns Publishers Co., 1964, p. 78) adds:

> The textual theories of W-H underlies virtually all subsequent work in NT textual criticism.

Scholarly books, articles and critical editions of the Greek New Testament are slowly abandoning the readings of Westcott and Hort in their 'Newest' Greek texts. Yet the pews are piled high with the W-H offerings like the NIV, NASB and *Living Bible.*

Wilbur N. Pickering, author of *The Identity of the New Testament Text* (Nashville: Thomas Nelson Publishers, 1980), pp. 38, 42, 96, 90) reveals:

> The dead hand of Fenton John Anthony Hort lies heavy upon us. (Colwell) The two most popular manual editions of the Greek text today, Nestles-Aland and U.B.S. (United Bible Society) really vary little from the W-H text. Why is this? Westcott and Hort are generally credited with having furnished the death blow [to the KJV and the Greek Text which was used for the previous 1880 years]. Subsequent scholarship has tended to recognize Hort's mistake. The W-H critical theory is erroneous at every point. Our conclusions concerning the theory apply also to any Greek text constructed on the basis of it [Nestle's-Aland, UBS etc.], as well as those versions based on such texts [NIV, NASB, *Good News for Modern Man*, NEB, L.B., etc.]

H.C. Hoskier's *A Full Account and Collation of the Greek Cursive Codex Evangelism 604* (London: David Nutt. 1890), Introduction, pp. cxv-cxvi) and *Codex B* and *Its Allies—A Study and an Indictment.* (2 vols. London: Bernard Quaritch Ltd., 1914) notes:

> The text printed by Westcott and Hort has been accepted as 'the true text', and grammars, works on the synoptic problem, works on higher criticism, and others have been grounded on this text. . .These foundations must be demolished.

Alfred Martin (former Vice President of Moody Bible Institute in Chicago) says:

> [M]any people, even today, who have no idea what the Westcott-Hort theory is. . .accept the labors of those two scholars without question. . .an amusing and amazing spectacle presents itself: many of the textbooks, books of bible interpretation, innumerable secondary works go on repeating the Westcott and Hort dicta although the foundations have been seriously shaken, even in the opinion of former Hortians.

Since Westcott and Hort are the 'basis' or foundation for the new translations, this chapter will document what objective secular historics say when inspecting these footings. The voices of Westcott and Hort, beckoning from their biographies, will further warn what's gone on 'underground'.

Hermes: Alias 'Satan'

As a Cambridge undergraduate, Westcott organized a club and chose for its name 'Hermes'.[8] The designation is derived from "the god of magic. . .and occult wisdom, the conductor of Souls to Hades,. . .Lord of Death. . .cunning and trickery."

> The medieval legend that witches made the sign of the cross upside down. . .began with worshippers of Hermes. . .To Hermes Trismegister, texts were added later to the growing body of semi-secret devilish arts which commanded more and more attention of European intellectuals. . .Hermes became the god within sought by all religious philosophers of the Gnostic period. Neoplatonist philosophers called Hermes 'the Logos'.[9]

(Westcott and Hort's neoplatonism will be discussed in Chapter 38.) In her *Secret Doctrine*, Luciferian H.P. Blavatsky identifies Hermes as Satan.

> Satan or Hermes are all one. . .He is called the Dragon of Wisdom. . .the serpent. . .identical with the god Hermes. .

> .inventor of the first initiation of men into magic. . .the author of serpent worship.[10]

Blavatsky's logo, a serpent biting its tail, represents Hermes. The portrait that history paints of Hermes looks remarkably like Westcott; they both, "succeed in charming the giant to sleep," "put lies into her mouth," "plunged the Greeks into slumber with the aid of his magic wand, with which he made drowsy the eyes of mortals."[11] Blavatsky's *Theosophical Glossary's* entry on 'Hermes' (which interestingly was written by a 'Brother Westcott') reveals him to be "the sacred **scribe** of the gods."[12]

Author of the *Occult Underground* cites Hermes as the entry point of scholars and philosophers into the occult.[13] Westcott's 'Hermes' club met weekly for three years from 1845-1848, discussing such topics as, the 'Funeral Ceremonies of the Romans', 'The Eleatic School of Philosophers', 'The Mythology of Homeric Poems', 'the Theramines' and numerous undisclosed subjects.[14]

Hermes was also the original 'hermaphrodite', the fusion of sexes in one person. Priests of Hermes wore artificial breasts and female garments.[15] Even thirty five years after his institution of this club, Westcott still presents this New Age concept of androgyny.

> There are differences between male and female character under which, we divine that there lies a real identity, and consequent tendency to fusion in the ultimate ideal.[16]

Were these young classicists perhaps following Plato's lead in his *Symposium*, where he describes homosexual love as the highest kind? One secular historian cites letters between members of Westcott's clubs and refers to the "intensity" of a "homosexual" relationship between members (i.e., Arthur Sidgwick, Frederic Myers); he comments, "I think that homosexuality was not rare among young classicists. . ."[17] The mummy of Hermes has come to life again stalking our generation. Today's cryptic *Metaphysical Bible Dictionary* notes, "The characteristics of man must therefore be masculine and feminine in one."[18] The School of Hermes is today listed as a New Age organization in the English New Age Network magazine.[19] Benjamin Creme, when identifying the New Age 'Christ', christens him 'Hermes' as does Blavatsky.[20]

A clue to the mind-set of Westcott's cohorts is seen in a letter written by Westcott to 'Frederic'. The note indicates Westcott knew Frederic was not at home because he did not smell cannabis, marijuana or hashish on the premises.

> [H]e certainly carried you off in fairy-like fashion. I am not quite sure that I will pardon you till I have a full account of the 'supernatural phenomenon' which must have accompanied your evanishment. It is but to say that I did not smell the odour of hempseed in the house.[21]

The use of mind altering drugs is not reserved to our generation. At this juncture in his life, Hort developed a passion for Coleridge, an opium addict. Blavatsky was addicted to hashish and Westcott was 'transported' by beer. Edmond Gerny, a protege of Frederic Myers, died of a drug-induced overdose; the same drug, chloroform, initiated turn-of-the-century Luciferian Anna Kingsford's delusions.

Channeled Bibles and Doctrines of Devils

The 1990's box office hit "Ghosts", with its all star cast, is steering a generation of movie goers to seances and mediums. The Stanford Research Institute reports that over half of Americans have had contact with ghosts. This figure will swell as federally funded projects, such as Confluent Education, instruct students to 'contact their spirit guide'.[22] The medium's darkened salon has been transformed into a brightly lit television studio which hypnotizes viewers, pulsating twenty fiendish frames per second. Today Los Angeles viewers watch Gerry Brown channel 'John the Apostle' every Sunday at midnight. Cable television in New York sports an entire show devoted to amateur channelers. Mini-series "Out on a Limb" featured channeler Kevin Ryerson. Emmy award winner Sharon Gless 'thanks' her channeler in front of millions of mesmerized viewers.[23] In tracing the recent revival of channeling, scores of history books, as we shall see, point to one origin: Westcott and Hort. These new version authors did not stop with their 'Hermes' Club, but went on to engage in spiritualism and to organize a society called the Ghostly Guild.

> Now the Spirit speaketh expressly that in the latter times some shall depart from the faith, giving heed to seducing **spirits** and doctrines of devils. I Timothy 4:1

The bitter fountain which springs forth from the new bible versions flows from the devils who 'seduced' the scribes. Drinking from the stream of spiritualism has infected these scribes, who in turn contaminate the pages of scripture with "doctrines of devils." The stream spills over blotting their 'bibles', washing away key words and diluting the 'blood' of Christ. The "doctrines of devils,"set forth by the new translations, are a mirror image of those reflected back from the still and stagnant pool filled by today's New Age channeled entities.

> . . .the **spirit** that now worketh in the children of disobedience: Ephesians 2:2

These entities, working the graveyard shift, show themselves to be ready scribes and tale-tellers. The seminal writings of the New Age movement were essentially born of channeling. "Blavatsky's two chief channeled works, *The Secret Doctrine* and *Isis Unveiled,* laid the foundation for the modern New Age belief system." Alice Bailey's twenty-five foundational works were also received from 'spirits'. Numerous other New Age 'bibles', such as the *Urantia Book* and *A Course in Miracles,* came from unfleshly fictionists. The New Age contracted its most recent tainted theology from channeler Jane Roberts who, like Westcott, "began doing research into psychic activity,"[24] and soon after, like Westcott, began writing a 'bible' for the New Age.

The Occult Underground: Address for New Bible Translators

To disentomb the truth about the scribes involved in these translations we will go underground to James Webb's classic *The Occult Underground.* This secular history unearths the roots of the New Age movement in the nineteenth century occult revival. In his opening chapter entitled "The Necromancers," he exhumes the sarcophagus of Westcott and Hort, still haunted by their 'Ghostly

Guild'. In his second chapter, his scholarly shovel shows us Philip Schaff, member of the 'New' Greek Text committee and also chairman for the *American Standard Version* (on which is based the *Living Bible* and the *New American Standard Version*). His photo there among the leaders of the Parliament of World Religions captures the shoulder to shoulder hopes of the New World Religion.(Chapter 33 elaborates.) It is noteworthy that a secular historian of the caliber of Webb, when presented the task of identifying *the* key events, people and organizations of the occult revival, included enterprises initiated by Westcott and Hort and endorsed by Schaff. Webb was perhaps unaware of the connection of these three men with the bible and called them as he saw them. Webb's third postmortem examination along this burial ground traces the monument markings of H.P. Blavatsky. Webb ties together the Western origins of the New Age movement with Blavatsky as one bookend and "the clerical eccentrics," as he calls them, as the other.

> [W]hat the occult was. . .[is] Madame Blavatsky's Theosophy, Eastern religion, astrology, geomancy, the Tarot cards, magic, secret societies. . .the clerical eccentricities over whom we have cast an eye. . .[All] form part of the occult complex. . .[25]

Blavatsky's writings, at the center of the New Age spider web, travel down the various radiating strands shadowing their prey—the seasoned New Ager. The concentric strands with their sticky coating tether the spider's unsuspecting victim—the naive Christian. The blatant occultist and subtle clergy weave Satan's web together to form the trap. Christians are haplessly being caught on the thread that runs through the new bibles. The previous and subsequent particulars offered by this book will hopefully unravel the network before it binds and finally strangles unsuspecting Christians.

The Ghostly Guild: Channeling's Lineage

Westcott and Hort were not only 'Fathers' in the Anglican church but, according to numerous historians and New Age researchers, appear to be among the 'Fathers' of the modern channeling movement. (The Fox sisters along with H.P. Blavatsky were the 'Mothers'.) The group referred to by James Webb as an element in the *Occult Underground* was 'The Ghost Club' or 'Ghostly Guild' launched in the 1850's by Westcott, Hort and Benson. Webb discloses:

> Ghost Society [was] founded by no less a person than Edward White Benson, the future Bishop of Canterbury. As A.C. Benson writes in his father's biography, the Archbishop was always more interested in psychic phenomena than he cared to admit. Two members of the Ghost Club became Bishops [Benson and Westcott] and one a Professor of Divinity [Hort].[26]

Hort writes of his and Westcott's work to set this apparition association in motion.

> Westcott, Gorham, C.B. Scott, Benson, Bradshaw, Laurd etc. and I have started a society for the investigation of ghosts and all supernatural appearances and effects, being all disposed to believe that such things really exist. . . Westcott is drawing up a schedule of questions.[27]

In the very *same* letter Hort chaffs that the bible, extant in his day as the *King James Version* from the Greek *Textus Receptus,* was 'Villainous'.[28] This letter, a foghorn sounded by Father Time to us today, testifies to the foreboding genesis of today's community of translations like the NIV, NASB, NKJV and NRSV. Westcott and Hort's position in the bloodline of the current New Age movement is conceded by Hort's son:

> Hort seems to have been the moving spirit of. . .'the Bogie Club', as scoffers called it, [it] aroused a certain amount of derision and even some alarm; it was apparently born too soon.[29]

Authors of *Ancient Empires of the New Age* see this trend without a son's bias noting, "Once the elite had closed their minds to Biblical revelation, they almost immediately began to fall for every spiritual con game and fringe teaching around."[30] Their contemporaries gave ample warning as Hort admits:

> . . .Macaulay is horrified at the paper. . .During the vacation I distributed some eight or ten 'ghostly papers'. . .I left a paper on my table the other evening when the Ray met here, and it excited some attention, but not, I think much sympathy. Dr. _____ was APPALLED to find such a spot of mediaeval darkness flecking light serene of Cambridge University in the nineteenth century. There were also grave smiles and civil questions; and finally several copies were carried off.[31]

Although Hort referred to evangelical Christians as "dangerous," "perverted," "unsound" and "confused," he was rabidly 'evangelistic' about his 'necromancy' as the bible calls it. Writing to a C.H. Chambers, Hort proselytizes:

> I sent you two 'ghostly' papers; you can have more if you want them, but I find they go very fast and the 750 copies which we printed go by no means far enough. We are promised a large number of well-authenticated private stories, but they have not arrived yet. Our most active members are however absent from Cambridge; to wit Westcott at Harrow and Gordon at Wells. . .[32]

Westcott's son writes, "Westcott took a leading part in their proceedings and their inquiry circular was originally drawn up by him. He also received a number of communications in response." Westcott's "Ghostly Circular" reads, in part:

> But there are many others who believe it possible that the beings of the unseen world may manifest themselves to us. . .Many of the stories current in tradition or scattered up and down in books, may be exactly true. . .[33]

The members apparently had their own 'experiences' and the circular was for eliciting "information beyond the limits of their own immediate circle."[34] Referring to 'the foundations' of the occult revival, another historian W.H. Salter, points to Westcott, Hort and Benson, their guild and circular.

> First mention should be made of spontaneous cases of haunts, apparitions and the like. . .[T]he founders of

> psychical research. . .The Cambridge 'Ghost Society' had collected them by circular.[35]

Toppling over the heap of secular histories which identify Westcott and Hort among the seeds of the present New Age thicket is *The Founders of Psychical Research*, by Alan Gauld. He lists their 'Guild' among the 'Founders'.

> In 1851 was founded at Cambridge a Society to conduct a 'serious and earnest enquiry into the nature of the phenomena vaguely called 'supernatural', and a number of distinguished persons became members.[36]

Pogo sticking through the index of *The Founders of Psychical Research* reveals the following 'company' in which our esteemed bible revisors find themselves.

> Automatic Writing, Benson, Biblical Criticism, Mme H.P. Blavatsky, Clairvoyance, 'Control' Spirit, Crystal-gazing, Charles Darwin, Sigmund Freud, **Ghost Club**, **F.J.A. Hort**, Hypnotism, **'Inspirational' writing and speaking in early British Spiritualism**, C.G. Jung, Levitation, **J.B. Lightfoot**, Mediumship, Mesmerism, Multiple Personality, Plato, Society for Psychical Research, Spiritualism, Swedenborne Society, Synthetic Society, Telepathy, Trance Medium, **B.F. Westcott.**

Westcott's son writes of his father's lifelong "faith in what for lack of a better name, one must call Spiritualism. . ." The subject was, he notes, "unintelligible or alarming to the general." In response to public disfavor regarding his esotericism and liberalism and in light of his position in the 'religious' community, Westcott determined that public involvement in the Ghostly Guild "led to no good."[37] In 1860 and 1861, Hort wrote to Westcott of their mutual concern in this regard.

> **[T]his may be cowardice—I have a sort of craving that our *text* ['New' Greek New Testament] should be cast upon the world before we deal with matters likely to brand us**

> **with suspicion. I mean a text issued by men already known for what will undoubtedly be treated as *dangerous heresy* will have great difficulties in finding its way to regions which it might otherwise hope to reach and whence it would not be easily banished by subsequent alarms. . .If only we speak our minds, we shall not be able to avoid giving grave offense to. . .the miscalled orthodoxy of the day.**[38]

Their subversive and clandestine approach continued, as seen ten years later when Westcott writes, ". . .strike blindly. . .much evil would result from the public discussion."[39] Westcott's son alludes to the shroud of mystery surrounding the continuation of the 'Ghostly Guild'. "[M]y father laboured under the imputation of being 'unsafe'. . .What happened to this Guild in the end I have not discovered."[40]

Rosemary's Baby: The Society for Psychical Research

Historians researching this period reveal that other 'Ghostly Guild' members became its 'front men'. Benson and Westcott were not above stalking their impressionable students to recruit members. Henry Sidgwick, a student of Westcott's and a cousin of Benson's "joined the Ghost Society before he took his degree in 1859; Westcott was then secretary [of the Ghostly Guild] and on his leaving Cambridge, Sidgwick appears to have succeeded him."[41] *The Founders of Psychical Research* reports how the Ghostly Guild spurred Sidgwick's "interest in the phenomena of Spiritualism" and incited his active involvement with them.[42] Sidgwick was among a number whose disillusionment with Christianity was spawned during Westcott's tenure at Trinity College in Cambridge. Author of *The Fabians*, a history of communism and socialism in England, writes:

> In this same period a group of young dons from Trinity College, Cambridge, were also turning to psychic research as a substitute for their lost evangelical faith. . .spiritism as a substitute for Orthodox Christian faith.[43]

Sidgwick himself explains, sounding much like an echo from one of Westcott's lectures.

> Recent historical and textual criticism had shown beyond doubt that most of the evidence for the New Testament miracles (not to mention the Old Testament) can not be unfairly described as remote and hearsay. . .[I]t is quite certainly far weaker than the evidence for, let us say, the miraculous events associated with modern Spiritualism.[44]

The Founders of Psychical Research notes the reaction of orthodox Christians to Westcott's 'crowd'.

> Christianity is about to die of self-inflicted wounds. . .It seemed to conservative Christians quite appalling that at a time when the impregnable rock of Holy Scripture was being undermined by Darwin and his allies, a group of those whose sacred duty should have been to shore it up again had **conspired** to hammer their wedge not under it, but into it. The reactions of the orthodox disgusted Sidgwick and those of his friends. . .He addressed a letter to *The Times* on the subject and was rather surprised that on 20th February 1861 it was published. [It said in part] 'Mr. Westcott expresses it, they love their early faith, but they love truth more.'[45]

The Occult Underground unfolds the flowering of the Ghostly Guild and its transformation through time into the Society for Psychical Research. *The Encyclopedia of Occultism and Parapsychology* lists 'the Ghostly Club' as one in which "members relate personal experiences concerned with ghosts." The snake uncoiled as the S.P.R. embraced "haunted houses. . .the divining rod . . .automatic handwriting and trance speaking. . .mediumship and communication with the dead."[46] Webb elaborates:

> It was a combination of those groups already working independently. . .of these the most important was that centered around Henry Sidgwick, Frederic Myers, and Edmond Gurney, all Fellows of Trinity College Cambridge and deriving its inspiration from the Cambridge University Ghost Society founded by. .

> .Benson.[Westcott and Hort]. . .The S.P.R. was a peculiar hybrid of Spiritualistic cult and dedicated rationalism; the S.P.R. fulfilled the function of Spiritualist Church for the intellectuals.[47]

Rosemary's baby, the S.P.R., concurs in its official history, *The S.P.R.: An Outline of Its History*. by W.H. Salter. It refers to the transmutation of "Westcott, Hort, Lightfoot and Benson's" "Ghostly Guild" into the S.P.R., calling the Ghostly Guild "the parent society," "a society from which our own can claim direct descent" and "the forerunner of so unorthodox a subject as ours." They list their interests as "telepathy, pure clairvoyance, communication from 'some spirit' in or out of the body. . .the nature and extent of any influence which may be exerted by one mind upon another. . .disturbances in houses reputed to be haunted. . .physical phenomena commonly called spiritualistic."[48]

The Ghostly Guild gave birth to the S.P.R. which the author of *Crash Course on the New Age* cites in the lineage of the New Age movement and current channeling craze.

> The evolution from traditional mediumship to contemporary channeling has been gradual. The original spiritualism had its start in 1848. . .Organizations like the Society for Psychical Research in Britain were formed. . .When Russian-born spiritualist medium Helena Petrovna Blavatsky founded Theosophy in 1875, the slow transition toward modern channeling began. . .her two chief works, *Isis Unveiled*, and *The Secret Doctrine* laid the foundation for the modern New Age belief system.[49]

Marilyn Ferguson, author of the *Aquarian Conspiracy*, also cites the S.P.R.'s impact on today's New Age movement.[50] Sidgwick predicted this saying, "I'm pretty confident that the whole scientific world will have accepted this [channeling] before A.D.2000."[51] 'Scientific' is not a word that could be used to describe the work of the Ghostly Guild or S.P.R. during Westcott and Hort's lifetime. "Grabbing the ectoplasm" at seances, as they put it, is no threat to the work of Duke University.[52]

> They had a number of sittings in the early part of 1874 mostly in private circles composed of their friends although occasionally with paid mediums.[53]

Like Benson and Westcott, the "friends" referred to did not all wish to be identified. For example, Sidgwick's fiance, Eleanor sister of England's Prime Minister-to-be, did not list her name on the active S.P.R. roll "for fear apparently that an open connection with so unorthodox a venture might prejudice" the professional position held. "Though not technically a member, I was entirely cognizant of the doings of the society and its councils from the beginning," she writes.[54]

Another 'friend' from the 'Ghostly Guild' was Alice Johnson. She wrote circular questions, learning directly from Westcott's adept example. Her contribution was, "Have you ever, when believing yourself to be completely awake, had a vivid impression of seeing or being touched by a living or inanimate object or of hearing a voice?" She went on from Westcott's 'Ghostly Guild' to become the secretary to S.P.R.'s President, Mrs. Sidgwick. Later Alice became editor of the *Proceedings of the S.P.R.* and finally in 1907 its Research Officer.[55] Other collaborators in the S.P.R. were Fredrick Myers, who wrote on the occasion of the suicide of his S.P.R. 'girlfriend', ". . .and strangely to myself I seemed a shade by shadowy Hermes led. . ." Edmond Gurney wrote for the Society, *Phantasms of the Living*, enumerating the "various psychological states that favour supernormal experiences." One such 'state', chloroform induced mediumship, caused his untimely death by overdose.[56]

Historians write of the importance of Westcott and Hort's 'training ground' provided in the form of the Ghostly Guild.

> It would have been impossible for the new society (S.P.R.) to undertake an inquiry of such a kind or on such a scale if several of its leading members had not already gained previous experience. . .[57]

Westcott's Cambridge cradle evidently nursed *Rosemary's Baby* to a long life. *The Encyclopedia of Occultism and Parapsychology* quips:

> There is a curious irony in the fact that the new premises of the American Society for Psychical Research are housed immediately behind the famous Dakota Apartments in Manhattan, the large Gothic building that was the setting for *Rosemary's Baby*.[58]

The Early S.P.R.'s Friends: Blavatsky and Westcott!

Man, Myth and Magic's prospectus on H.P. Blavatsky haunts us, raking up the past to cue us that the S.P.R. was "not unfavorable to theosophy [Lucifer worship] at the time of its beginning."[59] The S.P.R. historian details:

> In the summer of 1884 Mme. Blavatsky visited England and was interviewed by a committee of the S.P.R. appointed to investigate phenomena connected with the Theosophical Society. The committee was **considerably impressed** by the evidence of Mme. Blavatsky and her friends and in a report, circulated within the society but not published, declared. . .'it seems that there is a *prima facie* case. . .'[60]

A *prima facie* case, according to Webster is, "Evidence sufficient to raise a presumption of fact or establish the fact in question unless rebutted." *The Founders of Psychical Research* reports, "The Sidgwick group had at first been rather impressed with Madame Blavatsky."[61] She was, as documented in other sections of this book, an open Satanist. Her track record at that point (1884) included the occult tome *Isis Unveiled*, the institution of the Theosophical Society in 1875 and the editorship of its newsletter, *Lucifer*.

The One and the 'One Life'

"There is one life. . ."	"There is one life. . ."
B.F. Westcott[62]	H.P. Blavatsky[63]

You are not looking into a mirror. Or are you? Westcott's 'one life' was penned as late as 1891, long after he had finished the

'New' Greek text' and after Blavatsky had published her 'Holy Satan' bible (*The Secret Doctrine*). Their duet is further repeated in their explanation of this 'one life'. Blavatsky gives us the Reader's Digest version, while Westcott co-authors the clergymen's long-winded edition.

"[T]here is one life which has expression in many forms"[64] ". . .the one life is fulfilled in many parts. . ."[65] "To make of life one harmonious whole, to realize the invisible. "[66] Westcott	"There is one life, eternal, invisible."[67] Blavatsky

Chapter 5, 'The One', clarified for the reader what this 'one life' involves. Westcott reiterates by describing it as,

> [T]he connection by which we are bound one to another. . .is found to be more powerful and more far-reaching. It is the element—one element—in the idea of life which has been specially revealed to us in this age.[68]

Today Vera Alder repeats this for her New Age readers in *When Humanity Comes of Age.*

> [E]ach person's consciousness is a cell in the world mind. . .our minds are all linked together across the ethers, because we are all part of one great life and therefore one great mind. . .the one mind life.[69]

The circle of time closes as Alder recommends: 1) Lucifer Publishing Co. [Lucis Trust], publisher of Blavatsky's 'Holy Satan' and 2) Rudolf Steiner, author of *The Esoteric Basis of Christianity.* His comments on "the one life" lead readers to Blavatsky's newsletter *Lucifer*; then he closes the circle with "The Society of Psychical Research."[70]

Blavatsky and Westcott

"[T]hey love their early faith, but they love truth more."[71] B.F. Westcott	"There is no religion higher than Truth."[72] H.P. Blavatsky

To what can we attribute Blavatsky's and Westcott's repeated duets. The historian for the S.P.R. brings additional light on the source of this agreement.

> Two or more of them [Spiritualists] would at about the same time use very similar phrases or allude to the same topic or idea. This in itself would not have been remarkable and could easily have been explained by chance or coincidence if the phrase, ideas, or topics involved had been common place: but this they often were not. . .Moreover a reference to some topic would often be divided between two or more automatists. . .[The phrases come from] some mind or minds outside the group of automatists.[73]

Since both lived at the same time, at times in the same place, and shared common friends, familiarity with one another's works is assumed. Blavatsky refers to B.F. Westcott a number of times in her books, calling him "the best. . .the most erudite. . .such a learned commentator." She quotes his book, *On the Canon,* to support her bizarre beliefs. Blavatsky's main source of reference for denying the tenets of the Christian faith was a book called *Supernatural Religion.* Its support in many cases is Dr. Westcott's textual criticism.[74]

Bob Larson's *Book of Cults* details the tenets of Blavatsky's Theosophy as:

1. Universal brotherhood of mankind
2. Investigation of the unexplained
3. Comparative study of religion, science, and philosophy
4. The religion of self-respect[75]

After reading scores of books and letters written by Westcott, I can say without reservation that those four tenets summarized his belief system, *en toto*. It appears then that Westcott was a theosophist, of sorts, and Spiritualist.

Satan's 'Apostles'

During this period (the 1870's and early 1880's), the bond between the S.P.R.'s Henry Sidgwick and the bible revisors, Westcott, Hort and Lightfoot, became tighter. His sister Mary married Westcott's best friend, E.W. Benson (Ghostly Guild). Sidgwick, a man considerably "impressed" with an open Luciferian and himself experimenting with "automatic writing," was invited by both Westcott and Hort to join two other 'secret societies'. These societies were so exclusive that they both limited their membership to twelve. The first group, 'The Apostles', is listed in the index of *The Founders of Psychical Research* as "extremely select."[76] Hort joined in 1851. His son writes:

> [I]n June [he] joined the mysterious company of the Apostles. . .[H]e was mainly responsible for the oath which binds the members to a conspiracy of silence.[77]

In a letter to Rev. John Ellenton, Hort himself admits the questionable character of the group. He wrote, "I fear you scarcely tolerate my having joined 'the Apostles'." The letter further quips that 'one of the members does not believe *in matter*.' Sidgwick was elected to membership in 1857; *The Founders of Psychical Research* cite this membership as the cause of his rejection of his Christian upbringing. He describes the intensity of the group as "the strongest corporate bond I have known in my life."

> The spirit of the society gradually came to absorb and dominate Sidgwick completely and to influence the whole direction of his life.[78]

Another member, F.D. Maurice, admits 'the Apostles' "determined the course of his whole life also." This 'course' caused him to be expelled from his professorship because of "heresy" discovered in written correspondence between him and Hort.[79] (Chapter 38 will explore the *Encyclopedia of Religion and Ethics'* entry on "Alexandrian esotericism." It cites Maurice, Hort and Westcott as prime examples of "philosophical mysticism.")

Eranus

In 1872 Westcott started another group which he named the 'Eranus'. Sidgwick was, of course, one of the select members, as was another S.P.R. official, Arthur Balfour. Hort also belonged and his son said that it was a "senior Apostles" club. "The originator of the idea was the present Bishop of Durham's" [Westcott]; its members met regularly. Hort's room hosted meetings during 1877.[80]

During this period (the 1870's) Sidgwick was actively involved in seances at "Balfour's townhouse." These seances "composed of their friends," appear to be the same "group of intimate friends" described as the membership of 'the Apostles'.[81] *Who's Who* in 'the Apostles' and Eranus Clubs is as current as the direct mail Christian book catalogue received in my mail today. Members, such as Trench, Alford, Lightfoot, Westcott and Hort, all have books in print today, which the academic and seminary communities list as 'standard works' on the Greek text of the New Testament.[82]

The Council of Twelve

Sidgwick further comments, "The number of the club varied, but never exceeded twelve."[83] Groups of twelve have dominated esoteric organizations perennially. The Rosicrucians, for example, were directed by a council of twelve, of whom six were known and six remain unknown.[84] Today among New Agers, "The Council of Twelve" is being channeled.[85] *The New Age Dictionary* includes a citation for an occult book published in 1900 entitled *The Gospel of the Holy Twelve*.[86] This fixation on groups of twelve, led by a leader, permeates Vera Alder's New Age handbook, *When Humanity Comes of Age*. She sees in her crystal ball a group of twelve men, "of the highest spiritual training," reigning along with the Anti-Christ in the "New World Order." She writes:

> Thus the whole World Government would rest upon the ultimate guidance and influence of the Spiritual Cabinet. .

> .[based on] the Twelve Labours of Hercules, The Twelve Signs of the Zodiac and Christ and His Twelve Disciples.[87]

Westcott would have agreed wholeheartedly. He was chairman of the Christian Union for Promoting International Concord.[88] He saw "the spiritual" advancing to a complete sovereignty over the whole world."[89]

In the 1930's the Eranos Club would be seen as a platform for arch-Theosophist Alice Bailey and mother of the current New Age movement. Webb's *Occult Establishment*, in the chapter "The Hermetic Academy," cites this group's self-stated goals as the study of Theosophy, Mysticism, the esoteric sciences and Philosophies and all forms of spiritual research. He closes saying, "The Eranos Conferences are a compendium of all the elements of the Occult Revival."[90]

New World Order

> The spider taketh hold with her hands and is in kings palaces. Proverbs 30:28

If the false prophet's 'New World Religion', with its fusion of apostate churchmen and esoterics, was being launched into the twentieth century by this circle of comrades, to be sure, the Antichrist's autocracy was escorting the destroyer. Westcott himself writes of his hopes for a 'New One World Government',

> [O]ur hearts are moved when statesmen or students speak with glowing hope of the coming union of nations. . .[91]

The one world reign of the Antichrist is also the dream today of former Assistant Secretary General of the United Nations, Robert Muller.

> By the year 2000 we will be fully into the business of making a new world. . .narrow nationalism will shrink and countries will become like Vermont and California are now.[92]

Hort would agree, calling America as an independent nation, "a standing menace to the whole civilization." He wished, "the American union may be shivered in pieces."[93] Hort's 'Apostles' "had hoped that developments in the social sciences would before long make possible an equitable and frictionless society."[94]

This trial marriage of religion and government took place between Westcott, Hort and Lightfoot, as 'helpmeets'—and their consort in the Eranus Club, Arthur Balfour, upcoming Prime Minister of Great Britain. Balfour, "inspired by reports of human levitation" went on to take the leadership role in the Ghostly Guild's baby, the S.P.R..[95] *The Dictionary of National Biography* cites him as saying, "bring metaphysics back" and recalls his open declaration of his love for contacting 'the dead' and "in our power to communicate with them."[96]

Again we see historians pairing the Theosophical Society and the S.P.R.. *The Occult Underground* cites one historian who,

> . . .saw the early 1880's as a period filled with portents. The many organizations he saw founded—Hyndman's Democratic Federation, The Theosophical Society, The Vegetarian Society, The Society for Psychical Research [S.P.R.], The Anti-Vivisection movement—he characterized as 'tending toward the establishment of mystical ideas and a new social order.'[97]

Arthur Balfour, who was a member of Hort's Apostles, Westcott's Eranus, as well as President of the S.P.R., soon became *the* Prime Minister of England and instrumental in the first League of Nations. New Age planner Vera Alder writes recently:

> The embryonic World Government is potentially already there founded essentially upon the League of Nations.[98]

The temporal power and authority which can follow a league with seducing spirits is the subject of Luke 4:5-7.

> And the devil taking him up into an high mountain, shewed unto him all **the kingdoms of the world** in a moment of time. And the devil said unto him, All this **power** will I give thee, and the glory of them: for that is

> delivered unto me; and to whomsoever I will I give it. **If** thou therefore wilt **worship me**, all shall be thine. Luke 4:5-7

To fulfill this requisite—"worship me," Balfour not only headed the S.P.R., holding the seances at his home, but initiated a group called 'The Synthetic Society' whose goal was to create a 'one world religion'. He invited Frederic Myers of the S.P.R. to join and together they created "The preamble of all religions." It included the dogma, "departed spirits can communicate."[99]

'Synthetic Society' membership was reportedly dominated by proponents of Hegel's dialectical philosophy, which in practice became Marx's dialectical materialism.[100] These strange bedfellows, communism and occultism, are uncovered in *The Fabians*, a book detailing their interconnection in England. According to its authors, Edward Peace and Frank Podmore were instrumental in the genesis of both the S.P.R. and the various Marxist societies of London. Peace referred to the work of Westcott, Hort and Sidgwick's 'Ghostly Guild' and his own Marxist activities as "our common work."[101] Is there, perhaps, an unconscious understanding among these people of the alliance between Satan and those who would seek ruling power and authority?

> . . .and the dragon [Satan] gave him his power and his seat and his authority. Revelation 13:2

The mortar binding fiends and 'fellow travelers' comes into focus in "collective ventures between the S.P.R. and the Dialectical Society." Rather than "resort to a small group of persons called mediums" they "sought to educe supernormal faculties among members" by "thought-transference, table tilting and automatic writing." *The Fabians* mentions the complicity of two S.P.R. presidents, Arthur Balfour and his brother Gerald, with the Marxist harbingers of the day. This connection between England's Spiritualists and Socialists is further seen in Annie Besants *vitae* where the Oxford Movement (of which Westcott and Hort were in sympathy), "Friends of Russia," the Dialectical Society, and finally leadership of Blavatsky's Theosophical Society merge.[102]

Hort's crimson calligrapher's pen jabs of "[M]y deep hatred of democracy in all its forms."[103] "I have pretty well made up my mind to devote three or four years up here to the study of communism."[104] Today New Ager Benjamin Creme predicts, ". . .democracy will disappear."[105] The dialectical dream, with its thesis, antithesis, and synthesis seems to be taking form today with the breakdown of pure communism and pure democracy into a common world socialism. Westcott's dreams, set forth in his book, *Christian Socialism: What and Why,* are coming true.

Conspiracy buffs will prick up their ears to hear, not only of Balfour's esoteric comradeship with Westcott and Hort, but of his membership, beginning in 1881, in another 'secret society' with Cecil Rhodes, multimillionaire and founder of the famous Rhodes scholarship. This society is said to be the germination for the C.F.R. (Council on Foreign Relations). This fetal C.F.R. had an inner circle of three, followed by another circle of three, and so on.[106] The C.F.R., according to 'conspiracy' enthusiasts, blends politicians and international financiers in a brew which, though "reeling like a drunkard" at times, is propelling the nation states toward a one world government. (Bush is a member, as were half (28 of 59) of the major appointees of the Reagan administration.)[107]

The pet name given this sphinx is the 'New World Order', a phrase which peppers our daily diet at increasing rates. President Bush's nationally televised speech before Congress on September 11, 1990, during the Iraq crisis, hailed "The dream of a new world order." Representative Gephart's Democratic response encored these exact words again. United Nations leader Robert Muller continues the litany, calling for a "new world order." On the August 22, 1990 public television news, Henry Kissinger said that the Iraq regime was not cooperating with "the new world order." President Clinton *is* cooperating. As many have discovered, the Latin phrase 'New World Order' foots the U.S. one-dollar bill's all-seeing-eye of Horus (impersonator of Jesus Christ in Egyptian mythology).

The New Age chorus chimes in with esoteric leader Vera Alder's plan for "the building of a new world order."[108] Jeremy Rifkin's *Entropy* spins the new order across the pages of his book like a broken record. *Los Angeles Times* writer, Russell Chandler observes, "But New Agers believe a "New Order" is about to break out of the "old epoch of rationalism. . ." Editor of the *Christian Research Journal*[109] reiterates, "For some New Agers, the Age of

Aquarius is little more than a convenient symbol for the 'new order'.[110]

The 'religious' community 'faithfully' traces the words of this slogan. Pope John Paul II's June, 1990 speech in San Francisco booms this reprise, "Everything must change. Tolerance is the alpha and omega of a new world order."[111] Frighteningly, the NIV changes the words in Hebrews 9:10 from "until the time of reformation" to:

> "until the time of the new order." NIV

Neither the Greek words for "new" nor "order" are here in any manuscript. The Greek word implies 'an improvement', which is expressed well in the KJV. The NIV, more than any other translation I have collated, gives numerous chilling New Age renderings. This should not amaze the reader since the "NIV follows the critical Westcott and Hort text." And in this case, the 'spirit' of Westcott's "glowing hope of the coming union of nations" and his call for "the new order" haunts the NIV.[112]

Should we see as diabolical and prophetic, the inter-participation, inter-membership and philosophical agreement of 'spiritual' and government leaders? As John wrote "many false prophets are gone out into the world" and "there are many antichrists."[113] Baker Book author, Elliot Miller, poses a thought.

> As we consider the Western occult movements that have gathered momentum since the early nineteenth century, we must ask ourselves, if there might be a larger Satanic design than simply leading individual souls astray. While there is a temptation to dismiss these groups as 'fringe', it must be pointed out that:
>
> 1. Satan's objective is to unite the world under a man wholly given over to him, and
>
> 2. [T]he occult world is. . .uniquely Satan's domain then,
>
> 3. [I]t should not be surprising to find occult movements actively engaging in promoting such a world. . .[I]f there are enough. . .correspondences at critical points, his purpose will be furthered.[114]

Revelation 16:13 reveals the specific connection between the trio: 1.) Satan, 2.) the religious false prophet, 3.) the ruling Antichrist—*with* the 'spirits' of the 'Ghostly Guild' and S.P.R..

> [U]nclean **spirits** like frogs come out of the mouth of the **dragon** [Satan], and out of the mouth of the **beast** [Antichrist], and out of the mouth of the **false prophet**.

These frogmen, depending on this trident to prevail, are moving in the direction of the lake.

> And the beast was taken, and with him the false prophet that wrought miracles before him, with which he deceived them that had received the mark of the beast and them that worshipped his image. These both were cast alive into a lake of fire burning with fire and brimstone.
> Revelation 19:20

> And the devil that deceived them was cast into the lake of fire and brimstone where the beast and the false prophet are, and shall be tormented day and night for ever and ever.
> Revelation 20:10

Synopsis: A Family Affair and a Dog Named 'Devil'

The lake of fire for all false prophets and antichrists is a tragedy, for God is ". . .not willing that any should perish" (II Peter 3:9). The spyglass of numerous scholars has given us a birds-eye-view from the crow's nest of this corsair cruising toward 'the lake'. The interrelationship of these nineteenth century 'pirates' is uncanny.[115] It appears that this ship, flying the black flag of the British occult revival, has as its crew a group of friends who shared esoteric philosophies, joint membership in 'secret' societies, and *married one anothers sisters*. Due to Westcott's seniority, he appears to be 'the captain'. Their course is charted on page 690.

Fancy if you will, a shipboard holiday gathering in the galley of Westcott's rover. If everyone was in attendance, the 'secret society' pages *might* read:

ALL IN THE FAMILY!

In attendance was leading Theosophist Lady Emily Lutyens, wife of world renowned architect Sir Edwin Lutyens and granddaughter of occultist and author Bulwer Lytton, Grand Patron of the Rosicrucian Society of England, founded upon the doctrines of Hermes Trismegistus. H.P. Blavatsky called Lytton, "master of my dreams" and plagiarized much of his writings in her *Isis Unveiled*. Lady Emily, as you know, became a Theosophist after years of political activism for the legalization of prostitution. Her sister Constance was unable to attend, serving her fourth sentence in prison for such activism. Lady Emily's interest in Theosophy began when Sir Edwin peaked her curiosity about "a secret cupboard of books which one of his clients always kept locked."[116]

Emily sat next to her sister Betty and her brother-in-law Gerald Balfour, upcoming president of the S.P.R.. He is included in the recent *New Age Dictionary*. The three discussed Betty's recent letter to Emily regarding Emily's current position as 'foster-mother' to Krishnamurti, the Theosophist's would-be 'Christ'. The letter had relayed mutuality of intent. Betty wrote to Emily, "I long for the things you long for. I bless your aims and objects. I believe Krishna to be a very fine and holy being. . .trained from babyhood to believe the Christ *would* inhabit him. . .like the public baptism. . .and Pentecost." Gerald is "deeply interested."[117]

To the right of Gerald sat his sister Eleanor (Nora), also "a firm believer in communication between the living and the dead" and later to be named Honorable President of the S.P.R..[118] To her left was her husband Henry Sidgwick, first president of the S.P.R., Westcott's former student and member of Westcott's exclusive Eranus Club, Ghostly Guild, and Hort's twelve member 'Apostles'. Henry Sidgwick's sister Mary sat between him and her husband Edward White Benson, co-founder of the 'Ghostly Guild'.[119] Hort, on Benson's other side, asked him about a previous letter from Westcott to Benson regarding the possibility of communal living involving the Bensons, Horts, Westcotts" and a few other families."[120] [Westcott called this a "coenobium," a word Webster does not cite but quite predictably is listed in the recent *New Age Dictionary*.]

Arthur Balfour roosted across from his brother Gerald, their sister Eleanor, her husband Henry Sidgwick, [four S.P.R. Presidents], Henry's sister Mary and brother-in-law Edward White Benson. Flanking Arthur Balfour were Westcott and Lightfoot, Eranus comrades. Chides about Westcott's recent 'star status' as spokesmen in recent beer ads were overheard. Westcott talked about the letter[121] Balfour had written informing him of his son's selection, by Balfour, for a crown incumbency.[122] Settled next to her in-law Arthur Balfour, again we retrospect Blavatsky's initiate, Lady Emily.

Sleeping by the fireplace was Westcott's dog who he named "Mephistopheles." The name is that of 'the devil' in the literature of necromancy and magic of the late Middle Ages. [123] *Roget's Thesaurus* lists it among the few synonyms for 'the devil'. Westcott had written to his son, "The dog is far more than a dog to me. He is a symbol. . ."[124]

Holiday Gathering's Goblin Stories

Arthur Westcott recalls his father's tradition of reading Goblin stories at Christmas.[125] (Webster defines a Goblin as "an ugly, grotesque, evil, malignant being or spirit.") Gauld's "Spiritualism in England" explains Westcott's fascination with spirits sent to mesmerize their subjects.

> Along with the interest in mesmerism went an interest in the ghost stories which German occultists had regarded as tying in with the phenomena of mesmerism. . .In 1851 was founded at Cambridge a Society [Westcott's and Hort's]. . .[126]

Salter's S.P.R. history confirms this connection. "[T]hey explored. . .every conceivable type of phenomena which could be described in the words of its inaugural manifesto as mesmeric. . ."

They produced a book, *Phantasms of the Living*, which documented "accounts of apparitions seen or voices heard. . .the basis in fact of the time honored ghost story."[127]

(Historians place the revival of mesmerism directly antecedent to the nineteenth century occult revival. In 1666 a priest named Gassner used "magical powers" to heal. Interestingly, Blavatsky's original name for the Theosophical Society was the 'Miracle Club'; see Revelation 13:14, 16:14, 19:20, II Thessalonians 2:9. Gassner's work influenced Anton Mesmer who in 1766, working with a Jesuit named Hell, experimented with "fixing his eyes upon the subject while he waved the wand of magnets.")

Westcott took the wand and relayed it into the 20th century.[128] Occultist Emmanuel Swedenborg recognized 'spirits' as the source of hypnotic states rather than magnetism. Historians concur:

> Everywhere we find hypnotism and spiritualism identified with each other. . .[S]peaking in tongues and so-forth early formed a characteristic feature.[129]

New Ager Vera Alder sees this as a positive step toward uniting 'Christians' and esoterics.

> Much of this development everywhere has definite connection with the seven Gifts of the Holy Ghost,. . . [A]s man re-awakens to reality, they will be known again and with them he will build an integrated World Organism and a new world order.[130]

This giving over of one's consciousness to another is referred to as 'enchantment' or 'charming' in the bible. It is strongly condemned in Deuteronomy 18:10,11, Isaiah 19:3, 47:9,12, II Chronicles 33:6, II Kings 17:17, 21:6 and Leviticus 19:26. The 'mesmerism' of the nineteenth century became the hypnotism of this century. Scores of observers have witnessed the blank hypnotic stares of audience members at New Age meetings. As the snake charms its prey before the kill, gurus of today, much like Adolf Hitler, hold their audience spellbound.

TV 'GUIDE': Monday 6:30 or Mark 6:30

The reader may feel somewhat 'safe' from the Ghostly Guild's hypnotic 'spirits'. However, a review of the neurobiological "theory of cerebral dissociation" will cause one to pause. It appears television, with its "soothing and monotonous. . .sensory stimulus" coupled with "the fixation of the eyes" and repetitious sound, is a perfect instrument for producing a light hypnosis and thereby "causing highly increased suggestibility in the subject." Brain researchers disclose:

> The brain is composed of innumerable groups of nerve cells, all more or less closely connected with each other by means of nervous links or paths of variable resistance. Excitement of any of these groups, whether by means of impressions received through the sense organs or by the communicated activity of other groups will, if sufficiently intense, occasion the rise into consciousness of an idea. In the normal waking state the resistance of the nervous association paths is fairly low so that the activity is easily communicated from one neural group to another. Thus the main idea which reaches the upper stratum of consciousness is attended by a stream of other subconscious ideas, which *have the effect of checking the primary idea preventing its complete dominance.* Now the abnormal dominance of one particular system of ideas—that suggested by the operator—together with the suppression of all rival systems, is the principle fact to be explained in hypnotism. . .*the essential passivity of the subject* raises the resistance of the associated path. . .One neural disposition is thus isolated, so that *any* idea suggested. . .is free to work itself out in action without being submitted to the checks of the sub-activity of other ideas. . .a comparatively slight raising of resistance in the neural links suffices to secure dominance of the idea suggested by the hypnotizer.[131]

The sensory stimulus of television's pulsating flash of twenty frames per second, coupled with its unnatural and intense sound level, when experienced by a person who approaches its viewing in the typical passive relaxed state, creates neural suppression of the 'idea checking' pathways. For example, the viewer receives and stores the thought, "You deserve a break today," *uncoupled* with *factual* thoughts that normally might accompany its storage in the brain. The suggestibility caused by this state commends one to *extreme* caution given the renegade unregeneracy of most TV 'programming'. (Why do you think they call it 'programming'?)

(At the very least, its commercials have called forth Christian churches that 'satisfy the consumer' rather than those that teach Christians to be 'consumed with the Satisfier'. Many Christians can quote the line following "Monday 6:30" in their 'Guides' but few can quote Mark 6:30, "[A]nd the apostles gathered themselves together unto Jesus," not unto their televisions.[132] This departure into a discussion of television seemed appropriate due to the sad fact that *TV*, more than *NIV* or *NASV*, beckons the Christian from time in the word of God.)

Moving 'Pictures' and Mesmerism

The spiritual implications go beyond our heritage from Noah's son Japeth for 'the lusts of the eyes'. Scientist Sir John Eccles has written, 'the brain is a machine a **ghost** can run.' Disengaging what brain researchers call your 'executive controlling function' allows spirits to play their choice of keys, as it were, on your brain's neurons. The Antichrist will no doubt hypnotize the world, much like Hilter, but on a massive scale. The brain deadening mechanics of modern television will be his 'wand'. To facilitate this, two criteria must first be set in place.

Step One: Everyone needs a T.V.. The mandate for the New World Order states:

> [E]ducation will largely take place through the cinema and television. . .T.V., in color, should be included in the state fixtures supplied to every family.[133]

Step Two: Religious or cultural taboos discouraging this media (moving pictures) or its *modus operandi* (mesmerism) must be neatly tucked away in the archives.

Westcott's 'ghosts', haunting the New Age bibles (NIV, NASB, etc.) do just that. Numbers 33:52 (KJV) exhorts Israel to ". .

.destroy all their pictures and destroy all their molten images." Yet new versions omit 'pictures' and redundantly write, ". . .destroy all their figured stones and destroy all their molten images." Archaeologists and art historians will readily attest to the use of both pictures and three-dimensional images as a means of depiction. The silver laden images of the heathen and pigment laden images of the Middle Ages have been replaced by the filmmakers art. It combines silver, which produces the light reflecting qualities of film, with the colored images, evoking a "worship of the creature. . .more than the Creator."

New versions also eliminate the bible's censure of "enchantment" or "charming." The Hebrew words *cheber, nachash, lat,* or *lachash* may variously indicate such a phenomena. When these words appear in the text, the new translators feign sand blindness (caused by extended use of the Egyptian texts). The NASB committee sees a mirage, reading *gesem, migsam*, or *gasam,* and translate it 'divination'. However, they get 'caught' in II Kings 17:17 when the word 'enchantment' (*nachash*) appears with 'divination' (*gesem*) in the same sentence. Since they cannot say 'divination' twice, they bow to the reality of *nachash's* meaning here and translate it 'enchantment'.

The NIV also wrongly translates enchantment *(nachash)* variously as 'divination' *(gesem)*, 'sorcery' *(kashchaph)* and 'medium' (*ob*). In II Kings 21:6 they incorrectly translate *nachash* as 'divination'. In II Kings 17:17 they translate *nachash* as 'sorcery'. But when *nachash* appears in a sentence along with the *real* word for sorcery *(kashshaph)* or divination *(gesem),* as it does in II Kings 17:17, they translate *gesem* as 'divination' (which is correct) and *nachach* as 'sorcery'. If you care to follow the maneuvering here, you will be aghast at this shell game. Their highly calculated moves leave new version readers right where the New Age wants them—unable to move, "charmed" and "enchanted" by the serpent's moving "pictures." New version editors sit mesmerized too, under the spell of Westcott's Goblin stories in his 'new' Greek text.

THIRTY - ONE

The 'New' Greek Text and Ghosts

. . .the shadow has thickened into a substance[1]

The same Greek text-type was used in the translation of most English versions until the end of the nineteenth century," acknowledges John Kohlenberger III, co-author of *The NIV Complete Concordance.* He further concedes, "Because of numerical superiority, this text type is known as the Majority Text."[2] This is the Greek text from which the *King James Version* was translated. His remark, ". . .until the end of the nineteenth century," refers to the 'New' Greek Text brewed by Westcott and Hort, published in 1881, and used as the broth for the stew in subsequent translations (including Kohlenberger's NIV).

This 'new' text had a sinister start. In 1851, *the year* Westcott, Hort, and Lightfoot began the Ghostly Guild, they set in motion their notion of a 'New' Greek Text. Appendix A chronicles their 30 year involvement in secret esoteric activities *while* they were creating this 'New' text. In the *very* letter in which Hort hatched the 'New' Ghostly Guild, he christened 'villainous' the Greek Text which had, at his admission, been "the Traditional Text of 1530 years standing."[3] Like an echo of Hort's hammer, Westcott pounds:

> [I] am most anxious to provide something to replace them.[4]

'New Testament Scheme'

The words 'New Testament' fit with the word 'scheme' as poorly as the word 'Trinity' fits with the word 'ale'. Yet we shall see Westcott and Hort pairing them all. Hort's son reveals:

> About this time Mr. Daniel Macmillan [the publisher] suggested to him that he should take part in an interesting and comprehensive 'New Testament Scheme'. Hort was to edit the text in conjunction with Mr. Westcott; the latter was to be responsible for a commentary and Lightfoot was to contribute a New Testament Grammar and Lexicon.[5]

"[T]he much scheming" B.F. Westcott was a *soi-disant* used by Westcott to sign a letter. Hort's motive$ may have been a mite more mundane.

> [O]ne is perpetually spending huge sums on things which have no evident connexion with the necessities.[6]. . .This, of course, gives me good employment.[7]

Their correspondence elaborates 'the Scheme' cited in the previous chapter.

> I have a sort of craving that our text should be cast upon the world before we deal with matters likely to brand us with suspicion. I mean, a text, issued by men already known for what will undoubtedly be treated as dangerous heresy will have great difficulty finding its way to regions which it might otherwise hope to reach, and whence it would be banished by subsequent alarms. . .[I]f only we speak our mind, we shall not be able to avoid giving grave offence to. . .the miscalled orthodoxy of the day. . .Evangelicals seem to me perverted. . .There are, I fear still more serious differences between us on the subject of authority and especially the authority of the Bible. . .At present very many orthodox but rational men are being

> **unawares** acted upon by influences which will assuredly bear good fruit in due time if the process is allowed to go on **quietly**; but I cannot help fearing that a premature crisis would frighten back many into the merest traditionalism.[8]

Nip and Snip

The spirits of the Ghostly Guild were aided by spirits of another kind. During the thirty years in which they were laboring on this 'Scheme', their correspondence uncovers 'the spirits' midwifing the birth of the 'New' text. The word 'sober' is gone in new versions and was also missing from the lives of some editors. Did J.B. Phillips' daily doses of sherry incite his intemperate tirades against fundamentalists, calling them "perfervid," "firebreathing" "asses." Westcott's son admits his father was "much drawn to beer." Late in life, he divulged his intemperance and became a spokesman for a brewery.

> His picture together with some of the words spoken by him was utilized for the adornment of the advertisement of a brewer of pure beer. (See Appendix A)

Hort's letter to Lightfoot leaks their use of libation spirits and labile scripture (easily changed).

> But why did you send beer (Trinity Ale) instead of coming yourself. . .Dr. Tregelles. . .found in the possession of the Bible Society some extremely important palimpsest fragments [New Testament Greek manuscripts which have been erased and written over] of the first eleven chapters of St. Luke. . .The marginal catena (chiefly. . .Origen). . .[9]

The result was a 'New' Greek text in which the book of Luke, with its approximately 1000 verses shows 1000 or so changes. As they 'sip and snip', omissions become rampant. The entire text shows nearly 6000 places where 'the spirits' de-materialized the original Greek.[10] Consequently, today's readers of the NASB and NIV and other modern versions, picking up their bibles looking for a spiritual 'pick-me-up', become 'unconscious' of the doctrines which have been diluted or dowsed away.

Lest someone tell you the differences between the real Greek Text and 'New' Greek Text are minor, hear the conclusion of the carvers themselves. Hort crowns the changes in their chameleon with:

> I do not think the significance of their existence is generally understood. . .It is quite impossible to judge of the value of what appears to be trifling alterations merely by reading them one after another. Taken together, they have often important bearings which few would think of at first. . .The difference between a picture say of Raffaelle and a feeble copy of it is made up of a number of trivial differences. . .It is, one can hardly doubt, the beginning of a new period in Church history. So far the angry objectors have reason for their astonishment.[11]

This change in the standard Greek New Testament was very newsworthy upon its publication. Scholars of that time called it, "strongly radical and revolutionary," "deviating the furthest possible from the Received Text," "a violent recoil from the Traditional Greek Text," "the most vicious Recension of the original Greek in existence," a "seriously mutilated and otherwise grossly depraved NEW GREEK TEXT." They further yielded, "the passages in dispute are of great importance."[12]

Dr. G. Vance Smith, a Unitarian who denied the deity of Christ, the Trinity, and the inspiration of scripture, was invited to join Westcott and Hort in working on the revision. When furor arose regarding his participation, Westcott and Hort said they would resign if he was not included. Smith's book, *Texts and Margins of the Revised New Testament*, boasts of his strong influence upon the doctrinal changes in the 'New' text. He answers today's expositors who say the changes are inconsequential.

> [I]t has been frequently said that the changes of translation. . .are of little importance from a doctrinal point of view. . .[A]ny such statement [is]. . .contrary to the facts[13]

Most of these changes stand intact in the most recent versions. Of the underlying text E.W. Colwell, preeminent North American textual scholar and past president of the University of Chicago points out:

> The text thus constructed is not reconstructed, but constructed; it is an artificial entity that never existed.

John Burgon, who was Dean of Chichester and the preeminent Greek textual scholar of the day, said:

> For the Greek Text which they have **invented** proves to be hopelessly depraved throughout. . .[I]t was deliberately invented. . .[T]he underlying Greek. . .is an entirely new thing, is a manufactured article throughout. . .[T]he new Greek Text. . .is utterly inadmissible. . .Proposing to enquire into the merits of the recent revision of the bible, we speedily became aware that. . .the underlying Greek Text had been completely refashioned throughout. It was not so much a [new version] as a 'New Greek Text'. The New Greek Text. . .was full of errors from beginning to end: had been constructed throughout. . .
> [I]t was no part of your instructions to invent a new Greek Text, or indeed to meddle with the original Greek at all. . . [B]y your own confession—you and your colleagues knew yourselves to be incompetent. Shame on. . .[those] most incompetent men who—finding themselves in an evil hour occupied themselves. . .with falsifying the inspired Greek Text. . .Who will venture to predict the amount of mischief which must follow, if the 'New' Greek Text. . . should become used.[14]

Externalization of the Hierarchy

The New Age movement, as we know it today, had its germination in the rise of the spiritualism of the 1850's. Westcott, as we have seen, did his part to seed this virus. The blight began in the 1870's when, as New Agers tell us, the "hierarchy began the process of externalization."[15] (Christian translation: the doctrines of the devils conjured during the spiritualism of the 1850's were spreading.)

The conjurer, B.F. Westcott, did his share in spreading these diseased doctrines during the 1870's. In 1871, the three Ghostly Guild 'medicine men' were invited by the Church of England to lead a committee for the revision of the *King James Bible*. Hort's son calls Westcott, Hort and Lightfoot, 'The Three'; Hort writes to his wife of their invitation to join the bible Revision Committee.[16]

> Westcott. . .believes we ought to seize the opportunity. . .especially as we three [Ghostly Guild members] are on the list.[17]

The secrecy which hovered over the membership list of the recent NASB and NKJV committees, when they were under deliberation, does not spring from the life of Christ and the apostles; this canker was spawned by its 'Carrier' and the Committee of 'Apostles'. The 'secret societies' (or as Hort's son called 'the Apostles'—'the Secret Club') became the 'secret' Revision Committee.[18] Hort writes:

> We still do not wish it to be talked about. . .[19]

"Each member of the company had been supplied with a private copy of Westcott and Hort's [Greek] Text," writes Hort's son.[20] The 'New' Greek Text was marked 'Confidential'; members of the Revision Committee were all sworn to a pledge of secrecy. The Committee met secretly for ten years from 1871-1881. "An iron rule of silence was imposed."[21] A critic notes:

> The Revisors have. . .silently adopted most of those wretched fabrications which are just now in favor with the German School.[22]

The Revision Committee

The Church of England invited committee membership without regard to what "nation or religious body they may belong." One of the most esteemed Hebrew and Greek scholars of the day remarked that the committee members "are notoriously either tainted with popery or infidelity."[23] Hort's son records the rumor that "the revision was in the hands of a clique."[24] Another man of letters at that time conveys:

> The history of the 'New' Greek Text is briefly this: a majority of the Revisors. . .are found to have put themselves into the hands of Drs. Westcott and Hort.[25]

The liberalism of the members was evident in their approval of Westcott and Hort's substitution of the readings in the Vatican's Greek manuscript, *Vaticanus,* for the original Greek. Drs. Moberly, Pusey and Newman were invited to join, all three emissaries of the Roman Catholic Church. Member Dean Stanley believed, as did Westcott and Hort, that the word of God was also in the books of the other world religions. Bishop Thirwall was a follower of the liberal higher criticism of Schleiermacher. The reputations of the committee members were so tainted that Queen Victoria and her chaplain F.C. Cook refused to give it the official sanction awarded by King James to that esteemed body. Half of the members of the Church of England at the time declined involvement, as did its American branch, the Episcopal Church. Others, like Dr. Merival and the Bishop of St. Andrews, left after seeing the sinister character of the 'New' Greek Text. Like Judas, once the deed was done, many of the preeminent members expressed their remorse. Dean Burgon writes of this disenchantment of the committee in general.

> We can sympathize also with the secret distress of certain of the body, who now, when it is all too late to remedy the mischief, begin to suspect that they have been led away—overpowered.

Most noteworthy was the subsequent public exposure of the unholy and unscholarly character of the project by its official chairman Bishop Ellicott. He said, when comparing the credentials of the 1611 KJV committee to the scholars of his day:

> [W]e have certainly not yet acquired sufficient critical judgement for any Body of Revisors to undertake such a work as this.[26]

Hort writes of:

> . . .the abuse we are receiving. . .The crisis is a very grave one and we ought. . .to resist the Moderates in their attempts to carry out the demands of a noisy public opinion.[27]

As 'Planned', the pages of the new version propelled the 'falling away' in these last days. Consequently, today the 'noisy public opinion' can scarcely be heard, time broadening the hearing distance.

The New Age Christ

Upon the public release in 1881 of their 'New' Greek text and *Revised Version* , Hort's son says:

> [T]he work which had gone on now for nearly thirty years was perforce brought to a conclusion. . .[28]

Exactly thirty years earlier, in 1851, "the work" of the Ghostly Guild began. Is this text the minutes of the meetings, so to speak? Constance Cumby, author of the best selling *Hidden Dangers of the Rainbow* and *A Planned Deception* writes of 'the Plan' or work done during this period to prepare the world for the New Age Christ. The 1880's, she points out, were to be the climax of the "externalization of the hierarchy" and would touch off the preparation of the world for 'the Christ'.[29] Is it so surprising then that dozens and dozens of times their 'New' Greek and the subsequent versions which are based on it, drop the name 'Jesus' from the title Jesus Christ, leaving 'the Christ' for the New Age?

Why: Church of England and Bible Revision?

How can the participation of mesmerists and spiritualists, like Westcott, Hort and Lightfoot, in the Church of England's Bible Revision Committee be explained? Contemporaries of Westcott and

Hort, as well as secular historians, note the sinister silhouette of the Church of England when viewed at that juncture in history. Huxley, when voicing his sentiment on the 'spiritualism' and 'psychic activity' of his day, calls it, "the chatter of old women and curates in the nearest cathedral town." (Westcott was the curate of Durham Cathedral and Benson the curate of Westminster.) Secular historian James Webb discerned:

> The occult revival could often go hand in hand with Christian conviction. . .among the clergy of the Church of England proper there was in the early years of the century a measurable interest in Theosophy and occult matters.

It is not surprising that Westcott and Hort had a body of consensus on the revision committee for their 'New' Greek text. Sermon titles in the Church of England ran the gamut from Rev. W.F. Gerkie-Cobb of St. Ethelburga's Bishopsgate's "Theosophy and the Anglo-Catholic Ceremony" to Rev. L.W. Fearn of St. John's Westminster—"Reincarnation."[30] Cambridge University, where Westcott, Hort and Lightfoot had their affiliation, was in a similar state. During Westcott's tenure there, Cambridge produced Sir John Woodruff, author of the Hindu occult tomes *The Serpent Power* and *The Garland of Letters.*

Today's Church of England's members are the spiritual great-grandchildren of Westcott and Hort's 'transformed' Greek text. The New Age banner flies high over St. James Anglican Church off Piccadilly Square. There "Sufi Healing Order, Yoga Meditation Class, and Lifetime Astrology" are taught.[31] To train lay leaders for such esoteric meanderings, they begin with the occult spiritual exercises of Jesuit Ignatious Loyola. They follow up with a meditation ceremony celebrating the Birth of Buddha.[32]

Time magazine calls Westcott's successor, the current Bishop of Durham, "Britain's Doubting Bishop." It says "he prides himself in his heresy" denying the virgin birth, the resurrection and other dogmas. His superior replies, "There is room for everyone in the Anglican church."[33] Evidently so, as witnessed in their recent publication—*Life, Death and Psychical Research: Studies of the Church's Fellowship for Psychical and Spiritual Studies*.[34]

Even the Episcopalian Church, the American branch of the Church of England, has bred 'spirit' channeler Laura Cameron Fraser, their first woman priest. Their Bishop Pike, seance soothsayer of recent years, concedes he began his seminary education as a 'solid' believer, but it left him with "a mere handful of pebbles." Joseph Carr, author of *The Lucifer Connection,* aptly comments that involvement with spirits "should be taken as a warning that there is something wrong, with their theology—but it won't."[35] Morton Kelsey, whom Christian authors Reid, Virkler,and Morgan list as "the most significant spiritual leader in the church today, "recommends communication with the dead."[36] Josh McDowell frames the facts for us saying:

> In recent years there has been a denial of the cardinal doctrines of the Christian faith from those who occupy a position of leadership in the church. When the church waters down the gospel of Christ, the door to occult practices swings wide open.[37]

Necromancy or 'Communion of the Saints'?

> Regard not them that have familiar spirits, neither seek after wizards to be defiled by them. Leviticus 19:31

> There shalt not be found among you any one that maketh his son or his daughter to pass through the fire, or that useth divination, or an observer of times, or an enchanter, or a witch, or a charmer or a consulter with familiar spirits, or a wizard, or a necromancer. For all that do these things are an abomination unto the Lord and because of these abominations the Lord thy God doth drive them out from before thee. Deuteronomy 18:10-12

Webster tells us necromancy is ". . .communication with the spirits of the dead." It is forbidden in dozens of places in the bible, among them Galatians 5:20, Exodus 22:18, II Kings 23:24, II Kings 17:17, Deuteronomy 18:10, II Kings 21:6, Leviticus 19:26, and II Chronicles 33:6. New Bible 'fathers' Westcott and Hort, as well as

J.B. Phillips, author of the *New Testament in Modern English*, cloak their necromancy under the guise—"I believe in the communion of the Saints"—a phrase included in several church creeds. Westcott presented a speech on "The Communion of the Saints" as late as 1880, the final year of his life-long work on the 'New' bible. Describing his belief in the potential for intercourse with the dead, he "chatters,"

> [It] is independent of limitations of space and time. We are learning with the help of many teachers the extent and the authority of the dominion which the dead have over us. . .It is becoming clear to us that we are literally parts of others and they of us. . .We are bidden to enter the unseen. . .[T]here are many worlds. . .There is one life which finds expression in many forms. . .[I]ndividual fellowship with the spiritual world is quickened and guided [on]. . .All Saints Day.[38]
>
> And there is no limit to this inspiring communion. It encompasses the living and the dead. It acknowledges no saddest necessity of outward separation as reaching the region in which it is. . .[A]ll that is personal is gathered up without loss of personality in One. . .[39]

Westcott derides "the prevailing spirit of realism" saying, "[T]he world of sense is too much with us." He closes his speech admitting, "However strange the conception may be, it contains, I believe, some truths which we have not mastered."[40]

Josh McDowell unmasks Westcott's All Saints Day, uncovering "All Hallows Eve."[41] Westcott sees it as "the occasion through which individual fellowship with the spiritual world is quickened and guided."[42] His idea corresponds to what Satanists, Witches, and New Agers call the Samhain festival or Halloween, where "the spirits of the dead return to their former home to visit the living." "It is still considered by witches to be the night of their greatest power."[43]

The same 'Communion of the Saints' rhetoric is being restated today. New Age esoteric leader, Dominican priest and gay activist, Matthew Fox chants, "I don't believe in the Communion of the Saints. I KNOW it." He is referring to his 'communion' with dead occultist Meister Eckhart.[44] Moody Church's Erwin Lutzer hurdles the chatter of these wizards concluding,"No one ever communicates with the dead. . .Those who claim such encounters are either faking it or they are in communication with demons, wicked spirits who delight to deceive."[45]

J.B. Phillips: A Translator's Testimony

J.B. Phillips is author of the best selling MacMillan translation, *The New Testament in Modern English* and other recent translations of the bible. Their widespread distribution was evident on today's visit to the Kent State University Bookstore which housed a small stock of three bibles for sale, *one King James Version* and *two* Phillip's translations. He is also the author of the forward to *The NASB Interlinear Greek-English New Testament* published by Zondervan.

Phillips became involved in necromancy during a period in his life in which he felt horribly despondent, particularly at nighttime. God, he said, was not near to him and he sought comfort desperately. Bob Larson sounds the alarm: "Our post-Christian age has produced a biblically illiterate populace unaware of the scripture's stern denunciation of anyone who attempts to seek knowledge or comfort by contacting the spirit world."[46] However, in his biography, *Ring of Truth: A Translator's Testimony*, Phillips brags:

> Many of us who believe in what is technically known as the Communion of Saints must have experienced the sense of nearness, for a fairly short time, of those we love soon after they have died. This has certainly happened to me several times. But the late C.S. Lewis whom I did not know very well and had seen in the flesh once, but with whom I had corresponded a fair amount, gave me an unusual experience. A few days **after his death**, while I was watching television, **he 'appeared'** sitting in a chair within a few feet of me and spoke a few words which were particularly relevant to the difficult circumstances through which I was passing. He was ruddier in complexion than ever, grinning all over his face and as the old fashioned saying has it, positively glowing in health. The interesting thing to me was that I had not been thinking about him at all. I was neither alarmed or

> surprised. . .He was just there. . .larger than life and twice as natural. A week later, this time when I was in bed, reading before going to sleep, **he appeared again,** even more rosily radiant than before and reported to me the same message which was very important to me at the time. I was a little puzzled and mentioned it to a saintly Bishop. . .His reply was, 'My dear J.B., this sort of thing is happening all the time'.[47]

The message 'C.S. Lewis' gave to Phillips was identical to that given by all New Age channelers today. Elliot Miller reminds us, "Despite the tremendous diversity of these entities, there is a striking unanimity to their message."[48] C.S. Lewis merely told him in essence, "I'm OK, You're OK; Don't Worry. Be Happy (about your feelings of distance from God)." Phillips' despondency and 'distance' from God, as he describes it, was brought on by his faulty theology, to be discussed in Chapter 32.

NIV and NASB 'spirit'

Could their belief in contact with disembodied spirits have influenced their translation work? In Hort's commentary on I Peter (p.60) he remarks that the KJV rendition "the Holy Ghost sent down from heaven" should be "a holy spirit sent down from heaven." Again in Romans 8:15 the new versions (i.e., NASB, all Catholic bibles, Nestle/Aland Greek text, the UBS Greek, the Westcott and Hort Greek text and the Jehovah Witness bible) read "you have received a spirit" rather than the KJV and Majority text reading—"the Spirit."

This rejection of the personhood of the Holy Spirit is characteristic of New Age and cult cosmology. Cult leader Victor Paul Wierwille of The Way International writes, "The giver is God the Spirit. His gift is spirit." A characteristic of the Jehovah Witness bible, which was translated from the Westcott and Hort Greek text, is the consistent rejection of "the personality of the Holy Spirit."[49] Authors of *The Agony of Deceit* even notice this tendency in today's faith teachers remarking, "Like other spiritualists the faith teachers point adherents to their own inner spirit rather than to a Savior outside of them."[50] Could this come from their use of the NIV, NASB or Catholic bibles which read, "in his spirit he speaks mysteries" instead of "in the spirit." The word 'his' is added to these translations with no Greek support. Those familiar with Gnosticism and its focus on man's spirit, will recognize its resurrection with regard to the new versions' rendition of this verse.[51] The new version's substitution of 'a spirit' for the Holy Spirit was discussed in Chapter 28, 'The Godhead's Gone.'

What 'Spirit' prompted the NIV to substitute the word 'the Spirit' for 'the Holy Spirit'? The NIV's Virginia Mollenkott, in her book *Sensuous Spirituality*, lists "A Variety of Methods for Hearing the Spirit." Pages 13 through 19 list these as automatic writing through "a Spirit Guide," divination through the "use of the *I Ching* and Tarot" cards, the occult "A Course in Miracles," "psychotherapy and some mildly mystical experiences" and finally an "ongoing relationship" with the spirit of her dead mother.

THIRTY - TWO

Silenced Scribes Summon Psychology

Is it scriptural to believe God took men like Westcott, Hort, Lightfoot and Phillips and catapulted them to *the* position of greatest influence over the body of Christ, that of bible correctors? Scripture identifies them as God's *rejected*, not God's *chosen*.

> *DEATH*: A man also or woman that hath a familiar spirit or that is a wizard shall surely be put to **death**.
> Leviticus 20:27
>
> Because thou hast rejected the word of the LORD, he hath also **rejected** thee from being king.(I Samuel 15:23) So Saul **died** for his transgression which he committed against the LORD, even against the word of the LORD, which he kept not, and also for asking counsel of one that had a familiar spirit, to inquire of it (I Chronicles 10:13). And inquired not of the LORD: therefore he slew him. (I Chronicles 10:13,14)
>
> *CUT OFF*: And the soul that turneth after such as have familiar spirits, and after wizards to go a whoring after

them, I will even set my face against that soul and will **cut him off** from among his people. (Leviticus 20:6)

The Lord will **cut off** the man that doeth this, the master and **THE SCHOLAR**. (Malachi 2:12)

And when they shall say unto you, 'Seek unto them that have familiar spirits. . .it is because there is no light in them. (Isaiah 8:19,20)

Possessed?

G.W. Balfour, president of the Society for Psychical Research, characterized 'a spiritualist' or 'channel' as "a plurality of minds associated in a single organism."[1] Luke 8:30 and Mark 5:9-15 characterize this as possession by a 'legion' of devils. Symptoms of possession are shown in the New Testament. These include:

1. Profession (Imitation)
2. Obsession
3. Regression
4. Depression (Deliration)

These four evidences of 'influence' by spirits are manifested in the lives of the 'scribes' under investigation.

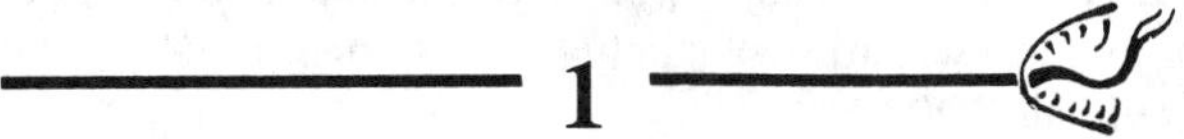

Imitation: They may know and proclaim Christian doctrine.

[T]wo possessed with devils. . .[said,] Jesus, thou Son of God Matthew 8:28,29

[A] certain damsel possessed with a spirit of divination. . .[said,] 'These men are the servants of the most high God and shew unto us the way of salvation.' Acts 16:16,17

[A] man with an unclean spirit. . .ran and worshipped him Mark 5:2-6

This 'imitation' profession is tenet number one of the Spiritualist Church. *The Encyclopedia of the Unexplained* lists their beliefs as follows:

1. "[T]he redemptive power of Jesus Christ." (This is true.)
2. "[T]he Fatherhood of God and brotherhood of man." (This is false.)
3. "[T]he eternal progress open to every soul."[2] (This is false.)

New version editor B.F. Westcott, described as a 'Spiritualist' by his son, echoes these 'unclean spirits' in his books.

1. The redemptive power of Jesus Christ. *Historic Faith*
2. The Fatherhood of God and brotherhood of man. *Religious Thought in the West*
3. "[T]he reality of the law of progress. . .and fellowship with the spiritual world."[3] *The Historic Faith*
   "Progress available to souls after death." *Commentary on St. John's Gospel*

These books were written before, during and after his tenure on the Bible Revision Committee. His *Introduction to the Study of the Gospels* was written *the* year he started the Ghostly Guild.[4] All of his books contain portions in which the language looks rather orthodox. At times it 'looks' like a sheep and 'feels' like a sheep. This jargon serves as the "sheep's clothing" of the false prophets described by Jesus Christ in Matthew 7:15:16.

> Beware of false prophets which come to you in sheep's clothing, but inwardly they are ravening wolves. Ye shall know them by their fruits.

The sheep's clothing cannot camouflage the cry of the wolf. Acts 20:29 warns that ". . .grievous wolves enter in among you." In order to get 'in' the sheepfold to attack the sheep, the clothing of a "righteous" sheep is required to avoid detection.

> And no marvel; for Satan himself is transformed into an angel of Light. Therefore it is no great thing if **his**

ministers also be transformed as the **ministers of righteousness**; whose end shall be according to their works. II Corinthians 11:14,15

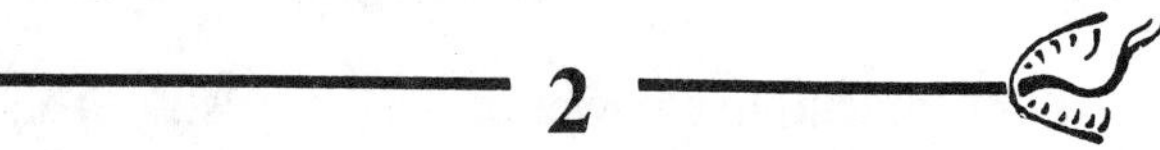

Obsession: A second manifestation of possession is a fixation with the dead. This was manifest in the demoniacs in Matthew 8:28 and Mark 5:2-17.

> . . .there met him two possessed with devils, coming out of the tombs

> . . .there met him out of the tombs a man with an unclean spirit, who had his dwelling among the tombs. . .

Westcott's Ghostly Guild and his writing which includes comments referring to "the dominion which the dead have over us," as well as Phillip's conversations with C.S. Lewis, "after his death" are symptomatic of an overall spiritual condition.

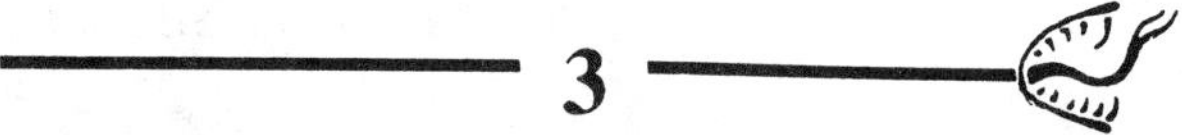

A peculiar phenomenon kept surfacing during my research into the life of these 'scribes'. God apparently 'cut off' their power to speak.

Regression: A third symptom which accompanies spirit possession in the bible is the inability to speak. It is called a 'dumb spirit' in Mark 9:17, 25 and Matthew 9:32, 33, 12:22, 15:30, 31. Those verses disclose the corresponding "frog" in the throat (Revelation 16:13) that accompanies unclean spirits of this kind.

> [H]e was casting out a devil and it was dumb. . .when the devil was gone out, the dumb spake. . . Luke 11:14

The Living Bible: Taylor

> The LORD shall cut off all flattering lips, and the tongue that speaketh proud things. Psalms 12:3

The popular press has made note of author, Kenneth Taylor's, loss of ability to talk. *Time* magazine, July 1972, states:

> Mysteriously half way through the paraphrase Taylor lost his voice and still speaks in a hoarse whisper. A psychiatrist who examined him suggested that the voice failure was Taylor's psychological self-punishment for tampering with what he believed to be the Word of God.

At least thirty million *Living Bibles* are in print, many now in the hands of children. Even the Introduction to the Catholic edition warns:

> [T]his translation cannot be used as a basis for Doctrinal or traditional disputes. . .People from various Doctrinal traditions may. . .be chagrined at the particular translations found within this volume.[5]

Even 'new bible' protagonist D.A. Carson says, "I distrust its looseness and dislike its theological slanting of the evidence."[6]

New American Standard Version

Let the lying lips be put to silence. Psalm 31:18

Also silenced was Philip Schaff, collaborator on the 'New' Greek Committee and director of the *American Standard Version*, which formed the foundation of the *New American Standard* and *The Living Bible*. (See chapter 33 for further discussion.) Paralleling Taylor's pathology, Schaff's son finds the same 'frog' in Philip Schaff's throat. Even as early as 1854, the warning was given, "his voice so affected that he could not speak in public so as to be heard." Finally by 1892. . .

> the power of articulated speech gone.[7]

A friend corresponds to Schaff, "It is with great sorrow that I have learned of the affliction which has befallen you." This malady followed his activity with Westcott and Hort on the RV committee and his *American Standard Version.* Still in 1893 his pathoses "deprived him of the power of speech."[8]

'New' Greek Text: Tregelles

Schaff himself writes of S.P. Tregelles, author of a 'New' Greek Text which preceded and strongly influenced the Westcott and Hort revision. Of Tregelles Schaff writes, he was "scarcely able to speak audibly."[9]

Westcott and Hort Greek Text:

(RV, NRSV, NIV, NASB, CEV, *New Century Version, GoodNews for Modern Man*, Jehovah Witness bible, *The Book*, *The Everyday Bible*, All Catholic bibles et al.)

Westcott's biographer cites that in 1858 "he was quite inaudible"[10] and by 1870 "His voice reached few and was understood by still fewer."[11]

The New Testament in Modern English: J.B. Phillips

> [T]he froward tongue shall be cut out. Proverbs 10:31

J.B. Phillips tells in his own autobiography, "I was still doing a fair measure of speaking in schools and churches until the late summer of 1961. And then quite suddenly my speaking, writing and communication powers stopped. I was not in panic but I was certainly alarmed, and when a few weeks rest brought no improvement I cancelled all speaking engagements for the rest of the year (age 55). *The Price of Success*, the title of his autobiography, is *apropos.*[12]

The speechless sphinx syndrome can even happen to a believer, as it did to Zacharias, because ". . .thou believest not my words" (Luke 1:20).

> What hast thou to do to declare my statutes or that thou shouldest take thy covenant in thy mouth? Seeing thou

hatest instruction and castest my words behind thee. Psalm 50:16-20

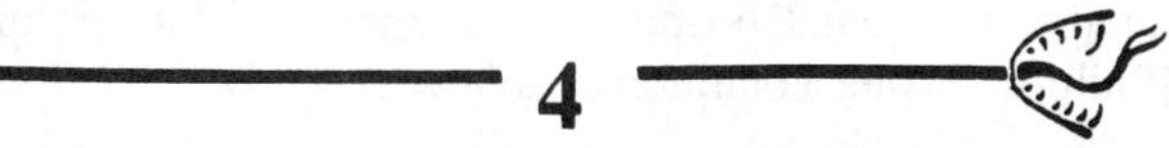

Deliration: Another symptom of possession or harassment by evil spirits is insanity or mental illness. Matthew 17:15-18 records:

> [H]e is lunatick. . .And Jesus rebuked the devil and he departed out of him. [Mark 9:17 adds that this was a 'dumb spirit' also.]

The 'dumb spirit' may plague its host with an accompanying 'lunacy'. J.B. Phillips' necromancy and the 'dumb spirit' it generated harassed Phillips with life-long bouts of insanity. (Yet author of the *NIV Concordance* and *Interlinear Hebrew Text*, John R. Kohlenberger, strongly endorses the J.B. Phillips' *New Testament in Modern English* calling it, "Certainly the most respected and arguably the best individual translation of the New Testament. . ."[13]) His mental illness is chronicled in his autobiography, *The Price of Success*. It began as what he calls a "nervous illness," after his ordination to the priesthood of the Church of England. He resigned a pastor's assistant job after a friend decided:

> [T]hat my trouble must be psychological and arranged for me to see the best psychologist I have ever met. . .He was a personal friend of Jung. . .Following the Jungian techniques I lay on a couch. . .[and] came to see for myself that the seeds of my present distress were sown in early childhood.[14]

Phillips describes his "clinical depression" in detail.

> I found the mental pain more than I could bear and I went as a voluntary patient to a psychiatric clinic. I was at the point of breakdown. . .which in popular parlance is called a nervous breakdown. . .The hardest thing of all to bear is what I can only describe as a nameless mental pain, which is, as far as I know, beyond the reach of any drug and which I have tried in vain to describe to anyone.One of the psychiatrists asked me to write down as far as I could the

nature of the almost intolerable pain. He was a distinguished man in his field and was about to visit a number of mental hospitals in a south London group. [Phillips lists his condition as follows:]

1. There is a slow but inevitable diminution of the self and it is apparently leading to self-extinction.
2. Familiar things become somehow touched with horror. . .[T]he sense of alienation means that one is not in one's own country or has strayed into a strange country by mistake.
3. [A] roaring galloping torrent of condemnation [is] directed against the self's achievements. With remorseless energy this particular 'demon' rushes to and fro up and down in one's mind and with savage cruelty exposes everything that the self has done as being useless and worthless.[15]

He closes his list with another "demon" and elsewhere writes:

[D]emon. . .the hellish torments of mind. . .utter despair. . .frightening experiences. . .seized by irrational panic. . . despite the use of drugs. . .the fears of childhood re-appear with monstrous force. . .The experiences are really evil and they sometimes are terrifyingly so[16]. . .[Y]ou may ask where does the Christian faith come in all this. The answer is that probably emotionally it is of little help at all[17] . . .God himself appears to be far away.[18] [He writes of] . . .praying to an empty heaven.[19]. . .I do not believe that there is any substitute for the long unhurried conversations between the sufferer and a compassionate trained psychiatrist.[20]. . .I set myself down for what must be a long siege and so it has proved. . .I never thought, for example, that I should ever know the type of despair that leads people to self-destruction. I know it now.[21]

Phillips can find "little help" in his own new version which is "swept" of Jesus Christ and the Holy Spirit. (e.g., John 1:1, Galatians 2:17, Luke 24:49) His "garnished" view of salvation, wherein "agnostics. . .are saved," leaves him in "despair."[22] Phillip's own instructions to "**empty** the mind of the. . .Authorized Version" left him with the "hellish torments of the mind" brought by the "demon" disguised as C.S. Lewis.[23]

> When he is come he findeth it **empty**, swept, and garnished. Then goeth he and taketh with himself seven other spirits more wicked than himself and they enter in and dwell there and the last state of that man is worse than the first. Matthew 12:43-45

The Jungian analysis on which Phillips relied can be as occult as his encounter with 'the dead'. Jungian analysis can include the use of spirit guides. Phillip's use of the word "demon" to describe the source of his psychosis is confirmed by Jung himself. Jung's *Collected Letters* Vol I records his discussion with the president of the American S.P.R., William James. He admits, spirits, not the unconscious, were the source of the psychic phenomenon he had experienced since he was three years old and living with his father, a medium and a minister. The official British *Proceedings of the Society for Psychical Research* (S.P.R.) published Jung's views about spirit phenomena in 1920. (This is cited in his *From the Life and Letters of C.G. Jung* and his memoirs.) Jung's experiences ranged from a six-year mental breakdown during which a spirit entity named Philemon began to channel writings through him, to seeing "the head of an old woman on the bed next to him when he opened his eyes."[24]

'Psychotic' is found near 'psychic', not only in the dictionary, but in the lives of the scribes. Phillips' autobiography refers to his E.S.P. so often the topic is listed in his index. (The term E.S.P. was coined by Westcott's offshoots in the American S.P.R.) Phillips boasts:

> I have known the gift of telepathy. [This term was first devised by Westcott's protege Fredric Myers.]. . .I have had first hand incontrovertible experiences of extrasensory perception and a little precognition. . .I had very occasionally extrasensory powers.[25]

He asked a palm-reader to read his palm, remarking:

> She had never seen me before in her life. At once and without hesitation she began to tell me some of the salient points of my life and to tell me my hopes and fears—This was, to say the least, uncanny and I said, 'Right, now tell me what I was thinking as I walked up the stairs. . .[W]ithout hesitation she told me that I had been worrying about a new car. This was perfectly true.[26]

His substitution of Jung for Jesus, the TV for the KJV and the 'spirit' of C.S. Lewis for the Holy Spirit makes him an apt translator for a generation of Christians who are unwarily following in his footsteps, leading as they do to mental problems.

Psychology: The Religion of the New Age

The word psychology means 'study of the soul' in Greek. The soul is God's domain; when humanists attempt its 'repair' without regard for its 'creator', spiritualism, without the Holy Spirit, is inevitable. Sigmond Freud, father of modern psychology, conceded he would "devote his life to psychical [occult] research" if he were to live over again. Carl Rogers, guru for this generation of psychologists, writes of his involvement with seances and communication with the dead.[27] Jung's "Answers to Job," in *Psychology and Religion: West and East*, published as part of New Ager Alice Bailey's Eranos Lectures, show this inevitable fusion of psychology and false religion.

When Humanity Comes of Age (which begins and ends with an endorsement of two Satanists, Blavatsky and Kingsford) says the "World Government" of the New Age, assisted by the "Spiritual Cabinet of 12 men," will be aided in *manipulation* of the masses by The Council for Psychology and Education—

> . . .providing the fundamentals of education, religion and psychology. Religion, spiritual ethics, or whatever it is called, will obviously be the basis upon which all education is founded. The second consideration will be the manner of its presentation and application. This will be planned in the sphere of practical psychology. . . The foundation of education should therefore be psychology

> interpreted through spiritual laws and spiritual lore. . . [using] enlightened pioneers, such as Jung. . .[28]

Another book *New Age Bible Interpretation* repeat the New Age focus and affinity for psychology.

> The education of the youth of the New Age will include a psychology which will deal with the power of thought. . .[29]

Psychology: The Religion of 'New' Christianity

The scriptures are like ladders raising the child of God above the tribulations and temptations of this life. Knocked down, they become fences barring the sheep from the "green pastures" of the shepherd. The removal of scores of comforting words and verses from the new versions leaves Christians hungry targets for the New Age bait of 'psychological counseling'. The 'New' Christianity is characterized by members who are overwhelmed by their inability to 'cope' with the small and large "tribulations" Jesus forewarned we would experience "in this world" (John 16:33). Television and radio ministries pop up in response offering a 'quick fix'. Generations of earlier Christians had responded, '*What* can I get out of this?'; panicked Christians today bark back at God, "*How* can I get out of this!" From these seeds of discontentment sprout depression and/or anxiety. As a consequence, at the 'New' Christian Carnival we see a new curiosity on the midway—'Christian Psychology'. Using Freudian, Jungian, or Rogerian darts you can hit 'trauma targets' in your past or subconscious and burst these balloons of anxiety and depression, walking away with the prize: self-esteem. Holding your prize, you move along to see yourself, not as God sees you, but in the distorted house of mirrors.

New Bibles—New Needs

Proponents, like Robert Schuller, tell us "theology has failed." To which Dave Hunt answers, "The obvious implication is that Christianity is somehow deficient and that psychology has found answers to spiritual problems that are missing from the bible."[30] His phrase, "*missing* from the bible" is the missing puzzle piece which, when set in place, gives us a complete picture of the problem. A speedy survey of churches, seminaries and pastors shows that the use of the 'New' versions runs hand in hand with a dependence on psychological techniques. As I was collating the new translations, red flags flashed frequently. Flies in the ointment replaced the balm of Gilead. I couldn't help but think these changes would leave unhealed and scarred, the Christian mind wounded by the daily "darts of the wicked." Not only do new versions remove what Paul calls "the patience and comfort of the scriptures"(Romans 15:4), but present in addition a theology of uncertainty. The peace and healing that previous generations gained from their bibles has been stolen by the thief in the battle for the mind.

My first glimpse down into this dark chasm full of Christians suffering from 'mental chaos' came via a distraught young Christian woman attending a campus bible study. On opening her bible to Luke 4:18 to find Jesus' words, "[H]e hath sent me to heal the broken-hearted," I found the entire sentence had been eliminated from her NASB. I later found it is also missing from the NIV, *Good News [?] for Modern Man* and all Catholic bibles. This omission is impossible since Jesus was in the synagogue reading from Isaiah 61:1,2, which contains the sentence in question. Its removal is censorship of the strangest kind since the sentence appears in *The Greek New Testament According to the Majority Text.* Its critical apparatus indicates the sigla of the German M, which according to Dallas Theological Seminary professor Zane C. Hodge, indicates the sentence is "one that is supported overwhelmingly." In this case 'overwhelmingly' is a modest estimation since *all* Greek manuscripts except two, *Aleph* and *B,* have it. Even *Alexandrinus* an ancient uncial has it. Tsk. . .Tsk to Nestle and his resurrected Westcott and Hort 'New' Greek text for leaving it out. NIV committeeman Ronald Youngblood *admits* his committee disregarded the majority text here.[31]

A second attempt to arm her (Ephesians 6:17) in her joust with the devil, found the NASB's sword sheathed hiding *the key* words, "on Thee."

NASB	KJV
The steadfast of mind Thou wilt keep in perfect peace	Thou wilt keep him in perfect peace, whose mind is stayed on thee Isaiah 26:3

Uncomforting Bibles

The *person* of 'the Comforter' has also been removed from all new bibles.(John 14:16, 14:26, 15:26, 16:7) He is replaced with 'the Helper' (NKJV, *New World* Jehovah Witness Version, NASB), the Counselor (NIV) and the Advocate or Paraclete (Roman Catholic versions). There is no semantic basis for this revision. The NASB translates the same kind of Greek word as "comfort" eighteen times elsewhere (e.g., Matthew 2:18 "she refused to be comforted") The NIV's 'Counselor', *bouleutes, sumboulos,* is not in *any* Greek manuscripts. The NKJV's word 'helper', or help,*boethos, antilepsis, epikouria,* is no where in the verse either, nor are words such as *antilambano, cheir, epilambano, antecho, propempo, huperetes,* or *prostatis,* all of which the new bibles translate as 'help' often.

Cults like the Jehovah Witnesses use "helper" since they deny the Trinity and the personhood of the Holy Spirit. *The Plain Truth* magazine explains why they too avoid the KJV and its 'Comforter'.

> [T]he Holy Spirit is not a person but the power God uses—much as man uses electricity[32]

The *New King James Version* and the *New American Standard Version* are in poor company rallying with, not only these two cults, but the New Age. Author of *Dark Secrets of the New Age* observes, "New Agers who communicate with Satan's demons see these spirit entities as their "helpers."[33] Vera Alder, for example, when referring to these entities uses the NASB and NKJV term.[34] (New versions are 'helping' to build the "semantic bridge" which Vera Alder and other New Agers said must be built between the New World Religion and existing sectarianism.)

The NIV removes 'the comfort' of the Holy Ghost in Acts 9:31. These versions have chopped out the word 'comfort' from Colossians 2:2, Colossians 4:11, I Thessalonians 5:11, I Thessalonians 5:14, Philippians 2:1, replacing it with the exact word chosen by the Jehovah Witness version.

The bride of Christ is no longer comforted with the salutation "Beloved," but met with "Dear Friend" in III John 2 (NIV). Ephesians 3:9 speaks of the intimacy of our fellowship with God. New Versions join the Jehovah Witnesses in replacing 'fellowship with the groom' with the coming 'new *age* administration'.

NASB	JEHOVAH WITNESS	NIV	KJV
And to bring to light what is the **administration** of the mystery which **for ages** hath been hidden in God who created all things.	And should make men see how the sacred secret is **administered** which has from **the indefinite past** been hidden in God, who created all things.	And to make plain to everyone the **administration** of this mystery which **for ages** past was kept hidden in God who created all things.	And to make all men see what is the **fellowship** of the mystery which from *the* **beginning of the world** hath been hid in God who created all things **by Jesus Christ.**

The Greek *Textus Receptus* has the word for "fellowship," while other Greek texts use a word which could easily be translated as such. The words "by Jesus Christ" are in the majority of Greek manuscripts and are out in only a few Egyptian manuscripts. Ephesians 3:9 is a microcosm of the new versions. They have: (1.) no comforting fellowship, (2.) a New Age world that had no beginning, but is cyclical and (3.) no Jesus Christ.

THIRTY - THREE

The Epitaph of Philip Schaff

"Ye shall conceive chaff" Isaiah 33:11

The 'New' *American Standard Version*

Venom from the fangs of the viper filled the fountain pen of Philip Schaff, staining every paragraph of his *American Standard Version.* The Westcott-Hort campaign to reframe the Greek and English bible sent Schaff, armed with his poison pen, to the front lines, as President of the American Old and New Testament Committees. The press had often protested his position, saying:

> We are at a loss to understand why such a man is permitted to be the big gun.[1]

If the biography of Philip Schaff, available in standard encyclopedias, appeared on the back jacket of the new versions, as author biographical sketches often do, his trial for heresy and active participation in *the* kick-off meeting for the New Age movement, would be only a few of the numerous aspects of his life which would cause Christians to reject his translations. His colleagues from the University of Berlin called him, "[T]he theological mediator between East and West."[2] Schaff chided Christians saying, "[T]hey vainly imagine that they possess the monopoly on truth."[3] As a result, "Shocked churchmen brought Schaff before the Pennsylvania Synod for heresy," notes one of his biographers.[4] Schaff's own son admits, "[T]he people associated all manner of doctrinal evil with [him]" and referred to him as a "traitor."[5] Referring to Schaff's theology, his son writes:

> [I]t was at that time considered by most [Christians] in the United States dangerous and by many heretical.[6]

The *Living Bible* and the *'New' American Standard Version*, which "sought to preserve" the ASV, are among the convoy carrying Schaff's deadly cargo forward to this generation.[7] They have taken custody of Schaff's 30,000 alterations to the text, each one a clang in his battle cry:

> [T]he church must adjust her. . .doctrinal statements. . .to natural science.[8]

These 'adjustments' disarm verses which defend miraculous or supernatural phenomenon, such as Christ's incarnation, deity, sinlessness, resurrection and ascension.[9] A cartoon mummy of his ASV is preserved today in *The Living Bible* by Kenneth Taylor. Its text is a direct paraphrase of the work of Schaff's paring knife. What now is 'fed' to children was considered poison by Shaff's contemporaries. "Parents were warned against sending their children to Mercersburg," admits Schaff's son, so he moved on to teach at Union Theological Seminary in New York City.[10] It was, Schaff said:

> . . .so liberal as to allow for all my dissenting views on these and other points.[11]

There in New York City, Schaff sought men, who shared what he called his "liberal outlook," for membership on his bible translation committee.[12] Rejected were those who believed in, what he called, "the moonshine theory of the inerrant apostolic autographs."[13] His monopoly of the translation later led committee members to admit that the 30,000 changes from the KJV are, "indebted to Philip Schaff more than to all others put together."[14] Schaff, however, gives credit to one member, a Unitarian layman. (They deny the deity of Christ and the Trinity.) Of him Schaff said, "No one took a deeper interest in the revision."[15] This 'interest' is evidenced in the Arianism seen in Schaff's text and footnotes (i.e., John 9:38, Micah 5:2 et al.) and now abounding in all new versions.

The Origin of the 1993 Parliament of World Religions

The event which Philip Schaff called, "the sum of my life and my theological activity," was also heralded as *the* debut of the New Age movement by today's editor of the *New Age Dictionary* and *East West Journal*.[16] Books exposing the New Age movement, like *Larson's Book of Cults*, Campus Crusade's *Mystical Maze*, Hunt's *America: The Sorcerer's Apprentice* and Chandler's *Understanding the New Age*, agree that Schaff's event, "The Parliament of World Religions," set the New Age movement in motion.[17] Larson calls it:

> The first surge of what was to be a transcendental tidal wave. In praise of the Hindu concept of God, theosophists [Luciferians] and *swamis* echoed the endorsement of 19th century luminaries. . .American Protestantism was jolted by the message of delegates to the Parliament who declare, 'All is one. Man is divine.'[18]

Schaff's "Parliament" even called itself, "Babel. . .the actual beginning of a new epoch." It was the first occasion since the tower of Babel to proclaim, "The Brotherhood of Man," "[T]he unification of the world in things of religion," and "the coming unity of mankind."[19] Conference speakers, "explicitly heralded the new age" and the "transforming touch of the new age." "Every voice has witnessed to the recognition of a new age," summarized one speaker.[20] These voices joined in a chorus of speeches, setting forth the theology of the One World Religion of the false prophet and Antichrist. Speech titles included:

"Theosophy and Modern Social Problems"(Annie Besant)
"Idealism the New Religion"(Dr. Brodbeck)
"Worship of God in Man"(Elizabeth Stanton)
"Christian and Hindu Thought"(Rev. Hume)
"Only Possible Method of Religious Unification"(Dr. Alger)
"Synthetic Religion"(Kinza Hirai)
"Sympathy of Religions"(T.W. Higginson)
"Brotherhood of Man"(Dr. Roberts)
"The Good in all Faiths"(Dr. Hugenholtz)
"Essential Oneness of Ethical Ideas"(Rev. Hultin)
"Elements of Universal Religions"(Dr. Hirsch)
"The Ultimate Religion"(Bishop Keane)
"Concessions to Native Religious Ideas(Rev. Slater)
"Swedenborg and Harmony of Religions"(Rev. Mercer)
"Sacred Books of the World"(Milton Terry)
"Buddha, The World's Debt to"(H. Dharmapala)
"Ethics of Christian Science"
"Hindus, Religious Belief of (Ni Dvivedi)
"Islam, The Spirit of (Mohammed Webb)
"Shinto"(Bishop of Japan)[21]

The apostasy of this Chicago meeting is evidenced by the conspicuous absence of Chicago's then leading Christian, D.L. Moody. Even the liberal Archbishop of Canterbury cautioned his clergy to avoid any involvement with the conference.[22] The impetus for the "Parliament" came from a committee which included, among others, a representative of the "New Church" of Emmanuel Swedenborg, a Universalist pastor (They believe all go to heaven.) and a Unitarian author.[23] To this list Schaff added his voice:

> I give you, with pleasure, the liberty of using my name in the list of those who recommend the holding of an international and interdenominational religious congress.[24]

The Unitarian author announced to the Parliament, "I see in vision the next Parliament." "The sum of my life," as Schaff called it, a drama where "Christians of different denominations [sat] side by side with Chinese, Brahmans, and Buddhists," was reenacted again in 1993 at the "World Parliament of Religions".[25] Its theme is "Religious Understanding and Cooperation in a Multicultural World." "Wiccan (witch) and neopagan brochures were everywhere," reports the enthusiastic *National Catholic Reporter* (9/10/93), along with "an exhibit announcing the coming of Maitreya, a person sighted in Africa and Europe, believed to be the Jewish Messiah, the risen Christ, and the Buddha of the Future." Speech titles paint a picture of Parliament leader Robert Muller's dream of a bible agreeable to the "new spiritual world order." The minds and momentum moving the 1993 meeting come into sharp focus with ALL CAP speech titles, reserved solely for the only participating organization which blatantly promotes the worship of Lucifer, Blavatsky's Theosophical Society.

> "Vocabulary for the 21st Century"
> "Language in Religion"
> "World Scriptures: Learning from Other Traditions"
> "Sikh Scriptures for Universal Text"
> "THEOSOPHIC WORLDVIEW"
> "The Problems & Hazards of Religious Pluralism"
> "UFO Abduction Phenomenon: What Could It Mean for the Human Future"
> "Journey From Fanaticism & Fundamentalism to Freedom"
> "Christianity 'Born Again' for a New Age"
> "Theosophical Perception in Christian Orthodoxy"
> "Establishing a Righteous Order Agreeable to All Religions"
> "Reconnecting with the Divine in Yourself"
> "The Witch as Shaman"
> "Spiritual Initiation"
> "Hindu Sanatana Dharma"
> "Satanism in West Texas"
> "The Viability of Pagan Theology"
> "The Theology of Icons"
> "The Christ for the 21st Century"
> "The Past & Future Oneness: Great Principles Shared by All Religions"

Efforts to have the United Nations declare 1993 "The International Year of Religious Understanding" have been made.[26] These strange bedfellows—religion and politics—were first married at the tower of Babel and are later depicted in the book of Revelation where "MYSTERY, BABYLON. . .THE MOTHER OF HARLOTS" is carried over the threshold by a beast portraying the Antichrist. A peek under the covers of Schaff's Victorian period bed again reveals the HARLOT embracing the government of the United States. The chambers of Congress cradled the sleeping souls of its members while the President babbled:

> I am disposed to believe that the Author of the Universe is preparing the world to become a single nation, speaking the same language, which will hereafter render armies and navies superfluous.[27]

Lulled members later voted, with the approval of the Senate and chief executive officer, to support the Parliament—a tower of Babel reaching far into the twentieth century. The theme of the Parliament, "union in the religions of different people," was transported around the globe by the U.S. State Department, as they solicited every country with which we have diplomatic relations.[28] Their official invitation aided Schaff's harlot to procure:

> . . .the representation of all faiths to aid us in presenting to the world. . .the religious harmonies and unities of humanity. . .and to contribute to those forces which shall bring about the unity of the race.[29]

<u>**Schaff**</u>	+	<u>**Delegates**</u>	=	<u>**Parliament**</u>
Samson		**Delilah**		**Philistines**

Three prominent delegates exemplify the three fold cord of Eastern Hinduism (Swami Vivekananda), Western esotericism (Blavatsky's successor Annie Besant) and apostate Christianity (Philip Schaff et al.), which will enchain the world and sustain the One World Religion of the Antichrist. Schaff became entangled, like Samson of old.

SAMSON & THE PHILISTINES	SCHAFF & THE PARLIAMENT
The Philistines, "bound him with fetters of brass." Judg. 16:21	The Parliament bound him with "the golden chain of brotherhood."[30]
"Let me die with the Philistines." Judg.16:30	"I want to die in the Parliament,"[31] said Schaff.

The Philistines sought to weaken the source of Samson's strength. The enemy now likewise seeks to destroy the source of a Christian's strength: "The **word** of his grace which is able to build you up." (Acts 20:32) So the Parliament's delegates, like Delilah, "pressed him daily with her words," until their captive said what she wanted him to say (Judges 16:16, 17).

HINDU SPEECH	LUCIFERIAN SPEECH	SCHAFF'S SPEECH
"[T]he world religions. . .come from the same truth adapting itself to the different circumstances. . .It is the same light coming through different colors."[32]	"All the saviors of the world were Christs though known by different names."[33]	"Unity in variety is the law of God . . .truth is many sided and all sided, and is reflected in different colors."[34]
HINDU SPEECH	**LUCIFERIAN SPEECH**	**NIV, NASB, et al.**
"Whatever comes to you is. . .the Blessed One."[35]	". . .as found in the. .New Testament."[36]	"the Blessed One" Mark 14:61
HINDUS	**LUCIFERIAN**	**NIV, NASB, et al.**
Exiled guru Bhagwan Shree Rajneesh calls himself "The Blessed One."[37] Collegians International Church members call themselves, "Sons of the One."[38]	"The Blessed Ones have never failed to send their representatives. . ."[39]	The Son of the Blessed One. Mark 14:61

The *Princeton Review* wrote of Schaff's "change of terminology" and admiration for men who held a "thoroughly pantheistic" philosophy.[40] They could not foresee the degree to which new versions would agree with Satan's New Age coterie.

The serpent's apt stenographer
made sure that bibles won't deter
the ones who worship Lucifer.

Parliament speeches about "the beginning of the new age," by new version 'scholars' like Charles Briggs and C.S. Goodspeed, would seed weeds that have choked new versions ever since with the religious 'new age' and the political 'new world order'.

MATT. 19:28 **THE REGENERATION (KJV)**	**HEB. 9:10** **REFORMATION (KJV)**
the New Age (GNB)	the new order (NIV)
the new age (CEV)	the new order (GNB)
the new age (NCV)	the New Order (TCNT)
the new age (AMP)	the complete new order (AMP)
the new age (NAB)	the new order (NAB)
the new age (NBER)	the new order (NBER)
the new world (RSV)	the new order (GSPD)
the new world (EASY)	**REV. 21:4** **THE FORMER THINGS (KJV)**
the new world (RV)	the old order (NIV)
the new world (MOFF)	the old order (TCNT)
the new world (LAM)	the old order (NEB)
the new order (WILL)	The old order (BARC)
	the former order (AMP)

II Cor. 5:17 **old things are passed away; behold all things are become new. (KJV)**
the old order has gone, and a new order has already begun. (NEB)
the old order has passed away, now all is new. (NAB)

PART TWO

The Manuscripts

THIRTY - FOUR

The Majority Text

The Scholar's Secrets

The arena of the average Christian rarely borders the sphere of the scholar. Sales in the bible market are too often the result of a hasty sifting through the bible advertisements in magazines such as the *Christian Herald,* not a lengthy "laboring in prayer" and a serious study of journals such as the *Harvard Theological Review.* World-class scholars comment on the mist of misinformation which leaves the average Christian in the dark about the version dilemma. Wilbur Pickering, author of the *Identity of the New Testament Text* and recipient of a TH.M in Greek Exegesis from Dallas Theological Seminary and M.A. and Ph.D. in Linguistics from the University of Toronto says:

> The distressing realization is forced upon us that the 'progress' of the past hundred years has been precisely in— the wrong direction—our modern versions and critical texts are found to differ from the Original in some six thousand places, many of them being serious differences. . .[They] are several times farther removed from the originals than are the A.V. and TR [King James Version and its foundation, the Greek *Textus Receptus*]. How

> could such a calamity have come upon us. . .much of the work that has been done is flawed. . .[1]

Dean John Burgon, the scholar who has collated the most early New Testament witnesses (87,000), says of the changes in one of the 'new' versions and Greek texts:

> Ordinary readers. . .will of course assume that the changes result from the revisor's skill in translating—advances which have been made in the study of Greek. It was found that they had erred through defective scholarship to an extent and with a frequency, which to me is simply inexplicable. . .Anything more unscientific. . .can scarcely be conceived, but it has prevailed for fifty years. We regret to discover that. . .their work is disfigured throughout by changes which convict a majority of their body alike of an imperfect acquaintance with the Greek language.[2]

Edward F. Hills, author of *The King James Version Defended* and graduate of Yale University, Westminster Theological Seminary and recipient of the Ph.D. from Harvard and the TH.M from Columbia University says:

> Modern speech bibles are unscholarly.[3]

The late E.W. Colwell, past president of the University of Chicago and *the* premier North American New Testament Greek scholar, authored scores of books, such as *Studies in Methodology in Textual Criticism of the New Testament.* He confesses his 'change of heart' concerning the reliability of readings in the new versions:

> . . .[S]cholars now believe that most errors were made deliberately. . .the variant readings in the New Testament were created for theological or dogmatic reasons. Most of the manuals now in print (including mine!) will tell you that these variations were the fruit of careless treatment. . .The reverse is the case.[4]

Zane Hodges, professor of New Testament Literature and Exegesis at Dallas Theological Seminary and co-editor of a Greek New Testament refers to new versions as,

> [M]onstrously unscientific, if not dangerously obscurantist. The average well-taught Bible-believing Christian has often heard the *King James Version* corrected on the basis of 'better manuscripts' or 'older authorities'. . .Lacking any kind of technical training in this area, the average believer probably has accepted such explanations from individuals he regards as qualified to give them.[5]

William Palmer, scholar and author of *Narrative of Events on the Tracts,* says:

> [O]rdinary Christians have little idea [concerning the new Greek text]. . .it rests in many cases on quotations which are not genuine. . .on passages which when collated with the original, are proved to be wholly inefficacious as proofs.[6]

'The' Original Greek

If you are convinced *most* Christians use a recently published version of the bible, such as the NIV, NASB, NKJB, *Living Bible*, etc.—what you really mean is—*most* that you have come in contact with, at your fellowship, in the nineteen nineties, in the U.S.A., use it. However throughout the 2000 year history of the New Testament, people using a text like those of the new versions, were in a mathematically infinitesimal minority. So, if you want to be lined up with *most* Christians 'when the saints go marching in', don't take a quick spin of the head (like the girl in *The Exorcist*) to see what's happening around you. Take a long look back through history and around the world. It is safer.

The survival of 'the' original Greek New Testament is a dream which dissolves with the discovery that no two manuscripts or critical editions are alike. Those applying this term to a Greek text on the bookstore shelf are unacquainted with the volatile state of the text.

There are over 5366 manuscripts of the Greek New Testament. Together they give a view of the text much like a shifting kaleidoscope. "They contain several hundred thousand variant readings. . .," notes Pickering.[7] In an attempt to marry these 'moody' manuscripts, the 'Wheel of Fortune' is whirled and readings are selected for inclusion in what scholars call a 'critical edition of the Greek Text'. There are more than two dozen of these texts, each a 'prize' stuffed with between 5000 and 8000 variations. As one scholar puts it, ". . .equally competent critics often arrive at contrary conclusions as to the same variation."[8]

Scholar's Sources

Evidence for the New Testament is composed of papyrus fragments and manuscripts, uncial and minuscule manuscripts (modified capitals and cursives) and lectionaries (books used in churches). Each of the 5366 manuscripts including 2209 lectionaries extant today are given a name, an abbreviation and/or a number.[9]

Papyri	1-88	(e.g., P66, P46, P75)
Uncials	01-0274	(e.g., Aleph, B, C, D)
Minuscule	1-2795	(e.g., 1-2795)
Lectionaries	1-2209	(e.g., 1 1-2209)

In addition to the above, numerous other language versions of the Greek text were made in the second century and those following. Those include the Old Latin, the Syriac, the Coptic, the Ethiopic, and score of others. These provide witnesses to the correct readings of the New Testament. Finally, scores of second, third and forth century personalities, such as John Chrysostom, Irenaeus, Tertullain, and Justin Martyr, to name just a few, have left writings containing citations of scripture verses, witnessing to the original readings of the New Testament. Dean John Burgon has extrapolated over 87,000 of these. Currently the manuscripts are being collated by the *Institut fur neutestamentiche Tereforschung* by Kurt Aland in Munster, Germany. Microfilms of many are housed in the archives of the Ancient Biblical Manuscript Center in Claremont, California. Should the reader wish to pursue their own investigation, a list of sources where copies of those manuscripts may be found is given in this footnote.[10]

The Majority Text

The overwhelming majority of these manuscripts, lectionaries, and writers agree generally with each other as to the readings of the New Testament. Manuscripts from the second century (P66) down through the Middle Ages (A.D.1500) attest to the readings of this 'Majority Text', as Kurt Aland terms it. Dean Burgon, who found this 'Majority Text' in most of the early writers collated, calls it 'The Traditional Text'. It is also called the Syrian Text, the Byzantine Text and the K (Kappa) or Common Text.

This text type is available today in English in the *Authorized Version*, or as it is called in the United States, the *King James Version*. It's 809,000,000 copies since 1611, in 300 languages, demonstrates the continuum of this 'Majority Text'. (Unfortunately, as we shall see, the new versions are *not* based on this 'Majority Text', but on the dissenting handful of manuscripts which disagree with the Majority.)

How It All Began

The cities receiving the actual Autographs were in the region of Asia Minor (Syria), Greece and Rome.

ASIA MINOR	GREECE	ROME
John	I & 2 Cor.	Mark
Gal.	Phil.	Rom.
Eph.	I & 2 Thess.	Heb.
Col.	Titus	
I & 2 Tim.		
Philem.		
I Pet.		
I, 2, & 3 John		
Rev.		
Luke (or Rome)		
Acts (or Rome)		
2 Pet.(or Rome)		
Matt. (or Palestine)		
James (or Palestine)		
Jude		

The scriptures themselves attest to the proliferation and early creation of a 'Majority' text.

Acts 6:7	"And the word of God increased."
Acts 12:24	"But the word of God grew and multiplied."
Acts 13:49	"[T]he word of the Lord was published throughout all the region"
Acts 19:20	"So mightily grew the word of God and prevailed."

Pickering explains the multiplication of the originals throughout history.

> [W]e may reasonably assume that in the earliest period of the transmission of the text, the most reliable copies of the Autographs would be circulating in the region that held the Autographs. With an ever-increasing demand and consequent proliferation of copies throughout the Graeco-Roman world and with the potential for verifying copies by having recourse to the centers still possessing the Autographs, the early textual situation was highly favorable to the wide dissemination of MSS in close agreement with the original text. . .It follows that within a relatively few years after the writing of the N.T. books, there came rapidly into existence a 'Majority text', whose form was essentially that of the Autographs. . .the science of statistical probability demonstrates that a text form in such circumstances could scarcely be dislodged from its dominant position. . .[I]n every age, from the apostolic to the nineteenth century, the text form in question. . .was the one that the church in general recognized, used, and transmitted.[11]

From the academic arena, world-class scholars express their unanimous agreement on the overwhelming dominance of this type of New Testament text in the early church and throughout history.

- Colwell calls it "[T]he uncontrolled popular edition of the second century."[12]

- Comfort says it, "became the most prevailing type of text throughout the Greek speaking world. . .it was nearly standardized. From then on, almost all MSS follow the Byzantine [Majority] text, including those MSS used by Erasmus in compiling the text that eventually would become the *Textus Receptus*." [The Greek Text type underlying the KJV.][13]

- Geerlings affirms regarding the Majority Text saying, "Its origins. . .go back to the autographs."[14]

- Hodges writes, "The Majority text, it must be remembered, is relatively uniform in its general character with comparatively low amounts of variation between its major representatives. . . [T]he majority of MSS in the transmission of any book will, *a priori* preserve the best text. Thus the Majority Text, upon which the *King James Version* is based, has in reality the strongest claim possible to be regarded as an authentic representation of the original text. . .based on its dominances in the transmissional history of the New Testament text."[15]

- *Harvard Theological Review* cites Kirsopp Lake's exhaustive examination of MSS which revealed, "the uniformity of the text exhibited by the vast majority of the New Testament manuscripts."

- Von Soden, who made the most extensive review of the text yet accomplished, calls it the Common (Kappa) text, showing that it was the Greek text type most commonly used throughout history.

- Kurt Aland's collation of 1000 minuscules in 1000 different passages shows that 90% contain the 'Traditional Text'. Work done at *The Institut fur neutestamentliche Textforschung* in Munster, Germany confirms this same 90%. When they include papyrus and uncials together with cursives the number remains above 80%.[16]

- Metzger agrees speaking of ". . .the great majority of the minuscule manuscripts on which the *Textus Receptus* rests."[17]

- Hills says, "The vast majority of these extant Greek New Testament manuscripts agree together very closely, so closely indeed that they may fairly be said to contain the same New Testament. This Majority Text is usually called the Byzantine Text by modern textual critics. This is because all modern critics acknowledge that this was the Greek New Testament text in general use throughout the greater part of the Byzantine Period (A.D.312-1453). For many centuries, before the Protestant Reformation, this Byzantine text was the text of the entire Greek Church, and for more then three centuries after the Reformation, it was the text of the entire Protestant Church. . .[It is] found in the vast majority of the Greek New Testament manuscripts. . .[T]he Traditional Text. . .is the true text because it is that form of the Greek New Testament which is known to have been used in the Church of Christ in unbroken succession. . .Thus the evidence which has accumulated. . .is amply sufficient to justify the view. . .that therefore the Byzantine text found in the vast majority of the Greek New Testament manuscripts is that true text."[18]

1881: The 1% Minority

[A] false balance is an abomination to the Lord.
Proverbs 11:1

The variations among the Majority Text are minor, like the varieties of doves. On the other hand, the remaining handful of manuscripts are as diverse as dogs and dragons. This handful, not only disagree with 'the Majority', as to what the New Testament says, but disagree among themselves. These include such manuscripts as Vaticanus (B), Sinaiticus (Aleph), Bezae (D), Papyrus 75 and a smattering of versions. Of the four uncials, Aleph, B, C, and D, Burgon writes:

> All four are discovered on careful scrutiny to differ essentially, not only from the 99 out of 100 of the whole body of extant manuscripts, but even from one another.[19]

In 1881 this 1% minority text type supplanted the Majority Text with its almost two millennia standing. A 'New' Greek Text, using the Vatican manuscript (B), was introduced by Westcott and Hort and has been used as the Greek Text for **all** subsequent versions.

Frederic Kenyon, the late Director of the British Museum and author of the most widely used textbooks on textual criticism, says of the Majority Text:

> This is the text found in the great majority of manuscripts, entrenched in print by Erasmus and Stephanus and known as the Textus Receptus or Received Text. . .**Until 1881**. . .it held the field as the text in practically **universal** use and when its position was then decisively challenged, a stiff fight was made in its defence by advocates such as Burgon. [This 'New' Minority-type Greek text] used predominantly. . .Aleph and B type readings. . .[The changes] amount to an **extensive modification** of the text. [It] has been the dominating influence in all modern critical editions. It is clear that. . .deliberate alteration. . .has been at work on a large scale in one text or the other. . .The Textus Receptus being habitually the longer and fuller of the two.[20]

Pickering reveals the continued use of this 1% text by the new version editors.

> [The new versions] ignore the over 5000 Greek MSS now extant. . .[T]he evidence cited does prove that aberrant

forms of the N.T. text were produced. Naturally some of those text forms may have acquired a local and temporary currency. Recall that the possibility of checking with the Autographs must have served to inhibit the spread of such forms. We have the Majority Text (Aland) or the Traditional Text (Burgon), dominating the stream of transmission with a few individual witnesses going their idiosyncratic ways. . .One may reasonably speak of 90% of the extant MSS belonging to the Majority Text type. . .[T]he remaining 10-20% do not represent a single competing form.

The minority MSS disagree as much (or more) among themselves as they do with the majority. We are not judging between two text forms, one representing 80% of the MSS and the other 20%. Rather we have to judge between 80-90% and a fraction of 1% (comparing the Majority text with P75 and B text form for example. . .) Or to take a specific case, in I Timothy 3:16 over 300 Greek MSS read 'God' [KJV]. . .7 Greek MSS read 'who' [NIV, NASB, etc.] So we have to judge between 97% and 2%. . .

It really does seem that those scholars who reject the Majority text are faced with a serious problem. . .They are remnants reflecting ancient **aberrant** forms. It is a dependence on such aberrant forms that distinguishes **contemporary** critical editions of the New Testament. . .I submit that due process requires us to receive as original that form of the text which is supported by the majority of witnesses. To reject their testimony in favour of our own imagination as to what a reading ought to be is manifestly untenable.[21]

Hodges describes the readings in the new versions.

[M]odern criticism repeatedly and systematically rejects majority readings on a large scale. . .[This is] monstrously unscientific. . .[I]f modern criticism continues its trend toward more genuinely scientific procedures, this question will once again become a central consideration. . .[T]he Textus Receptus was too hastily abandoned. . .[22]

Alexandria's Allegories

These manuscripts comprise not only a minority of witnesses but represent only one geographical area—Alexandria, Egypt. The Majority text, on the other hand, comes from manuscripts from Greece, Constantinople, Asia Minor, Syria, Alexandria, Africa, Gaul, South Italy, Sicily, England, and Ireland. The professionals' platform notes the following:

- Pickering states, "[A] reading found in only one limited area cannot be original. . .if a reading died out in the fourth century, we have the verdict of history against it."[23]

- Hodge contends that because most of the early manuscript discoveries, all of the non-Byzantine text-type, have come from Egypt, therefore they probably represent a textual tradition, pertaining only to that geographical area.[24]

- Zuntz notes that the agreement between our modern editions does not mean we have recovered the original text. It is due to the simple fact that their editors. . .follow one narrow section of the evidence, namely the non-Western Old Uncials.[25]

- K.W. Clark adds, "All are found on the same Egyptian recension."[26]

'Recension', according to Webster, means "revision." *The NASB Interlinear Greek-English New Testament* refers to its 'Greek text' as a "recension."[27] Wouldn't you really rather have 'the original'?

The Alexandrian Apologists

Like ostriches, new version editors and those who unbraid the KJV have their heads buried in the Egyptian sand—seeing B and P75 to the exclusion of the thousands of other witnesses. When confronted with the shaky stance of this sword balancing on its tip, a variety of weak responses ensue. Some yield the problematic stance they have taken. Kenyon writes:

> There are those who are uneasy on account of the immense numerical preponderance of the witnesses of this [Majority text] class, which they think must outweigh the small body of dissident testimony.[28]

Some admit the minority position they hold. Comfort admits:

> [S]cholars look to the. . .**fewer** MSS in their work to recover the original wording of the Greek Text. . . Generally speaking, a reading belonging to the Alexandrian text type is given considerable weight—more so than a reading found in the MSS belonging to the Western type (D) and definitely more so than a reading found in a Byzantine MSS [Majority type].[29]

A few give contradictory statements in their own writing, giving the truth in some places and false impressions in others.

☑ Carson pretends,
"The textual base of the T.R. [KJV Greek] is a small number of haphazardly collated and relatively late minuscule manuscripts."

☑ [Chapters later he admits] "95% of the MSS belong to the Byzantine tradition. . .[That is] the textual tradition which in large measure stands behind the KJV. . .[T]here are far more manuscripts extant in this tradition than in the other three combined [Caesarian, Western, and Alexandrian]."

> [Then he disregards reason and concludes,]
> "God, it is argued, has providentially preserved the Byzantine tradition—That is true. . .God preserved the Byzantine-text type for at least a millennium, during which time the others were unknown. . .True enough. . . [Is] everything that takes place under divine providence morally good or necessarily true? To say this is not to ascribe evil to God. Divine sovereignty is so all embracing that it stands behind all things, including. . . Adolf Hitler."

Then he sheepishly adds:

> "Of course one should be very careful and humble before dogmatically disagreeing with what the majority of believers have held to be true."[30]

We can safely conclude from scholars on both sides of the issue that the vast majority of manuscripts agrees with the readings in the *King James Version.* New versions, such as the NIV, NASB, NEB, TEV, *Living Bible*, *New Century Version*, CEV, RSV, NRSV, JB, NJB, NAB, et al. are based on readings from, as Pickering states, ". . .a fraction of 1%" of the extant manuscripts. Not only does the KJV have a firmer foundation numerically, but also geographically. It comes from numerous localities, as opposed to the minority texts, which come only from Alexandria, Egypt. Finally, as we will see, the KJV readings represent *the earliest* known manuscripts (i.e., P66 A.D.175); the new versions are based on later alterations of the original, extant in the form of P75 (A.D.200)and Aleph and B (A.D.350).

THIRTY - FIVE

The Earliest Manuscripts

The Papyrus Manuscripts

Before the discoveries of the papyri and their exhaustive collation by scholars such as Colwell, Sturz, Zuntz, and Pickering, some scholars of the nineteenth century believed that the 'Majority text' was a fourth century recension and did not represent *the earliest* manuscripts. In 1881 Hort contended,". . .all distinctively Syrian readings may be set aside at once, certainly originating after the middle of the third century."[31] This idea of 'the lateness' of the Majority text was repeated in textbooks like Kenyon's, who in 1937 echoed, "The relatively late date. . .must now be taken as established. The [Majority] text may be dismissed from further consideration." However he added, "If it can be shown, that the readings which Hort called 'Syrian' existed before the fourth century, the keystone would be knocked out of the fabric of his theory."[32]

Out it comes! Harvard scholar, Hills writes, "This. . . [theory] has been abandoned by most present day scholars."[33] The ninety-six papyri (with the exception of P3, 4, 7, and 14) were all discovered *after* 1890. Pickering observes:

> In Hort's day. . .the early papyri were not extant—had they been the W-H theory could scarcely have appeared. . . Each of the early papyri (A.D.300 or earlier) vindicates some Byzantine [KJV] reading. . .Bodmer II shows some Syrian readings to be anterior to corresponding [Aleph and B] readings. . .[T]he early papyri vindicate Byzantine readings in 660 (or 885) places where there is a significant variation.[34]

Pickering cites H.A. Sturz, *The Byzantine Text-Type and New Testament Textual Criticism,* and summarizes his research concerning the superiority of the KJV text-type, based on the discoveries in the papyri.

> H.A. Sturz. . .surveyed all the available papyri. . .each new MS discovered vindicated added Byzantine readings. . . The magnitude of this vindication can be more fully appreciated by recalling that only about 30% of the New Testament has early papyri attestation. . .[I]f we had at least three papyri covering all parts of the New Testament, all of the 5000+ Byzantine readings rejected by the critical (eclectic) texts would be vindicated by early papyrus. . . Henceforth no one may reasonably or responsibly characterize the Byzantine text-type as being. . .late. . . [A]lthough modern editors continue to reject these readings, it can no longer be argued that they are late.[35]

A.F.J. Klijn, in his book *A Survey of the Researches into the Western Text of the Gospels,* compared Aleph and B (fourth century) readings with the papyri (second century). Pickering added to his research and compared the *Textus Receptus* to Aleph and B. He concluded that the KJV readings (TR) dominated the early papyri to a *greater* percentage than the readings of Aleph and B, seen in the new versions.

PAPYRI	ALEPH	B	TR
P45	19	24	32
P66	14	29	33
P75	9	33	29
P45,66,75	4	18	20
P45,66	7	3	8
P45,75	1	2	2
P66,75	0	8	5
P45	2	1	1
P66	2	3	5
P75	2	3	4
Total	60	124	139

John 1-14							
	W	D	C	A	Aleph	B	TR
P75	45%	38.9%	48.5%	45.6%	44.6%	50.4%	51.2%

*(Note: Even P75 which is touted as the great ally of Aleph & B, agrees here with the TR to a *greater* extent.)

SUMMARY			
P45 has	TR 33 places	B 25 places	Aleph 21 places
P66 has	TR 38 places	B 32 places	Aleph 16 places
P75 has	TR 33 times	B 36 times	Aleph 11 times
Total	104	93	48

Together P45, 66, and 75 have:	TR	20 places
	B	18 places
	Aleph	4 places
Two of these papyri agree with the:	TR	20 places
	B	13 places
	Aleph	8 places
One of these papyri follows:	TR	69 places
	B	62 places
	Aleph	36 places

Pickering concludes, "[T]he TR has more early attestation than B and twice as much as Aleph—evidently the TR reflects an earlier text than either B or Aleph."[36]

Other scholar's findings reveal results which vindicate the KJV readings, which in the 1870's were considered 'later'.

- G. Zuntz in *The Texts of the Epistles* writes, "[KJV type] readings previously discarded as late are [in] P46. . .[A]re all Byzantine readings ancient?. . .G. Pasquali answers in the affirmative. . .Papyrus 46 and 45 support the Majority text readings. . ."[37]

- Metzger says, "Papyrus 75 supports the majority text dozens of times. In relation to the [majority] text, P46 (about A.D.200), shows that some readings. . .go back to a very early period. . .P66 [has] readings that agree with the [majority]. . . text type."[38]

- Hills notes, "Byzantine readings which most critics have regarded as late, have now been proved by Papyrus Bodmer II to be early readings."[39]

- *The Journal of Theological Studies* (London: Oxford University Press) N.S., vol.II, 1960) p. 381 says, "Papyrus 66 supports the readings of the Majority text."

- Comfort writes, "[S]ome of the N.T. papyri that have been discovered show remarkable similarity with later MSS. In fact, several of the extant early papyri are related to many later MSS (fourth century and beyond) or at least share a common ancestor."[40]

- Carson, a KJV detractor who felt 10% of its readings were late now concedes, "with new discoveries this percentage is still falling."[41]

- Colwell found that as early as A.D.200 scribes were altering manuscripts, changing them from a Majority-type text to a minority type. He notes, "The Bodmer John (P66) is also a witness to the early existence of many of the readings found in the [KJV]. Strangely enough to our previous ideas, the contemporary corrections in that papyrus frequently change a [KJV] reading to a. . .[new version type]. This indicates that at this early period readings of the. . .[new version type] were supplanting the. . .[KJV type]."[42]

Colwell's discovery that *the earliest* manuscript, P66, had corrections on it, which change a KJV type reading to a new version type reading, shows that the KJV was anterior to the minority type text.

The following are but a handful of the verses in which the earliest manuscripts, the papyri of the first, second, and third century, side with the Byzantine Majority-type KJV readings, rather than the minority Aleph and B (fourth century) readings of the new versions.

VERSE	KJV	NEW VERSIONS
Mark 5:42	Majority plus P45	Aleph & B
Mark 7:35	Majority plus P45	Aleph & B
Luke 13:2	Majority plus P75	Aleph & B
Luke 24:47	Majority plus P75	Aleph & B
John 4:29	Majority plus P66, 75	Aleph & B
John 5:37	Majority plus P66	P75, Aleph & B
John 7:39	Majority plus P66	P75, 66 & Aleph
John 10:19	Majority plus P66	P45, 77, Aleph & B
John 10:31	Majority plus P66	P75, Aleph & B
John 11:22	Majority plus P45, 66	P75, Aleph & B
John 12:9	Majority plus P66, 75, B2	Aleph

VERSE	KJV	NEW VERSIONS
John 14:14	Majority plus P66, Aleph	P75, B
John 7:41	Majority plus P66, Aleph	P66, 75, B
John 9:6	Majority plus P66, 74, Aleph	B (Hort follows B)
John 13:36	Majority plus P66, Aleph	B
I Cor. 9:21	Majority plus Aleph C, P46 verb	Aleph & B
2 Cor. 7:14	Majority plus P46, Aleph C	Aleph & B
John 8:51	Majority plus P66	P75, Aleph & B
John 9:28	Majority plus P66	P75, Aleph & B
John 11:21	Majority plus P45, P66 (word order)	P75, Aleph & B
John 11:32	Majority plus P45	P66, 75, Aleph & B
John 14:5	Majority plus P66	B
I Pet.5:8	Majority plus P72	B

(Expanded Appendix B is included at the end of this book citing some of the thousands of instances in which the earliest papyri discoveries reveal KJV readings, while the new versions have readings from later manuscripts.)

A typical example of the use of the earliest manuscripts by the KJV is seen in the last chapter of Luke. In this chapter, the NASB omits or brackets nearly 100 words based on *one* fifth century manuscript, D, and Westcott's now defunct 'theory of interpolation'. These verses are in all of the other manuscripts, including the second century P75, the fourth century Aleph, B, and W, as well as A, C, L, and 33. The witness of the Majority text coupled with the early attestation of second to fourth century uncials certainly outweighs *one* highly corrupt fifth century manuscript. The NASB footnote, when explaining its gaps says, "Some manuscripts insert. . ." A more accurate footnote would read, "All manuscripts insert. . .except one."

Attesting to the deity of Christ and his post-resurrection appearances, Matthew 28:17 records, "they worshipped him, but some doubted." In Luke's last chapter, the NASB 'doubters' removed, 1.) "they worshipped him," 2.) his Ascension and 3.) two eyewitness accounts of his resurrection and the record of his care for them. The 'doubters' doubt if verses 12 and 40 really happened.

LUKE 24	NASB OMITTED	NASB ADDED
verse 1	". . .and certain others with them"	
verse 5		"One"
verse 12	[Then arose Peter and ran unto the sepulchre and stooping down, he beheld the linen clothes laid by themselves, and departed, wondering in himself of that which was come to pass.]	
verse 17	"and are sad?"	
verse 26		"the" (to Christ)
verse 36	"and said unto them Peace be unto you" Footnote mistakenly says, "Some ancient MSS insert."	
verse 40	["And when he had said this, He showed them his hands and his feet."] Footnote mistakenly says, "many manuscripts do not contain this verse."	
verse 42	"and of a honeycomb"	

LUKE 24	NASB OMITTED	NASB ADDED
verse 44	switches "the" to "My" contradicting John 12:49, 50; 17:8	
verse 51	"And carried up into heaven"	
verse 52	"And they worshipped him"	
verse 53	"blessing"	

Within the confines of just one chapter, the NASB lines up in queue with standard New Age teaching. Historians admit manuscript D was truncated by Marcion, Mme. Blavatsky's mentor, and has now been resurrected in the last days for the religion of the Antichrist. Note the following five New Age doctrines taught in Luke 24 by the NASB.

1. God becomes the *impersonal* "One" of Hinduism; he is not concerned if you are "sad," nor would he greet your fearfulness with the calming, "Peace be unto you." (He would probably appear saying—"Boo"—.)

2. "Christ" becomes "the Christ," a position not a person.

3. Jesus did not ascend; he was just a man. He left them to travel to India (or, as the Mormons insist, to America.)

4. Since he was just *a man*, they did not worship him.

5. The "suffering for sins" evident by the nail-prints, is 'doubted by *some*', lining up with the bloodless creeds of the New Age.

If you want to follow manuscript D in Luke, as the NASB and old Nestle's do, get your pen and cross out another 121 words from the last chapter, another 229 words from the last three chapters, 1,552 of the 19,941 words in Luke altogether, and another 4,000 words in the Gospels and Acts. Conforming to D, you will make 13,781 changes in your New Testament, perhaps more, depending on which of the 10 correctors of D you follow. Be sure to remember to change to D's Gnostic Ebionite reading in Luke 3:22. Here the first century New Agers changed the verse so that 'the Christ' pole descends on Jesus at his baptism and leaves him on the cross. This is why manuscript D must change Luke 24. You'll now be in company with Madame Blavatsky, the senior New Age Luciferian, who thinks D should be followed, because it was sculpted by Marcion.

Other Early Witnesses

In addition to the second and third century papyri, which show that the KJV text-type dominated the early church, codex W (fourth century) and Codex A (fifth century) support the KJV. In addition, the Sinaitic Syriac Version (third century), the Gothic Version (fourth century) and the Peshitta Syriac (now dated much earlier than the fifth century) agree with the KJV. One scholar reminds the new version editors:

> You talk of 'Antiquity'. But you must know very well that you actually mean something quite different. You fasten upon. . .two perhaps three. . .documents of the IV and V century. . .[T]hose are 1, 2, 3, or 4 specimens of Antiquity, not antiquity itself. . .[Y]ou use Aleph and B, why not A, C or D, [you] use the old Latin or the Coptic, why not the Peshitta or the Sahidic. [You] quote Origen or Eusebius, why not Didymus, Athanasius, Epiphanius, Basil, Chrysostom, Theodoret, the Gregories, or the Cyrils. . .The Traditional Text receives more support from the early Church Fathers than does the critical text.[43] [at a ratio of 2:1 before A.D.350 and 3:1 for important passages.]

The following writers pre-date Aleph and B and attest to KJV-type readings in the *early* church.

A.D.				
100-150	**150-200**	**200-250**	**250-300**	**300-400**
Didache Diognelus Justin Martyr	*The Gospel of Peter* Athenagouis Hegesippus Irenaeus	Clement Tertullian Origen Clementinus Hippolytus	Gregory of Thaumaturgus Novatian Cyprian Dionysius Achelaus	Athanasius Macarius Magnus Eusebius Hilary Didymus Basil Titus of Bostra Cyril of Jerusalem Gregory of Nyssa Apostolic Canons & Constitutions Epiphanius Ambrose

"Men of High Degree. . ."

> Men of high degree are a lie: to be laid in the balance they are altogether lighter than vanity. Psalm 62:9

New version editors exhibit gross unfamiliarity with recent papyrological scholarship (i.e., the oldest papyrus in the world, P66 has predominantly KJV readings). They appear also to be in the dark concerning the numerical preponderance of the Majority Text. Repeating the rhetoric of their timeworn 1937 edition college textbook, they pass passé accounts on to the unwary. Edwin Palmer, chief editor of the NIV, delivers his unversed version of the facts.

> The KJV translators. . .all they had to work with was a handful of copies of the Greek manuscripts of the New Testament books. These were very late copies dating from a thousand (!) years after the New Testament was written. . .many more Greek manuscripts had been

> preserved and were subsequently discovered—in fact, more than five thousand of them. . .even to about A.D.200.[44]

(!) to use his style. Is he unaware that : 1.) Of these 5000, all but a fraction of 1% agree with the KJV against his NIV and 2.) The A.D.200 manuscript also agrees with the KJV against his NIV. Proof—the Greek text used by the NIV (Nestle's 25th/UBS 1st, 1963) was later changed in nearly 500 places in the 1979 Nestle's 26th/UBS 3rd edition—to agree with the KJV. The NIV committee foresaw some of these but ignored many others.

Other new version editors also voice their 'varnished' view of the facts:

- Calvin Linton, NIV Committee member repeats Palmer's varnished version: "[T]he first ancient Greek manuscript of the New Testament was not available in English until 1628."[45]

- Ralph Earle, another NIV committee member discloses his sciolism by stating, the KJV ". . .is a text based primarily on late medieval manuscripts. Fortunately now we have a little over 5000 Greek manuscripts. . .[W]ith thousands of Greek manuscripts of the N.T. now at our disposal, we can reach a high degree of certainty with regard to the probability of the best text."[46]

- Lewis Foster, NIV and NKJV committee member echoes, "But we have great assurance of knowing what the originals said because of the number of copies of the Bible available. . .[M]ore manuscripts are known today than were used in the making of the KJV. Today's judgement is better because we have more information. . .[47]

But they choose to ignore the vast "number" of manuscripts and the latest "information."

Why, as we have seen, do world-class scholars refer to the new versions and their editors as "unscientific," "unscholarly," "incompetent" and far adrift from the realities of manuscript history.[48] Even Hort, chief architect of their 'New' Greek text, admits in a letter to a friend:

> I am afraid I must have talked big and misled you when you were here, for I really know very little of Church History.[49]

Actually, the members of new version committees are selected by their chief editors to show a broad representation of denominations, thereby broadening their versions' market. Those chosen may be Greek grammarians, but most are in no sense eminent paleographers, papyrologists, codicologists, historians (or most importantly, Spirit-led Christians). The NASB committee list remained a closely guarded secret for over 30 years, lest conservative Christians catch a glimpse of the liberal membership. (However, Dr. Frank Logsdon has renounced his participation. At numerous speaking engagements he denounced his part in what he now perceives to be a heretical version. "I may be in trouble with God" because of it, he confesses.) The editors of the new versions are not qualified by the endless hours of pouring over the ancient manuscripts, as were Burgon, Colwell, Hoskier, and scores of others. In fact, as committee member Lewis Foster admits, they are not involved with actual manuscripts or facsimiles at all:

> The New Testament translators may choose to differ from the decision founded in the Greek text [i.e. Nestles/UBS] he is using, but he does not deal with the manuscripts themselves. He works indirectly through the use of the modern Greek text.[50]

Moving from a discussion of the Majority and minority type manuscripts themselves, we now move on to the critical editions of the Greek N.T. or as Foster called it 'the modern Greek text'. These reduce the hundreds of thousands of variant readings in the Greek manuscripts to a 'manageable' 6000 or so variants.

THIRTY-SIX

The Modern Greek Editions

The Battle in the Bookstore: The Critical Greek Text

The action is in the aisles of the bookstores in this spiritual war, where two highly disparate types of critical Greek Texts are available today. The first, representing the Majority text is the *Textus Receptus,* from which the KJV was translated. (*The Greek New Testament According to the Majority Text* by Hodges and Farstad must be rejected since it follows von Soden's collation of *only* 414 of the 5000+ manuscripts and ignores the older Andreas line of Revelation manuscripts.)

The agent in the aisle, representing the minority type text, is called the Nestle-Aland twenty-seventh edition or the United Bible Societies fourth edition. The Nestle's and UBS editions differ from the *Textus Receptus* in nearly 6000 places. This skimpier 'Raider's Digest' version scuttles enough words, verses and chapter sections to crowd a complete anthology on Christian creeds.

Nestle's Makes the Very Best. . .

. . .Chocolate, not Greek texts. Hort's heir was Eberhard Nestle, who in 1898 cloned the text for the next generation. In 1927 his son Erwin became warden, reforming its critical apparatus in minor ways and making a dozen or so changes in the text, yet guarding the minority 'spectre' of Hort's kin. In 1950, custody was transferred to Kurt Aland, who with the help of Matthew Black, Bruce Metzger and Allen Wikgren, today recommit allegiance to the Westcott-Hort text type.

A verbatim translation of the Nestle-Aland text, with all of its deletions, would shock even the most liberal reader and could never be sold as a 'New Testament'. [The closest actual translation of it are the super-liberal NEV, TEV, NRSV and Catholic Bibles, all of which use many of Nestle's manuscript D readings.] Consequently, other versions which are based on Nestle's, such as the NASB, 'borrow' some 'Majority' readings from the *Textus Receptus* in order to be marketable (e.g., John 7:53 and 8:1-11). Nestle's own statement, in his preface, cautions the reader that it is *not* the 'Traditional' Greek Text but a "Kind of New Textus Receptus."[51] Its advocates even caution the unlettered, who would take such a text and pronounce, "The Greek says. . ." For example, Philip Comfort, collaborator on *The New Greek-English Interlinear New Testament—NRSV* yields:

> This text however is by no means 'inspired' or 'infallible' as many scholars will readily attest. In fact, some scholars have openly criticized UBS3/NA26 as trying to gain the reputation of being the new 'Textus Receptus'; and other scholars are discouraged that this **new** text still looks so much like the Westcott-Hort text.[52]

Of the UBS3/NA26, other researchers conclude:

> [It is] the Greek text pieced together.[53]

> [T]he edition Nestle-Aland is clearly non-Byzantine.[54]

> It is of utmost importance to the true text of the Bible to oppose their minority Greek text and to support the traditional Greek text which basically is the text

> underlying the *King James Version* of the New Testament.[55]

Changes in both the Nestle's text and the critical apparatus have been made over the years. The NASB is based loosely on Nestle's 23rd edition (1959), but the *NASB Greek Interlinear* is marketed with Nestle's 21st edition (1951). In the recent Nestle's twenty-sixth edition (1979) the chameleon becomes a cobra with a whopping 712 changes in the Greek text. These drastic changes were a response to the cry of scholars who saw the mounting evidence of the papyri discoveries stacking up on the side of the KJV. Consequently, nearly 500 of these changes were 'white flags', retreating back to the pre-Westcott and Hort *Textus Receptus* readings. Now every third page reflects some sort of back-to-the *King James Version* reading. This about-face leaves Greek-o-philes footless, often armed only with their 1951 NASB-Nestle's Interlinear.

Resting on this Achilles heel, their case is further crippled by the new Introduction to Nestle's 26th edition. It no longer boasts of *Theta, Vaticanus, Sinaiticus*, or *Caesarean* families of manuscripts. Verses which had previously been discarded based on 'conflation', 'assimilation' or 'harmonization' suddenly pop back into the text. "The body of the Lord Jesus" even pops in in Luke 24:3. "The age of Westcott and Hort is definitely over," the Introduction says.[56] Scholars are aware of this shift, yet the pews are still piled high with NIV's, NASB's, NKJV's, *Living Bibles, New Jerusalem Bibles*, NRSV's, etc.. Comfort's extensive collation for his recent book, *Early Manuscripts and Modern Translations of the New Testament* prompted him to say:

> Although the NASB translators had claimed consideration was given to the latest available manuscripts with a view to determining the best Greek text (cited by Kubo and Specht in *So Many Versions?*, 173), the evidence does not bear this out. On the contrary, the NASB does not reflect the impact of the latest available manuscripts.[57]

The Apparatus Criticus

Kenneth W. Clark, noted textual scholar and author of "The Theological Relevance of Textual Variations in Current Criticism of the Greek New Testament" in the *Journal of Biblical Literature,* warns dabblers, as well as seasoned translators, of "pursuing the retreating mirage of the originals."[58] Yet pastors with post-graduate degrees, too sophisticated to use a bookstore variety Greek interlinear, are clutching their Greek edition published by the British and Foreign Bible Societies or by *Privilegierte Wurttembergische Bibelanstalt.* These contain a critical apparatus, that is, footnotes which enumerate which manuscripts attest to or omit a certain questionable reading. This gives the pastor, teacher or translator *a sense* that they can judge for themselves which reading is best, based on their (typically limited) exposure to the manuscripts themselves. Comfort talks about this teeter-tottering.

> For example some translators may have used a specific edition of the Nestle's text, but they deviate from the text at will choosing to follow here and there a variant reading cited in the apparatus.[59]

The swaying state of the new versions and their minority text is caused, in part, by this random rocking back and forth to the apparatus, not content to 'nestle' in the text.

Another crisis has now been uncovered as their 'critical' cushion crashes to the concrete, leaving unsupported, fans of the eclectic minority text. Colwell, University of Chicago's late President, gives us a frightening peek behind the closed doors of a meeting of the Society of Biblical Literature as he reports on the *discovery* by the International Greek New Testament Project (IGNT) of the 'sorry' state of the critical apparatus.

> [C]areful study shows that the textual evidence in these editions cannot be used in the IGNT apparatus, since they fail to cite witnesses completely, consistently or accurately.[60]

Other noted scholars have concluded "the critical apparatus. . . misleads the user and presents a distorted view of the evidence."[61] Eberhard Nestle's son, Erwin, said, "My father knew quite well that a certain one sidedness adhered to his text." This new version critical apparatus cites only 7% of the cursives, .02% of the lectionaries, 24% of the church fathers and 33% of the versions.

The crumbling cause of the minority text mounts debris in the margin, as each subsequent *printing* of the Nestle's 26th edition shows changes in the critical apparatus. Its eighth printing affected Hebrews 6:7-9, 15-17, Ephesians 1 and 2, and Thessalonians 1. Comfort says, "In future printings, we should see. . .[affected] John 18:36-19:7, John 2:30-37, 46-3:2, John 13:15-17, Acts 2:30-37, 46-3:2, John 5:26-29, 36-38."[62]

These changes are due to the historically weak foundation on which Nestle's readings lie. Nestle's omission of Matthew 21:44 is a typical example. It is based on three witnesses—D (fifth century), 33 and Lucifer of Cagliari. (The latter is not a legitimate witness since he quotes verse 43, not 42, 44, or 45.) The verse in question is in every known Codex, five from the second and third century, eight from the fourth, seven from the fifth and all other manuscripts following. It is in the ancient Syrian, Coptic, Armenian, Ethiopic, Curetonian, Harkleian, Peshitto, Old Latin and Vulgate versions. A few other brief examples represent the irrational judgements which have abounded in various editions of Nestle's Greek text.

> • Each of the gospels had at least six instances in which Nestle's ignored the oldest manuscripts. It disregarded the oldest readings in such places as Luke 16, Romans 5,8,9,12,15, Matthew 22,27, I Corinthians, II Corinthians, Galatians 1, 2, 3, Ephesians 3, Colossians 1, and Revelation 11 (e.g., I Corinthians 13:3 in Nestle's reads like manuscript C (5th century) rather than P46, Aleph, B (2nd and 4th century) and the Majority.
>
> • "Jesus" was omitted scores of places, such as Matthew 4:23, where its omission is based on only one manuscript; *all* other MSS have Jesus.
>
> • Based on D (5th century) alone, 38 critical words (15%) were omitted from the last chapter of Luke. Nestle's followed 'D' alone many times. Ironically, however, D *has* John 5:34, yet Nestle's *omits* them.

United Bible Society: UBS 3rd & 4th Edition

The uncertainty, rampant in the state of these critical editions, is further evident in the UBS 3rd & 4th edition, *The Greek New Testament.* The disputability of their text is even 'codified' by their editors in the Introduction.

> By means of the letters A, B, C, and D, enclosed within 'braces' { } at the beginning of each set of textual variants, the Committee has sought to indicate the **relative** degree of certainty, arrived at. . .The letter A signifies the text is virtually certain, while B indicates that there is **some** degree of doubt. The letter C means there is a **considerable** degree of doubt whether the text or the apparatus contains the superior reading, while D shows that there is a **very high degree of doubt** concerning the reading for the text.[63]

Much like Nestle's dramatic turn around, the UBS third edition was forced to make 500 changes from its second edition. Since there were *no* manuscript discoveries in that interim, Pickering observes, "It is hard to resist the suspicion that they are guessing." *The New International Version* (NIV) followed the UBS first edition (1966), thereby missing hundreds of updates.

"A New Age in the Church"

Who are these guessers? The UBS Vice President is Roman Catholic Cardinal Onitsha of Nigeria. The executive committee includes Roman Catholic Bishop Alilona of Italy. Among the editors is Roman Catholic Cardinal Martini of Milan. In the past, Catholics would not work with Protestants in the work of bible translation, because Catholics translated using the Greek manuscript Vaticanus (B) as seen in Jerome's Latin Vulgate. Protestants, until 1881, used the Majority Greek Text. Now that liberal Protestants are using the Vatican Manuscript also, Catholics are saying (Vatican II):

> Catholics should work together with Protestants in the fundamental task of biblical translation. . .[They can] work very well together and have the same approach and

> interpretation. . .[This] signals a **new age** in the church. . .[64]

This began in 1943 when Papal encyclical *Divino Afflante Spiritu* called for an ecumenical bible. It said:

> [T]hese translations [should] be produced in cooperation with separated brothers.[65]

Subsequently, Jesuit scholars moved on to editorial positions in the previously Protestant *Journal of Biblical Literature*. Their work on the UBS/Nestle's text and influence in biblical scholarship has biased so many 'new' readings that the recent Catholic *New American Bible* was translated directly from UBS/Nestle, rather than the traditional Catholic Latin Vulgate. Its introduction notes:

> In general, Nestle's-Aland's *Novum Testamentum Graece* (25th edition, 1963) was followed. Additional help was derived from *The Greek New Testament* (editors Aland, Black, Metzger, Wikgren) produced for the use of translators by the United Bible Societies in 1966.[66]

Since both the Catholic and 'New' Protestant bibles are now based on *the identical* critical Greek texts (UBS/Nestle's,) which are based on the same 1% minority Greek Manuscripts (*Vaticanus, B*), the Catholic doctrinal bend in the NIV and NASB and other 'New' bibles is substantial. (This is documented in Chapter 8.) Hand-in-hand, Catholics and unwary Protestants, with their Gnostic Vatican manuscript under their arm, are being steered into the waiting arms of the one world church of the Antichrist. Dean Stanley, a member of one of these corrupt translation committees, applauds this subtle work of the new versions in preparing for 'amalgamation'.

> [T]he revision work is of the utmost importance. . .in its indirect effect upon a closer union of the different denominations.[67]

New Inconsistent Versions (NIV, NASB, NEB, etc.)

To determine the consistency of manuscript use in the new versions, six verses were selected at random from within the short compass of a few pages of the bible, that is, the last nine chapters of I Corinthians. My collation of the manuscript evidence shows new version editors using Majority or KJV readings when *no* doctrinal issues are involved (three out of three verses). This might be expected since a large part of even new versions must contain the traditional bible readings in order to be sold as 'bibles'. However, they used random minority text type readings when an opportunity arose to present New Age philosophy or demote God or Christ. The inconsistent choice of witnesses throughout these six verses will be evident upon study by the reader. Note particularly that the favored manuscripts in item four and five are diametrically opposite.

NEW VERSIONS	MANUSCRIPTS	DOCTRINES
1. I Cor. 7:15	**Ignores**: Aleph **Follows**: P46, B and Majority	
2. I Cor. 8:3	**Ignores**: Aleph, B and Majority **Follows**: P46	P46 reads, "If any man loves he is known" rather than the other reading "If any man loves God, he is known by him."
3. I Cor. 10:9	**Ignores**: P46 and Majority **Follows**: Aleph and B	Denies deity of Christ by not identifying him as the rock that accompanied the Israelites in the desert.
4. I Cor. 11:24	**Ignores**: Majority **Follows**: P46, B, and Aleph	Denies Christ was "Broken for you."
5. I Cor. 13:3	**Ignores**: Aleph, B and P46 **Follows**: Majority	
6. I Cor. 14:38	**Ignores**: P46, Majority, B **Follows**: Aleph	

Again we see the New Age menu of 'brotherly love', the denial of the perpetual deity of Christ and his sacrifice for sins, served to unsuspecting Christians. In I Corinthians 10:9, new versions, following old editions of Nestle's Greek, use "Lord" despite the earlier and weightier attestation of "Christ." The recent switch in the Nestle's 26th edition to the KJV, P46 and Majority text reading of "Christ", marks the new versions as obsolete. New version collaborator, Philip Comfort, comments concerning the apparent doctrinal bias:

> Some scribes from the fourth century onward must have had a theological problem with the reading 'Christ' and thus tried to neutralize it to 'Lord' or 'God'. I say fourth century because not one witness prior to the fourth century attests to the reading 'Lord' or 'God'. The earliest MS, P46 and several church fathers attest to the reading of 'Christ'. Later MSS and later church fathers attest mainly to the reading 'Lord'. However a majority of MSS persist in keeping the reading Christ.[68]

By randomly extending the investigation a few more pages, **over half** of the new version verses are seen to have followed the **exact opposite** evidence as the other half. The remainder exhibit gross inconsistency in the use of witnesses. (The "accepted principles of the science of textual criticism" used to justify this 'shell game', are hardly worth the printer's ink to list them. They are illustrations of Timothy's "science, falsely so called" and can be summarized in one sentence—"I believe the writer is probably more likely to have said this."

NEW VERSIONS	MANUSCRIPTS
7. I Cor. 15:49	**Ignores**: P46, Aleph, and Majority **Follows**: B
8. I Cor. 15:54	**Ignores**: P46 and Aleph **Follows**: Aleph (Corrector) and B
9. 2 Cor. 1:10	**Ignores**: P46 **Follows**: Aleph and B

NEW VERSIONS	MANUSCRIPTS
10. 2 Cor. 1:11	**Ignores**: P46 and B **Follows**: Aleph
11. 2 Cor. 1:12	**Ignores**: Majority **Follows**: P46, Aleph and B
12. 2 Cor. 2:1	(NIV) **Ignores**: Aleph and Majority **Follows**: P46 and B (NASB) **Ignores**: P46 and B **Follows**: Majority
13. 2 Cor. 2:17	**Ignores**: P46 **Follows**: Aleph and B
14. 2 Cor. 3:2	**Ignores**: Aleph **Follows**: P46 and B
15. 2 Cor. 3:9	(NASB) **Ignores**: B and Majority **Follows**: P46 and Aleph (NIV) **Ignores**: P46 and Aleph **Follows**: B and Majority
16. 2 Cor. 8:7	(NASB) **Ignores**: Aleph and Majority **Follows**: P46 and B (NIV) **Ignores**: P46 and B **Follows**: Aleph and Majority
17. Gal. 1:3	**Ignores**: P46 and B **Follows**: Aleph
18. Gal. 1:8	(NIV) **Ignores**: P51 and B **Follows**: Aleph (NASB) **Ignores**: Aleph **Follows**: P51 and B

NEW VERSIONS	MANUSCRIPTS
19. Gal. 1:15	(NIV) **Ignores**: P46 and B **Follows**: Aleph (NASB) **Ignores**: Aleph **Follows**: P46 and B
20. Gal. 4:25	**Ignores**: P46 and Aleph **Follows**: B
21. Gal. 4:28	**Ignores**: Aleph and Majority **Follows**: P46 and B
22. Gal. 6:2	(NASB) **Ignores**: P46 and B **Follows**: Aleph and Majority (NIV) **Ignores**: Aleph and Majority **Follows**: P46 and B
23. Gal. 6:13	**Ignores**: P46 and B **Follows**: Aleph

Not only do they choose to follow different manuscripts half of the time, but the NIV and NASB disagree as to which ones to follow.

"The Original Greek says. . ."

The next time this fictitious phrase is flipped at you, by a modern day Ananias, attempting to advance his ascendency and authority, simply say:

> "Save you too be 'slain in Spirit' like Sapphria, tell me—which Greek? In Matthew 13:28, we see the following disparity:
>
> •Nestle's follows Manuscript C
> •UBS follows Manuscript B

•*Textus Receptus* follows Manuscripts L, W, 1, 13, pm, vg, sy.

So, which Greek? Aleph1, Aleph2, Aleph3, B1, B2, B3, C, L, W, *Textus Receptus*, Westcott and Hort, Scrivener's, Alfred, Griesbach, Elzevir, Erasmus, Tischendorf, Lachman, Souter, von Soden, Hodge-Farstad, Nestle's-Aland, (If so which edition between 1 and 26?, which printing of the 26th?) UBS-Aland, Black, Metzger, Wikgren (Which edition between 1 and 4?) or the Greek-English Diglot for the Use of Translators.

A complete list of manuscripts and critical texts will bury the boaster in words, with the epitaph, "It's Greek to me.."

In conclusion, recent scholarship demonstrates that the majority of manuscripts, as seen in the traditional Greek *Textus Receptus* and its translation, the *King James Version*, represent the earliest, broadest (numerically and geographically) and most consistent edition of the New Testament. On the other hand the new versions and their underlying unsettled Nestle's-Aland type eclectic text, use later readings, representing a narrow "fraction of 1%" of the extant manuscripts, from one locale. They typify Satan's meager and shaky attempt to counterfeit the written "word of God" (II Corinthians 2:17, Hebrews 4:12)—just like he tries to counterfeit the living "Word of God" (Revelation 19:13, Isaiah 14).

THIRTY - SEVEN

Inspiration & Preservation

Have it your way

". . .hold the pickle. . .and the ascension." The diversity of 'opinion' and preference in relation to the readings in the minority Greek text is symptomatic of the subjective relativism which has swept into the church from a world brimming over with it. New Ager Vera Alder says of the 'New' world religion:

> It is likely that a new kind of religion will develop in which each man will discover and work out his own sermons for himself.[1]

Perhaps Matthew 17:21, 18:11, Acts 8:37, Romans 16:24, and scores of other verses are not in your sermon (or your NIV). The Old Testament lament, ". . .every man did that which was right in his own eyes," still sounds today. Seth, an entity now being channeled in New Age circles echoes: "There is no authority superior to the guidance of a person's inner self."[2] This wizard 'peeps' as cultists and textual scholars 'mutter' the same monotonous declamation. Hare Krishna devotees listen to see if a bible verse has a "ring of truth."[3] Hort used his "instinctive" powers to determine if a verse had a "ring of genuineness."[4] J.B. Phillips touts the reader of his forward to the *NASB Interlinear Greek-English New Testament* to "try to make his own translation," looking for *The Ring of Truth* (the title of his autobiography). Westcott recommends using your "intuitive powers" as a sounding board.[5] For your first try, the following verses are given with their corresponding manuscript variations (on the left) and manuscript evidence (on the right).

Colossians 2:2

του Θεου χαι Πατρος χαι του Χριστου	Byz D^c K *pm* Lect
του Θεου χαι Πατρος του Χριστου	$Aleph^b$ Ψ *pc* sy^h
του Θεου Πατρος χαι του Χριστου	0208 1908 sy^p
του Θεου Πατρος του Χριστου	A C it^{pt} sa^{pt} bo
του Θεου Πατρος Χριστου	Aleph 048
του Θεου Χριστου	P^{46} B (alone of MSS)
του Θεου	D^b H P 436 1881 sa^{pt}
(at least seven further variations)	

Matthew 10:3

Θαδδαιος	Aleph
και Θαδδαιος	B *pc* vg cop
και Λεββαιος	D 122 d k
και Λεββαιος ο επικληθεις Θαδδαιος	Byz C^2 K L W X Δ Θ Π 1 *pl* sy $^{p, h, pal}$

Matthew 13:28

οι δε αυτω λεγουσιν	B 157 *pc* cop
οι δε δουλοιειπονaυτω	Byz L W Θ 1 13 *pm* vg sy^h
οι δε δουλοι αυτω λενουσιν	C (NESTLES)
λεγουσιν αυτω οι δουλοι	D it (sy $^{c, s, p}$)
οι δε δουλοι λεγουσιν αυτω	Aleph (UBS)

Matthew 15:14

οδηγοι εισιν τυφλοι τυφλων	Byz C W X Δ Π 0106 *pm* q
οδηγοι εισιν τυφλοι	Aleph cop sy^c
οδηγοι εισιν τυφλων	B D 0237
τυφλοι εισιν οδηγοι	Aleph ^{c} L Z Θ 1 13 33 *al* lat $sy^{p,h}$
τυφλοι οδηγοι εισιν τυφλων	K pc sy^s

Mark 12:17

και αποκριθεις	W 258 *al*
ο δε Ιησους	Aleph B C L Δ Ψ 33 pc sy $^{(p)}$cop
και αποκριθεις ο Ιησους	Byz P^{45} A N X Γ Π Φ1 13 *pm* sy $^{(s), h}$
αποκριθεις δε ο Ιησους	D 700 *pc* lat
αποκριθεις δε	Θ 565

Romans 6:12

αυτη	P^{46} D E F G d f g m
ταις επιθυμιαις αυτου	Aleph A B C *al* lat cop
αυτη εν ταις επιθυμιαις αυτου	Byz K L P Ψ pm

I Thessalonians 3:2

και διακονον τον θεον	Aleph A P Ψ pc lat cop
και συνεργον	B 1962
και συνεργον τον θεον	D 33 b d e mon
διακονον και συνεργον τον θεον	G f g
και διακονον τον θεον και συνεργον ημων	Byz K *pl* sy^{p,h}

Luke 9:10

τοπον ερημον	Aleph al sy^{c}
κωμην λεγομενην Βηδσαιδα	D
πολιν καλουμενην Βηδσαιδα	P^{75}
πολιν καλουμενην Βηθσαιδα	Aleph^{c} B L Ξ 33 *pc* cop
τοπον ερημον πολεως καλουμενης Βηθσαιδαν	Byz A C W (1) 13 *pm* sy(p),h
κωμην καλουμενην Βηθσαιδαν εις τοπον ερημον	Θ

Luke 12:18

παντα τα γενηματα μου	Aleph D it (sy^{s,c})
παντα τον σιτον και τα αγαθα μου	P^{75c} B L 070 1 (13) *pc* cop
παντα τα γενηματα μου και τα αγαθα μου	Byz A Q W Θ Ψ *pm* vg sy^{p,h}

John 8:51

τον λογον μου	433 *pc*
τον εμον λογον	P^{75} Aleph B C D L X W Ψ 0124 33 *al* cop
τον λογον τον εμον	Byz P^{66} E G K Γ Δ Θ Λ Π 1 13 *pm* lat syr

One might not actively give voice to Shirley MacLaine's, "We are not under the law of God. We are the law of God!" But picking and choosing what should be in God's bible is tantamount to following Luciferian David Spangler who said:

> The evolution of the race is for every man not to learn to obey the law but to be the law. . .We can take all the scriptures. . .and have a jolly good bonfire. . .Once you are the truth, you do not need it externally represented.[6]

So. . .maybe we Christians only throw in the fire several dozen scriptures relating to the deity of Christ or Acts 8:37 on the eunuch's salvation. These flares may not make a bonfire, but will smolder in our spirits, searing the soul toward God and parching our spiritual progress.

> How great a matter a little fire kindleth. James 3:5

"The word is very nigh unto thee"

It is obvious that the word of God in its perfect state does not reside in any one of the *ancient Greek manuscripts* extant today. Even Bruce Metzger admits:

> [T]he disquieting possibility remains that the evidence available to us today may, in certain cases be totally unrepresentative of the distribution of readings in the early church.[7]

The carnal spirit of Gnosticism, that is, the desire for hidden knowledge others do not have, is prevalent in the New Age *and* the church. New Agers try to get a word from 'God' through some 'hidden' wisdom from 'far off' gurus living 'beyond the sea'. Christians search for the 'hidden' meaning of a word in Greek lexicons from 'far off' Egyptian manuscripts from 'beyond the sea'. But the Lord has said:

> For this commandment which I command thee this day, it is not **hidden** from thee, [in ancient Greek, which you

> don't understand] neither is it **far off** [in the 5000 or so manuscripts held in the Vatican or in museums around the world]. It is not in heaven, that thou shouldest say Who shall go up for us to heaven and bring it unto us, that we may hear it and do it? Neither is it **beyond the sea** [buried in some yet to be found papyri] that thou shouldest say, Who shall go over the sea for us and bring it unto us that we may hear it and do it? But the word is very nigh unto thee, in thy mouth [Is the Greek in your mouth?] and in thy heart, that thou mayest do it.
> Deuteronomy 30:11-14

"The word is very nigh unto thee. . .that thou mayest do it." However, by pushing the scriptures out of our laps and back into a yet undiscovered dirt mound from the first century, we avoid the "sharp" pruning of the word of God. We prune it—before it prunes us.

Preservation Promised

The bible repeatedly speaks of God's promise to preserve his word—not, however the paper on which the Autographs were written, nor early copies of these originals. God commanded Jeremiah to throw his 'originals' in the river! (Jeremiah 51:63)

> Heaven and earth shall pass away but my words shall not pass away. Matthew 24:35

> The grass withereth, the flower fadeth: but the word of our God shall stand for ever. Isaiah 40:8

> Now go, write it before them in a table and note it in a book that it may be for the time to come for ever and ever. Isaiah 30:8

> My words which I have put in thy mouth shall not depart out of thy mouth, nor out of the mouth of thy seed, nor out of the mouth of thy seed's seed, saith the Lord from henceforth and forever. Isaiah 59:21

> . . .the word of God which liveth and abideth forever.
> I Peter 1:23

The word of God was not only preserved after those pieces of fragile paper were destroyed, it *precedes* them.

> For ever, O LORD, Thy word is settled in heaven. Psalm 119:89

> For I have given unto them the words which thou gavest me. John 17:8

> The Father which sent me, he gave me a commandment, what I should say, and what I should speak. . .Whatsoever I speak therefore, even as the Father said unto me, so I speak. John 12:49-50

Muslim Mentality Mounting

The Christian doctrine of the preservation of scriptures is at striking odds with the beliefs of the New Age and pagan sects. The first doctrine of Buddhism is 'the doctrine of Impermanence', *anicca, Pali*, which says, "All things are impermanent."[8] The Hindu and Gnostic world view, particularly as seen in today's New Age movement, shows a disdain for matter and the material world, calling it *maya*, an illusion. Skeptical translators and diffident church doctrinal statements scoff at the doctrine of the preservation of scripture—just like the Khomeini.

AYATOLLAH KHOMEINI OF IRAN	CALVIN LINTON NIV TRANSLATOR
"No translation accurately transmits the messages of the Koran only the original is infallible."[9]	"No translation can be a perfect reproduction of the original."[10]

Like doubting Thomas, they say, "Except I see in *my* hands the prints of the *originals*. . .I will not believe." The error of this stance is rooted in an inacquaintance with the biblical definition of 'scripture'. When used, the term always refers to copies, not the original paper. Timothy (II Timothy 3:15), the Bereans (Acts 17:11) and the eunuch (Acts 8:32) did not have the original in their possession yet they "searched" and "knew" "the scriptures."

The new versions themselves deny that God's promise of perfect preservation extends beyond the originals. Although the verb "is" occurs in the following verse in every Greek manuscript, *The Living Bible* concurs with the Khomeini.

> All scripture **is** given by inspiration of God. KJV

> The whole Bible **was** given to us from God. LB

Observe how new versions dismantle the following verse attesting to God's promise to preserve a "pure" bible "for ever."

> The words of the LORD are **pure** words. . .Thou shalt keep them, O LORD, thou shalt **preserve** them from this generation **for ever**. Psalm 12:6,7 KJV

> O LORD, you will keep us safe and protect us from such people forever. NIV

> Thou wilt preserve him from this generation forever. NASB

Inspiration and the KJV

It appears the case for the inspiration of the KJV is mounting. Recent discoveries in the Ugaritic language have prompted recent translators to return to the KJV Old Testament renderings in some places. In Psalm 68, the KJV's "rideth upon the heavens," was found in the Ugaritic. The NASB retains the outdated, "rides through the deserts." (This sounds more like the Antichrist!) The NIV translators update to the KJV rendition and note, the KJV reading, "must have been a 'guess' from the context since this word normally signifies desert." In Isaiah 41, the lexicons previously indicated *'tishta'* meant 'see'; now the Ugaritic shows that it means 'fear'—the KJV reading all along. Larry Walker, NIV translator, comments on the KJV's dismissal of the lexicons saying, ". . .it is merely coincidence that the KJV and NIV came out with the same translation, because the NIV translators had access to this information unknown to the KJV translator."[11] Even the italics in the KJV are being vindicated by recent discoveries. Its ten italicized words in I John 2:23 were discovered hundreds of years later in what scholars perceive to be the most accurate ancient Greek manuscript.. Several ancient MSS have the italicized 'the church' in I Peter 5:13.[12] 'Guesses' or God, fear or faith, haughty or humble. These are the perpetual options for the Christian.

PART THREE

Back to the Future

THIRTY - EIGHT

The Western Roots of the New Age & New Versions

EGYPT:	PANTAENUS
	SACCAS
	PHILO
	CLEMENT
	ORIGEN
GREECE:	PLATO
ROME:	EUSEBIUS

The Men Behind the Manuscripts

Why do new versions agree with the New Age movement? *Who* originated the philosophies of today's New Age movement? *Who* originally wrote or influenced the few corrupt ancient manuscripts behind today's *New Age Versions*? The answer—the same men created both the manuscripts and the message.

The western roots of the New World Religion of the false prophet can be found in the philosophies of Egypt, Greece and Rome. The esoteric meanderings of philosophers such as Saccas, Philo and Origen spring from Egypt into the books of today's New Agers. The Greek philosophies of Plato provide the perfect broth for blending East and West in the New Age caldron. Moving further north yet, the Rome of Constantine and Eusebius, with their merger of Christianity and paganism, cradled the infantile crossbreed which today is Satan's seasoned scarlet woman. (Revelation 18)

Looking down into this poisoned well of the past reveals: 1.) the reservoir of 'ideas' spawning much of the 'New' Age and 2.) the course of contamination found in the 'New' versions. The well fed by Egypt, Greece, and Rome is today 'dished out' to New Agers and New Christians alike. The 'New' versions agree in many particulars with the 'New' Age because they flow from the same source. We will examine the philosophies of six men: Saccas, Philo, Plato, Clement, Origen and Eusebius—to see *why* new versions have New Age leaven. We will trace the origin of the handful of ancient papyrus and uncial New Testament manuscripts which were altered to agree with the esoteric philosophies of these men. These manuscripts (Aleph, B, D, P75, etc.) were resurrected by Westcott and Hort to 'correct' the Traditional Greek text. New versions are based on this corrupted Greek text. First we will look at these men and then their manuscripts.

The Return to Egypt (Exodus 13:17)

In 4B.C., Asoka, the emperor of India, sent Buddhist missionaries to Egypt. His coolies, Saccas, Philo, and Origen, carried the 'New' Age doctrine one step closer to our Western corridor. Now the Egyptian sand from spiritually arid Alexandria is choking both 'New' Ager and 'New' Christian with the words of Saccas, Philo and Origen. Secular scholars add Westcott and Hort to this Alexandrian sand storm which is blinding so many. Looking through the window of any city library in Small Town, U.S.A. will reveal the secular *Encyclopedia of Religion and Ethics*. Our duo, Westcott and Hort, is found in it under "Alexandrian Theology." In tracing the history of the mysticism of Alexandria, Egypt the *Encyclopedia* begins with a discussion of Philo, moves on to Clement and Origen, and ends with Westcott and Hort! They summarize this 'Theology' saying, "Those who would oust metaphysics from theology can have but scanty sympathy with the Alexandrian."[1]

On the next shelf, *Man, Myth and Magic: An Illustrated Encyclopedia of the Supernatural* points to the same "Alexandrian Theology" as the source of the New Age! They begin with Philo and end with Blavatsky.

> At Alexandria the philosophies of Philo Judaeus joined the ideas of Plato with Judaism in a theosophic system. It persisted in the Cabala and Neo-Platonism—all taught the essential base of theosophy. In modern times the name is associated with the system set out in the nineteenth century in the book by H.P. Blavatsky. . . [O]ccult feats made her salon a magnet for a wide variety of people.[2]

Blavatsky's Luciferian 'theosophy' is "Alexandrian Theology." The Theosophical Society's publication *Theosophy Simplified* reiterates the encyclopedia's remark.

> Saccas of Alexandrea coined the word Theosophia. Theosophy [was] first used by Saccas of Alexandria.[3]

We see from those two encyclopedias that 1.) Alexandria was a prime source for the philosophy of the New Age and 2.) Westcott, Hort and Blavatsky were its nineteenth century proponents. We are beginning to uncover *why* there is concurrence between the New Age and the new versions.

Just as Pharaoh's chain of bondage held the children of God, this Egyptian chain attempts to link the New Age with Judeo-Christian beliefs through men like Origen, Westcott and Hort. After the plague of flies Pharaoh said, "I will let you go. . .only ye shall not go very far away."(Exodus 8:28) Truly these men have not moved far from Egyptian philosophy.

Alexandria, Egypt was the crossroad where Eastern and Western culture and religious beliefs collided and became entangled. When Christianity came to Egypt to untangle the spiritual wreckage, it was assimilated and conjoined to Egypt's pagan heritage—the fate of scores of religions before it. Westcott boasts:

> Alexandria was a meeting place of east and west. . .[I]deas were discussed, exchanged and combined. When the east and west enter a true union then the canon [New Testament] is found perfect.[4]

Emperor Hadrian gives us a clearer picture and it was not 'perfect'.

> There is [at Alexandria] no ruler of the synagogue among the Jews, no Samaritan, no Christian who is not also an astrologer, soothsayer. . .Money is their god.

Hadrian's objectivity is missing from today's New Age movement. Their current preeminent monthly magazine is, in fact, called the *East West Journal*. One of its most vocal leaders, Benjamin Creme, "tells us that the New World Religion will fuse East and West. . ."[5] His sister soothsayer Alice Bailey writes of the one world religion as being "the factual solidarity of the Eastern and Western approaches to God."[6] Westcott is not alone among new version editors who seek the union of "east and west." Philip Schaff ('New' Greek Text, ASV and its offshoots the NASV and *Living Bible*) helped organize the 'World Religion Parliament'. Its keynote speaker, a Hindu named Vivekananda told attendees, "The East must come to the West."[7]

Philo: East Meets West

Philo (20B.C.-A.D.42) produced a philosophic ideology by coalescing the Old Testament (for which he "expressed contempt for the literal narrative") and the Greek philosophies of the Stoics and Heracleitus. Philo held that the scriptures held an occult or hidden meaning. Hort's personal letters disclose his penchant for Philo. His biographer said, "There are no writers on whom Dr. Hort spent more time than Josephus and Philo." Hort writes:

> I'm glad you are working on Philo's psychology. . .I lay on the sofa and read. . .Clement. . .wrote a piece of Introduction to the text [his 'New' Greek text]. . .took my manuscript book. . .and references from Philo. . .dinner came. . .then a good piece of Shakespeare. . .more Introduction. . .a little Philo at night and some Bible.[8]

While Philo was influencing Hort's work on his 'New' Greek New Testament Text, Madame Blavatsky was penning quotes from Philo in her occult tome, *The Secret Doctrine.* There she cites Philo to explain her odd beliefs, like "Satan is a God, of whom even the Lord is in fear."[9] In her *Theosophical Glossary*, she states that Philo, ". . . was a great mystic and. . .in esoteric knowledge he had no rival."[10]

Not only did Philo's philosophy influence the revisors of the 'New' Greek, but *his own* codex was used to alter the NIV in Luke 1:78. Papyri #4 was discovered *in* the binding of a codex of Philo's. Needless to say, this is not a 'repository' of truth. In Luke 1:78 his papyrus reads, he "will come to us." It uses a future tense verb, rather than he "hath visited" us, the reading seen in the Majority Greek Text and consequently the KJV.[11] This denial that Christ has come in the flesh is the mark of antichrist as described in I John 4:2.

Plato: 19th Century Revival

Man, Myth and Magic concluded that Blavatsky's nineteenth century New Age religion was a fusion of the philosophies of Philo of Alexandria, Egypt and Plato of Greece; so also the *Encyclopedia of Religion and Ethics* names Plato as the fountainhead for all of the "Alexandrians" from Philo to Westcott.

> Jewish and Christian Platonism, as developed at Alexandria. . .[has] three representative names. . .Philo, Clement, and Origen. . .Among later developments of Christian Platonism. . .it is necessary to mention. . .the Cambridge Platonists of the seventeenth century, and in our day the theology of F.D. Maurice [Hort's 'Apostles'] and Westcott. . .Alexandrianism has been revived by modern thinkers. . .Westcott. . .Hort.[12]

So we have Blavatsky resuscitating 'Alexandrianism' and Plato for the inner circle of New Agers and Westcott and Hort recasting the New Testament in light of Plato's "ideas" for the outer circle. Westcott calls Plato a "prophet" whose works are a "treasure" "in some danger of being forgotten."[13] Plato's ideas have rightly escaped the mind of most Christians but run into the waiting arms of Madame Blavatsky. She summoned him nearly one-hundred times in her writings to act as oracle for her New Age and Luciferian blasphemy. Westcott thinks Plato has a clear source of "truth," which for us is "blurred and dim." He writes that this "truth" stems from Plato's,

> . . .communion with a divine and super-sensuous world,. . .[with] those beings who occupy a middle place between God and man. . .[A]ll fellowship which exists between heaven and earth is realized through this intermediate order. . .These spirits are many and manifold.[14]

Westcott's Ghostly Guild activities were no doubt aimed at garnering 'truths' from this 'world'. *The Encyclopedia* cites a tendency of all of these 'Alexandrian' mystics to call in intermediary powers such as spirits.[15]

One of Plato's most well-known philosophies is his concept of 'the Idea' wherein the outside form of things merely veils 'the idea', which alone is real. Westcott expresses this Eastern and Gnostic world view saying,

> There is. . .a serious danger in the prevailing spirit of realism which leads us to dwell on the outside form, the dress of things, to the neglect of 'ideas' which are half-veiled. . .Eternal life is. . .the potential fulfillment of the 'idea' of humanity.[16]

Plato: 20th Century Revival

The T.V. mini-series *The Power of Myth* 'programmed' potential New Agers with Plato's concept of 'the Idea'. Joseph Campbell, its author, also wrote *Hero with a Thousand Faces.* Both try to popularize Westcott's Platonic idea that, as Westcott says, God appears, "not in one form, but in many."[17] [Buddha, Krishna, Mary] If you missed the mini-series reruns, your college psychology class will present the same concept under the guise of Carl Jung's 'archetypes' welling up from the 'universal unconscious'. Following these links in the chain, which attempts to keep the world close to spiritual Egypt, brings us to the current library of the New Ager. Authors Pride and de Parrie note:

> The similarities between [Plato] and the utopias proposed by the New Agers. . .are not coincidental.[18]

These authors find the *Dialogues of Plato* being promoted through New Age bookstores. New Age authors, like Lola Davis, cultivate interest in Plato citing his initiation into the Egyptian and Pythagorean mysteries. Plato is their hero because he broke his vow of secrecy to promote 'New Age' consciousness among the masses.[19]

In a typical New Age bookstore, Westcott and Hort and Schaff's grandchild, the NASB might be found alongside the *Dialogues of Plato*. The preface to the New Age *Metaphysical Bible Dictionary* says, "[T]his [NASB] version is used and recommended by the Unity School of Christianity."[20] I happened to read a small booklet, *What's Wrong with Unity School of Christianity* by Louis Talbot, *while* researching Platonism and reading the biographies of Westcott and Hort.[21] Like images in a three way mirror, this 'New Age' Unity Church, Platonism, and the Alexandrian mysticism of Westcott and Hort, are recognizable as reflections of the same approaching New World Religion.

When the Antichrist and False Prophet initiate their World Religion, they may simply quote Plato's *Republic* or *Dialogue* which recommends, "[A]ll religion and religious doctrine [is] to be state controlled." Plato advocated that this dominion begin at birth so that "no parent is to know his own child." Westcott and Hort's 'coenobium' was planned to be, as Hort wrote in 1869, "an artificial family as a substitute for a natural family." Socialist and communist regimes have historically used this ploy. And it is being imported to America in the sometimes careless use of day care centers. (Some mistake the price tag on the VCR or BMW for the actual price. The hidden cost is the soul of their child. Much too expensive, I venture.)

Plato's vision for the state control of children is rooted in his 'ideate' of the "*summum bonum*" or greatest good. He said, "join me in the search for the good." Scholars say that the Platonic dialogue concerning 'What is good' was inserted by Gnostics into Matthew 19:16,17 in several ancient New Testament manuscripts. It now appears in the Unity recommended NASB, as well as other new versions.[22]

> NIV
> Teacher, what good thing must I do to get eternal life? Why do you ask me **what is good**, Jesus replied. There is only One who is good:

Its inclusion in the new versions is based on two fourth century manuscripts from Alexandria, Egypt, *Aleph* and *B*. It is also seen in the writings of Origen and Eusebius, who will be discussed shortly. The new versions witness against themselves because this same story is told again in Mark 10:17 and Luke 18:18 where the new versions render it correctly. The majority of Greek texts and the KJV agree in all three locations. Testimony earlier than *Aleph* and *B*, agrees with the Majority Text; this includes Justin Martyr (A.D.150), Irenaeus (A.D.180), Hippolytus (A.D.200), the Sahidic and Peshitta Versions and D, the third oldest uncial. The manuscript evidence overwhelmingly agrees with the KJV, as usual.

> Good Master, what good thing shall I do that I may have eternal life? And he said unto him, why callest thou me good? there is none good but one, that is God:

Jesus was saying, in essence, 'Do you recognize that I am God? The new versions change this from a discussion of the deity of Christ to a philosophical argument. The internal disagreement within these versions destroys the harmony of the gospels.

Heresy: Then and Now

The appearance of this Platonic dialogue in the Westcott and Hort 'New' Greek Text came from their use of the two Alexandrian manuscripts. It can further be explained by unfolding Hort's letter to Mr. A. MacMillan, the publisher. In it he announces that Plato was "the center of my reading" while creating the New Greek text.[23] His biography further speaks of his fascination "with Plato and Aristotle to say nothing of more modern speculations."[24] This led Hort to translate the whole works of Plato in 1857. He comments:

> . . .the great Greeks. Sometimes I have a yearning to read nothing else and often think of assigning them a fixed number of hours per week. . .[M]y old fondness for philosophy makes me anxious to make it a serious and constant study.[25]

Platonic speculations found in Hort's correspondence with F.D. Maurice, (his "idol" and the "most powerful element in his religious development") caused Maurice's dismissal from his professorship at Cambridge.[26] Heresy which caused dismissal one hundred years ago is the *status quo* today. It has almost become 'heresy' to use the word 'heresy' in the 'New' church.

> For I know this, that after my departing shall grievous wolves enter in **among you**, not sparing the flock. Also **of your own selves** shall men arise, speaking perverse things, to draw away disciples after them. Therefore watch, and remember, that by the space of three years I ceased not to warn every one night and day with tears. Acts 20:29,30

The Moody Press publication, *The Agony of Deceit*, in reviewing the apostasy in the church today, expresses the same concern.

> Throughout history Christianity has had to fight Platonizing tendencies even within its own orthodox ranks. What concerns us here is not Platonizing tendencies but the adoption of Platonic Heresies—the

> same heresies that became central in the Gnostic cult against which the apostles fought so vigorously.[27]

The heresy which is being assimilated into the church today is being tolerated under the same guise as it began. *The Encyclopedia of Religion and Ethics'* section on "Heresy" describes "the men" and "the method" dominant *then* and *now*.

> [T]he danger was increased through the combination of Oriental forms of imagery with Greek Christian thoughts.[28]

Today the New Age still bombards the church with its Oriental and Greek philosophy. Paul warned the Colossian church most clearly:

> Beware lest any man spoil you through philosophy and vain deceit, after the tradition of men, after the rudiments of the world, and not after Christ. Colossians 2:8

Hort disagreed holding, "Greek philosophy. . .seems full of precious truths."[29] The NIV agrees saying, "hollow philosophy" is to be avoided, not *all* philosophy. (Colossians 2:8) The NIV translators ignore the order of the Greek words here, as they often do.

Westcott also chose to ignore the scriptural admonition against philosophy; he even wrote an entire book, *Religious Thought in the West,* showcasing Plato, Aeschylus, Euripides, Dionysius, Origen and others. This book was not written during a mental hiatus from his position in the Anglican church, but between 1866-1883—*the* very years in which his *Revised Version* was taking shape. He thinks that through philosophy the seeker can,

> . . .learn as perhaps he can in no other way what the apostolic message is.[30]

As late as 1891 he conceded that "some of the lines of thought which I have endeavored to indicate. . .may be strange, but I know they are worth following." He contends that God has revealed truths to the heathen which he has hidden from the Christian.

> He has made some parts of his will clearer than to us. . . The noblest speculations of men who have not the Faith are thus unconscious prophecies. . .In such writings the Spirit manifested in many strange ways and unexpected quarters, lies our guidance. The last word of God is not yet spoken. . .[M]en will hereafter see truths which have not been made known to us, truths brought from many fresh springs.[31]

Today's New Age International Cooperation Council concisely echoes Westcott in their 'Declaration of Independence'.

> [R]espect the teachings of the prophets and sages at all time and in all cultures.[32]

Alexandria's "Grievous Wolves": Clement and Origen

You may not have heard of Clement of Alexandria, but your children have been exposed to his philosophies if they have seen the Hanna-Barbera video cartoon 'The Nativity" or read *The MacMillan Book of 366 Bible Stories* for children. Both present Clement's eccentric notion that Jesus Christ was born in a cave. 'Lambs' are born in stables; bats and wolves are born in caves. Scholars identify Clement and Origen of Alexandria, Egypt as two of the "grievous wolves" of Paul's warning. *The Encyclopedia of Religion and Ethics* follows the tracks of the wolf pack down to the twentieth century:

> Clement and Origen, by which. . .Platonism. . .was incorporated into Christianity. . .[M]odern thinkers, for example Westcott, are in sympathy with Clement and Origen.[33]

The Encyclopedia closes its article on 'Alexandrianism' citing Hort's opinion of Clement:

> In Clement, Christian theology, in some important respects, reaches its highest point. . .There was no one whose vision of what the faith of Jesus Christ was intended to do for mankind was so full and so true.[34]

The chart at the end of this chapter reveals Clement and Origen, not as high points, but as low points reaching down into the New Age pit for their doctrines. *The History of Heresy* calls Origen a 'Christian Gnostic' who was pronounced a 'heretic' by a series of general synods.[35]

The philosophical school, based in Alexandria, had seen as its head Pantaenus, a pagan gnostic, followed by Clement, who was succeeded by Origen. Like Philo, these scholars attempted to cross the young Christian cub with the wailing wolf of the 'hidden wisdom' of paganism. Philip Lee, author of *Against the Protestant Gnostics* and graduate of Princeton and Harvard Divinity Schools observes:

> The Alexandrian school was indeed one of the historical moments in the church's closest proximity to gnostic heresy. . .[For] Clement and Origen. . .gnosis [hidden wisdom], far from being a forbidden word, was a basic tenet of their system. . .[T]he word gnosis is the key to Clement's work.[36]

Ammonius Saccas also taught at this school and is often called 'the Father of the New Age religion'. The encyclopedia *Man, Myth and Magic* lists Ammonius Saccas of Alexandria as the founder of Madame Blavatsky's Luciferian Theosophy and the foundation of the New Age philosophy. Westcott seems to share Blavatsky's ardor for Saccas when writing:

> His success shewed that he had some neglected forms of **truth** to make known; and Origen became one of his hearers. . .There can be no doubt that Origen was deeply influenced by the new philosophy.[37]

Blavatsky summons Origen dozens of times in her *Isis Unveiled* to pander her occult doctrines. Her *Theosophical Glossary* places him where he belongs, as a "disciple" of neo-platonism at the Alexandria School of Ammonius Saccas.[38] She sees Clement and Origen as apologists for her occult world view:

> It is maintained on purely historical grounds that Origen. . .and even Clement had themselves been initiated into the Mysteries, before adding to the Neo-Platonism of the

> Alexandrian school that of the Gnostics, under a Christian veil.[39]

She calls it 'a Christian veil'; Jesus called it 'wolves clothing'. Blavatsky is not alone among New Agers in seeing Clement and Origen as 'fellow-travelers'. Even today's favorite New Age psychologist, Carl Jung, records "channeling" one of Origen's students.[40] New Age books, like *The Hidden Wisdom in the Holy Bible,* quote Origen at length with such blasphemies as, "[T]he laws of men appear more excellent and reasonable than the laws of God."[41] Rudolf Steiner's *The Esoteric Basis of Christianity*, a book teeming with positive references to Lucifer, says:

> The divinity of man, of all men, was taught. . .from the writings of Origen and Clement. Plato is saturated with it.[42]

The *McClintock and Strong Encyclopedia* records Origen as saying, "[T]he scriptures are of little use to those who understand them as they are written." *Hidden Wisdom* vaults Origen's allegorical method of bible interpretation saying:

> Disciples of Saccas and the neo-platonists of Alexandria and their successors [Clement and Origen] down to this present day [Westcott, Hort, and Blavatsky] have all regarded world scripture as being largely, but not entirely allegorical. The hidden sense lies concealed.[43]

Note how the following New Agers must weave Origen's web of allegory around the scriptures to promote their 'private' interpretation.

Unity Christianity:	"New Thought, Christian Science, and Unity. . .spiritualize every truth in the Word of God. . .[T]he Scriptures become an allegory."[44]
Alice Bailey:	"[T]he entire Gospel story. . .contains little except symbolic details."[45]

H.P. Blavatsky:	"It is well known that Origen, and Clement. . .confessed that. . .the Bible were veiled and secret books"[46]
Corrine Heline author of *New Age Bible Interpretation*:	Cites Origen and his belief that "[T]he entire bible is written so that it has one meaning for the masses of the people and another for occult students."[47]

Westcott repeats the *New Age Bible Interpretation*'s view almost verbatim.

> It must be remembered that the book (Origen's *On First Principle*) was not for simple believers but for scholars—for those who were familiar with the teachings of Gnosticism and Platonism. . .questions which. . .become urgent when men have risen to a wide view of Nature and life. He aimed at presenting the higher knowledge.[48]

(In Matthew 7:13 Jesus calls the "wide view of Nature and life"—"the broad way. . .that leadeth to destruction.") Westcott's son tells us that, "For many years the works of Origen were close to his [Westcott's] hand and he turned to them at every opportunity." For this reason Westcott was selected to write the section on Origen in the *Dictionary of Christian Biography*.[49] He also reserved a large section in his book, *Religious Thought in the West*, to present Origen views. Westcott uses Origen's allegorical approach to scripture to dismiss its literal narrative:

> We transfer. . .the language of earth. . .to an order of beings to which it is wholly inapplicable. We have not yet made good the position which he marked out as belonging to the domain of Christian Philosophy. . .They are in danger of being forgotten. . .He has left us the duty of maintaining his conclusions in a later age.[50]

Rest assured, the "later age" or New Age 'Christian' scholar will not leave it buried or "forgotten". Theologians like Emmanual

Kant exhumed the allegorical method for Westcott's generation. The author of the recent *New Directions in New Testament Study* points his reader to the new trend of applying "Clement and Origen's biblical alchemy and mysterious language of symbols," using the views of "Freud" [atheist], "Jung" [occultist], "Eliade" [shamanist] and "Erikson" [humanist], to interpret the bible.[51]

Dr. Henry Krabbendam, in his "Twisting Scriptures" section of the recent Moody Press book *The Agony of Deceit,* explains the error of the allegorical approach.

> The Bible's narrative portions are not allegorical. . .[T]he allegorical method. . .sought to interpret the text in terms of something else, whether that something else was a philosophical system [The Alexandrian] or a doctrinal position.[52]

Moody's Alfred Martin agrees saying, "Origen's. . .influence in promoting the spiritualizing method of Bible interpretation has done untold damage. Hort relied on him perhaps more than any Father."[53]

The church declared Origen a heretic because he held the following beliefs:

1. The Logos is subordinate to the Father and has some characteristics similar to the Logos of the Gnostics.
2. The soul is preexistent; Jesus took on some preexistent human soul.
3. There was no physical resurrection of Christ nor will there be a second coming. Man will not have a physical resurrection.
4. Hell is nonexistent; purgatory, of which Paul and Peter must partake, does exist.
5. All, including the devil, will be reconciled to God.
6. The sun, moon and stars are living creatures.
7. Emasculation, of which he partook, is called for for males.

Westcott stands at odds with the church saying, "[H]is practical conclusions remain unshaken."[54]

Alexandrian Manuscripts

The beliefs of the Alexandrian school, particularly those of Origen, are of critical interest to us because scores of scholars, tracing the history of the transmission of the text of the bible, see the hand of the Alexandrian scribes in the corruption of certain ancient copies of the text. Today these corrupt codices and papyri are being resurrected by 'Alexandrians', like Westcott and Hort, to reshape the bible to match their delusions. As a result, those 'falling away' (II Thessalonians 2:3) will be *prepared* to fall into the waiting arms of Blavatsky's New Age; hence the pages of *New Age Journal* read like the pages of the *New American Standard.* The following shows the consensus of opinion among many scholars, both ancient and contemporary, concerning the corruption of some ancient bible manuscripts.

☐ Tertullian (A.D.160-220) writes of how Alexandrians corrupted manuscripts.

☐ Dr. Philip Comfort, author of *Early Manuscripts and Modern Translations of the New Testament* states:

> [T]he early manuscripts exhibit some very significant differences in the wording of the New Testament, text-differences pertaining to the titles of the Lord Jesus Christ, Christian doctrine and church practice as well as significant word variations. . .[T]extual corruption happened at such an early date. . .Origen was the first New Testament critic.[55]

☐ Dr. David Fuller, Princeton scholar finds:

> Many of the important variations in the modern versions may be traced to the influence of Eusebius and Origen.[56]

☐ Dr. Edward Hills, Harvard and Yale scholar, relays:

> Origen. . .was not content to abide by the text which he received but freely engaged in the boldest sort of conjectural emendations. And there were other critics at Alexandria. . .who deleted many readings of the original

> New Testament text and thus produced the abbreviated text found in the papyri and in the manuscripts Aleph and B [the Greek manuscripts used to create the recent new versions].[57]

☐ World renowned scholar Hermann Hoskier, (scholars say his collation of New Testament manuscripts is unsurpassed in quality and quantity) feels:

> We do not necessarily recover Origen's manuscripts when we are inclined to follow Aleph and B [basis for new translations], but very likely only Origen himself.[58]

☐ John Burgon, author of scores of scholarly books on the transmission and corruption of the original Greek manuscripts said:

> I am of the opinion that such depravations of the text [as found in Aleph and B] were in the first instance intentional. Origen may be regarded as the prime offender. . .the author of all the mischief. . .[Clement used] 'hopelessly corrupt' versions of the New Testament which there is in these last days an attempt to revive and palm off on an unlearned generation the old exploded errors.[59]

☐ Even Westcott admits,

> Origen, in a word, laid down the lines of systematic. . . criticism.[60]

☐ Alfred Martin, former Vice-President of Moody Bible Institute calls Origen "aberrant" and says:

> [H]e seems to have been so saturated with the strange speculations of the early heretics. It is manifest that Origen is not a safe guide in the textual criticism any more than in theology.[61]

The Alexandrian Papyri

Some of the most ancient witnesses of the Greek New Testament exist in the form of papyrus fragments. The early papyri, with the exception of P52 (A.D. 100-115), which contains only a few fragmentary verses, were all written during the life and influence of Origen and came from the circumference of his school. The Chester Beatty papyri came from Aphroditopolis (city of the goddess Aphrodite), a mere ninety miles from 'the Alexandrian School'. Thirty two other papyri came from Oxyrhynchus, which was one hundred and fifty miles away.[62] Colin H. Roberts in his *Manuscripts, Society and Beliefs in the Early Christian Egypt* comments that, "[T]here was a healthy flow of communication between scholars who lived in upper and middle Egypt and those who lived in Alexandria." Comfort cites E.G. Turner's study of the papyri stating, "[S]cholars from Oxyrhynchus were exchanging notes with other Alexandrian scholars. . .[S]everal Alexandrian scholars lived in Middle and Upper Egypt."

The dating of the papyri coincides perfectly with the dates of the Alexandrian school. Turner writes, "[T]he scribes of Middle and Upper Egypt probably knew of Alexandrian scriptoral practices as early as A.D.180."[63] This period would have included the tenure of the pagan gnostic Pantaenus as head of the school. Herbert Hunger dates P66 "not later than the middle of the second century." This period saw Clement as a teacher and head of this school. Gordon Fee asserts that P66, "offers us first-hand evidence of a kind of official editorial activity going on in the church in Alexandria at the time of Clement."[64]

E.G. Turner, however, dates P66 "A.D. 200-250." Origen was a student of Saccus, Pantaenus, and Clement. He became the head of the Alexandrian school by A.D.213 at age eighteen. Westcott concedes, "Origen completed nobly the work which Clement began. . .He professes only to rèpeat the teachings which he received."[65] Scholars such as K.W. Clark, W. Bousset and Kenyon, author of *The Text of the Greek Bible,* have asserted that a text alteration or 'recension' occurred at Alexandria in the third century [A.D.200-300]. Fee writes, "It has been frequently posited that Origen was the philological mind behind the production of the Egyptian recension."[66] Publication in 1961 of P75, dated A.D.175-200 by some and "early third century" by Metzger, only serves to move the date of this recension into the earlier part of Origen's career or the later part of Clement's or Pantaenus'. Evident in Origen's writings is his awareness of, as Hoskier in *Codex B and Its Allies* states, "both the original and the altered text." Princeton professor, Bruce Metzger agrees, commenting that Origen was familiar with "each of the main families of MSS that modern scholars now isolated."[67]

Consequently, we can conclude that the papyri now being used to *alter* the Traditional Greek Text were the product of Clement and Origen's philosophies. It appears that the stew in today's new versions was construed by Saccas and Pantaenus, brewed by Clement and spewed by Origen. Lucifer said, "I will ascend. . .north."(Isaiah 14:13) Like 'a carrier' of the plague, Satan brought his Sahidic or Coptic papyri 'New' Testament north to Caesarea (modern day Syria) via Origen. These manuscripts in turn were carried further north to Rome where the virus was contracted by the sickly regime of Constantine. These manuscripts got another northward boost in apostate Germany with its institution of the 'science' of 'textual criticism'. Their last stop was a northward push to London were 'Alexandrians' Westcott, Hort and Blavatsky meet, as she called them, "the Egyptian group of the Universal Mystic Brotherhood." *Even* KJV detractors, such as D.A. Carson admit, this text type [new versions] probably originated in Egypt and may have been brought to Caeserea by Origen.[68]

New World Order: Rome 4th century

The New World Order, with its union of the Antichrist and a religious false prophet, has historical precedence, not only in England with Westcott and Balfour, but around the world and back throughout history. As Erwin W. Lutzer in his booklet *The Antichrist's New Age Roots* reminds us:

> We must remember that Satan does not know when Christ is scheduled to come back to earth. He knows *what* will happen, but he does not know *when*. Consequently he must always have someone in place to play the role of Antichrist [and false prophet] should the need arise.[69]

We will examine how the bible 'created' by Westcott and Hort and used today to 'soften up' the unsuspecting, received its substructure from another amalgamation of religion and politics, that of Constantine and Eusebius in the 4th century. They needed a 'world bible' to smooth out cultural and religious differences in their highly heterogeneous Roman Empire. Origen's 'corrected' version, which espoused his synthetic Alexandrian, East meets West doctrine, fit the bill perfectly.

Constantine's predecessor Emperor Diocletian had cleared the shelves, so to speak, of real bibles. Just as Herod ordered the destruction of the 'young' living Word, so:

> Emperor Diocletian in A.D.302 ordered all sacred manuscripts to be destroyed. In this bitter and determined attempt to destroy Christianity, the penalty of death was inflicted upon all who harbored a copy of the Christian scripture.[70]

For this reason, no *early* copies of the true *Greek* New Testament are extant today. Remaining only are the corrupted Egyptian papyri and their ancestors *Aleph* and *B* (protected, like the Egyptian babies, from Pharaoh's murder mandate against the seed of Abraham.) God has none the less preserved "the incorruptible seed. . .the word by which the gospel is preached unto you" (I Peter 1:23-25), just as he protected Moses from Pharaoh and Christ from Herod.

Constantine: 'Man of Peace'

> [H]e shall magnify himself in his heart and by peace shall destroy many Daniel 8:25

Rome was 'ungovernable'—still "drunken with the blood of the saints, and with the blood of the martyrs of Jesus." Revelation 17:6 records what Rome did to Peter, Paul and those martyred later by Diocletian. Constantine saw that the division between pagans and 'Christians' "menaced the future of the state."[71] The adage of this Antichrist antetype was,

> Let us cherish peace and forbearance. . .for it would be truly disastrous that we should assail one another. Let us banish strife.[72]

This 'Peace' banner is a ploy of the Antichrist; consequently the word 'peace' in Daniel 8, God's warning flag to future generations, has been torn down in recent versions by the enemy troops. The spear that pierced the side of the living Word still assails the written word. Historians, such as the author of *The Spear of Destiny,* record that the ruler who possesses the spear that pierced Christ's side, including forty-five men from Constantine to Adolf Hitler, will have occultic sovereignty.[73] The spear is now housed in Austria, the site of a new United Nations center.

Eusebius, like the false prophet of the book of Revelations and Daniel, "magnifies" Constantine, proclaiming that his power came from a supernatural source. Constantine was, he says:

> . . .interpreter to the Word of God. . .invested as he is with heavenly sovereignty. . .whose character is formed after the Divine original. . .Hence is our emperor perfect.[74]

Together Constantine and Eusebius called for religious toleration, which is invariably followed by amalgamation. To placate both Christian and heathen, they took a 'middle of the road' position regarding the deity of Christ. Consequently Arianism and semi-Arianism, the doctrine that Jesus was "the eldest and highest of creatures," rather than 'God manifest in the flesh', was adopted by Constantine in 330 A.D.[75] (The proliferation of this doctrine in the new versions and New Age literature is treated in Chapter 23.) So in A.D.331 Constantine asked Eusebius to create bibles which presented this somewhat de-deified Christ and ecumenical theology. Origen had much in his writings to suggest the subordination of the Son; his amalgamation of heathen and Christian doctrine—smoothing out differences thereby allowing for unity—was perfect for Constantine's purposes. So Constantine,

> . . .charged Eusebius with preparing fifty copies. . . written on prepared skins with the help of skillful artists.[76]

Scholars agree on the role of Origen and Pamphilus, a scribe, as the authors of these fifty corrupt copies. Jerome (A.D.325-420) records that Pamphilus, a friend of Eusebius and an apologist of Origenism, "copied with his own hand the chief part of the work of Origen." Even Westcott tells us that the bible texts used by Eusebius to create these bibles were "compared with accurate copies of Pamphilus of Caesarea contained in the library of Eusebius."[77] In the textbook, *Ancestry of the English Bible*, Ira Price summarizes:

> Eusebius of Caesarea. . .assisted by Pamphilus. . .issued with all his critical remarks the fifth column of Origen's Hexapla. . .The Emperor Constantine gave orders that fifty copies of this edition should be prepared for use in the churches.[78]

Numerous scholars, including Bruce Metzger, contend that *the* two Greek manuscripts, *Aleph* and *B* (used as the basis for the new versions), may have been two of these fifty. Tischendorf noted that parts of *Aleph* and *B* were written by the same scribe. Their dating, vellum skins and artistic style confirm this. It was a common practice of scribes to add their name and the place and date of their work at the end of manuscripts or books. *Aleph* contains such inscriptions, indicating "the hand" of "Pamphilus" copying and "correcting" "Origen's own copy" of his Hexapla. Metzger therefore describes *Aleph* as, "only one step removed from Origen himself."[79] The writings of "aberrant" Origen were penned and reshapened by his student Pamphilus, for Eusebius, a semi-Arian. The two copies remaining today, called *Aleph* and *B*, are the foundation of the critical Greek texts used as a basis for the new versions. (The differences between *Aleph* and *B* do not negate their common ancestry. When bibles disagree, an "interpreter to the Word of God" like Constantine is needed.)

Headlines read—"ACCUSED OF, AMONG OTHER THINGS, ADULTERY ON THE EVIDENCE OF A PROSTITUTE." This was not a reference to the dalliances of today's T.V. evangelists, but to the meanderings of Eusebius, as recorded in *The History of Heresy*. Because of this, he was cut from his leadership role, like those pandering 'his' bible version today. Corrupt bibles, with their loose doctrine, seem to create loose living in A.D.333 *and* the 1990's.

When the sheep's clothing slips, revealing the wolves' wild hair, "the beast" is no longer of any use in the wolf pack. (The second beast of Revelation 13:11, also called the false prophet, has "two horns like a lamb" but "he spake as a dragon.")

New Age authors like Vera Alder and Lola Davis recognize Constantine and Eusebius as prototypes of an "alliance between a head of government and the Church, which began a long series of such agreements." New Agers hope one such agreement will culminate soon in a One World Religion and Government. Constantine expected the new bibles to be a unifying force in his empire, writes Vera Alder. Her coming Antichrist does too. Like Constantine and Eusebius, New Agers hope an ecumenical bible will assist in this unification. Former Assistant Secretary General of the United Nations, Robert Muller, writes of the new bible-new world order synchrony in his book, *The New Genesis.*

The Roman Empire's persecution and suppression of the true text was only necessary until a 'New' text was in the making—its amalgamating powers foreseen. The Russian government's long-standing suppression of bibles remained in place until the demise of the true text and the dominance of the 'New' text was on the horizon. This allows the Antichrist's new versions to proliferate, preparing the way for his reign of 'peace' and destruction.

Origen and the Old Testament

The Septuagint (LXX), a Greek translation of the Old Testament, is used today by textual critics, in many instances, to determine the wording of new versions. It appears that Origen was the author of this A.D. document. The NIV translators admit they use the O.T. text which was "standardized early in the third century by Origen."[80] Hence, Origen's six column Old Testament, the Hexapla, is used as the LXX today. It is freely drawn from by new translation editors to alter the Masoretic Hebrew Text. Recall, the colophon at the end of Sinaiticus (*Aleph*) stated that it was 'the Hexapla' of Origen. Hort concedes in his *Introduction to the New Testament in the Original Greek* that the LXX,*Aleph* and *B* are "the same manuscript Bibles."[81] Therefore, some New Testament quotes match the LXX because, as Carson writes, "[S]cholars have argued that Vaticanus [B] came from the same hand [as the LXX]."[82] Jerome, a contemporary of this 'revision', agreed.

The New International Version (NIV) might more realistically be called Old Origen's Oracles (OOO). NIV committee members, like Bruce K. Waltke, *miss* the historical background and see the agreement of *Aleph*, *B* and the LXX as evidence of their accuracy![83]

Even the edition of *The Septuagint* marketed today points out in its preface that the stories surrounding its B.C. creation and existence are fables.[84] All of the LXX manuscripts cited in its concordance were written after A.D. 200. The *Encyclopedia of Religion and Ethics* elaborates calling "the Letter of the pseudo-Aristeas, a manifest forgery and the fragments of Aristobulus, which have also been highly suspect."[85] The existence of an entire Greek Old Testament predating the life of Christ has no extant documentation. In fact, only scraps containing a few Old Testament chapters in Greek have ever been found.

'Alexandrianism' is evident throughout Origen's 'Septuagint' as the *Encyclopedia's* scholars note:

> [T]he translators frequently modify the naive anthropomorphisms of the Old Testament, substituting, *e.g.*, the power for the 'hand' of God and His 'glory' for his 'robe' [train] in Isaiah 6:1. In Genesis 1:2 they seize the opportunity to introduce the Platonic distinction of matter and form and in Psalm 51:12 the Stoical [your spirit instead of God's spirit]. . .intrudes itself.[86]

The latter Stoical rendering appears in the new versions, which seem determined to have man succeed with his *own* spirit, rather than God's. Students of Gnosticism, Eastern mysticism and 'The Force' will recognize in the *Encyclopedia's* comments, the substitution, by the Septuagint, of a 'New Age god' for the God of the Old Testament. Numerous changes in the new versions are simply Origen's neo-platonic 'corrections' of the true Old Testament.

Among translators of the New Testament, we find die-hard 'Origen Fans' on the committee of the *New Jerusalem Bible*, *New English Bible* and *Revised Standard Version*. Even though Pamphilus "corrected" Origen's reading of John 11:25 for *Aleph* and *B*, based on P66 and P75 type-texts, these new versions retain Origen's truncated "I am the resurrection" rather than "I am the resurrection and the life." This is done based on Origen and P45, which is notorious for omissions. Origen has provided through his Septuagint Old Testament and New Testament documents, a vehicle for the propagation of the 'East meets West' religion for the 'New' Age.[87]

The following charts unearth the roots of the nine major New Age philosophies. This corrupt 'tree of knowledge' is rooted in Platonism and branched out to reach Philo, then Clement and finally Origen. Its twisted branches cast a centuries long shadow over today's new versions and 'New' Age Movement. They have sent out seeds which have found soft soil in the 'me' generation. (Quotations are taken from Westcott's *Religious Thought in the West* or *The Encyclopedia of Religion and Ethics*: "Alexandrian Theology.")

MONISM
Plato: Called God "One" and "the Good." Believed [the planet] "was endowed with life and reason." [V]iewed the universe or the individual. . .[as] the instinctive power of which it is the expression." "[It s]trives necessarily toward unity—the unity of the single being or the unity of the sum of being." Believed "The universe is the thought of the universal mind or the One."
Philo: "God is not a being who can feel anger, jealousy, or repentance."
Clement: "God is a Being. . .beyond even the One and the Monod." "God knows reality not as external to Himself."
Origen: "Sun, moon and stars are animated and rational, the temporary body of souls which shall hereafter be released from them and finally be brought into the great unity when God shall be all in all. . .the sum of finite being as unity." "The Individual. . .exists only as part of the cosmos."
New Versions: God is the 'One' or 'One and Only' instead of masculine pronoun. See chapter 5.
New Age: God is 'the One' or 'One and Only'. See chapter 5.

OFFICE OF CHRIST
Plato: "He called into being Time and the bright Gods of heaven and to them he gave charge of peopling the world. . . Thereupon the Supreme Father reposed in his eternal rest and His children fashioned the body of many, imitating as best they could the laws which their Father had followed."
Philo: "In the hierarchy of Powers, the Logos of God is second to God himself." "The Logos is the constitutive principle of human individuality; he himself is not an individual." "[T]he first God" (Logos of Stoics not John's gospel.)
Clement: "[T]he Son is a creature." "[There is a] dependance of Clement on Philo as regards his conception of the Logos." "[H]e taught two, Logoi. . .[as] a power or energy of God."
Origen: "[T]he Son is less than the Father." "In the Incarnation, the son united Himself with a soul which had remained absolutely pure in its preexistent state."
New Versions: Teach: 1) Christ is a creature, a begotten God, "ranked" beneath God. 2) Separate 'the Christ' (the Logos) from Jesus, calling Christ "itself" not himself.
New Age: Teach: 1) Christ is a creature, a begotten God, "ranked" beneath God. 2) Separate 'the Christ' (the Logos) from Jesus, calling Christ consciousness "itself" not himself.

NEW AGE SPIRITUAL HIERARCHY
Plato: Writes of "hierarchy of beings," "intermediate orders," "interest in oracles and demons." Says "[T]he universe contains many beings more divine than man-daemons and gods, who are daemons of a superior order."
Philo: Believes there are "powers to intermediate." These "powers or ideas are not of equal rank. The highest of them is the Logos."
Origen: "Some by diligent obedience have been raised to the loftiest places in the celestial hierarchy."

New Versions: Call devils, 'demons'. Present a spiritual ranking system with Christ as the highest "rank." Teach salvation by diligent "obedience." Say Jesus was a "son of the gods."

New Age: Calls devils, 'demons'. Presents a spiritual ranking system with Christ as the highest "rank." Teaches salvation by diligent "obedience." Says there is a plurality of "gods."

ELEVATES MAN

Plato: Believes God said, "[I] make them (mortal creatures), they will be like Gods." "[T]he divine principle in me departs in me to unite itself with the divine in the universe."

Clement: "The aim of the Gnostic is to become like God." (The *Encyclopedia* refers to Clement as a Gnostic.)

Origen: "Their variety tend to the one end of perfection." "All things were made for the sake of man." "The end of life then. . .is the progressive assimilation of man to God."

New Versions: Replaces the Godhead with a "divine nature." Says man is only "a little lower than God."

New Age: Replaces the Godhead with a "divine nature." Says man is only "a little lower than God."

ILLUMINATION AND INITIATION

Philo: Said, "[I]mmediate communion with 'the first God' in visions, is the result of personal experience."

Clement: "[T]rue gnosis. . .[is] initiating them first into the lesser and then to greater mysteries." "[M]ystical philosophy [is that]. . .which could not be fully imparted or even made intelligible to the public." "[I am] initiated by the laver of illumination into the true mysteries."

Origen: Westcott says Origen "[A]imed at presenting the higher knowledge." Believed, "[T]he scriptures are of little use to those who understand them as they are written." "[B]elieved himself to be illuminated."

New Versions: Present a second God, begotten as a God, by the "first" God. "Visions he has seen" are included. Present a progressive salvation.

New Age: Presents a second God, begotten as a God, by the "first" God. "Visions he has seen" are included. Presents a progressive salvation.

REINCARNATION VS. RESURRECTION

Plato: "At their first embodiment, [they]. . .would be born a man. . .If he succeeds, he would pass to a home in his kindred star. If he failed at this, at his second birth, he would be a woman, next an animal."

Philo: "The resurrection of the body has no place in his creed." "[H]eaven and hell are within us."

Clement: "[L]ike Origen" ". . .inclined to believe it [reincarnation]."

Origen: Believed, "[T]he position of each has been determined in accordance with previous conduct."

New Versions: Deny the bodily resurrection of Christ. Transliterate "hell" so that the reader is free to choose his own doctrine regarding the afterlife. Degrades women.

New Age: Denies the bodily resurrection of Christ. Rejects the belief in hell. Teaches progressive evolution and reincarnation.

MAYA (i.e., allegorism,sacramentalism, archetype, Plato's 'ideas'.)

Plato: Wrote that "The universe is the thought of the universal mind or One." "Ideas" "Shadows"

Philo: "Platonic idealism." "The Blessed One must not come into contact with. . .matter and this is why he used the Immaterial Powers; whose real name is ideas.

Clement: "[The] earthly life of Christ as a grand symbolic drama."

Origen: The "bible is an analogy; compared to a ladder, literal facts are the lowest rung." He "expresses contempt for the literal narrative." Said, "There is an Eternal Gospel which the actual Gospel is only a shadow."

New Versions: Write of, "The Blessed One." Their editors believe the bible is only "the wrong side" of a beautiful tapestry.

New Age: Write of 'the Blessed One." Express contempt for the "literal" bible.

TIME IS CYCLICAL (No Hell/New Age)

Plato: "[T]he Cosmos. . .has been subject to the laws of cyclic change." God "recreates the world over and over."

Clement: "Matter is timeless." "[T]here were many worlds before Adam."

Origen: "World grows out of world, so to speak, till the consummation is reached." "[I]t had no beginning. . ." "[A]ge is linked with age. . .stages in a majestic progress." "[M]ore of the total powers of humanity. . .are brought from age to age."

New Versions: Deny a "beginning" of the world. Present a series of "ages." Deny a final judgement.

New Age: Deny a "beginning" of the world. Present a series of "ages." Deny a final judgement.

PROGRESSION VS. NEW BIRTH

Plato: Wrote of, "that which is always becoming."

Philo: Wrote of, "the potentiality of becoming."

Clement: Wrote of, "salvation as an educational process." (Baptism begins the process.)

Origen: Wrote of, "the progressive training, purifying, and illumination of men. . .passing from sphere to sphere. . .Lower phenomena are successively exclaimed to them and higher phenomena are indicated." There is "progressive and gradual revelation." (Baptism begins the process.)

New Versions: Teach progressive salvation.

New Age: Teach progressive salvation.

THIRTY - NINE

The 1% Manuscripts: Aleph & B

Is there anything whereof it may be said, 'See, this is new? It hath been already of old time which was before us. Ecclesiastes 1:10

The *New International Version*, *New American Bible*, *New American Standard*, *New Jerusalem*, *New English Bible*, and *New Revised Standard* are not so 'New' as we have seen, but are merely an encore of the 'New' Age esotericism of Plato, Saccus, Clement and Origen, set on the stage of the Egyptian papyri and Eusebius' *Aleph* and *B* manuscripts.

> Then the **chief captain** came near and took him and commanded him to be bound with **two chains**. . .And as Paul was to be led into the castle, he said unto the chief captain, May I speak unto thee? 'Who said, **canst thou speak Greek?** Art not thou that Egyptian. . .' But Paul said, 'I am a man which am a Jew. . .[then] he spake unto them in the Hebrew tongue. . . Acts 21:33-40

Today the Greek manuscripts *Aleph & B*, produced under the 'authority' of Constantine's Rome, attempt to hold captive those like

Paul, who want to speak the word of God in the language of the people. The 'chief captains' of the new version translation committees would open any discussion with 'canst thou speak Greek?' You will be bound by their two chains, Aleph & B, unless you can identify the weak links. Vaticanus, designated 'B', and Sinaiticus, designated 'Aleph', were used by Westcott, Hort and subsequent editors to alter the traditional Greek text. Manuscript expert Sir Herman Hoskier writes:

> The text of Westcott and Hort is practically the text of Aleph & B.[1]

Westcott and Hort's *Introduction to the New Testament in the Original Greek* affirms:

> [R]eadings of Aleph & B should be accepted as the true readings. . .[They] stand far above all documents. . .[are] very pure. . .excellent. . .and enjoyed a singular immunity from corruption.[2]

The Corruption of Aleph & B

Many scholars today disagree with Westcott and Hort, noting the poor character of these minority manuscripts. Moody Vice President, Alfred Martin, calls Aleph & B "depraved."[3] Dean John Burgon writes:

> I have convinced myself by laborious collation that they are the most corrupt of all. They are the depositories of the largest amount of fabricated and intentional perversions of truth which are discoverable in any copies of the word of God. They exhibit a fabricated text. . . [and are] shamefully mutilated.[4]

Since, on occasion, the editors of the 'new' versions depart from the readings of Aleph & B, they too comment on the errors inherent in these manuscripts. Hort admits, they ". . .reached by no means a high standard of accuracy."[5] Bruce Metzger, co-author of the recent Greek text, has observed, "[N]on-Byzantine readings, for example, in the Codex Vaticanus, can be explained from the tendency of scribes to assimilate and simplify the text."[6] E.W. Kenyon, noted textbook author on the subject, feels they are "disfigured."[7] Gordon Fee points out that they were copied from an [altered] papyrus much like P75; he brings us up to date and reveals the dilemma in which textual scholars find themselves today.

> [T]he recensional [altered] nature of 'B' has become a byword in NT textual criticism. The recent text-critical handbooks and NT introductions, as well as articles on 'trends' and on text-types, are almost unanimous in their concurrence with Kenyon's conclusion that the Egyptian text is now generally regarded as a text produced in Alexandria under editorial care. . .Hence our dilemma, for as long as our critical texts [Nestle's Greek, UBS Greek, etc.] continue to look much like a text that is generally acknowledged to be edited,. . .our dilemma seems to be that we know too much to believe the old. . .[8]

Lest someone tell you that the NIV, NASB, NRSV, etc. were translated using the eclectic method and not the text of Westcott and Hort, Fee points out:

> The dilemma of contemporary NT textual criticism relates directly to the labors of Westcott and Hort. On the one hand, there has been an open disavowal—one might call it a debunking—of Westcott and Hort's methodology and textual theory, while at the same time critical texts issued since Westcott and Hort have generally continued to have a clearly 'Hortian' face. In fact the recent United Bible Society's *Greek New Testament* (UGT), which was produced by the so-called eclectic method, has moved even closer to Westcott and Hort than subsequent critical issues.[9]

Aleph & B: The New Version Manuscripts

Listen to the clang of the two chains as today's chief captains approach to constrain and control this generation.

- Edwin Palmer, Executive Secretary of the NIV committee, writes that *Aleph & B* are "more reliable and accurate."[10]

- Ronald Youngblood, NIV translation committee member agrees, "[T]he readings found in. . . *Vaticanus* [B] and *Sinaiticus* [Aleph] of the fourth century A.D. are to be preferred."[11] Other committee members, such as Kenneth L. Barker, have expressed agreement.

- J.B. Phillips, author of the forward to the *NASB Interlinear Greek-English New Testament*, as well as numerous other new translations says, it is "the most reliable Greek Text." (Recall, he is the voiceless, necromancer, who suffered from 'clinical' psychosis.) The Introduction to this interlinear credits Tregelles, another voiceless conspirator, for a major role in this Greek text.[12]

- Lewis Foster, member of both the *New King James Committee* and the NIV Committee says, "The most highly valued manuscripts. . .[and the most] dependable. . .are the *Codex Vaticanus* [B] and the *Sinaiticus* [Aleph]."[13]

- The Introduction to Nestle's Greek New Testament, *Novum Testamentum Graece,* cites the use of *Aleph & B* as the basis for its text saying, ". . .the precedence of the Vaticanus will be justified."[14]

Consequently the footnotes in the NIV and other new versions (i.e., Mark 16:9-20), when referring to "the most reliable" manuscripts, mean *Aleph & B.*

Scholar's Shocked

No man on the previous list has come near, in scholarly collation of actual manuscripts, Dean John Burgon, the author of *The Causes of Corruption of the Traditional Text*, *The Traditional Text* and *The Revision Revised.* Because of his extensive hand collation of the major ancient uncials, Aleph & B included, as well as his monumental collation of the evidence in other New Testament witnesses (86,489 citations), his well-educated opinion of such translators and their new versions bears hearing.

> What does astonish us, however is to find learned men. . . freely resuscitating these long-since forgotten critics [Aleph & B] and seeking to palm them off upon a busy and careless age, as so many new revelations. . .[I]t is sometimes entertaining to trace the history of a mistake which, dating from the second or third century, has remained without patron all down the subsequent ages until at last it has been taken up in our own times. . . palmed off upon an unlearned generation as the genuine work of the Holy Ghost. What. . .of those blind guides. . .who would now, if they could, persuade us to go back to those same codices of which the church has already purged herself.[15]

Dr. Wilbur Pickering's recent research of the ancient papyri revealed the superiority of the KJV text over the new versions. (John Wenham of the *Evangelical Quarterly* says of Pickering's book, "It is not often that one reads a book which reorients one's whole approach to a subject, but that is what this has done for me.") Pickering says of Aleph, B and the new versions:

> To judge by the circumstances that codices like Aleph and B were not copied, to speak of, that the church by and large rejected their form of text, it seems they were not respected in their day. . .If readings. . .died out in the fourth or fifth century we have the verdict of history against it. . .They [Aleph & B] are remnants of the abnormal transmission of the text reflecting ancient aberrant forms. It is dependency upon such forms that distinguishes contemporary critical editions of the NT. . .

> [T]heir respectability quotient hovers near zero. . .In particular, I fail to see how anyone can read Hoskier's *Codex B and its Allies* with attention and still retain respect for Aleph & B as witnesses to the New Testament . . .[T]he modern critical and eclectic texts are based precisely on B and Aleph and other early manuscripts. . . [T]hey have been found wanting. . .[T]he result will be the complete overthrow of the type of text currently in vogue.[16]

Dr. Herman C. Hoskier's extensive collation of Vaticanus (B), unsurpassed to this day, leads him to conclude that the new version editors are guilty of an ". . .incomplete examination of documentary evidence. . .[working] without due regard to scientific foundation."

> My thesis is then that B (Vaticanus) and Aleph (Sinaiticus) and their forerunners, with Origen who revised the Antioch text [KJV], are Egyptian revisions current between A.D. 200-400 and abandoned between 500 and 1881, merely revived in our day. . .[17]

Harvard and Princeton textual scholar, Dr. Edward Hills, summarizes:

> Old corrupt manuscripts, which had been discarded by the God-guided usage of the believing church were brought out of their hiding place and re-instated. . .and today thousands of Bible-believing Christians are falling into this devils trap through their use of modern speech versions.[18]

Aleph & B: A Closer Look

What have the paleographers seen when actually collating Aleph and B that cause these scholars to reject versions such as the NIV and NASB and their foundation Aleph & B?

Vaticanus (B)

1. The use of recent technology such as the vidicon camera, which creates a digital form of faint writing, recording it on a magnetic tape and reproducing it by an electro-optical process, reveals that B has been altered by at least two hands, one being as late as the twelfth century. Metzger admits, "A few passages therefore remain to show the original appearance of the first hand." The corrector "omitted [things] he believed to be incorrect."[19]

2. B agrees with the *Textus Receptus* only about 50% of the time. It differs from the Majority Greek in nearly 8000 places, amounting to about one change per verse. It omits several thousand key words from the Gospels, nearly 1000 complete sentences, and 500 clauses. It adds approximately 500 words, substitutes or modifies nearly 2000 and transposes word order in about 2000 places. It has nearly 600 readings that do not occur in any other manuscript. These affect almost 1000 words.

3. Linguistic scholars have observed that B is reminiscent of classical and Platonic Greek, not the Koine Greek of the New Testament (see Adolf Deissman's *Light of the Ancient East*). Nestle concedes he had to change his Greek text when using Aleph & B, to make it 'appear' like Koine.

4. Codicologists (scientists who study the make-up of ancient book forms) note that B was written on vellum scrolls, (skin ". . .obtained from animals not yet born") not papyrus codices, as were used among "the early Christians."[20]

5. B does not consider the following as part of the bible: Revelation, Phil., Titus, I and II Timothy, large parts of Samuel, Kings, Nehemiah, the Psalms, and Genesis. B omits crucial parts of Mark and Luke. In their place it adds apocryphal books such as Bel and the Dragon, Tobit, Judith and the Epistle of Barnabas. In Job, for example, it has 400 'half-verses' of Theodotian, a follower of Blavatsky's 'friend' Marcion.[21]

6. Protestant theologians question its lack of use by anyone for 1300 years—then its sudden 'discovery' in the Vatican in 1481. Its immediate use to suppress the Reformation and its subsequent release in 1582, as the Jesuit-Rheims Bible, are logical, considering the manuscript's omission of anti-Catholic sections and books (i.e., Hebrews 9:14, Revelation, etc.). Its Catholic 'tone' is evidenced by the fact that at Vatican Council II, each bishop was given his own copy with an introduction by Jesuit priest, Carlo Martini.[22] Protestant researchers have never been permitted to examine the actual manuscript and work only from copies provided by the Vatican.

7. It agrees essentially with Origen's Hexapla, omitting the deity of Christ frequently and making other Gnostic or Arian alterations.

Sinaiticus

1. Princeton Professor, Bruce Metzger's recent *Manuscripts of the Greek Bible* reveals:

> In the light of such carelessness in transcription, it is not surprising that a good many correctors (as many as nine) have been at work on the manuscript. . .Tischendorf's edition of the manuscript enumerates some 14,800 places where some alteration has been made to the text. . .[With] more recent detailed scrutiny of the manuscript. . .by the use of ultra-violet lamp, Milne and Skeat discovered that the original reading in the manuscript was erased. . .[in places].[23]

See also *Scribes and Correctors of the Codex Sinaiticus* (British Museum, 1938).

2. F.H.A. Scrivener's *Full Collation of the Codex Sinaiticus with the Received Text of the New Testament* and other researchers (see Dean Burgon's *The Revision Revised*) find:

- There are about 9000 changes in this text from that of the Majority and Traditional Text, amounting to one difference in every verse. It omits some 4000 words from the Gospels, adds 1000, repositions 2000 and alters another 1000. It has approximately 1,500 readings that appear in no other manuscript; this affects nearly 3000 words. The following omissions are just a few examples.

- The end of Mark and John.
- Thirty-nine words from John 19:20, 21; twenty words from John 20:5,6; nineteen words from Mark 1:32-34; fourteen words from Mark 15:47.
- John 5:4, Matthew 16:2,3, Romans 16:24, Mark 16:9-20, I John 5:7, Acts 8:37, Genesis 23:19-24,46, Numbers 5:27-7:20, I Chron. 9:27-19:27.
- Exodus, Joshua, I and II Samuel, I and II Kings, Hosea, Amos, Micah, Ezekiel, Daniel, and Judges.
- In Luke 8, for example, 19 out of 34 words are changed. In Matthew chapter one, sixty words are changed.
- It adds Apocryphal books, such as Bel and The Dragon, Tobit, Judith, The Epistle of Barnabas and The Shepherd of Hermas, among others.

When using this manuscript to 'alter' the new versions, Greek editors must choose between *Aleph* A, *Aleph* B, and *Aleph* C, the three principle correctors. Because of its blatant omissions and alterations, it lapsed into a wastebasket in a monastery, where it was 'discovered' by Constantine von Tischendorf in the mid-eighteen hundreds. It was kept by the Russian government from 1859 until 1933. Eastern Germany and Russia, however, still retain portions of it. The fact that some pages were written on sheepskin and some on goatskin is a telling sign of its part -Christian, part-heathen character.

Vaticanus Meets Sinaiticus

> For many bare false witness against him but their witness agreed not together. Mark 14:56

False witnesses spoke against Jesus Christ, the living Word, but as history tells us, their 'versions' did not correspond. The written word had two such witnesses against it and they too do not agree with the Majority of manuscripts, *or with each other*.

1. Metzger says that Sinaiticus and Vaticanus do not agree with the majority of manuscripts.[24]
2. Not only do they disagree with the Majority of manuscripts, but they do not agree with each other. The 8000 changes in B and the 9000 changes in Aleph are not the same changes. When their changes are added together, they alter the Majority text in about 13,000 places. This is two changes for every verse. Together they omit 4000 words, add 2000, transpose 3500, and modify 2000.
3. They disagree with each other a dozen times on every page.
4. Colwell says they disagree 70% of the time and in almost every verse of the gospels. Burgon says, "It is easier to find two consecutive verses in which these manuscripts differ than two in which they agree.[25]

FORTY

The Final Bible!

Is the Antichrist's *final* bible already here,waiting in the wings in new version manuscripts Vaticanus (B) and Sinaiticus (Aleph)? New Age leader Vera Alder's *When Humanity Comes of Age* betrays the method by which 'the Christ' will create the bible for his one world religion.

> [T]he World Government and its Spiritual Cabinet of 12, headed by 'the Christ' will study all archaeological archives. . .From it, the Research Panel would develop the 'New' Bible of a World Religion which would be the basis of future education.[1]

Texe Marrs, New Age researcher, observes how the words 'Research' and 'archaeology' are woven into this web of deception.

> For centuries Satan has inspired scientists and pseudo-scientists to label Christians as unsophisticated and behind-the-times. Many of these. . .secular humanist arguments will become part of the New Age Bible. The bible that is developed by the Antichrist will be applauded as fully in keeping with a high-tech age. Furthermore, New Age citizens will be told that the New Age scriptures

> can be changed whenever new scientific discoveries suggest revisions are needed.[2]

The Antichrist's ploy has its precedence in the prefaces of the new versions which boast of their use of "recent discoveries of Hebrew and Greek textual sources"[3] or "linguistic discoveries in this century."[4] The RV of 1881 used Aleph & B. The RSV added 16 papyrus, the NASB added 13 more, the NIV added another 10 and the NRSV another 18. (It should be noted these *additional* sources in most cases caused the *subtraction* of words, phrases or sentences.) As Comfort's and my collation have shown, these sources were used very haphazardly. *U.S. News and World Report* (11/8/93) reveals plans by Canon Seminar scholars for a "radical revision of the New Testament" that will replace the Book of Revelation with "Other writings. . .[previously] dismissed by church leaders as unauthentic or heretical." "We're saying to the church, 'If you think you have everything you need in your Bible. . .we don't think that's true.'" They "hope their new canon eventually will work its way into the churches' major Christian denominations."

When the Antichrist's bible comes, it too will boast a resurrection from the 'archaeological archives'—or is it already here? A word-for-word translation of Vaticanus (B) or Sinaiticus (Aleph) with its Apocrypha will serve Satan's purposes perfectly. I can just see the ads—"More accurate. . .closer to the originals."

Antichrist's Apocrypha

The book of Revelation gives God's version of the 'end of the story'. Both Aleph and B give a *different* ending to the story, ignoring God's warning.

> If any man shall add unto these things, God shall add unto him the plagues that are written in this book: And if any man shall take away from the words of the book of this prophecy, God shall take away his part out of the book of life, and out of the holy city, and from the things which are written in this book. Revelation 22:18,19

Neither Aleph nor B ends with the book of Revelation.

Vaticanus (B) completely *eliminates* Revelation, thereby disobeying God's command not to "take away from the words of the book." Sinaiticus (Aleph) *adds* two books after Revelation, both written in the same handwriting as the remainder. Hence this manuscript is guilty of adding "unto these things." The addition of these two books presents an ending to the story that lines up, word-for-word with the scenario Satan would like to see. (Since the exegesis of most apostate Christian teachers regarding the book of Revelation puts it in the setting of the fall of the Roman Empire, the two added books will easily be used to form a manual for the *New* Age.) These two books, *The Shepherd of Hermas* and *The Epistle of Barnabas,* spell out in detail the entire New Age scenario, including commands to do the things God specifically forbids, such as:

1. Take 'the name' of the beast.
2. Give 'up to the beast'.
3. Form a one world government.
4. Kill those not receiving his 'name'.
5. Worship female virgins.
6. Receive 'another spirit'.
7. Seek power.
8. Believe that God is immanent in his creation, as a pantheistic, monistic Hindu god.
9. Avoid marriage; permit fornication.
10. Abstain from fasting.
11. Subscribe to the New Age Root Race Theory.
12. Be saved by being baptized and keeping the 'twelve' mandates of the Antichrist.

About-Face to the Arcane Apocrypha

Like the TV advertisements selling 'faux' diamonds (French for 'false'), 'New' versions are now being advertised as containing the 'Apocrypha' (Greek for 'false'). The NRSV, RSV, TEV, NEV and *Revised English Bible* have abandoned their previously Protestant moorings and added these 'false Rocks'. This might be expected since the two foremost New Testament scholars value the Apocrypha very highly. F.F. Bruce cites the Muratorian Canon which "implies that its [*The Shepherd of Hermas*] right to a place in the canon could be maintained on the strength of its prophetic quality. . ."[5] Bruce Metzger, American mastermind behind the UBS *Greek New Testament*, believes the Apocrypha is a part of the bible.[6]

They are not alone, but are not in good company. The Ghostly Guild duo, Westcott and Lightfoot, and their specters from the past, Clement, Origen and Eusebius, called these added books, "divinely inspired and very useful," "remarkable" and "Theologically . . .of the highest value."[7] Our bible revisors, Bruce, Metzger and Westcott, are here in common cause with Mme. Blavatsky, who sees these added books as vehicles for her Luciferian doctrines. She snickers in her book, *Isis Unveiled,* of Westcott's ardor for this material, recognizing it as the domain of the occult world. She recognizes (the contents of *The Shepherd of Hermas*) as direct excerpts from pagan literature, "concocted from those Pagan predecessors. . .such as the *Kabala*, the *Sohar*, Hindu and Gnostic writings."

> [T]he best men, the most erudite scholars even among Protestant divines, but too often fall into [our]. . .traps. We cannot believe that such a learned commentator as Canon Westcott could have left himself in ignorance as to Talmudistic and purely kabalistic writings. How then is it that we find him quoting, with such serene assurance. . .passages from the work of *The Pastor of Hermas*, which are complete sentences from the kabalistic literature?. . . [N]early everything expressed by the pseudo-Hermas. . .is a plain quotation, with repeated variations, from the *Sohar* and other kabalastic books. [They]. . .are not only purely kabalistic without even so much as a change in expression, but Brahmanical and Pagan.[8]

She gives several pages of quotes showing the parallels between Aleph's apocryphal *Shepherd of Hermas* and occult writings. (She not only shows these added books to be occultic, but throws in Lightfoot himself, who she quotes to support her views on magic.

> Lightfoot assures us that this voice [which]. . .responded from the mercy-seat within the veil. . .was indeed performed by magic art [vol. ii., p. 128].[9])

The Shepherd of Hermas & the Antichrist!

A 1991 advertisement in a Christian bookseller's brochure called Lightfoot's translation of the *Shepherd of Hermas* "indispensable. . .for a new generation."[10] Professor Gaiser, a Lutheran pastor, tells students in his 'Christian Bible' class at Kent State University that the *Shepherd of Hermas* should be in the bible and the book of James should not. Verses from this added ending to Aleph will send chills down the spine of the average Christian who is versed in the biblical facts regarding the last days. If, after reading the following pages, the reader finds manuscript Aleph to be 'most reliable', 'accurate', 'preferred', 'the most highly valued', and of 'preeminent excellence', as new version editors assert, then I've got a membership card for you in the Ghostly Guild too.

The right hand column is an abstract of *The Shepherd of Hermas*. Any student of the bible will recognize it as a picture of the false shepherd foretold by Jeremiah's prophecy. The left column exposes how *The Shepherd* contradicts the real bible and fulfills the picture of the Antichrist's regime, as foretold in the bible and anticipated in New Age literature. (The numbers in the right column refer to items in the left column.) If you think the readings of Aleph & B should be used instead of the Majority text, then add the following verses to the end of your bible. If you are too busy, just wait, the Antichrist will do it for you![11]

FACTS	NEW VERSION MANUSCRIPT PART I
1. **Arcadia** is the home of Pan, the Greek god of flocks, a false shepherd. Pan is one of the names of the devil. Findhorn, a New Age center, hosts visits by 'Pan', who concede he is 'the devil'. The root word of 'Arcadia' is 'arcane', which means 'secret'; consequently New Age leader Alice Bailey calls her teaching 'the Arcane School'.	And **he** took me away into **Arcadia (1)**

FACTS	NEW VERSION MANUSCRIPT
2. Luke 4:5 identifies "**he**" as ". . .the devil taking him up into an high **mountain shewed** unto him. . .the **world**."	to a certain rounded **mountain** and set me on the top of the mountain and **shewed** me. . .twelve **mountains**. . .a great white rock. . .it could contain the whole **world**. **(2)**
3. Zech. 11:16 identifies the **shepherd** as "the foolish shepherd"; Jer. 50:6 describes further, "their **shepherds** have caused them to go astray. . .on the **mountains**."	[T]welve virgins. . .four that stood at the **corners (6)** and the **shepherd (3)** saith to me. . .
4. The **deep** is the home of "the serpent," the dragon, leviathan (Isa. 27:1, Job 41:1, Ps. 148, Isa. 30:33). "The beast. . .shall **ascend** out of the bottomless pit" (Rev. 17:8) "[T]here **arose**. . .out of the pit. . .faces.. .as the faces of men.". . .[and] the angel of the bottomless pit." (Rev. 9)	[A]nd there went up **ten (5,7) stones**. . .[T]he virgins laid the first ten stones that **rose out of the deep (4)**. . .the **corners** of the stone. **(6)**
5. Dan. 2:41, 42, 7:7, 20, 24, and Rev. 17:12 identify the **ten** nation base of the Antichrist's power.	Those **ten** stones then were **joined together, (5)**
6. Jer. 51:23-26 reveals God's judgement on this false shepherd. "I will also break in pieces with thee the **shepherd** and his flock. . .Behold I am against thee O destroying **mountain**,	and they covered the whole rock and these formed a **foundation (6)** for the building of the **tower. (7)** The stones ceased coming up from the deep. And again the **six** men ordered the multitude of the people

FACTS — NEW VERSION MANUSCRIPT

saith the Lord, which destroyeth all the earth. . .and they shall not take of thee a **stone** for a **corner** nor a stone for **foundations** but thou shalt be desolate forever saith the Lord."

to bring stones from the mountains (6) for the building of a tower.

7. Rev. 17:12 says, "**ten** kings. . .these have **one mind** and shall give their power and strength unto the beast."

8. Gen. 11:4,8 shows the creation and destruction of the first one world government. "And they said, Go to, let us build us a city and a **tower**, whose top may **reach** unto heaven. . .and they **left off to build** the city."

And when the various stones were placed in the building they **all became alike (7,8)** and white and they lost their various colors. And the building was finished on that day, yet was not the **tower** finally complete, for it was to be carried up still higher and **there was a cessation in the building. . .**

9. Are these the **six** kings which remain in league with the Antichrist? (Dan.7:24)

And the **six (9)** men ordered the builders to retire for a short time. . .'How is it, Sir, say I, 'that the building of the tower was not complete? The tower, saith he, cannot yet be finally completed until its master come. . .a man of such lofty stature. . .[A]nd the six men who superintended the building walked with him. . .[T]he glorious man who was lord of the whole tower called the shepherd to him and **delivered unto him (10)** all the stones.

10. Luke 4:6 records, "the devil said. . .that is **delivered unto me**."

FACTS	NEW VERSION MANUSCRIPT
11. Mme. Blavatsky resurrected a 'Root Race Theory' from ancient occultism. It asserts that this current Piscean Age or Black Age is led by the Black Lodge (Christians, Jews and dark skinned peoples). She believed her occult White Lodge will prevail in the 'New Age'.	And so commencing first we began to inspect the **black (11)** stones; and the shepherd ordered them to be removed from the tower. . .[M]any among them were found **black**. . .Then he began to inspect those that were half white and half **black**, and many of them were now found black; and he ordered those. . .cast aside. But all the rest were found white. . .for being **white** they were fitted by them into the building. . .
12. This was discussed in chapter 9. "Neither repented they of their fornication. . ." (Rev. 9:21); "[T]he great whore which did corrupt the earth with her fornication. . .and she repented not." (Rev. 19:2, 2:21)	[A]nd she that seemed to be the chief of them began to kiss and embrace me and others seeing her embrace me, they too began to kiss me. . .and to sport with me. . .and I stayed the night with them. **(12)**
13. This is Arian heresy. Jesus Christ is eternal, not a created being. This 'begotten God' occurs in John 1:18 in all new versions. They took it from Sinaiticus (Aleph) which also contains this *Shepherd of Hermas*. Blavatsky comments that this line is taken from the occult Codex "Onomasticon" which reads, ". . .the most excellent who is older by	The Son of God is **older** than all His creation, so that he became the Father's advisor in His creation. Therefore also he is ancient. **(13)**

FACTS — NEW VERSION MANUSCRIPT

birth." She says the remainder of the sentence comes from the *Vedas* which say, "Brahma holds council with Parabrahma as to the best mode to proceed to create the world." (*Isis Unveiled* Vol. II, p. 246)

14. This Calvinistic predestination statement appears in numerous new versions, particularly the NIV. Edwin Palmer, its Executive Secretary, wrote *The Five Points of Calvinism*. The gate referred to here is the "wide **gate**. . .that leadeth to destruction" (Matt. 7:13) and the "gates of hell" (Matt.16:18). Blavatsky boasts that this is the Gate of Metatron, which is one of the names of Satan. (*Isis Unveiled* Vol. II, p. 245)

The **gate** was made recent that they which are **to be saved** may enter. . . **(14)**

15. Rev. 13:16, 17 says the Antichrist will cause "all both small and great, rich and poor, free and bond to **receive** a mark in their right hand or in their foreheads: And that no man might buy or sell, save he had the mark, or **the name** of the beast or the number of **his name**."

Didst thou see, saith he, the six men and the glorious and mighty man in the midst of them, him that walked about the tower. . .whosoever shall not **receive His name (15)** shall not enter the kingdom of God.

FACTS	NEW VERSION MANUSCRIPT
16. Since *The Shepherd of Hermas* was reportedly authored under Pope Pius (A.D.140-165) or Pope Zephyrinus (A.D.197-217), (and scholars agree that it came from Rome), **'the Church'** (capital C) refers to the Roman Catholic or 'universal' one world church.	'The tower', saith he, 'why this is **the Church**. **(16)**
17. Chapter 6 discussed the identity and worldwide worship of 'virgins', which may accompany the religion of the Antichrist.	And these **virgins (17)** are holy spirits; and no man can otherwise be found in the kingdom of God, unless these shall **clothe him(18)** with their garments; for if thou **receive** only **the Name**, but **receive** not the garment from them, thou profitest nothing. . .
18. Those who are familiar with the obscene secret Mormon temple ceremonies will recognize this procedure (see *The God Makers* by Dave Hunt).	
19. Words referring to the 'New Age' God are capitalized in all occult writings and new versions (e.g., His, Name).	For these virgins are powers of the Son of God. . .If thou **bear the name** and bear not **His** power, thou shalt bear **His (19) name** to none effect.
20. I John 4:1 warns, "believe not every spirit. . ." Ephesians 4:4 tells us "There is. . .one Spirit." I Corinthians 12 says, "the same spirit," which is according to I Pet.1:11 "the spirit of Christ." These other 'spirits' are called "foul spirits" (Rev.	And the stones, saith he, which thou didst see cast away, these bare **the Name**, but clothed not themselves with the raiment of the virgins. . .The names themselves, saith he, are their raiment. Whosoever **beareth the Name** of the Son of God ought to bear

FACTS	NEW VERSION MANUSCRIPT
18:2), "**spirits of devils**" (Rev. 16:14), "unclean spirits" (Rev. 16:13) and "the spirit that now worketh in the children of disobedience." (Eph. 2:2) We are warned, "as the serpent beguiled Eve. . .if ye **receive another spirit**, which ye have not received." (2 Cor. 11:3,4)	the names of these also; for even the Son of God himself beareth the names of these virgins. . .clothe themselves in these **spirits. . .(20)**
21. See note 7.	[T]hey had the **same mind. . .(21)**
22. Speaking of the Antichrist, Dan. 11:37 says, "Neither shall he regard. . .the **desire of women**."	These men should repent and **put away their desire for women (22)** and return unto these virgins and walk in their power. . .He Himself then is become their foundation. . .they are not ashamed to **bear His name. . .**the names of the more powerful virgins, those that are stationed at the four corners. . .Power. . .Cheerfulness, Truth, Understanding, Concord, Love. . .[T]he names of the women [are] Disobedience. . .
23. Rev. 13:1 records John saw, "a **beast rise** up out of the **sea**" and "the first beast whose **deadly** wound was **healed**." (Rev. 13:12) Rev. 17:7,8 records, "I will tell thee the mystery of the	Wherefore, Sir, say I, did these **come up from the deep. . .**It was necessary for them, saith he, to **rise** up through **water. . .**[W]hen he received the seal, he layeth aside his deadness and **resumed life. (23)**

FACTS	NEW VERSION MANUSCRIPT
woman and of the beast that carrieth her. . .The beast that thou sawest was and is not; and shall **ascend** out of the bottomless **pit** and go into perdition." 2 Thess. 2:3 says the antichrist is, ". . .the man of sin, the son of perdition." John 17:12 says, [Judas] "the son of perdition."	
24. Baptism, as an initiation rite of the New Age is discussed fully in chapter 14; Apostate Christianity, along with 'ancient mystery cults', believe baptism itself imparts spiritual life.	The seal then is the water; so they go down into the water dead, and they come up alive. . .**(24)**
25. The New Age scenario calls for a **one** world government 'divided' into **twelve** segments. (See Vera Alder's *When Humanity Comes of Age*.) Also see Dan. 11:39 where the Antichrist will "divide the land for gain."	These twelve tribes which inhabit the whole world are **twelve nations. (25)**
26. Genesis records ". . .And the LORD said, Behold the people is **one. . .**So the LORD scattered them. . ."	These twelve tribes which inhabit the whole world are twelve nations and they are various in understanding and in mind. When their stones were set into this building [tower, they] became **one (26)** like the stones that had come up from the deep. Because all the nations that dwell under heaven, when they heard
27. New versions repeatedly substitute 'believe' for "believe in him." Gen. 11:4 records the first one	

FACTS | NEW VERSION MANUSCRIPT

world government: ". . .and let us make a **name**, lest we be scattered abroad upon the face of the whole earth. . ."

28. Rev. 19:20 says ". . .them that had **received the mark** of the beast. . .were cast alive into a lake of fire burning with brimstone."

29. Rev. 17:13, referring to the followers of the Antichrist, says, "These have **one mind**. . ."

30. See note 11.

31. Rev. 20:4 says, "I saw the souls of them that were beheaded for the witness of Jesus, and for the word of God and which had not worshipped the beast, **neither his image neither had received his mark** upon their foreheads or in their hands." Jesus said the Antichrist "shall cause them to be **put to death**." (Mark 13:12)

32. Rev. 13:16, 17 says, "And he causeth all both small and great, rich and poor, free and bond, to

and **believed**, were called by **one name (27)**. . .so having **received the seal (28)** they had **one** understanding and **one mind. . .(29)** and one faith. . .[T]hey **bore** the spirits of the virgins along with **the Name**. . .

[S]ome . . .were cast out from the society. . .hath a certain punishment. . .delivered over to evil spirits. . .For these there is no repentance, but there is **death**. **(31)** For this cause also they are **black**; for their **race (30)** is lawless. . . [B]ut some repented and **believed (27)** and submitted themselves to those that had understanding. . .but if not, ye shall be delivered unto him to be **put to death. (31)**.

Now all these have been found white who have **believed** and who shall **believe (27)**, for they are

FACTS	NEW VERSION MANUSCRIPT
receive a mark in their right hand, or in their foreheads. And that no man might **buy or sell**, save he **that had the mark**." Daniel 8 and 11 say, "He shall enter **peaceably**. . .he shall **scatter** among them the. . .**spoil** and **riches** and by **peace** shall destroy many. . .But he shall have power over the treasures of gold and silver. . ." Isaiah 10:13-14 adds, "I have removed the bounds of the people, and have robbed their treasures. . .and my hand hath found. . .the riches of the people. . .have I gathered all the earth."	of the same kind. Blessed is this kind. But the other which. . .have **not received the seal** have been replaced. . .**their possessions must be cut off (32)** them. The Lord dwelleth in men that love **peace**, for to Him **peace (32)** is dear, but from the contentious. . .this thy deed punish thee with **death**. **(33)**
33. See note 31.	
34. Dan.7:25, referring to the Antichrist, warns, ". . .he shall. . .think to change. . .laws: and they shall be given into **his** hand."	This shepherd. . .walk in **his commandments. (34)**
35. "[N]o man might buy or sell save he that had the mark."	For if thou keep his commandments,. . .this world shall be subject unto thee, moreover success **(35)** shall attend thee. . .
36. Dan. 7:23-27 says, "he shall devour the **whole earth**". . .dominion. . . under the **whole** heavens." Rev. 13:7 repeats, "power was given him over all kindreds, and tongues, and nations."	[T]ell it out unto all men. To him alone in the **whole world** hath **authority**. . .**(36)**

FACTS	NEW VERSION MANUSCRIPT
37. The Holy Spirit is called a **'Helper'** in the new versions instead of the 'Comforter'.	[S]peak these words to others. . .[C]ontinue. . .unto the end. . .Thou hast them [holy spirits of these virgins] as **helpers. (37)** Whosoever therefore shall walk in these commandments, shall live. . . [W]hosoever shall neglect them shall not live. . .[T]he tower will be complete. . ."

PART II

FACTS	NEW VERSION MANUSCRIPT
1. The New Age and new versions encourage 'visions'. Col. 2:18 is changed from "things which he hath **not** seen" to "**visions** he **has seen**."	**VISION** ONE **(1)**
2. The "**queen** of heaven" of Jer.7 and 44, the "**lady**" of Isa. 47:7, "the **goddess**" of I Kings 11:5, 33 and Acts 19, coming from "the **East**" in Ezek. 8:16, is identified as Mystery Babylon. God calls this false religion an "abominable thing" and "wickedness."	Now while I prayed, the **heaven** was opened and I see the **lady (2)**. . .saying, 'Good Morning **Hermas'. (3)**. 'Did I not always regard thee as a **goddess**?' . . .she finished. . .and departed toward the **East**.
3. The name "Hermas" comes from the Latin root for the Greek 'Hermes'. His occult roots were covered in the chapter 'The Necromancers'.	

FACTS	NEW VERSION MANUSCRIPT
4. 2 Cor. 11:4 warns of "another Spirit." Eph. 4:4 says, "[T]here is. . .one Spirit."	VISION TWO '. . .**a Spirit (4)** taketh me. . .[G]ive me the little book'. . .'[E]ndure patiently the great tribulation that cometh.'
5. Contradicts Rev. 4:11 "for thou [Jesus Christ] hast created all things, and for **thy** pleasure they are and were created."	The Church. . .she was created before all things and. . .for **her sake (5)** the world was framed. . .[W]alk in simplicity. . .
6. **Sibyl** was a fortune teller of Greek and Roman mythology who gave oracles by which "a god or daemon revealed hidden knowledge."	I saw a vision. . .thought it was **Sibyl (6)**. . .[W]rite two little books, send one to **Clement (7)**. . .[s]o Clement shall send to the foreign cities for this is his duty. . .Behold tribulation cometh. . .
7. *The Shepherd of Hermas* was written during the life of **Clement** of Alexandria.	
8. This is the 'magic wand' used in high magic and witchcraft.	VISION THREE The third vision. . .and lifting up a certain **glistening rod (8)** she saith to me,
9. Rev. 17:1, 15 warns of "the great whore that sitteth upon many **waters**."	'Look thou; doest thou not see in front of thee a great tower being built **upon the waters. (9)**
10. The baptismal regeneration of apostate Christianity and ancient mystery religions is repeatedly taught in this document (Aleph).	Now the tower was being built. . .by six young men. . .some of them from the deep. . .The tower which thou seest building is myself the Church. . .Hear then why the tower is builded upon waters; (it is because your life is **saved. . .by water**). . .**(10)**

FACTS	NEW VERSION MANUSCRIPT
11. Luke 4:6 reveals the fallen '**angel**' to whom the world was delivered: "[T]he devil said. . .that is **delivered** unto me."	[I]t is strengthened by unseen power. . .'who are they, lady?' 'These are the holy **angels** of God. . .unto whom the Lord **delivered (11)** all His creation. By
12. 'Simplicity', 'Love' and 'Share' are words central to the New Age agenda.	their hand therefore the building of the tower will be accomplished '. . .the circle
13. Rev. 17:5 tells of MYSTERY, BABYLON, THE GREAT, THE **M O T H E R** OF HARLOTS. See the discussion of 'the mother' in chapters 6 and 7.	of the tower'. 'Seest thou seven women round the tower. . .This tower is supported by them. . . .one is **Simplicity. . .Love. . .(12)** [W]hen thou shalt do the works of their **mother (13)** thou cast live. . .
14. Luke 4:6 reveals the source of this power: "[T]he devil said unto him, All this **power** will I give thee. . ."	[W]hat **power (14)** each of them possesses. . .
15. Isaiah 3:12 says, "women rule over them." The Ecumenical Movement will culminate in the Antichrist's one world religion.	[W]hosoever therefore shall serve these **women (15)**. . .shall have his dwelling in the tower. . .Here now concerning the stones that go into the building. The stones that are squared and white and fit together. . .these are the apostles and bishops and teachers and deacons. . .they **always agreed (15)** with one another,
16. Dan. 8:25 cautions that the Antichrist "by peace shall destroy many."	[T]hey both had **peace (16)** among themselves and listened to one another. . .

FACTS	NEW VERSION MANUSCRIPT
17. The plan of the New Age (see Lucis Trust literature) and international socialism is the 'even' distribution of wealth. In the Antichrist's cashless society, he controls all resources.	[T]hey that are rich in this world, unless their riches be cut away, cannot become useful **(17).**
18. The connection between false baptism and 'the mark' is discussed chapter 14.	[B]e baptized into the name **(18)** . . .[Y]our life is saved and shall be saved by water. . .[T]hese stones that were rejected. . .shall be fitted into another place much more humble, but not until they have undergone torments. . . [I]f he refrain from every evil desire, he shall inherit eternal life. . .whensoever therefore the tower shall be finished, the end cometh.
19. New Age spokesperson Benjamin Creme calls for the "just sharing of resources" (see *Hidden Dangers of the Rainbow* p. 218).	**[S]hare. . .(19)**.also with those that are in want. . .share. . .[T]hese divisions of your deprive you of your life. I asked her to reveal to me concerning the three forms in which she had appeared to me. There appeared unto me a young man. . .ask me revelations. . .the impending tribulation.
20. See Rev. 13, 14, 15, 16, 17, 19, and 20 i.e., "I saw a woman sit upon a. . . beast" "If any man worship the beast and. . .receive his mark. . .he shall be tormented with fire." "And the beast was taken and with him the false prophet. . .These both were cast	VISION FOUR His great and glorious **Name**. . .sufficient for thee are these revelations. . .I see a cloud rising. . .I suspected that it was something supernatural. . .I see a huge **beast (20)** like some **sea monster (21)** and from its mouth fiery **locust** issue forth. . .

FACTS | NEW VERSION MANUSCRIPT

alive into a lake of fire burning with brimstone."

21. Isa. 27 describes "leviathan" as "the piercing serpent (Genesis 3). Job 41:34 reveals the sea monster to be Satan, "king over all the children of pride." Rev. 9:2-7 says, "And he opened the bottomless pit. . .there came out of the smoke **locust**. . ."

22. Giving up to the beast is in opposition to Rev. 15:2 which says Christians "had gotten the victory over the beast. . .having the harps of God."

23. New Age cosmology has a cyclical series of ages. It asserts that we are entering, the 'New' Age of Aquarius.

24. False gospels are notoriously sent by 'angels', as forewarned in Gal. 1:8: "But though we, or an **angel** from heaven , preach any other gospel unto you than that which we have preached unto you, let him be accursed." New Agers believe

I took courage and **gave myself up to the beast (22)**. . .

[T]here meeteth me a virgin. . .she said, '[B]elieve that thou canst be saved by nothing else but by His great and glorious **Name**. . .[T]he tribulation. . .if ye be willing, it shall be nought. . .[T]he white portion is the coming **age. (23)**

REVELATION FIVE

Therefore entered a glorious man. . .white skin. . .in the garb of a shepherd 'I was sent by the most holy **angel (24)**, that I might dwell with thee the remaining days of thy life. . .

FACTS	NEW VERSION MANUSCRIPT
Lucifer is the **angel** of this planet's evolution. Mohammed's Muslim religion came from a supposed visit by 'Gabriel'. The Mormon religion stems from a visit by the 'angel' Moroni. An Assembly of God pastor authored the heretical *Angels on Assignment*.	
25. The United Nations uses the term 'Mandate'.	Write down my commandments.' MANDATE THE FIRST **(25)**
26. The god of the New Age/new versions is a pantheistic, monistic 'One', who replaces the male God of the bible. See chapter 5.	1. First of all, believe that God is **One**. **(26)**
27. This is the motto of Blavatsky, Westcott and the New Age Unity-in-Diversity Council, (They ignore Jesus Christ who said, "I am the way, the **truth** and the life." John 14:6)	MANDATE THE SECOND 2. Keep simplicity. MANDATE THE THIRD 3. Love **truth**. **(27)**
28. Rev.13:14 says the Antichrist and false prophet "deceiveth them that dwell on the earth by the means of those **miracles**. . ." Rev. 16 and 19 say, "they are the spirits of devils working **miracles**" and "the false prophet that wrought **miracles. . .**" 2 Thess. 2:9 says, "Even him, whose coming is after the working of Satan, with all	MANDATE THE FOURTH 4. There is **One** who is able to give **healing; (28)**

FACTS	NEW VERSION MANUSCRIPT
power and **signs** and lying **wonders**. . ." Rev. 13:12 tells of the "beast, whose deadly wound was **healed**. . ."	
29. I Tim. 4:1 tells of "seducing spirits and doctrines of devils. . .**forbidding** to **marry**. . ."	[I]t is he who hath authority over all things. . .[T]here is no other repentance save that which took place when we went down into the water and obtained remission of our former sins. . .[T]o me was given the authority over this repentance. . .[I]f he **remain single (29)**,
30. Dan. 11:21 The Antichrist does "obtain the kingdom by flatteries" and "corrupt by flatteries." (Dan.11:32)	he investeth himself with more exceeding **honour**. **(30)**
31. Dan. 11:37 says of the Antichrist, "Neither shall he regard. . .the **desire of women.**"	MANDATE THE FIFTH They were all justified by the most holy angel. . .remain always. . .tranquil. . .walk in the way. MANDATE THE SIXTH There are two angels with a man. . .the angel of wickedness. . .[brings] the **desire of women**. **(31)**
32. Acts 26:18: "the **power** of Satan" Luke 4:6: "the devil said unto him, All this **power** will I give thee. . ." Rev. 13:2-4: "the dragon gave him his **power**. . .the dragon which gave **power** unto the beast"	MANDATE THE SEVENTH Thou shalt be **powerful. (32)** thou shalt be master over the devil. For in whom is no power. MANDATE THE EIGHTH [S]how me the power of **'the good'. (33)** that doing them it may be possible for me to be saved. . .show yourselves more submissive.
33. This Platonic concept, 'the good', is introduced in the new versions in Matt.19:17.	

FACTS	NEW VERSION MANUSCRIPT
34. Faith is not 'a power' in the sense taught by the current positive confession teachers. This concept that what you 'think' (mind power) or 'say' will come to pass is classical occultism. On the contrary, Lam. 3:37 says, "Who is he that saith, and it cometh to pass, when the Lord commandeth it not."	MANDATE THE NINTH Ask of the Lord and thou shalt receive all things. . . Faith. . .hath great power. . . [S]erve that faith which hath power. . .**(34)**
35. In Matt. 26:38 Jesus said, "My soul is exceeding sorrowful. . ." Isa. 53:3 says Jesus was "a man of sorrows." Zeph. 3:18 records, "I will gather them that are sorrowful." 2 Cor. 6:10 says the apostles were "as sorrowful, yet always rejoicing." 2 Cor. 7 says, "ye sorrowed to repentance: for ye were made sorry after a godly manner. . .For godly sorrow worketh repentance to salvation. . ."	MANDATE THE TENTH Put away sorrow from thyself. . .**[S]orrow (35)** is more evil than all the spirits. . .[I]nvestigate concerning deity and truth. For the intercession of a sad man hath never any time power to ascend to the altar of God.
36. 'a' is an indefinite article and is used when 'one' of many is indicated, as opposed to 'the' a definite article meaning 'having no fellow or equal'. New versions repeatedly substitute 'a spirit' or 'Spirit' for the Holy Spirit; they also replace 'the Godhead' with 'deity' or 'a divine being'.	MANDATE THE ELEVENTH How then. . .shall a man know who of them is a prophet and who is a false prophet? By this test. . .he that hath [the divine] Spirit. . .is. . .tranquil. When then the man who hath the divine Spirit cometh into an assembly of. . .men who have faith in ***a* divine Spirit**. . .then the angel of the prophetic spirit who is

FACTS — NEW VERSION MANUSCRIPT

attached to the man, filleth the man. . .speaketh to the multitude. . .In this way the Spirit of the deity shall be manifest. . .when he comes into an assembly full of. . .men who have **a (36) Spirit** of deity. . .[T]he divine Spirit coming from above is powerful. This Spirit therefore trust. . .

MANDATE THE TWELVTH

Luxury is foolish. . .and brings death. . .

He completed the twelve commandments. . .For I will be with thee and will compel them to **obey** thee. . .[I]f thou keep them not. . .thou shalt not have salvation. . .He created the world **for man's sake**. . .**(37)** Nothing is easier than these commandments. . .ye that walk after the commandments of the devil, the commandments which are so difficult. . .Ye shall have power to master the works of the devil. Hear me therefore and fear him who is able to do all things, to save and destroy and observe these commandments and ye shall live. . .

PARABLES

But perform thine own task and thou shalt be saved. . .For they that busy themselves overmuch, **sin**. . .[B]y so **fasting (38)** unto God thou shalt do nothing for righteousness. . .eat. . .

37. See note 5, 17, 19. The word 'obey' is repeatedly substituted for "believe" in new versions.

38. Contradicts I Cor. 7:5 which says, "give yourselves to **fasting**." The new versions remove 'fasting from Mark 9:29 and Matt. 17:21.

FACTS	NEW VERSION MANUSCRIPT
39. Matt. 20:25-28 says "Ye know that the princes of the Gentiles exercise dominion over them, and they that are great exercise authority upon them. But it shall not be so among you: but whosoever will be great among you, let him be your minister; And whosoever will be chief among you, let him be your **servant**: Even as the **Son** of man came not to be ministered unto, but to minister, and to give his life a ransom for many."	[T]he **Son** is not represented in the guise of a **servant (39)**, but is represented in great power and lordship. He created the people and delivered them over to his Son. And his Son placed the angels in charge of them,. . .He therefore took the son as adviser. . .
40. Gal. 2:16 says, "for by. . .the law shall no flesh be justified. . ."	[T]he commandments. . .were able to **save (40)** a man's soul. . .
41. Saffron is an Indian plant used to make dye. It is seen in the saffron robes of the Hindu swamis. God wears white (Daniel 7:9, Mark 9:3, etc.).	He showed me a young man, a **shepherd** clothed in a light cloak of **saffron (41)** colour. . .great and glorious angel **Michael**, who hath the power over this people and is their **captain (42). . .**
42. Heb. 2:10 says "the **captain** of their salvation" is Jesus Christ. Only Jehovah Witnesses believe Michael has this role.	[T]raitors to the church. . .ashamed of the Name. . .These then perish altogether. . .From men of this kind life departed. . .never at peace among themselves but always

FACTS	NEW VERSION MANUSCRIPT
	causing dissension. Life is for all those that keep the commandments. . .but others of them were double-minded, not hoping to be saved by reason of the deeds that they had done. . .[T]he Holy Spirit, which spake with thee in the form of the Church. . .In fair and seemly manner hast thou seen all things, as it were by a virgin.

The Epistle of Barnabas

This Apocryphal book sits between the book of Revelation and *The Shepherd of Hermas* in manuscript Aleph (Sinaiticus). It is written in the same handwriting as the rest of Aleph, by someone who apparently believed it to be inspired. Lightfoot, as translator, makes the following comments regarding this 'epistle'.

1. "The author is an uncompromising antagonist of Judaism."
2. "The author believed the ordinances [of] circumcision and the Sabbath. . .were never intended to be observed, but had a. . .mystical significance."
3. "It was written in Alexandria. . .[and] cited by Origen and Clement."[12]

Compare its teachings, (in the right column to New Age doctrines in the left column).

DOCTRINE OF NEW AGE AND APOSTATE CHRISTIANITY	*THE EPISTLE OF BARNABAS*
1. Salvation by works; regeneration by baptism.	1. "[H]oping to be saved" (Ch. 1) "[T]hou shalt work with thy hands for a ransom for thy sins." (Ch. 19) "[B]aptism which bringeth remission of sins. . ." (Ch. 11).
2. God is the monistic "One."	2. "the Active One" (Ch. 2)
3. II Corinthians 4:4 says Satan is the "god (small g) of this world." I Corinthians 8:5 says "[T]here be gods many and lords many." I Timothy 6:15 says Jesus Christ is "Lord of lords" (small l for the false 'lords'). Satan can never be Lord (capital L).	3. "Satan. . .is Lord." (Ch. 18)
4. New Age Root Race theory teaches that Christians, Jews, and certain 'dark' races are the 'Black Lodge'. In reference to this group, the New Age 'Great Invocation' prays, "seal the door where evil dwells."	4. "The Black One is crooked and full of a curse." (Ch. 19) "[O]ffer resistance that the Black One may not effect an entrance." (Ch. 19)
5. The lamb is a type of Christ; Satanists have adopted the goat as the type of Satan.	5. ". . .when they shall see Him coming then they may be astonished at the likeness of the goat. . .the type of Jesus. (Ch. 7)
6. Jesus has servants; Satan has slaves (See chapter 12 of this book.)	6. "[B]eing your devoted slave. . ." (Ch. 4)
7. This teaches amillennial, postmillennial or dominion/restoration theology.	7. "[B]e lords of the earth. . ." (Ch. 6)

Papyri Problems

In addition to these heresies in Aleph's Apocrypha, there are 'New Age' readings in the papyri which are yet to be adopted. New version editors join New Agers in scavenging these documents to produce a 'final bible'.

Although the papyri show that KJV readings existed and dominated in the early church, they also contain some minority text readings. P75, in Luke and John, and P46, in Ephesians, Colossians, and the epistles, sometimes support the omissions in the new versions. P75, however, agrees with the (KJV's *Textus Receptus*) 51% of the time in most of John. P66 supports the KJV most of the time and is older than P75. What this data indicates is that both the real text and its corruption existed in the early church period. As Paul warned in the first century, "[W]e are not as those which corrupt the word of God."

> Eldon Epp has suggested. . .there was in the beginning two distinct textual streams. . .[T]he papyri have not solved the problem as to why there were two competing texts.[13]

The papyri that have been discovered are very unreliable as absolute sources of New Testament readings. C. H. Roberts notes, it was a Jewish custom to bury heretical scripture, not to preserve them, but because they might contain the name of God and therefore could not be destroyed. The papyri that have been discovered are intact because they are such *poor* manuscripts. The fragility of papyrus causes its disintegration if used, as normal scriptures would be. Since there was no printing, many people would use one MS. Many of the recent discoveries were from the city garbage heaps, accompanied by such New Age apocryphal material as the *Gospel of Thomas* and the *Sayings of Jesus*. P46, used heavily for the readings of the NRSV and NEB, has such New Age readings as "if anyone loves, he is known," rather than the Majority text's, "But if any man love God, the same is known of him." (I Corinthians 8:3)

So we see, the oldest manuscripts are not necessarily the best, although Hodges notes, "This argument is the one most likely to impress the ordinary person."[14] As Aland in his article "The Significances of the Papyri" notes, "We need not mention that the oldest manuscript does not necessarily have the best text."[15]

The weak character of the papyri is indicated below in E.W. Colwell's article, "Scribal Habits in Early Papyri: A Study in the Corruption of the Text." It notes the following:[16]

•**P66:** Contains portions of the Gospel of John
(900 errors in John)
200 nonsense readings
400 itacistic spellings
216 careless readings
482 singular reading
269 correctors
54 leaps forward; 22 backward

Pickering notes it has "Roughly two mistakes per verse."

•**P75:** Contains portions of Luke and John
145 itacisms
257 singular readings
27 leaps forward; 10 backward
57 careless readings

Pickering notes, ". . .scarcely a good copy."

•**P45:** Contains small portions of all four Gospels.
90 itacisms
275 singular readings
20 careless readings

•**P46:** Contains some of John, Acts and Paul's epistles.
Zuntz says, "Is by no means a good manuscript."

The errors in these ancient manuscripts are important to note, because liberal scholars hope to recast the bible in a mold *closer* to these manuscripts. Harnack writes of the "yet to be published" papyri. Comfort hopes:

> It is my **hope** that future editions of the Greek text will incorporate even more of the readings found in the early papyri. . .Undoubtedly more Oxyrhynchus NT papyri will be published for the papyrologists have not yet worked their way through all the papyri discovered there.[17]

Kenyon hopes:

> [I]f so many discoveries have been made in our generation, there is every reason to **hope** that more discoveries may still be awaiting in the sands of Egypt.[18]

The NIV translators say, "[T]he work of translation is never wholly finished."[19] The New Age boasts of their plans for a new bible from the "archaeological archives."[20] The stage is set for the Antichrist to pull back the veil and launch *his final version* of the story.

FORTY - ONE

The Black Lodge: Christians

The Shepherd of Hermas said:

> [T]he shepherd ordered. . .the black stones removed [and] cast aside. . .they are black; for their race is lawless. [They] shall be delivered unto him to be **put to death**. The Black One is crooked. . .offer resistance that the Black One may not effect entrance.

The "black" stones, which are to be "put to death" are those Christian martyrs which Christ said will be "put to death" during the tribulation (Matthew 10:21). Like lines taken from a New Age script, the dicta in the new version manuscripts, *The Epistle of Barnabas* and *The Shepherd of Hermas* (and also seen in the word choices in the new versions) refers to the Hindu Root Race theory. In it race is seen as an outward manifestation of one's spiritual 'evolution'. As an extension of this, many New Age groups assign spiritual connotations to the terms 'black' and 'white'. Religious groups, such as born-again Christians, who do not subscribe to New Age assertions, are called 'The Black Lodge' or 'Black Forces'.[1] New Agers also call the period since the birth of Christ—'The Black Age'. Vera Alder tells her readers:

> [T]he Black Age. . .the Piscean Age, as you know, lasts 2000 years or so. Its inception marked the beginning of the Christian era. It is passing out of manifestation now, as the new Aquarian Age is coming in.[2]

Luciferian, Rudolf Steiner wrote that the 1890's were a turning point in the 'Black Age'.[3] Alice Bailey said "the final break or division between the so-called black and white forces, for this particular world cycle, will take place during the period of the sixth root race."[4] New Agers believe this is immanent.

New Agers christen their most highly developed members—'The Great White Brotherhood'. These include 'the Christ' and his 'Ascended Masters' of the Seventh Root Race, who communicate through today's channelers. Popular New Age books, such as the *Keys of Enoch*, profess to be 'transmitted' in code language from this 'White Lodge'. Rare treatises, like *The Ultimate Frontier*, acknowledge the analogy between 'The Great White Brotherhood' and 'The Luciferian Brotherhood'.[5] The New Age Church Universal and Triumphant boasts that their book, *The Forbidden Mysteries of Enoch*, is a direct transcription from contact with the Great White Brotherhood.

Root Race Roots

As Blavatsky boasted, the material in *The Shepherd* and *The Epistle* comes from esoteric sources. So when Hermas writes, "[T]heir race is lawless," he is using the term 'race' as it was used in the Septenary Law of the ancient mystery schools. These laws may have been written by the light skinned, pointed nosed Aryans (from whence we get the names Iran and Ireland) who migrated from the fertile crescent to India. They brought with them the Babylonian mysteries, as well as their worship of 'The Heavenly One' or 'The Divine Father'—thereby creating the basis for Hinduism. These Arya created a caste system, based on color, to subjugate the native, dark skinned Dravidians. To provide a religious rationale for the castes, they developed the theory of karma, which resigned a reincarnating soul to a body representative of its spiritual development. The Root-race theory, still held today by the Jains of India, is described by one Hindu scholar:

> Each Root Race is said to be a phase of human unfoldment in which a new sense is developed and a new level of consciousness. The first Root-race has only the sense of hearing. . .The third Root-race, known as Lemurian, produced. . .speech, sight. . .mentality, emotion. The fourth Root-race, the Atlantean, is marked by the development of lower mind. . .The fifth Root-race, the Aryan or Indo-European. . .has seen the awakening of the higher mind. . .The sixth Root-race will develop intuition and clairvoyance; the seventh, the faculty of direct perception and clairaudience.[6]

Blavatsky popularized the Root Race Theory, seen profusely in all of her books:

> Mankind is obviously divided into God informed men and lower human creatures. The intellectual differences between the Aryan and others is inexplicable on any other grounds. No amount of culture could raise such specimens as the Bushmen, the Veddas of Ceylon, and some African tribes to the same intellectual level as the Arian. . .The tide and wave of incarnating Egos has rolled past them to harvest experience in more developed and less senile stock, and their extinction a Karmic necessity. . . When the close of the Kali Age shall be nigh. . .that divine Being shall descend upon Earth. . .he shall give birth to a race who shall follow the laws of the Krita Age.[7]

Blavatsky's Theosophical Society and its spokesman Annie Besant continues the rhetoric:

> Take any savage of the lowest type, the aborigines of Australia, the Veddhas of Ceylon, the hairy men of Borneo—these are scarcely human, yet they are human. . . he has practically no mind and no morals, only the germs of them.[8]

New Agers and the Root Race Theory

The following chapter will examine how new version architect

Gerhard Kittel and Hitler worked together to hawk the Root-race theory to the last generation. This generation's New Agers are buying it—buried in books about 'New Age Consciousness'. (See chapter 42) Today the book, *New Age Bible Interpretation* gives their installment:

> Seven Root-Races succeed one another in the racial evolution on a planet. . .the Lemurians (i.e., Ethiopians) were the first root race, followed by the Atlantians (i.e., Mongolians and Red Indian Race) and finally the Aryan (i.e., Hindu, Persian, Greco-Roman, Celtic, and Anglo-Saxon-Teutonic). The soul incarnates periodically in gradually improving bodies.[9]

The New Age *Metaphysical Bible Dictionary* says, "Ethopians represent the undisciplined and undeveloped thought forces."[10] Lola Davis says, "Each one of us [has] a national, racial, and family karma."[11]

The recipe for the Antichrist's regime, detailed in *When Humanity Comes of Age*, remits the final installment of this theory. Chapter ten entitled, "Racial and Planetary Psychology" reveals:

> The Central World Council. . .will study collective racial psychology very carefully working with the International Council. They will together build up a chart assessing the particular characteristics, qualities, and potentialities of each race. . .[12]

This 'assessment' will no doubt determine that the 'qualities' of leadership and even survival are held by *their* new 7th Root-race, the Homo Neoticus. This term is used by New Agers to describe their members who will replace the old 6th Root race, the Homosapiens. As New Age writer John Randolf Price boasts, New Agers are "part of a new race that will someday rule the planet."[13]

Racey New Bibles

The 'New Bibles' of the Antichrist's 'Central World Council' will no doubt keep pace with their 'racial assessment'. The fact that neither the KJV nor any Greek manuscript contains the word 'race' is ignored by new version editors. They continue to allow the pages of their versions to be used as semantic stepping stones to the New World Religion. To accomplish this the NIV, NASB, *Living Bible* and other versions mistranslate Greek and Hebrew words such as 'seed', 'brethren' and 'generation', as '*race*'. To try to put some reality into their Root-race reverie, New Agers will no doubt latch on to I Peter 2:9 in the NASB; it reads, "But you are a chosen race." The Greek word here is *genos* from the root word *ginomai*, which means 'to come into being'. The KJV translates all such words as 'generate', 'generation', or 'Genesis'. The NASB translates a total of ten *different* words as 'race'. (e.g., Acts 7:19, Mark 7:26 and elsewhere) In Zechariah 9:6, the NASB introduces the 'mongrel race' of Hermas 'half white and half black' stones. The Hebrew word is really 'seed' which they correctly translate hundreds of other times. (e.g., Genesis 1:22 "the tree yielding fruit whose seed. . .") The NASB also gives the reader a "Chosen race" or "holy race" pitted against a 'mongrel race'—just like the New Age 7th Root race is pitted against the earlier races.

The NIV mistranslates 'brethren' as 'race' in Romans 9:3, giving the reader the Root-race distinction, "Those of my own race." Commentators, tainted with New Age ideology, even suggest that Matthew 24:34 could be translated, "This race shall not pass away until all things be fulfilled."[14]

Editors and 'Race'

Editors of new versions, commentaries, and lexicons rationalize their use of the word 'race', citing a handful of instances in which Greek mystery initiates such as Plato and Socrates, use the word 'race'. They perhaps are unaware of the Root-race theory which was very much a part of the esoteric philosophy of these men. Plato wrote much about the third Root-race, the Atlantians. Westcott picked up on it, writing in his books of scientific proof for the existence of Atlantis. He said the 'Lost Continent of Atlantis' was destroyed because, "the divine element within was overpowered by human passion."[15] 'The divine element within' and 'Atlantis' are two theories being promoted in New Age books such as *The Golden Thread* by

Natalie Banks. Ramtha, an entity being channeled today, says he comes from Atlantis. It was also on Hitler's 'hit parade' of topics for discussion.

Root-race rhetoric is evident in the writings of Origen, Westcott and Hort, showing further their sympathies with 'the tares'. Origen wrote that the 'outer darkness' of which the bible speaks is a "black body of flesh."[16] Knowing that Origen, the Platonist, wrote the first draft of Sinaiticus (Aleph) helps clarify the meaning of Hermas 'black ones'. Hort's hours spent in Plato give rise to his comment:

> [T]he niggers themselves. . .they have surely shown themselves only as an immeasurably inferior race, just human and no more, their religion frothy and sensuous, their highest virtues those of a good Newfoundland dog.[17]

The S.P.R., Westcott's grandchild, had four categories of people: "educated persons, Asiatics, the lower races and children."[18] Westcott echoes calling Africans, Hindus and Muslims "childlike races."[19] It seems participants in this Root-race heresy derive support from mutual affirmations of the fable.

Saddam Says:

The global universality of this theory is seen in the Muslim ceremony called *Wudia* in which Muslims wash their faces and say:

> O God, make my face white on the day of Judgement when sons are resurrected with white faces and others with black faces.[20]

The notion that racial evolution is at the root of behavior is even seen in comments by the 'good guys', like General Schwartzkopf. His comment that those who committed the atrocities in Kuwait, "are not a part of the same human race," likely did not frame well his intentions. But it represents unregenerate man's attempt to circumvent the biblical view of the problem. Genesis, the book of roots, not a root-race theory, reveals the skeletons of rebellion at the source of the "desperately wicked" (Jeremiah 17:9) nature of all men.

NIV Whitewash

If New Agers use the word 'black' to describe Christians who disagree with them, it is likely that the word will *disappear* from any *positive* bible context, such as Song of Solomon 1:5,6. In the NKJV and NIV, the Hebrew word *shachor* stays 'black' for 'hairs' and 'horses', but *not* for the "Black" one whom New Agers and NIV manuscript *Sinaiticus* describe as "crooked" but Christ describes as "my love" and "my spouse" (Song of Solomon). The NIV whitewashes 'black' with 'pale', *Roget's Thesaurus*' synonym for 'white'.

NIV et al.		KJV
every face grows pale	Nahum 2:10	faces of them all gather blackness
every face turns pale	Joel 2:6	all faces shall gather blackness
Dark am I	Song of Sol. 1:5	I am black
I am dark	Song of Sol. 1:6	I am black
I mourn	Jer. 8:21	I am black
Our skin is hot	Lam. 5:10	Our skin was black
darkness, gloom	Heb. 12:18	blackness, darkness
dark of night	Prov. 7:9	black and dark night
OMIT	Jer. 14:2	black
grow dark	Jer. 4:28	be black
darkness	Is. 50:3	blackness
darkened	Job 6:16	blackish
porphyry	Esther 1:6	black

FORTY - TWO

Lucifer's Lexicons

The root-race theory has resulted, not only in rhetoric, but in the red-handed holocaust of its prey. It has been the purpose of this book to bring to light to this generation of Christians what time and indifference have obscured. The 'Nazi connection' will shock Christians of even nominal sensitivities. Adolf Hitler's name is a household word, used synonymously with the consummate evil of this century. Gerhard Kittel's name is a household word—among New Testament Greek scholars. It would seem the chasm between two such men would be monumental. Kittel edited the ten volume standard reference work used in New Testament Greek word studies, the *Theological Dictionary of the New Testament.* The NIV translators relied on its judgements when selecting words, as do all translators.[1] When a pastor or 'media preacher' elaborates with reference to 'the Greek', it is virtually certain he is citing a judgement about the correct meaning or choice of a word from this dictionary or an abridged compendium which has adopted its citations. Editors remark regarding this ten volume set:

> *The* standard. . .This set is a necessity for the serious Greek student. . .the best New Testament dictionary ever completed. . .Every serious Greek student dreams of owning a set. . .[2]

The late nineteenth century saw B.F. Westcott, Balfour and Blavatsky shadowing the unholy trinity of Revelation—the false prophet, the Antichrist, and Satan. Projecting upon the background of the next generation, the shadow grew even darker as the silhouettes of Kittel, Hitler and Blavatsky merged and became indistinguishable. History repeats itself. We saw how Westcott's New Age Ghosts were summoned the same year the apparition of a 'New' Greek text began to gather substance. Kittel's labors on his ten volume Greek New Testament dictionary also began *the same year* he became Hitler's 'hired man'.

Kittel's trial, conviction and imprisonment for his key part in the extermination of two thirds of Europe's Jewish population is a harsh fact, hidden to those pridefully seeking 'hidden' meaning in the Greek. This same pride impels New Age mystics in their pursuit of hidden 'gnosis' or knowledge. Both, when raising this rock, will be met by the resident rattler.

The Seed and the seed

> And Haman said unto king Ahasuerus, There is a certain people scattered abroad and dispersed among the people in all the provinces of thy kingdom; and their laws are diverse from all people; neither keep they the king's laws: therefore it is not for the king's profit to suffer them. If it please the king, let it be written that they may be destroyed. Esther 3:8-9

The enmity foretold in Genesis 3, between the serpent and 'the seed', is seen in the actions of Haman, Herod, Hort, and Hitler. Like the unceasing hiss of the snake, they hammer to break the seed of Israel and the "incorruptible seed" of the word of God, lest the 'tender plant' of Isaiah 53:2 become 'the vine' of John 15:1. Just as Balak, the king of Moab, hired the false prophet Balaam to curse the seed of Israel when they were living in his country, so Adolf Hitler hired Kittel to curse the seed of Israel in Germany. The apostle Peter warns of these 'false prophets' and 'false teachers' who are "gone astray following the way of Balaam. . .who loved the wages of unrighteousness. . .[T]hey speak great swelling words of vanity." (II

Peter 2:1, 15) A more apt description of Kittel's dictionary and his diatribe against the Jews could not be penned.

Kittel's Pen: Instrument of Death

In Gerhard Kittel, Satan found a man who could destroy both the seed of Israel and the "incorruptible seed." His writings penned between 1937 and 1943 caused the physical death of millions of Jews and spiritual death for untold others. Using the cloak of 'Christianity' and 'science', Kittel was the chief architect of the so-called 'racial science' and 'Christian base' for Hitler's anti-Semitism. Scholar Robert Erickson, winner of the 1987 Merit of Distinction from the International Center for Holocaust Studies writes, "He established a solid Christian foundation for the opposition to the Jews."[3] Kittel called himself "the first authority in Germany in the scientific consideration of the Jewish question."[4] William Foxwell Albright, a prominent archaeologist and Semitic scholar, writes:

> Kittel is. . .even darker and more menacing. . .than Goerring or Goebbels. . .[He credits Kittel with]. . .the grim distinction of making extermination of the Jews theologically respectable.[5]

This spiritual treason by the 'Christian' academic and theological community, provides the answer to the weighty question, 'How could civilized young men of a modern culture brutally torture and murder their fellow man and why did a whole generation of Germans sit by and allow it?' Author Joseph Carr answers: "Satan's gospel of racial hatred had been preached loudly in Germany for more than a decade. . ."[6] This war of words preceded World War II, preparing the minds of some Germans for their unholy betrayal of humanity. Scholars explain:

> [T]here was a cancer in 19th century Germany. The German theologian. . .had deteriorated to an unbelieving liberalism. . .Understanding the moral treason of churchmen required knowledge of the doctrinal state of much of Europe during the first four decades of this century. . .the satanic influence.[7]

Erickson says further:

> [T]he elder Kittel's (Rudolf) feet were firmly planted in nineteenth century liberal academia. The younger Kittel. . .was [even] more easily swept along with the prevailing winds, which after 1918 meant irrationalism, volkish mysticism and anti-Semitism.[8]

The NKJV and all new versions have abandoned the traditional Old Testament Hebrew, *Ben Chayyim Masoretic Text*, and follow Rudolph Kittel's 1937 corruption, *Biblia Hebraica,* which follows Leningrad Ms B 19a.

Bedchamber to Gaschamber

What was the source of these bizarre notions of 'Aryan' superiority and Jewish inferiority? Kittel's 'volkish' mysticism and Hitler's occultism were at the root of their mutual anti-Semitism. The U.S. Army discovered Hitler's library of personally marked occult books and noted that he kept a copy of Blavatsky's *The Secret Doctrine* by his bedside! Its fables of the new fifth root race of 'divine' Aryans, battling the inferior old Jewish root race, coupled with its call for the open worship of Lucifer over Jehovah, (who Blavatsky identifies as 'Satan'), explains this monstrous phenomenon. Without an awareness of the contents of Hitler's bedside reading, his actions would remain a strange mystery. Blavatsky's book was also used by the mystical societies of Germany after World War I and was perhaps a source for Kittel's anti-Semitism as well. One writer notes:

> [M]ost of these groups used the writings of Madame Blavatsky as their bible.[10]

Blavatsky's Theosophical Society was at one time called The Aryan Theosophical Society.[11] Her anti-Semitic pamphlet and quotes, similar to the following, provided fuel for the crematoriums. Hitler read in *The Secret Doctrine*:

> [T]he Semites. . .The Sacred Spark is missing and it is they who are the only inferior race on the Globe, now

> happily-owing to the wise adjustment of nature which ever works in that direction—fast dying out. . .Here again one perceives the immense chasm between Aryan and Semitic religious thought, the two opposite poles, sincerity and concealment.[12]

Numerous books, even some written prior to 1941, have exposed occultism as Hitler's driving force. One major book club selection, *Beyond All Belief,* calls Hitler, "the theosophist's most notorious proxy-disciple."[13] One writer concurs:

> Adolf Hitler was a disciple of Madame Blavatsky and was initiated into the meaning of the secret doctrine.[14]

Karl Haushofer gave Hitler his initial initiation into the secret doctrine. This was followed by a final initiation by occultist Dietrich Eckart who wrote:

> Follow Hitler, He will dance, but it is I who will call the tune. I have initiated him into *The Secret Doctrine*.[15]

Hitler's *Mein Kampf* was dedicated to Blavatsky's disciple, Dietrich Eckart and contained much anti-Semitism. His 'Master Race Theory' mirrored clearly Blavatsky's Root Race Theory. As early as 1909 Hitler joined the Anti-Semitic Union. His speeches of 1919 and 1920 were peppered with this poison. And finally, on January 30, 1939, he told the world, "In a New World, the Jewish race in Europe will be destroyed."[16] This 'New World' oratory of the Fuehrer and today's international leaders cannot fashion the "new earth" (Revelation 21) of which it is only a counterfeit.

The Fuehrer's False Prophet

'Voices' told Hitler before 1920 that he had been selected 'by God' to be Germany's messiah, saving the nation from "the claws of international Jewry."[17] Erickson notes that "Kittel. . .did see God's hand in the elevation of Hitler to power." Kittel's defense, during his trial for war crimes, included his assertion that his actions had been "imposed upon him 'by God'." The God, heard by both, was the "god of this world." Blavatsky's doctrines of devils were delivered by Hitler, an antichrist, then sanctified by his 'scribe' Kittel and finally served to the SS and Satan's other unwary servants.

With Hitler's totalitarian regime, came the Nazi takeover of the church, under the new name *Deutche Christen.* Kittel, unlike theologians Karl Barth and Dietrich Bonhoeffer, urged:

> [A]greement with the state and Fuhrer was obedience toward the law of God.[18]

Theologian Martin Buber responded publicly that he was not surprised to see Kittel acting as pied piper for the Fuehrer.[18] Erickson notes further:

> Theologians who stressed gospel. . .tended to be immune to Hitler's charms. Kittel's work cannot be seen as anything but a satanic distortion of Christianity.[19]

Foreshadowing the final false prophet, Kittel promoted a 'New' bible version for Hitler's 'New' church, to replace Luther's traditional German Bible, *Die Heilige Schrift,* based on the Majority Text.[20] Luther's bible was about 400 years old during Hitler's generation. 'Archaic'. . .Kittel said. (The KJV will be 400 years old during our generation. Archaic. . .some say. Is it a coincidence that God closed the Old Testament canon 389 years before Christ's first coming. And now, he gives us the 1611 KJV in these last days', in the world's universal language, 389 years before his second coming in the 6000th year. The 4000th year Christ came the first time. The fourth day he created the sun, a type of Christ. The 7th day God rested, prefiguring his millenial reign during the 7000th year.)

In 1933 Kittel joined the Nazi party and his mystical maze hit a turning point. That same year he also began work on the *Theological Dictionary of the New Testament*, a work he hoped would give theology a more secular substructure. One *secular* historian notes:

> The potential for trouble suddenly became concrete in 1933. Ego involvement. . .must have played a role in Kittel's career after 1933. After 1933 Kittel's work changed in tone. Before 1933 Kittel defended Judaism,

> afterward he attacked it. Kittel produced a body of work between 1933 and 1944 filled with hatred and slander toward Jews. . .The bulk of Kittel's research between 1933 and 1945 was devoted to a rigorous and harsh anti-Jewish stance. . .[I]t corresponded to the worst of Nazi propaganda.[21]

In 1933 Kittel wrote a book and gave speeches entitled, "*Die Judenfrage.*" It's first edition states:

> We must not allow ourselves to be crippled because the whole world screams at us of barbarism. . .How the German Volk regulates its own cultural affairs does not concern anyone else in the world.[22]

Between 1933 and 1944, as Kittel was cranking out volume after volume of the lengthy *Theological Dictionary*, he was also taking a leadership role in the *Forschungsabteilung Judenfrage*, a Nazi organization and publication. Rudolf Hess, one of the earliest members of the Occult Thule Society and Hitler's right hand man, attended the opening ceremonies, which were followed by newspaper headlines pronouncing the organization as, "[T]he scientific weapon in the Nazi fight against the Jews."[23] Kittel became the most frequent contributor to this journal, writing 6 of the 8 volumes, the last being cut short by the end of the war and Kittel's imprisonment for war crimes. (The same fate fell to his closing work on the *Theological Dictionary*.)

Kittel's pseudo-'science' and 'research' for this journal stooped to the ridiculous. For example, he would show ancient drawings of men with "large hooked noses" having sex with women who had small noses. These drawings, he purported "proved" scientifically that historically "inferior" Jewish men had attempted to mate with "superior" Aryan women in order to improve their racial stock. Kittel's vulgarity included slander and name-calling, using terms such as, "refuse," "depraved" and "enemies of humanity." He wrote of "readiness to speak in racial. . .terms" and of the Jews being "justly ruined." He recommended all German Jews be dismissed from their jobs, stripped of their German citizenship and their property confiscated. He said, "[T]hough this would cause hardship it was a necessary price to pay for past excesses."[24] Doesn't this sound like the Antichrist's plan for the 'unevolved' non-compliant Christians who refuse to take 'the Name' of the beast? The same plan comes from the same source—Satan.

Holocaust

Dr. Josef Goebbels, Minister of Propaganda and Enlightenment, believed Hitler was the reincarnation of Jesus Christ. Goebbels and his SS began the first mass murder of German-Jewry on November 9 and 10, 1938. In 1939, Kittel closed one of his speeches with a tribute to Hitler calling him the, "saving force which stemmed the tide of Jewish infiltration."[25] "Knowledge of the killings was widespread within Germany itself," notes one observer. As early as 1942, the London Times reported the mass murder of Jews; Swedish diplomat Baron von Otter also publicly reported mass gassings. The B.B.C. reported the massacre by A.M. and short wave radio. "They all knew what was going on."[26] Even with such clear awareness of what was going on, Kittel continued to write for the Fuehrer. In 1943, Goebbels asked Kittel to write for his *Anti-Judische Aktion* (Anti-Jewish Action), a publication laced with Goebbels' astrological predictions about a German victory in the war. Kittel admitted knowing "about Jewish murders" and wrote of his support for Adolf Hitler's actions.

> [T]oday many harsh things do occur and must occur. . .[I]t was not despotic brutality or barbarism. . .[for] the Fuhrer. . .in his radical resolve. . .to place the Jewish problem on a wholly new foundation . . [T]he radical suppression. . .carried out by National Socialism is not, as almost the entire world maintains, an unheard of cruelty against the Jews.[27]

To what was Kittel referring when he said, "radical suppression. . .unheard of cruelty"?—Mass Murder. As late as 1944, Kittel was lecturing at the University of Vienna, speaking of the "depraved" Jews who were the cause of the fall of the Roman Empire."[28] His writing showed attempts to rationalize the murder of Jews by twisting Talmudic thoughts. Kittel writes:

> . . .full freedom to murder. . .just as you should smash the brains of even the best snake . . .[This is] justification for the most anti-Jewish acts.[29]

. . .knowing good and EVIL

> But unto the wicked God saith, What hast thou to do to declare my statutes, or that thou shouldest take my covenant in thy mouth? Seeing thou hatest instruction and castest my words behind thee. . .Thou givest thy mouth to EVIL and thy tongue frameth deceit. Thou sitteth and speakest against thy brother; thou slanderest thine own mother's son. Psalm 50:16-20

The pen of the Psalmist painted a perfect portrait of Kittel. Jerusalem is our mother (Galatians 4:26) and the Jews, the sons of Jerusalem. Erickson concludes:

> The picture of Kittel which emerges is not that of a devout Christian. . .He refurbished it with a touch of contemporary racial mysticism.[30]

That "refurbishing touch" of the paw of the wolf in sheep's clothing, massaged the meanings in the *Theological Dictionary* and is manipulating a new generation of Christians, when they touch their new versions.

> *Kittel*: "Yea, hath God said. . ."
> *Blavatsky*: "Ye shall be as gods. . ."
> *Hitler*: ". . .knowing good and EVIL."
> Genesis 3

First—we question God's word. Its authority is moved out of the way. Then, our "impressions," "feelings," "reasonings" or "associates" become our authority. We have now moved to step two and become our own gods. Then the EVIL comes. It is a shorter route than one might imagine. Erickson points out:

> [W]e cannot rely upon intelligence or rationalism to protect us from error. We must further acknowledge that

> neither rationalism, intellectualism or Christian [?] values protected Kittel. . .from supporting Hitler [and mass murder]. This is a disturbing conclusion and one which requires careful consideration if we desire that the Hitler phenomena not recur.[31]

Being Deceived?

> But evil men and seducers shall wax worse and worse, deceiving and being deceived. II Timothy 3:13

If you feel that perhaps you have been deceived, you are not alone. At the very end of Kittel's life, he confessed that the years of his editorship of the *Dictionary* and his propaganda 'ministry' for Hitler,

> . . .was based upon the most bitter deception of my life.[32]

His lack of spiritual discernment or his "diseased conscience," as Erickson calls it, seems to have been accompanied by a defect in his scholarship. In citing an error in Kittel's work, Erickson writes,

> This example throws a shadow of doubt on all of Kittel's research. . .Kittel's factual base may not always have been strong enough to support the conclusions he drew.[33]

What are these conclusions? Perhaps you will hear some this week from the pulpit, the radio or television preachers, *or* as you read a 'New' version.

The Wizard of Ahs

The next time you hear a pastor proclaim, "The Greek here *really* means. . .," (yea hath God said?), be forewarned that his pronouncements are an echo from history past. Their hollow sound is one of Kittel's spiritually bankrupt grammatico-historico method of exegesis used by today's lexicons. Carson reveals:

> I have heard pastors with two or three years of Greek behind them explain to their congregation what a certain Greek word means by citing all the entries in some lexicon.[34]

Hiding behind a curtain of words, today's Wizard of Ahs bluff, because as Kohlenberger reveals, they are taught only "basic grammar" and even:

> [T]hose who have concentrated on biblical languages have not taken as many courses or translated as much literature as would be required for a bachelor's degree in liberal arts.[35]

The Greek and Hebrew Lexicons and dictionaries are written by men, "most of whom are unbelievers," writes Princeton and Yale scholar Edward Hills. A few examples will suffice: 1) *The New Brown-Driver-Briggs Hebrew-English Lexicon's* editor (Briggs) was defrocked by the 'liberal' Presbyterian Church for his 'liberalism'. 2) Trench, author of the much used *Synonyms of the New Testament,* was a member of Westcott's esoteric clubs, as was Alford, whose Greek reference works are still used. 3) J. Henry Thayer, author of the *New Thayer's Greek Lexicon,* was a Unitarian who vehemently denied the deity of Christ. (Thayer was also the dominant member of the ASV committee!) His Lexicon contains a seldom noticed warning by the publisher in its Introduction (p. vii). It cautions readers to watch for adulterations in the work relating to the deity of Christ and the Trinity. 4) The acclaimed A.T. Robertson's *Greek Grammar* also sends up a red flag in its preface saying, "The text of Westcott and Hort is followed in all its essentials." 5) Conclusions drawn by Kurt and Barbara Aland of the *Nestles-Aland Greek New Testament* elicit the response by Phillip Comfort that "the Alands' designations must be taken with caution."[36] 6) James Strong, author of *Strong's Concordance* was a member of the corrupt ASV Committee. Hills summarizes:

> Undeniably these unbelievers know a great many facts by virtue of God's common grace. They misrepresent these facts, however because they ignore and deny God's revelation of Himself in and through the facts.

Just as *Black's Law Dictionary* switched definitions to match progressively liberal legal interpretations, likewise most Greek and Hebrew dictionaries and interlinears have now adopted definitions based on Kittel's expanded dictionary, or the like, which define words based on citations by ancient Greeks like Plato, Socrates, Aristotle and other pagan sources. When applied to bible words, these pagan interpretations serve, not as a magnifying glass, as most suppose, but as a glass darkened by the shadow of fallen men. One example will suffice. The word 'love', if defined from the daises of our day, would elicit a definition embracing such connotation as 'a feeling', 'an emotion' or perhaps a sexual sentiment. We have all heard bible teachers, following a Kittel-like Lexicon cite *phileo* and *agapao*, as the two Greek words which are translated 'love' in the New Testament. *Phileo*, according to their grammatico-historico method of exegesis, would mean 'to be a friend'; *agapao* would mean 'an unselfish God-like love'. These definitions, garnered from the secular Greek writers of the time, *do not* represent God's use of the terms. Former seminary professor, Dr. Samuel Gipp, has observed the inefficacious employment of this method, which is exposed by the following verses.

PHILEO		***AGAPAO***	
John 5:20	the Father loveth the Son	I Pet.3:10	he that will love life and see good days
John 16:27	the Father. . . loveth you	I John 3:10	neither he that loveth not his brother
I Cor. 16:22	if any man love not the Lord Jesus Christ	I John 4:20	that loveth not his brother
Titus 2:4	women. . .love their husbands	Eph. 5:25, Col. 3:19	love your wives
Titus 3:4	and love of God our Saviour	Eph. 5:28	So ought men to love their wives

"Every word of God is pure" and "given by inspiration of God"; reference works are not. The bible calls us to "compare spiritual things with spiritual " things (I Cor. 2:13). Studying the context of other verses which also contain the word (listed in a concordance) will reveal God's definition of the word. ('Love', for example, is defined in I John as "keep his commandments." We are to 'act' in love, not to 'feel' love. Going along with the New Age, new versions render Mark 10:21, "felt a love for" rather than "Jesus loved him.") New versions hid this key to understanding bible words by mistranslating I Cor. 2:13. They say, "combining (or expressing) spiritual thoughts with spiritual words." The NASB italicizes *'words'* and *'thoughts'* because they do not occur in the Greek. The command in all Greek MS is "comparing," not 'combining' or 'expressing'.

The congregation travels down the yellow brick church aisle, like the tin man, hoping to get a heart, and the scarecrow, hoping for a brain. The Wizard of Ahs, with all of his bravado, can only give a bogus 'brain' and a heart heavy with histrionics.

Nineties Neo-Holocaust

> They have said, Come and let us cut them off from being a nation; that the name of Israel may be no more in **remembrance**. Psalm 83:4

News magazines in the nineties are reporting, "[T]he anti-Semitism that lay dormant. . .has sprung back to life."[37] *Newsweek* and *Time* report of an anti-Semitic organization in Russia today called 'Remembrance', whose membership vows to kill one Jew each day. Magazines publish accounts of a French political movement, the 'National Front', which has incited the desecration of scores of Jewish burial grounds, a situation not seen since the 1300's when the French government itself confiscated all Jewish property after banishing them from the nation. As the New Age movement mantles the globe we see a pattern of anti-Semitism emerging. Carr notes:

> The Nazi worldview and major elements of the NAM [New Age Movement] worldview are identical. They

> should be, after all, for they both grew out of the same occult root: theosophy. . .the teachings of Helena P. Blavatsky (*The Secret Doctrine* and *Isis Unveiled*).[38]

Blavatsky's anti-Semitism is not characteristic of the entire New Age movement. Participants in the 'Save the Earth' movement, for example, see the cultivated 'green' carrot top. But beneath 'the earth' lies Blavatsky's bitter wild root and the harvest hell hopes to bear. Many New Age gurus, however, recognize their Hindu congruity with this Root-race theory. Swami Svalantrananda has seen this sharp spindle-shaped root and approves:

> Hitler was a mahatma, almost like an avatar. . .[H]e was the visual incarnation of Aryan polity.[39]

The heartland of America was pierced to find it harbored a large crematorium with bleacher seats in the now abandoned multimillion dollar ashram of the exiled guru, Rajneesh. Their spokesman chaffed to Constance Cumby, "[It is] for Jews, for Christians." New Age books, such as *Return of the Bird Tribes* (p. 62), *Revelation: The Birth of a New Age* (pp. 63-65) and *Prophecies and Predictions* (pp. 57, 58), all predict an upcoming "cleansing action" to purify "the race." *Sane Occultism*, another New Age tome, says: "The Beast whose number is 666. . .[tells us] we must not forget that destruction is always the first phase of construction."[40]

Cosmic Countdown says, "[T]hese people will eventually be replaced by a new root race about to make its appearance in a cleansed world."[41] College students and 'intellectuals' find this theory presented in such 'classics' as Richard Bucke's *Cosmic Consciousness: A Study in the Evolution of the Human Mind.* He says:

> In civilized man, especially in the Aryan race,. . .the mental faculties. . .have for some millennium developed with great rapidity.[42]

For those who will never read Alice Bailey's books, which accuse the Jews of having "bad national karma. . .for their sin of non-response to the evolutionary process," influential figures, such as India's Gandhi, echo to a broader audience, "The Jews would have died anyway."[43] Chiming along to the tune of the times, new bible versions inject anti-Semitic notes to this occult overture.

New Version Anti-Semitism

"Strength through Joy" Hitler
"The Way of Joy" Kenneth Taylor (L.B.)
"The Joy of Brotherhood" Lord Maitreya[44]

Kent State University English professor, Diana Culbertson, writes of her research which reveals that one new version,

> [I]ncludes not only theological distortions, additions and mistranslations, but numerous examples of anti-Semitism. The bad news is that many readers are buying a shoddy version of the text. *The Living Bible* is not just a harmless, bland paraphrase. It is a slanted version of the scripture. . .Those reading *The Book* should know what has happened to the texts and to doctrine in this hyped best seller. [45] [Note her following examples.]

	KJV	LB
John 1:17	For the law was given by Moses	Moses gave us only the Law with its rigid demands and merciless justice
Matt.12:45	this wicked generation	this evil nation
Gal. 4:3	were in bondage under the elements of the world.	We were slaves to Jewish laws and rituals.

Her last citation rings like the new version manuscript Aleph's *Epistle of Barnabas*. Its author's anti-Semitism is exposed by such statements as, "The whole Old Testament sacrificial and ceremonial institution are the devil's work." Aleph, and B as well, have numerous instances of anti-Semitism. New versions, based on Aleph and B in I Thessalonians 2:15, say the Jews killed "the prophets" rather than just "their own prophets," as cited in the KJV and Majority text. New versions echo Kittel's 1943 speech which purported there was a Talmudic Jewish mandate to kill Gentiles in general. Supporting Kittel's claim of a murderous spirit among Jews, new versions change Acts 26:17 from "Delivering thee from the people" to "from the Jewish people." No Greek support exists for adding the word 'Jewish'. Again, in Acts 23:12, the NIV and NASB have *all of* "the Jews" conspiring "under a curse" to kill Paul, whereas the verse really says "certain of the Jews." In addition, Mark 12:33, in the *New Jerusalem Bible,* directly transliterates the word 'holocaust' in a positive context, in spite of its contemporary negative associations.

Did Jesus forgive the Jews? Not according to the new versions. The NASV, NAB and *Living Bible* add "the guilt of" to Matthew 23:35, words which appear in no Greek manuscript. In addition, the verse, "Father forgive them; for they know not what they do" (Luke 23:34) is "probably not in the original writings," according to the *New American Bible*, the *NASB Interlinear Greek-English New Testament*, Nestle's Greek and the Jehovah Witness *New World Translation*.[46] The NIV casts doubt on its inclusion with a marginal note. The verse is found in the vast majority of manuscripts, even the early uncials such as Aleph, A,C, L, N, as well as the Old Latin, Curetonian, Peshitta, Harclean, and Philoxenia versions. Scholars believe its omission was caused by Marcion, who was anti-Jewish in all his sentiments. (Williams, *Alterations to the Text* p. 9) "Marcion expunged his copies of the Gospel according to Luke of all references to the Jewish background of Jesus," notes another scholar.[47] "Paul's favorable remarks about Israel posed a problem for Marcion who simply excised those passages," says still another.[48] New version editors who question its inclusion are in the beleaguered company of Marcion, the Vatican Manuscript , Westcott and Hort.

> The precious sons of Zion comparable to fine gold, how are they esteemed as earthen pitchers. . . Lamentations 4:2

New versions (i.e., *Living Bible*) deny any special place for the Jews—going so far as to remove the entire salutation from James 1:1. It begins, "to the twelve tribes of Israel." All new versions stop the book of Mark twelve verses short. This omission is based on *Aleph*, whose author would rather have you read the *Shepherd of*

Hermas. Some feel the verses in question designate special signs given to the Jews and hence their omission.

Bloodbath

> [N]oblest blood. . .toiled to benefit the Aryan race; performing surgery without anesthesia.[49]

The bizarre balladeer who sang this stanza was Def Jam, in the title song "Auschwitz, The Meaning of Pain," from their latest rock album entitled *Slayer: Reign in Blood*. Songs like this are stepping stones to sway the sentiments of yet a new generation, preparing them to persecute the Jews during the tribulation. Def Jam's reference to "the noblest blood" recalls the 1935 Nuremberg Blood Laws enacted in Nazi Germany to halt the intermarriage of Gentiles and Jews. Carr tells us:

> In Nazi racial doctrine blood was intimately related to the concept of race, race defilement. . .To the Nazi, the prime capital crime of the Jewish people was race defilement, which meant intermingling blood lines [50]

Kittel's propaganda reinforced this belief, as seen in his writings:

> [T]heir. . .blood results in decadence. . .[I]t weakens and infects. . .[I]t is poison. . .[T]here was a moral right to throw stinkbombs.[51]

This idea was rooted in Blavatsky's writings which asserted that the Jewish people were created by "Jehovah, an inferior god" and therefore are not of "the same essence" as the Aryan race.[52] Acts 17:26 disagrees saying, God "hath made of one blood all nations of men for to dwell on all the face of the earth." Now new versions join Blavatsky, Aleph and B, omitting the word "blood." The omission leaves an awkward sentence so some versions substitute the word 'man', although it does not occur in any Greek manuscripts, even Aleph and B.

The Synagogue of Satan

> I know the blasphemy of them which say they are Jews and are not, but are the synagogue of Satan.
> Revelation 2:9

Given this caution in Revelation, it is no surprise that New Agers and some Christians assert that "they are Jews." Elizabeth Claire Prophet claims her 'revelations' are a "fulfillment of the prophecy of Jeremiah concerning his covenant with the house of Israel."[53] Some 'Christians' believe the church replaced Israel. In Christ's words, this positions such people in the pews in "the synagogue of Satan." Origen and Eusebius were the headspring of this heresy. The cascade down to this century was carried by Augustine and Calvin. Hort and Westcott were the watercourse to this generation. Hort wrote in his commentary on I Peter, "The Christian Church is the true Israel."[54] Westcott calls the church the "New Israel and St. Peter, the leader of the New Israel."[55] The riptide crests today with the Reconstruction, Kingdom Now, Dominion, and Identity theology movements, spotlit on Bill Moyer's three part television series. Their sentiments are represented by men such as James McKeever who says:

> It is vitally important for the body of Christ to realize that they are Israel.[56]

Haman's disregard for 'the seed' is now seen in books such as Bill Hamon's *The Eternal Church* and David Chilton's *Days of Vengeance* which states, "[T]he Kingdom has been transferred to His new people, the Church." Consequently Earl Paulk disagrees with those who "continue to be sympathetic toward national Israel."[57]

The siege on the seed of Israel and the "incorruptible seed" has been unrelenting. In 1300 the Inquisition set its sights on the Jews and the bible, banishing both from Spain. The Crusades attempted to conquer Jerusalem in 1099. Saddam sent 40 skuds. Misguided Gentiles "the number of whom is as the sands of the sea" will continue their attempt to seize scriptures—and the throne of David until—

Thy Kingdom Come

Whose kingdom do we preach—that of the Antichrist or the "kingdom of God"?

Verses, such as Revelation 20:6, which state, "[They shall be priests of God and of Christ and reign with him a thousand years" speak of the coming reign of Jesus Christ on the earth. However, having a kingdom without *the* King is the vision of these amillennial, postmillennial and New Age millenarians looking for the Greek Golden Age, Maharishi's Thousand Years of Peace or even Hitler's Thousand Year Reich. Lola Davis says New Agers must work "in materializing the Kingdom of God on earth."[58] Vera Alder agrees calling the coming New Age, "Heaven on earth which we have been promised."[59] Christians such as Gary North agree calling for us to "rebuild our apostate civilization into the kingdom of God."

To discover the real King is omitted from his kingdom in the new versions is no surprise. Origen, Westcott, Hort, and the authors of the most widely used Greek reference works (Trench, Thayer, Machen, Warfield, Nestle, Vincent, Gregory, etc.), as well as many new version editors, subscribe to the postmillennial or amillennial view. As a result, a shift in scripture is strongly evident in the new versions.

NIV, NASB, et al.	**KJV**
preaching the kingdom	preaching the kingdom **of God** Acts 20:25
His kingdom	kingdom **of God** Matt. 6:33
his kingdom	the kingdom **of God** Luke 12:31
OMIT	Set him over the works of thy hand Heb. 2:7
good news of God	the gospel of the kingdom Mark 1:14

1. The NIV omits, "for thine is the kingdom, and the power and the glory; forever. Amen." Their footnote says, "some late mss add." Their definition of "some" defies Webster's, since 492 MSS include the verse and only 8 omit it.

2. *The Living Bible*, NASB, NAB and Jehovah Witness Bible remove the highly critical word 'now' from John 18:36, ". . .now is my kingdom not from hence." It is in all Greek manuscripts. Sounding clearly New Age, new versions read, "My kingdom is not of this realm."

3. *The Amplified Bible* spiritualizes Amos 9:11, a verse clearly indicating the restoration of David's kingdom under the Messiah. It also alters I Thessalonians 2:16 in this regard.

4. The NIV and NASB spiritualizes Revelation 11:15, omitting the plural in "The kingdoms of this world are become the kingdoms of our Lord."

5. The NASB's rendition of Luke 17:21, "The kingdom of God is in your midst," presents a visible 'Kingdom Now' theology not seen in the KJV's "the kingdom of God is within you."

Christians will no doubt be killed for 'treason' during the tribulation for not worshipping the 'emperor' in a visible kingdom, but seeking the kingdom "within." NIV Committee leader Edwin Palmer cites a dozen instances in which he changed the word "judgment" to "justice" because he saw the need for social action *now*, not judgment later.[60]

6. Revelation 1:6 in the NASB reads, "He has made us to be a kingdom" rather than "made us kings."

7. New versions render Matthew 24:22, Revelation 15:3 and scores of other verses in the past tense. This is typical of the post and amillennial denial of the coming tribulation. Numerous new version verses, such as I John 2:18, Rev. 11:18 and several others in Revelation, give the amillennial and postmillennial impression that judgement and tribulation are over and pertained to the destruction of Rome. (e.g., New versions say, "The day of the Lord has come" rather than "The day of Christ is at hand." (II Thess. 2:2) They also say, "unless those days had been cut short no life would have been saved," instead of "except those days should be shortened, then should no flesh be saved." (Matthew 24:22)

Luciferian David Spangler's book, *Revelation: Birth of a New Age,* says Christ's appearing is past tense. Agreeing with him are the NIV, NASB and the Jehovah Witness Bible, all based on the 1% corrupt Greek texts. Note, for example, II Timothy 4:8 which new versions render as "have loved his appearing" instead of "love his appearing." Some pick a point in time. For the JW's it was 1914, for the New Agers "Christ has been back on earth since 1977," for followers of Guru Maharaj Ji it was in 1971 on flight 761 "in the clouds." For most of the misinformed, it is a process, not a past or future moment of time. Note how the new versions editors parallel the New Age rhetoric—exactly!

NEW AGE	NEW VERSION EDITOR
"[T]he Christ is not Jesus. In the history of all races the Cosmic Christ has incarnated in him—Buddha, Moses, Elijah. . .However in this New Age, the Cosmic Christ will come into millions of men and women who are ready to receive it. This will be the second coming of Christ for them."[61]	"The Coming of Christ is not one but manifold. We may—recognize comings of Christ in. . .Boniface,. . .Colet. . .Loyola. . .Francis of Assisi. . .Through them Christ is coming to us."[62]
"It is not the personal and visible Jesus who returns but rather Christ Consciousness that descends into the minds of all earthly inhabitants."[63] "The Second Coming refers not to the return of Jesus, but to the awareness by an individual that he is a god."[64]	"The Apostolic expectations were mistaken. We must take warning from their disappointment against indulging in visionary and vain hopes. . .We know that all things are full of God."[65]
"Instead of speaking of God having become incarnate, it is more appropriate to speak of God as becoming incarnate. Jesus as the Christ must be seen as processively coming into existence."[66]	"Revealing the law of progress. . .he will come socially in the secret spiritual forces. . .The appearing of Jesus Christ may be a long and varying process."[67]

As an extension of the editor's views, new versions concur by deleting or spiritualizing the second coming of Christ.

- 2 Tim.4:1 KJV's "at his appearing" becomes "and by his appearing." ('at' is a point in time)

• Matt. 25:13	KJV's "Watch therefore, for ye know neither the day nor the hour wherein the Son of man cometh (last 6 words omitted).
• Rev. 7:15	KJV's "He shall. . .dwell among them" becomes "He shall. . .spread his tabernacle over them."
• Titus 2:13	KJV's "the glorious appearing" becomes "the appearing of the glory."
• Phil. 4:5	KJV's "The Lord is at hand" becomes "The Lord is near." The former is a reference to time, while the latter is a reference to space.
• 2 Thess. 3:5	KJV's "Waiting for Christ" is omitted by new versions.

The final chapter of the *New Age Version* of the story finds the pens of the scribes lining up a barricade against the second coming of Jesus Christ. Their banter serves as a battering ram, opening hell's door to unleash persecution of those who are saved during the seven year "kingdom" of the Antichrist. Both barricade and battering ram will break when—

KJV		**NIV, NASB et al.**
[T]he Son of man cometh	Matt. 25:13	Is this in your version?

EPILOGUE

Beneath the habit of a harlot—whether humanist's cap and gown or sage's saffron robe—is a heart hiding from God. The documentation herein—whose cumulative force is formidable—has uncloaked their cover. The evidence demonstrates that the naivete is *not* on the part of KJV believers, but on the part of those who "professing themselves to be wise. . .became fools." (Romans 1:22)

The new versions are sweeping the church like an uncontrolled brush-fire, propelled by a high wind from the "prince of the power of the air." God framed a fire-wall to forestall its spread. It read: "Mark them which cause divisions and offenses contrary to the doctrine which ye have learned and avoid them." (Romans 16:17) Instead, the saints said, "Mark them which cause division. . .and avoid them."

Smitten by the sentimentality sent on Cupid's darts, they harden their hearts and court the whore. They forget that Cupid (the *Roman* god of 'love') was the son of Venus (Lucifer) and the 'lover' of *Psyche* (mind, psychology). Today, on a worldwide scale, churches follow this tale in every detail. To keep little cupid afloat, some say, "Why throw the baby out with the bath water?" Dave Hunt's reply to a similar decry bears repeating. "I searched for that baby in the bath water and found it was *Rosemary's Baby*."[1]

The harlots haunting the new cults, new age, new versions, 'new' Christianity and new One World Religion are like the five fingers on a hand. Each varies in purpose, but Satan is waving the hand, moving the fingers and 'reaching out' to choke the church. One scholar concludes:

> For if the true New Testament came from God, whence came the erroneous variant readings ultimately save from the evil one.[2]

It is safer to live without the answers to some questions than to have quick answers that may be harmful in the end. God's method for understanding the bible is described in Appendix C. Its spiritual demands lead some, like King Saul, to seek information *about God* from someone who has contacted familiar spirits. (I Samuel 28:7) Because of this, Saul fell in battle, smitten by an archer's bow and his own sword. This same temptation also leaves New Testament "kings" (Revelation 5:10) unable to stand up under "the fiery darts of the wicked." We see them falling all around us. Satan is no respecter of persons. He seeks to devour all.

Remember when you first heard the gospel you thought, "How narrow! *One* man, who lived hundreds and hundreds of years ago. . ." The timeworn tale of "one mediator between God and man" does not fit into our 'new' and pluralistic view. Could it be that Jesus Christ is calling you again to, "*One* book, written hundreds and hundreds of years ago. . .?" You kept an open mind about Christ, investigated the facts and are thankful today. Perhaps you need to humble yourself *again* and *grow* in grace. The churches of Christ are continually in need of correction, as recorded in the book of Revelation. There Jesus said, "As many as I love, I rebuke and chasten; be zealous therefore, and repent." (Revelation 3:19) Brethren, do you "tremble at his word," the bible? If you will, God promises joy:

> Hear the word of the LORD ye that tremble at his word; Your brethren that hated you, that cast you out for my name's sake, said, 'Let the LORD be glorified': but he shall appear to your joy, and they shall be ashamed. Isaiah 66:5

The lines of the bible, laid end to end, form a centuries long lifeline, linking souls to their Saviour. When severed, souls slip into the pit. God has taken the lines of the *Authorized King James Version* and strung beautiful jewels upon them. One new version editor admits, it is a "miraculous," "amazing" "mystery."

> It remains a mystery how a committee of 50 scholars produced a unified level of prose beauty that ever since has permeated English literature like a rich die. It is an amazing fact. Some have not hesitated to use the term miraculous.[3]

When the hand of man cuts this miraculously woven thread, the jewels spill. Some are lost in the process. The remaining broken stones, when set on a new version page, form a muddled mosaic. Some may see Jesus Christ in the distorted Picasso-like picture. But gone are the stepping stones on God's high road. This book has sifted out only a small portion of the stumbling stones which lie on *every* line of these versions.

> Finally, brethren, **pray** for us, **that the word of the Lord may** have free course,and **be glorified**, even as it is with you. II Thessalonians 3:1

APPENDIX A

A Summary: Westcott and Hort

A peek into the private thoughts of the men who wrote the Greek text underlying the new versions (Westcott and Hort) can be had by reading their personal correspondence preserved in their biographies. The following chart chronicles the concurrent thoughts and activities of these men *while* they were preparing the 'New' Greek Text and the Revision of the New Testament. (emphasis mine) Their exploration of necromancy and esoteric clubs and individuals was occurring while they were deciding what does and does not belong in the bible. (e.g., On a trip to view a N.T. manuscript, Westcott made a pilgrimage to a shrine of the Virgin commenting that "God appears in many forms.")

> [S]o can no fountain both yield salt water and fresh.
>
> James. 3:12

THEIR 'NEW' AGE HERESIES	THEIR 'NEW' GREEK TEXT
1840	
". . .he took a strange interest in Mormonism. . .procuring and studying the Book of Mormon." (Westcott, Vol 1, p. 19)	
1842	
"In the evening I go with Tom to the wizard; but he does not dare perform before us." (Westcott, Vol. 1, p. 9)	
1845	
Westcott, Hort, and Benson start the 'Hermes' Club.	
1846	
". . .his diary tells of a walk to Girton with C.B. Scott in which metaphysics was discussed." (Westcott, Vol. 1, p. 42.) [R]efers to evangelicals as "dangerous" and "unsound." (Westcott, Vol 1, pp. 44-45.) "New doubts and old superstitions and rationalism, all trouble me. . .I cannot determine how much we must believe; how much in fact is necessarily required of a member of the church." (Westcott, Vol. 1, pp. 46-47.)	

1847	
"So wild, so skeptical am I; I cannot yield." (Westcott, Vol 1, p. 52.)	
In speaking of heretic Dr. Hampden, he says, "If he be condemned, what will become of me?" (Westcott, Vol. 1, p. 52.)	
1848	
Hort refers to the ". . .fanaticism of bibliolaters." He remarks, "The pure Romish view seems to me nearer and more likely to lead to truth than the evangelical." (Hort, Vol. 1, pp. 76-77.) "Protestantism is only parenthetical and temporary." (Hort, Vol II, p. 31.)	
1850	
Hort speaks of ". . .confused evangelical notions. . ." He says, "I spoke of the gloomy prospect should the Evangelicals carry on their present victory." (Hort, Vol. 1, pp. 148, 160.)	Westcott was, "troubled in thought about this passage" (blasphemy against the Spirit)." (Westcott, Vol. 1, p. 109)
1851	
Hort joins the 'Philosophical Society' and comments, "Maurice urged me to give the greatest attention to Plato and Aristotle and to make them the center point of my reading." (Hort, Vol. 1, pp. 202, 93.)	Hort refers to, "the common orthodox heresy: Inspiration." (Hort, Vol. 1, p. 181.)

Westcott, Hort, and Benson start the 'Ghostly Guild'. Westcott was ordained a 'priest' in the Anglican church. Hort also joins 'the Apostles', a secret club.	
1852	
Westcott and Hort distribute 'Ghostly Guild' literature.	Westcott, in speaking of Revelation, admits, "On this, my views are perhaps extreme." (Westcott, Vol. 1, p. 225.) Referring to the Traditional Greek Text, then currently in use, Westcott says, "I am most anxious to provide something to replace them." He admits the drastic changes he plans and calls it, "our proposed *recension* of the New Testament." (Westcott, Vol 1, p. 229.)
1853	
Hort "was diligently preparing for his ordination" into the Anglican priesthood.	"It was during these weeks with Mr. Westcott, who had come to see him, [Hort] at Umberslacle, that the plan of a joint *revision* of the text *of the Greek* Testament was first definitely agreed upon." (Hort, Vol. 1, p. 240.) "About this time Mr. Daniel Macmillan suggested to him [Hort] that he should take part in an interesting and comprehensive 'New

	Testament *Scheme*'. Hort was to edit the text in conjunction with Mr. Westcott, the latter was to be responsible for a commentary, and Lightfoot was to contribute a New Testament Grammar and Lexicon." (Hort, p. 241.) "He and I are going to *edit* a Greek text of the New Testament some two or three years hence if possible." (Hort, Vol. 1, p. 250.) "We came to a distinct and positive understanding about *our* Greek Text and the details thereof. We still do not wish to be talked about but are going to work at once and hope we may have it out in a little more than a year. This of course gives good employment." (Hort, Vol. 1, p. 264.)
1855	
"How certainly I should have been proclaimed a heretic." (Westcott Vol. 1, p. 233.)	
1856	
"Campbell's book on the Atonement. . .unluckily he knows nothing except Protestant theology." (Hort, Vol. 1, p. 322.)	"I hope to go on with the New Testament Text more unremittingly." (Hort, Vol. 1, p. 355.)

1857	
"I am just now chiefly occupied about a proposed Cambridge translation of the whole of Plato. . .another scheme likely to be carried out if a publisher can be found." (Hort, p. 349.)	
1858	
"But no doubt there was an element of mystery about Westcott. He took his turn preaching in chapel, but he dreaded and disliked the duty and he was quite inaudible." (Westcott, Vol I, p. 198.)	"The principle literary work of these years was the *revision* of the Greek Text of the New Testament. All spare hours were devoted to it." "Evangelicals seem to me perverted. . .There are, I fear, still more serious differences between us on the subject of authority, especially the authority of the Bible." "At present many orthodox but rational men are being *unawares* acted upon by influences which will assuredly bear good fruit in due time if the process is allowed to go on *quietly*; but I fear that a premature crisis would frighten back many into the merest traditionalism." (Hort, Vol. I, p. 400.)
1859	
"I shall be very glad to learn what are the objectionable parts in my sermon: I fancied that I kept wonderfully within the limits	"My dear Lightfoot, thank you very much for your kind present. But why did you send *beer* instead of coming yourself? I have

of orthodoxy: but I trust that my object was rather to say what I felt rather than square what I say with some scheme." (Westcott, Vol. I, p. 208.)	another question to ask about palimpsest fragments of the first seven chapters of St. Luke. . .I can testify to the high value of the MS." (Hort, Vol. I, pp. 403-404.)
1860	
"If only we speak our minds, we shall not be able to avoid giving *grave* offense to. . .the miscalled orthodoxy of the day." (Hort, Vol. 1, p. 421.)	"If you make a decided conviction of the absolute infallibility of the New Testament a *sine qua non* for cooperation, I fear I could not join you." (Hort, Vol. 1, p. 420.) "[M]y doubts about infallibility [remain]." Lightfoot wants you to take Hebrews, if it does not go to *Benson* [Ghostly Guild]." (Hort, Vol 1, p. 422.)
"I. . .looked at the *Christian Observer['s]*. . .condemnation of my heresy." (Westcott, Vol. 1, p. 241.)	"I reject the word infallibility of Holy Scriptures overwhelmingly." (Westcott, Vol 1, p. 207.) "I am also glad that you take the same provisional ground as to infallibility that I do. . .In our rapid correspondence about the New Testament, I have been forgetting Plato." (Hort's letter to Lightfoot, Hort, Vol. 1, p. 424.)
1861	
". . .imputations of heresy and the like against me." (Westcott, Vol. 1, p. 222.)	**"[T]his may be cowardice—I have sort of a craving that our text should be cast upon the world before we deal with matters likely to brand us with suspicion. I mean, a**

	text issued by men who are already known for what will undoubtedly be treated as dangerous heresy will have great difficulty in finding its way to regions which it might otherwise hope to reach and whence it would not be easily banished by subsequent alarms." (Hort's letter to Westcott regarding their writing other things.) (Hort, p. 445)
1862	
	"English Clergy are not compelled to maintain the absolute infallibility of the bible." (Hort, Vol. 1, p. 454.)
1864	
	"Westcott talks of our keeping pace with the printers."
1865	
"[T]he idea of La Salette [appearances of the Virgin] was that of God revealing Himself, *now*, not in one form, but in many." (Westcott, Vol. 1, p. 251.)	During his trip to visit the shrine of the Virgin he stopped in Milan to make "examination of the Muritorian Fragment of the Canon." (Westcott, Vol. 1, p. 254.)
1866	
"All the questionable doctrines which I have ever maintained are in it." (Westcott, Vol. 1, p. 290.)	

1869	
	"We must somehow contrive. . .some way of adding to income." (Hort, Vol II, p. 108.) "Westcott urges me to try what writing will do." (Hort, Vol. II, p. 110.)
1870	
"Dr. Butler calls him [Westcott]. . .mysterious. . .His voice reached but a few and was understood by still fewer." (Westcott, Vol. 1, p. 272.)	"Dr. Westcott and myself have for about seventeen years been preparing a Greek text. . .we hope to have it out early next year." (Hort, Vol II, p. 137.) ". . .strike blindly. . .much evil would result from the public discussion." (Westcott, Vol. 1, p. 229.)
1871	
"I shall aim at what is transcendental in many peoples eyes. . .I suppose I am a communist by nature." (Westcott, Vol. 1, p. 309.)	Westcott, Hort, and Lightfoot were invited to join the Revision Committee of the New Testament. "Westcott. . .believes we ought to seize the opportunity especially since *we three* are on the list." (Hort, Vol. 2, p. 133.)
1872	
Westcott, Hort and Lightfoot begin the Eranus Club (the "we three" of the Ghostly Guild). Sidgwick and Balfour, of upcoming Society for Psychical Research, also join Eranus.	[Work on New Testament revision continues, 1871-1881.]

1873	
"Truth is so wonderfully large." (Westcott, Vol. 1, p. 333.)	
1877	
Eranus meet in Hort's room.	
1881	
"Our Bible as well as our Faith is a mere compromise." (Westcott, *On the Canon of the New Testament: A General Survey*, p. vii)	"[T]he work which has gone on now for nearly 30 years was brought to a conclusion." (Hort, Vol. II, p. 234)(*The Revised Version* and 'New' Greek are published; or is he talking about the Ghostly Guild, which also began exactly 30 years ago and inspired the S.P.R. in 1882?)
1882	
"The truth seems to me to be so overwhelmingly vast and manifold that I shrink from drawing any outline except provisionally." (Westcott, Vol. II)	
1889	
"Life and truth grow more and more mysterious." (Westcott, Vol. II, p. 61.)	
1893	
"He sometimes with much seriousness professed to be much drawn to **beer**. . ." (Westcott, Vol. II, p. 178.) "His zeal in the cause of pure **beer** involved him in a correspondence which was published in the newspapers in the later part of	

1893 and **his picture** together with some of the following words spoken by him, **was utilized for the adornment of the advertisement of a brewer of pure beer**." "My idea is that they might have a public house in which good **beer** alone would be sold.. . .I consider pure beer. . .to be an innocent and wholesome beverage. . .[S]ubstitutes for malt. . .is not what the purchaser demands nor expects." [Westcott's letter written to Brewer's Society in complaint against inferior **beer**] (Westcott, Vol. II, pp. 218-219, 177.)	
1896	
"The Prohibitionists once more showed themselves to be unstatesmanlike. . ." (Westcott, Vol. II, p. 238.)	
1899	
"But from my Cambridge days I have read the writings of many who are called mystics with much profit." (Westcott, Vol. II, p. 309.)	

You can fool some of the people
all of the time
And all of the people
some of the time, but. . .

You Can't Fool Mom: Hort

Hort's mother appears to have been an evangelical Christian. Her influence seems to have provided the Christian branch of his syncretistic tree. Hort's biography states, he "outgrew the Evangelical teaching which he came to regard as "sectarian . .fanaticism. . . perverted." Of his mother, Hort's biography states:

> Her religious feelings were deep and strong. . .[H]is mother was . . .an adherent of the Evangelical school and she was to a certain degree hampered by it. . .She was unable to enter into his theological views which to her generation seemed a desertion of the ancient way; thus pathetically enough, there came to be a barrier between mother and son. The close intercourse on subjects which lay nearest to the hearts of each was broken. . . [Concerning] her different point of view,. . .he. . .had to recognize that the point of view *was* different. She studied and knew her bible well.[1]

His mother wrote to him, pleading that he would not be "missing" from,

> . . .the many mansions of our Heavenly Father's House and my darling, Now happy it will be if we all meet there; no one missing of all our household.[2]

As Hort's career progressed, he retained his distaste for Evangelicals who held tenaciously to the "articles of the Christian faith." Hort writes to Lightfoot mocking an Evangelical Bishop:

> . . .Claughton's fierce denunciation of everyone who questions an article of the Christian faith as an enemy of God and holiness.[3] [There are] serious differences between

> us on the subject of authority, and especially the authority of the bible.[4]

The "fanaticism of bibliolaters," Hort bemoans.[5] His son writes, "Hence he was led to seek firmer foundation than he could find in the Evangelical position."[6] His shift from his evangelical upbringing was prodded by membership in the Philosophical Society and by his grandfather, an Archbishop who wanted to "interpret the Bible in a manner agreeable to the principles of Philosophy."[7]

Fourteen years after his instigation of the 'Ghostly Guild' with Westcott and Benson, Hort writes:

> During the last 15 years my thoughts and pursuits have grown and expanded but not considerably changed. In Theology itself I am obliged to hold a peculiar position, belonging to no party, yet having important agreements and sympathies with all. . .I perhaps have more in common with the Liberal party than with others. . .I look upon freedom and a wide toleration as indispensable. . .[8]

Of Westcott a friend wrote:

> What a theology it was—how broad. . .anti-dogmatic; how progressive.[9]

The errors in the 'New' Greek Text and new versions, stemming from the liberal and hypocritical lives of Westcott and Hort, are leaving a generation of souls hungry. God foretold this in Isaiah 32.

> The vile person shall no more be called liberal. For the vile person will speak villainy and his heart will work iniquity, to practice hypocrisy and to utter error against the Lord, to make empty the soul of the hungry. . .to destroy the poor with lying words. . .the liberal diviseth liberal things.

Hort Haunts Today's Pulpits

If Hort were applying for the position of pastor in your church, he might reply as he did in 1871, when asked by the Bishop of Ely's to be a chaplain. (This was the very year he joined the New Testament Revision Committee.)

> I doubt greatly whether I possess some of the qualifications. . .in views, and still more in sympathies. I do not sufficiently conform to any of the recognized standards. . .on what might be called the details of even these matters of faith, I am not sure that my views so far as they are fixed would be generally accepted. . .[T]o give an instance, there are certain parts of the Old Testament. [Mr. Maurice's books] have led me to doubt whether the Christian faith is adequately or purely represented in all respects in the accepted doctrines of any living school . . I have. . .a keen interest in philosophy, a conviction that their vigorous and independent progress is to be desired for the sake of mankind, even when for the time they seem to be acting to the injury of the faith. . .[A] fundamental difference in the subject of the Atonement, **if it existed**, would place me in a false position as your examining chaplain. . .I have friends of various creeds and creedless, from whom I believe I should do wrong to dissociate myself. It is quite possible that I might wish to write papers or books in which some of these facts would unavoidably come to light.[10]

Webb wrote of the dismal state of the Church of England at this time; it is evidenced in the fact that, in spite of Hort's admission of 'heresy', he *was hired* as chaplain! His son writes:

> [F]or the next six years [he] lectured to the theological students at Emmanuel College. The subjects were Origen. . .Clement. . .etc. . .[h]is lecturing which exercised a kind of spell over the more thoughtful listener. . .[T]here has grown up. . .a kind of cult around him. There is something mysterious about those lectures.[11]

And those bibles.

APPENDIX B

The KJV & the Earliest Manuscripts

The following are just a few samples of the thousands of instances in which the earliest papyri support the KJV, while new versions ignore the earliest MSS. (Note the changes in Nestle's latest 26th edition *Greek New Testament* to KJV readings based on the most recent findings.)

VERSE	EARLIEST MANUSCRIPTS
Matt. 26:27	"the cup" of the KJV has been vindicated by P37 and P45 and is *now* used in Nestle's 26, NJB, NEB. The NASB follows the old Nestles.
Mark 2:22	"is put," of the KJV has been vindicated by P88 but was not used in the NASB. It was put into the NIV. The sentence has no predicate as used in the NASB.
Mark 7:4	Nestle's 26 had to change to agree with KJV.
Mark 7:28	Nestle's 26 had to change to agree with KJV.
Mark 9:29	"and fasting" of the KJV has been vindicated by P45, Aleph 2, A, C, D.

VERSE	EARLIEST MANUSCRIPTS
Luke 10:42	"but one thing is needful" is now vindicated by P45 and P75. Yet NJB, NASB and old Nestles, (before 26) still have "few things are needful ."
Luke 15:21	P75 supports the Majority text against Aleph and B.
Luke 24:51	P75 supports the KJV.
John 4:1	Nestle's 26 changed from a P66, P75, A, B, NIV, NASB reading to an Aleph and B reading.
John 7:8	P66, P75 and B support the KJV reading "yet". This word is critical because without it Jesus becomes either a liar or confused and contradictory. Yet Nestle's 26 and the NASB leave it out. Comfort (p.113) refers to the KJV reading as the one "that puts Christ in a better light."
John 13:2	P66 supports the Majority text and KJV reading. In spite of this, all other translation follow Aleph and B.
John 14:4	P66 (the original) wrote the KJV rendering. A corrector changed it and now all the new versions follow the "corrector".
John 16:22b	NIV follows P5, in spite of the testimony of P66, P22, Aleph, A and C (and KJV).
John 16:27	NASB is out of date again, not following P66 and P5.
John 8:16	P39, 66, 75, Aleph and B have "Father who sent me." The NASB, NJB and NEB have "he who."
John 8:39	NASB follows P66 and B. NIV follows P75 and Aleph.
Acts 11:11	NASB follows P74. NIV follows P45.
John 10:16	P66 and Aleph supports KJV; however Nestle's 26 changed ***from P66*** and KJV reading in Nestle's 25 ***to P45*** reading in Nestle's 26. This is a weaker foundation.

VERSE	EARLIEST MANUSCRIPTS
John 10:18	Nestle's change verb tense ***from P45*** in Nestle's 25 ***to P66*** in Nestle's 26, now matching the KJV. (Note Nestle's inconsistency in verse 16 and 18.)
John 10:29	Nestle's 26 ignores P66, P75 and the Majority text to follow one of the correctors of manuscript B.
Acts 10:30	P50 supports the KJV "and fasting," which all new versions omit.
Acts 11:11	P45 supports the KJV and NIV reading; the NASB is again out of date.
Acts 23:12	P48 supports the KJV against the new versions. This verse is an example of the anti-Semitism of the new versions.
Rom. 1:1	P26 and the Majority Text support the KJV against the new versions.
Rom. 12:14	Nestle's 26 changed to the KJV reading.
(see previous analysis of Corinthians and Galatians, pp. 499 to 502)	
Eph. 1:14	"Holy Spirit of promise, *which* is the earnest" is supported by P46. This is in line with the Greek word for Spirit which is always neuter throughout the N.T. . Nestle's 26 and the NRSV changed from "who," to the KJV "which". Here the NJB, NIV, and NASB still have the outdated "who" based on Aleph and D. They ignore B and P46 which they follow elsewhere.
Eph. 3:9	Nestle's 26 changed to the KJV based on P46 and B, yet the NASB still omits "all men."

VERSE	EARLIEST MANUSCRIPTS
Eph. 4:28	The reading "own" in the NIV, NASB, NEB, and NJV is not supported by P46, P49 or B. The KJV has the earliest reading. It is bracketed in Nestle's.
Eph. 5:2	P46 supports the KJV "loved us," yet the NASB reads "loved you."
Eph.5:9	P46 supports the KJV "fruit of the Spirit," whereas all new translations have "fruit of the light."
Phil. 1:14	P46 supports the KJV, yet NIV and NASB ignore this early attestation. Nestle's 26 changed to the KJV reading.
Phil. 3:13	P46 supports the KJV, so Nestle's 26 changed to follow them. Yet the NIV and NASB still have the outdated reading.
Col. 1:7	P46 supports the KJV; Nestle's 26 changed to follow them. Yet all new translations ignore the finding.
Heb. 11:4	P13 has "to God" with the KJV; all new versions go with the later MS Aleph (Hebrews 9:11 also).
Heb. 11:11	P13 has "herself received strength to conceive seed" along with the KJV. New versions follow D (fifth century) saying "he received power to beget."
Heb. 11:37	NIV omits "they were tempted," yet it is in P13, Aleph, D, and KJV.
I Pet.1:22	All new translators have "a heart." Nestle's 26 changes to the P12 and KJV reading which is "a pure heart."

VERSE	EARLIEST MANUSCRIPTS
I Pet.5:2a	KJV, P72 and the new Nestle's have "oversight." Yet the NASB omits this because, as Comfort notes, "[T]hey had the misconception that elders could not function as overseers. At that time [and now in the Roman Catholic and other liberal churches] the offices of elder and overseer (i.e., bishop) were differentiated. The overseer or bishop had been elevated to a rank above elder—though this deviates from the situation in the N.T. in which overseers and elders were two functions of the same individual (Titus 1:5, 7)."
2 Pet.2:4	P72, Nestle's 26 and KJV have "chains," yet all new versions follow the outdated "pits" of Aleph and B.
Rev.14:13	Nestle's 26 moved to KJV readings.

APPENDIX C

The Seven Seals: How to Understand *The King James Bible*

The transition from the *Authorized King James Bible* to a recent version is usually based on the contention that the KJV is old and difficult t o understand. The *real* gap is one of distance between God and man, not a lapse between us and 'Father Time'. Since the fall (Genesis 3), man has moved off to a corner of the universe, out of reach of God's voice. Now powerless to penetrate God's spiritual realm, he moves madly through man-made word-mazes, in version after version, defiantly determined never to look up to God or delve within his own misdirected heart.

The spiritual chasm is so vast that even those close to Jesus could not understand him. He was not speaking archaic Aramaic to Mary and Joseph yet, "they understood not the saying which he spake unto them." Obsolete words were not the obstacle when he asked Peter, "Are ye also yet without understanding? Do not ye yet understand?" Later, Peter again fell under the darkening spell of sin saying, "I know not, neither understand I what thou sayest."

God tells us man's inability to understand the bible has a number of causes, none of which is a limitation in his vocabulary.

The bible is not difficult to understand—it is impossible—unless God's criteria are met. The verses and checklists to follow should help the reader look within his heart for the start of the knot, and then look up to God for the unraveling.

The bible is a sealed book.

For the LORD hath poured out upon you the spirit of deep sleep, and hath closed your eyes. . .and the vision of all is become unto you as the words of a book that is sealed, which men deliver to one that is learned, saying, Read this, I pray thee: and he saith, I cannot; for **it is sealed**. Isaiah 29:10, 11

Man's sin casts a shadow which darkens his understanding of each verse.

Who is worthy to open the book and to loose the seals thereof?. . .no man was found worthy to open and to read. Revelation 5:2,4

The LORD looked down from heaven upon the children of men, to see if there were any that did **understand,** and seek God. They are all gone aside, they are all together become **filthy**. . .Have all the workers of iniquity **no** knowledge. Psalm 14:2-4

Why do ye **not understand** my speech? . .Ye are of your father the **devil**. John 8:43,44

[N]one of the **wicked** shall **understand**. Daniel 12:10

A **scorner** seeketh wisdom and findeth it **not:** but knowledge is easy unto him that **understandeth**. Proverbs 14:6

[T]he **wicked**. They know **not,** neither will they **understand**. Psalm 82:4,5

A **brutish** man knoweth **not**; neither doth a fool **understand** this. Psalm 92:6

Evil men **understand not** judgment. Proverbs 28:5

[T]he people. . .the Pharisees. . .they **understood not** what things they were which he spake unto them. John 8:2,3, 10:6

Understand, ye **brutish** among the people: and ye fools, **when** will ye be wise? Psalm 94:8

And even as they did not like to retain God in their knowledge, God gave them over to a reprobate mind. . . Being filled with all **unrighteousness**, fornication, wickedness, covetousness, maliciousness; full of envy, murder, debate, deceit, malignity; whisperers, Backbiters, haters of God, despiteful, proud, boasters, inventors of evil things, disobedient to parents, **Without understanding**, covenant breakers, without natural affection, implacable, unmerciful: Who knowing the judgment of God, that they which commit such things are **worthy of death**. . .Romans 1:28-32

Even man's mind cannot penetrate the deep, dark shadow which blackens 'the book'.

[F]or the wisdom of their **wise** men shall perish, and the **understanding** of their **prudent** men shall be **hid**. Isaiah 29:14

For it is written, I. . .will bring to nothing the **understanding** of the **prudent**. I Corinthians 1:19

But the natural man receiveth not the things of the Spirit of God: for they are foolishness unto him: neither can he know them, because they are **spiritually discerned**. I Corinthians 2:14

The shadow is shaped like the profile of a heart jagged with sin.

[W]alk not as other Gentiles walk, in the vanity of their mind, Having the **understanding darkened**. . .because of the blindness of their **heart**. Ephesians 4:17, 18

[Y]e shall hear, and shall **not understand**. . .For the **heart** of this people is waxed gross. . .lest they should. . .**understand** with their **heart**. Acts 28:26,27

[Y]e fools, be ye of an **understanding heart**. Proverbs 8:5

[T]hou hast **hid** their **heart** from **understanding**. Job 17:4

They have not known nor understood: for **he hath shut** their eyes, that they cannot see; and their **hearts,** that they cannot **understand**. . .a **deceived heart** hath turned him aside. Isaiah 44:18-20

And they understood none of these things: and this saying was **hid** from them. Luke 18:34

[W]here is the place of **understanding**? Seeing it is **hid** from the eyes of all living. Job 28:20-21

There is 'a way' of understanding the bible and that way is Jesus Christ.

The preface to the KJV says,"**He** removeth the scales from our eyes, the veil from our hearts, opening our wits that we may understand His word."

Weep not: behold, the Lion of the tribe of Judah, the Root of David, hath prevailed to open the book. . .for thou wast slain, and hast redeemed us to God by thy blood. Revelation 5:2, 4, 5, 9

[G]o in the way of understanding. Proverbs 9:6

Jesus saith unto him, I am the way. . .John 14:6

The man that wandereth out of the way of understanding shall remain in the congregation of the dead. Proverbs 21:16

Hearken unto me everyone of you, and **understand**. Mark 7:14

Then opened he their understanding, that they might **understand the scriptures**. Luke 24:45

And we know that the Son of God is come, and hath **given** us an **understanding**. . .I John 5:20

Christ; In whom are hid all the treasures of wisdom and knowledge. Colossians 2:2

Great is our Lord, and of great power: his understanding is infinite. Psalm 147:5

[H]e hath counsel and understanding. Job 12:13

[W]ho hath given **understanding** to the **heart**? Job 38:36

[T]he **Almighty giveth** them **understanding**. Job 32:8

Only **the LORD give** thee wisdom and **understanding**. I Chronicles 22:12

[T]he Lord give thee **understanding** in all things. II Timothy 2:7

[T]he LORD made me understand. I Chronicles 28:19

[E]very wise hearted man, in whom **the LORD put** wisdom and **understanding**. Exodus 36:1

I have **given** thee a wise and an **understanding** heart. I Kings 3:12

Pharaoh said unto Joseph. . .thou canst **understand**. . . And Joseph answered Pharaoh, saying, It is not in me: **God** shall **give** Pharaoh an answer of peace. Genesis 41:15,16

God gave them knowledge. . .Daniel had **understanding** in all visions and dreams. Daniel 1:17, 18

And **God gave** Solomon wisdom and **understanding** exceedingly much, and largeness of heart. I Kings 4:29

The Seven Seals

1. A New Heart

When we receive Jesus Christ as our Saviour, he gives us a new heart where the Spirit of God can dwell. Have you received him?

I will put a new spirit within you; and I will take the stony heart out of their flesh, and will give them an heart of flesh. Ezekiel 11:19

I have filled him with **the spirit of God**, in wisdom, and in **understanding**. . .Exodus 31:3

[T]he **God** of our Lord Jesus Christ, the Father of glory, may **give** unto you **the spirit** of wisdom and revelation in the knowledge of him: The eyes of your **understanding** being enlightened. . .Ephesians 1:17-18

Except a man be **born again,** he cannot **see** the kingdom of God. . .Except a man be born of water and of the **Spirit**, he cannot enter into the kingdom of God. John 3:3, 5

I thank thee, O Father,. . .thou hast **hid** these things from the **wise** and prudent, and hast revealed them unto **babes**. . .for so it seemed good in thy sight. Matthew 11:25

And the spirit of the LORD shall rest upon him, the **spirit** of wisdom and **understanding**. . .And shall make him of quick **understanding**. Isaiah 11:2,3

They also that erred in **spirit** shall come to **understand**. Isaiah 29:24

[U]nderstand the words that I speak unto thee. . .from the first day that thou didst set thine **heart to understand,** and to chasten thyself before thy God, thy words were heard. Daniel 10:11,12

[B]e ye of an **understanding heart**. Proverbs 8:5

[T]hey, which in an **honest and good heart,** having heard the word, keep it, and bring forth fruit with patience. Luke 8:15

2. *Pray*

Do you pray before you study the bible?

If any of you lack **wisdom**, let him **ask** of God. James 1:5

Ask, and it shall be given you. Luke 11:9

Give me **understanding**. Psalm 119:34, 73, 144, 169

[G]ive me **understanding,** that I may know thy testimonies. Psalm 119:125

Make me to **understand** the way of thy precepts. Psalm 119:27

Give therefore thy servant an **understanding** heart. I Kings 3:9

[H]ast **asked** for thyself **understanding**. I Kings 3:11

I was. . .**praying**, and confessing my sin. . .and presenting my supplication before the LORD. . .then

Gabriel. . .said. . .thou art greatly beloved: therefore **understand** the matter. Daniel 9:20, 23

[W]e. . .do not cease to **pray** for you, and to desire that ye might be filled with the knowledge of his will in all wisdom and spiritual **understanding**. Colossians 1:9

3. Read and Hear

Are your senses (seeing and hearing) saturated with the bible, or are they filled with other things such as television, videos, radio, books, newspapers, magazines, or gossip? (Even 'Christian' media and materials can block out the word of God.)

Wisdom [the bible] is **before** him that hath **understanding**; but the eyes of a fool are in the ends of the earth. [TV, magazines, catalogues, etc.] Proverbs 17:24

The heart of him that hath **understanding** seeketh knowledge: but the mouth of fools **feedeth** on foolishness. Proverbs 15:14

[U]nderstanding put forth her voice? . .She crieth. . . **Hear**. Proverbs 8:1, 3, 6

A wise man will **hear,** and will increase learning; and a man of **understanding** shall attain unto wise counsels. Proverbs 1:5

My son, **attend** unto my wisdom, and bow thine **ear** to my **understanding**. Proverbs 5:1

[A]ttend to know **understanding**. Proverbs 4:1

[G]et **understanding**. . .neither decline from the words of my mouth. Proverbs 4:5

Do you attend church regularly to hear those whom God has given the ministry of teaching?

And I will give you **pastors** according to mine heart, which shall feed you with knowledge and **understanding**. Jeremiah 3:15

And Philip ran thither to him, and heard him read the prophet Esaias, and said, **Understand** thou what thou readest? And he said, How can I, except some **man** should guide me? Acts 8:30,31

When I thought **to know** this, it was too painful for me; Until I went into the **sanctuary** of God; then **understood** I their end. Psalm 73:17

[T]he Levites, caused the people to **understand** the law. . .So they read in the book in the law of God distinctly, and gave the sense, and caused them to **understand** the reading. Nehemiah 8:7,8

Do the teachers you hear (church, media, books) gain their understanding of the scriptures from following God's criteria or man's (degrees, commentaries, consensus)?

[H]e that followeth vain persons is **void of understanding**? Proverbs 12:11

[S]ome having swerved have turned aside unto vain janglings; Desiring to be **teachers** of the law; **understanding neither** what they say, nor whereof they affirm. I Timothy 1:7

As also in all his epistles, speaking in them of these things; in which are some things hard to be **understood**, which they that are **unlearned** and **unstable** wrest, as they do also the other scriptures, unto their own destruction. II Peter 3:16

4. Seek

Do you pursue an understanding of the bible daily?

I am **understanding**. . .those that **seek** me early shall find me. . .Blessed is the man that heareth me, watching **daily** at my gates. Proverbs 8:14, 17, 34

Redeeming the **time**, because the days are evil. Wherefore be ye not unwise, but **understanding** what the will of the Lord is. Ephesians 5:16, 17

[T]hey that **seek** the Lord **understand** all things. Proverbs 28:5

There is none that **understandeth**, there is none that **seeketh** after God. Romans 3:11

Have you studied the bible to the same extent that you have studied books for school, career, or hobbies—for the approval of men?

Study to shew thyself approved unto God, a workman that needeth not to be ashamed, rightly dividing the word of truth. II Timothy 2:15

[K]nowledge of the holy is **understanding**. Proverbs 9:10

Do you pursue further study of the bible to understand portions which are unclear or do you give up easily or rely on commentaries which may or may not be correct?

[N]ot in the words which man's wisdom teacheth, but which the Holy Ghost teacheth; **comparing spiritual things with spiritual.** I Corinthians 2:13

Through **thy precepts** I get **understanding.** Psalm 119:104

The entrance of **thy words giveth** light; it giveth **understanding** to the simple. Psalm 119:130

Are you expecting to understand the bible at a level beyond your chronological or spiritual level of maturity? (The bible is a book for an entire lifetime.)

When I was a child,. . .I understood as a child. I Corinthians 13:11

Brethren, be not children in understanding. . .but in understanding be men. I Corinthians 14:20

[W]ith the **ancient** is wisdom; and in length of days **understanding.** Job 12:12

These things **understood** not his disciples **at the first.** John 12:16

As newborn babes, desire the sincere **milk of the word,** that ye may grow thereby. I Peter 2:2

I have fed you with milk, and not with **meat**: for hitherto ye were not able to bear it neither yet now are ye able. I Corinthians 3:2

[T]he first principles of the oracles of God; and are become such as have need of milk, and not of **strong meat**. For everyone that useth milk is unskilful in the word of righteousness: for he is a babe. Hebrews 5:12, 13

But **strong meat** belongeth to them that are of **full age.** . .Hebrews 5:14

Whom shall he teach knowledge? and whom shall he make to **understand** doctrine? them that are weaned from the milk, and drawn from the breasts. For precept must be upon precept. . .line upon line; **here a little**, and **there a little**. Isaiah 28:9,10

5. *Delight*

How do you delight yourself? Are your 'delights' related to the flesh or the spirit? Self or God?

[H]is **delight** is in the law of the LORD; and in his law doth he meditate day and night. Psalm 1:2

How much better is it to get wisdom than gold! and to get **understanding** rather to be chosen than silver! Proverbs 16:16

A fool hath no **delight** in **understanding**, but that his heart may discover itself. Proverbs 18:2

6. *Memorize and Meditate*

Do you think about scripture verses you have memorized or do you think about other things?

I have more **understanding** than all my teachers: for thy testimonies are my **meditation**. Psalm 119:99

[T]he **meditation** of my heart shall be of **understanding**. I will incline my **ear** unto a parable. Psalm 49:3,4

7. Obey

Do you obey the light God has already given you? Do you think he will give you more understanding if you do not follow that which he has already shown you?

Whoso. . .will **observe** these things, even they shall **understand**. Psalm 107:43

I **understand** more than the ancients, because I **keep** thy precepts. Psalm 119:100

[A] good **understanding** have all they that **do** his commandments. Psalm 111:10

[D]o them; for this is your wisdom and your **understanding**. Deuteronomy 4:6

Have you allowed sin to creep into your life?

[Y]et made we not our prayer before the LORD our God, that we might turn from our **iniquities**, and **understand** thy truth. Daniel 9:13

For **my people** is foolish, they have not known me; they are **sottish** children, and they have **none understanding**. Jeremiah 4:22

Be ye not as the horse, or as the mule, which have **no understanding**. Psalm 32:9

Are you open to correction?

All scripture is given by inspiration of God, and is profitable for. . .reproof, for correction, for instruction in righteousness. II Timothy 3:16

He that refuseth instruction despiseth his own soul: but he that heareth reproof getteth **understanding**. Proverbs 15:32

[R]eprove one that hath understanding, and he will **understand** knowledge. Proverbs 19:25

[A] **rod** is for the back of him that is void of **understanding**. Proverbs 10:13

☑ **Do you believe what you are reading is the "pure" and "preserved" word of God?** (Psalm 119:140, 12:7, Proverbs 30:5)

O ye of little **faith**. . .Do ye not yet understand. . .How is it that ye do not **understand**. Matthew 16:8, 9, 11

Through **faith** we **understand**. Hebrews 11:3

[W]hatsoever is not of faith is sin. Romans 14:23

☑ **What is your motive for wanting to understand more of the bible? Do you seek to exalt self or God with this knowledge?**

Knowledge **puffeth up**. I Corinthians 8:1

☑ **Are you willing to pay the price to remain humble once you have this understanding?**

And lest I should be exalted above measure through the abundance of the revelations, there was given to me a thorn in the flesh, the messenger of Satan to buffet me, **lest I should be exalted** above measure.
II Corinthians 12:7

Finally

Are you expecting to understand more than God has chosen to reveal to man now? There is much a godly person will not understand in this life.

[GOD]	Hast thou considered my servant **Job**, that there is none like him in the earth, a **perfect and an upright** man, one that feareth God, and escheweth evil? Job 1:8
[JOB]	[T]herefore have I uttered that I **understood not**. Job 42:3
[PAUL]	[W]e are **perplexed**, but not in despair. 2 Cor. 4:8 For now we see through a glass, darkly. . .now I know **in part**. I Cor. 13:12

Is the portion of the bible that you cannot understand prophetic in nature and, as such, will not be clear until it is fulfilled?

And I heard, but **understood not**. . .[T]he words are closed up and **sealed** till the time of the **end**. Daniel 12:8,9

But they **understood not** this saying, and it was hid from them, that they perceived it not. Luke 9:45 (Concerning Christ's betrayal into the hands of sinners.)

But they **understood not** that saying. Mark 9:32 (about Christ's death and resurrection)

Summary: The Seven Seals

SALVATION	**My son, if** thou wilt receive my words,
MEDITATE	[A]nd **hide my** commandments with thee;
READ	So that thou incline thine **ear** unto wisdom, and **apply thine heart** to understanding;
PRAY	Yea, **if** thou criest after knowledge, and **liftest up thy voice** for understanding;
SEEK	**If** thou **seekest** her as silver, and **searchest** for her as for **hid** treasures; **Then** shalt thou understand the fear of the Lord, and find the knowledge of God. For the Lord giveth wisdom: out of his mouth cometh knowledge and understanding.
OBEY	He layeth up sound wisdom for the **righteous**; he is a buckler to them that **walk** uprightly. He keepeth the paths of judgment, and preserveth the way of his saints. **Then** shalt thou understand righteousness, and judgment, and equity; yea, every good path.
DELIGHT	**When** wisdom entereth into thine heart and knowledge is **pleasant** unto thy soul; Prov. 2:1-10

INTRODUCTION

[1] Arthur Westcott, *The Life and Letters of Brook Foss Westcott*, Vol II (London: Macmillan and Co., Limited, 1903), p. 252.

[2] Edwin Palmer, *The Holy Spirit* (Grand Rapids, Michigan: Baker Book House, 1974), p. 83.

[3] Kenneth Barker, *The NIV: The Making of a Contemporary Translation* (Grand Rapids, Michigan: Zondervan Corporation, 1986), p. 143.

[4] David Schaff, *The Life of Phillip Schaff* (New York: Charles Scribner's Sons, 1897), p. 467; Alex Jack, *The New Age Dictionary* (Brookline, Mass.: Kanthaka Press, 1976), p. 11.

[5] *The Life of Schaff*, pp. 427-428.

CHAPTER 1

[1] Lola Davis, *Toward A World Religion for a New Age* (Farmdale, N.Y.: Coleman Publishing, 1983), p. 7.

[2] Robert Muller, *A New Genesis: Shaping A Global Spirituality* (Garden City, New York: Doubleday and Co., Inc., 1982), pp. 17, 75, xiii.

[3] *The Terrytown Letter*, June/July, 1983, "Jean Houston: The New World Religion" (an interview) p. 5, as cited in *The Seduction of Christianity*, p. 53.

[4] Texe Marrs, *Dark Secrets of the New Age* (Westchester, Ill.: Crossway Books, 1987), p. 59.

[5] Alice Bailey, *Externalization of the Hierchy*, pp. 453-454, as cited in Constance Cumby, *Hidden Dangers of the Rainbow* (Shreveport, Louisiana: Huntington House Inc., 1983), p. 74.

[6] *Hidden Dangers of the Rainbow*, p. 73.

[7] *The Encyclopedia of Occultism and Parapsychology* (Detroit, Michigan: Gale Research Co., 1978), p. 81.

[8] *Toward A World Religion for a New Age*, p. 224.

[9] Elliot Miller, *A Crash Course on the New Age* (Grand Rapids, Michigan: 1989), p. 35.

[10] Russell Chandler, *Understanding the New Age* (Dallas, Texas: Word Publishing, 1988), p. 207.

[11] Dave Hunt, *America: The Sorcerer's New Apprentice* (Eugene, Oregon: Harvest House Publishers, 1988), p. 45.

[12] Alex Jack, *The New Age Dictionary* (Brookline, Mass.: Kanthaka Press, 1976), p. 16.

[13] Ibid., pp. 84, 53, 83, 174, 123, 67, 122 et al.

[14] Dave Hunt, *Beyond Seduction* (Eugene, Oregon: Harvest House Publishers, 1987), p. 176.

[15] Bob Larson, *Larson's Book of Cults* (Wheaton, Ill.: Tyndale House Publishers, Inc., 1982), p. 32.

[16] *Dark Secrets of the New Age*, p. 150.

[17] *A Crash Course on the New Age*, p. 26.

[18] Charles Filmore, *The Metaphysical Bible Dictionary* (Lee Summit, Mo.: Unity School of Christianity, 1950), p. 522.

[19] *The Encyclopedia of Occultism and Parapsychology*, p. 551.

[20] *Religion in the Age of Aquarius*, p. 62.

[21] *The Encyclopedia of Occultism and Parapsychology*, p. 631.

[22] *The Encyclopedia of Religion and Ethics*, ed. James Hastings (New York: Scribner's and Sons, 1926), p. 233.

[23] *Dark Secrets of the New Age*, pp. 212, 205, 181, 183, 177, 189, 190, 224.

[24] Lewis Foster, *Selecting a Translation of the Bible* (Cincinnati, Ohio: Standard Publishing Co.), pp. 21, 76.

[25] John Kohlenberger, *Words About the Word* (Grand Rapids, Michigan: Regency Reference Library, 1987), p. 89.

[26] *Larson's Book of Cults*, p. 32.

[27] Josh McDowell, *Understanding the Cults* (San Bernardino, Ca.: Here's Life Publishers, 1982), p. 50.

28 *Larson's Book of Cults*, p. 321.
29 Texe Marrs, *Mystery Mark of the New Age* (Westchester, Ill.: Crossway Books, 1988), p. 210.
30 *Dark Secrets of the New Age*, p. 218.
31 Michael Horton, ed. *The Agony of Deceit* (Chicago: Moody Press, 1990), p. 53.
32 Joseph Carr, *The Lucifer Connection* (Lafayette, Louisiana: Huntington House Inc., 1987), p. 151.
33 *The Hidden Dangers of the Rainbow*, p. 223.
34 *Crash Course on the New Age*, p. 126.
35 *Toward A World Religion for a New Age*, pp. 187, 188.
36 *Crash Course on the New Age*, p. 127.
37 *Dark Secrets of the New Age*, p. 179.
38 *The Lucifer Connection*, p. 145.
39 Wanda Marrs, *New Age Lies to Women* (Austin, Texas: Living Truth Publishers, 1989), p. 205.
40 *Dark Secrets of the New Age*, p. 213.
41 *The Lucifer Connection*, p. 16.
42 *Understanding the New Age*, p. 47.
43 *The New Age Dictionary*, p. 11.
44 Vera Alder, *When Humanity Comes of Age* (New York: Samuel Weiser, 1974), p. 11.
45 *The Encyclopedia of the Unexplained*, ed. Richard Cavendish (New York: McGraw Hill, 1974), s.v. "Theosophy".
46 H.P. Blavatsky, *Isis Unveiled* Vol. II (London: The Theosophical Publishing House, 1923), pp. 125, 252.
47 *Isis Unveiled*, Vol. II, pp. 125, 252.
48 James Webb, *The Occult Establishment* (La Salle, Ill., Open Court Press, 1976), p. 472.
49 *Words About the Word*, p. 54.
50 *The NIV: The Making of a Contemporary Translation* ed. Kenneth L. Barker (Grand Rapids, Michigan: Zondervan Publishing House, 1986), p. 37.
51 *Christianity Today*, as cited in Barry Burton, *Let's Weigh the Evidence* (Chino, Ca.: Chick Publications, 1983), p. 13.
52 Alfred Marshal, *The NASB Interlinear Greek-English New Testament* (Grand Rapids, Michigan: Zondervan Publishing House, 1984), p. ii.
53 *Isis Unveiled*, Vol. II, p. 495.
54 *The NIV: The Making of a Contemporary Translation*, p. 142.
55 *The Secret Doctrine*, Vol. II, p. 504.
56 Ibid., p. 142.
57 Ibid., p. 111.
58 *Larson's Book of Cults*, p. 36.
59 *When Humanity Comes of Age*, p. 39.
60 *Toward A World Religion for a New Age*, as cited in *Dark Secrets of the New Age*, p. 182.
61 Bruce Metzger, *A Textual Commentary On the New Testament* (Stuttgart, Germany: German Bible Society, 1975), p. 198.
62 *Dark Secrets of the New Age*, p. 193.
63 *When Humanity Comes of Age*, p. 30 et al.
64 *New Age Dictionary*, p. 11; B.F. Westcott, *The Historic Faith* (London: Macmillan and Co., 1885), pp. 146-147.
65 Constance Cumby, *A Planned Deception* (East Detroit, Michigan: Pointe Publishers, Inc., 1985), p. 162.
66 *Understanding the New Age*, p. 123.
67 *Words About the Word*, p. 55.
68 Dean John Burgon, *The Revision Revised* (Paradise, Pa.: Conservative Classics, orig. 1883), p. 109.
69 *Selecting a Translation of the Bible*, p. 57.

CHAPTER 2

1 *"praying to a new god,"* recorded by Wang Chung from the *Warmer Side of Cool* album. Geffen Records 9130 Sunset Blvd., Los Angeles, California, 1989.

2 The NIV drops "new gods" in Deuteronomy 32:17 and writes "gods who recently appeared." The preface to the NIV promises that this new translation in "contemporary" English was needed to aid "memorizing" and for "ease of reading." I suspect Wang Chung would disagree.

3 *The NIV: The Making of a Contemporary Translation*, p. 66.

4 *The Secret Doctrine*, p. 517.

5 F. L. Cross (ed.), *Oxford Dictionary of the Christian Church* (N.Y.: Oxford University Press, 1974), p. 841.

6 The use of the word "pierced" in Isaiah 14:19 in the NASB seems to reinforce the notion that this chapter refers to Jesus Christ rather than Lucifer. References such as Psalm 22:16, "they pierced my hands and my feet" and Zechariah 12:10, "they shall look upon me whom they have pierced," allude to the death of Jesus Christ. The Hebrew word here is *taan*, meaning to be thrust through, not *kur* of Psalm 22:6 or *daqar* of Zechariah 12:10.

7 R. Swineburn Clymer, *The Science of the Soul* (Quakertown, Pennsylvania: The Philosophical Publishing Company, 1944), pp. 44-45.

8 Texe Marrs, *Mystery Mark of the New Age* (Westchester, Illinois: Crossway Books, 1988), p. 97.

9 H. P. Blavatsky, *Isis Unveiled*, Vol. II (London: The Theosophical Publishing House, 1923), p. 86.

10 H. P. Blavatsky, *The Theosophical Glossary* (Los Angeles, California: The Theosophy Company, 1971), p. 192 (originally published in 1892); *The Secret Doctrine*, Vol. II, pp. 542, 569.

11 Constance Cumby, *A Planned Deception* (East Detroit, Michigan: Pointe Publishers, Inc. 1985), p.246.

12 *The Revision Revised*, p. 214; Westcott's Commentary on 1-3 John, p. 106; Hort's commentary on Revelation, p. 27.

13 *Isis Unveiled*, Vol. II, p. 14.

14 *The Theosophical Dictionary*, p. 192.

15 Texe Marrs, *Dark Secrets of the New Age* (Westchester, Illinois: Crossway Books, 1987), pp. 240-241.

16 Joseph Carr, *The Lucifer Connection* (Lafayette, Louisiana: Huntington House, Inc., 1987), pp. 133 and 137.

17 Charles Filmore, *The Metaphysical Bible Dictionary* (Lees Summit, MO.: Unity School of Christianity, 1950), s.v. daystar.

18 Gustav Davidson, *Dictionary of Angels*. (N.Y.: Free Press, 1971), p. 176.

19 Livesey, *Understanding the New Age*, p. 71.

20 Joseph Carr, *The Lucifer Connection*, pp. 84-85.

21 Kurt Koch, *The Devil's Alphabet*, p. 7.

22 *The Secret Doctrine*, Vol. II, p. 798.

23 *Selecting a Translation of the Bible*, pp. 18, 21.

24 Constance Cumby, *A Planned Deception*, p. 74.

25 Herbert Lockyer, *All the Doctrines of the Bible* (Grand Rapids, Michigan: Zondervan, 1963), pp. 133, 135.

26 Helena P. Blavatsky, *The Secret Doctrine*, Vol. II (London: The Theosophical Publishing House, 1893), pp. 171, 225, 255.

27 David Spangler, *Reflections on the Christ* (Scotland: Findhorn Publications, 1982), pp. 36-39.

28 Constance Cumby, *Hidden Dangers of the Rainbow* (Shreveport, Louisiana: Huntington House, Inc. 1983), p. 95.

29 Texe Marrs, *Mystery Mark of the New Age* (Westchester, Illinois: Crossway Books, 1988), p. 209.

30 Constance Cumby, *Hidden Dangers of the Rainbow*, p. 143.

31 H. P. Blavatsky, *The Secret Doctrine,* Vol. II, p. 350.
32 H. P. Blavatsky, *The Secret Doctrine,* Vol. I, p. 106.
33 Ibid, p. 493.
34 Ibid., p. 610.
35 *The Two Babylons,* p. 93.
36 H. P. Blavatsky, *Isis Unveiled,* Vol. II, p. 207.
37 H. P. Blavatsky, *The Secret Doctrine,* Vol. I, pp. 215, 216, 220, 245, 255, 533.

CHAPTER 3

1 Alice Bailey, *The Reappearance of the Christ* (New York: Lucis Publishing Company, 1948), p. 32.
2 Eliphas Levi, *Dogma and Ritual of High Magic,* Vol. II, p. 88.
3 H. P. Blavatsky, *Isis Unveiled,* Vol. II (The Theosophical Publishing House Ltd., reprint 1923), pp. 476, 593.
4 Ibid., p. 168.
5 Corrine Heline, *New Age Bible Interpretation* (New York: The New Age Press, 1935), p. 82.
6 *Philosophumena,* vi. p. 42.
7 H. P. Blavatsky, *The Secret Doctrine,* Vol. I (New York: The Theosophical Publishing Company, 1893), p. 376.
8 H. P. Blavatsky, *Isis Unveiled,* Vol. II, pp. 159-168.
9 H.P. Blavatsky, *The Secret Doctrine,* Vol. I, p. 375.
10 *Anti-Nicene Fathers,* Vol. I, pp. 434-435.
11 Dean John William Burgon, *The Revision Revised* (Collingwood, New Jersey: The Bible For Today, Inc., 1981), pp. 34-35.
12 Ibid.
13 *The Secret Doctrine,* Vol. II, p. 241.
14 Eliphas Levi, *Dogma and Ritual of High Magic,* p. 639.
15 H. P. Blavatsky, *The Secret Doctrine,* Vol. II, p. 254.
16 H. P. Blavatsky, *Isis Unveiled,* Vol. II, p. 505.
17 H. P. Blavatsky, *The Secret Doctrine,* Vol. II, p. 107.
18 H. P. Blavatsky, *Isis Unveiled,* Vol. II, p. 561.
19 H. P. Blavatsky, *The Secret Doctrine,* Vol. II, p. 569.
20 Alice Bailey, *Reappearance of the Christ,* pp. 70, 71, 9, 26.
21 R. Swinburn Clymer, *The Science of the Soul* (Quakertown, Pennsylvania: The Philosophical Publishing Company, 1944), p. 280.
22 Charles Filmore, *Metaphysical Bible Dictionary,* p. 349.
23 Benjamin Creme, *The Reappearance of the Christ and Masters of Wisdom* (London: The Tara Press, 1980), p. 135 as cited in Texe Marrs, *Dark Secrets of the New Age* (Westchester, Illinois: Crossway Books), p. 81.
24 Bob Larson, Larson's Book of Cults (Wheaton, Illinois: Tyndale House Publishers, Inc., 1982), pp. 214, 218.
25 Harold Sherman, *How to Use the Power of Prayer,* p. 137.
26 Texe Marrs, *Dark Secrets of the New Age,* p. 256.
27 Leslie Shepherd, *Encyclopedia of Occultism and Parapsychology* (Detroit, Michigan: Gale Research Company, 1978), p. 641.
28 *The Life of Westcott,* Vol. I, p. 353 et al.
29 H. P. Blavatsky, *The Secret Doctrine,* Vol. I, p. 301.
30 Ibid.
31 Corrine Heline, *New Age Bible Interpretation,* p. 82.
32 Charles Filmore, *Metaphysical Bible Dictionary,* p. 518.
33 Eliphas Levis, *Dogma and Ritual of High Magic,* Vol. II, p. 88.

[34] Alice Bailey, *The Reappearance of the Christ*, pp. 38-39.

[35] J. J. Hurtag, *The Keys of Enoch* (Los Gatos, California: The Academy for Future Science, 1977), p. 242 as cited in Texe Marrs, *Mystery Mark of the New Age*, p. 145.

[36] Bob Larson, *Larson's Book of Cults*, p. 230.

[37] Kathryn Paulsen, *The Complete Book of Magic and Witchcraft* (New York: New American Library/Signet Books, 1980), p. 24 as cited in Texe Marrs, *Dark Secrets of the New Age*, p. 88.

[38] Anna Kingsford, *Perfect Way* (New York: Macoy Publishing and Masonic Supply Company, 1912), XV, pp. 366, et seq..

[39] Corrine Heline, *New Age Bible Interpretation*, p. 82.

[40] H. P. Blavatsky, *The Secret Doctrine*, Vol. II, p. 544.

[41] See Edwin Palmer's *The Holy Spirit* p. 20 or *The Five Points of Calvinism*, p. 20.

[42] *The Encyclopedia of Religion and Ethics.*

[43] *The Agony of Deceit*, p. 116.

[44] *The Reappearance of the Christ*, pp. 151, 152.

[45] *The New Genesis*, pp. 46, 124.

[46] "Credence Cassettes," *The National Catholic Reporter* (Kansas City, MO, Winter/Lent, 1991), p. 19.

CHAPTER 4

[1] Werner Keller, *The Bible as History* (N.Y.: Bantom Books, 1982), pp. 303, 315.

[2] *The NIV: The Making of a Contemporary Translation*, p. 162.

[3] *Mystery Mark of the New Age*, p. 154.

CHAPTER 5

[1] Naomi Goldberg, *Changing of the Gods* (author is professor of religion at University of Ottawa in Ontario, Canada).

[2] Douglas R. Groothius, *Unmasking the New Age* (Downers Grove, Illinois: InterVarsity Press), p. 51.

[3] *The Encyclopedia of Mysticism and Mystery Religions*, p. 136.

[4] See *The Secret Doctrine*, Vol. I pp. 102, 125, 104, 105, 144, 145, 592, 614; Vol. II pp. 580, 612, 613, 617, 614.

[5] Ibid., pp. 257, 585.

[6] *Isis Unveiled*, Vol. II, p. 413.

[7] Ibid., p. 387.

[8] *The Aquarian Gospel*, p. 16 as cited in *The Hidden Dangers of the Rainbow*, p. 31.

[9] Bob Larson, *Larson's Book of Cults* (Wheaton, Ill.: Tyndale House Publishers, Inc., 1982), p. 109.

[10] Edward Rice, *Eastern Definitions* (Garden City, New York: Doubleday and Company, Inc., 1978), p. 55.

[11] Texe Marrs, *Mystery Mark of the New Age* (Westchester, Ill.: Crossway Books, 1988), p. 78.

[12] *Isis Unveiled*, Vol. II, p. 298.

[13] *Larson's Book of Cults*, p. 243.

[14] Keith Brooks, "Spirit of Truth and the Spirit of Error" (Moody Press, 1985).

[15] *Mystery Mark of the New Age*, p. 49.

[16] *Larson's Book of Cults*, p. 153.

[17] Constance Cumby, *A Planned Deception* (East Detroit, Michigan: Pointe Publishers, Inc., 1985), p. 241.

[18] *Mystery Mark of the New Age*, pp. 175, 157.

[19] *Larson's Book of Cults*, p. 191.

[20] Ibid., p. 273.

21 Lola Davis, *Toward a World Religion for the New Age*, p. 42.
22 *Secret Doctrine*, Vol. I, p. 73; Vol. II, pp. 405, 573, 247 ; *Sensuous Spirituality*, p. 11.
23 Ibid., Vol. I, p. 38.
24 *Unmasking the New Age*, p. 11.
25 *Secret Doctrine*, Vol. I, p. 40.
26 "Spirit of Truth and the Spirit of Error " ; *Sensuous Spirituality*, p. 126.
27 *Secret Doctrine*, Vol. I, p. 314.
28 Ibid., Vol. II, pp. 294-296.
29 *Secret Doctrine*, Vol. II, p. 632.
30 *Isis Unveiled*, Vol. II, p. 282.
31 Ibid., Vol. II, p. 282.
32 *Secret Doctrine*, Vol. II, p. 607.
33 *The NIV: The Making of a Contemporary Translation*, p. 143.
34 Layard's *Babylon and Ninevah* (London, 1853), p. 605.
35 See MACROBIUS, Saternalia (Sanct. Colon, 1521) lib. i, cap. 17, 23, pp. 65, c, 1, 2 as cited in *The Two Babylons*, pp. 276, 279.
36 "Asiatic Researches," Vol. vii (London, 1806), p. 293 as cited in *Two Babylons*, p. 16.
37 *The Two Babylons*, p. 16.
38 Harnack, *History of Dogma*, "Arianism," p. 776.
39 Shepard, Leslie, *Encyclopedia of Occultism and Parapsychology*, Vol. II (Detroit, Michigan: Gale Research Company, 1978), p. 899; also see *Websters Collegiate Dictionary* (Springfield, Mass: G and C Merriam Co., Publishers, 1938), p. 1007.
40 *Eastern Definitions*, pp. 269, 431, 268, and note 4.
41 *Unmasking the New Age*, p. 115.
42 *Understanding the New Age* , p. 28.
43 Pat Means, *The Mystical Maze* (Campus Crusade for Christ, 1976), pp. 202, 203.
44 David L. Johnson, *A Reasoned Look at Asian Religions* (Minneapolis, Minn.: Bethany House Publishers, 1985), pp. 98-100.
45 Benjamine Creme, *The Reappearance of the Christ and the Masters of Wisdom*, p. 150.
46 *Unmasking the New Age*, p. 97; Westcott agrees. See *Historic Faith*, p. 22.
47 *The Mystical Maze*, p. 220.
48 Alice Bailey, *The Reappearance of the Christ*, p. 150.
49 *Isis Unveiled*, Vol. II, p. 96; *The Secret Doctrine*, Vol. I, p. 596.
50 *Eastern Definitions*, p. 375; see also "the One Life" in Luciferian Rudolf Steiner's *The Esoteric Basis of Christianity*, p. xli.
51 *The Reappearance of the Christ*, pp. 70, 71.
52 *Religious Thought in the West*, p. 357 ; *Sensuous Spirituality*, pp. 10-11.
53 *The Life of Westcott*, Vol. II, pp. 232, 242, 263, 147, 148, 239; Westcott refers to the Living One in his *Gospel of the Resurrection*, p. 63.
54 *The Life of Hort*, Vol. I, p. 246; Vol. II, pp. 231, 330; *Christian American*, Feb. 1994, p. 19.
55 *The NIV: The Making of a Contemporary Translation*, p. 102.
56 *The National Catholic Reporter* "Credence Cassettes," (Kansas City, MO. Winter-Lent 1991).
57 *The Secret Doctrine*, Vol. I, pp. 380, 620.
58 *The Life of Hort*, Vol. I, p. 246.
59 *The Secret Doctrine*, Vol. I, pp. 259, 620.
60 *The Life of Westcott*, Vol. I, pp. 249-255, 164; Vol. II, p. 306. *Historic Faith*, p. 258; *The Gospel of the Resurrection*, p. 63; *Religious Thought in the West*, p. 106.
61 *A Reasoned Look at Asian Religions*, p. 88.
62 *The Five Points of Calvinism*, pp. 77, 78; *The Holy Spirit*, p. 161.
63 *The Holy Spirit*, p. 24; *The Five Points of Calvinism*, pp. 75, 22, 23, 78, 55.

64 *Isis Unveiled*, Vol. II, p. 123; *The Secret Doctrine*, p. 443.
65 *The NIV: The Making of a Contemporary Translation*, p. 150.
66 *A Reasoned Look at Asian Religions*, p. 157.
67 *The Mystical Maze*, p. 46.
68 *Unmasking the New Age*, p. 153.
69 *Dark Secrets of the New Age*, p. 140
70 *The Reappearance of the Christ*, pp. 64, 188.
71 *Dark Secrets of the New Age*, p. 89.
72 *The Secret Doctrine*, Vol. I, pp. 468-469; Vol. II, pp. 411, 105.
73 *Science of the Soul*, p. 5.
74 *The Secret Doctrine*, Vol. I, p. 391.
75 *Toward a World Religion for the New Age*, p. 6.
76 *A Planned Deception*, p. 251.
77 *Hidden Dangers of the Rainbow*, p. 96.
78 *Eastern Definitions*, p. 279.
79 Higley, *Sunday School Lesson Commentary* (Winnona Lake, Indiana: Lambert Huffman, Publishers), p. 289.
80 *Mystery Mark of the New Age*, p. 240.
81 Elizabeth Clare Prophet, *The Great White Brotherhood* (Los Angelos, California: Summit University Press, 1975), p. 140 as cited in *Mystery Mark*, p. 173.
82 *Mystery Mark of the New Age*, p. 50; also see *Reappearance of the Christ*, p. 65 et al.

CHAPTER 6
1 Trumpet Ministries, 510 Main St. #4, Cottage Grove, Oregon 97424. *Akron Beacon Journal*, June 5, 1994, p. H2.
2 Shanks, *The Dead Sea Scrolls After Forty Years*, pp. 22,23,24,34,36,58,60, et al. Gaster, *The Dead Sea Scriptures*, pp. 29, 38, 57, 85, 121, 181, et al.
3 *When Humanity Comes of Age*, p. 8.
4 *A Reasoned Look at Asian Religions*, p. 21.
5 *The Secret Doctrine*, Vol. I, p. 324.
6 Sir John Sinclair, *The Alice Bailey Inheritance* (Wellingborough, Northamptonshire, England: Turnstone Press Ltd. 1984, p. 103; *The Rays and the Initiations*, p. 80, as cited in *Mystery Mark of the New Age*.
7 *Hidden Dangers of the Rainbow*, p. 77.
8 Alice Bailey, *The Destiny of Nations* (London: Lucis Press, Ltd., 1982), p. 19.
9 *The Lucifer Connection*, p. 171.
10 *Hidden Dangers of the Rainbow*, p. 77.
11 Robert J. Mandell, "Some Insights into Psychic Ability," *Los Angelos Times*, 5 June 1981, part 5.
12 Edward Rice, *Eastern Definitions* (Garden City, N.Y.: Doubleday and Company, Inc., 1978), pp. 61, 62, 308.
13 Alexander Hislop, *The Two Babylons* (Neptune, New Jersey: Loizeaux Brothers, 1916), p. 77.
14 *Mystery Mark of the New Age*, p. 52.
15 H.P. Blavatsky, *The Secret Doctrine*, Vol. I (London: The Theosophical Publishing Society, 1893), pp. 495-496.
16 H.P. Blavatsky, *The Secret Doctrine*, Vol. II (London: The Theosophical Publishing Society, 1893), p. 537.
17 Tomislav Vlasic and Slavko Barbaric, *Open Your Heart to Mary Queen of Peace* (Milan, Italy: The Association of the Friends of Medjugorje, 1985), p. 14.
18 "Why All Our Statues Moving," *The Sunday Tribune*, September 15, 1985, Vol. 5, No. 37, p. 9; see also June Levine, *Sunday Independent*, Middle Abbey Street, Dublin 1, Sept. 15, 1985, p. 10.

19 *The Secret Doctrine*, Vol. I,p. 232.
20 *The Life of Westcott*, Vol. I, p. 251.
21 Emily Lutyens, *Candels in the Sun*, pp. 124-125 et al.
22 *The Life of Westcott*, Vol. I, p. 255; *Religious Thought in the West*, p. 337.
23 *New Age Lies to Women*, see Ch. 8.
24 *The Two Babylons*, p. 263.
25 Michael P. Carroll, *The Cult of the Virgin Mary* (Princeton, New Jersey: Princeton University Press), pp. 28-29.
26 Ibid., pp. 22-27.
27 Robert Burrows, "America Gets Religion in the New Age," *Christianity Today*, 16 May, 1986, p. 19.; Susan Cyre, "Fallout Escalates Over Goddess Sophia Worship", p. 74, Spring 1994.
28 Ralph Woodrow, *Babylon Mystery Religion* (Riverside, Ca., Ralph Woodrow Evangelistic Association, Inc., 1966), p. 25.
29 Hislop, *The Two Babylons*, pp. 78, 802.
30 *Beyond Seduction*, p. 196.
31 *The Unchangeable Church*, Vol. I (New York: John Duffy Publisher, 1910), p. 140.
32 Vlasic and Slavco, *Open Your Heart to Mary Queen of Peace*, p. 86.
33 H.P. Blavatsky, *Isis Unveiled*, Vol. II (London, England: The Theosophical Publishing House, Ltd., 1923), p. 556.
34 Alan Schreck, *Catholic and Christian* (Ann Arbor, Michigan: Servant Books, 1984), p. 167.
35 Ibid., pp. 185-187.
36 *The Hidden Wisdom in the Holy Bible*, p. 129.
37 *Life of Hort*, Vol. 2, p. 50.
38 *The Cult of the Virgin Mary*, p. 19.
39 William P. Barker, *Everyone in the Bible* (Old Tappan, New Jersey: Fleming H. Revell Company, 1966), pp. 229-230.
40 *Open Your Heart to Mary Queen of Peace*, p. 65.
41 Ibid., p. 81.
42 Ibid., p. 88.
43 Ibid., pp. 88, 34.
44 Ibid., p. 50.
45 Ibid., p. 122.
46 Ibid., p. 140.
47 Ibid., p. 56.
48 Ibid., p. 62.
49 Ibid., p. 137.
50 Ibid., p. 86.
51 *The Science of the Soul*, p. 257.
52 *The Cult of the Virgin Mary*, pp. 176, 189, 203, 213.
53 *Mystery Mark of the New Age*, pp. 101, 135, 136, 148, 165, 169.
54 *The Two Babylons*, p. 672.
55 Brooke Foss Westcott, *History of Religious Thought In The West* (London: McMillan and Co., 1891), p. 2; see also pp. 45, 46, 48, 185-186.
56 *The Hidden Wisdom in the Holy Bible*, p. 9.
57 *Catholic and Christian*, p. 48.
58 *The Church Divided*, pp. 69-76.
59 *Life of Westcott*, Vol. I, p. 51.
60 *Open Your Heart to Mary Queen of Peace*, p. 63.

CHAPTER 7

1 *Christian Information Bulletin*, (Camarillo, Ca., June, 1989, Vol. 5, No. 6.)

2 William C. Standridge, *What's Happening in the Roman Church* (Greensboro, N.C.: Independent Faith Missions, 1975), pp. 4, 20, 21, 65.

3 *The Secret Doctrine*, p. 539.

4 Cardinal St. Alphonse di Liguori, *The Glories of Mary*, pp. 130, 137, 141, 143, 169, 170.

5 Ibid., pp. 180-181; see also *Serafino Faluo's L'ora della Spirito Santo*, pp. 186, 197.

6 *The Occult Establishment*, p. 448.

7 June Levine, *Sunday Independent* (Middle Abbey Street, Dublin, Ireland, Sept. 15, 1985), p. 10.

8 Rose Marie Slaubs, "Andrew's Sisters," *OMNI* (October 1987), p. 28.

9 *Eastern Definitions*, p. 308.

10 *The Secret Doctrine*, Vol. I, pp. 375-376.

11 *The Living Bible* (Wheaton, Ill.: Tyndale House, 1971), p. 586.

12 Chandler, *Understanding the New Age*, p. 121.

13 *The Two Babylons*, p. 85.

14 *Eastern Definitions*, p. 105.

15 *The Secret Doctrine*, Vol. II, p. 537.

16 *Eastern Definitions*, p. 258.

17 *The Two Babylons*, pp. 31-32.

18 Helen Barnes, "Olimpo," *Interior Design*, April 1987, pp. 264-265.

19 Chandler, *Understanding the New Age*, p. 124.

20 *Harper's Dictionary of Classical Literature and Antiquity*, (New York: Cooper Square Publishing Co., 1963), p. 605.

21 *The Secret Doctrine*, Vol. II, pp. 415, 416, 429, 430.

22 *Harper's Dictionary of Classical Literature and Antiquity*, pp. 136-137.

23 *The Oxford Classical Dictionary* (Oxford: Clarendon Press, 1970), p. 127.

24 *Harper's Dictionary of Classical Literature and Antiquity*, pp. 136-137.

25 *The Two Babylons*, pp. 30, 822.

26 Marilyn Ferguson, *The Aquarian Conspiracy* (Los Angelos, Ca.: J.P. Tarcher, 1980), as cited in *The Lucifer Connection*, p. 94.

27 *Larson's Book of Cults*, p. 94.

28 *Inside the New Age Nightmare*, p. 17

29 *The Encyclopedia of Occultism & Parapsychology*, p. 335.

30 *Larson's Book of Cults*, p. 109.

31 *The Cult of the Virgin Mary*, p. 64.

32 *Larson's Book of Cults*, p. 79.

33 See *Webster's Dictionary* citation "asceticism."

34 *Larson's Book of Cults*, pp. 169-170.

35 *The Cult of the Virgin Mary*, p. 97.

36 *Ancient Empires of the New Age*, p. 41.

CHAPTER 8

1 *The Catholic Encyclopedia* (Thomas Nelson Publishers, 1976) as cited in *Whatever Happened to Heaven?*

2 *Whatever Happened to Heaven*, pp. 146, 149.

3 *New Dimensions in New Testament Study*, pp. 125-126.

4 Coleman J. Berry, O.S.B., (ed.), *Readings in Church History*, Vol. I, *From Pentecost to the Protestant Revolt* (The Newman Press, 1960), pp. 438-439, 466, as cited in *Whatever Happened to Heaven*, pp. 151, 153.

[5] *The New Genesis: Shaping a Global Spirituality*, pp. 111, 114, 149.
[6] *A Planned Deception*, p. 48.
[7] *Reappearance of the Christ and the Masters of Wisdom*, p. 46.
[8] *The Lucifer Connection*, p. 169.
[9] *When Humanity Comes of Age*, p. 38.
10 Constance Cumby, *New Age Monitor*, May 1991, p. 3.
[11] *Crash Course on the New Age*, p. 164.
[12] Livesey, *Understanding the New Age*, p. 12.
[13] *L'Observatore Romano*, February 10, 1986, "Spiritual Vision of Man," p. 5; as cited in C.I.B. Bulletin, Vol. 6, No. 9, September, 1990, p. 1.
[14] *National Catholic Reporter Publishing Company, Inc.*, "Credence Cassettes" (Kansas City, MO) Winter/Lent 1991.
[15] *Hidden Dangers of the Rainbow*, p. 39
[16] Livesey, *Understanding the New Age*, p. 125.
[17] See National Catholic Reporter note 14.
[18] *The NIV: The Making of a Contemporary Translation*, pp. 45, 46, 89, 111, 115, 118.
19 *Isis Unveiled*, Vol. II, pp. 496, 630; The Secret Doctrine, Vol. I, p. 301.
[20] *The New Age Dictionary*, p. 17.
[21] *New Directions in New Testament Study*, p. 240.
[22] *The NIV: The Making of a Contemporary Translation*, p. 23.
[23] Ibid., p. 111.
[24] *The Secret Doctrine*, Vol. I, p. 152.
[25] *New American Bible*, preface.
[26] *The NIV: The Making of a Contemporary Translation*, p. 53.
[27] *The New American Standard Bible*, pp. v, vi.
[28] *The New American Bible*, p. ix.
[29] *The Lifè of Phillip Schaff*, pp. 428, 427, 478.
[30] Ibid., pp. 115, 108, 114, 131.
[31] Ibid., pp. 488, 489.
[32] Ibid., p. 266.
[33] Don A. Schanche, "Pope Offers Olive Branch to Lutherans," *Los Angelos Times*, Part 1, p. 5, May 4, 1987 as cited in *What Ever Happened to Heaven?*, p. 194 and see also p. 193.
[34] *Battle Cry*, Nov./Dec. 1987 citing an article in the *Los Angelos Herald Tribune*.
[35] Livesey, *Understanding the New Age*, p. 210.
[36] "The Scandal Crisis: Is it Over," *Christian Herald* (Chappaqua, N.Y.: Christian Herald Association, Inc.) Vol. 112, No. 2, February 1989, p. 21.
[37] *The Life of Westcott*, Vol. II, p. 274.
[38] *The Life of Hort*, p. 99.
[39] *The Life of Schaff*, pp. 119, 217.
[40] *Conversion-Initiation and the Baptism of the Holy Spirit*, pp. 82, 98, v.
[41] *The Reappearance of the Christ*, p. 80.
[42] *New Directions in New Testament Study*, p. 213.

PART 2
1 *The Life of Hort*, Vol. I, pp. 262-263.
2 *Historic Faith*, p. 11.
3 Richard Roberts, *From Eden to Eros: Origins of the Put Down of Women* (San Anselmo, California: Vernal Equinox Press, 1985), p. 65 as cited in *New Age Lies to Women*.
4 *Dark Secrets of the New Age*, p. 175.

CHAPTER 9

1 *Larson's Book of Cults*, p. 153.
2 *The New Genesis*, p. 7.
3 *A Reasoned Look at Asian Religions*, p. 87.
4 Ibid., p. 114.
5 *The Mystical Maze*, p. 221.
6 *The Aquarian Conspiracy*, p. 316.
7 *Dancing in the Light*, p. 209.
8 *Revelation: The Birth of the New Age*, p. 13.
9 *Satan's Evangelistic Strategy for this New Age*, p. 161.
10 Richard Baer, "Parents, Schools and Values Clarification," *The Wall Street Journal*, April 12, 1982.
11 "American Teens Even More Sexually Active Than Thought," *Baptist Bible Tribune*, June 28, 1989, p. 31.
12 January 28, 1988
13 August 8, 1990
14 Lanny Buettner, "Ethics in Contemporary Psychic Experience: A Descriptive Analysis," M.A. thesis, University of Southern California, 1984, pp. 65-67 as cited in Chandler, *Understanding the New Age*.
15 "The Goddess Goes to Washington," *Fidelity*, December 1986, p. 42; Mathew Fox, *Original Blessing* (Sante Fe, New Mexico: Bear and Company, 1983), pp. 282-283 as cited in *New Age Lies to Women*.
16 Chandler, *Understanding the New Age*, p. 18.
17 *Revelation: The Birth of a New Age* as cited in *Dark Secrets of the New Age*, p. 196.
18 *The Agony of Deceit*, p. 126.
19 Lehman Strauss, "Holy Living," *Confident Living*, Sept. 1986.
20 "Quelques Variantes Importantes de P. Bodmer III et Leur Accointance avec la Gnose," by Ed. Massaux, *New Testament Studies*, vol. 5, 1959, pp. 210-212.
21 *The NIV: The Making of a Contemporary Translation*, p. 129.
22 Pat Robertson, *Answers*, Christian Broadcasting Network, Partner's Edition (Virginia Beach, Virginia: CBN, 1984), p. 155.
23 Paul Crouch, *Praise* (Trinity Broadcasting Network newsletter), May, 1987.
24 Gloria Copeland, *God's Will is Prosperity* (Harrison House, 1978), p. 60 as cited in *Beyond Seduction*, p. 23.
25 *The Mystical Maze*, p. 174.
26 *What's Wrong with Unity*, p. 49.
27 John Randolf Price, *The Superbeings* II (Austin, Texas: Quartins Books, 1981), pp. 101-103 as cited in *Dark Secrets of the New Age*.
28 *What's Wrong with Unity*, p. 49.
29 *Inside the New Age Nightmare*, p. 140.
30 *Occult Encyclopedia*, p. 550.
31 *Answers*, p. 76.
32 Kenneth E. Hagen, *Faith Food for Winter* (Tulsa, Oklahoma: Kenneth Hagin Ministries), p. 58.
33 *A Planned Deception*, p. 258.
34 *Dark Secrets of the New Age*, p. 193.
35 *Historic Faith*, p. 13.
36 Robert Wise et al, *The Church Divided* (South Plainfield, N.J.: Bridge Publishing, Inc., 1986, pp. 73, 76, 81-86.
37 *Occult Encyclopedia*, p. 551.
38 *The Infiltration of the New Age*, p. 26.
39 *Conversion/Initiation and the Baptism in the Holy Ghost*, pp. 82, 94.
40 *A Reasoned Look at Asian Religions*, p. 112.
41 *Hidden Dangers of the Rainbow*, p. 217.
42 *The NIV: The Making of a Contemporary Translation*, p. 153.
43 *The Life of Schaff*, pp. 366-377.
44 See *Ring of Truth* and *Price of Success*, p. 163.
45 *A Crash Course on the New Age Movement*, p. 207.
46 *When Humanity Comes of Age*, p. 201.
47 Livesey, *Understanding the New Age*, p. 103.
48 *America: The Sorcerer's New Apprentice*, p. 48.
49 "Mad About Moon," *Time*, November 10, 1975, p. 44.

CHAPTER 10

1 *The Infiltration of the New Age*, pp. 58-59 et al.
2 *The Seduction of Christianity*, pp. 192, 195.
3 *The Two Babylons*, p. 25.
4 *Ancient Empires of the New Age*, p. 26.
5 Robert Schuller, *Self-Esteem: The New Reformation* (Word, 1982), pp. 57, 74 et al. as cited in *Beyond Seduction.*
6 *The Theological Dictionary of the New Testament*, Vol. III, p. 646; Vol. I, p. 227.
7 *Inside the New Age Nightmare*, p. 129.
8 *Toward AWorld Religion for the New Age*, pp. 95-96.
9 Norman Vincent Peal and Smiley Blanton, *Faith is the Answer* (Fawcett Crest, 1950), p. 41 as cited in *Beyond Seduction.*
10 *Hidden Dangers of the Rainbow*, iv.
11 *Toward AWorld Religion for the New Age*, p. 58.
12 *Towad A World Religion for the New Age*, p. 180 et al.
13 *Where Was God When Pagan Religions Began?*, p. 106; see also Hammerskjold's *Markings*, p. xvi and Muller's *Genesis.*
14 *Reflections on the Christ*, p. 25.
15 Paul Billheimer, *Destined for the Throne* (Minneapolis: Bethany House, 1983), pp. 35, 37.
16 "Why Where You Born," (Worldwide Church of God, Pasadina, Ca.) pp. 21-22; also David Hill "Why is God the Father called a Father," *Tomorrow's World*, Sept. 1970, p. 27.
17 *Dancing in the Light*, p. 412 et al.
18 "Praise the Lord," Trinity Broadcasting Network, July 7, 1986, January 10, 1986; Casey Treat, "Believing in Yourself," tape 2 (Seattle Christian Center), September 1983; Kenneth Copeland, "Take Time to Pray," *Believers Voice of Victory*, February 1987; *Believer's Voice of Victory*, March 1982, p. 2; "The Force of Love," tape BCC-56 (Fort Worth, Texas: Kenneth Copeland as cited in *The Agony of Deceit*, pp. 119, 91, 114, 92.
19. Maharishi Mahesh Yogi, *Meditations of Maharishi* (N.Y.: Bantom Books, 1973), p. 178; The Science of Being and the Art of Living, 1967, p. 276.
20. Robert Tilton, *God's Laws of Success* (Word of Faith, 1983), pp. 170-171 as cited in *The Seduction of Christianity*, p. 84.
21 Krishnamurti, *At the Feet of the Master*, p. 10.
22 *Meditations of Maharishi*, p. 177.
23 *Toward A World Religion for the New Age*, p. 9.
24 Annie Besant, *Is Theosophy Anti-Christian?* (London: Theosophical Publishing Society, 1901), p. 16.
25 Shirley Mac Laine, *Out on a Limb* (New York: Bantom, 1983), pp. 209, 347, et al.
26 *The Agony of Deceit*, p. 41.
27 *New Dimensions in New Testament Study*, p. 282.
28 *The Reappearance of the Christ*, p. 30.
29 *Transcendental Meditation*, p. 58.
30 John White, *Everything You Wanted To Know About TM—Including How To Do It* (New York: Pocket Books, 1976), p. 103.
31 *Historic Faith*, pp. 111, 105, 253, *The Epistles of St. John: The Greek Text With Notes and Addenda*, p. 70; *The Gospel According to St. John: The Authorized Version With Introduction and Notes*, p. 246.
32 Kenneth E. Hagin, *Zoe: The God-Kind of Life* (Tulsa, Oklahoma: Faith Library, 1981), p. 1 as cited in *The Agony of Deceit*, p. 44.
33 *Beyond Seduction*, p. 163; *Self-Esteem*, p. 21.
34 *The Agony of Deceit*, p. 263.
35 *Beyond Seduction*, p. 163.
36 *Historic Faith*, pp. 258-259; The Gospel of St. John, pp. 66, 46.
37 Kenneth Copeland, *Believer's Voice of Victory*, August 1988, p. 8 as cited in *The Agony of Deceit.*
38 Josh Mc Dowell, *His Image, My Image* (San Bernardino, California: Here's Life, 1984), p. 106.
39 Ibid., p. 34.
40 Robert Schuller, address at Unity Village, Unity tape, as cited in *The Seduction of Christianity*, p. 153.
41 Margot Adler, *Drawing Dawn the Moon* (Boston: Beacon Press, 1979), p. viii.
42 Robert Schuller, Address at Unity Village, Unity tape.

43 *Dark Secrets of the New Age*, p. 52.
44 Robert Schuller, address at Unity Village, Unity Tape.

CHAPTER 11

1 O.T. Allis, *Revised Version Or Revised Bible*? (Philadelphia: Presbyterian and Reformed Publishing Co., 1953), p. 51 as cited in Introduction to the RSV Old Testament.
2 *Selecting a Translation of the Bible*, p. 94 et al.
3 *The NIV: The Making of a Contemporary Translation*, p. 101.
4 *The Life of Westcott*, Vol. II, p. 127.
5 *Larson's Book of Cults*, p. 287.
6 Hermann F. von Soden, *Die Schriften des Neuen Testament* (Gottingen: Vanderhoeck and Ruprecht, 1911), p. 486.
7 *The King James Version Defended*, p. 155.

CHAPTER 12

1 H. P. Blavatsky, *The Secret Doctrine*, Vol. II, p. 61, 502; Vol. I, p. 353.
2 *Webster's Collegiate Dictionary*, 5th Edition (Springfield, Massachusetts: G & C Merriam Co., Pub., 1938).
3 Leslie Shepherd, *The Encyclopedia of the Occult and Parapsychology*, p. 395.
4 H. P. Blavatsky, *Isis Unveiled*, Vol. II, pp. 283-285, 257.
5 *The Encyclopedia of Occultism and Parapsychology*, p. 395.
6 *The NIV: The Making of a Contemporary Tranlsation*, p. 58.
7 Webster's Collegiate Dictionary, 5th Edition (Springfield, Massachusetts: G & C Merriam Co., Publishers, 1938), pp. 934, 908.
8 Raul Ries, "Demon Possession: 1986" *Passport Magazine*, Oct./Nov. 1986, pp. 12,13.
9 H. P. Blavatsky, *The Secret Doctrine*, Vol. II (London: The Theosophical Publishing House, 1893), p. 394.
10 Ibid, p. 255.
11 Ibid, Vol. I, pp. 585, 439.
12 R. Swinburn Clymer, *The Science of the Soul* (Quakertown, Pennsylvania: The Philosophical Publishing Company, 1944), pp. 283, 281.

CHAPTERS 13-17

1 *The NIV: The Making of a Contemporary Translation*, pp. 13, 48.
2 *Words About the Word*, p. 161.
3 Edwin Palmer, *The Holy Spirit* (Grand Rapids, Michigan: Baker Book House, 1974), p. 83.
4 *Religious Thought in the West*, p. 77.
5 Edwin Palmer, *The Five Points of Calvinism* (Spring Lake, Michigan: The Men's Society of the Christian Reformed Church, 1954), p. 18.
6 Ibid., p. 5; *The Holy Spirit*, p. 191 et al.
7 Ibid., p. 30.
8 Ibid., p. 30.
9 Ibid., pp. 30-33, 45.
10 *The NIV: The Making of a Contemporary Translation*, p. 150; *The Holy Spirit*, p. 83.
11 *The Causes of Corruption*, p. 22. *The Revision Revised*, pp. 41-47, 341, 421.
12 *The NIV: The Making of a Contemporary Translation*, p. 48.
13 Ibid., p. 148.
14 Ibid., p. 139.
15 *The Ring of Truth*, p. 67.
16 *The Life and Letters of B.F. Westcott*, Vol. II, pp. 101, 226; Vol. I, pp. 231, 209; *Religious Thought in the West*, p. 228.
17 *The Life and Letters of F.J.A. Hort*, Vol. II, 158, pp. 373, 334, 401, 224, 57. Vol. I, pp. 428-430," F.J.A. Hort, *The First Epistle of St. Peter 1:1-2:17: The Greek Text with Introductory Lecture, Commentary and Additional Notes* (Minneapolis, Minn: James and Klock Publishing Co., reprint 1976), p. 77.
18 Dr. Louis T. Talbot, *What's Wrong With Unity School of Christianity* (Findlay, Ohio: Dunham Publishing Company, 1956), p. 34.

19 *The Hidden Dangers of the Rainbow*, p. 67.

20 *Inside the New Age Nightmare*, pp. 107, 132.

21 Rudolf Steiner, *Initiation, Eternity and the Passing Moment* (Spring Valley, N.Y.: The Anthroposophical Press, 1980), pp. 118-124.

22 *Reflections on the Christ*, pp. 36-45.

23 *Towards a World Religion for the New Age*, p. 24.

24 *The Reappearance of the Christ*, pp. 86, 87.

25 Howard M. Ervin, *Conversion-Initiation and The Baptism of the Holy Spirit* (Peabody, Mass: Hendrickson Publishers, Inc., 1984), p. 157.

26 *Hidden Dangers of the Rainbow*, p. 141.

27 *Mystery Mark of the New Age*, p. 132.

28 *Hidden Dangers of the Rainbow*, p. 79.

29 Rudolf Steiner, *Esoteric Christianity* (New York: Anthrosophical Press, 1962), pp. 164-173.

30 *Conversion-Initiation and the Baptism of the Holy Spirit*, pp. 22, 99, 158, 108, 101.

31 *The Secret Doctrine*, Vol. II, p. 598; Vol. I, p. 337.

32 James D. G. Dunn, *Baptism in the Holy Spirit* (Philadelphia: The Westminster Press, 1977), pp. 95, 145, 214, 217.

33 *Hidden Dangers of the Rainbow*, p. 67.

34 *Dark Secrets of the New Age*, p. 29.

35 *Satan's Evangelistic Strategy for This New Age*, pp. 100, 48.

36 *A Planned Deception*, p. 133.

37 *The Encyclopedia of Religion and Ethics*, p. 314; see also *Religious Thought in the West*, pp. 115-118 and *Historic Faith*, pp. 202, 197, 133; *The Life of Westcott*, Vol. I, p. 160.

38 *The Life of Hort*, Vol. II, p. 86.

39 *The NASB Interlinear Greek-English New Testament*, p. vii.

40 *The NIV: The Making of a Contemporary Translation*, p. 17.

41 *Catholic and Christian*, pp. 38, 39.

42 *The Revision Revised*, p. 160; see also *Forum*, June, 1887, p. 357.

43 *Selecting a Translation of the Bible*, p. 90.

44 *The Life of Westcott*, Vol. I, p. 235; "Lazaris," "Do Not Ignore Your Responsibility to be Free. . .," *Psychic Guide*, September 1, Oct 1987, pp. 52-53.

45 F. Aster Barnwell, *The Meaning of Christ for Our Age* (St. Paul, Minn: Llewelyn Publications, 1984), as cited in *Dark Secrets of the New Age*, p. 211.

46 *Larson's Book of Cults*, p. 184.

47 "Why Were You Born," (Pasadena, Ca.: Worldwide Church of God), p. 11.

48 See *Newsweek*, Dec. 20, 1976.

49 *The Science of the Soul*, p. 155.

50 Charles Filmore, *The Twelve Powers of Man* (Lee's Summit, MO: Unity), p. 162.

51 *Crash Course on the New Age*, pp. 230, 188.

52 *New Directions in New Testament Study*, pp. 207-210; Understanding the New Age, p. 250.

53 *Religious Thought in the West*, p. 13.

54 *The Encyclopedia of Religion and Ethics*, p. 314.

55 *The Occult Establishment*, p. 170.

56 *The Secret Doctrine*, Vol. I, pp. 278, 301; *The Metaphysical Bible Dictionary*, p. 347.

57 *B. F. Westcott, The Gospel According to St. John: The Authorized Version with Introduction and Notes* (Grand Rapids, Mich.: Wm. B. Eerdmans Publishing Company, reprint 1975), p. 219; B. F. Westcott, *The Epistle to the Hebrews the Greek Text with Notes and Essays* (Grand Rapids, Mich: reprint 1974), p. 179.

58 *New Age Lies to Women*, p. 156.

59 Robert Muller, *New Genesis: Shaping a Global Spirituality* (Garden City, New York: Doubleday and Co., 1982), p. 70.

60 *Ancient Empires of the New Age*, pp. 95, 99 et. al.
61 *Understanding the Occult*, p. 38.
62 *Reflections of the Christ*, p. 39.
63 *Hidden Dangers of the Rainbow*, p. 67.
64 Abstracted from tract no. 101, Fellowship Tract League, P.O. Box 164, Lebanon, Ohio, 45036.
65 Gerhard Friedrich (ed.) *Theological Dictionary of the New Testament* , Vol. 6 (Grand Rapids, Mich.: Wm. B. Eerdmans Pub. Co., 1968), p. 11.
66 *The Agony of Deceit*, pp. 140-141.
67 *The Science of the Soul*, p. 179.
68 *Toward a World Religion for the New Age*, p. 94.
69 *The Life of Westcott*, Vol. II, p. ?.
70 *Agony of Deceit*, p. 247.
71 John Vasconcellos and Mitch Saunders, "Humanistic Politics," in AHP Perspective (Association for Humanistic Psychology), July 1985, pp. 12-13, as cited in *Beyond Seduction*, pp. 161-162.
72 *The Life of Westcott*, Vol. II, p. 72; *Religious Thought in the West*, p. 358; *Historic Faith*, p. 54.
73 *Mystery Mark of the New Age*, p. 194.
74 *Reappearance of the Christ*, p. 59.
75 La Vedi Lafferty and Bud Hollowell, *The Eternal Dance* (St. Paul, Minn.: Llewelyn Publications, 1983), p. 503.
76 *The NIV: The Making of a Contemporary Translation*, pp. 17-19.
77 Ibid., p. 34.
78 Ibid., pp. 111, 117.
79 *The Ring of Truth*, p. 150.
80 *The Identity of the New Testament Text*, p. 211.
81 *The Life of Westcott*, Vol. II.
82 *The Life of Hort*, Vol. I, pp. 422, 424.
83 *Back to Godhead Magazine*, Vol. II, No. 7 (Los Angelos, Ca.: International Society for Krishna Consciousness), p. 1.
84 *A Planned Deception*, p. 245.
85 *When Humanity Comes of Age*, p. 55.
86 *Dark Secrets of the New Age*, p. 146.
87 *Science of the Soul*, p. 176.
88 Thomas H. Trapp, "Ecumenical," The Northwestern Luthern, October 15, 1985, p. 32 as cited in *Dark Secrets of the New Age*, p. 221.
89 *Dark Secrets of the New Age*, p. 59.
90 *Reappearance of the Christ*, p. 41.
91 *Larson's Book of Cults*, p. 77.
92 *The Lucifer Connection*, p. 174.
93 *Science of the Soul*, pp. 40, 157.
94 *Larson's Book of Cults*, p. 352.
95 *Eastern Definitions*, p. 203.
96 *New Age Lies to Women*, pp. 148-149.
97 *Dark Secrets of the New Age*, p. 147.
98 *Understanding the Occult*, p. 165.
99 *Toward a World Religion for the New Age*, p. 177.
100 *The Revision Revised*, p. 155.
101 *A Reasoned Look at Asian Religions*, p. 103.
102 *The Life of Westcott*, Vol. 1, pp. 251, 223.
103 Rodney Romney, *Journey to Inner Space: Finding God-In-Us* (Nashville, Tenn.: Abingdon Press, 1980), pp. 106-107 as cited in *The Hidden Dangers of the Rainbow*, p. 179.
104 *Earthkeeping*, p. 165.
105 *Science of the Soul*, pp. 234, 16.
106 Mark and Elizabeth Clare Prophet, *The Science of the Spoken Word*, p. 73 as cited in *Dark Secrets of the New Age*, p. 287.

107 Benjamin Creme, *Reappearance of the Christ and the Masters of Wisdom* (North Hollywood, Ca.: Tara Center, 1980), p. 25.
108 Levi Dowling, *The Aquarian Gospel of Jesus The Christ* (Marina del Rey, California: DeVorss, 1982), p. 52.
109 Beyond Seduction, p. 70.
110 F.J.A. Hort, *The First Epistle of St. Peter 1:1-2:17: The Greek Text with Introductory Lecture, Commentary and Additional Notes* (Minneapolis, Minn.: James and Klock Publishing Co., 1898), p. 54. *Christian American*, 'PC Promotes Goddess Worship', Feb. 1994, p. 19.
111 Maharishi Mahesh Yogi, *The Meditations of Maharishi Mahesh Yogi* (New York: Bantam Books, 1968), pp. 177, 178, 123, 124.
112 William Peterson, *Those Curious New Cults* (New Canaan, Ct.: Keats Publishing Co., 1973), pp. 43, 44.
113 *The Mystical Maze*, p. 68.
114 Suzuki, D.T., *Mysticism, Christianity and Buddhist* (New York: Harper and Row, 1957), p. 149.
115 Virginia Smith, "Oprah Winfrey Reveals Secret of Her Invisible Success," *Examiner*, July 14, 1987, p. 29 as cited in *Mystery Mark of the New Age*, p. 20.
116 *Occult Underground*, p. 93.
117 *Toward a World Religion for the New Age*, p. 10.
118 Foster Bailey, *Things to Come* (New York: Lucis Publishing Company, 1974), p. 114 as cited in *Mystery Mark of the New Age*, p. 26.
119 *Toward a World Religion for the New Age*, p. 125.
120 *Reincarnation, Edgar Cayce and the Bible* (Downers Grove, Ill.: Intervarsity Press, 1975), pp. 27, 28.
121 Emile Cady, *Lessons in Truth* (Lee's Summit, MO.: Unity), pp. 37-39.
122 *New Genesis: Shaping a Global Spirituality*, p. 105.
123 David Spangler, *Revelation: The Birth of a New Age* (Middleton, Wis.: Lorian Press, 1976), pp. 156, 178.
124 *The Life of Westcott*, Vol. II, p. 22; *Religious Thought in the West*, p. 351; *The Gospel According to St. John: The Authorized Version with Introduction and Notes* (Grand Rapids, Michigan: Wm. B. Eerdmans Publishing Co., reprint 1975), p. 159.
125 *Reappearance of the Christ*, p. 32.
126 *New Genesis: Shaping a Global Spirituality*, p. 43.
127 *Articles of Faith*, pp. 85, 91, 162.
128 Theodore M. Hesburg, *The Human Impetative* (New Haven, Conn.: Yale University Press, 1974), p. 11 as cited in *The Hidden Dangers of the Rainbow*, p. 151.
129 *Historic Faith*, p. 8; B.F. Westcott, *The Epistle to the Hebrews: The Greek Text with Notes and Essays* (Grand Rapids, Michigan: Wm. B. Eerdmans Publishing Company, reprint 1974), p. 44; *The Life of Westcott*, Vol. II, p. 241; *The Gospel According to St. John*, p. 52; The Epistles of St. John, p. 70; *Religious Thought in the West*, p. 357.
130 James Sire, *The Universe Next Door* (Downers Grove, Ill.: InterVarsity Press, 1976), p. 231.
131 *What's Wrong with Unity Christianity?*, p. 10.
132 *Eastern Definitions*, pp. 105, 107.
133 *Larson's Book of Cults*, p. 88.
134 *A Reasoned Look at Asian Religions*, pp. 44, 49, 50.
135 *Eastern Definitions*, p. 354.
136 Ibid., pp. 166-167.
137 Ibid., p. 153.
138 Alice Bailey, *The Rays and the Initiations* (New York: Lucis Publishing Company, 1960), p.80; *Reappearance of the Christ*, p. 30.
139 *New Age Bible Interpretation*, p. 137.
140 Da Free John, *Dawn Horse Testament* (San Rafael, Ca.: Dawn Horse Press, 1985), p. 733.

141 Paul Twitchell, "ECK and Music" (Menlo Park, Ca.: ECKANKAR, 1971), as cited in *Larson's Book of Cults*, p. 272.
142 Ibid., p. 178.
143 *Journey to Inner Space: Finding God-In-Us*, p. 30 as cited in *The Hidden Danger of the Rainbow.*
144 *Science of the Soul*, pp. 68, 279.
145 *A Reasoned Look at Asian Religion*, p. 28.
146 *Eastern Definitions*, p. 91.
147 Ibid., pp. 91, 369.
148 H.P. Blavatsky, *The Keys to Theosophy* (Point Loma, Ca.: Aryan Theosophical Press, 1913), p. 63.
149 *Eastern Definitions*, p. 90.
150 *The Life of Westcott*, Vol. II, p. 110; *Historic Faith*, p.152; *Religious Thought in the West*, 346, 232, 26.
151 *A Reasoned Look at Asian Religions*, p. 107.
152 Mary Baker Eddy, *Science and Health*, Ch. 456: 27 and 28.
153 *A Planned Deception*, p. 12.
154 *The New Genesis: Shaping a Global Spirituality*, p. 183.
155 *Religious Thought in the West*, p. 194.
156 *The Life of Westcott*, Vol. II, p. 69.
157 *The Life of Hort*, Vol. I, pp. 78, 414-416.
158 *Omni*. Dec. 1984, p. 650.
159 Charles Filmore, *Mysteries of Genesis* (Lee's Summit, MO.: Unity), p. 13.
160 *The Revision Revised*, p. 208.
161 "Ramtha" with Douglas James Mahr, *Voyage to the New World* (Friday Harbor, Wash.: Masterworks, 1985), p. 61.
162 *F.J.A. Hort, The Apocalypse of St. John 1-3: The Greek Text with Introduction, Commentary, and Additional Notes* (Minneopolis, Minn.: James & Klock Publishing Co., 1976 reprint), p. 27; *The Life of Hort*, Vol. 1, p. 118.
163 *The Life of Westcott*, Vol. II.
164 Gerhard Kittle, *The Theological Dictionary of the New Testament*, Vol. 1 (Grand Rapids, Mich.: Wm. B. Eerdmans Publishing Company, 1964), pp. 197-209.
165 *Religious Thought in the West, p. 22; Some Lessons on the Revised Version*, pp. 186, 187.
166 *Journey to Inner Space: Finding God-In-Us*, pp. 74-75 as cited in *The Hidden Danger of the Rainbow*, p. 178.

CHAPTER 18
1 H.P. Blavatsky, *Isis Unveiled*, Vol. II, pp. 506-507.
2 *The NIV: The Making of a Contemporary Translation*, pp. 58-71.
3 Ibid., pp. 95-105.
4 *Tomorrow's World*, April 1971, pp. 14, 18.
5 *The NIV: The Making of a Contemporary Translation*, pp. 58-71.
6 *Let God Be True* [1952], p. 99
7 *New World Bible*, appendix , p. 1157.
8 *The NIV: The Making of a Contemporary Translation*, pp. 58-71.
9 Ibid.
10 *Toward a World Religion for the New Age*, p. 10.
11 R. Swineburn Clymer, *The Science of the Soul and Spiritual Ethics for the New Age* (Quakertown, Pa.: The Philosophical Publishing Co., 1944), p. 273.
12 *Isis Unveiled*, Vol. II, p. 11.
13 Leslie Shepherd, *Encyclopedia of Occultism and Parapsychology* (Detroit, Michigan: Gale Research Company, 1978), p. 60.

[14] *The Life of Hort,* Vol. II, pp. 336-337.
[15] *The Life of Schaff,* p. 346.
[16] *De Civit Dei,* I, xxi, c. 17.
[17] Walter Houghton, *Parliament of World Religions* (Chicago, Ill.: F.T. Neely, 1893), p. 720.
[18] See Hort's *Commentary on I Peter.*
[19] See *Ring of Truth* and *The Price of Success,* p. 10.
[20] *Historic Faith,* pp. 76-78.
[21] *The Life of Westcott,* Vol. II, p. 49; *Historic Faith,* pp. 150-151; *Religious Thought in the West,* p. 247.
[22] *The Mystical Maze,* p. 164.
[23] *Metaphysical Bible Dictionary,* p. 266; *Teach Us To Pray,* p. 72.
[24] *Larson's Book of Cults,* p. 386.
[25] *The Revision Revised,* p. 207.
[26] *Historic Faith,* pp. 149-151.
[27] Morgan, *The Plan of Salvation,* p. 8.
[28] *The Life of Hort,* Vol. I, p. 149.
[29] *Today's World,* April 1971, p. 14.
[30] *Christian Healing,* p. 114.

CHAPTERS 19-27
[1] *Satan's Evangelistic Strategy For This New Age,* p. 71.
[2] *Early Manuscripts and Modern Translations of the New Testament,* pp. xvii, 6.
[3] *Which Bible,* p. 37.
[4] *A Reasoned Look at Asian Religions,* p. 145.
[5] See *The Reappearance of the Christ.*
[6] *The King James Version Debate,* p. 63.
[7] A random survey of 21 KJV verses on the deity of Christ showed 18 from the Majority Text, 2 from the Textus Receptus and 1 with no Greek basis. In the rare instances when the KJV follows the T.R. alone or has a narrow Greek base, it always elevates Christ; conversely, new versions frequently follow a narrow Greek bases which always demeans Christ or orthodox Christian doctrine.
[8] *Historic Faith,* p. 62; *The Gospel According to St. John: The Authorized Version With Introduction and Notes,* pp. 297, 16.
[9] *The First Epistle of St. Peter 1:1-2:17: The Greek Text with Introductory Lecture, Commentary and Additional Notes,* p. 52.
[10] *The NIV: The Making of a Contemporary Translation,* p. 143.
[11] *The Apocalypse of St. John 1-3: The Greek Text with Introduction, Commentary and Additional Notes,* p. 13.
[12] *Isis Unveiled,* Vol. II, p. 193.
[13] *The Agony of Deceit,* pp. 101, 102, 114.
[14] Bruce Metzger, *A Textual Commentary on the Greek New Testament* (Federal Republic of Germany: Biblia-Druck GmbH Stuttgart, 1975), p. 193.
[15] *Larson's Book of Cults,* p. 144.
[16] *Crash Course on the New Age,* p. 29.
[17] *Texts and Margins,* p. 47.
[18] *Crash Course on the New Age,* p. 29.
[19] Kurt Koch, *Occult ABC* (Germany: Literature Mission Aglasterhausen, 1978), pp. 209, 210.
[20] *Dark Secrets of the New Age,* p. 17.
[21] *The Epistle to the Hebrews and the Greek Text,* p. 122; *The Gospel According to St. John,* pp. 184, 297; *Historic Faith,* p. 47.
[22] *Isis Unveiled,* Volume II, pp. 544, 479; *The Secret Doctrine,* Vol. I, p. 157.
[23] *The Esoteric Basis of Christianity,* p. xliii; see also Foster Bailey, *Things to Come* (New York: Lucis Publishing Co., 1974), pp. 116, 117.

[24] *Science and Health* (Boston, Mass: Christian Science), 473: 9-16.
[25] Annie Besant, *Esoteric Christianity* (Wheaton, Ill.: Theosophical Publishing House, 1953), p. 96.
[26] Philip Swihart, *Reincarnation, Edgar Cayce and the Bible* (Downers Grove, Ill.: InterVarsity Press, 1975), p. 18.
[27] Emmett Fox, *Diagrams for Living: The Bible Unveiled* (New York: Harper and Row, 1968), pp. 158-159.
[28] Noel Langley, *Edgar Cayce on Reincarnation* (New York: Castle Books, 1967), p. 167.
[29] *Hidden Wisdom in the Holy Bible*, p. 115; *Eastern Definitions*, p. 318.
[30] *The Epistle to the Hebrews*, p. 315.
[31] *Hidden Dangers of the Rainbow*, p. 149.
[32] *New Dimensions in New Testament Study*, p. 220.
[33] *The Gospel According to St. John*, p. 200.
[34] *Revelation: The Birth of a New Age*, p. 150; *Reflections on the Christ*, p. 40; *The Secret Doctrine*, p. 569; *Bhagavad-Gita*, Chapter 10.
[35] *Dark Secrets of the New Age*, p. 99.
[36] *Larson's Book of Cults*, p. 386; see also J. Yutaka Amato and Norman Geisler, *The Infiltration of the New Age* (Wheaton, Ill.: Tyndale House, 1989), p. 142.
[37] *The Secret Doctrine*, Vol. II, p. 815.
[38] *Christian Healing*, p. 27; *The Metaphysical Bible Dictionary*, p. 150.
[39] *Teach Us To Pray*, p. 79, *Christian Healing*, pp. 217, 27; *The Metaphysical Bible Dictionary*, p. 150.
[40] *Historic Faith*, p. 53; *The Epistles of St. John: The Greek Text*; p. 73.
[41] H.P. Blavatsky, *Studies in Occultism* (London: Theosophical University Press), p. 134.
[42] *Reflections on the Christ*, p. 29.
[43] *The Epistle to the Hebrews: The Greek Text*, p. 133. *The Epistles of St. John: The Greek Text*, p. 42.
[44] *Larson's Book of Cults*, p. 139.
[45] *What Ever Happened to Heaven?*, p. 260.
[46] *Catholic and Christian*, p. 18.
[47] Livesey, *Understanding the New Age*, p. 23.
[48] Harriet and F. Homer Curtis, *Coming World Changes* (Albuquerque, N.M.: Sun Publishing, 1981), as cited in *Mystery Mark*, p. 60.
[49] *Reappearance of the Christ*, pp. 17, 67, 82, 86.
[50] *Isis Unveiled*, Vol. II, p. 152; see also Theodore H. Gaster, *The Dead Sea Scriptures* (Garden City, N.Y.: Anchor Books, 1976), pp. xii, 6, 9.
[51] *Reappearance of the Christ*, pp. 102-106.
[52] *The Eternal Dance*, p. 2 as cited in *Dark Secrets of the New Age*, p. 60.
[53] *Larsons Book of Cults*, pp. 140-142.
[54] *Ancient Empires of the New Age*, p. 89.
[55] *The NIV: The Making of a Contemporary Translation*, p. 147.
[56] *The First Epsitle of St. Peter*, p. 31.
[57] *Reappearance of the Christ*, pp. 158-159.
[58] *The Lucifer Connection*, p. 67.
[59] *Dark Secrets of the New Age*, p. 264.
[60] *Reappearance of the Christ*, pp. 59, 67.
[61] *The Mystical Maze*, p. 171.
[62] *A Reasoned Look at Asian Religion*, p. 22.
[63] *The Lucifer Connection*, p. 153.
[64] *The Theological Dictionary of the New Testament*, Vol. II, p. 162.
[65] Benjamin Creme, *Messages from Maitreya*, as cited in *Mystery Mark of the New Age*, p. 63.
[66] *When Humanity Comes of Age*, p. 188.

67 *Satan's Evangelistic Strategy for the New Age*, p. 320.
68 Marilyn Ferguson, *The Aquarian Conspiracy* (Los Angelos: J.P. Tarcher, Inc., 1980), pp. 373, 379, 377.
69 *A Reasoned Look at Asian Religions*, p. 104.
70 Jessie Penn-Lewis, *War on the Saints* (Parkstone, Poole, Dorset BH 14 OHJ England: The Overcomers Literature Trust, Ltd.), pp. 1, 72, 73, 74, 115, 122, 116; available through Christian Literature Crusade P.O. Box 1449 Fort Washington, PA 19034.
71 *Ancient Empires of the New Age*, p. 147.
72 Michael Doan, "A Unisex Bible: Reformers Run into a Storm," *U.S. News and World Report*, Dec. 17, 1984, p. 70.
73 *Understanding the Cults*, p. 138.
74 *The Revision Revised*, p. 180.
75 *The Theological Dictionary of the New Testament*; Vol. IV, p. 469; for early church citations see Chrys, Thdrt, also F. Vigouroux, *Dict. de la bible*, IV (1908), p. 713.
76 John White, "A Course in Miracles: Spiritual Wisdom for the New Age," *Science of Mind*, March 1986, pp. 10-14, 80-88 as cited in *Dark Secrets of the New Age*, p. 107.
77 Edward F. Hills, *Believing Bible Study* (Des Moines, Iowa: The Christian Research Press, 1977), p. 77.
78 *The Encyclopedia of Religion and Ethics*, pp. 231-241.
79 *The Causes of Corruption*, pp. 216-218, 956.
80 *The Apocalypse of St. John*, p. 36.
81 *The Encyclopedia of Religion and Ethics*, p. 240.
82 Ibid., pp. 313-314.
83 *The History of Heresy*, pp. 45-55; *The Causes of Corruption*, p. 956.
84 *A Textual Commentary on the Greek New Testament*, p. 198.
85 *The Person and Ministry of the Holy Spirit: The Traditional Calvinistic Perspective* (Grand Rapids, Mich.: Baker Book House, 1974), pp. 15, 16.
86 *The Life of Schaff*, pp. 320, 743.
87 *The Gospel According to St. John*, p. 159; *Historic Faith*, p. 204.
88 Bruce M. Metzger, "The Jehovah Witnesses and Jesus Christ" *Theology Today* 15:80 April, 1953.
89 *The NIV: The Making of a Contemporary Translation*, p. 162.
90 *The New American Bible*, p. 528.
91 Mo Letters (The Children of God, no. 631, May 18, 1975), p.14.
92 *Make Sure of All Things* (New York: Watchtower Bible and Tract Society, Inc., 1965), p. 207.
93 *Let God Be True* (New York: Watchtower Bible and Tract Society, 1952), p. 33.
94 Ibid., p.88.
95 *Larson's Book of Cults*, p. 177.
96 Ibid., p. 251.
97 *The Agony of Deceit*, p. 100.
98 *The Theological Dictionary of the New Testament*, Vol. IV, p. 739.
99 *Understanding the New Age*, p. 309.
100 Doctrinal statement of the Unification Church filed with the Korean Government, p. 185.
101 *The Aquarian Gospel of Jesus the Christ*, pp. 240-241.
102 *The King James Version Debate*, p. 92.
103 *The NIV: The Making of a Contemporary Translation*, p.123.
104 Ibid., pp. 119-126.
105 *The Secret Doctrine*, p. 566.
106 *The Person and Ministry of the Holy Spirit*, p. 15.
107 *Larson's Book of Cults*, p. 161.
108 *The NIV: The Making of a Contemporary Translation*, p.124.

109 McConkie, *Morman Doctrine,* p. 192, Talmadge, *Doctrine and Covenants,* p. 472 as cited in Keith L. Brooks *The Spirit of Truth and the Spirit of Error* (Chicago, Ill.: Moody Press, 1990).

110 *The NIV: The Making of a Contemporary Translation,* pp. 119-126.

111 *The King James Version Debate,* p. 92.

112 *The History of Heresy,* p. 39.

113 *The NIV: The Making of a Contemporary Translation,* p. 126.

114 *Toward a World Religion for the New Age,* p. 101.

115 Elizabeth S. Turner, *What Unity Teaches* (Lee Summit, Mo: Unity, pp. 6, 7, 8.

116 Annie Besant, *Esoteric Christianity* (Wheaton, Ill.: Theosophical Publishing House, 1953), p. 96.

117 Alice Bailey, *The Destiny of the Nations* (London, England: Lucis Press, Ltd., 3rd paperback edition, 1982), p. 19 as cited in *Mystery Mark of the New Age,* p. 121.

118 *Hidden Dangers of the Rainbow,* p. 66.

119 *The Lucifer Connection,* p. 169.

120 *The Secret Doctrine,* p. 566.

121 *Dark Secrets of the New Age,* p. 43; Donald Cole, November 24, 1987, Moody Broadcast "Open Line."

122 The Bob Larson Show, June 30, 1989.

123 *Historic Faith,* p. 47; *The Epistle to the Hebrews: The Greek Text,* pp. 25, 26.

124 Levi Dowling, *The Aquarian Gospel of Jesus the Christ* (Marina del Rey, California: DeVorss, 1982), p. 261.

125 *The Lucifer Connection,* p. 158.

126 Hayward Coleman, quoted by Susan Woldenberg, "Mime Yoga: Meditation in Motion," *Yoga Journal,* July/August 1986, pp. 23-24.

127 John White, "A Course in Miracles: Spiritual Wisdom for the New Age", *Science of Mind,* March 1986, pp. 10-14, 80-88.

128 La Vedi Lafferty and Bud Hollowell, *The Eternal Dance,* p. 503 as cited in *Dark Secrets of the New Age,* pp. 123, 128, 107.

129 *The Aquarian Gospel of Jesus the Christ,* pp. 14, 15.

130 *The Gospel According to St. John,* p. 23.

131 *Larson's Book of Cults,* p. 371.

132 *Hidden Wisdom in the Holy Bible,* pp. 129, 130.

133 *Baptism in the Holy Ghost,* pp. 24, 40.

134 *Isis Unveiled,* Vol. II, p. 566.

135 *The Metaphysical Bible Dictionary,* p. 150; *The Unity Treasure Chest,* p. 49.

136 *When Humanity Comes of Age,* p. 91.

137 *A Textual Commentary on the Greek New Testament,* p. xviii.

138 *The Revision Revised,* p. 515.

139 *Which Bible,* p. 108.

140 *The Lucifer Connection,* p. 46.

141 *Nestle's Greek New Testament,* p. 44.

142 Christian Book Distributers, Peabody, Mass..

143 *Make Sure of All Things,* p. 426.

144 *Isis Unveiled,* Vol. II, p. 526.

145 Ernest C. Wilson, *Have We Lived Before?* (Lee Summit, MO: Unity), pp. 65-99.

146 *If You Die, Will You Live Again?* (Pasadena, Ca.: Worldwide Church of God), p. 6.

147 *Religious Thought in the West,* pp. 244, 37, 39; *The Life of Westcott,* Vol. II, p. 77; *The Gospel According to St. John,* pp. 168, 109, 42; *The Epistle to the Hebrews,* p. 185.

148 *Science and Health,* p. 593:9.

149 *Declaration of Principles,* Nos. 7 and 8 as cited in *Spirit of Truth, Spirit of Error.*

150 Charles Filmore, *The Science of Being and Christian Healing* (Lee Summit, MO.: Unity), p. 206.

151 H. Spencer Lewis, *The Mystical Life of Jesus,* 8th ed., 1948, pp. 283, 289.
152 *Reappearance of the Christ*, pp. 80, 43, 113.
153 *Hidden Danger of the Rainbow*, pp. 96, 97.
154 *U.S.A. Today, Jan. 12, 1987.*
155 *Reappearance of the Christ*, p. 43.
156 *Reappearance of the Christ and the Masters of Wisdom*, pp. 54, 46.
157 *Dark Secrets of the New Age*, p. 96.
158 *A Textual Commentary on the Greek New Testament*, p. 124.
159 *The Revision Revised*, pp. 36, 37.
160 Ibid., p. 283.
161 *The Lucifer Connection*, p. 49.
162 *The King James Version Debate*, p. 65.
163 *Dake's Annotated Reference Bible*, p. 37 N.T..
164 *The Gospel According to St. John*, p. 35.
165 *The Agony of Deceit*, p. 108.
166 *Science of the Soul*, p. 156, 9.
167 *The NIV: The Making of a Contemporary Translation*, pp. 153, 42; *The King James Version Debate*, p. 42.
168 See *Words about the Word*, p. 75, *The KJV Debate*, p. 148.
169 *Selecting a Translation of the Bible*, p. 78.
170 *Understanding the Cults*, p. 23.

CHAPTER 28

1 *The Secret Doctrine, Isis Unveiled*, Vol. II, pp. 535, 40.
2 *The NIV: The Making of a Contemporary Translation*, p. 107.
3 For example see *A Greek-English Lexicon of the New Testament* by J. H. Thayer, *A Greek-English Lexicon*, by Liddell and Scott, *A Greek and English Lexicon to the New Testament*, by J. Parkhurst.
4 *The Metaphysical Bible Dictionary*, p. 332.
5 *Isis Unveiled*, p. 169, *The Secret Doctrine*, pp. 87, 535.
6 *The Secret Doctrine*, Vol. II, pp. 405-406.
7 Ibid, pp. 444, 446, 101; *The Secret Doctrine*, Vol. I, p. 501.
8 Adapted from *CIB Bulletin* (Camarillo, CA: Christian Information Bureau, Oct. 1989, Vol. 5, No. 10), pp. 1-2.
9 Recorded in Bob and Gretchen Passantino's *Witch Hunt* (Nashville, Tennessee: Thomas Nelson, Inc., 1990), pp. 20-21.
10 *Words About the Word*, p. 47.
11 *Understanding the Cults*, p. 81.
12 *The Kingdom Interlinear Translation of the Greek Scriptures*, pp. 3-5.
13 Charles Taze Russell, *Studies In Scripture* (Brooklyn: International Bible Student, 1912), p. 54.
14 Victor Paul Wierwille, *Jesus Christ Is Not God*, p. 3.
15 Talmadge, *Articles of Faith*, p. 40; *Morman Doctrine*, p. 670.
16 *The Agony of Deceit*, p. 43.
17 *The Spirit of Truth and The Spirit of Error.*
18 *The Life of Hort*, Vol. II, p. 128.
19 *The NIV: The Making of a Contemporary Translation*, p. 56.
20 *Isis Unveiled*, Vol. II, p. 177.
21 *The NIV: The Making of a Contemporary Translation*, p. 56.
22 *A Textual Commentary on the Greek New Testament*, p. 715.
23 Ibid., p. 716.

[24] K. Aland, "The Significance of the Papyri for Progress in New Testament Research," *The Bible in Modern Scholarship,* ed. J.P. Hyatt (New York: Abingdon Press, 1965), p. 340.
[25] Taskier, R.V.G. (ed.) *The Greek New Testament* (Oxford: Oxford University Press, 1964), p. viii.
[26] *Notes on Vindication of I John 5:7* (London: Trinitarian Bible Society, Article No. 17, July 1980), p.2.
[27] *When Humanity Comes of Age,* p. 196.
[28] *The Aquarian Gospel of Jesus the Christ,* p. 15.
[29] *The Revision Revised,* p. 124.

CHAPTER 29
[1] *Dark Secrets of the New Age,* p. 258.
[2] *The Identity of the New Testament Text,* p. 11.
[3] *Satan* (Phil., Pa: Sunday School Times Co., 1932), p. 73.
[4] *Dark Secrets of the New Age,* p. 21.
[5] *A Reasoned Look at Asian Religions,* p. 87.
[6] *Whatever Happened to Heaven?,* p. 303.
[7] *The Seduction of Christianity,* p. 145; *Beyond Seduction,* p. 45.
[8] *Selecting a Translation of the Bible,* pp. 18, 21, 77, 78, 48.
[9] *The N.I.V.: The Making of a Contemporary Translation,* pp. 128, 167.
[10] *Words About the Word,* pp. 54, 74.
[11] *The K.J.V. Debate,* p. 65.
[12] *The Causes of Corruption of the Traditional Text,* p. 89.
[13] *The Lucifer Connection,* p. 165.
[14] *The Seduction of Christianity,* p. 144.

CHAPTER 30
[1] John R. Kohlenberger, *Words About the Word* (Grand Rapids, Michigan: Zondervan Publishing House, 1987), p. 42.
[2] Ibid., p. 34.
[3] D.A. Carson, *The King James Version Debate* (Grand Rapids, Michigan: Baker Book House, 1979), pp. 41, 75.
[4] Edward F. Hills, *The King James Version Defended* (Des Moines, Iowa: The Christian Research Press, 1979), p. 229.
[5] Philip W. Comfort, *Early Manuscripts and Modern Translations of the New Testament* (Wheaton, Illinois: Tyndale House Publishing, Inc., 1990), p. 21.
[6] Robert Young, *Analytical Concordance to the Bible* (Grand Rapids, Michigan: Wm. B. Eerdmans Publishing Company, 1970), p. 18.
[7] Henry H. Halley, *Halley's Bible Handbook* (Grand Rapids, Michigan: Zondervan Publishing House, 1965), p. 747.
[8] Arthur Westcott, *Life and Letters of Brooke Foss Westcott,* Vol. I (London: Macmillan and Co., Limited, 1903), p. 47.
[9] Barbara G. Walker, *The Woman's Encyclopedia of Myths and Secrets* (San Francisco: Harper and Row Publishers), pp. 395-398.
[10] H.P. Blavatsky, *The Secret Doctrine,* Vol. II (London: The Theosophical Publishing Society, 1893), see pp. 30, 381, 472, 473, 558, 660.
[11] *Dictionary of Greek Mythology,* pp. 93, 101, 124
[12] See note 128 in this section; H.P. Blavatsky, *The Theosophical Glossary* (Los Angelos, Ca.: The Theosophical Society, 1971), p. 140; also see preface; originally published in 1892.
[13] James Webb, *The Occult Underground* (La Salle, Illinois: Open Court Press, 1974), p. 222.
[14] *Life of Westcott,* Vol. I, p. 47.
[15] *The Woman's Encyclopedia of Myths and Secrets,* p. 395.

[16] Brooke Foss Westcott, *The Historic Faith* (London and Cambridge: Macmillan and Co., 1885), p. 234.
[17] Alan Gauld, *The Founders of Psychical Research* (New York: Schocken Books, 1968), pp. 90-91.
[18] Charles Filmore, *The Metaphysical Bible Dictionary* (Lees Summit, MO: Unity School of Christianity, 1950), p. 516.
[19] Constance Cumby, *Hidden Dangers of the Rainbow* (Shreveport, Louisiana: Huntington House, Inc., 1983), p. 28.
[20] J. Yutaka Amano and Norman Geisler, *The Infiltration of the New Age* (Wheaton, Illinois: Tyndale House Publishers, Inc., 1989), p. 115; also see footnote 10.
[21] *Life of Westcott*, Vol. I , p. 230.
[22] Edwin W. Lutzer and John F. DeVries, *Satan's Evangelistic Strategy for This New Age* (Wheaton, Illinois: Victor Books, 1989), p. 137.
[23] Russell Chandler, *Understanding the New Age* (Dallas, Texas: Word Publishing, 1988), pp. 81, 88.
[24] Elliot Miller, *A Crash Course on the New Age* (Grand Rapids, Michigan: 1989), pp. 146, 147, 148, 163.
[25] *The Occult Underground*, p. 155.
[26] Ibid., p. 8.
[27] Arthur Hort, *The Life and Letters of Fenton John Anthony Hort*, Vol. I (New York: Macmillan and Co., 1896), p. 211.
[28] Ibid.
[29] Ibid., pp. 171, 177.
[30] Paul de Parrie and Mary Pride, *Ancient Empires of the New Age* (Westchester, Illinois: Crossway Books, 1989), p. 182.
[31] *Life of Hort*, Vol. I, pp. 219, 220.
[32] Ibid.
[33] *Life of Westcott*, Vol. I, pp. 117, 118.
[34] Ibid.
[35] W.H. Salter, *The Society for Psychical Research: An Outline of Its History* (London: The Society for Psychical Research, 1948), p. 8.
[36] *The Founders of Psychical Research*, pp. 66-67.
[37] *Life of Westcott*, Vol. I, p. 119.
[38] *Life of Hort*, Vol. I, pp. 445, 421.
[39] *Life of Westcott*, Vol. I, p. 229.
[40] Ibid., pp. 119, 235.
[41] *The Society for Psychical Research*, p. 6.
[42] *The Founders of Psychical Research*, p. 88.
[43] Norman and Jeanne MacKenzie, *The Fabians* (New York: Simon and Schuster, 1977), p. 18.
[44] *The Founders of Psychical Research*, p. 53.
[45] Ibid., pp. 50-51; also see *Life of Westcott*, Vol. I, pp. 215, 233.
[46] Leslie Shepard, *The Encyclopedia of Occultism and Parapsychology* (Detroit, Michigan: Gale Research Company, 1978), pp. 372, 847.
[47] *Occult Underground*, pp. 36-40.
[48] *The Society for Psychical Research*, pp. 5, 6, 13, 41.
[49] *Crash Course on the New Age*, pp. 145-146.
[50] Dave Hunt and T.A. McMahon, *The Seduction of Christianity* (Eugene, Oregon: Harvest House Publishers, 1985), p. 44.
[51] *Founders of Psychical Research*, p. 322.
[52] *The Society for Psychical Research*, p. 22.
[53] *Founders of Psychical Research*, pp. 104, 107.
[54] *The Society for Psychical Research*, p. 14.

55 Ibid., pp. 18, 27.
56 *Founders of Psychical Research*, pp. 123, 18.
57 *The Society for Psychical Research*, p. 8.
58 *Encyclopedia of Occultism and Parapsychology*, p. 787.
59 *Man, Myth and Magic: An Encyclopedia of the Supernatural*, Vol. 20 (New York: Marshall Cavendish, 1970), p. 2814.
60 *The Society for Psychical Research*, p. 21.
61 *The Founders of Psychical Research*, p. 203.
62 *The Historic Faith*, see all of pp. 249-255.
63 Edward Rice, *Eastern Definitions* (Garden City, New York: Doubleday and Company, Inc., 1978), p. 375.
64 Ibid.
65 B.F. Westcott, *Essays in the History of Religious Thought in the West* (London: Macmillan and Company, 1891), p. 357.
66 Westcott motto; often used to end or start his books.
67 *Eastern Definitions*, p. 375.
68 *Historic Faith*, p. 148.
69 Vera Alder, *When Humanity Comes of Age* (New York: Samuel Weiser, 1974), pp. 191, 198, 201.
70 Rudolf Steiner, *The Esoteric Basis of Christianity*, pp. xli, 137; see also latter third of his book for repeated positive references to Lucifer. This open Luciferian was at the root of the Homeopathy movement. It is based on 'sympathetic magic'—not natural healing. He also founded the Waldorf Schools for young children. Both are growing in popularity and have his philosophy at their core.
71 *The Founders of Psychical Research*, pp. 50-51.
72 Blavatsky's motto used to begin or end her writings.
73 *The Society for Psychical Research*, pp. 33-37; see *Isis Unveiled*, pp. 243, 161 for examples of her comments on Westcott.
74 *Supernatural Religion*, see pp. 811, 753, 286, 364.
75 Bob Larson, *Larson's Book of Cults* (Wheaton, Illinois: Tyndale House Publishers, Inc., 1982), p. 321.
76 *The Founders of Psychical Research*, p. 48.
77 *Life of Hort*, Vol. I, pp. 170, 171, 198.
78 *The Founders of Psychical Research*, p. 48.
79 *Life of Hort*, Vol. I, pp. 196, 42.
80 Ibid., Vol. II, pp. 184-185; also see *Life of Westcott*, Vol. I, p. 385.
81 *Founders of Psychical Research*, pp. 105, 104, 48.
82 Did someone say, "you can publish and still perish?"
83 *Life of Hort*, Vol. II, pp. 184-185; also see Life of Westcott, Vol. I, p. 385.
84 *Occult Underground*, p. 170.
85 Randall N. Baer, *Inside The New Age Nightmare* (Lafayette, Louisiana: Huntington House, Inc., 1989), p. 103.
86 Alex Jack, *The New Age Dictionary* (Brookline, Massachusetts: Kanthaka Press, 1976), p. 85.
87 *When Humanity Comes of Age*, pp. 28, 36; see also chapter 2, 3, and 4.
88 *Life of Westcott*, Vol. II, pp. 18-23.
89 *Historic Faith*, p. 116.
90 James Webb, *The Occult Establishment* (La Salle, Illinois: Open Court Press, 1976), pp. 396-397; the root of the word used for Westcott's and Bailey's Club means 'club'.
91 *Historic Faith*, p. 108.
92 Robert Muller, *New Genesis: Shaping a Global Spirituality* (Garden City, New York: Doubleday and Company, Inc., 1982), p. xv.
93 *Life of Hort*, Vol. I, pp. 458-459.

[94] *Founders of Psychical Research*, p. 317.
[95] Ibid., pp. 86-87.
[96] *The Dictionary of National Biography* (London: Oxford University Press, 1937), pp. 42-43.
[97] *The Occult Underground*, p. 359.
[98] *When Humanity Comes of Age*, p. 24.
[99] *Founders of Psychical Research*, pp. 305-307.
[100] Ibid., p. 306.
[101] *The Fabians*, pp. 18, 316.
[102] Ibid., pp. 18, 299, 298, 53, 377; see also Salter's *The Society for Psychical Research*, p. 10.
[103] *Life of Hort*, Vol. II, p. 34.
[104] *Life of Hort*, Vol. I. p. 130
[105] *Hidden Dangers of the Rainbow*, p. 98.
[106] Roy Livesey, *Understanding the New Age* (Chichester, Endland: New Wine Press, 1989), p. 146.
[107] *The Seduction of Christianity*, p. 50.
[108] *When Humanity Comes of Age*, pp. 13, 218, 221, 222.
[109] *Understanding the New Age*, p. 31.
[110] *A Crash Course of the New Age*, pp. 28-33.
[111] *Orange County Register*, (June 6, 1990), p. 1 as cited in Dave Hunt, *The C.I.B. Bulletin*, Vol. 6 No. 10 (October, 1990), p. 1.
[112] *Historic Faith*, p. 146.
[113] I John 4:1, I John 2:18
[114] *Crash Course on the New Age*, p. 134.
[115] Webster defines piracy as "literary theft"; the missing words and verses in the new bibles elicits my choice of this name; slander is not intended.
[116] Lady Emily Lutyens, *Candels in the Sun* (Soho Square: London, 1957), p. 14.
[117] Ibid., p. 143.
[118] Ibid., p. 143 footnote; see also *Society of Psychical Research*, p. 47.
[119] *Occult Underground*, p. 105; also see *Encyclopedia of Occultism*, Vol. 2, pp. 847-848.
[120] *Life of Westcott*, Vol. I, pp. 264-265.
[121] Ibid., Vol. II, pp. 177-178, 218-219.
[122] *Life of Westcott*, Vol. II, pp. 335; also see pp. 210 and 330.
[123] *Dictionary of Gods, Goddesses, Devils, and Demons* (London: Routledge and Kegan), p. 230.
[124] *Life of Westcott*, Vol. II, p. 147.
[125] Ibid., p. 185.
[126] *Founders of Psychical Research*, pp. 66, 67.
[127] *Society for Psychical Research*, p. 16.
[128] The articles on Hermetic doctrine in Blavatsky's *Theosophical Dictionary* "were contributed at the special request of H.P.B. by Brother W.W.Westcott." She mentions B.F. Westcott, the subject of this past chapter, several times in her other books. B.F. Westcott's son points out that his father's signature was almost always read as W., not B., preceeding his last name. (See *Life of Westcott*, p. 450.) The similar identity of these two is not a matter of historical record. W.W. Westcott was the name given by the London Hermetic Order of the Golden Dawn as its founder. *The Encyclopedia of Occultism and Parapsychology* [p.983] when discussing this organization writes, "This is the official story of the foundation of the famous Golden Dawn. . .He published a short number of books or pamphlets on occult or mystical subjects including. . .The Pymander of Hermes." *The Encyclopedia of the Unexplained* elaborates [p.105],"[T]he Order's origins have been surrounded with mystery. . .a secret society." A member wrote of the "Secret Chiefs of the Society". . ."I do not even know their earthly names. I know them only by their secret mottos." Strangely W.W. Westcott's motto "Vincit omnia veritus" (Truth conquers all things) rings like B.F. Westcott's "they loved truth more" and Blavatsky's "There is no religion higher than truth." This encyclopedia further states,

> The Order was founded upon a series of ingenious fabrications. . .the G.D.'s teachings have greatly influenced the theories and work and to a lesser extent the internal organization of many occult groups in English-speaking counties. . .it was in fact a prototype magical order. . .The G.D. was to some extent a by-product of several related factors in the social history of 19th century England. The Spiritualists movement attracted a widespread public interest and following between about 1850 and 1890. Dissatisfied with Spiritualism, with its many fraudulent mediums and unproven hypothesis, some men and women turned to the study of 'refected knowledge'. . .It was not a Masonic lodge but rather the equivalent of a literary society. . .Westcott conceived his plan for a secret and highly exclusive occult order only a few months after H.P. Blavatsky settled permanently in London in 1887. . .Westcott clearly intended that the Golden Dawn project should. . .based firmly on Western hermetic tradition. . .Westcott, who knew his hermetic literature well. . .envisaged nothing more than a cosy little secret society of occultists. . .Outer Order members were not allowed to know of its existence, who belonged to it. . .He was also a leading member of and an associate of Madame Blavatsky and Anna Kingsford. (. . .the reviver of the idea of esoteric Christianity. . .wife of a Shripshire [Church of England] clergyman. . .[Through] the constant use of chloroforms. . .spirits began speaking to her. . .the doctrines of the Neo-platonists). He translated the *Sefer Yetsirah* and the Chaldean *Oracles of Zoroaster* into English. [p. 273]

B.F. Westcott's Ghostly Guild had as its off-shoot the Society for Psychical Research. Its President at one point was Henri Bergson whose sister Mina married the co-founder of the Golden Dawn, S.L. Mathers.
Another S.P.R. president's (Balfour) sister-in-law, Emily Lutyens, was granddaughter of Lord Lytton, Grand Patron of the Rosicrucian Society of England "based on the doctrines of Hermes. . ." of which W.W. Westcott was Grand Patron before starting his Golden Dawn. The connection between B.F. Westcott and the activities attributed to the possible allonym W.W. Westcott are speculation on my part.

129 *Encyclopedia of Occultism and Parapsychology*, pp. 453, 927; see pp. 448-454. Many esoteric groups speak in tongues imitating the Apostolic gift (i.e., Mormons, the Way).

130 *When Humanity Comes of Age*, p. 224.

131 *Encyclopedia of Occultism and Parapsychology*, pp. 453.

132 Advertisements now have further amplified TV's hypnotic ability by alternating a series of very dark frames with a series of very bright frames. The level of hypnosis enduced disengages the executive controlling function to a level similar to that of drugs or alcohol.

133 *When Humanity Comes of Age*, pp. 65, 70.

CHAPTER 31

1 Dean Burgon, *The Revision Revised* (Paradise, Pa.: Conservative Classics), p. 277.

2 John R. Kohlenberger III, *Words About the Word* (Grand Rapids, Mich.: Zondervan Publishing House, 1987), p. 42.

3 *The Life of Hort*, p. 211; B.F. Westcott and F.J.A. Hort, *Introduction to the New Testament in the Original Greek* (Peabody, Mass.: Hendrickson Publishers, 1988, originally published by Harper and Brothers, New York, 1882), p. 92; *The Revision Revised*, p. 364.

4 *Life of Westcott*, Vol. I, p. 229.

5 *Life of Hort*, Vol. I, pp. 241, 240.

6 *Life of Hort*, Vol. II, p. 106.

7 *Life of Hort*, Vol. I, pp. 264.

8 *Life of Hort*, Vol. I, pp. 445, 421, 400.

9 *Life of Hort*, p. 403; see also *Ring of Truth*, p. 67 and *Price of Success* (pp. 144, 163 et al.).

10 *The Revision Revised*, p. 403.

11 *Life of Hort*, Vol. II, pp. 102, 138, 139.

12 *The Revision Revised*, pp. 114, 109; David Otis Fuller, *Which Bible?* (Grand Rapids, Michigan: Grand Rapids International Publication, 1984), pp. 294, 300.

[13] Vance Smith, *Texts And Margins*, p. 45.
[14] *The Revision Revised*, pp. 114-122, 273, 509, 107, 235, xi, 135, 245.
[15] *The Lucifer Connection*, p. 91.
[16] *Life of Hort*, Vol. II, p. 370.
[17] Ibid., p. 133.
[18] *Life of Hort*, Vol. I, p. 171.
[19] Ibid., p. 264.
[20] *Life of Hort*, Vol. II, p. 237.
[21] *Which Bible*, pp. 257-258.
[22] *The Revision Revised*, p. 236.
[23] David Otis Fuller, *True or False* (Grand Rapids, Michigan: Grand Rapids International Publishers, 1983).
[24] *Life of Hort*, Vol. II, p. 55.
[25] *The Revision Revised*, p. 40.
[26] "Considerations on Revision," May 1870, p. 44, as cited in *The Revision Revised*.
[27] *Life of Hort*, Vol. II, p. 145.
[28] Ibid., p. 234.
[29] Constance Cumby, *A Planned Deception* (East Detroit, Michigan: Pointe Publishers, Inc., 1985), p. 152.
[30] *Occult Underground*, pp. 36, 128, 131.
[31] *The Seduction of Christianity*, p. 71.
[32] *Understanding the New Age*, pp. 129-130.
[33] Texe Marrs, *Dark Secrets of the New Age* (Westchester, Illinois: Crossway Books, 1987), p. 219.
[34] Josh McDowell and Don Stewart, *Understanding the Occult* (San Bernardino, California: Here's Life Publishers, Inc., 1982), p. 103.
[35] Joseph Carr, *The Lucifer Connection* (Lafayette, Louisiana: Huntington House, Inc., 1987), p. 123.
[36] Dave Hunt, *Beyond Seduction* (Eugene, Oregon: Harvest House Publishers, 1987), p. 203.
[37] *Understanding the Occult*, p. 20.
[38] *Historic Faith*, pp. 249-255.
[39] Ibid., pp. 258-259.
[40] Ibid., p. 257.
[41] *Understanding the Occult*, p. 174.
[42] *Historic Faith*, pp. 252, 255.
[43] *Understanding the Occult*, p. 174.
[44] *Dark Secrets of the New Age*, p. 77.
[45] *Satan's Evangelistic Strategy for This New Age*, p. 83.
[46] *Larson's Book of Cults*, p. 317.
[47] J.B. Phillips, *Ring of Truth: A Translator's Testimony* (New York: The Macmillan and Company, 1967), p. 119.
[48] *A Crash Course on the New Age*, p. 156.
[49] Josh McDowell and Don Stewart, *Understanding the Cults* (San Bernardino, California: Here's Life Publishers, Inc., 1982), pp. 149, 73.
[50] Michael Horton (ed.), *The Agony of Deceit* (Chicago: Moody Press, 1990), p. 146.
[51] Patrick Henry, *New Directions in New Testament Study* (Philadelphia: The Westminster Press, 1979), pp. 98-99.

CHAPTER 32

[1] *Society for Psychical Research*, p. 38.

[2] *The Encyclopedia of the Unexplained*, ed. Richard Cavendish (New York: Mc Graw Hill, 1974), p. 46.

[3] *The Historic Faith*, p. 96.

[4] See also *Life of Westcott*, Vol. II, pp. 18-23, 114.

[5] *Words About the Word*, p. 89.

[6] *King James Version Debate*, p. 84.

[7] David S. Schaff, *The Life of Phillip Schaff* (New York: Charles Scribner's Son's, 1897), pp. 171, 446.

[8] Ibid., p. 492.

[9] Ibid., p. 246.

[10] *Life of Westcott*, Vol. I, p. 198.

[11] Ibid., p. 272.

[12] J.B. Phillips, *The Price of Success* (London: Hodder and Stoughton, 1984), see pp. 163-196.

[13] *Words About the Word*, p. 100. This section is not meant to imply that all mutism or mental illness is caused by 'spirits'; many have a physiological, biochemical or nutritional base. Nor does it imply that there has not developed in the field of psychology a few 'common sense' observations about human behavior (e.g., Glasser's Reality Therapy) which can sometimes be shared with an overwhelmed or socially deviant individual. I also recognize the validity of certain aspects of scientific inquiry which have wrongly come under the heading of psychology (e.g., behavioral mapping, cognitive behavior). As generally practiced, however, it usurps the role of 'Christ' as 'Counselor' (Isaiah 9:6) and his word as the vehicle (Psalm 107:20).

[14] *The Price of Success*, pp. 71-78.

[15] Ibid., pp. 197, 203.

[16] Ibid., pp. 201, 197, 196, 200, 203, 205, 210.

[17] Ibid., p. 205.

[18] Ibid., p. 215.

[19] Ibid., p. 196.

[20] Ibid., pp. 203.

[21] Ibid., pp. 210, 213.

[22] *Ring of Truth*, p. 67.

[23] *The Price of Success*, p. 141.

[24] Dave Hunt, *America: The Sorcerer's New Apprentice* (Eugene, Oregon: Harvest House Publishers, 1988), pp. 107-121.

[25] *The Price of Success*, p. 120, 133.

[26] Ibid., p. 119.

[27] *America: The Sorcerer's New Apprentice*, pp. 107, 115.

[28] *When Humanity Comes of Age*, pp. 31, 176, 68, 70.

[29] Corrine Heline, *New Age Bible Interpretation*, p. 132.

[30] *Beyond Seduction*, p. 132.

[31] Kenneth L. Barker, *The NIV: The Making of a Contemporary Translation* (Grand Rapids, Michigan: Zondervan Corporation, 1986), p. 112.

[32] B. McDowell, "Is the Holy Spirit a Person?" *Tomorrow's World*, September 1990, p. 31.

[33] *Dark Secrets of the New Age*, p. 105; Changing the name of the Holy Ghost puts new version authors in company also with Muhammed who did likewise. See Surah LXI, 6.

[34] *When Humanity Comes of Age*, p. 36.

CHAPTER 33

[1] David Schaff, *The Life of Schaff* (New York: Scribner's Sons, 1897), p. 132 quoting the *Pennsylvania Telegraph of Philadelphia*, Sept. 1853.

[2] Ibid., p. 467.

[3] Ibid., p. 352.

[4] Charles Wetzel;, "Schaff," (NY: *McGraw-Hill Encyclopedia of World Biography*, Vol. 9, 1973), pp. 434-435. See also Ibid. pp. 114-120.
[5] *The Life of Schaff*, pp. 105, 131.
[6] Ibid., p. 117.
[7] *New American Standard Bible* (La Habra, Calif: The Lockman Foundation, 1960), preface.
[8] *The Life of Schaff*, p. 488; Walter R. Houghton (ed.) *Neely's History of the Parliament of Religions* (Chicago: F.T. Neely, 1893), 3rd edition, p. 715.
[9] See Chapters 19-27 of this book.
[10] *The Life of Schaff*, p. 105.
[11] Ibid., p. 287.
[12] Ibid., pp. 351, 357.
[13] Ibid., p. 439; see also pp. 434-435.
[14] Ibid., p. 385.
[15] Ibid., p. 340.
[16] Ibid., p. 486, *New Age Dictionary*, preface.
[17] *Larson's Book of Cults*, p. 12; *Mystical Maze*, p. 20; *America: The Sorcerer's Apprentice*, p. 63; *Understanding the New Age*, p. 48.
[18] *Larson's Book of Cults*, p. 12.
[19] *Neely's History of the Parliament of Religions*, cover, pp. 861-862.
[20] Ibid., pp. 821, 976.
[21] Ibid., see index pp. 993-1000.
[22] Ibid., p. 978.
[23] Ibid., pp. 23, 24, 856.
[24] *The Life of Schaff*, p. 484.
[25] Ibid., p. 486.
[26] Livesey, *Understanding the New Age*, p. 170.
[27] *Neely's History of the Parliament of Religions*, p. 629.
[28] Ibid., pp. 17, 18.
[29] Ibid., p. 24.
[30] Ibid., p. 10.
[31] *The Life of Schaff*, p. 486.
[32] *Neely's History of the Parliament of Religions*, p. 444.
[33] Ibid., p. 927.
[34] Ibid., pp. 713, 714.
[35] David L. Johnson, *A Reasoned Look at Asian Religions* (Minneapolis, Minn.: Bethany House Publishers, 1985), p. 107.
[36] *Neely's History of the Parliament of Religions*, p. 927.
[37] *Larson's Book of Cults*, p. 191.
[38] *Dark Secrets of the New Age*, p. 123.
[39] *The Secret Doctrine*, p. 619.
[40] *The Princeton Review* (Princeton N.J.: Princeton University Press, January 1854), pp. 153, 169-170.

CHAPTERS 34-36

[1] Wilbur Pickering, *The Identity of the New Testament Text* (Nashville: Thomas Nelson Publishers, 1980), pp. 149, 150, 237.
[2] Dean John Burgon, *The Revision Revised* (Paradise, Pa: Conservative Classics), pp. 54, xi, 270-277.
[3] Edward F. Hills, *The King James Defended* (Des Moines, Iowa: The Christian Research Press, 1973), p. 219.

[4] E. W. Colwell, *What is the Best New Testament?* (Chicago: The University of Chicago Press, 1952), pp. 53, 49.

[5] *The Identity of the New Testament Text,* p. 160; David Otis Fuller, *Which Bible* (Grand Rapids, Michigan: Grand Rapids International Publications, 1984), p. 25.

[6] Ibid., p. 265.

[7] *The Identity of the New Testament Text,* pp. 16-18.

[8] B.F. Westcott and F.J.A. Hort, *Introduction to the New Testament in the Original Greek* (Peabody, Mass.: Hendrickson Publishers, Orig. 1882), p. 21.

[9] Bruce Metzger, *Manuscripts of the Greek Bible* (Oxford: Oxford University Press, 1981), p. 54.

[10] Ibid., pp. 4-5. The following directories will lead to the location of all of the New Testament manuscripts so that facsimiles can be obtained. *The Palaeography Collection in the University of London Library* (Boston, 1968) Vol. 1 and Vol. 2; Library of Congress, Washington D.C. will give you copies of the Mt. Sinai and Mt. Athos manuscripts; John L. Sharp's Checklist of Collections of Biblical and Related Manuscripts on Microfilm, *Scriptorium,* XXV (1971), pp. 97-109; Paul Canart, 'Les inventaires specialises de manuscrits grecs', *Scriptorium* xxiv (1970), pp. 112-116; Marcel Richard's *Repertoire des bibliotheques et des catalogues de manuscrits grecs,* 2nd ed. (Paris, 1958); *Bursians Jahresbericht uber die Fortschritte der klassischen Altertumswissenschaft;* Gerard Garitte, 'Manuscrits grecs, 1950-55, *Scritporium,* XII (1958) pp. 118-48; Jean Irigoin, 'Les manuscrits grecs, 1931-1960, in *Lustrum,* vii (1962) pp. 1-93, 332-5; Paul Canart and Vittorio Peri, *Sussidi bibliografici per i manoscritti greci della Biblioteca Vaticana* (Studi e testi, 261; Vatican City, 1970), xv + 709 pp; Kurt Aland *Repertorium der griechischen Christlichen Papyri;* i, *Biblische Papyri* (Berlin and New York, 1976)

[11] The *Identity of the New Testament Text,* pp. 116-120, 237.

[12] *Studies in Methodology in Textual Criticism,* p. 53, as cited in Philip W. Comfort, *Early Manuscripts and Modern Translations of the New Testament* (Wheaton, Illinois: Tyndale House Publishers, 1990), p. 13.

[13] Ibid., pp. 13-14.

[14] J. Geerlings, *Family E and Its Allies in Mark* (Salt Lake City: University of Utah Press, 1967), p. 1.

[15] *Which Bible,* p. 37; *King James Version Debate* (Grand Rapids, Mich.: Baker Book House, 1979), p. 48.

[16] *The Identity of the New Testament Text;* p. 160.

[17] Bruce Metzger, *Manuscripts of the Greek Bible* (Oxford: Oxford University Press, 1981), p. 86.

[18] *Which Bible,* pp. 104, 89, 90.

[19] *The Revision Revised,* p. 12.

[20] Frederic Kenyon, *The Text of the Greek Bible* (London: Gerald Duckworth and Co. Ltd., 1958), pp. 197-204, 224, 231.

[21] *The Identity of the New Testament Text,* pp. 114-120, 25, 149, 150, 237.

[22] Ibid., pp. 159-179.

[23] *The Identity of the New Testament Text,* pp. 143-144.

[24] *The King James Version Debate,* p. 49.

[25] G. Zuntz, *The Text of the Epistles* (London: Oxford University Press, 1968), p. 8.

[26] K. W. Clark, "Todays Problems with the Critical Text of the New Testament," *Transitions in Biblical Scholarship,* ed. J.C.R. Rylaarsdam (Chicago: The University of Chicago Press, 1968), p. 166.

[27] Alfred Marshall, *The NASB Interlinear Greek-English New Testament* (Grand Rapids, Mich.: Zondervan Publishing House, 1984), p. vi.

[28] *The Text of the Greek Bible,* p. 202.

[29] *Early Manuscripts and Modern Translations of the New Testament,* p. 14.

[30] *The King James Version Debate,* pp. 26, 36, 50, 55.

[31] *Introduction to the New Testament in the Original Greek,* p. 117.

[32] *The Text of the Greek Bible,* pp. 203-212, 321-322.

[33] *King James Version Defended,* p. 179.

[34] *The Identity of the New Testament Text*, p. 224.
[35] Ibid., pp. 77, 184, 202.
[36] Ibid., pp. 55-56, 220.
[37] *The Texts of the Epistles*, p. 55.
[38] *Manuscripts of the Greek Bible*, pp. 64, 108.
[39] Dean Burgon, *The Last Twelve Verses of Mark*, p. 54.
[40] *Early Manuscripts and Modern Translations of the Bible*, p. 11.
[41] *The King James Version Debate*, p. 111.
[42] E.C. Colwell, "The Origin of Texttypes of New Testament Manuscripts," *Early Christian Origins*, ed. Allen Wikgren (Chicago: Quadrangle Books, 1961), pp. 128-138.
[43] *The Revision Revised*, pp. 245, 70.
[44] Kenneth L. Barker (ed.), *The NIV: The Making of a Contemporary Translation* (Grand Rapids, Mich.: Zondervan Publishing House, 1986), p. 142.
[45] Ibid., p. 27.
[46] Ibid., p. 54, 57.
[47] Lewis Foster, *Selecting a Translation of the Bible* (Cincinnati, Ohio: Standard Publishing), pp. 15, 66.
[48] See notes 2, 3, and 5 et al.
[49] Arthur Hort, *The Life and Letters of Fenton John Anthony Hort*, Vol.I, p. 233.
[50] *Selecting a Translation of the Bible*, pp. 14, 15.
[51] Nestle, Ervin and Aland, Kurt, *Novum Testamentum Graece* (Stuttgart: Privilegierte Wurttembergische Biblelanslalt, 1960), pp. 40, 41.
[52] *Early Manuscripts and Modern Translations of the New Testament*, p. 24.
[53] *The Identity of the New Testament Text*, p. 221.
[54] Jacob Van Bruggen, *The Ancient Text of the New Testament* (Winnipeg: Premier, 1976), p. 33.
[55] D.A. Waite, *Heresies of Westcott and Hort* (Collingswood, New Jersey: The Bible For Today, 1979), p. 41.
[56] *Novum Testamentum Graece*, p. 43.
[57] *Early Manuscripts and Modern Translations of the New Testament*, p. 195.
[58] K.W. Clark, "The Theological Relevance of Textual Variation in Current Criticism of the Greek New Testament," *Journal of Biblical Literature*, LXXXV (1966), p. 15.
[59] *Early Manuscripts and Modern Translations of the New Testament*, p. 16.
[60] E.C. Colwell, "The International Greek New Testament Project: A Status Report," *Journal of Biblical Literature*, LXXXVII, 192 note 13 as cited in *The Identity of the New Testament Text*, p. 237.
[61] Ibid., p. 223.
[62] *Early Manuscripts and Modern Translations of the New Testament*, p.23.
[63] Aland, Kurt, Black, Matthew, Martini, Carlo M., Metzger, Bruce M., and Wikgren, Allen (eds.), *The Greek New Testament* (New York: United Bible Societies, 1966), p. x-xi.
[64] Patrick Henry, *New Directions in New Testament Study* (Philadelphia: The Westminster Press, 1979), pp. 232-234.
[65] *New American Bible* (New York: The World Publishing Co., 1970), p. vii.
[66] Ibid., p. ix.
[67] David Schaff, *Life of Philip Schaff* (New York: Charles Scribner's Sons, 1897), p. 378.
[68] *Early Manuscripts and Modern Translations of the New Testament*, p. 142-143.

CHAPTER 37

[1] Vera Alder, *When Humanity Comes of Age* (New York: Samuel Weiser, 1974), p. 209.
[2] Texe Marrs, *Dark Secrets of the New Age* (Westchester, Ill.: Crossway Books, 1987), p. 196.
[3] *The Mystical Maze*, p. 156.
[4] *Introduction to the New Testament in the Original Greek*, p. 66; *The Life of Hort*, p. 227.
[5] *History of the Canon*, p. 56, *Religious Thought in the West*, pp. 204, 78. *The Life of Westcott*, Vol. 1, p. 2.

[6] Russell Chandler, *Understanding the New Age* (Dallas, London: Word Publishing, 1988), pp. 285-286.

[7] *The Identity of the New Testament Text*, p. 217.

[8] David Johnson, *A Reasoned Look at Asian Religions* (Minneapolis, Minn.: Bethany House Publishers, 1985), p. 123.

[9] Ibid., p. 151.

[10] *The NIV: The Making of a Contemporary Translation*, p. 18.

[11] Ibid., pp. 97-98.

[12] *Early Manuscripts and Modern Translations of the Bible*, p. 176.

CHAPTER 38

[1] *The Encyclopedia of Religion and Ethics*, ed. James Hastings (New York: Scribners and Sons, 1926), see pp. 308-318.

[2] *Man, Myth and Magic: An Illustrated Encyclopedia of the Supernatural*, ed., Richard Cavendish Vol. 20, "Theosophy" (New York: Marshall Cavendish, 1974), p. 2814.

[3] Irving Cooper, *Theosophy Simplified* (Wheaton, Illinois: The Theosophical Press, 1964).

[4] B.F. Westcott, *A General Survey of the History of the Canon of the New Testament* (Cambridge and London: Macmillan, 1881), p. 396;
B.F. Westcott, *Essays in the History of Religious Thought in the West* (London: Macmillan, 1891), pp. 191, 196.

[5] Joseph Carr, *The Lucifer Connection* (Lafayette, Louisiana: Huntington House, 1987), p. 145.

[6] Alice Bailey, *The Reappearance of the Christ* (New York: Lucis Publishing Company, 1948), p. 45.

[7] Edward Rice, *Eastern Definitions* (Garden City, N.Y.: Doubleday and Company, Inc., 1978), p. 398.

[8] Arthur Hort, *Life and Letters of Fenton John Anthony Hort*, Vol. 2 (London: McMillan and Co., 1896), pp. 8, 358, 485.

[9] H.P. Blavatsky, *The Secret Doctrine*, Vol. II (London: The Theosophical Publishing Society, 1893), p. 501.

[10] H.P. Blavatsky, *The Theosophical Glossary* (Los Angelos, Ca.: The Theosophical Press, 1971), p. 253.

[11] Philip Comfort, *Early Manuscripts and Modern Translations of the New Testament* (Wheaton, Illinois: Tyndale, 1990), pp. 33, 89.

[12] *The Encyclopedia of Religion and Ethics*, pp. 318, 319.

[13] *Religious Thought in the West*, p. 47.

[14] Ibid., pp. 2, 7, 12.

[15] *The Encylcopedia of Religion and Ethics*, p. 309.

[16] B.F. Westcott, *The Historic Faith* (London and Cambridge: Macmillan and Co., 1885), pp. 74, 136, 143; see also his commentary on I John.

[17] Arthur Westcott, *The Life and Letters of B.F. Westcott*, Vol. I (London: Macmillan and Co., Limited, 1903), p. 251.

[18] Paul de Parrie and Mary Pride, *Ancient Empires of the New Age* (Westchester, Illinois: Crossway Books, 1989), p. 125.

[19] Lola Davis, *Toward a World Religion for a New Age* (Farmdale, N.Y.: Coleman Publishing, 1983), p. 149.

[20] Charles Filmore, *The Metaphysical Bible Dictionary* (Lees Summit, MO: Unity School of Christianity, 1950), preface.

[21] Louis Talbot, *What's Wrong with Unity School of Christianity* (Findlay, Ohio: Dunham Publishing Co., 1956); see *Life of Hort*, Vol. II, p. 106 for a discussion of the Platonic 'Coenobium'.

[22] *Religious Thought in the West*, p. 241 also see Rendel Harris "Codex Bezae," *Texts and Studies* (Cambridge, England: Cambridge University Press, 1891), p. 229.

[23] *The Life of Hort*, Vol. I, p. 425; Westcott also would "dwell on subjects such as the myths of Plato" to prepare candidates for confirmation. See *Life of Westcott*, Vol. I, p. 192.

[24] Ibid., p. 97.

[25] *Life of Hort*, Vol. II, pp. 69, 79.

26 *Life of Hort*, Vol. I, pp. 42, 266, 92.
27 Michael Horton (ed.), *The Agony of Deceit* (Chicago: Moody Press, 1990), p. 131.
28 *The Encyclopedia of Religion and Ethics*, p. 615.
29 *Life of Hort*, Vol. I, p. 449.
30 *Religious Thought in the West*, p. 4.
31 Ibid., pp. 397, 360.
32 Constance Cumby, *Hidden Dangers of the Rainbow* (Shreveport, Louisiana: Huntington House, 1983), p. 213.
33 *Encyclopedia of Religion and Ethics*, p. 318.
34 Ibid., p. 319.
35 David Christie-Murray, *The History of Heresy* (Oxford: Oxford University Press, 1976), p. 6.
36 Philip Lee, *Against the Protestant Gnostics* (Oxford: Oxford University Press, 1987), p. 50.
37 *Religious Thought in the West*, p. 207.
38 *Theosophical Glossary*, p. 17.
39 *The Secret Doctrine*, Vol. I, p. 27.
40 *The Lucifer Connection*, p. 110.
41 Geoffrey Hodson, *The Hidden Wisdom in the Holy Bible* (Adyar, Madras 20 India: The Theosophical Publishing Society, 1963), p. 34.
42 Rudolf Steiner, *The Esoteric Basis of Christianity*, p. 149.
43 Ibid., pp. 24, 27.
44 Unity publication, p. 13; see also Bob Larson, *Larson's Book of Cults* (Wheaton, Illinois: Tyndale Publishing House, 1985), p. 174.
45 J. Yutaka Amano and Norman L. Geisler, *The Infiltration of the New Age* (Wheaton, Illinois: Tyndale Publishing House, 1989), p. 108.
46 *The Secret Doctrine*, pp. 100, 565.
47 Texe Marrs, *Dark Secrets of the New Age* (Westchester, Illinois: Crossway Books, 1987), p. 214; Corrine Heline, *New Age Bible Interpretation* (New York: The New Age Press, 1935), p. 32, republished by New Age Bible and Philosophy Center, Santa Monica, Ca., 1984.
48 *Religious Thought in the West*, pp. 225; see also *Life of Westcott*, Vol. I, p. 320.
49 Patrick Henry, *New Directions in New Testament Study* (Philadelphia: The Westminster Press, 1979), p. 277.
50 *Historic Faith*, pp. 74; *Religious Thought in the West*, pp. 319, 247, 252.
51 *New Directions in New Testament Study*, pp. 221, 222.
52 *The Agony of Deceit*, p. 74.
53 David Otis Fuller, *Which Bible* (Grand Rapids, Michigan: Grand Rapids International Publications, 1975), p. 146.
54 *A General Survey of the History of the Canon of the New Testament*, p. 360.
55 *Early Manuscripts and Modern Translations of the New Testament*, pp. xvii, 8.
56 *Which Bible*, p. 3.
57 Edward F. Hills, *The King James Version Defended* (Des Moines, Iowa: The Christian Research Press, 1973), p. 144.
58 *Which Bible*, p. 140; also see Wilbur Pickering, *The Identity of the New Testament Text* (Nashville: Thomas Nelson, 1980), p. 49.
59 John Burgon, *Causes of Textual Corruption* (London: George Bell and Sons, 1896), pp. 95, 108; John Burgon, *The Revision Revised* (Paradise, Pa.: Conservative Classics), p. 336.
60 *Religious Thought in the West*, pp. 212, 213.
61 *Which Bible*, p. 164.
62 *The Early Manuscripts and Modern Translations of the New Testament*, pp. 18, 221.
63 Ibid., p. 10.

[64] Bruce Metzger, *Manuscripts of the Greek Bible: An Introduction to Greek Palaeography* (Oxford: Oxford University Press, 1981), pp. 66, 68; also see E.G. Turner's *Greek Manuscripts of the Ancient World*, p. 108; *Anzeiger des phil-hist Klasse der Osterheichischen Akademie* der Wissenschaften, 1960, No. 4, pp. 12-23; *New Dimensions in New Testament Study*, eds. Richard N. Longenecker and Merrill C. Tenney (Grand Rapids, Michigan: Zondervan Publishing House, 1974), p. 30.

[65] *A General Survey of the History of the Canon of the New Testament*, p. 358.

[66] *New Dimension in New Testament Study*, p. 28. Fee ignores the all too obvious facts and choose to posit that Origen could not have been involved because he did not have the 'type' of "mind" required.

[67] Gunther Zuntz, *The Text of the Epistles* (London: Oxford University Press, 1953), p. 152.

[68] D.A. Carlson, *The King James Version Debate* (Grand Rapids, Michigan: Baker Book House, 1979), p. 27.

[69] Erwin W. Lutzer, *Coming to Grips with The Antichrist's New Age Roots* (Chicago: Moody Press, 1990), p. 12.

[70] *A General Survey on the History of the Canon of the New Testament*, p. 47.

[71] Dave Hunt, *What Ever Happened to Heaven* (Eugene, Oregon: Harvest House Publishers, 1988), p. 11.

[72] *A General Survey on the History of the Canon of the New Testament*, p. 428.

[73] Trevor Ravenscroft, *The Spear of Destiny* (York Beach, Me.: Weiser, 1982), p. 64. See also Inman: *Ancient Pagan and Modern Christian Symbolism*, p. 84 for the Church of Rome's involvement.

[74] *What Ever Happened to Heaven*, p. 115.

[75] *The History of Heresy*, p. 45; *A General Survey*, pp. 414, 416, 419.

[76] Ibid., p. 426.

[77] Ibid., p. 398.

[78] Ira Price, *The Ancestory of the English Bible*, p. 70 as quoted in *Which Bible*, p. 3.

[79] Bruce Metzger, *Manuscripts of the Greek Bible* (Oxford: Oxford University Press, 1981), p. 77; see also Wilhelm Bousset, *Texte and Untersuchungen* as cited in Harnack's *Textual Studies in the New Testament*, 1894, p. 45.

[80] Kenneth L. Barker (ed.), *The NIV: The Making of a Contemporary Translation* (Grand Rapids: Zondervan Publishing House, 1986), pp. 50, 89.

[81] F.J.A. Hort, *The Introduction to the New Testament in the Original Greek* (Peabody, Massachusetts: Hendrickson Publishers, 1988), p. 264; first printed by Harper Brothers, New York, 1882.

[82] D.A. Carlson, *The King James Version Debate*, p. 53.

[83] *The NIV: The Making of a Contemporary Translation*, p. 89.

[84] *The Septuagint*, Zondervan Publishing Co., 1970, (Samuel Bagster and Sons, London).

[85] *The Encyclopedia of Religion and Ethics*, p. 309.

[86] Ibid.

[87] *The Septuagint* (LXX) cannot be the word of God for several other reasons:

1. It contains apocryphal books such as *Tobit, The Prayer of Manasses, Second Esdras, Wisdom, Ecclesiasticus, Baruck, I and II Maccabee*; there are also additions to Esther and Daniel. Jesus never quoted the Apocrypha and the Jews rejected it also.
2. The "fable" of its origin states that it was written under orders of the king of Egypt (Ptolemy) around 250 B.C. by 72 Jews. The word Septuagint, however, means 70. The "fable" further states that six Jews from each of the twelve tribes wrote it. However, only the tribe of Levi were permitted by God to write the scriptures (I Chronicles 16:4).
3. Any Jew living in or returning to Egypt was in direct disobedience to God's command in Deuteronomy 17:16. "But he shall not. . .cause the people to return to Egypt forasmuch as the LORD hath said unto you, Ye shall henceforth return no more that way."
4. Origen's six column Old Testament, the Hexapla, parallels O.T. versions by Theodotian, Symmachus, and Aquilla, all three Gnostic occultists.

CHAPTER 39

1 David Otis Fuller, *Which Bible* (Grand Rapids, Mich.: Grand Rapids International Publications, 1984), pp. 135, 136.

2 B.F. Westcott and F.J.A. Hort, *Introduction to the New Testament in the Original Greek* (Peabody, Mass.: Hendrickson Publishers, Orig. 1882), pp. xxii, 225, 212, 220, 239, 210.

3 *Which Bible*, p. 150.

4 *The Revision Revised*, pp. 16, 520, 318.

5 *Introduction to the New Testament in the Original Greek*, p. 233.

6 Jakob Van Bruggen, *The Ancient Text of the New Testament* (Winnipeg: Premier, 1976), pp. 30-31.

7 Frederic Kenyon, *The Text of the Greek Bible* (London: Gerald Duckworth and Co. Ltd., 1958), p. 308.

8 Richard N. Longenecker and Merrill C. Tenney, *New Dimensions in New Testament Study* (Grand Rapids, Mich.: Zondervan Publishing House, 1974, p. 23.

9 Ibid., p. 19.

10 Kenneth L. Barker (ed.), *The NIV: The Making of a Contemporary Translation* (Grand Rapids, Michigan: Zondervan Publishing House, 1986), p. 143.

11 Ibid., p. 112.

12 Alfred Marshall, *NASB Interlinear Greek-English New Testament* (Grand Rapids, Mich.: Zondervan Publishing House, 1984), intro.

13 Lewis Foster, *Selecting a Translation of the Bible* (Cincinnati, Ohio: Standard Publishing Co.), p. 16.

14 Nestle, Erwin and Aland, Kurt, *Novum Testamentum Graece* (Stuttgart: Privilegierte Wurttembergische Biblelanstalt, 1960), intro.

15 *The Revision Revised*, pp. 94, 151, 334-335.

16 Wilbur Pickering, *The Identy of the New Testament Text* (Nashville: Thomas Nelson Publishing Co., 1980), pp. 120, 136, 145, and back cover.

17 *Which Bible*, pp. 134-143.

18 Edward F. Hills, *The King James Version Defended* (Des Moines Iowa: The Christian Research Press, 1973).

19 Bruce Metzger, *Manuscripts of the Greek Bible* (Oxford: Oxford University Press, 1991), p. 74.

20 Ibid., p. 14; Philip W. Comfort, *Early Manuscripts and Modern Translations of the New Testament* (Wheaton, Ill.: Tyndale Publishing House, 1990), p. 5; see also *Cambridge History of the Bible* Vol. I, "Books in the Graeco-Roman World and in the New Testament."

21 *Manuscripts of the Greek Bible*, p. 74.

22 Ibid., p. 74.

23 Ibid., p. 77.

24 Ibid., p. 78.

25 *The Revision Revised*, p. 12; *The Identity of the New Testament Text*, p. 220.

CHAPTER 40

1 Vera Alder, *When Humanity Comes of Age* (New York: Samuel Weiser, 1974), p. 39.

2 Texe Marrs, *Dark Secrets of the New Age* (Westchester, Ill.: Crossway Books, 1987), p. 193.

3 *The New International Version* (Grand Rapids, Mich.: Zondervan Bible Publishers, 1973), preface.

4 *The New American Version* (Philadelphia: A.J. Holman Company, 1960), preface.

5 *New Dimensions in New Testament Study*, p. 16.

6 *Manuscripts of the Greek Bible*, p. 74.

7 B.F. Westcott, *A General Survey of the History of the Canon of the New Testament* (London: Macmillan and Co., 1881), pp. 196, 198.

8 H.P. Blavatsky, *Isis Unveiled*, Vol. II (London: The Theosophical Publishing House, 1923), p. 243.

[9] Ibid., p. vii.

[10] Christian Book Distributors (Peabody, MA; January-February, 1991), p. 13.

[11] See J.B. Lightfoot and J.R. Harmer (eds.) *The Apostotic Fathers* (Grand Rapids, Mich.: Baker Book House, 1988, from 1891 edition published by Macmillan and Co. London), pp. 291-483.

[12] Ibid., see pp. 239-288.

[13] *Early Manuscripts and Modern Translations*, pp. 12, 13, 21.

[14] *Which Bible*, p. 27.

[15] Kurt Aland, "The Significance of the Papyri for Progress in New Testament Textual Criticism," *The Bible in Modern Scholarship*, ed. J.P. Hyatt (New York: Abingdon Press, 1965), p. 333.

[16] E.C. Colwell, "Scribal Habits in Early Papyri: A Study in the Corruption of the Text," *The Bible in Modern Scholarship*, ed. J.P. Hyatt (New York: Abingdon Press, 1965), pp. 370-389.

[17] *Early Manuscripts and Modern Translations*, pp. 18, 201.

[18] *The Text of the Greek Bible*, p. 256.

[19] *The New International Version*, p. x.

[20] *When Humanity Comes of Age*, p. 39.

CHAPTER 41

[1] Texe Marrs, *Mystery Mark of the New Age* (Westchester, Ill.: Crossway Books, 1988), p. 192.

[2] Vera Alder, *The Initiation of the World* p. 245, as quoted in *Mystery Mark of the New Age*, p. 188.

[3] Rudolf Steiner, *The Esoteric Basis of Christianity*, p. 177.

[4] Alice Bailey, *Treatise on White Magic*, pp. 543-544, as quoted in *Hidden Dangers of the Rainbow*, p. 76.

[5] Texe Marrs, *Dark Secrets of the New Age* (Westchester, Ill.: Crossway Books, 1987), p. 75.

[6] Edward Rice, *Eastern Definitions* (Garden City, New York: Doubleday and Company, Inc., 1978), p. 376.

[7] H.P. Blavatsky, *The Secret Doctrine* Vol. I, (London: The Theosophical Publishing House, 1893), pp. 404-405, Vol. II, pp. 439-445, 824-825 .

[8] *Eastern Definitions*, p. 377.

[9] Corinne Heline, *New Age Bible Interpretation*, p. 355.

[10] Charles Filmore, *Metaphysical Bible Dictionary* (Lees Summit, MO.: Unity School of Christianity, 1950), p. 209.

[11] Lola Davis, *Toward a World Religion for a New Age* (Farmdale, N.Y.: Coleman Publishing, 1983), p. 184.

[12] Vera Alder, *When Humanity Comes of Age* (New York: Samuel Weiser, 1974), p. 77.

[13] John Randolph Price, *The Superbeings* (Austin, Texas: Quartus Books, 1981), p. 1 as cited in *Dark Secrets of the New Age*, p. 18.

[14] Elliot Miller, *A Crash Course on the New Age* (Grand Rapids, Mich.: Baker Book House, 1989), p. 236.

[15] B.F. Westcott, *Essays in the History of Religious Thought in the West* (London: Macmillan & Co., 1891), pp. 25, 211.

[16] Origen, *De Principis*, Book II, Ch. 11, par. 8; also see *A History of the Christian Church* (New York: Charles Scribner's Son, 1918), pp. 164-165.

[17] Arthur Hort, *The Life and Letters of F.J.A. Hort*, Vol. I (New York: Macmillan &Co., 1896), p. 458.

[18] Alan Gould, *The Founders of Psychical Research* (New York: Schocken Books, 1968), p. 366.

[19] *Religious Thought in the West*, p. 343.

[20] *Eastern Definitions*, p. 178.

CHAPTER 42

1 *The NIV: The Making of a Contemporary Translation*, pp. 166, 110; *Selecting a Translation of the Bible*, p. 17.

[2] Christian Book Distributors, (Peabody, Mass., Jan-Feb 1991, pp. 7-8 et al.).

3 Robert Erickson, *Theologians under Hitler* (New Haven: Yale University Press, 1985), p. 54.
4 Ibid., p. 37.
5 William Foxwell Albright, *History Archaeology and Christian Humanism* (New York, 1964), pp. 229-230.
6 Joseph J. Carr, *The Twisted Cross* (Lafayette, Louisiana, Huntington House Inc., 1985), p. 165.
7 Ibid., pp. 198, 262, 263.
8 *Theologians Under Hitler*, pp. 45-46.
10 *The Twisted Cross*, p. 104.
11 James Webb, *The Occult Establishment* (La Salle, Ill.: Open Court Press, 1976), p. 287.
12 *The Secret Doctrine*, Vol. I, p. 411, Vol. 2, pp. 439-445.
13 Peter Le Mesurier, *Beyond All Belief* (Salisbury, Willshire, England: Clement Books Ltd., 1983), as cited in *A Planned Deception*, p. 85.
14 *The Twisted Cross*, p. 282.
15 Ibid., p. 87.
16 Rita Thalmann and Emmanuel Feinermanne, *Crystal Night, 9-10 November, 1938* (New York: Holocaust Library, 1974).
17 Robert G. L. Waite, *The Psychopathic God—Adolf Hitler* (New York: Basic Book, 1977), as cited in *The Twisted Cross*, p. 36.
18 *Theologians Under Hitler*, p. 25, 41, 48, 59.

19 Ibid., pp. 25, 70.
20 Ibid., p. 70.
21 Ibid., pp. 54, 61, 74, 75.
22 Gerhard Kittel, *Die Judenfrage* (Stuttgart, 1933), p. 39.
23 'Deutsche Wissenschaft and Judenfrage - "Forschungsabteilung Judenfrage" des Reichsinstituts Geschichte des neuen Deutschlands eroffnet,' *Volkischer Beobachter*, 325. Ausgabe, 49. Jahrgang (20 Nov. 1936), Munich edition, p. 1.
24 *Theologians Under Hitler*, pp. 34-37, 45, 49.
25 Gerhard Kittel, 'Die Behandlung des Nichtjuden nach dem Talmud', *Archiv fur Judenfragen*, vol. 1, Group A, (Berlin, 1943), p. 7.
26 *The Twisted Cross*, p. 190, 149.
27 Gerhard Kittel, 'Die Entstehung des Judentums und die Entstehung der Judenfrage', *Forschungen zur Judenfrage*, vol. 1 (Hamburg, 1936), p. 63; Gerhard Kittel, 'Das Konnubium mit den Nicht-Juden im Antiken Judentum', Forschungen zur Judenfrage, vol. 2 (Hamburg, 1937), p. 62.
28 Gerhard Kittel, 'Die Entstehung des Judentums' (Theological Library of the University of Tubingen, lecture delivered March 22, 1943), p. 5.
29 Gerhard Kittel, 'Die Behandlung des Nichtjuden nach dem Talmud', *Archiv fur Judenfragen*, vol. 1, Group A1 (Berlin, 1943), p. 7.
30 *Theologians Under Hitler*, p. 76.
31 Ibid., pp. 26, 27.
32 Gerhard Kittel, *Meine Verteidigung* (Tubingen Library Archives, November-December, 1946), p. 67.
33 *Theologians Under Hitler*, p. 62.
34 *The King James Debate*, p. 89.
35 *Words About the Word*, p. 62.
36 *Early Manuscripts and Modern Translations of the New Testament*, p. 7.
37 *Time*, May 28, 1990, "An Outbreak of Bigotry," p. 35.
38 *The Twisted Cross*, pp. 278-279.
39 *Update*, September 1982, Johannes Aagaard, "Hindu Scholars, Germany and the Third Reich," as quoted in Dave Hunt, *America: The Sorcerer's New Apprentice* (Eugene, Oregon: Harvest House Publishers, 1988), p. 100.

[40] Dion Fortune, *Sane Occultism* (London: *The Aquarian Press*, 1967), pp. 80-81.

[41] *Hidden Dangers of the Rainbow*, p. 190.

[42] Richard Bucke, *Cosmic Consciousness: A Study in the Evolution of the Human Mind* (New York: E.P. Dutton and Co., Inc., 1901), pp. 55, 59.

[43] Richard Grenier, *The Ghandi Nobody Knows* (Nashville: Thomas Nelson, 1983), p. 79.

[44] Wm. Kerr, *The Living Bible: Not Just Another Version* (Tyndale Publishers), p. 5; see also *Hidden Dangers of the Rainbow*, p. 14.

[45] *Akron Beacon Journal*, letter to the editor.

[46] *The NASB Interlinear Greek-English New Testament* (Grand Rapids, Mich.: Zondervan Publishing House, 1984), p. wiii.

[47] Wilbur Pickering, *The Identity of the New Testament Text* (Nashville: Thomas Nelson Publishers, 1980), p. 41.

[48] *New Directions in New Testament Study*, p. 42, see also *New Dimensions in New Testament Study*, p. 154.

[49] *Spin*, September 1986, p. 32.

[50] *The Twisted Cross*, p. 44.

[51] Gerhard Kittel, *Die Judenfrage* (Stuttgart, 1933), p. 34.

[52] *The Secret Doctrine*, Vol. II, pp. 439-445.

[53] Wanda Marrs, *New Age Lies to Women* (Austin, Texas: Living Truth Publishers, 1989), p. 159.

[54] See F.J.A. Hort, *Commentary on I Peter*, pp. 7, 16, 116.

[55] See *Religious Thought in the West* p. 313; B.F. Westcott's *Commentary on John* (1:12).

[56] *End-Times News Digest*, December 1987 (James McKeever Ministries Newsletter), p. 3 as quoted in Dave Hunt, *What Ever Happened to Heaven* (Eugene, Oregon: Harvest House Publishers, 1988), p. 251.

[57] Ibid., p. 249, 95.

[58] *Toward a World Religion for a New Age*, p. 181.

[59] *When Humanity Comes of Age*, p. 93.

[60] *The NIV: The Making of a Contemporary*, p. 146.

[61] Emmett Fox, *Diagrams for Living: The Bible Unveiled* (New York: Harper and Row, 1968), pp. 158-159 as cited in *Dark Secrets of the New Age*, p. 209.

[62] *Historic Faith*, pp. 91-99.

[63] Randall N. Baer, *Inside the New Age Nightmare* (Layafette, Louisiana, Huntington House, Inc., 1989), p. 91.

[64] John Randoph Price, *The Planetary Commission*, p. 28 as cited in *Dark Secrets of the New Age*, p. 37.

[65] *Historic Faith*, pp. 89,99.

[66] Eugene Fontinelli, *Cross Currents*, "Toward a Reconstruction of Religion," (West Nyack, New York, 1979), as cited in *Hidden Dangers of the Rainbow*, p. 148.

[67] *Historic Faith*, p. 948; see Hort's *Commentary on I Peter*, pp. 44,45.

EPILOGUE

[1] *The Lucifer Connection*, p. 104.

[2] *Which Bible?*, p. 97.

[3] *The Five Points of Calvinism*, p. 252.

APPENDIX A

[1] Arthur Hort, *The Life and Letters of Fenton John Anthony Hort*, Vol. I (London: Macmillan Press, 1896), pp. 7, 41, 77.

[2] Ibid.

[3] Ibid., Vol II, p. 116.

[4] Ibid., Vol. I, p. 400.

5 Ibid., p. 77.
6 Ibid., p. 61.
7 Ibid., p. 2.
8 Ibid., Vol. II, p. 63; also see p. 92.
9 Arthur Westcott, *The Life and Letters of Brook Foss Westcott*, Vol. II (London: Macmillan and Co., 1903), p. 32.
10 Ibid., pp. 155-159; see also Vol. I, p. 252.
11 Ibid., Vol. II, pp. 172, 368, 377.
12

HERMAS CLUB

WESTCOTT

A. SIDGWICK   FREDRIC MYERS

GHOSTLY GUILD

A. JOHNSON   WESTCOTT   HORT   BENSON (Married H. Sidgwick's Sister, Mary)   LIGHTFOOT   H. SIDGWICK (Westcott's Student Married Gerald Balfour's Sister, Eleanor)

SOCIETY FOR PSYCHICAL RESEARCH

(SOCIETY WAS "FAVORABLY IMPRESSED WITH MME. BLAVATSKY")

A. JOHNSON   ELEANOR BALFOUR SIDGWICK   FREDRIC MYERS   H. SIDGWICK

ED GURNEY   ARTHUR BALFOUR   GERALD BALFOUR (Married Betty, Sister of Emily Lutyens, Luciferian initiate and Granddaughter of Blavatsky's Mentor Rosecrucian Founder Bulwer Lytton); Gerald is Eleanor B. Sidgwick's Brother)   HENRI BERGSON (Sister Mina married S.L. Mathers, co-founder of the Godlen Dawn with W.W. Westcott; see pp. 676-677)

APOSTLES

ARTHUR BALFOUR   HORT   H. SIDGWICK

ERANUS

ARTHUR BALFOUR   WESTCOTT   HORT   H. SIDGWICK

SYNTHETIC SOCIETY

ARTHUR BALFOUR   FREDRIC MYERS

CFR/LEAGUE OF NATIONS

ARTHUR BALFOUR/CECIL RHODES

REV. 16:13

THE DRAGON (OCCULTISTS LIKE H. SIDGWICK, G. BALFOUR, F. MYERS)
THE BEAST (A. BALFOUR, PRIME MINISTER OF ENGLAND)
THE FALSE PROPHET (WESTCOTT, HORT)
"UNTIL THE TIME OF THE NEW ORDER" (HEB. 9:10 NIV)

ATALOGUE
1-800-435-4535

New Age Bible Versions

by G.A. Riplinger

$14.95

30% discount off 5 or more ($10.50 ea.)
40% discount off case of 14 ($135.00 includes shipping)

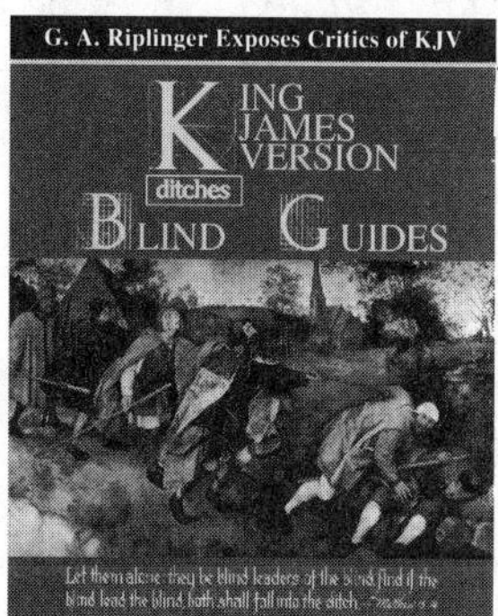

NEW RELEASE

Blind Guides by G.A. Riplinger

$5.95

30% discount off 5 or more ($4.20 ea.)

False accusers, breathing out the dragon's fire, are sending up a smokescreen to hide the unholy new bible versions from the scrutinizing light of the bestseller *New Age Bible Versions*. The author exposes, one by one the tissue of lies printed by the critics.

VIDEOS

Nationally syndicated Christian program with G.A. Riplinger; excellent teaching series for church or sharing with friends.

- **Night Line,** Feb. 27, 1995 (2 hrs.) **$19.95**
- **Action Sixties,** Feb., 1995/1994 (4 hrs.) **$35.95**
- *Call for additional programs*

AUDIO TAPES

- **KNIS Radio Interview** with G.A. Riplinger **$3.00**
- **New Age Bible Versions Album** *(8 tapes)* **$19.95**

Interviews with the author by Texe Marrs and Southwest Radio Church

- **New Age Bible Versions Album** *(16 tapes)* **$49.95**

Includes all nine tapes above plus 15 other interviews by talk show hosts across the country.

TRACTS

- **Verse comparison chart** *(folds out to 11"x17")* **20¢**

New Releases

Which Bible Is God's Word?

by

G.A. Riplinger

$8.95

30% discount off 5 copies or more ($6.30 ea.)

40% discount off case of 14 ($80.00 includes shipping)

Transcript of the series of interviews with G.A. Riplinger by Noah Hutchings of the nationally syndicated program Southwest Radio Church. Answers these and many other common questions concerning bible versions.

- How do new versions change the gospel?
- How do the NIV and NASB support New Age philosophy?
- What about the NKJV, KJ[21], and others which say they merely update the KJV?
- Where was the bible before the KJV 1611?
- What errors are the KJV critics making?

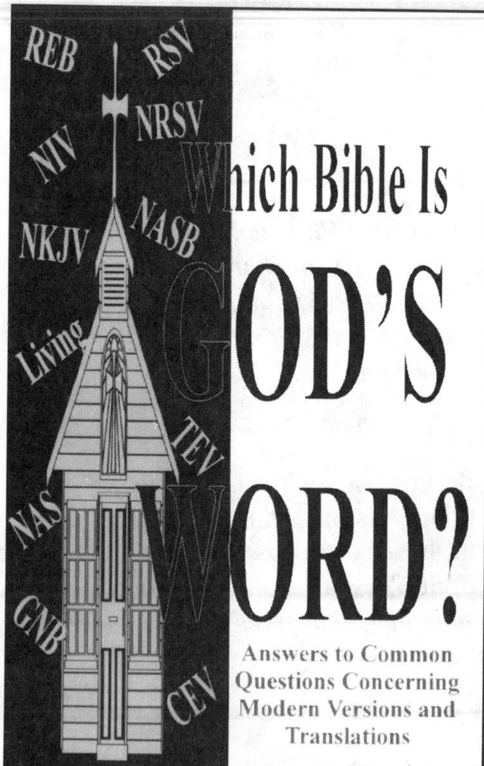